Web 101

Making the 'Net Work for You

Web 101

Making the 'Net Work for You

Wendy. G. Lehnert

University of Massachusetts, Amherst

Addison
Wesley

Boston San Francisco New York
London Toronto Sydney Tokyo Singapore Madrid
Mexico City Munich Paris Cape Town Hong Kong Montreal

SENIOR ACQUISITIONS EDITOR:	Susan Hartman Sullivan
ASSISTANT EDITOR:	Elinor Actipis
SENIOR PERMISSIONS EDITOR:	Mary Boucher
EXECUTIVE MARKETING MANAGER:	Michael Hirsch
COPYEDITORS:	Laura Michaels and Roberta Lewis
PROOFREADER:	Holly McLean Aldis
COMPOSITION AND ART:	Gillian Hall, The Aardvark Group
DESIGN MANAGER:	Gina Hagen
TEXT DESIGN:	Leslie Haimes and Gillian Hall
COVER DESIGN:	Gina Hagen
COVER ILLUSTRATION:	Susan Cyr
PREPRESS AND MANUFACTURING:	Caroline Fell
MEDIA PRODUCER:	Jennifer Pelland

Access the latest information about Addison-Wesley computer science titles from our World Wide Web site: http://www.awl.com/cs

The programs and applications presented in this book have been included for their instructional value. They have been tested with care, but are not guaranteed for any particular purpose. The publisher does not offer any warranties or representations, not does it accept any liabilities with respect to the programs or applications.

Library of Congress Cataloging-in-Publication Data

Lehnert, Wendy G.
    Web 101: making the net work for you / Wendy G. Lehnert.
        p. cm.
    ISBN 0-201-70474-9 (alk. paper)
    1. World Wide Web. 2. Internet. I. Title.

 TK5105.888.L435 2001
 025.04--dc21

                                              00-044798

2345678910-CRW-04030201

For Mark, Michael, Kate, and Annelise

Preface

The year 2000 marked a turning point for the Internet. For the first time, over 50% of all American homes and more than 90% of all American college students had Internet access. As a group, college students are relatively savvy about the Internet, quick to exploit online resources and eager to embrace technological innovations. Out of necessity, most students have learned what they know about the Internet on their own. They've learned by word-of-mouth, by browsing the Web, and by asking friends for help. This hit-or-miss process works to some extent, but it does have its limitations. For one thing, it takes a long time to cover the basics when your lesson plan relies on serendipity. In addition, some things are likely to be learned the hard way, and the school of hard knocks can be downright painful when it comes to computers.

This book is for anyone who wants to learn more about the Internet. These pages cover all the basics for those who are just starting out, but they also include more advanced and optional topics for those who want to expand their knowledge in specific directions. At all times, our emphasis is more practical than technical, although we aim for a level of understanding that is more general than the operation of specific software applications.

FROM NEWBIES TO NETIZENS

In these chapters you will find a solid foundation of basic concepts and practical know-how for everyone from the novice to the self-taught expert. You don't have to have any experience with the Internet to get started with this book—we explain it all from scratch. On the other hand, if you've been online for a few years and think you know everything, you might be surprised to find out how much you still have to learn. This book was written for a range of readers, from Internet newcomers (the "newbies") to seasoned regulars (the "Netizens").

In order to address a wide range of readers, we have structured our topics in a way that makes it easy to pick and choose. Each chapter is written in two parts: The first part contains core topics that cover the basics. A newbie could cover just these core topics and learn enough to make the Net a valuable asset. The second part is easily identified by sections titled "Above and Beyond" the core topics. This material is for those who already know the basics and want to dig a little deeper.

WHAT'S IN THE BOOK

Chapter 1 starts by explaining some basic computer and computer networking concepts as a foundation for all that follows. We develop a working vocabulary in Chapter 1 before moving on to an in-depth tour of the Internet. Chapter 2 surveys important pitfalls and precautions before the real hands-on learning begins—we don't want anyone to get into trouble, and there is danger out there. Starting with Chapter 3 on e-mail management, we encourage readers to dive right in and use the Net. E-mail is a good place to start because many people have an e-mail account and are already familiar with at least one e-mail program.

No book about the Internet would be complete without an introduction to Web-page construction. We cover the basics of HTML in Chapter 4 for beginners. Chapter 5 concentrates on dynamic Web-page elements through the use of JavaScript and Java applets. We explain how to find and install existing scripts and applets, and we demonstrate what can be done at this level without any knowledge of computer programming.

Although the Internet is clearly about computers, computer networks, and computer software, the Internet is also about information, people, and human communication. We cover online search strategies (Chapter 6), virtual communities and hackers (Chapter 7), software downloads and installations (Chapter 8), software for the Internet (Chapter 9), e-commerce (Chapter 10), encryption for the Internet (Chapter 11), telecommuting, careers in information technology, and Internet addiction (Chapter 12). To be knowledgeable about the Internet also means being educated about a wide range of contemporary issues, including intellectual property law, the First Amendment, personal privacy in a digital age, digital wiretapping legislation, self-regulation in American business, and consumer profiling practices. These topics are all introduced and discussed, with advice and guidelines for all Internet users.

WHAT'S ON THE WEB

As one of the reviewers for this book commented, timely Internet topics have the "half-life of a May fly." As soon as you put something about the Internet into print, it's out of date. This is true of the technology that drives the Net, the software we use to tap the Net, and all the information that lives on the Net. Any book about the Internet is not just a shot at a fast-moving target; it's also a shot at a shape-shifting target as well.

With so much in flux, it makes sense to turn to the Net itself for updates. Each chapter of this book contains pointers to resources on the Net. The most important pointers are grouped inside special sections titled "Where Can I Learn More?" Others are scattered throughout the text but printed in blue to help you spot them. You can visit our Web site and find links to all of the online resources referenced throughout these pages:

```
http://www.awl.com/lehnertweb101/
```

Many of the Web sites mentioned throughout this book are accompanied by URLs, but not all. Web page addresses are notoriously short-lived and require frequent updates. We cannot update a URL that appears in these pages, but we can update the links at our Web site. We will update any URLs at the Web site as needed in order to keep these resources readily available. You will also find a software index with links to software sites, documentation, and tutorials (if available) for all of the software mentioned in this book.

SOFTWARE THAT STUDENTS CAN USE

It is impossible to discuss software without showing examples of specific software packages in action. This is tricky in an educational text because we are not trying to endorse specific products, we just want some concrete examples for good pedagogy. We are also aware that it can be discouraging for students to see software that they cannot afford, and many popular software titles (e.g., Web-page construction kits) may be out of reach for a large number of students. In an effort to avoid commercial endorsements and pricey software, this book emphasizes the use of freeware (with two or three exceptions where no good freeware was available).

This policy may perplex some instructors and experienced Netizens, who may find themselves wondering why the book showcases an obscure piece of freeware instead of a popular shareware alternative. In all cases, I have tested each of these freeware options myself and have found them to be largely comparable to their better-known $20–$30 counterparts. When it comes to software, high prices and high quality do not always go hand in hand. Some students need to cut corners, and software is one place where students can exploit the Internet to great advantage.

For those who prefer to see a perfect match between the software in front of them and blow-by-blow instructions in a textbook, I would suggest putting more emphasis on the underlying functionality of comparable software packages and less emphasis on software-specific details. There is nothing terribly unique about most Internet software applications. The underlying functionality of a Web browser, an FTP client, or a download manager does not vary a great deal from program to program. It's a rare piece of software that distinguishes itself with truly original operations and features. This is good news for users: If you master one application, you can master any other application of the same type without much trouble. The menus and check boxes won't be identical, but the basic commands and preferences will all be there.

Software is constantly being upgraded and replaced, just like everything else on the Net. If we publish detailed instructions for a particular software exercise, there is an excellent chance those instructions will be obsolete within a year. Once again, it makes sense to focus on the basic functionality of an Internet application rather than on specific command lists and instructions. We do illustrate selected preference settings with screenshots for the sake of having some concrete examples, but no attempt has been made to provide comprehensive coverage at this level of detail.

HANDS-ON LEARNING

We may steer clear of in-depth software tutorials, but we emphatically stress that there is no substitute for hands-on software experience. No one can learn about the Internet without getting online and working with Internet software applications. To facilitate software mastery, many chapters have software checklists that enumerate the most important things you should be able to do with a given piece of software. We do not tell you how to do them, just that you should be able to do them. For readers who have trouble with a software checklist, solutions for all of the most popular software applications are available at `http://www.awl.com/lehnertweb101/checklists/`. In this way, readers using different software can still tackle a software checklist and get the help they need—not from the book, but from the book's Web site. When the software changes, we will update our checklist solutions with solutions for new software releases or entirely new software packages as needed. Additional opportunities for first-hand software experience will be found in exercises that have been marked **[Hands on]**.

PEDAGOGICAL FEATURES

Each chapter is divided into two sections: a section containing core topics, followed by a separate section containing optional topics. At the end of each core section you will find:

Things to Remember—Facts, tips, and reminders

Important Concepts—Key terminology and definitions

Where Can I Learn More?—URLs for relevant Web sites

Problems and Exercises, Including three special types of questions:

- **[Find It Online]**—Find the answer on the Web
- **[Hands On]**—Gain experience with software
- **[Take a Stand]**—Present and defend an opinion

Optional chapter topics follow the core material: Each optional section is titled **Above and Beyond**. These topics augment or complement the core chapter material, and give students an opportunity to further enrich their understanding of the Internet. At the end of the optional section is a second set of exercises, **Above and Beyond: Problems and Exercises**, which covers only the optional material.

Throughout the text, we also distinguish notable material using a system of five reference boxes:

Tips and Tricks—Useful information of practical value

Definitions—Definitions for important terms or phrases

Checklists—Do-it-yourself software checklists

For Your Information—Related facts or background material

Quotations—Relevant quotations by Internet experts

Glossary Terms

Important words and phrases appear boldfaced throughout the text. A glossary of the most important terms is also included at the end of the book for easy reference.

Web Sites to Visit

References to Web sites are printed in blue. Links for all of these Web sites can be found at `http://www.awl.com/lehnertweb101/`.

Color Insert

These colored pages illustrate some key ideas for Web-page authors, including glossy image compression, tiling patterns for Web-page backgrounds, the use of transparent GIFs to create special effects, color samplers, and the use of tables and frames to control Web-page layouts. All these concepts come alive with color, enhancing the exposition of Chapters 4 and 5.

Index

A comprehensive index makes it easy to track down all references to specific terms or concepts.

TOPICS AND CHAPTER SELECTION

Getting Started - Chapter 1

To get off the ground, we introduce the Internet in Chapter 1. Most importantly, we use this chapter to introduce a core vocabulary which will be used throughout the book. We cover important Internet concepts and practical tips for working with Web browsers. Most of this material should be familiar to a seasoned Netizen, but the newbies will find Chapter 1 an important prerequisite for everything that follows.

Optional topics include a brief history of the Internet, an introduction to packet switching, and a discussion of file compression.

Staying Safe Online - Chapter 2

There are some very real dangers online. Many will be discussed in great detail throughout the book. But we have devoted Chapter 2 to the topic of personal safety so you'll have everything you need to know in one place. If you master Chapter 2, you'll steer clear of the most serious mistakes that people make online. Optional topics include intellectual property laws for the Internet, notice and consent policies, how cookies work, safeguards for computers with broadband connections, and a brief history of computer hacking.

Coping with E-Mail - Chapter 3

Everyone uses e-mail these days, but not everyone has it under control. Chapter 3 begins with the basic operations of any good e-mail program and covers the rules of e-mail netiquette that everyone should know. We look at different e-mail services (POP, IMAP, HTTP) and discuss the pros and cons of each service. Then we move on to filtering, routing, and some general mail-management tips. Optional topics include spam, the challenge of managing multiple e-mail accounts, a tutorial on "raggy" text (how to prevent it), and uuencoded mail messages.

Basic Web-Page Construction - Chapter 4

Web pages are easy to create and can be a lot of fun. Chapter 4 introduces HTML, the language of all Web pages. We explain and illustrate the elements of beginning HTML, concluding with a presentation of tables and frames. With this level of knowledge, students can construct a recreational Web page, spruce up a seller's listing at eBay, or add some pizazz to an e-mail newsletter. For those who want to learn more, this is a good foundation for intermediate tutorials and more advanced topics in Web-page construction. Optional topics include download optimizations, hit counter services, and fair use guidelines for multimedia.

Advanced Web-Page Construction - Chapter 5

Many people are drawn to the Web because of its graphics; they want to work with photographs, special effects, and animation. Others are interested in interactive Web pages; they want to add a guestbook or an opinion poll to their Web pages. In Chapter 5 we'll give you a taste of what can be done with image maps, JavaScript, and Java applets. We show how nonprogrammers can add existing scripts and applets to their Web pages, drawing from extensive script and applet archives for Web-page developers. Some students will want to learn JavaScript or Java in order to pursue advanced Web-page construction in depth. Others will be content to exploit "plug-and-play" Web-page enhancements from a developer's archive. In either case, this chapter shows everyone how to get started with image flips, data-driven text displays, site mappers, and other advanced Web-page features. Optional topics include CGI scripts and RAD editors.

Searching for Information Online - Chapter 6

You might be wasting a lot of time if you keep going back to the same old search engine every time you need to hunt down information on the Net. Chapter 6 presents a systematic approach to online searching. We describe three different types of search tools, and explain which tools are best for what types of questions. We show how to use successive query refinement to get the best possible results, and we finish up with a discussion of quality assessment. Optional topics include concepts in information retrieval and the difficulty of indexing the entire Web.

Virtual Communities - Chapter 7

People are social animals. We grow up in a family, we hang out with friends, and we talk to anyone who will listen. On the Internet, our social selves take on whole new personas. No longer limited to nearby neighbors and face-to-face contact, we can reach out to fellow Netizens across the country or around the world. People tend to look for others with common interests, and the Internet is one huge, never-ending college mixer (minus the bodies and the body language). Once you learn where to look, you can find entire communities of people who share some of your interests and enjoy talking about them. Chapter 7 covers mailing lists, Web-based discussion groups, Usenet newsgroups, online chat, and instant messaging. Optional topics include censorship on the Net, privacy safeguards, and Internet telephony.

Getting Software from the Net - Chapter 8

Once you learn how to download software from the Internet, you may never visit a software retail outlet again. Excellent software can be obtained (without stealing) for free, and other software is available for a free evaluation—you can give it a test drive on your own computer before you buy. Then if you still want to invest in shrink-wrapped software, you can use a "shopping bot" to shop around for the best prices in a snap. Chapter 8 spells out everything you need to know to find, download, and install software from the Internet. Optional topics include the open-source software movement and Trojan horses.

Power Tools for the Internet - Chapter 9

One of the big differences between an Internet newcomer and an experienced old hand is the software he or she uses. A plain vanilla Web browser is fine for a beginner, but anyone who spends a lot of time on the Web would probably benefit from a customized version of that same browser. Chapter 9 introduces Web accelerators, ad filters, download managers, password managers, desktop portals, alternative Web browsers, and advanced FTP features. Optional topics include cookie managers, firewalls, Net monitors, and Telnet clients.

E-commerce - Chapter 10

A well-designed e-store makes it easy to shop online, but an educated consumer has to know more than any e-store can be expected to explain. Chapter 10 tells you what you need to know about SSL, digital certificates, certificate authorities, and online auctions. This background will help you to understand and assess the level of risk associated with any e-store or auction site on the Web. Optional topics include the hacker threat, digital telephony, digital convergence, and Internet appliances.

Encryption on the Net - Chapter 11

Encryption offers a solution to a lot of problems on the Internet, including system security, private communication, and verifiable authentication for documents, software and Web sites. Although specific encryption techniques cannot be described in detail to a nontechnical audience, general approaches can be described to a general audience. Chapter 11 explains both private and public-key encryption, how digital signatures work, and the difference between strong and weak encryption. Optional topics include PGP, privacy-enhanced e-mail, encryption as a tool for law enforcement, and U.S. export restrictions.

Putting It All Together - Chapter 12

Once you know the basics, it's time to get down to business. Chapter 12 talks about the discipline needed to work online productively, what it takes to be a successful telecommuter, preparation for a career in information technology (IT), and the danger signs of Internet addiction.

CHAPTER SELECTION FOR DIFFERENT COURSES

This book was written for students enrolled in a course devoted to the Internet, as well as students in computer-literacy courses or other courses in which the Internet is only part of the curriculum. A curriculum based on all the core sections of this book will easily fill a 15-week course aimed at (non-CS) undergraduates. A 15-week curriculum based on both the core and optional sections would be appropriate for an undergraduate (non-CS) honors course. Other combinations of chapters with or without the optional sections can be combined to support concentrations, intersession workshops, or independent projects (see below).

- A 15-week course devoted to the Internet:
  Chapters 1–12 skipping some small number of selected core sections if need be.
- A 15-week honors course devoted to the Internet:
  Chapters 1–12 including all optional Above and Beyond (A&B) sections.

- An intensive (6-week) Internet concentration within a computer-literacy course:
  Chapters 1, 2, 3, 3A&B, 4.1–4.5, 4.9, 6, 7.1–7.4, 10

- A short (4-week) Internet concentration within a computer-literacy course:
  Chapters 1, 2, 3.1–3.4, 4.1–4.5, 6.1–6.6, 7.1–7.4

- An intensive (3-week) Internet concentration in an introductory computer-science course:
  Chapters 1, 1A&B, 2, 2A&B, 6.1–6.3, 7.1–7.6, 8, 8A&B, 11, 11A&B

- A workshop or independent project on Web-page construction:
  Chapters 1, 1A&B, 2, 2A&B, 4, 4A&B, 5, 5A&B

- A workshop or independent project on Internet search techniques:
  Chapters 1, 2, 6, 6A&B, 7, 8.1–8.6, 9.2, 9.7

- A workshop or independent project on software downloads:
  Chapters 1, 1A&B, 2, 2AB, 8, 8A&B, 9, 9A&B

- A workshop or independent project on social and legal issues:
  Chapters 2, 2A&B, 3.9.1, 3.9.2, 4.10, 4.11.3, 7.8, 7.9.1, 7.9.2, 8A&B, 10, 10.7.1, 11, 11A&B

A NOTE TO THE STUDENT

As the Internet evolves, we all have to struggle to keep up, and the first step is a solid foundation. Seemingly mundane activities such as a trip to an e-store can turn into a regrettable undertaking if you don't know how to spot a secure Web server, how to protect personal information from data resellers, or to expect the unexpected. Other problems creep in over time. For example, e-mail is a breeze until you start getting 100 messages a day. Then you need to get organized and take advantage of specialized tools for e-mail management.

Ignorance of computer security is another pitfall for newcomers to the Internet. Each time you connect to the Internet, you open the door to possible hacker attacks. If you visit a poorly designed e-store, your credit-card number could be stolen. Spend some time at another site, and highly personal or sensitive information can wind up in countless databases. You can break the law by downloading the wrong file, or you could find yourself visited by the FBI, or on the receiving end of a lawsuit for speaking candidly about the wrong subject in an online forum.

There is more to understanding the Internet than self-preservation and self-defense. For example, remarkable software is available on the Net—and much of it is free. But you have to know how to find it and how to move it onto your computer. There are some important do's and don'ts when it comes to free software, and all the basics are here. Then when you're ready to take advantage of all the Net has to offer, we'll show you some downloads that can transform your whole Internet experience.

Whether you expect to use the Net personally or professionally, this book will give you the skills you need to make the Net a real asset. No one can say what the Internet will be like five or ten years from now, but the people who are using the Internet today will help shape the Internet of tomorrow. In a very real way, this technology belongs to you and is yours to mold. Every week, some Congressional hearing in Washington touches on the Internet in one way or another. Children need to be protected. Consumers need to be protected. Musicians and artists need to be protected. A burgeoning e-commerce needs to be nurtured, and a digital divide between the rich and the poor needs to be crossed. Learn about the Internet today, and you will get the Internet you want tomorrow.

A NOTE TO THE INSTRUCTOR

If you've taught an Internet course before, you know the Internet is not your only moving target. Your students are changing at least as fast as the Net itself, and it may be necessary to take their collective pulse two or three times a year. We know that college students tend to be very interested in music: Many students already know how to find and download music files from the Net. Some students have mastered the know-how needed to find and download software from the Net because they've investigated their MP3 player options (the software needed to play music files found on the Net). These same students have probably been using e-mail for at least a year or two, they may have dabbled in Web-page construction, and they have probably purchased at least one item online. We know that online chat is also quite popular among students, and a growing number of students are learning to use the Internet to make long-distance phone calls at reduced rates. We hope that students are also using the Internet to enhance their education and find valuable information. Evidence suggests this is true: We know that 80% of all students graduating in 1999 used the Internet to search for a job or research a prospective employer.

The Digital Divide

If you conduct a survey of your students, you will find that many are knowledgeable about e-mail and Web browsers, others are very experienced with a wide range of Internet resources and applications, and a few have managed to miss out on everything and are desperate to catch up. This wide range of expertise is a major challenge facing all instructors of the Internet. You need to hold the interest of the more experienced students while getting the less experienced students off the ground. If the digital divide is dramatically apparent in your classroom, your syllabus must be flexible and your assignments must somehow accommodate everyone.

In the Instructor's Manual (IM) that accompanies this text, I address the very real problem of the digital divide. Students who do not have their own computers will not be able to do some of the hands-on chapter exercises, even if computing facilties are available to your students in computer labs. Security concerns usually prohibit students from downloading and installing software from the Internet in educational computer labs, and this will be a problem for some of the exercises in Chapters 8 and 9. I have some suggestions in the IM for handling this, as well as other problems related to the digital divide.

Wizards in the Classroom

Courses about the Internet are usually fun for both students and teachers, but neither should underestimate the amount of work involved. Everyone is struggling to keep abreast of the most valuable Internet tools and resources. You should expect to find at least one or two students who are more experienced than you are with some aspects of the Internet (the "wizards"). I tell you how to identify these individuals early on and give you some suggestions on how to turn their expertise into a classroom asset.

With each new class, an instructor should always revisit the question of where to start, how fast to move, and how much material to cover. In the case of the Internet, initial class assessments are even more important. In the IM, I show you how to assess your class with a few casual questions during your first class meeting. Not only can you benchmark your class in general, but you can smoke out the wizards right from the start.

The Instructors Manual

The IM also contains all the usual things you hope to find in an IM:

- Solutions to all the problems and exercises in the book
- A large archive of test questions, indexed by chapter and section
- Chapter notes and teaching tips
- Suggested classroom demonstrations
- Suggested class projects
- A checklist of things to do at the start of the semester
- A sample class syllabus (with variations)

All recipients of the IM are also welcome to join my Internet 101 Mailing List for Internet instructors (see http://www.awl.com/lehnertweb101/ for instructions on how to subscribe). Members are welcome to post questions, ask for advice, report on classroom experiments, and look for inspiration in our collective classroom experience.

I've had a lot of fun teaching undergraduates about the Internet, and I have written the IM for both the inexperienced first timer as well as for the experienced teacher who is looking for ways to improve an existing course offering. Students bring considerable enthusiasm to the subject of the Internet; all you have to do is sustain it. The Internet itself is always a plentiful source of timely Internet-related news items.

Plus, students who have been online for a year or more have probably had their own first-hand learning experiences. If you draw from the news as it happens, and encourage selected students to participate in your class presentations, you can sustain a high level of interest and involvement (your own included) for an entire semester.

WHY THE IGUANA?

For those who are curious about the cover of this book, I suppose I should say a few words about the iguana. The green iguana is a fitting symbol for everything that is unique and wonderful about the Internet. Iguanas are surprisingly popular in the United States as pets, especially among college students and the 20- or 30-something crowd. Unfortunately, much published misinformation is available to a prospective iguana owner about what constitutes a healthy diet or how an iguana should be housed. Luckily for the iguana, many iguana enthusiasts are active on the Internet and talking to each other. Questions from beginners are being answered in great detail by herpetologists and experienced iguana owners. Thanks to the Internet, this native inhabitant of tropical rain forests now thrives in Arizona, Alaska, and all kinds of intemperate regions. The iguana community is not a place you will find on any map, but it is alive and well on the Internet!

ACKNOWLEDGMENTS

Many people helped make this book possible. First and foremost, I am indebted to my colleagues in the Computer Science Department at the University of Massachusetts who encouraged me to develop an undergraduate course on the Internet. I am also deeply indebted to the many undergraduate students who have taken my course and given me valuable feedback on my choice of topics, exercises, and examples. The enthusiasm and achievements of my students have kept me interested in the challenge of teaching the Internet to non-Computer Science majors in spite of all the work that necessarily accompanies a moving-target curriculum. There are also many individuals behind the scenes who have also worked to make my classroom efforts pay off. Just as I was starting this book, Steve Cook, Director of the Computer Science Computing Facility at UMass-Amherst, orchestrated a move of 500 computers, along with 300 faculty, staff, and graduate students, into a new Computer Science building without missing a beat (an astonishing achievement that made the mere writing of a textbook look thoroughly straightforward). For many years now, Terrie Kellogg has managed my educational UNIX accounts and suggested useful accommodations for my command-mode-challenged Internet students. I also continue to benefit from the just-in-time interventions of my lab manager, David Fisher, who has inexplicably resisted the lure of big bucks in order to serve his alma mater and keep me functional. And last, but not least, the departmental technical support staff at UMass have given me invaluable support by making it a point to answer any and all questions as quickly as possible.

My best defense against inaccuracies and outright errors were my many reviewers, who were remarkably generous in providing me with detailed feedback, corrections, and suggestions. My reviewers assisted me greatly in my humble attempt to produce a manuscript that is free of errors and omissions. Heartfelt thanks to Jeffrey R. Brown (Montana State University—Great Falls), Janet Brunelle (Old Dominion University), Jack Brzezinski (DePaul University), Peter G. Clote (Boston College), Paul De Palma (Gonzaga University), Michael Gildersleeve (University of New Hampshire), Martin Granier (Western Washington University), Stephanie Ludi (Arizona State University), Jayne Valenti Miller (Purdue University), Lori L. Scarlatos (Brooklyn College—CUNY), and Scott Tilley (University of California—Riverside). This book benefited greatly from their expertise. With all of this excellent assistance, any errors that may have found their way onto these pages are mine and mine alone.

Many thanks also to everyone at Addison Wesley who supported me in this endeavor. This book would never have been written without the support and encouragement of Acquisitions Editor Susan Hartman Sullivan, whose enthusiasm and confidence kept the project on target in spite of an accelerated production schedule. Assistant Editor Elinor Actipis marshalled reviewer feedback, kept an eye on all the copyright permissions, answered all my questions, and helped me keep my priorities straight when too many deadlines began to get the better of me. Production Editors Helen Reebenacker and Patty Mahtani tackled the unenviable job of putting it all together and remaining cool in the face of upstream delays (mea culpa). Joe Vetere managed the graphics for our color insert, courageously assuming responsibiliy for the iguana photograph which mysteriously morphed from brown to red to green depending on the printer. Mary Boucher, Senior Permissions Editor, gave us invaluable support by handling the copyright permission requests for over 400 screen shots. My copy editor, Laura Michaels, moved through a remarkable amount of text in short order, sorting out the mess produced by imperfect typing and speech-recognition software. Webmaster Jennifer Pelland takes full credit for the design of the Web site that accompanies this text. I am grateful to Regina Hagen, who designed the book cover, and especially to Susan Cyr, our cover artist, whose fertile imagination produced a thoroughly believable iguana with a taste for MP3's.

Special thanks go to my husband, Mark Snyder, who contributed to these chapters by poring over my text and suggesting countless improvements. Finally, I want to thank my whole family for putting up with the ambiguous shadow of a mother who was simultaneously there and not there for the six months it took me to write this book. Unexpected life forms flourished in the fridge, dust bunnies roamed the hallways with confidence, and the kids acquired important macaroni and cheese survival skills. As the mathematician in *Jurassic Park* remarked, "Life finds a way . . ."

Wendy Lehnert (August 2000)

Contents

CHAPTER 4   Basic Web Page Construction   157

CHAPTER 7   Joining a Virtual Community   379

CHAPTER 8   Software on the Internet   457

First Things First

CHAPTER GOALS

- Understand the purpose of your computer's CPU, RAM, and hard drive.
- Learn about bits, bytes, kilobytes, megabytes, and gigabytes.
- Find out how the Internet is structured and how computers become part of the Internet.
- Discover how IP and DNS addresses are used.
- Master the basic navigational features of your Web browser.

1.1 TAKING CHARGE

As a college student, you have probably spent quite a few hours on the *Internet*, also called the *Net*, even if you don't own a computer. In 1999, over 90% of U.S. college students had access to the Net, and 80% of graduating college students used it to search for a job or research a prospective employer. It's time to set aside all of the hype about how the Internet is changing everything—the ability of the Internet to transform our lives is a given. Now we need to get down to the serious business of really putting the Internet to work for us.

Each of us brings our own interests and needs to the Internet. By using Internet resources intelligently, we can be better informed, better connected to others who share our interests, and better able to pursue our goals. However, attaining this ideal won't happen automatically. We can easily spend too much time socializing in chat rooms or surfing for entertainment or exploring online games. In order to make time online productive and professional, we must begin by learning about the Internet and software applications for the Internet.

Most people do not fully appreciate how many choices color our experience of the Internet. Surveys show that most Internet users start with one Web browser (typical-

1

ly the one that came with their computer) and never experiment with alternative browsers. Chances are, these people have never bothered to think about their browser options and whether they're working with the browser that's best for them. However, the choice of a browser is simply one in a long list of software options that can make the difference between a productive Internet experience and an ineffective or frustrating one.

The Internet has evolved rapidly in recent years, and this pace will likely continue well into the future. Keeping up with it can divert us from other interests and goals that deserve attention. However, the Net can be tamed and put to good use if we are serious about using it wisely. The trick is to figure out when we are using the Net effectively and when we are floundering. Then, we can take charge, of our expectations and of our time, in order to maintain the right balance between our online activities and the rest of our lives.

Taking charge means cutting a swathe through the overwhelming number of choices and options that the Net offers. Our lives are shaped by choices that we make at each step along the way. We each choose our friends, our interests, and our beliefs. We also choose clothes, cars, hair styles, music, meals, pets, and insurance plans. The list is long, and at times, overwhelming. The Internet can help us make better choices by showing us available options, useful facts, and provocative opinions. The Internet also puts us in direct touch with a dizzying rate of technological change unparalleled in human history. We are clearly dealing with a transforming technology. The trick is to make sure that we stay in charge of the transformation.

Much of the challenge before us comes down to plain old time management and the realization that the Internet can be a time sink just as easily as it can be a time-saver. We can conserve and optimize time, in part, by making informed selections of Internet software, based on a practical understanding of the Internet and its resources. For example, if you dial into the Internet over a telephone line, a *Web accelerator* (see Section 9.3) might cut in half the amount of time that you spend waiting for Web pages to download. If you are dealing with large amounts of e-mail, you can take steps to save time and manage those mountains of messages more efficiently (see Section 3.7). If you download a lot of files and a download needs to be resumed or scheduled during off-hours, a good download manager (see Section 9.5) can free you to concentrate on other things. And if you spend a lot of time tracking down information using search engines, some powerful browser enhancements can speed you through those searches by cutting through all of the garbage (see Sections 6.7 and 6.8). Of course, when you're still learning it's hard to know what you need to know. That's why it pays to take some time to learn about the Internet software options available for Internet users today.

This book is a good place to start. It will introduce you to the most powerful Internet tools that every Internet user should know about. It will also prepare you to choose your Internet tools wisely regardless of how you intend to use the Internet: for work, for pleasure, or both.

Before we start, let's make sure that we're all speaking the same language. Computer jargon is a stumbling block for many Internet newcomers (often called *newbies*) because they've never bothered to learn the basics. This chapter will help you demystify the most commonly encountered jargon. Computers are typically characterized by the software that they run, how fast that they run, and the amount of memory that they contain. We will tell you what you need to know about computer software, computer speed, and computer memory in the next section.

1.2 COMPUTER BASICS

1.2.1 The Operating System

The heart of any computer is its operating system. An **operating system (OS)** is a large program that starts whenever you turn on your computer. The most important program running on your computer, the OS is necessary for other programs, called *application programs*, to run. It is like a computer's nervous system. It recognizes input from the keyboard and mouse, keeps track of files, updates the time display, tells you when you have a problem—it generally is there to respond to your input. Without an OS, your computer cannot perform any of the fundamental tasks that make it useful. If something is wrong with your OS, you have major problems.

The world of *personal computers* has long been divided into two camps based on the OS that they run: *Microsoft Windows*™ or *Apple's OS for the Macintosh*. The vast majority of personal computer users run Windows. However, other OSs are available. For example, **Linux** (a version of *UNIX*) is popular primarily with programmers and experienced computer users, but it is gaining a foothold in business environments as an increasingly popular alternative to Windows. Another alternative OS is *BeOS*. A computer that runs Windows is often called a **PC (personal computer)** to distinguish it from a Macintosh computer, called a Mac for short. For simplicity, this book uses the term *personal computer* to mean both PCs and Macs. When it comes to the Internet, PCs and Macs are largely indistinguishable, although software is generally written for one or the other: As a rule, software written for a PC will not run on a Mac and software written for a Mac will not run on a PC. We will explain why in the next section. Throughout this book, you will find many examples of Internet software in action. These examples are based on software for PCs, but if you have a Mac, don't worry. Whenever you hear about a piece of PC software, there is something analogous for Macs. In Chapter 8 we will show you how to find and select software for personal computers (both PCs and Macs).

A newly purchased computer usually comes with an OS already installed. Upgrading to a new version of the OS is usually easy, although you'll want to set aside half a day for the process. Switching to an entirely new OS is a major project and is best managed with a second computer on hand so that you can revert to your old OS if needed.

1.2.2 The Central Processing Unit

The part of the personal computer that performs instructions is the **central processing unit** (**CPU**). The hardware unit that houses the CPU in a personal computer is called a **microprocessor** (the Pentium III and the G4 are two examples of microprocessors). Microprocessors normally contain additional hardware that supports the CPU, but the two terms are often used interchangeably in casual conversation. The CPU is the brain of the computer—it is where most of the computation takes place. In terms of computing power, it is the most important part of the computer—in general, the faster the CPU, the faster the computer. A CPU is distinguished by three characteristics:

- its speed (called the *clock speed*)
- its instruction set
- bandwidth (the amount of information it can manipulate at one time)

A CPU's **clock speed** determines how many instructions per second that it can execute. Clock speed is given in megahertz (MHz), a unit that refers to one million cycles per second, where a **cycle** is the smallest unit of time recognized by the computer's internal clock. A CPU running at 800 MHz goes through 800 million processing cycles in one second. You may also see descriptions of CPU speed in terms of MIPS (1 MIPS = 1 million instructions per second) although this measure is less meaningful because different instructions require a different number of cycles. CPU speeds in personal computers get faster and faster each year. If your computer is three years old, its CPU is probably running at less than a third or even a quarter of the CPU speed of personal computers sold today. You can do little to speed up an old CPU. As a result, used computers are not in great demand, unless they are relatively new.

Moore's Law

Computers double in speed at least every 18 months and do so without any increase in cost.

A CPU is also distinguished by its instruction set. An **instruction set** (also called **machine instructions**) describes the collection of operations that the CPU can execute. One instruction may be used to negate an integer, while a different instruction is used to add two integers. While instructions like these are standard fare, other instructions may be specific to a particular microprocessor. As a result, a Motorola CPU runs a different instruction set than does an Intel CPU. At the lowest level, all software operates by executing operations in a specific instruction set. For example, Macs use a Motorola CPU because the Mac OS relies on the Motorola instruction set. To run Windows, you need an Intel CPU (or another brand that supports the Intel instruction set) because Windows relies on the Intel instruction set. It is possible to simulate the Intel instruction set on a Motorola CPU and therefore run

Windows on a Mac. However, OS simulations tend to run slowly because the target instruction set has to be simulated by the native instruction set. For this reason, OS simulations are never as satisfactory as an OS running on native hardware (the microprocessor that runs the required instruction set directly).

Computer engineers can achieve significant speed-ups by increasing the **bandwidth** (sometimes called the *data width*) of a microprocessor. More bandwidth means that a CPU can receive, manipulate, and return more data during each processing cycle. Instruction sets need to be modified so they can keep up with larger data transfers—it will do no good to hand a CPU a larger block of data if all of its instructions are still designed to handle smaller amounts of data. CPU speed, instruction sets, and bandwidth all work together to determine the overall computing power of your computer.

1.2.3 Memory

A computer's memory is its internal storage area and consists of several different types, including

- random access memory and
- long-term memory.

Random Access Memory The memory that the CPU uses when it executes its machine instructions is **random access memory** (**RAM**), also called **main memory**. RAM is often called **fast memory** because the CPU can write to and read from it very quickly, thereby enabling the CPU to perform its operations as quickly as possible. RAM is also *volatile* memory: when you turn off your computer, all data in RAM is lost.

RAM is sometimes described as a computer's version of human short-term memory. That is, the amount of space is limited and the information that it contains doesn't stay there for long. However, it is a crucial gateway to your computer; much of the information going in and out of your computer moves through its version of short-term memory.

Each program that you run on your computer requires some minimal amount of RAM. When running more than one program at a time, your computer allocates a fixed amount of the available RAM to each program. If there is enough RAM to go around, everything works as it should. But if those running programs collectively require more RAM than is available, then the OS resorts to various *memory management strategies*, which might or might not work very well. Your computer might respond very slowly when it is working with less RAM than it needs or might crash more often when you try to run too many programs at once. It is usually a good idea to buy as much RAM as you can afford (although all computers do have limits on the amount of RAM that can be installed). When you buy a new computer, never settle for the minimal RAM configuration. Research the software you want to run and then ask for at least twice as much RAM as the various software manufacturers say you should have. If you already have a computer that tends to crash when you open too many applications, check to see if your computer has room for more RAM. An ailing computer can often be made healthy with a RAM upgrade.

Long-Term Memory A different type of memory is used for long-term storage. Sometimes called **slow memory**, this is the memory on your hard drive. Whereas data in RAM disappears when the power goes off, data saved on the hard drive remains in long-term memory. The hard drive can be used to save, for example, computer programs, word processing files, and spreadsheet data, as well as that partially completed tax return. The larger your hard drive, the more files you can save and the more programs you can store on your computer. Whereas a lot of RAM can help your computer run faster, a large hard drive allows you to install many applications, such as word processors and games.

Personal computers may contain other types of memory and microprocessors. For example, some CPUs include their own built-in short-term memory that is faster than RAM (for example, the L1 cache in Power Macintosh computers). In addition, most computers contain a **floating-point unit** (**FPU**), a special microprocessor designed to handle floating-point arithmetic, which is crucial for speedy graphics displays. However, for the purposes of this book the most important hardware components are the CPU, RAM, and the hard drive as described here.

Computer Checklist: Get to Know Your Computer

Find out the hardware specs for your home computer:

1. How much RAM do you have?
2. How large is your hard drive?
3. How fast is your CPU?

If you don't know the answers, consult the Help feature for your OS and look for information about your *system resources*. Depending on your OS, you might need to find the answers in a few different places.

1.3 UNITS OF MEMORY

As people have become increasingly enamored with the Internet, many applications have surfaced to enhance the online experience. Many of these enable multimedia communication (audio and video) over the Internet. Software designers are always pushing the envelope regarding what can be done on available hardware. In turn, hardware manufacturers labor to produce faster CPUs and larger hard drives at affordable prices. Many leading-edge software applications tend to stress all but the most current and powerful computers, but software manufacturers know that hardware advances will make these products more accessible in a year or two—at least for those users who have access to the latest computers.

To understand how computing limitations can affect your experiences on the Net, you need to understand how files work. A **file** is a collection of data that has a name (the filename). Almost all the information stored in a computer is stored in a file. Thus the file is the building block of everything that we see and hear online. Files are constantly being moved across that Net, and different software applications work with different types of files. The size of a file often determines how long you must wait for an application to do something with the file, so it is important to know how big your files are. Files come in all sizes, from tiny to gigantic. In the next two sections we will explain how file sizes can be described with great precision.

1.3.1 The Bit

The smallest unit of measurement for computer data is called the bit. A **bit** is a memory unit that can hold one of two possible values: 0 or 1. All data inside of a computer is represented by *patterns* of bits. Small amounts of information can be represented by a small number of bits and larger amounts of information require more bits. The value of a bit stored in RAM or on your hard drive can be changed by software. When your CPU executes an instruction, it often stores a bit pattern in RAM, performs some manipulation on that pattern, and produces a new bit pattern as the result of the instruction. When you write over old files on your hard drive, you erase old patterns of bits and replace them with new patterns of bits. By contrast, read-only media such as a read-only CD-ROM or DVD disc consists of bits that cannot be changed.

What Is a 32-Bit System?

If you are a Windows user, you might have seen references to a *32-bit system* or *32-bit software*. The number of bits refers to the amount of memory that a CPU can reference by naming specific memory locations (also known as *addresses*). The range of addresses that a CPU can reference is called an *address space*. In a 32-bit system, both the OS and the CPU can work with 2^{32} memory locations (this is called a *32-bit address space*) by chunking 32 bits into a single unit that can be moved in and out of the CPU in a single cycle. Video game consoles have progressed from 8-bit CPUs (for example, the original Nintendo game) to 128-bit CPUs (for example, the Sega Dreamcast system).

Software described as 32-bit has been programmed to take full advantage of a 32-bit CPU. Windows 95/98/NT (Win95/98/NT) are 32-bit OSs; Windows 3.1 was a 16-bit OS. Applications for Win95/98 can be either 16-bit or 32-bit, but a 32-bit application will run faster because it can move twice as much information in and out of the CPU in a single cycle. The Macintosh G4 computer is a 128-bit system.

The actual speed of a computer depends on, as mentioned earlier, the CPU's clock speed, the intrinsic power of the CPU's instruction set, the number of bytes that can be transferred into and out of the CPU in a single instruction, as well as other features not described here.

1.3.2 The Byte and Beyond

The next level up from the bit is the byte. A **byte** is a pattern of 8 bits, for example 00101110. Patterns of bits are used to represent the letters of the English alphabet (among others). It takes only 5 bits to create 32 (= $2 \times 2 \times 2 \times 2 \times 2$) distinct patterns, more than enough to code the letters A through Z. Only 7 bits are required to code both lowercase and uppercase characters, numerical digits, and punctuation marks, with room to spare. Even the extra bit is put to good use for something called *error checking*, which makes it possible to detect transmission errors when bytes are moved from one computer to another. Therefore a byte is quite convenient when you want to represent all of the symbols that a keyboard can produce.

Interestingly, Japanese was initially a problem for software designers because Japanese characters could not be adequately represented using 8-bit bytes. To handle the Japanese language, computers had to be programmed to work with 16-bit patterns (sometimes called *16-bit words*).

The set of visible characters that you can type on a standard keyboard are referred to as **ASCII characters** because they are represented by a code for encoding 128 characters called the **ASCII character code** (see Figure 1.1). **ASCII text files** are files that contain only ASCII characters. **Binary files** contain additional characters not found on any keyboard (these files are usually generated by computer programs). The size of a file (either ascii or binary) is measured by the number of bytes used to represent its contents. This number is more or less equivalent to the number of characters in the file. For example, a page of text that contains 60 lines of text, and 110 characters per line, contains 6,600 characters, which consumes 6,600 bytes of memory.

Kilobytes, Megabytes, and Gigabytes For easy reference, bytes are grouped into larger units. For example, a **kilobyte (KB)** consists of 1,024 bytes. (In casual writing, you might see the abbreviation K instead of KB.) Although the term *kilo* means 1,000, a kilobyte contains 1,024 bytes rather than 1,000 bytes as might be expected. This is because the arithmetic of computers works with binary (*base-2*) representations for numbers—recall that a bit can hold either of only two values: 0 or 1. This contrasts with a base-10 system, such as the decimal system that is used to represent numbers throughout the industrialized world. Just as the number $1,000_{(base\ 10)}$ = 10^3 is a nice round number in the decimal system, The number 1,024 is a nice round number in base-2 because $1,024_{(base\ 10)} = 1,000,000,000_{(base\ 2)} = 2^{10}$. When you need only a rough estimate, you can think of a kilobyte as being 1,000 bytes. However, for precision, use 1,024 bytes. Thus one page of text that contains 6,600

Figure 1.1:
The ASCII Character
Set

	0	1	2	3	4	5	6	7	8	9	A	B	C	D	E	F
0	NUL	SOH	STX	ETX	EOT	ENQ	ACK	BEL	BS	HT	LF	VT	FF	CR	SO	SI
1	DLE	DC1	DC2	DC3	DC4	NAK	SYN	ETB	CAN	EM	SUB	ESC	FS	GS	RS	US
2	SPC	!	"	#	$	%	&	'	(	)	*	+	,	–	.	/
3	0	1	2	3	4	5	6	7	8	9	:	;	<	=	>	?
4	@	A	B	C	D	E	F	G	H	I	J	K	L	M	N	O
5	P	Q	R	S	T	U	V	W	X	Y	Z	[	\	]	^	_
6	`	a	b	c	d	e	f	g	h	i	j	k	l	m	n	o
7	p	q	r	s	t	u	v	w	x	y	z	{	|	}	~	DEL

bytes consumes approximately 6.6KB of memory, or, more precisely, 6.45KB (rounded to the nearest hundredth).

The Sinclair Computer

One of the first personal computers sold in the late 1970s, the Sinclair ZX81 came with 1KB of RAM and cost $100. If you could afford it, you could spend an additional $100 and add an extra 16KB of RAM. This was considered a tremendous amount of memory in those days.

If you need to deal only with text, you can go far with just kilobytes. For really large numbers of bytes, however, a more convenient unit to work with is the megabyte. A **megabyte** (**MB**) is 2^{20} = 1024KB—roughly 1,000KB, if you need only a quick estimate. Therefore 1,000 pages of text formatted like the previous example will require 6,445KB of memory or 6.4MB approximately and 6.3MB (rounded) precisely. Most of us do not need such large amounts of memory for our text files, but megabytes are a useful unit when referring to RAM. The new larger and more powerful computer programs can consume many megabytes of RAM, and RAM installations have been increasing to handle them (see Figure 1.2).

In addition, large amounts of RAM are needed to handle the many complicated graphics that are commonplace on the Net. Compared to text, graphical images require significantly larger amounts of memory. Whoever said that a picture is worth a thousand words was lowballing the amount. One thousand words that consist of approximately 5,600 characters require an estimated 5.5KB of memory. For graphics, this would be enough memory for only one black-and-white drawing of, say, Dilbert or perhaps a small, colored arrow on a Web page. Larger images can consume 60KB or more of memory, and a high-resolution photograph (see I-1 in the color insert) can eat up as much as 600KB if nothing clever has been done to con-

Figure 1.2:
Typical RAM
Configurations for
New Computers

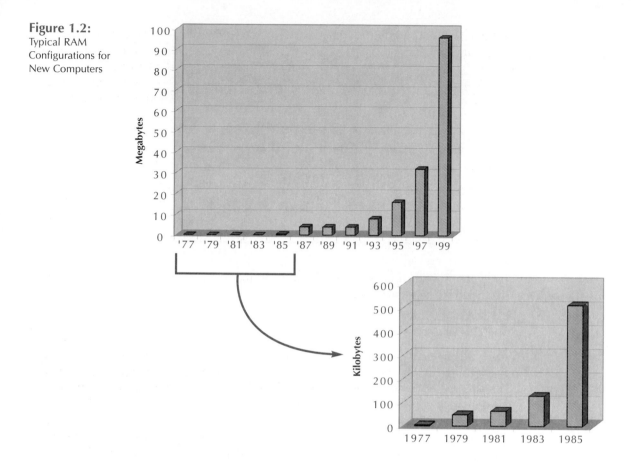

serve memory. Three large photographs might be too big for a 1.44MB **floppy disk** (although that same floppy can hold 200 pages of plain ASCII text).

As people started working more with graphics on their personal computers, they began to need larger storage devices for handling many large files. In 1995, the storage capacity of hard drives for high-end personal computers crossed the line from megabytes to gigabytes. A **gigabyte** (**GB**) is 2^{30} bytes = 1,024MB. During the same period, floppy disks began giving way to **zip disks**, which can hold 100MB to 250MB per disk, and to **jazz disks** (1GB to 2GB per disk), and to writeable **CD-ROMs** (640MB).

At the time of this writing, entry-level computers are typically configured with 13GB hard drives and high-end computers come with 40GB hard drives. Some people can easily fill up 10 GB in only a few months; heavy users, in only a few weeks. Where does all of that long-term memory go? Figure 1.3 shows a few benchmarks. Win98 requires 100MB all by itself. A large collection of screen savers could eat up another 100MB. A family photograph album can easily consume 100MB. A Web accelerator (see Chapter 9) for your Web browser requires a minimum of 200MB (you can opt to give it as much as 3GB if your appetite for the Web tends toward insatiable). With what else can you fill up a 13GB hard drive? A photographer or an artist would have no trouble using that amount of memory. Neither would the average college student.

Figure 1.3:
Where Does All
the Memory Go?

One page of plain ascii text (54 single-spaced lines, 10pt)	5KB		One Iomega Zip Disk	100MB
One color cartoon on a Web page	50KB		Three minutes of video (compressed MP3 format)	400MB
One high-resolution photograph	500KB		One CD-ROM	640MB
One floppy disk (high density—double sided)	1.44MB		A hard drive for a new PC (in the year 2000)	13GB
Three minutes of music (compressed MP3 format)	3MB		One DVD disc	4.7–17GB
One medium sized Web site (text and graphics)	50MB			

A Music Revolution Massive amounts of long-term memory in countless dormitory rooms on hundreds of college campuses across the country are consumed by something that was a college preoccupation long before computers became a standard fixture: music. Music is a true memory hog. For example, a 3-minute music file can require from 3MB to 45MB, depending on how it's stored. To minimize a hefty music file without sacrificing its content, you can use any of various *file compression techniques*. File compression is discussed in more detail in the Above and Beyond section. Without compression, for example, 10GB on a hard drive can store the equivalent of 15 audio CDs. With compression, that 10GB will store a respectable music library of approximately 200 audio CDs.

You can listen to this music on your computer, or you can invest $200 on an *MP3 player* (see the box, What Is File Compression?) designed to play digital audio files wherever you go (the programmable equivalent of a Walkman).

All of this indicates that a music revolution is underway, fueled by digital technology. And where do we get these audio files? The Internet, of course.

What Is File Compression?

Large files can be stored either in their original format or in a *compressed format* to save space. Different types of file compression are used for different types of files, such as text, graphics, and audio. You usually can reduce a large file by at least 50%, depending on the type of file and the type of compression.

In the case of audio files, for example, the **MP3 (MPEG audio layer 3)** format can be used to reduce audio files by as much as 90% to 93%. Bigger is never better when you're trying to move a large file across the Net.

Other ways to fill a 13GB hard drive include storing video files. These files require even more long-term memory than do audio files. Currently, few people collect video files from the Internet because they are so memory intensive. However, the introduction of Apple's iMac DVD SE, with its easy-to-use video editor designed for family use, is making personal computers and camcorders a powerful combination. Long-term memory requirements for video and audio files are driving consumer demand for larger hard drives on personal computers. As the cost of a hard drive continues to drop, users can be counted on to find new ways to use all of the long-term memory on their computers. In a culture in which you can never be too rich or too thin, you also can never have too much computer memory.

1.4 ▌ SPEED AND BOTTLENECKS

You will also encounter bits and bytes on the Internet. When you "go online," or connect your computer to the Internet, you create a communication channel between your computer and other computers. Data is exchanged between computers at the rate of *bits per second (bps)*. If you're connecting to the Internet from your home, you're likely dialing in over a telephone line or using a special service, such as ISDN, DSL, or cable. If you are connecting from your outside work office or a computer laboratory at school, you might have an Ethernet connection. The actual rate of data flow between any two computers on the Internet will vary, depending on competing traffic.

If you don't have broadband, then your Internet connection probably acts sluggishly sometimes. You might be feeling the effects of too much traffic on a specific server or of other traffic patterns on the Net. To find out why your connection is bogged down, you can visit the **PC Pitstop** and take the *ping test* (see Figure 1.4). Pinging is discussed in further detail in the Above & Beyond section. For now it's enough to know that a ping is a way to measure the speed of a data transmission between two computers. Ping values between 200 and 300 milliseconds (ms) are typical for computers connected via phone lines. The PC Pitstop displays test outcomes in this range with a yellow background. Unusually fast times and unusually slow times are shown with green and red backgrounds, respectively. If all of the ping test sites come back red, your ISP is probably having difficulties. If the tested sites are all green or yellow, these slowdowns are probably due to overworked servers. A mix of colors might indicate a routing problem on the Net or that some servers are overloaded. To find out what's normal for your type of connection and your ISP, take your computer's "pulse" by taking the ping test at different times of the day and on a few different days.

Figure 1.4:
Testing Your Internet
Connection at the
PC Pitstop

Test your Internet connection - Microsoft Internet Explorer

| Back | Forward | Stop | Refresh | Home | Search | Favorites | History | Mail | Print | Edit | Copernic |

Address | http://www.pcpitstop.com/pin | Go | Links » | File » | Flyswat Off | Search! (?)

PC Pitstop

PC Pitstop Home
Test My PC
Check Disk Health
Test Internet Connection
Test ActiveX
Anti-Virus
FAQ
Glossary
Statistics
Privacy
Safety
Support
Press
About Us
Store

Starting at $1599
The Gateway Performance 700 pentium... intel inside

Test Your Internet Connection

This test starts automatically and will take approximately 70 seconds to complete. You may exit it at any time by going to another page.

Can't get results? Seeing error messsages? See frequently asked questions.
Like to know more about this test? See Notes.

Site	Round-Trip Time (ms)		
	Min	Max	Avg
www.pcpitstop.com	154	189	172
www.mheller.com	187	236	207
www.byte.com	234	277	251
www.cern.ch	276	339	302
internic.net	165	1000	261
yahoo.com	220	1072	327
www.unisa.edu.au	514	1000	705

Done

http://www.pcpitstop.com/press.asp   Internet

For most home users, the major bottleneck is the computer's modem and the telephone line. A 28.8K modem can transfer data at a maximal rate of 28,800 bits per second, or 28 kilobits per second (28.8 kbps). A 56K (56 kbps) modem is capable of 56,000 bits per second. However, achieving true 56K exchange is not possible because no telephone line can keep up with that rate. A poor-quality telephone line can slow you down to about 20 kbps no matter what your modem can do. The best transmission rate you can hope for with a 56K modem is probably in the 40 kbps to 45 kbps range.

K (1,024) vs. k (1,000)

Why does 56K when referring to modems mean 56 × 1,000 bits per second (56 kbps), whereas 56KB (often written as 56K) of memory means 56 × 1,024 bytes? The ambiguity surrounding the letter "K" results because the same symbol is being used to represent both a base-10 (decimal system) kilo (1,000) and a base-2 kilo (1,024). In the context of data transmissions, K always means 1,000. In the context of computer memory, K always means 1,024. You need to know in which context the K is being used.

Some authors are careful to use a lowercase "k" for the decimal system version (as in kbps) in an effort to distinguish the two usages. However, you will see Kbps as well as kbps (with both meaning 1,000 bits per second). Further, modem speeds are often described in terms of K (as in a 56K modem), even though what is meant is kbps.

Most authors are careful at least to keep their bits (b) and their bytes (B) straight, although context is useful here, too. Usually, bits (b) describe data transmission rates, whereas bytes (B) describe quantities of computer memory. If this is too confusing, simply remember that most of the time, K means KB (1,024 bytes), unless you are talking about transmission speeds, in which case K means kbps (1,000 bits per second).

As an example, Figure 1.5 shows a status window from an Internet application called **LeechFTP**. This application transfers files between computers via the Internet. At the time of this snapshot, LeechFTP was transferring data at an average rate of 2.33 kbps.

The Windows Dial-Up Networking™ window in Figure 1.6 shows a connection made over a 56K modem which is operating at a maximal speed of 44 kbps.

Figure 1.5:
LeechFTP Moving a File across the Internet at 2.33 kbps

| Queue | Threads | Downloads | Failures |

5 ⬍ max threads

2 Threads running, total transfer speed is 2.33 kb/s

🔄 [MainThread] Host: ren.cs.umass.edu
Idle for 432 sec

⬆ Host: ren.cs.umass.edu
Uploading bookbak1.zip with 2.33 kb/s, 828444 of 1056791 bytes, 00:01:37 sec left

---

Downloading and Uploading Files

The terms *download* and *upload* refer to file transfers across a network. You **download** a file when you move a copy of a file from a computer at a remote location to your local computer. You **upload** a file when you move a copy of a file on your local computer to a computer at a remote location.

Figure 1.6:
The Maximal Speed
of an Internet
Connection

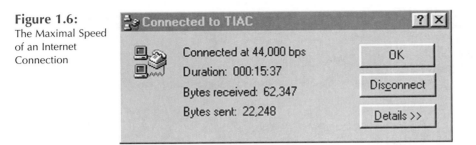

The amount of data that can be moved through a digital device during a fixed period of time is called **bandwidth**. The greater the bandwidth, the faster the data exchange. A file in one computer will travel to another, remote, computer over various communication channels, ranging from copper telephone wires to optical fiber. **Broadband channels**—that is, *high bandwidth* channels—might move the file at 1 billion bits per second, but that doesn't mean that they will arrive at the same rate. Data transfer on the Internet is ruled by the dictum "hurry up and wait." A 1MB file can cross the United States in only seconds. However, it will hit a major bottleneck when it meets a 56K modem, which can transfer 1MB in, at best, 3 minutes. This is why it takes the average home personal computer at least an hour to download a 20MB file such as Microsoft Internet Explorer™ (MSIE).

Traffic patterns on the Net vary from time to time and place to place. To view current traffic conditions, you can visit **The Internet Weather Report** (see Figure 1.7). There, you can choose from the available maps either a global view or a more detailed regional view. A large circle indicates where servers are showing slower response times—these times are also called **latencies**. Nested circles indicate more congestion than does a single circle. Such maps show that the most favorable traffic conditions are at 6 A.M. Eastern Standard Time (EST).

1.5   THE INTERNET

The earlier discussion of speed spoke casually about computers exchanging data over the Internet. Thus one might imagine that the Internet is a massive network similar to that used for telephone communications, except with computer-to-computer connections instead of telephone-to-telephone connections. Any two computers connected to the Internet can establish a communication link between them via telephone lines. However, a look at the nature of Internet communication shows that Internet connections are fundamentally different from telephone-to-telephone connections even when the computers involved access the Internet via telephone lines. If this sounds confusing, read on—it takes a little explaining.

The **Internet** is more than a network of computers. It actually is a network of networks. *Internet* stands for **inter**networked **net**works. Computer networks have been

Figure 1.7:
A "Weather Report"
for the Internet

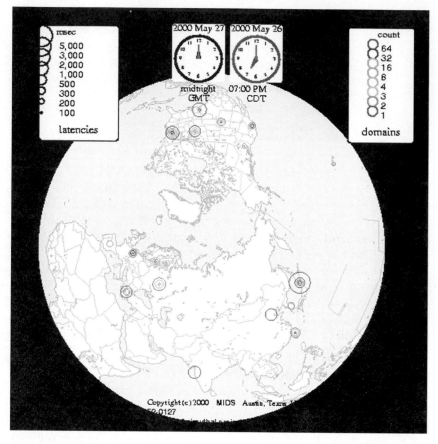

around for decades. The first were geographically close to one another, often within a single building. Called a **local area network** (**LAN**), these networks were used by large companies for in-house data processing long before the arrival of the Internet. Universities used LANs for administrative, educational, and research purposes. Libraries used LANs to hold their card catalogs. In time, university research LANs and commercial research LANs began to create communication links so that computers in different LANs could share information. Then government networks and corporate networks joined the mix. Eventually, commercial networks were created for the sole purpose of giving consumers access to this rapidly expanding infrastructure, this Internet, of computer-based communication. The Internet now reaches into more than 185 countries, connects more than seventy thousand computer networks, and is used by over three hundred million people worldwide.

The Internet's structure is largely heterarchical (the correct word is probably "heterogenous" but computer scientists insist on saying "heterarchical"). In a **heterarchical network**, the members, or *nodes*, of the network are interconnected randomly, with no node occupying a position of greater importance than any other node. This is done to ensure robust communication. By contrast, some communication networks are designed as a **hierarchy**. A hierarchical network is organized in the shape of a pyramid and always includes a unique *root node* that is superior over all other nodes. Two nodes that want to exchange data within a hierarchy must use a path that passes through some node that is superior to them. The shortest such path is unique and will always be a part of any path between the same two nodes. In other words, to get from one location to another inside of a hierarchy there is always one critical path for doing so (see Figure 1.8).

A hierarchical network is much less robust than a heterarchical network. This is because removing the root node from a hierarchy destroys the only communication paths available to nodes that are not close to each other within the hierarchy. The more nodes that are removed from the top regions of the hierarchy, the more communication that is disrupted. In a heterarchy, by contrast, many ways are possible to get from one node to another. You can reduce the speed of communication within a heterarchy by removing nodes; however, you would have to remove a great many nodes in order to disrupt communications completely.

The original research that formed the foundation for today's Internet was motivated by concern for robust network communications: If one part of the network failed, the rest would continue to function. This could be accomplished only if more than one way was available for information to get from point A to point B. Network designers decided that the standard means of moving data across the Internet would be **dynamic routing**. A **dynamic route** is a route that is selected at the time of trans-

Figure 1.8:
Heterarchies and Hierarchies.

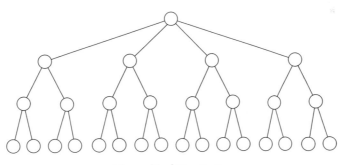

Hierarchical Structure

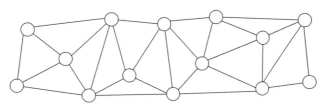

Heterarchical Structure

mission and based on current network conditions. The ability to select such a route is distributed throughout the network so that no one essential site is responsible for the operation of the entire network. The computers that decide how to route data across the Internet are called **routers**. The Internet has thousands of routers.

1.6   HOST MACHINES AND HOST NAMES

Each computer on the Internet is called an **Internet host**, or a **host machine**. Each host machine has a special *Internet protocol address*, called an **IP address**, that identifies that host uniquely. IP addresses were never designed for human eyes; they were created by computer programmers for the sake of computer programs. Computers handle numbers well, so each IP address consists of numbers, four integers separated by periods. For example, one host machine at the University of Massachusetts at Amherst has the IP address `128.119.240.41`. Some Internet hosts have their own permanent IP addresses, whereas others "borrow" IP addresses for use temporarily. For example, when you connect to the Internet over a telephone line, your home computer is assigned a temporary IP number for the duration of that Internet session.

Although IP addresses are fine for computer communications, most people can't easily remember long strings of numbers. To make life easier for people, most host machines have a symbolic **Domain Name Service (DNS) address** in addition to their IP address. Following are some examples of IP host addresses and their corresponding DNS addresses.

IP Host Address	IP Host DNS Address
128.119.240.41	freya.cs.umass.edu
18.92.0.3	mitvma.mit.edu
204.71.200.33	ns1.yahoo.com

Each DNS address contains a **host name** followed by a **domain name**, as illustrated in the following chart.

DNS Address	Host Name	Domain Name
freya.cs.umass.edu	freya	cs.umass.edu
mitvma.mit.edu	mitvma	mit.edu
ns1.yahoo.com	ns1	yahoo.com

Each domain name consists of two parts: the **institutional site name** and the **Top-Level Domain name** (**TLD**). For example, `cs.umass` is an institutional site name that represents the Department of Computer Science at the University of Massachusetts and `mit` represents the Massachusetts Institute of Technology. An example of a TLD name is `edu`, which refers to an *educational* site. The TLD name identifies the type of site at which the host machine resides. The most common TLD names are given in the following chart.

TLD Name	Type of Organization
`.com`	A commercial organization
`.edu`	An educational site in the United States
`.gov`	A government agency in the United States
`.mil`	A military site in the United States
`.net`	A network site
`.org`	A nonprofit organization

Other TLD names identify geographical locations by country, as illustrated in the following partial list.

TLD Name	Country
`.au`	Australia
`.ca`	Canada
`.dk`	Denmark
`.fr`	France
`.de`	Germany
`.uk`	Great Britain
`.hk`	Hong Kong
`.hu`	Hungary
`.ie`	Ireland
`.il`	Israel
`.es`	Spain
`.lk`	Sri Lanka

TLD names have been the subject of much discussion in recent years. The current names will continue to be used, but they will probably be augmented by names that represent a set of new domains that better describe the various types of commercial (`.com`) sites. Likely contenders include `.firm`, `.shop`, `.web`, `.arts`, `.rec`, `.info`, and `.nom`. Once you've learned some institutional acronyms, you'll be able to recognize and unravel DNS addresses quickly on your own.

Although each host machine has a unique IP address, some hosts have more than one DNS address. An alternative name for a host machine is an **alias**. Heavily used host machines are often assigned an alias. A host may have any number of aliases.

No one polices the aliases that a machine can use or the selection of DNS names beyond making sure that each DNS address is unique. Anyone can register a host machine under any, unclaimed, address. Be cautious about making assumptions based on a host machine's DNS address. For example, Figure 1.9(b) shows the Web page at the address `http://www.gwbush.com`. This page looks like it could have been the address for the official George W. Bush campaign Web site for the 2000 presidential election. Actually, it was set up by a counterfeit operation that had posted a satirical Web page. The legitimate Bush campaign site was found at the address `http://www.georgewbush.com`, as shown in Figure 1.9(a).

Figure 1.9:
Which Is the
Legitimate Site and
Which Is the Spoof?

(a)

(b)

An official-sounding DNS address might be what you think it is, or it might not. If you're not sure what you are looking at, proceed with caution.

DNS addresses need to be translated into IP addresses. This essential function in the Internet's operation is handled by **domain name servers** (also shortened to DNS). If the database used by a DNS is corrupted, all Internet service moving through that server will be affected. DNS's are managed with great care, have many levels of redundancy, and have carefully designed fallback plans.

1.7   THE CLIENT/SERVER SOFTWARE MODEL

When you read about Internet software, you inevitably will encounter the terms *client* and *server*. The **client/server software model** is the basic design for all Internet applications. It is based on a simple idea. That is, a host machine can act as either a client or a server. Client/server interactions underlie all communication on the Internet and the model is a de facto standard for network-oriented computing.

Generally, a host acting as a client is an information consumer and when acting as a server is an information provider. The server acts as a resource for all of its clients and provides a service for those clients. For example, a **Web server** provides information on the Internet by housing publicly accessible Web pages. A host running a **Web browser** acts as a client that is capable of moving from one server to another based on a single mouse click.

A host acting as a server typically interacts with multiple clients at one time (see Figure 1.10). As a result, heavily utilized servers are sometimes overwhelmed by client requests. For example, when the Starr Report was initially released on the Internet in 1998, a Cable News Network (CNN) Web server that posted the report handled more than 30,000 client requests per minute—a lot of traffic for a single server. However, even this did not set a record. Some DNSs routinely receive an average of 42,000 requests per minute.

In a client/server interaction, client software interacts with server software so that both the client's host machine and the server's host machine share the total computing load. Clients and servers are designed to form a seamless computing environment. Thus the user typically has no idea which machine is performing which operations, and, indeed, the exact division of labor is irrelevant to the user.

Figure 1.10:
One Server
Interacting with
Many Clients

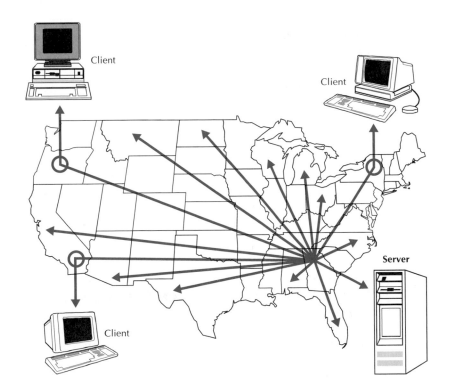

1.7.1 Web-Based Software Hosting

Sometimes proprietary software is made available to the public through the client/server model. For example, a keyword search engine for the Web might reside on a server that can be accessed on demand by many remote clients. Therefore many people can use the server's software without having to install copies of that software on their own host machines.

Several companies currently are exploring commercial markets for *Web-based software hosting*. Standard office applications such as spreadsheet and word processing programs are being made available on Web servers by **Application Service Providers** (**ASPs**). Subscribers to an ASP will not need to install software applications on their own computers and will not have to upgrade or patch that software in order to keep it up to date. They will simply "rent" the applications that they need and let the ASP handle everything else.

If a suitable selection of ASP software were available, more of the online computing load would shift from the client side of the client/server equation to the server side. Such a shift would require more-powerful servers while reducing the amount of computational muscle needed for client machines. The ASP model also depends on very fast, reliable Internet connections. Although it's too early to predict the future size of the ASP market, AT&T announced plans in 2000 to build 26 data hosting centers worldwide. The relationship between clients and servers is constantly changing as people create new business models for distributed computing on the Internet.

F
Y
I

Versionless Software

In 1999, **McAfee.com** released a suite of services that gives users access to various personal computer utilities via the Web. Called McAfee Clinic, it allows subscribers to scan their local drives for viruses, tune system settings, and rid directories of unneeded files, simply by clicking a few buttons on a Web page. Additional services support online collaborations, a "smart" Web navigation toolbar, and online shopping. Minimal software downloads are required to support the service, and subscribers automatically access the most recent software releases each time that they log on. McAfee was one of the first ASPs to pioneer *versionless software*. As a result, their site is the second most-visited software site on the Web (Microsoft is number one).

The client/server model is a very powerful framework for sharing computational resources over a computer network. By making the computational power of a host available for public use, a software designer can maximize the number of users of the software (who might also be paying customers), while retaining maximal control over the software.

1.8   THE WORLD WIDE WEB AND WEB BROWSERS

The **World Wide Web**—or, simply, the **Web**—is the premier Internet application. It has made the Internet widely accessible to millions of people, from children to senior citizens. Its most remarkable feature is the ease of working with it. Many people think that the Web is the same as the Internet. This is not true, although the confusion is understandable. The Web is only one software application that uses the Internet. It actually is a newcomer to the Internet. However, it is the application that integrates resources from other Internet applications. This contributes to some confusion about where the Web stops and everything else begins.

A **Web browser** is a piece of software that enables users to view information on the Web. The essential mechanics of all Web browsers are very simple—learn two or three navigational commands, and you are off and running. Because a Web browser can support other Internet activities in addition to Web browsing, it is an excellent starting point for Internet exploration. The most popular Web browsers can handle the most commonly used Internet resources. Even though the Web is not the same as the Internet, many users will find that all their Internet needs can be adequately addressed by using the right Web browser.

The Web consists of hypertext interspersed with multimedia elements such as graphics, sound clips, and video clips. **Hypertext** is a dynamic variation on traditional text that allows you to digress as you read to view related documents. A hypertext document contains *pointers* to other hypertext documents, called **hyperlinks**, or **links**, that you click with your mouse. Hyperlinks on a Web page might be underlined, boldfaced, or a different color (usually blue) so that you can easily see them. Different browsers use different display conventions. Clicking hyperlinks allows you to easily weave through multiple documents according to your interests and preferences. You decide whether you want to digress and visit related documents. In fact, you can jump from document to document and never return to the original at the start of the chain. Figure 1.11 shows a Web page of interest to authors of Internet books.

A **Web page** is an online document that is viewed with a Web browser. A Web page may contain any number of words. When a page is long, you can scroll it up and down, typically by pointing to arrows on the scroll bar that runs vertically along the right-hand side of the page. Most documents on the Web contain hyperlinks to other Web pages. The process of reading Web pages and traversing links to more Web pages is called **browsing**. You can browse Web pages casually for entertainment or with a serious goal in mind. Either way, when you don't know beforehand exactly where a link is going to take you, then you are browsing. Browsing is an exploratory process. It's a lot like daydreaming: You simply go where your interests lead you.

You can traverse many links in only a few minutes of browsing. If you want to return to a Web page that you left twenty links ago, you might find this difficult to do.

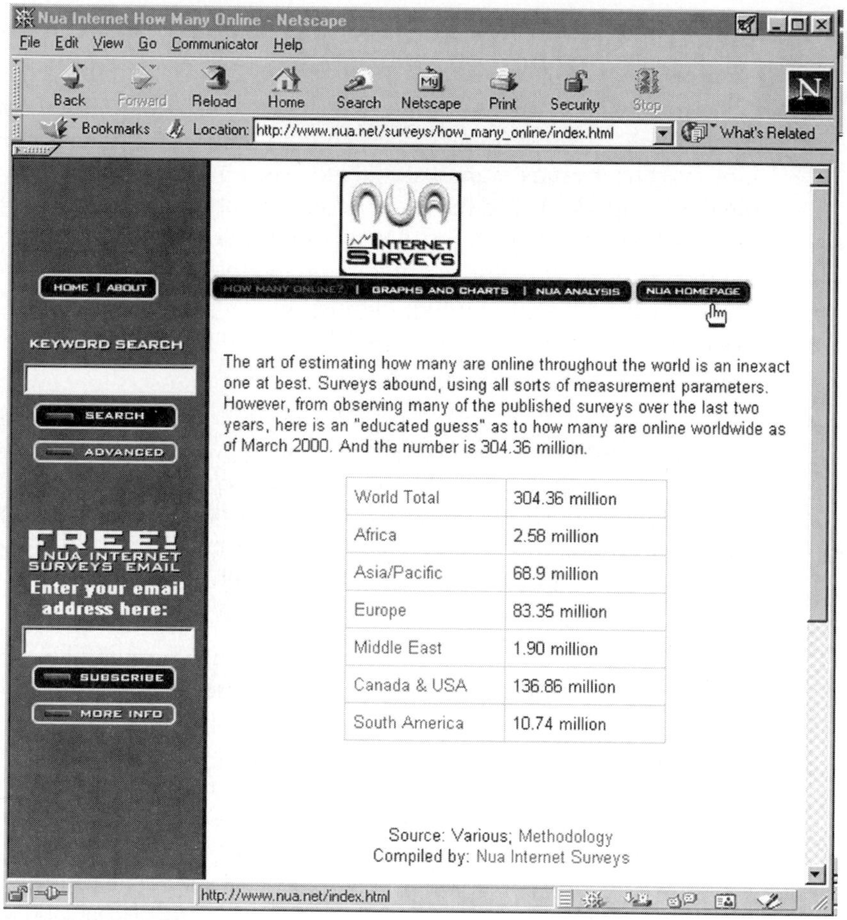

Figure 1.11:
A Web Page That
Requires Frequent
Updates

Fortunately, all Web browsers make it easy for you to return to earlier pages by maintaining a **history list** of all visited pages. You simply ask the browser to pop up the history list. Then you can retrace your steps—it's a little like following a trail of breadcrumbs that you left along the way. Or, you can use the browser's **Back button** to retrace the pages in the history list one step at a time. Also, you can use the **View History command** to view the complete history list and the links to any pages that you may have put on hold while you were distracted by promising links and other Web pages. The history command is especially useful when you've wandered far from familiar territory and you just want to return to an earlier starting page without having to revisit each visited page.

Each time that you start your Web browser, you begin from a **default home page**. Your Web browser probably came configured with a default home page, such as **Netscape Navigator's NetCenter**. You can change this default Web page, selecting any Web page that you want. The most useful choice is one that shows you links to places that you like to visit each time that you get onto the Web.

Each Web page is located at a unique global address called a **uniform resource locator** (**URL**). By referencing the URL, you can jump directly to that page at that URL no matter where you currently are on the Web. All Web browsers let you jump directly to a URL. In Netscape Navigator (Navigator), for example, you type a URL in a Location text box and hit Enter or Return to jump to the desired page.

1.9 HOW TO GET ONLINE

Before you can do anything online, you must have access to the Internet. Students at colleges and universities can usually obtain an educational account. Check whether your school has an Office of Information Technology or a Computer Services Office that maintains educational accounts for students. If you do not have access to an educational computing facility, you will need to use a commercial **Internet service provider** (**ISP**), a company that provides access to the Internet. To find directories of ISPs to help you research the available options, go online at a local public library (or a friend's house or your place of work) and visit **The List** or **ISPs.com** (see Figure 1.12). Some points to consider when selecting an ISP are discussed in Appendix A.

When you work from an educational computing lab, all of the necessary software to get online will be in place and ready to go. To use your own personal computer for Internet access, you will need to install some special software. Your ISP can recommend preferred system configurations, including memory requirements. They will set up a personal user identification (**userid**) and password for you and give you a telephone number to dial to connect your computer to the Internet. Your ISP also will help you to obtain and install the software that you need. Many provide conveniently bundled software that has step-by-step instructions for installation and start-up. If you are fairly new to computers (most Internet users are beginners), follow the ISP's recommendations. It's the ISP's job to get its customers up and running as quickly and easily as possible.

When you have difficulties with your Internet software, ask the service provider's **technical support staff** for assistance. If you are using an ISP, technical support is one of its services that you pay for. If you are a student at a university or college using an educational account, look for a **Help Desk** service where you first signed up for your account. *Do not* go to your school's Computer Science Department for technical support. These departments are not responsible for campuswide computing facilities; their technical staffs are paid to handle other problems. While it's important to know that you can ask for help when you need it, be sure that you're talking to the right people. (See Appendix B for more tips on how to talk to technical support staff when you have a problem.)

Figure 1.12:
Directories to Help
You Shop for an ISP

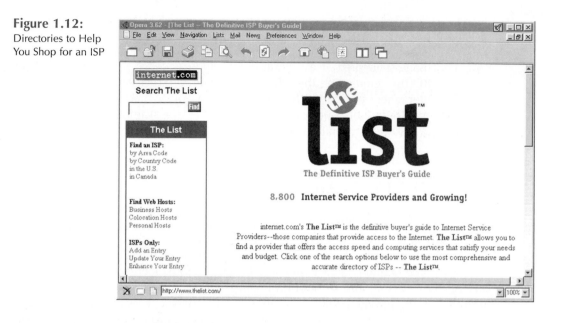

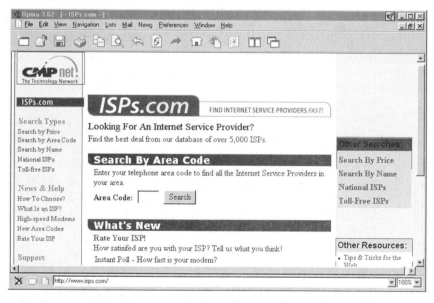

1.10 BROWSER TIPS AND TRICKS

Web browsers are very easy to use with only a small amount of instruction. However, some simple tips can make your browsing sessions more productive and less time-consuming. This section focuses on some key browser features and includes specific instructions for Navigator. Additional tips and tricks, as well as instructions for MSIE, can be found at **CNET's Browser Help Center**. This section discusses the following tips.

- Select your own default home page.
- Use the Find command.
- Use your history list.
- Use bookmarks.
- Add bookmarks with care.
- Abort a download if you get stuck.
- Turn off graphics.
- Don't let a "404 Not Found" stop you dead
- Avoid peak hours.

1.10.1 Select Your Own Default Home Page

Each browser is configured to display a default home page every time that you start the browser. Very likely, that default home page is not the best for you. A better alternative is a Web page that contains many links to places that you like to visit each time that you get on the Web.

To change your default home page in Navigator, follow these steps:

1. From the Options menu, click General Preferences.
2. Click the Appearance tab, and then click Home Page Location.
3. Click the Home Page Location text button, and type the URL of the page that you want to use.
4. Close the dialog box by clicking OK.

1.10.2 Use the Find Command

If you know exactly where you want to go, you often can use the Find command to take you there immediately. Most browsers have a Find command that lets you enter a text string and go directly to the first instance of that string on the current Web page.

The Find command can be useful on long Web pages when you are interested in a specific topic and want to read only about that topic. In addition, some browsers have a Find Next command, which will take you to the next occurrence of that same text string.

Keyboard Shortcuts

These shortcuts work for both Navigator and MSIE.

What You Want to Do	What to Type
Pop up the dialog box for a Find command	Ctrl + F
Jump to the end of a Web page	Ctrl + End
Jump to the top of a Web page	Ctrl + Home
Open a new browser window	Ctrl + N
Close the current browser window	Ctrl + W

Note: Macintosh users, type the Command key (⌘) instead of Ctrl.

1.10.3 Use Your History List

To save time while on the Web, you need to master some navigational tricks associated with hyperlinks. For example, you might find that you easily wander down a path of links on some digression that takes you deeper into a region of the Web that is irrelevant to your original topic. Eventually, you decide to return to business and need to retrace a lot of links back to some page that you were on 10 or 20 minutes ago (possibly an hour ago, if you have no sense of time). You could do this by hitting the Back button a dozen times. Or, you could look at your history list. All browsers have a History command that takes you to a list of all the pages that you visited. Consult this list, and click an address to return to an earlier page. Experiment with your history list and get into the habit of using it whenever you need to retrace a lot of steps. It might save you from getting distracted all over again on your way home.

1.10.4 Use Bookmarks

If you spend much time on the Web, you'll likely find many Web pages that you'll want to revisit regularly. You could start a listing of their URLs and some notes about each one. Or, you can take advantage of your browser's *bookmark feature*. A **bookmark** is pointer to a Web page that you expect to revisit. You can add a bookmark whenever you are viewing the page that you want to mark.

Setting up a bookmark in Navigator takes two steps:

1. Visit the page that you want to mark.
2. From the Communicator menu, select Bookmarks and then select Add Bookmark (or type Cmd + D).

Your bookmark file will display each entry along with a link to its URL. Once a bookmark has been added to the bookmark file, you simply click the bookmark entry whenever you want to return to that particular page.

You also can edit bookmark entries. Follows these steps to edit a bookmark entry in Navigator:

1. From the Windows menu, click Bookmarks.

2. Highlight the bookmark entry.

3. From the Item menu, click Edit Bookmark. A window will appear showing the name of the bookmark, its URL, when you added it to your bookmark file, and when you last visited it.

4. Add a more detailed description of the site or change its name, as desired.

The bookmark file can grow very quickly and get out of control. Your browser should allow you to delete bookmark entries. You should periodically review your bookmark file and weed out entries that you no longer use. A good browser also will let you organize and categorize your bookmarks in a hierarchy for easier reference. To do this in Navigator, follow these steps:

1. From the Bookmark window, click Item/Insert Folder. A dialog window opens.

2. In the window, name the new folder. The name will be inserted at the top level of your bookmark list.

You can place bookmarks in the folder or put the folder inside of another folder by using drag-and-drop operations inside of the bookmark window. If you collect a lot of bookmarks, your bookmark window will become an extensive URL directory. Keep it well-organized, and don't hesitate to prune it as your information needs change.

1.10.5 Add Bookmarks with Care

You might be tempted to save in your bookmark file everything that could ever be of interest to you. However, doing this will result in an unwieldy bookmark file. Decide if a Web page deserves to be in your bookmark file because you really do intend to revisit the page. If a pointer is good to save but you expect it to be useful only for infrequent visits, then it is better to store it elsewhere.

Keyboard Shortcuts

These shortcuts work for both Navigator and MSIE.

What You Want to Do	What to Type
Display your bookmarks	Ctrl + B
Add the current page to your bookmark file	Ctrl + D
View the history window	Ctrl + H
Quit the browser session (close the application)	Ctrl + Q

Note: Macintosh users, type the Command key (⌘) instead of Ctrl.

1.10.6 Abort a Download If You Get Stuck

Sometimes, your browser might appear to stick during the downloading of a page. If your browser has a status line showing the progress of the download, you will sometimes see it freeze and appear to be dead. Stuck downloads happen for various reasons, and they happen with all browsers. Check your browser for a command button that aborts downloads. In Navigator, it is the Stop button. With some browsers, issuing this abort command will make the page mysteriously appear (as if it had been waiting for you to ask). With Navigator, the page will sometimes pop up if you click the same link again right after aborting.

Browser Checklist: Get to Know Your Browser

1. Change your default home page to something new. When does it make sense to change your default home page?

2. Locate your history list. Does it contain entries for only the current browsing session or also entries from previous browsing sessions? How much control do you have over your history list? (Check your preference settings to see what preferences you can change.)

3. Locate your bookmarks. Add a new bookmark. Create a new folder for only that bookmark, and move the bookmark into the new folder. Can you add a comment to this bookmark? Delete the new bookmark and the new folder. Where does your browser store your bookmarks? Can you back up your bookmark file for safekeeping?

4. Try out five keyboard shortcuts that you like. Do they all work? Is it hard to remember them? Work with them for a session or two until you can use them easily. Do they save you time?

If you don't know how to do everything on this checklist, consult your browser's Help menu. Different browsers will have slightly different procedures, but all support these standard features.

1.10.7 Turn Off Graphics

When the Web gets pokey, you'll find that pages with lots of graphics are always the slowest to load. This is because graphics files are relatively large and consume a fair amount of bandwidth. If you don't have a fast modem or enough memory on your machine or if the Internet is very busy, you might find yourself too often waiting for some Web pages. This is no fun if you are accustomed to faster performance or you are in a hurry. You can speed up things by trading in the graphics for faster downloads. Sometimes you don't need to see the graphics; they might be purely cosmetic. Or you might have already seen a page a number of times, and the graphics are no longer important to you.

All browsers enable you to turn off graphics. Because your browser never requests the graphic's file, you don't have to wait for that graphic to appear. When graphics

Figure 1.13:
Internet Traffic
Patterns Online

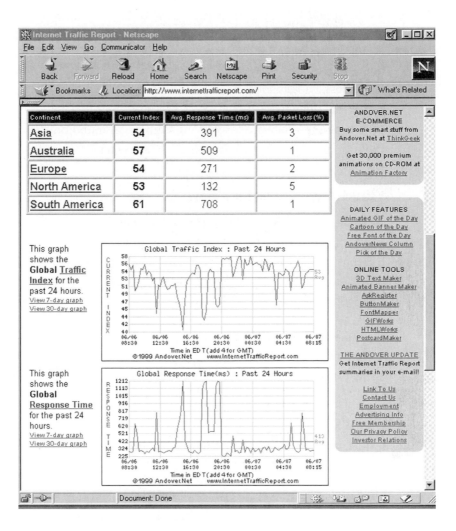

Important Concepts

bandwidth—the maximal rate of data transmission over a given communication channel.

client—an Internet host that consumes information from the Net.

DNS address—a symbolic name for an Internet host.

dynamic routing—a strategy for finding the best pathway between two hosts, when given current conditions on the Net.

heterarchical structure—a connected structure in which no nodes are more central or more important than any other nodes.

hierarchical structure—a connected structure in which all nodes have a common ancestor (the root node).

host—a computer connected to the Internet.

IP address—a numerical name for an Internet host.

server—an Internet host that serves information on the Net.

Web browser—software for viewing Web pages found on Web servers.

Web server—an Internet host that offers Web pages for public consumption.

Where Can I Learn More?

Webopedia—http://www.webopedia.com/

PC Pitstop—http://www.pcpitstop.com/

Internet Traffic Report—http://www.internettrafficreport.com/

NUA Internet Surveys—http://www.nua.net/surveys/

CNet's Browser Help Center—http://www.help.com (Click "Internet" and then "Browsers.")

Internet Errors Explained—http://coverage.cnet.com/Resources/Tech/Advisers/Error/

How MP3 Files Work—http://www.howstuffworks.com/mp3.htmb

Problems and Exercises

1. In 1993, an Intel 486 CPU ran at 40MHz. and by the end of 1999, the fastest Intel Pentium III chips were running at 733 MHz. Are these CPU speeds consistent with Moore's Law? Assume that the cost of a personal computer was constant during the 1990s.

2. Does clicking a link on a Web page begin a file download or upload? Can you see the Web page on your computer monitor before the file transfer is complete? Explain your answer.

3. If a kilo means 1,000, why doesn't 10KB equal 10,000 bytes? When does "K" mean 1,000, and when does "K" mean something else?

4. If you connect to the Internet with a 56K modem, what is the fastest transmission rate that you can expect?

5. Is the Internet heterarchical or hierarchical in its overall design? Explain the difference between a heterarchical network and a hierarchical network. Why was the Internet's networking design adopted?

6. What is dynamic routing, and how is it used on the Internet?

7. If you connect to the Internet over a telephone line, what can you say about your computer's IP address?

8. Match up the items in the left-hand column with their most likely memory requirements in the right-hand column.

1. one floppy disk	a. 700KB
2. one sentence	b. 10GB
3. one small drawing	c. 1 byte
4. one large photograph	d. 10KB
5. one zip disk	e. 4 bytes
6. 200 audio CDs	f. 640MB
7. the MSIE browser	g. 100MB
8. one CD-ROM	h. 65 bytes
9. 32 bits	i. 1.44MB
10. the letter "A"	j. 20MB

9. How many bits are needed to represent an alphabet that contains 300 different characters?

10. Explain the difference between an IP address and a DNS address.

11. List six top-level domain names, and explain what they mean.

12. When music is recorded on a CD, a digital recording device samples the sound 44,100 times per second. Each sample is 2 bytes (16 bits) long, and a separate sample is taken for each of the two speakers in a stereo system. Therefore each second of sound on the CD requires $44{,}100 \times 2 \times 2 = 176{,}400$ bytes of memory. How much memory is this in bits? Using these figures, determine how many megabytes of memory are needed to store a 3-minute song. If you could attain the maximal MP3 file reduction of 93%, how much memory would this 3-minute song consume as an MP3 file?

13. What does a domain name server do?

14. Which of the following are clients, and which are servers?

  a. A Web browser

  b. A Web site where you can access a general search engine

  c. A Web site that tells you the correct time

  d. A program that displays news headlines on your desktop

  e. A Web site that tells you the speed of your Internet connection

  f. A program that tracks stock prices and displays a customized stock ticker for you

15. Who initiates a client/server interaction: the client or the server?

16. How many client requests per second do the busiest Web servers handle?

17. What is an Application Service Provider? Who might want to use one? What advantages does using one offer?

18. Explain the difference between a history list and a bookmark file. When do you use the history list? When do you use a bookmark?

19. What is the first thing that you should do when you see a 404 Not Found error message? What can you try after that?

20. Do you notice different response times when you are on the Net? Which times of day tend to give you the fastest file downloads? Which times are the worst? If you haven't noticed any patterns, try logging on at different times of the day, watch for fast connections and slow connections, and see if you can find any patterns. You might find it useful to keep a log on which you can record the times of day and one or two actual download times that you can monitor each time that you log on.

First Things First: Above and Beyond

A Little History

The Internet can be described in terms of the hardware infrastructure that supports it, the demographics of the people who populate it, and the software that facilitates it. Although it is natural to think of the Internet in terms of computers and communication links between computers, the real force that shapes the Internet is the people who use it. Until the early 1990s, the Internet was used by scientists and academics pursuing long-distance collaborations and scholarly research. Computer science students and professional programmers also used the Internet for more casual communications and have been responsible for much of the enabling software. In 1994, widespread distribution of a graphical browser for the Web triggered mainstream America's explosive interest in the Internet. Commercial service providers quickly materialized, offering Internet access to anyone who had a personal computer and a telephone line.

The Internet wasn't discussed by the popular press much before 1990. However, its origins date to 1970 when four computers were first hooked up to each other over telephone lines—one computer at each of the Stanford Research Institute, the University of California at Los Angeles, the University of California at Santa Barbara, and the University of Utah at Salt Lake City. Twenty years of concerted effort by computer scientists and engineers resulted in today's all-purpose global network for high-speed digital communication. That same 20-year period also witnessed the creation and commercialization of personal computers, which made it possible for people to hop on the Internet from the convenience of their own homes.

Famous Visionaries

I think there is a world market for maybe five computers.
—Thomas Watson, Chairman of IBM (1943)

There is no reason anyone would want a computer in their home.
—Ken Olson, Chairman/Founder of DEC (1977)

No one in 1970 could have imagined the Internet of today. There was never a master plan in place to guide all of the contributing technologies. However, a sense of limitless possibilities attracted a generation of scientists and technicians to the field of computer science, in which innovation is a way of life and nothing stands still for very long. In 1983, what was to become the Internet was a computer science experiment used primarily by scientists and consisting of only 562 computers. In 1993, it was a global infrastructure with important implications for the business world and telecommunications industries. By then the number of connected computers had grown to over 1,200,000. By 1996, that number exceeded 12 million. Over the last

15 years, the number of computers on the Internet has doubled every 12 to 14 months. Figure 1.14 shows the growth rate of computers on the Internet.

Figure 1.14:
Growth of the Internet

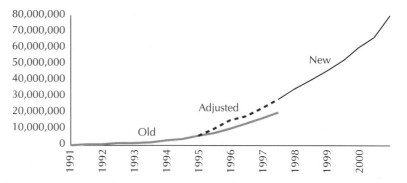

One critical component underlying today's Internet is the software that supports network communications. In the Internet's early days, network software was not particularly user-friendly. The only people who used it were computer scientists, who didn't care about user-friendly interfaces. The software that they designed was somewhat difficult to use, although it served its intended user community very well. Two of the earliest Internet applications became standards among computer scientists long before home computers were a commercial concern. **Telnet** was created in 1969, and the **File Transfer Protocol** (**FTP**) was first used in 1971. Both were designed long before anyone began to think about point-and-click user interfaces. However, Telnet and FTP are still in use.

Telnet and FTP

Telnet allows a user on one host to log on to a computer account on a remote host and work on that remote host as if it were the local machine. Computer scientists with accounts at different universities and research laboratories use Telnet to run software on and work on computers that might be thousands of miles away.

FTP makes it possible to move files from one computer account to another, no matter where the computers are located. Files can be either uploaded or downloaded via FTP. To do either, the user must have access privileges for the computers involved in the transfer.

Although the Web is the fastest-growing segment of the Internet, the most popular software application on the Internet has always been **e-mail** (electronic mail). More people have access to e-mail than to the Web, and e-mail messages are gradually replacing traditional mail correspondence and telephone conversations for a new generation of workers and private citizens. In 1995, the Internet, for the first time, delivered more mail messages than the United States Postal Service. E-mail software now sports user-friendly interfaces, and Internet communication via e-mail is very easy.

However, some people are using e-mail for more than friendly greetings and business correspondence. In recent years, e-mail also has become a highly effective vehicle for spreading *computer viruses*. Viruses and other dangers of going online are discussed in Chapter 2.

How Fast Are Different Internet Connections?

Some readers might be disturbed by the use of the term *speed* to describe the movement of data over the Internet. The speed with which something moves is normally described as a ratio of distance to time, as in "the fastest elevator in the world is in Yokohama and travels at over 40 feet per second." However, when talking about speed on the Internet, people do so in terms of bits per second (bps) or, sometimes, bytes per second (Bps), neither of which have anything to do with distance. Even so, these rates tell how long it takes to view a Web page or download a file, so we naturally think of this as the speed of the data transmission.

If you investigate very many discussions of speed on the Internet, you might encounter the term *baud rate*. It is often confused with bits per second. The earliest modems ran at 300 baud, which meant that the modem could process 300 electrical signals per second. At slow speeds (fewer than 1,200 baud), one bit of data is encoded in one electrical signal, so, for example, 300 baud is the same as 300 bps. However, at higher speeds more than 1 bit might be encoded in each electrical signal. For example, a 4,800 baud modem can transfer data at a rate of 9,600 bps. In fact, a 9,600 bps modem running at only 2,400 baud is possible. Although data transmission rates are currently described in terms of bits per second, you might still see baud rates mentioned in the context of older computer hardware.

The rate of data transmission is often called its **data rate** or **throughput**. High levels of throughput on the Internet are achieved by fast carrier technologies, such as optical fiber, and the use of multiple data channels, called **multiplexing**. Analog telephone lines rely on copper wires (also called **twisted-pair wiring**) to provide **Plain Old Telephone Service** (**POTS**). Twisted-pair wires used to support a single channel are limited to 56 kbps. But it is possible to achieve some degree of multiplexing with twisted-pair wiring, and thereby raise the throughput to 512 kbps. This is the basis for ISDN and ADSL services that are available to telephone customers in some areas of the country.

A communication connection that supports many channels is called a **broadband connection**. Broadband technologies are used within ISP networks and for the most heavily traveled routes within the Internet, the backbones of the Internet. Figure 1.15 shows a number of communication technologies that are used to support the Internet.

FIGURE 1.15:
Different
Throughput Rates
for Different Types
of Communication
Links

POTS	56 Kbps	**cable modem**	512 Kbps–52 Mbps
ISDN	64–128 Kbps	**T3**	44.736 Mbps
IDSL	128 Kbps	**OC-1**	51.84 Mbps
satellite	400 Kbps	**FDDI**	100 Mbps
T1	3.152 Mbps	**E5**	565.148 Mbps
DSL	512 Kbps–8 Mbps	**gigabit ethernet**	1 Gbps
ethernet	10 Mbps	**OC-256**	13.271 Gbps

A cable connection can support up to 52 megabits per second (Mbps). That number describes the rate at which service to *multiple* customers can be delivered. A single personal computer user cannot handle more than 10 Mbps due to the current limitations of personal computer ports. However, throughput rates above 10 Mbps are useful in large corporations or ISP networks. An E5 connection, which relies on optical fiber, can support up to 7,680 simultaneous voice conversations and even more simultaneous Internet connections. Visit **MSN Computing Central's "How Fast"** (see Figure 1.16) to see how different Internet connections compare for speed. You also can test your own connection at the **Speed Test** page to find out exactly how fast or how slow your on-ramp to the Internet really is.

Communication on the Internet tends to be **bursty**, that is, the traffic ebbs and surges. You might be able to see the effects of a heavy surge of traffic on a single download if you are monitoring its transmission rate. During a single download, throughput can slow to a crawl, although it will continue. No one is ever denied access to the Internet because it is too busy. Telephone users are sometime denied service when telephone lines are overloaded because no more open channels are available. When that happens, you get a "trunk" busy signal. Internet users are never shut out because of traffic conditions, although limited resources can result in no access at specific locations. For example, a dial-up connection to an ISP is always limited by the number of available telephone lines running into the ISP's servers, and a specific server might be limited as to the number of connections that it can support. Occasionally, you'll see a busy signal for a Web server, as depicted in Figure 1.17. However, when encountering a busy server a client usually will repeatedly attempt to connection until it connects, so you will rarely see a server that is too busy to respond for very long.

POTS allocates one dedicated line for each telephone call. As long as there are enough lines to satisfy demand, this system works well. Dedicated lines are not shared, so once you have a call in place, your connection is not affected by how many other users are trying to call in. Internet users, however, do not depend on dedicated lines. On the Internet, many users can share a single channel. This is why busy traffic on the Net can perceptibly affect throughput. But unlike the old telephone party lines, on which people could eavesdrop on each other's conversations, Internet communications are kept distinct and separate through a system called *packet switching*. Packet switching is explained in the next section.

Figure 1.16:
Click on the Mouse
and See How
Different
Throughput Rates
Compare

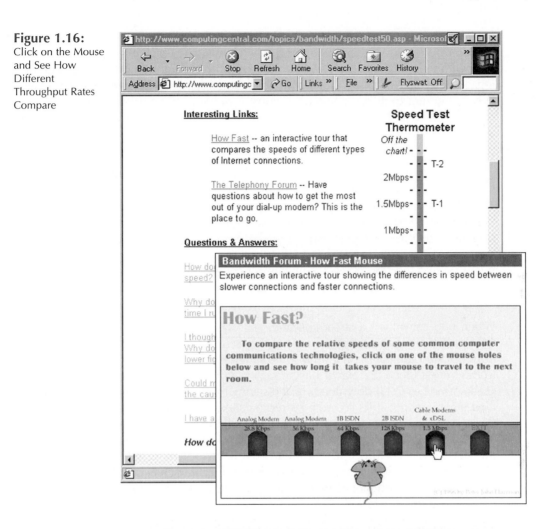

Figure 1.17:
A Web Server's
Busy Signal

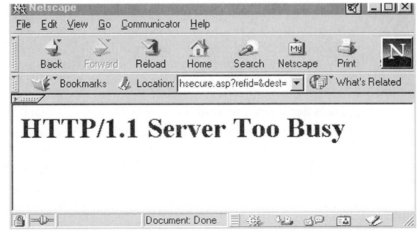

Although throughput is growing to meet demand, what can be achieved by using hardware alone is limited. Bottlenecks will always be a problem. Further, high-bandwidth applications such as video-on-demand and full-motion videoconferencing are more than today's telecommunications technologies can manage easily. When it comes to digital communications, however, software can sometimes push one step beyond the capabilities of current hardware limitations. One example of this is in the distribution of audio and video files over the Internet, as discussed next.

Streaming Media   Audio and video files are extremely bandwidth-intensive. Digital radio broadcasts in real time are hampered by bottlenecks and Internet traffic patterns, yet they are within the reach of users with 28.8 kbps and 56 kbps modems. Even video conferencing can be attempted, if you don't mind the stop-and-go images that aren't always quite in sync with the audio. These communications are possible today because of streaming media. **Streaming media** is a strategy for playing very large multimedia files in real-time while the file is downloading over a bursty Net connection. Special software is needed to handle streaming media. Real Networks, the creator of RealPlayer, was a major pioneer in the development of streaming media.

When you download a streaming audio file, your audio player starts to save the front-end of the file in a temporary holding area, called a **buffer**. The audio player does not start to play the file until some suitable amount of that file has been saved to the buffer. Once the player has enough data buffered, it begins to play it, while at the same time, still downloading and saving more of the file. Buffer space is recycled whenever possible, so room for more data is always available. The hope is that the player will never process its data faster than the Net connection can fill the buffer. If the player does manage to get ahead of the buffer, a break in the song or the video display will occur, and then you'll have to wait for the music or video to restart. However, with a large enough buffer you usually can smooth out the expected variations in throughput that would interfere with a real-time rendering of the data if no buffers were involved.

Using streaming audio, you can hear, for example, a 60-minute radio show without having to wait for hours to complete a massive download. If your network connection is severely stressed, the quality of the audio playback might not be acceptable (there might be too many breaks in the stream). However, streaming media works well under the right conditions. It enables you to hear and view multimedia materials that otherwise would be beyond the reach of most Internet users.

How Data Is Sent over the Internet

Two computers can communicate with each other only if they can agree to speak a common language. A common language that computers share is called a **communication protocol**. Different Internet applications use different protocols.

One of the earliest Internet applications was Telnet (see the Above and Beyond section in Chapter 1). Users who wanted to use Telnet had to negotiate a correct protocol each time that they initiated a Telnet connection. Sometimes, the protocol negotiations were less than successful and the resulting text displays looked like communications from aliens (see Figure 1.18).

Figure 1.18:
Sabotaged Computer Communications by Using the Wrong Protocol

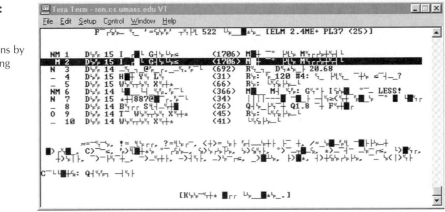

When computer scientists set out to create computer networks, their first challenge was to find a common communication protocol for different types of computers running different OSs. All of the computers needed to speak a common language. First, the **Internet Protocol** (**IP**) was adopted as a universal addressing system for all computers on the Internet. Second, the **Transmission Control Protocol** (**TCP**) was designed to work closely with IP by preparing the data for the trip from one Internet host to another. All computers on the Internet run these two protocols, called **TCP/IP**, which are available for all computer platforms. These protocols for network communication prevented the Internet from becoming a Tower of Babel.

Packets and Packet Switching At the TCP level, bytes are organized into **packets** before they leave home for a trip on the Net. Once they arrive at their intended destination, TCP is then responsible for unpacking the packets and reconstructing the original file or command. Each Internet host must run TCP in order to send and receive data over the Net. Packets can vary in size, but the average is about 1.5KB. Each is stamped with the IP address of its destination and the IP address of its origin.

No one wants to resend an entire 1MB file just because 1 byte of the file was corrupted. Fortunately, packets lost or damaged in transit can be resent without the need to resend the entire set of packets that comprise the complete transmission. This feature makes TCP/IP an efficient protocol when large files are sent across poor-quality communication channels, such as noisy telephone lines.

Before reassembly, packets are examined at the receiving end by error correction techniques to determine whether they are healthy. These techniques, however, while very effective, are not 100% effective. So you can still receive a corrupted file over the Internet. If this happens repeatedly with the same file, that file is probably corrupted on its original host as well.

Each packet is stamped with a unique identifier to help the receiving host reassemble the complete transmission. In this way, confusion is eliminated if packets for different jobs are received at the same time. Thus a single communication channel can carry packets for many users. This system of shared communication channels in combination with TCP/IP is called **packet switching**. Packet switching is responsible for the Internet's robustness and reliability. When demand for a channel exceeds the channel's maximal throughput, packets are set aside in a holding area (something like a waiting room) called a **buffer**. If all available buffers become full, additional packets will be dropped for lack of space. These packets are considered *lost* during transmission. This is no great tragedy, however, since lost packets can always be resent to finish an incomplete data transfer. The complete transfer will simply take a little longer. This is why heavy traffic on the Internet slows transmission times.

Pinging Computer programmers who write code for the Internet often find it useful to *ping* the host machine before a network transmission to make sure that the other host is available and listening to the Net . A **ping** is a request for a fast reply. When one computer pings another computer, it establishes contact, as well as checks to see how long it takes for the reply. A few pings can determine the condition of the network between the two hosts. A lot of traffic (packets) competing for limited bandwidth will lengthen the ping's round-trip between the two hosts.

Some OSs include a ping program. For example, Windows uses ping in a troubleshooting dialog. To try this out, search for "ping" under the Start Menu's Help and pretend to be having trouble with a URL with your browser. Alternatively, you can ping by using freeware obtained off of the Net (see Chapter 8). Figure 1.19 shows a ping report generated by CyberKit v2.5 for Windows.

The figure shows a host sending five pings to a distant computer to see if conditions are favorable for communication over the Net. The responding host returned four of five pings in less than 250 milliseconds—a good response time between these two hosts.

Slight variations in network conditions produce minor variations in the time required—this indicates normal network conditions. Sometimes, unusual fluctuations are found in a ping report. Large fluctuations in ping response times indicate unstable network conditions—this is not a good sign.

Traceroute Reports Another diagnostic tool for examining network conditions is a traceroute report. A **traceroute report** shows the precise pathway across the Net that a ping (or any other network transmission) will follow. It identifies each host machine along the way and reports how many milliseconds it takes to get a reply from each host on the path (very much like a ping report for each intermediary host). Figure 1.20 shows a traceroute report between the two computers pinging in Figure 1.19.

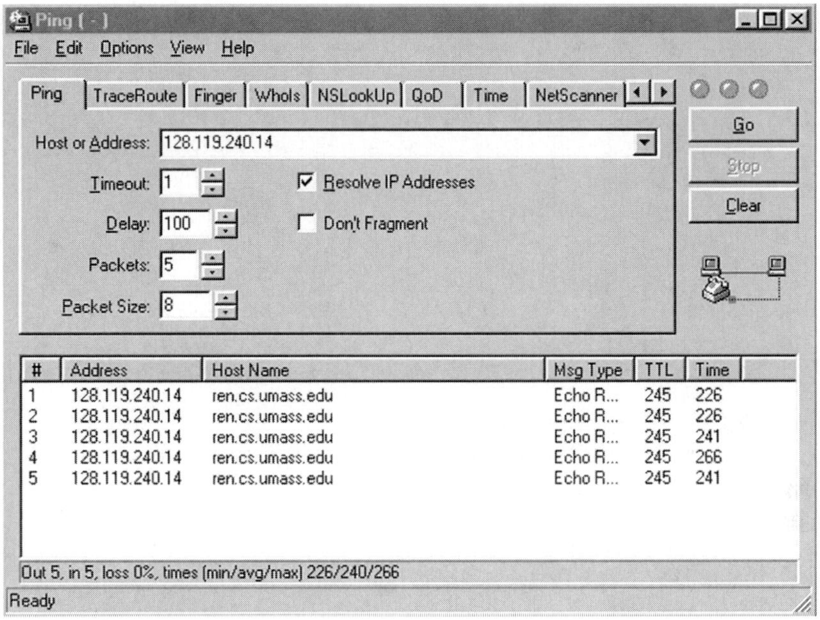

Figure 1.19:
Five pings to a com-
puter named `ren`

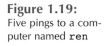

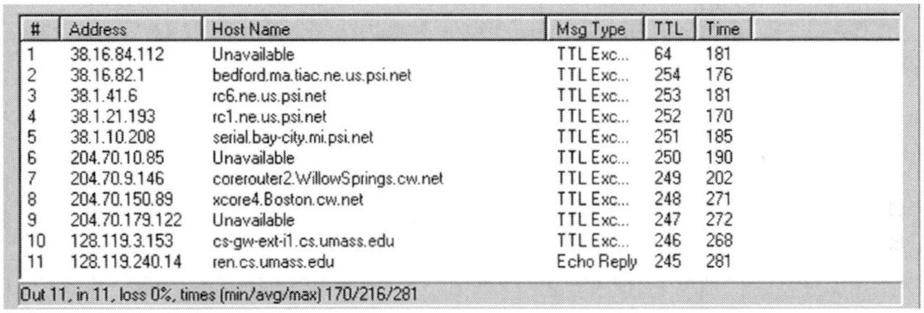

#	Address	Host Name	Msg Type	TTL	Time
1	128.119.240.14	ren.cs.umass.edu	Echo R...	245	226
2	128.119.240.14	ren.cs.umass.edu	Echo R...	245	226
3	128.119.240.14	ren.cs.umass.edu	Echo R...	245	241
4	128.119.240.14	ren.cs.umass.edu	Echo R...	245	266
5	128.119.240.14	ren.cs.umass.edu	Echo R...	245	241

Out 5, in 5, loss 0%, times (min/avg/max) 226/240/266

Ready

Figure 1.20:
A Traceroute Report

#	Address	Host Name	Msg Type	TTL	Time
1	38.16.84.112	Unavailable	TTL Exc...	64	181
2	38.16.82.1	bedford.ma.tiac.ne.us.psi.net	TTL Exc...	254	176
3	38.1.41.6	rc6.ne.us.psi.net	TTL Exc...	253	181
4	38.1.21.193	rc1.ne.us.psi.net	TTL Exc...	252	170
5	38.1.10.208	serial.bay-city.mi.psi.net	TTL Exc...	251	185
6	204.70.10.85	Unavailable	TTL Exc...	250	190
7	204.70.9.146	corerouter2.WillowSprings.cw.net	TTL Exc...	249	202
8	204.70.150.89	xcore4.Boston.cw.net	TTL Exc...	248	271
9	204.70.179.122	Unavailable	TTL Exc...	247	272
10	128.119.3.153	cs-gw-ext-i1.cs.umass.edu	TTL Exc...	246	268
11	128.119.240.14	ren.cs.umass.edu	Echo Reply	245	281

Out 11, in 11, loss 0%, times (min/avg/max) 170/216/281

Each host along the traceroute can slow a transmission if it is overloaded, so a large number of hops between hosts is likely to result in slower response times. However, a trip of, say, 3,000 miles might require no more hops than a trip of 50 miles. As a result, time and travel on the Internet tend to be counterintuitive. That is, geographical distances might not predict transmission speed.

When you are having trouble connecting to another computer on the Internet, you can use traceroute to pinpoint the source of a problem. Technical support personnel will understand if you talk to them about something that you saw in a traceroute report. Figure 1.21 shows a snapshot of a CyberKit traceroute report that was taken when `ren.cs.umass.edu` could not be reached.

If you want to play with ping and traceroute, download CyberKit for Windows (it's free if you send the author a thank you note on a postcard). However, first wait until you've learned how to download software in Chapter 8. Although many traceroute

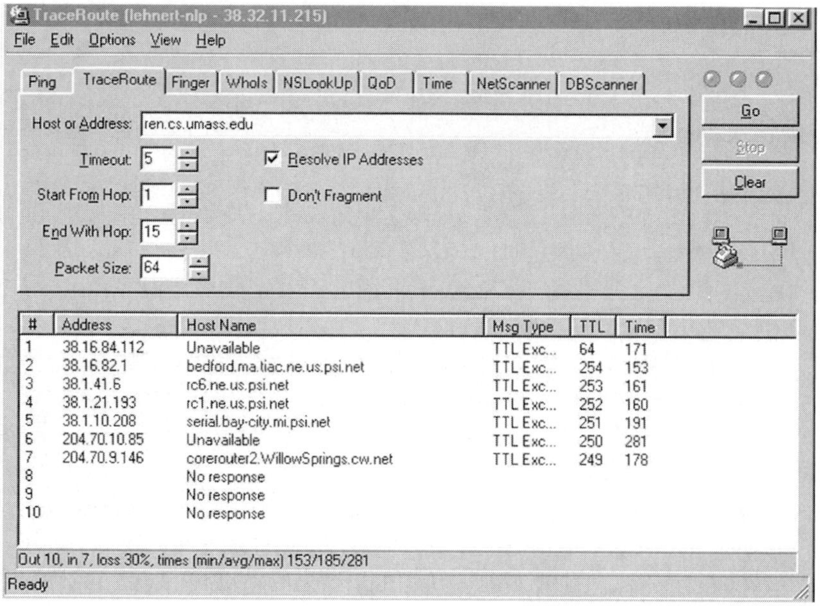

Figure 1.21:
Traceroute
Pinpointing a
Communication
Breakdown

clients are available on the Net, CyberKit comes with unusually informative online documentation. You can learn a lot by reading its Help files.

How File Compression Works

Different types of files require different *compression techniques*. One technique for compressing text is based on the use of a document-specific dictionary that contains only the words found in that file. Each word in the dictionary is indexed by a number, and the original document is encoded as a list of indices that represent those dictionary entries. For a medium-sized document, the space needed to store the dictionary and the index list will be less than the space needed to store the ASCII-text encoding of the original document. A very long text file that contains many instances of repeated words might be reduced by as much as 50% to 60% of its original size.

The MP3 audio files use a different set of compression techniques. Audio CDs are recorded by sampling data from a recording device 44,100 times per second. Each sound sample is digitized and encoded using 2 bytes (16 bits). Separate sample sets are taken for each speaker in a stereo system. Audio CDs therefore require 1,411,200 (44,100 × 16 × 2) bits, or about 175 KB for each second of sound. A 3-minute song therefore consumes about 32MB of space. No one with a 56K modem would want to download music from the Internet if it took two hours to download 3 minutes of music. This is why MP3 files are so important for the distribution of music over the Internet. When music is stored using the MP3 format, the original audio file is reduced by a factor of from 10 to 14 without a perceivable loss in sound quality. This can mean a huge difference, for example a 3MB file rather than a 32MB file.

Perceptual Noise Shaping The technique that makes this possible is **perceptual noise shaping**. Characteristics of the human ear are brought into play in order to reduce storage requirements without sacrificing the quality of the recording. For example, some sounds captured on a digital recording might fall outside of the range of sounds that people can hear; therefore these frequencies can be omitted without any perceptible loss of sound quality. In addition, under certain conditions, when two sounds are played together one sound might mask the other so that only the one is heard.

Temporal masking effects due to threshold effects also occur. For example, a loud sound effectively erases softer sounds of the same frequency for a period of 200 ms after the loud sound stops. Thus there is no reason to record sounds that exist but are never perceived by our ears.

Knowledge of human hearing is being exploited whenever music is compressed in an MP3 file. Your dog might be able to hear the difference, but as long as you can't, the MP3 version of your favorite song is fine.

Hypertext: Changing How People Read

The Internet affects interpersonal communication, formal education, and all sorts of long-distance collaborations, not to mention the political process, the economy, and global communication. The multitude of decision points inherent in richly linked hypertext documents and the fast interactive nature of the Web clearly cater to individual interests and varying attention spans. This is likely to have implications not only for how people read, but also how they live their lives in every aspect.

It is not unreasonable to imagine that a generation raised with user-centric technology will be less inclined to wait for answers, less tolerant of information that is deemed irrelevant, and less able to tolerate social situations that do not offer immediate gratification. Once you adapt to e-mail, incoming telephone calls begin to feel obtrusive and unreasonably demanding. Once you become accustomed to finding information on the Web, trips to the library become quaint and tedious.

Growing Up Wired

Now, the very fabric of my existence is threatened by the Internet. By being exposed to so much information, and so quickly, I seek such stimulation in real life, and find real life to be lacking. Classes drag on, and the simple commutes between classes take a surprising amount of time . . . . I am not afraid of a high-strung, technology-obsessed culture. I welcome it for the same reason everyone younger than me does; it's more exciting than real life.

—Jacob Glazeski , University of Nebraska

The next time that you pick up a textbook at your campus bookstore, drop by the Comparative Literature section and see how many of those texts are about cyberspace. Literary scholars are very interested in the impact of the Internet on written communication. Hypertext accelerates attention shifts and can therefore reinforce short attention spans. Readers who are not sufficiently stimulated by the text on a Web page can simply click a link in search of more immediate gratification.

If television was the medium that lulled children into zombie-eyed couch potatoes, the Web is a perfect match for attention deficit disorder. With television, people make decisions about their viewing preferences once an hour. With the Internet, similar decisions can be made about once a minute. If we allow the Internet to replace books and all forms of printed matter, unpredictable consequences will likely result. The choice is ours. It is easy to feel helpless in the face of such a rapidly evolving technology. Further, the excitement and momentum of such a transformational technology can overwhelm competing concerns. However, we must take a deep breath and conduct our lives with thoughtful deliberation in the face of this ongoing communication revolution. We can still buy books, read novels, and study great literature. We can still pick up the telephone or write a letter on stationary. We can still shop the brick-and-mortar stores and seek the advice of close friends over dinner instead of strangers on the Net. None of these low-tech activities get much media attention or create sensations on Wall Street. However, the existence of high-tech options need not make low-tech options obsolete. We simply need to be conscious of our choices and act accordingly.

Above and Beyond: Problems and Exercises

A1. When did the Internet begin? How many computers were connected at that time?

A2. Explain the difference between FTP and Telnet.

A3. What is the most popular Internet application?

A4. Explain the difference between a baud rate and bits per second. When are you likely to see references to baud rate?

A5. If your home computer is connected to the Internet through a cable service, what is the maximal throughput that you can expect?

A6. What is a dedicated communication line? Give an example of a communication medium that uses dedicated lines.

A7. How does streaming media work, and when is it used?

A8. What is TCP/IP, and why is it important for the Internet?

A9. What does it mean to *lose* a data packet on the Internet? What happens when a packet is lost?

A10. If a small portion of a large file is corrupted during a file transfer over the Internet, does the entire file have to be resent? Explain your answer.

A11. Explain how a ping report is used to evaluate network conditions. How can a ping report tell you if problems exist on the Internet?

A12. When is it useful to see a traceroute report? What can you learn from such a report?

A13. How are text files compressed? Why can larger text files be reduced to a greater extent than smaller text files? Can you think of a way to construct a text file so that it could not be compressed?

A14. How does MP3 compression reduce the size of audio files so much without hurting the quality of the music?

CHAPTER 2

Personal Safety Online

CHAPTER GOALS

- Understand the importance of acceptable use policies, passwords, and constant vigilance while online.
- Learn how your computer is not secure on the Internet unless you make it secure.
- Discover what you can do to protect your computer and personal data while you are online.
- Know when your own online activities violate copyright or software piracy laws.
- Become aware of privacy issues, and learn what you can do to protect your personal privacy.
- Find out how to separate fact from fiction when you see warnings and advice on the Net.

2.1 TAKING CHARGE

The Internet gives you access to a very public space. It might not feel particularly public when you dial in from the privacy of your own home. However, each time that you connect you enter a public space. This means that your conduct will be visible to others, as well as monitored by various network administrators (and others) who may be invisible to you. You have rights as well as responsibilities. To be a good *Netizen* of the Internet, you need to act responsibly. And because of aggressive data collection, intrusive advertisers, underhanded business practices, and malicious miscreants, you need to protect your rights.

Being online is not so very different from being offline. When you visit a large city, you plan your trip, tuck your wallet in a safe pocket, obey the law, and use common sense. Going online is much the same. When you log on to the Internet, you need to understand and follow the behavioral codes that are specific to the Net, and you need to minimize your personal risk. The same laws that constrain your behavior in real life still apply when you are on the Internet. However, the extremely public nature of the Internet can amplify and broadcast your actions to a potentially large audience. Some rules (the cyberspace equivalent of parking tickets) can be broken with little or no consequence. Others (the ones that protect the rights of others) might arouse the attention of law enforcement agents. Just as in real life, some actions will have consequences for only you. In any case, it is always wise to anticipate the potential consequences of your actions. Your taking the time to read this book will help: we cover everything you need to know to be a good Netizen.

Note that the technology that enables you to access the Internet assumes no moral or legal responsibility regarding how you use that technology. Simply because some software enables a person to easily reproduce an image or distribute a document does not mean that anyone has the legal, or moral right to do so. Many newcomers to the Internet, sometimes called **newbies**, mistakenly assume they have this right. Such assumptions derive from unrealistic expectations about software. Read the licensing agreement that accompanies your software. You'll discover that the software manufacturer assumes no responsibility for any consequences that might arise from the use of its software (see Figure 2.1). Only you can be responsible for your actions. ***Software doesn't break laws; people break laws.***

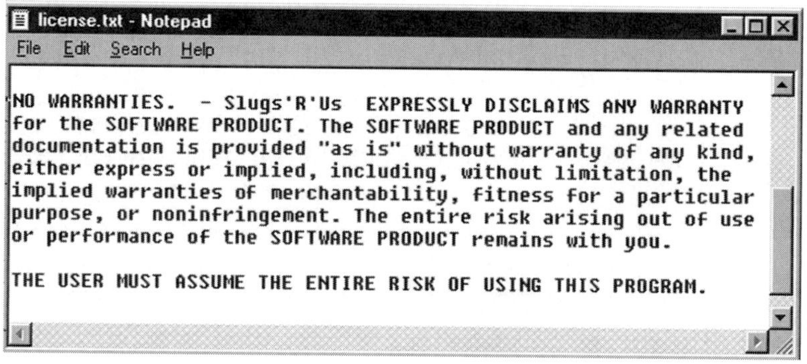

Figure 2.1:
Sample Software
Manufacturers
Licensing
Agreement

```
license.txt - Notepad
File   Edit   Search   Help

NO WARRANTIES.  - Slugs'R'Us  EXPRESSLY DISCLAIMS ANY WARRANTY
for the SOFTWARE PRODUCT. The SOFTWARE PRODUCT and any related
documentation is provided "as is" without warranty of any kind,
either express or implied, including, without limitation, the
implied warranties of merchantability, fitness for a particular
purpose, or noninfringement. The entire risk arising out of use
or performance of the SOFTWARE PRODUCT remains with you.

THE USER MUST ASSUME THE ENTIRE RISK OF USING THIS PROGRAM.
```

2.2 ACCEPTABLE USE POLICIES

All computer accounts and some public Internet servers are subject to an **acceptable use policy** (**AUP**), a policy that outlines appropriate use of the Internet and that is enforced by system administrators. Your Internet access privileges can be withdrawn if you violate the rules and restrictions specified by the AUP. AUPs are posted on the Web and should be easy to locate.

The restrictions that pertain to ISP accounts are often called **terms of service (ToS)**. Whenever you open a computer account or join an online discussion group, take the time to locate and read the AUP that governs your use of those facilities. University AUPs typically prohibit the use of university resources for commercial profit, any form of academic dishonesty, and ongoing communications with other individuals that are deemed to be harassment. Some schools might also prohibit the use of specific Internet services, such as **Napster**, a software program designed to facilitate audio file sharing among Internet users (see Section 2.12), because they do not have enough bandwidth to support the demand for the service. Check your AUP periodically to see if any new restrictions have been added. *You are expected to know your AUP and any of its restrictions that apply to your online activities.*

2.3　PASSWORD SECURITY

Your first line of defense against all kinds of mischief and misery is your password. You probably don't have a password for your personal computer, and that's fine. It's the password on your Internet access account that needs to be handled with care. Someone who breaks into your university account or ISP account is probably hoping to break into more than only your account. Starting from your account, a digital trespasser might be able to break into other accounts and acquire access privileges normally reserved for system administrators. You must protect your computer account not only for your own sake but also for that of everyone in your immediate computing environment.

In a secure computing environment, passwords are stored by using special techniques so that no one, including the most powerful system administrator, can retrieve a password for a given account. No system administrator will ever need to know your password for the sake of legitimate system maintenance and will never ask for it. Privileged administrators can bypass the usual password protocol if an appropriate circumstance justifies it. Any stranger who asks you for your password is up to no good. No matter what someone tells you, no matter how forceful their argument, don't buy it.

Further, if you ever receive an e-mail message from some official-sounding person, with an official-looking return address, that includes a request for your password, realize this is a ruse. Hackers who want to break into computer accounts often use elaborate scenarios in an effort to take advantage of the unwary. This is called **social engineering**. Never give your password to *anyone*, including your own mother. As soon as you share your password with another person, that person also becomes a potential target for social engineering, and you are no longer in control of your own computer account.

Beware of Social Engineering

Any request for your password from a stranger should be reported to a system administrator as soon as possible. If it comes to you via e-mail, forward the message to your system postmaster with the Subject: field containing URGENT: PASSWORD THEFT ATTEMPT. Alerts to postmasters are covered in the Above and Beyond section in Chapter 3.

People can also steal passwords without resorting to social engineering. Computer programs can run through a full dictionary of the English language in an effort to "guess" your password. Dictionaries of common names are also used for the same purpose. You can foil these programs by carefully creating passwords that are not words in a dictionary or proper names. Examples of bad passwords are "television" and "Jessica." An example of a good password is "fiNallY93."

Finally, never use the same password at more than one Web site. Chapter 9 covers this in more detail when it discusses password managers.

A safe, secure password always contains the following elements:

- At least six characters (eight is better)
- Both lowercase and uppercase letters
- At least one numeric character

Passwords and Underwear

Passwords are like underwear. Change them often. Don't share them with anyone. Not even friends.

—Seen on Usenet

Regardless of how carefully you create your passwords, you still should change them every month or two. Passwords can be "sniffed out" by software that is designed to eavesdrop on your Internet communications.

Tips for Good Password Security

- Never tell anyone your password. Ever.
- Don't write your password where someone can find it.
- Change your password about every month or two.
- Don't use the same password in many different places.

2.4 ▮ VIRUSES, TROJANS, AND WORMS

Computer security experts worry about software that can be used maliciously to put computer users at risk. Over the years, they have found it useful to distinguish different classes of software that are often associated with security problems. Mainstream news outlets tend to call such software a *virus*. However, many fast-spreading troublemakers are actually *worms*, and one of the most insidious forms of software attack is the *Trojan horse*.

Is Your Front Door Open?

As soon as you connect your home computer to the Internet, financial records and other personal information stored on your computer become potential targets of cyberattacks. All computers are at some risk if appropriate steps have not been taken to limit access to them. Computers operating over broadband connections are especially susceptible to attack.

Failure to take steps to secure your computer and its most sensitive files is like leaving the front door of your home wide open.

A **virus** is an executable program that attaches itself to a host program and whose purpose is to replicate itself via files that are transferred from one computer to another. They can propagate via shared floppies or other media and need a host program in order to propagate. Some viruses are benign, doing nothing more than leaving the equivalent of their initials on a file somewhere. Others, however, are extremely destructive, capable of destroying files or even entire file systems.

A **Trojan horse** is an executable program that slips into a system under the guise of another program. To qualify as a Trojan horse, the program must do something that is undocumented and intended by the programmer that the user would not approve of. Deception is a key characteristic of all Trojan horses. You think that you've installed only a particular program, but you end up getting more than you expected. Some Trojan horses are designed to record every key that you hit, including the credit card account number that you use when online shopping. Your keystrokes might be monitored by the program's author in real time, or they might be saved to a log file which can be sent back to the program's author at a later time. Other Trojan horses allow a stranger to take control of your computer and issue commands remotely. If this is done cleverly, sensitive files can be uploaded to a remote host without your knowledge.

A **worm** is very similar to a virus but differs in its reproductive habits. Whereas viruses propagate via shared floppies or other media and need a host program in order to propagate, a worm depends on active network connections in order to multiply and needs many different hosts that are running the same software. Sophisticated worms can have multiple parts, or segments, that run on different machines, do different things, and communicate with each other over a network. Some are programmed to act maliciously, whereas others are merely resource hogs that pull down entire networks by tying up too much memory or too many CPU cycles.

If you can't remember how these three differ from each other, just remember that everyone who uses computers is vulnerable to attack and must take precautions. There are some that you can take to protect your system. Once you know the ropes, good computer security doesn't have to take a lot of your time.

The Price of Malicious Code

A 1997 study reported that computer viruses had been discovered at 99% of all medium-sized and large organizations in North America and that 33% of those sites fell victim to a costly computer virus incident. During 1999, malicious code attacks on business computers cost an estimated $12 billion in damaged data and lost productivity.

- **Use antivirus software.** Antivirus software should contain a virus scanner with has a memory-resident option that runs in the background, checking every new file that enters your computer no matter where it comes from (whether a floppy drive, a CD-ROM drive, an Internet download, or elsewhere). Set the software to scan all program files on your computer whenever you turn it on, and make sure that it is always running in the background. You might have to turn off the scanner during a software installation (see Chapter 8). If so, make sure that you turn it back on again after the installation is complete.

- **Update your antivirus software regularly.** You should update at least once a month the data files that contain information about particular viruses, Trojan horses, and worms (see Figure 2.2). If you can't do this regularly, use versionless antivirus software instead, which is updated for you automatically over the Internet (see Section 1.7.1).

- **Keep floppy diskettes out of your floppy drive unless you are actively working with the files on a floppy.** Boot sector viruses hide on floppies. They are triggered when your machine routinely checks to see whether it should run its startup sequence from the floppy drive. If the floppy's boot sector is infected, its virus will kick into action.

  If you need to work without a virus scanner running continuously in the background, then you must remember to manually scan each file before opening or executing it. Don't take someone else's word that a file is safe. Always check for yourself.

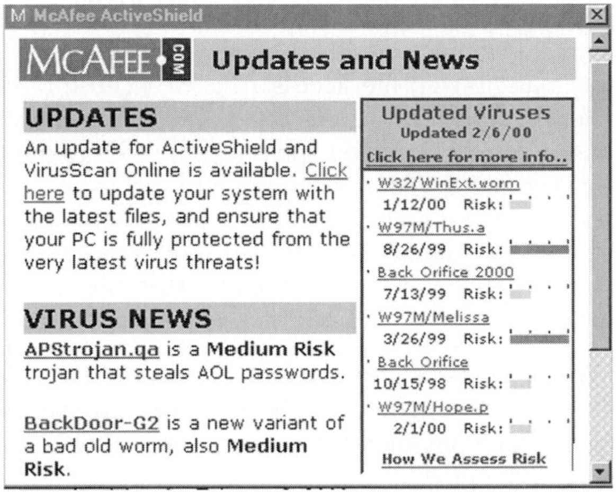

Figure 2.2:
Updating Antivirus
Software

■ **If you are not running a virus scanner in the background, disable Java and JavaScript in your Web browser** (see Figure 2.3). Java and JavaScript both can contain **applets**, small executable programs that can be attached to a Web page. By disabling Java and JavaScript, you prevent malicious applets from infecting your system.

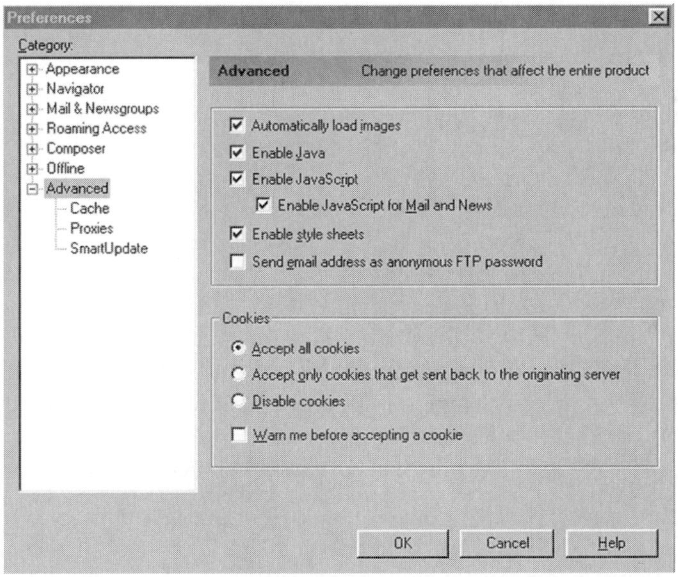

Figure 2.3:
Uncheck the
Appropriate
Preferences to
Disable Java and
JavaScript

■ **For maximal safety,** *encrypt* **all files that contain sensitive information** (see Chapter 11) **or store them offline on floppies or other removable media.**

- **Do not leave your computer connected to the Internet any longer than necessary.** A computer connected to the Internet via a 56K modem is not an attractive target for unauthorized file access. This is because breaking into systems that have faster Net connections is easier. However, your computer could still be compromised, especially if you leave it connected to the Net for long intervals of time. Disconnect whenever you don't need to access online resources. In general, the longer you stay online, the easier it is for someone to break into your system over your Internet connection. The amount of time that you spend connected to the Net is more of a risk factor than the speed of your Net connection.

Sophisticated Web pages are another avenue of attack that must be scanned by antivirus software that is configured to check all downloaded Web pages. Some Web pages contain small computer programs that are automatically executed by a Java-enabled or Javascript-enabled Web browser. Most of these programs are harmless, but it is possible to visit a Web page that contains a malicious program which will be automatically executed upon download. Treat *all* incoming files with suspicion, no matter their source.

Running with Scissors

Automatically executed content is like running with scissors; it may be fun, but sooner or later someone's going to get hurt.

—Peter Ciccarelli

You might have heard that Macs are safe from viruses and therefore don't need antivirus software. This is partly true because most viruses "in the wild" (see "Viruses in the Wild") are designed to attack Windows installations and 90% of personal computers run Windows. However, the most commonly found viruses today are *macro viruses.* A **macro** is a small computer program that executes in response to a specific combination of keystrokes or clicking a particular icon. Macros allow power users to customize personalized keyboard commands, and they can also be set up to automatically execute whenever a document is opened. A **macro virus** is a virus written inside a macro, which typically executes as soon as the document containing the macro is opened. Of all virus incidents reported in 1997, 80% were the work of macro viruses. Further, macro viruses are platform-independent—a macro virus will strike a Mac as easily as a Windows-based machine.

Computers running the UNIX or Linux OS generally are safe from viruses. If you decide to install Linux on your personal computer, ensure that you know what you're doing, as a proper Linux installation is a significant undertaking. Recall that Linux is an offshoot of UNIX, and UNIX was designed with professional system administrators in mind; it was never intended for computer novices.

Viruses in the Wild

Virus specialists have identified more than 16,000 computer viruses, but most of these exist only in research laboratories. Currently, fewer than 300 computer viruses are **in the wild**, that is, on computers not associated with virus research.

If you have installed a memory-resident virus scanner on your machine, you can determine if your scanner is working correctly by testing what it does when it finds a virus. Do this by introducing on your computer a harmless test virus called EICAR. With a text editor, type the following line into a file:

`X5O!P%@AP[4\PZX54(P^)7CC)7}$EICAR-STANDARD-ANTIVIRUS-TEST-FILE!$H+H*`

Make sure that this is the file's first, and only, line and that the line contains no blanks or tabs. Then save the file anywhere you want, naming it `eicar.com`. Next, use your antivirus program to scan your system. It should recognize the EICAR virus when it scans `eicar.com` and display a virus alert, as McAfee's antivirus software does, depicted in Figure 2.4.

Figure 2.4:
A Virus Scanner Passing the EICAR Virus Test

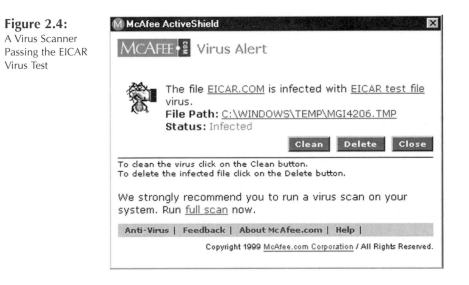

Under certain circumstances, when *file sharing*—giving others access to your files—is turned on, sensitive files on your hard drive can be made publicly available to anyone on the Internet. On a personal computer that runs Windows, you can protect yourself from a relatively trivial attack by ensuring that the File and Printer Sharing setting is turned off. To turn this off, follow these steps:

1. From the Start menu, select Settings, and then the Control Panel.
2. Double-click the Network icon.

3. Under the Configuration tab, click the File and Print Sharing button. Make sure that the two checkboxes displayed in the top of the next window are *not* checked (see Figure 2.5).

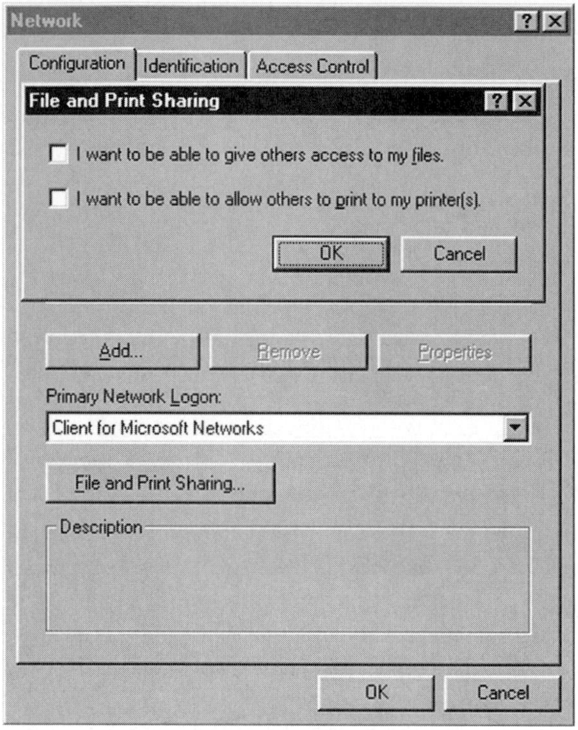

Figure 2.5:
Turning Off File and Printer Sharing on a Windows Personal Computer

Network

Configuration | Identification | Access Control

File and Print Sharing

☐ I want to be able to give others access to my files.

☐ I want to be able to allow others to print to my printer(s).

OK   Cancel

Add...   Remove   Properties

Primary Network Logon:

Client for Microsoft Networks

File and Print Sharing...

Description

OK   Cancel

Antivirus Software Facts

Here are some tips to use your antivirus software effectively:

- Good commercial antivirus software watches for Trojan horses, worms, and malicious applets, as well as viruses.

- Multiple virus scanners can interfere with one another. Don't install more than one.

- No virus scanner can guarantee 100% safety, but keeping your scanner up-to-date will minimize your risk.

- Don't take unnecessary chances. Avoid suspicious executables from unknown sources.

2.5 ▌ E-MAIL VIRUSES

Periodically, you'll see warnings on the Internet about viruses in e-mail messages. The most famous one is the Good Times virus, but many others exist. These warnings typically tell you to never read anything with a specific Subject: field content (such as Good Times or Pen Pal Greetings) and to be sure to pass this warning along to everyone you know. **Such warnings are hoaxes. You cannot get a computer virus from reading a plain text mail message.** If you see such a virus warning, you can check whether it is a known hoax by visiting the **Computer Virus Myths Web site**. Whatever you do, don't forward the message to all of your friends and coworkers. If there is a real virus on the loose, leave it to the professionals in technical support to distribute appropriate warnings.

E-mail messages that contain *mail attachments* are a different story. **Mail attachments can carry viruses, and reading a mail attachment can cause a virus to swing into action.** If you read your mail on a UNIX or Linux host, don't worry about viruses in mail attachments. However, if you are reading your e-mail on a Mac or a Windows machine (or any other platform with Windows software installed), be careful about mail attachments. You should first save the file to your hard drive *before* you open it (see Figure 2.6) and then check it with a virus scanner before you read it. If an up-to-date scanner detects no viruses, then the file is 99.99% safe to open. (You still might receive a new virus before the antivirus software vendor has had a chance to add it to its scanner's data files.) For 100% safety, read on.

Figure 2.6:
Saving an
Attachment to the
Hard Drive from
Outlook Express

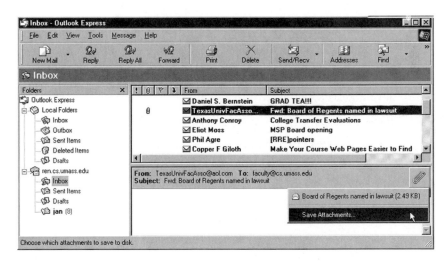

Mail attachments are a problem because they are not always only data files. Some mail attachments contain executable code in the form of scripts. A **script** is a small computer program written in a scripting language such as Microsoft's Visual Basic™

(VB). Other mail attachments contain executable code in the form of *macros*. Your first line of defense against malicious mail attachments is to make sure that your e-mail client, also called a mailer, is not configured to open one of these files for you automatically.

Making Sure That No Mail Attachments Are Opened without Your Consent

If you use Outlook:

Follow these steps to turn off the auto-execution of attachments. Doing this will not only prevent auto-execution of most attachments, including VB scripts (such as the LoveLetter), but also warn you when you try to open the attachment.

1. Select Tools menu, the Options menu item, and then the Security tab.
2. In the Secure Content section, click the Attachment Security button.
3. Set the security to High.

If you use Outlook Express:

Outlook Express doesn't provide a simple mechanism for preventing auto-execution of attachments. Consider upgrading to Outlook.

If you use Netscape Communicator:

1. Select Edit menu and then Preferences.
2. From the Navigation menu, select Navigator and then Applications (see Figure 2.7a).
3. Scroll down to the Winword File entry that specifies a `.doc` file extension (see Figure 2.7a).
4. Click the Edit button, and in the Handled By section, select Save to Disk (see Figure 2.7b).

If you use Eudora Pro:

1. Select Tools menu, the Options menu item, and then the Viewing Mail (icon).
2. In the "HTML content" section, uncheck "Allow executables."
3. Edit your `eudora.ini` file to add (or modify) the following lines:

```
WarnLaunchProgram=1
WarnLaunchExtensions=exe|com|bat|cmd|pif|htm|do|xl|reg|lnk|
```

2.5.1 Macros Viruses

In recent years, macros in Microsoft Word™ documents have been the single greatest source of computer viruses; Microsoft Excel™ spreadsheet documents are also frequent carriers. Opening a Word file that comes to your mailbox from an unknown party is definitely asking for trouble. But it is not enough to know and trust the person who sends you the attachment. ***Word and Excel users can pass a macro virus on to friends and co-workers without realizing it.***

The Melissa Virus

(The Melissa virus was the first e-mail attachment virus designed to exploit the user's e-mail address book in order to propagate itself.)

On Friday, March 26, 2000, CERT/CC received initial reports of a fast-spreading new MS Word macro virus called Melissa. Once loaded, it used the victim's MAPI-standard e-mail address book to send copies of itself to the first 50 people on the list. The virus attached an infected document to an e-mail message bearing the subject line, "Important Message From <name>," with <name> that of the inadvertent sender. The e-mail message read, "Here is that document you asked for … don't show anyone else ;-)," and included an infected MS Word file as an attachment. The original infected document, list.doc, was a compilation of URLs for pornographic Web sites.

—1999 Infosecurity Year-in-Review

Trusting recipients recognized the return address on the Melissa mail and let down their guard, just as Melissa's author intended. The message was not what it appeared to be, even though it did come from the indicated source.

Determine whether your mail program includes an option that allows you to save Word file attachments to your hard drive. Then you can scan them before opening them with Word. Figure 2.7 shows this preference setting for Netscape Communicator's e-mail client. In addition, **never configure your mail program to automatically open a Word attachment for you**. See Section 2.5 for more details on how to use antivirus software. Many macro viruses are relatively subtle and can easily go unnoticed by a casual user. This allows the virus to migrate freely within a large population of relatively inexperienced e-mail users.

Avoiding Macros by using RTF

Macros cannot be saved in a **Rich Text Format (RTF)** file. RTF files consist of ASCII text, so they can be inserted *into* e-mail message bodies as an alternative to attaching a file.

Word documents can be saved as RTF files. To convert an RTF file back into a Word document, save the RTF file to your hard disk and then open it in Word. Opening an RTF file that is inside of a plain text message body is always safe.

If everyone saved their Word files in RTF format and never opened Word documents that were not in RTF format, macro viruses in Word documents would go away. Figure 2.8 shows a document saved in both RTF and Word's `.doc` formats. Files that contain graphics, however, are much larger in RTF than in Word's `.doc` format. So reserve the RTF format for documents that contain only text or mostly text.

Figure 2.7:
Setting Software
Preferences for
Word Documents

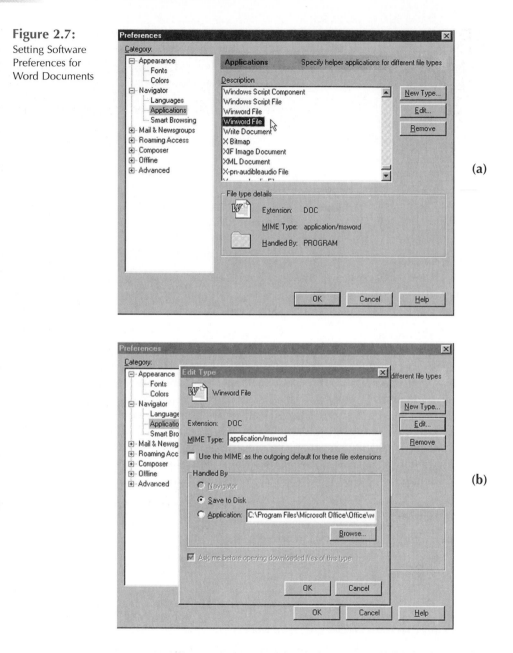

(a)

(b)

Macro viruses affect primarily Word users and spread rapidly for two reasons.

1. Microsoft's domination of the office application market results in many users (potential victims) who share documents that are in a common format.

Figure 2.8:
Files Saved in RTF
and .doc Formats

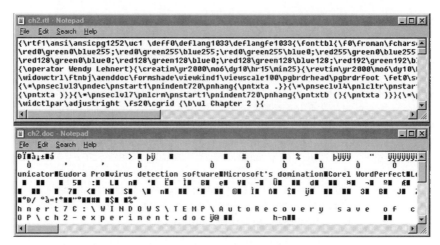

2. Microsoft's decision to allow powerful programming instructions, in the form of macros, to be *embedded* within documents. Other software manufacturers that support macro capabilities store their macros in separate files, for example Corel WordPerfect and Lotus WordPro. However, 90% of all home computers run Windows, and a large percentage of those run Word. (Word is also available for the Mac, where it enjoys a substantial user community as well.)

Because of Word's widespread popularity, combined with the routine use of e-mail attachments for document distribution by largely naive newbies, a highly successful class of computer viruses has emerged. We can blame those who create the viruses, questionable software design decisions, or the users who embrace sophisticated software without adequate training or preparation. In fact, a macro virus needs all three of these in order to create widespread chaos.

How Word Macro Viruses Infect a Computer

Word templates allow users to customize various settings for different types of documents. A number of predefined templates for business letters, faxes, professional resumes, and other document types are available. To see these templates, select File and then New and then click the various tabs in the pop-up window. Most people who use Word rely on its default template, `normal.dot`, for most documents. Word uses this template when you create a new document using [Ctrl] + [N] or the new document icon in Word.

Recall that a crucial feature of macros is that they can be set up to execute automatically whenever a document is opened. Anyone can create a Word macro by recording a sequence of Word commands using Word's *macro recorder*. Programmers who know VB can create Word macros that are not limited to operations available as Word commands. User-defined macros are associated with specific templates. A Word document moved from one computer to another takes its template with it, along with any macros associated with that template. When you open a Word file whose template is new to your system, Word installs the new template for you. This usually means overwriting an existing template file to make new macros available to you.

Macro viruses most often are passed to new systems by their overwriting of the `normal.dot` template. A macro virus in the `normal.dot` template will be attached to all of your Word files that use `normal.dot`, both new and old. If you pass on a Word file that uses this template to someone else, it will overwrite that person's version of `normal.dot`—and the macro virus will have claimed another computer. The `normal.dot` template is the foundation template for all other Word templates, so you can't stop a macro virus by using a different template for your Word documents. In addition, a macro added to the `normal.dot` template will infect all of your Word documents.

Virus protection measures are effective against macro viruses for the most part. However, a computer programmer can easily take an existing macro virus and alter it so that virus scanners will no longer recognize it. Some users protect themselves simply by refusing to open any documents that contain macros. If you use Word 97 or 2000, you can set an option so that Word will warn you whenever you attempt to open a document that contains a macro (see Figure 2.9) and thereby give you the opportunity to disable it. To set up the macro alert, follow these steps:

1. Select Tools, Options, and then the General tab.
2. Make sure that the "Macro virus protection" check box is checked.

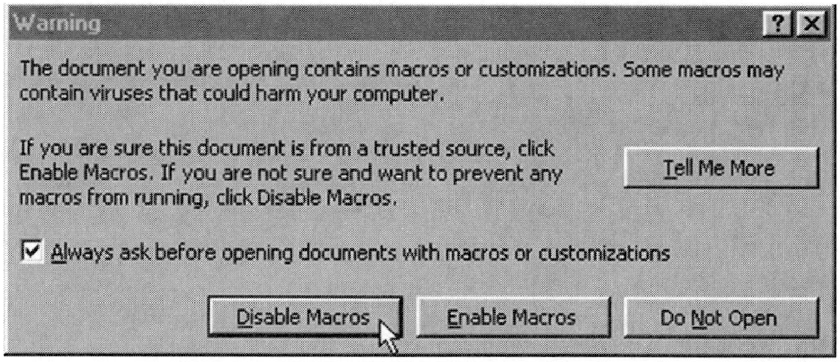

Figure 2.9:
Instructing Word to Warn You When a Document Contains a Macro

In addition, Word 2000 introduced new security options that check for *trusted digital signatures* whenever a document contains a macro. Chapter 11 discusses how digital signatures can be used to validate the actual source of an e-mail message. If everyone sending e-mail placed a digital signature on their outgoing mail, then you could simply ignore any e-mail attachments that don't have a signature. Until that happens, however, you can disable all macros that do not come from a trusted source by setting the macro security option to "High." This will protect you from viruses in documents from unknown or untrusted sources. Of course, a trusted source that is already infected can unknowingly pass on a macro virus to you, so you still must be watchful.

Deception and Trickery

6.11.99 The Explore.Zip worm appeared as an attachment to e-mail masquerading as an innocuous compressed WinZip file. The executable file used the icon from WinZip to fool people into double-clicking it, at which time it began destroying files on disk.

9.20.99 A couple of new Y2K-related virus/worms were discovered in September. One e-mail Trojan, called Y2Kcount.exe, claimed that its attachment was a Y2K-countdown clock; actually, it sent user IDs and passwords out into the 'Net by e-mail. Microsoft reported finding eight different versions of the e-mail in circulation.

The other Y2K virus, named W32/ Fix2001, came as an attachment (ostensibly from the system administrator) and urged victims to install the "fix" to prevent Internet problems related to the Y2K transition. Actually, the virus/worm would replicate through attachments to all outbound e-mail messages from the infected system.

—1999 Infosecurity Year-in-Review

What to Do When You Receive an E-mail Attachment

1. If you receive an unsolicited e-mail attachment from an unknown person, delete it without opening it first.

2. If you receive an e-mail attachment accompanied by an empty message body, delete it. Even if you recognize the return address, the absence of a message is very suspicious (or, given the potential dangers associated with e-mail attachments, very rude).

3. If you receive an unexpected e-mail attachment from someone you know and the message body looks generic, contact the sender to make sure that the sender sent the e-mail message to you.

4. If you do decide to open any mail attachment, make sure that you scan it with antivirus software first, even if you have confirmed its authorship and you trust the source.

5. To be 100% safe, disable all macros before opening any Microsoft Office™ document.

When possible, avoid using e-mail attachments in your outgoing e-mail messages.

What to Do When You Have to Send an E-mail Attachment

If you must attach a file to an e-mail message, be considerate of your recipient.

- Include a personalized message body that only you could send. If your message body looks too generic, your recipient will be (should be) suspicious.
- Describe the purpose and content of your attachment in the message body.
- If the file you are attaching contains no graphics, save it as an RTF file. A knowledgeable recipient will know that RTF files do not need to be scanned.

2.5.2 Script Attacks

Although attachments are the primary source of e-mail risk, e-mail clients that render message bodies into Web-like page displays (complete with clickable links and graphics) can also be susceptible to malicious attacks. This happens if the content of a message body is allowed to trigger scripts.

BubbleBoy

11.08.99 In early November, a worrisome new worm called BubbleBoy appeared on the scene. This proof-of-concept worm was sent to Network Associates, which immediately posted a free software patch and alerted the FBI of the danger. The problem with this worm was that it would infect a host if an MS-Outlook user merely highlighted the subject line of the carrier e-mail message—no double-clicking was required. The worm's payload was mild—changes to the Registry and a simple display screen—but experts warned that the same techniques could carry much more dangerous payloads in future variations. The worm spread by mailing itself to every e-mail address on the infected system's address list, thus posing an even greater potential danger than the Melissa virus. This attack again demonstrates the foolishness of allowing automatic execution of code by e-mail and word-processing packages.

—1999 Infosecurity Year-in-Review

In 2000, two new e-mail attachment attacks targeted users of Outlook and Outlook Express. The LoveLetter and NewLove viruses—technically speaking, these were worms, not viruses—were spread via VB scripts passed along as e-mail attachments. Each script deleted files on the target host and then sent itself on to new targets, using addresses in the Outlook address book. Users who knew to scan all e-mail attachments before opening them and to keep their antivirus software up-to-date should have been safe. However, in the case of the LoveLetter virus it spread too quickly and the damage that it caused was not immediately obvious, so the antivirus protection software companies were slow to catch it and alert their customers about it. The effects of the NewLove virus were more immediately obvious; this kept it from spreading too far, too fast.

Microsoft and Security Patches

If you use Outlook or Outlook Express, be on the lookout for software patches and system upgrades whenever a new security hole is discovered. Patches and upgrades for all Microsoft products are available from the **Microsoft Download Center**. Microsoft has repeatedly refused to add stronger security safeguards to its e-mail clients. However, it does issue patches for specific problems as they arise (which is fairly often). To avoid having to deal with frequent software updates, shop around for a different e-mail client.

2.6 ▌ SHOPPING ONLINE

Purchasing merchandise online does pose some risk, but you can take precautions to protect yourself. For example, be aware that ***using credit cards is safer than using personal checks and money orders***. When you send someone a check or money order as payment, you might have no recourse if your order is damaged, not as requested, or lost in transit. When you use a credit card, you can always complain to the credit card issuer for help with an unresolved dispute with the vendor. Credit card issuers are required by the federal Fair Credit Billing Act to limit your potential loss to $50 when disputed charges are made on your credit card, provided that you report such charges in a timely manner. Retailers and credit card issuers absorb the bulk of any losses incurred resulting from theft of a credit card or its account number.

Note that bank debit cards *do not* afford you the same protections as do credit cards. Be careful not to confuse the two. Credit cards are much safer than debit cards for online transactions.

Risks Are Everywhere

Over the past four years, there has been an enormous amount of publicity about the dangers of credit card fraud on the Net . . . . Yet, as many savvy Internet shoppers now know, the reality is that it's actually much safer to enter your credit card number on a secure online order form than it is to give your credit card to a waiter at a restaurant. After all, what's to stop the waiter from writing down your credit card number and placing orders on the phone with it later? And research shows that the rate of fraudulent purchases made by cell phones is much higher than credit card fraud on the Net.

—Internet ScamBusters

If you want to buy something online, make sure that the address of the page on which you are to enter your credit card account information begins with `https://`. The "s" means that the page is **secure**, that is, protected by the **Secure Sockets Layer (SSL)** encryption protocol—an effective safeguard against anyone who might want to steal your card information in transit. SSL and encryption are discussed in detail in Chapters 10 and 11.

In addition, your browser should display a special icon to indicate whether the Web page is secure, either a key or a padlock. Look in the lower left-hand corner of your browser window for this icon. An unbroken key or unlocked padlock indicates that the page is secure. Figure 2.10(a) shows a locked padlock—the page is secure—and Figure 2.10(b) shows an unlocked padlock—the page is not secure.

Figure 2.10:
Padlock Icon That Indicates Whether a Web Page Is Secure or Unsecure

(a)   **(b)**

Although you can examine a Web page to see if it is secure, you unfortunately have no way of knowing how secure the computers are that store your order history and billing data. If your order is *encrypted* during transit (see Chapter 11), but then stored without encryption on a public server that is not properly maintained, your order history and billing data might be at risk long after your transaction has been completed.

Maintaining a secure server and monitoring network activity for possible security breaches requires the services of a professional system administrator. If an e-store outsources their storefront operation to a reputable, professionally managed e-commerce service, they are paying that service to manage their storefront security. But some e-stores try to handle their storefront operation inhouse. In that case, a full-time professional system administrator represents a non-trivial payroll expenditure, and many small business operators may not realize that this is a necessary business expense. Smaller companies that cannot afford experienced system administrators pose the greatest risk. However, even large corporations with no prior experience in e-commerce will go through a settling-in period where mistakes may be made. Most companies try to cut corners wherever possible, and some view the costs associated with top-rate system security as unnecessary. Unfortunately, consumers can't know if any given e-store operation is being managed by professionals who are knowledgeable about computer security. A large corporation with a thriving e-commerce operation is more likely to hire the necessary technical personnel to keep its servers safe from cyberattacks. A small or medium-sized company that is trying out Web-based sales for the first time may be much less secure. See Section 10.2 for more advice on how to evaluate an e-store operation. But before you get too caught up in risk assessments, remember to put these risks in their proper perspective. Whenever you use a credit card in a restaurant or over the phone, you are subjecting yourself to comparable risks. The only difference is that you are probably not worrying about it in those more familiar contexts.

Acceptable Levels of Risk

Before you enter your credit card account number on a Web page, check whether the Web page is secure. If it is, your risk is very small. If you feel safe placing a credit card order over the telephone or if you allow store clerks to discard credit card impression carbons without their tearing them up in front of you first, you have no reason to worry about using Navigator and MSIE for credit card transactions. All of these scenarios carry some amount of risk, but most people live with such risks in exchange for the convenience of fast transactions.

If you do a lot of shopping online, you'll end up with accounts at different sites so that you can track your orders. Some sites support the convenience of **one-click shopping** for repeat customers. This is a convenient service designed to speed you through your purchase, and your account information is protected by a password. Most people pick the same userid and the same password for each new e-commerce site with which they do business. This is like using the same key for your home, your office, your car, and your safe deposit box. It might be more convenient, but you stand to lose a lot if someone steals that key. You should always select a new password for each site. You can easily manage multiple passwords for various online merchants if you install a *password manager* to help you out, as discussed in Section 9.6. A good password manager is easy to use and can be obtained online for free.

When You Shop Online, Remember These Tips

1. Use a credit card instead of checks, money orders, or debit cards.
2. Examine the URL for the beginning `https://`, and check for a locked padlock or unbroken key icon before entering any credit card account information.
3. Do business with reputable companies that have been selling online for at least a year.
4. Do not use the same password for all of your e-commerce accounts.
5. Save a copy of all purchase orders and confirmation numbers for your records.
6. Review your credit card billing statement each month, and report any questionable charges immediately to the credit card issuer.

These basics will get you started. Safe e-commerce practices are discussed in more detail in Chapter 10. In Chapter 11, you'll learn about how sensitive information such as credit card account numbers is encrypted for maximal safety.

2.7   PROTECTING YOUR PRIVACY

Sometimes people don't appreciate what they have until it's gone. Privacy is like that. Consumer data has always been valuable for marketing purposes, but the Internet has created opportunities for data collection on a scale never before encountered. Imagine a man following you around all day, taking notes. He jots down which television shows you watch and how many times you leave the room while the television set is on. He pays attention to how much time you spend on the telephone and to whom you talk. He follows you when you go shopping, recording which stores you visit, how much time you spend looking at specific items, and which items you purchased. He notes which magazines and newspapers you read, as well as exactly which articles catch your eye. He knows when you wake up and when you go to bed. He does this every day—and then he sells this information to anyone who wants it!

This level of surveillance might seem an unthinkable invasion of privacy, but this is what can happen each time that you take your Web browser for a spin. Any Web page can be programmed to collect information about, for example, when you visited the page and how many times, which links you clicked on the page, and how long it took before you clicked them. Consumer privacy is not protected by the U.S. Constitution or by federal law, so it's up to each of us to protect ourselves, if we care about keeping our private lives private.

Never fill out a form on a Web page that asks for personal information unless that information is required for a credit card transaction; for example, your home address is needed for shipping purposes. ***Under no circumstances should you divulge your social security number, age, income, or other sensitive information.*** This information is used only for profiling purposes (see Section 9.4) and should not be required by any company, online or offline.

Before you complete a site's form as part of a credit card transaction, check the site's **privacy policy** (see below). Companies are required by law to divulge computer records under court order and need not obtain your permission before releasing your personal data to law enforcement agencies. However, they are not required by U.S. law to obtain your permission in order to sell your personal data. So, read the policy to find out if the company plans to sell or distribute your personal information to third parties or its business partners.

Privacy Policies

A responsible e-commerce site points to its privacy policy via a link at the bottom of its home page. Many sites display a **TRUSTe** icon; click the TRUSTe icon to see the site's privacy policy (see the Above and Beyond section in Chapter 7). If a company does not make finding its privacy policy easy, or it hasn't posted a privacy statement, assume the worst. This is one case in which no news is bad news. Sites that take your privacy seriously will go out of their way to reassure you that your data is safe.

Sometimes a company will offer you a customized service of some sort in exchange for information about your interests and other background information. This is a big feature for portal sites and online news delivery services. You might feel that a personalized Web page is exactly what you need. In such cases, collecting personal information might be necessary. For example, to receive a regional weather report, you must reveal where you live. However, be aware that the same information needed to customize a service for you can also be used by banner advertisers, junk e-mail operations, and direct mail companies, if the site chooses to sell that information. In these cases, be especially careful to check for a privacy policy and weigh the pros and cons before giving away your personal information. Once it goes up for grabs, you will not be able to call it back.

Few privacy laws have been passed to protect personal data. The proposed privacy legislation in the United States that does exist is being drafted slowly and piecemeal. However, thanks to the Child Online Protection Act, information collected from children on the Internet requires prior parental permission.

In addition, the 1999 Electronic Privacy Bill of Rights Act attempts to establish more comprehensive guidelines that are on par with the more stringent European regulations. Yet as of this writing, this legislation is still pending and might never make it through Congress. For the most part, U.S. companies are self-regulating regarding consumer privacy policies. That is, they can do as they please with the information that they collect.

You can study more about privacy safeguards by visiting **PrivacyScan's Privacy Tips** and reading more about privacy in the Above and Beyond section. You need to do protect your personal information; no one else will do that for you.

2.8 INTERNET SCAMS

The famous saying "There's a sucker born every minute" dates from 1869 and was never actually said by the famous P. T. Barnum (it was said by someone named David Hannum, but that's another story). However, since the advent of the Internet, it might be more accurate to say, "There are 1,000 suckers born every minute." Scam artists are nothing new. The Internet has simply made it easier than ever for them to reach a huge pool of potential pigeons. The **Internet Fraud Watch** site has compiled a complete index of commonly encountered Internet frauds and scams. You can also read the **Internet ScamBusters** newsletter or research classic scams in the **ScamBusters archive** of back issues.

If something sounds too good to be true, it probably is—and if you saw it on the Internet, you can be sure of that. Here are some tips for avoiding scams on the Net.

- Beware of get rich quick offers, especially if they show up in your e-mail inbox as unsolicited e-mail messages.

- Don't trust an operation only because it offers a slick-looking Web site.
- Be wary of anyone who pressures you to respond fast.
- Never send cash. When buying something from a private individual over the Net, try to arrange for a cash on delivery (COD) payment to protect yourself. Any operation that lists only a P.O. box address could disappear tomorrow without a trace. If you must send someone a check or money order, don't spend more than you are prepared to lose.

Further, watch out for any e-mail offer that promises you any of the following:

- Money by pulling in additional "investors"
- Money by stuffing envelopes at home
- Money playing the currency exchange markets
- Free goods once you pay a membership fee
- Miracle health cures and diet formulas
- Your credit record repaired for a fee
- Insider investment advice for a fee
- Free cable service by using a descrambler (these are illegal)
- Guaranteed loans or credit
- Vacations as a prize

Con artists and criminals have greater reach and more opportunities than ever before. As more people go online, the potential audience for scams and rip-offs grows as well. A scam artist can set up shop in cyberspace and then quickly vanish to stay clear of the law. However, law enforcement agencies are getting wise to online crime. If you believe that a scam artist or fraudulent business has victimized you or you become aware of any suspicious communications or criminal activities, contact the **National Fraud Information Center**. It might not be able to resolve your complaint, but it will forward your report to a relevant law enforcement agency that can initiate an investigation.

2.9 ONLINE AUCTIONS

Online auctions link buyers with sellers who might never find each other any other way. Hard-to-find items might be no further away than the right search query, and prices are subject to the simple rules of supply and demand. When all goes well, the seller is happy, the buyer is happy, and everyone will tell you how a particular online auction site, such as eBay, has changed their lives. Millions of transactions take place at online auctions every day (see the Above and Beyond section in Chapter 10).

Participating in online auctions also involves risk. Online auction sites have topped **Internet Fraud Watch**'s list of popular Internet scams since its inception in 1997. In

1999, the Federal Trade Commission (FTC) received almost 11,000 complaints about Internet auctions, a dramatic increase from only 107 in 1997. The FTC, Justice Department, U.S. Postal Inspection Service, and other federal agencies have filed almost three dozen law enforcement actions concerning online auction fraud.

Watch Out for Highly Popular Items

Popular collectibles attract a lot of bidders at online auction sites. They also attract a lot of scam artists. In the typical set up, a buyer pays for an item that is never delivered. Documented complaints have exposed operators who have collected as much as $50,000 from victims without delivering merchandise to any. The top three states for reported cyberfraud operations are California, Florida, and Texas. Personal checks are the most common method of payment in fraudulent Internet transactions, with money orders ranking second.

Before buying an item at an online auction, do some homework first and proceed with caution. On your first visit to an auction site, browse to find out how it operates. Most sites are just fancy bulletin boards for public notices. The site assumes no responsibility for the accuracy of its posts or the integrity of its sellers. Look for sites that post fraud warnings and offer the following features:

- Escrow services (see later in the chapter)
- Feedback areas
- Easy-to-follow complaint procedures
- A policy to remove problem vendors

If you see an item that interests you, find out anything you can about the seller. If it's a company, contact the **Better Business Bureau** (BBB) and see if any complaints have been filed. Be aware, however, that not all legitimate companies are members of a BBB. Also, no record at the BBB means only that no one has filed a complaint against a company; it doesn't mean that no complaints exist against that company. If the auction site offers online feedback from other customers, check out what they say. Note, however, that feedback comments come with no guarantees; for example, a seller can post bogus messages to bolster the seller's image. Further, a seller who has never sold items at that site will have no track record.

Sales by private sellers are riskier than are sales by companies. Consumer protection laws apply only to commercial businesses, so if you have problems with a private seller, you are on your own. A legitimate private seller should be happy to provide you with his or her name, street address (don't accept a P.O. box address), and telephone number. Avoid transactions that can't be backed up with this much information.

Never pay for an item in cash unless you can first examine the item. Paying with a credit card gives you the greatest protection should you need to return the item.

However, many sellers at an online auction are not merchants and therefore can't process a credit card transaction. In this case, use an **escrow service**, which will withhold your payment from the seller until you've received your item and deemed it acceptable. You might also be able to arrange for a COD shipment.

Some Sellers Are Honest

On March 6, 1998, I threw caution to the wind and sent off a $27 check to someone selling Beanie Baby™ toys online. This was at the height of the Beanie Baby™ feeding frenzy, with people lining up outside of stores for hours when new shipments of the toy were expected. I was happy to take a chance buying two of the toys from a seller on the Net. However, I had had no prior contact with the seller and I found no recommendations from any other satisfied customers. So I was pleased, and mildly surprised, when Iggy and Gobbles actually arrived at my house on March 14. They had been sent via insured U.S. Postal Service Priority Mail and were in excellent condition (see Figure 2.11). Despite the risks, I felt reassured by two facts.

1. The seller replied to me from a `.edu` mail address. This told me that the mail account had not been set up primarily for an Internet scam. I would have been much more suspicious of a free Web-based mail account.

2. I was given a residential mailing address to which to send payment. Had the address been a P. O. box, I probably would have backed off.

However, I still knew I could get burned. Negotiating with unknown individuals over the Internet is always a gamble, despite precautions.

Figure 2.11:
Iggy and Gobbles, Delivered Promptly and in Excellent Condition

Until you become better educated about how online auctions work, follow these tips:

- Begin with inexpensive items.
- Work with large well-known auction sites.
- Deal with sellers who are willing to give you their telephone numbers.
- For expensive items, always use an escrow service.

If you have trouble with a transaction, report the incident to the **National Fraud Information Center**, which will relay the report to appropriate federal, state, or local law enforcement agencies.

2.10 LIBEL AND LAWSUITS

Libel is any written or pictorial statement that damages a person or organization. Posting libelous statements on the Net can result in legal actions against the poster. Some large corporations monitor Web pages and online discussions in public forums in an effort to discover potentially damaging statements about corporate services or products. Libel is not a criminal offense, so you can't be sent to jail for it. However, you can be sued for damages in civil court.

Statements about a company's products or services could be considered libelous if they result in lost revenues for the company. The Internet offers ample opportunity for people to make damaging misrepresentations that could have widespread negative consequences. ***A person who disseminates information that is deemed harmful to a company can be the target of a lawsuit even if the information is accurate.*** If the claims can be verified, the lawsuit will fail, but the ensuing legal process can be very costly and time-consuming. Most people do not want to risk a lawsuit even if they know their defense is solid.

Statements about individuals can also be considered libelous, under certain conditions, although individuals are less likely to initiate lawsuits. However, if the person libeled is a public figure, no lawsuit is likely. This is because in 1988, the U.S. Supreme Court held that public figures can be publicly ridiculed, even if that ridicule borders on libel. For example, Bill Gates, the founder and former CEO of Microsoft, is considered to be a public figure and therefore a safe target. If Bill Gates won a civil suit each time that someone said something nasty about him on the Internet, he could probably collect enough money to buy out all of his company's shareholders. However, care should be taken regarding people who are less famous. In a libel dispute, a private individual who has not opted for public life has stronger rights than does a public figure.

Information is difficult to contain on the Internet. All digital communication can be easily reproduced and distributed without your permission, so you can't be sure that a private e-mail communication will remain private. Before you send anything out onto the Internet, ask yourself how you would feel if your message turned up on the front page of the local newspaper. If that thought makes you sweat, reconsider posting your message. ***Any online communication can be easily transformed into a very public document,*** either by its intended recipient or by someone who has broken system security and has covertly intercepted your outgoing e-mail.

2.11   THREATS AND HARASSMENT

Children used to scream "I'm going to kill you!" on playgrounds and schoolyards all over the country, and with total impunity. However, that was before grade-school children started carrying handguns—and following through on their threats. Our society takes threats of deadly force more seriously these days.

Threats posted to chat rooms or contained in e-mail messages are likely to arouse serious attention. There is no such thing as a casual threat on the Internet, even when said in jest and between close friends. Online stalking and hate mail incidents are a reality. One chilling Web site detailed the emotional breakdown of a teenage user who eventually carried out his murderous fantasies about a 15-year-old girl who had spurned his advances.

The Internet fosters online attacks in which anonymity and geographical distance seem to turn some seemingly normal people into raving lunatics, engaging in flame wars. A **flame** is an e-mail or newsgroup message in which the writer attacks another person with uninhibited hostility. A **flame war** is an exchange of flames between two or more participants. It can be very easy to write off any online display of rage as just another flame. Who can say when the rage is pathological and when it's just another flame? This makes many people nervous, since it's impossible to know much about the people behind the words in an Internet communication.

Regardless of the social climate, U.S. criminal laws make issuing threats on or off the Internet illegal. Anyone who threatens the President of the United States will be investigated by the Secret Service and can be both fined and jailed for the offense (18 USC Sec. 871). Any threat of kidnapping or causing bodily harm that crosses state lines can be punished with a $250,000 fine and five years in jail (18 USC Sec. 875). How do state lines apply to the Net? A packet moving through an out-of-state server might qualify even if it contains an e-mail message that has a source address and destination address in the same state.

Consider as an example the eighteen-year-old Florida student who made threatening remarks to a student in an Internet chat room in December 1999 (see Figure 2.12). The second student attended Columbine High School in Littleton, Colorado. Those threats resulted in Columbine High School's closing down for two days while the FBI investigated the threat and tracked down the author. In April 1999, two Columbine students, Eric Harris and Dylan Klebold, killed 12 fellow students and a teacher at their school, before killing themselves. Once identified, the Florida youth publicly apologized for his chat room fantasy play. No firearms were found in his possession, and there was no evidence that he intended to carry out his threats. His words were nevertheless a felony offense worthy of an FBI investigation and subsequent arrest under the Interstate Communications statute (18 USC Sec. 875).

Figure 2.12:
A Chat Session That Prompted an FBI Investigation

Soup81: Listen, I can't tell you who I am because you know me... Do me a favor, don't go to school tomorrow.

Student: Why?

Soup81: Please, I trust in you and confide in you.

Student: I have to go. I can't miss school.

Soup81: I need to finish what begun and if you go I don't want blood on your hands.

Student: Please don't do this. You are really scaring me.

Soup81: There is nothing to be scared about, just don't go to school and don't tell anyone. If anyone finds out, you'll be the first to go.

Student: Please don't do this.

Soup81: Time magazine has brought more chaos and I need to strengthen this. This is what they wanted and people need to know what is really going on here. Don't go to school.

Student: What am I going to tell my parents when they wonder why I didn't go to school?

Soup81: Pretend you're sick! But don't tell anyone because you and only one person knows now. I had to tell someone before the big day.

Student: Well, what about my two best friends?

Soup81: It was nice to know you. I only wish I could tell you who I really was and to let you know how much I liked you. But I'm a nobody, and soon everyone will know who I am. Goodbye. Good to evil and evil to good.

Student: Please don't do this. You are really scaring me.

Harassment in the workplace is another potential trouble area for Internet users. Title VII of the 1964 Civil Rights Act changed the workplace dramatically. Since Title VII, you can't hang up a Penthouse calendar in your office and you can't make a racist joke with impunity. Similarly, offensive materials available on the Internet have no business in the workplace. If an employee is looking at a Web page that contains sexually (or religiously or racially) offensive material, and a coworker happens to see it while walking by, the employer could be cited for harassment. An employee who receives an e-mail that contains religiously or sexually or racially offensive jokes and forwards the e-mail to the whole department could be the target of a lawsuit.

Companies have become increasingly vigilant about Title VII infractions because they are legally liable if an employee chooses to initiate a lawsuit based on a civil rights violation in the workplace. In an effort to avoid lawsuits, many companies have installed pornography filters on their Web browsers and mail monitors on their e-mail servers. Employees are subject to stringent AUPs and can be terminated for noncompliance of them (see Section 2.2). Free speech in the workplace takes a back seat to Title VII. Employees must understand that an employer who is trying to comply with Title VII can curb their freedom.

It is often said that e-mail communications are more like postcards than letters: Anyone can read the writing on a postcard that is in transit. It's safer to think of e-mail in the workplace like posting a notice on a billboard. Not only is your e-mail very visible to anyone who wants to look, but you can be fairly sure that someone is looking regularly. Similarly, your employer might be keeping a log of all of your browser activities in an effort to maintain a proper workplace environment. If you want to exercise your First Amendment rights on the Internet, do it on your own time, from your own personal computer, using a commercial ISP. When it comes to the workplace, you are subject to a different set of behavioral codes than the ones that apply after hours (see also Section 2.13).

Students are similarly constrained by the AUPs of their educational institution, although colleges and universities are somewhat more reluctant to enforce rules that could interfere with the free expression of ideas. Schools nevertheless can be fined for Title VII violations and therefore must walk a fine line regarding what is considered to be offensive material in student e-mail and graphical displays on computers in public areas.

2.12　SOFTWARE PIRACY AND COPYRIGHT INFRINGEMENTS

Software piracy is the willful reproduction or distribution of one or more copies of one or more copyrighted works that collectively have a total retail value of more than $1,000. It is a criminal offense punishable by a jail term and a fine. Newcomers to the Internet often mistakenly think that copyright violations can be prosecuted only if the materials being distributed are sold for profit. This is not true; the person performing the piracy need not profit from the action in order to be found guilty of software piracy (see the Above and Beyond section in Chapter 2 for more details). The seriousness of a copyright violation is measured by how much the copyright owner's potential income has been harmed.

When you purchase commercial software, you do not become the owner of that software. Rather, you purchase only *licensee rights* to that software. Software licenses grant you only the right to *use* the software, subject to specific restrictions. It is your responsibility to understand the applicable licensing restrictions of the commercial software that you use. For more information about software piracy and answers to commonly asked questions, visit **Microsoft's Anti-Piracy Web site**.

Be especially careful about software that is distributed over the Internet. Legitimate software is always accompanied by a licensing agreement, even when distributed for free. *If you obtain any software that does not come with a licensing agreement, discard the software.*

Software Piracy Is Big Business

From *1999 Infosecurity Year-in-Review*:

- Worldwide, software piracy costs industry $11 billion a year.
- More than 90% of all software used in Bulgaria, China, Indonesia, Lebanon, Oman, and Russia is pirated software.
- 60% of the software sold via online auctions is sold illegally.

In August 1999, a 22-year-old University of Oregon senior became the first person convicted under the 1997 No Electronic Theft (NET) Act for software piracy and other copyright violations on the Internet. This student used his university computer account to publicly post on the Web a large number of MP3 files, as well as software applications, games, and movies. Under this law, acts of software piracy are either felonies or misdemeanors, depending on the value of the materials distributed. A felony conviction is punishable by up to three years in prison and a $250,000 fine.

While the U.S. Justice Department is poised to make Internet piracy a law enforcement priority under NET, the Recording Industry Association of America (RIAA) is taking matters into its own hands when it comes to illegal MP3 file distributions. RIAA is a trade association whose members create, manufacture, or distribute approximately 90% of all audio recordings produced in the United States. The Anti-Piracy division of the RIAA investigates the illegal production and distribution of these recordings. According to the RIAA, increased access to CD-R (Compact Disk-Recordable) drives are responsible for the surge in the number of illegal audio CDs created during 1999. The RIAA reports that in the first six months of 1999, 165,981 counterfeit audio CDs were seized by law enforcement agents. This compares to only 23,858 in all of 1998.

RIAA Bounty Hunters

In 1999, RIAA announced the CDReward program against CD-R pirates. Under this controversial policy, the RIAA will award up to $10,000 to an individual who provides the RIAA with information regarding illegal CD-R drive manufacturing locations.

RIAA is presumably looking for the big fish—the people who run large MP3 distribution sites on the Web or who manufacture CDs on order. However, anyone who downloads illegal MP3s from the Internet is also engaging in a criminal activity. The RIAA could stage a well-publicized lynching of a lowly user just to make a point.

The routine distribution of illegal MP3 files on the Internet presents an ethical dilemma for college students. Some universities are stepping in to protect themselves when copyright infringements are brought to their attention. For example, in 1999, university officials at Carnegie-Mellon University shut down Internet access accounts for 71 students who posted music files and other copyrighted material on the campus computer system.

When Is It Against the Law to Copy a Music File?

Some music files on the Internet are freely available from artists and record companies that are looking for maximal exposure. Downloading these files for personal use is legal. Other music, however, typically music recorded by major record companies, cannot be downloaded from the Internet without violating copyright protections. Many commercial MP3 sites are careful to post only legal MP3 files for public downloads. Other sites, usually private sites run by students or hackers, post MP3 files illegally. ***If you download an audio file that is being distributed illegally, you are guilty of copyright infringement.***

Your legal status is somewhat more complicated if you have purchased the music in question on a CD (however, bootlegged CDs are not legitimate). The Copyright Act of 1971 prohibits anyone but the copyright owner from making a copy of a recording. However, the Audio Home Recording Act of 1992 protects consumers from lawsuits by record companies when they make copies of personal recordings for their own use. Under this act, people may copy cassette tapes and CDs onto computer files as long as the original source material was acquired legally and the copies are made for personal use only. Is it illegal to download a file from an Internet site if you have a legal right to create that file on your own through other means? The courts have not yet had an opportunity to rule on this issue. RIAA is not likely to prosecute anyone who legitimately paid for the right to enjoy a piece of music produced and distributed by RIAA member companies. RIAA is more concerned with blatant copyright infringements, since those activities pose a serious threat to the recording industry.

Converting CD Tracks to MP3 Files

The 1992 Audio Home Recording Act gives you the legal right to convert CD tracks to MP3 files as long as you are the legitimate owner of the CD that you want to copy. Converting the tracks depends on your having the right software. You need a CD ripper to copy the tracks into a `.wav` file format and an MP3 converter to translate the `.wav` file into an MP3 file. Details, as well as pointers to freeware for doing this, can be found on the Internet. mp3.com has good tutorials for beginners (if the RIAA hasn't shut it down by the time that you read this).

2.13 PORNOGRAPHY AND OTHER LAPSES IN GOOD TASTE

For those who enjoy off-color jokes or have an interest in "blue" material (pornography), the Internet might appear to be a haven in which anything goes. This is not quite true. The FBI has launched many successful sting operations on the Internet to trap child pornography rings, while in 1999, 22 employees of *The New York Times* newspaper were fired for sending offensive e-mail messages from work.

The First Amendment protects against the censorship of pornography and prosecution of those who create or distribute pornography. These protections also extend to pornography on the Internet. As a result, attempts to outlaw "bad" language online have so far been unsuccessful. For example, the well-publicized federal law, the Communications Decency Act of 1996, was overturned by the U.S. Supreme Court in 1998 for violating the First Amendment. Although the First Amendment does limit the powers of government, exclusions to it apply. For example, pornography involving adults is generally protected (as long as it doesn't cross a mysterious line that separates the merely pornographic from the genuinely obscene), but owning or distributing child pornography in the United States is a felony.

When Your Personal Computer Is Not

Ronald F. Thiemann, Dean of the Harvard Divinity School, resigned from his post in 1998 "for conduct unbecoming a dean." Apparently, Thiemann had a healthy collection of explicit pornography on his personal computer—equipment that actually was the property of Harvard University. When he asked university technical support personnel to transfer his files to a larger hard drive, the collection was discovered and brought to the attention of Harvard's president, Neil L. Rudenstine.

Although Thiemann had done nothing illegal, his resignation was accepted presumably to minimize public embarrassment for Harvard. Thiemann still holds a tenured faculty position at the university.

Chances are, your proclivities are more mainstream. Who hasn't passed along a raunchy joke or made a sexist statement (in jest, if not in earnest), perhaps in an e-mail message to a friend or relative from work? Be aware that personal e-mail on a company computer is less private than a personal telephone call on an office telephone. Employers cannot legally monitor personal calls on company telephones, but they can monitor e-mail messages that pass through company computers. If company policy prohibits offensive materials on office computers, a raunchy joke or a sexist statement could cost you your job. The First Amendment affords you no protection in such situations.

Workplace Rules

Computer communications must be consistent with conventional standards of ethical and proper conduct, behavior and manners and are not to be used to create, forward or display any offensive or disruptive messages, including photographs, graphics and audio materials.
—From a policy document for employees of *The New York Times*

Your employer determines your rights and freedoms in the workplace. Even though *The New York Times* allows its employees "reasonable" personal use of company e-mail, its management fired 22 workers for sending offensive e-mail messages. The *Times* justified the firings as necessary in order to minimize its legal liability in the face of potential harassment lawsuits.

When it comes to offensive materials in the workplace, legal liability is the bottom line. In 1995, offensive e-mail played a key role in a case involving a subsidiary of Chevron Corp. An e-mail message entitled "25 reasons beer is better than women" was used as supporting evidence in a sexual harassment claim that cost the company a $2.2 million settlement. Given this legal climate, some companies use sophisticated software to spy on employee e-mail. Although employees might feel that they deserve more privacy in the workplace, the courts generally find that companies are justified in monitoring the use of their computer equipment. The right to free expression is squaring off against the right to a harassment-free workplace—and free expression is losing. If you must be off-color, save it for after work hours and keep it out of your office e-mail. Note that if the computer in your home is owned by your employer, you should treat it as you would any computer in the office. The same company policies apply at 2 A.M. in your own bedroom if the computer that you are using is company property (see Section 2.11).

Search engines make finding adult content online easy, and all sorts of kinky characters can be found in chat rooms devoted to pornography. Indulge if you must, but if you want to stay out of trouble you need to understand what lines you can and cannot cross.

2.14 HOAXES AND LEGENDS

The Internet is a source of valuable information and, unfortunately, much misinformation. This section discusses the long-standing tradition of Internet hoaxes and urban legends that never fail to snare innocent new victims year after year.

Don't Be Naive

You can't believe everything that you read, especially if you read it on the Internet.

The Internet is particularly effective at propagating misinformation designed to alarm people and generate panic among the uninitiated. Once you start getting e-mail, you might begin to see earnest computer virus alerts and possibly chain letters that promise to turn your life into a living hell (or possibly heaven on Earth) if you don't send the letter on to other people. These notices always ask you pass the information along to all of your friends, relatives, and coworkers. Since there are always enough newbies on the Net who helpfully comply out of ignorance and goodwill, the Net will probably never be rid of these things. The virus warnings tend to come and go, and come again, whenever enough collective ignorance is available to breath life into them one more time. This problem will go away only when everyone becomes educated about the Internet. You can do your part by checking out the **Computer Virus Myths** Web site.

Although the Internet is a fertile breeding ground for frauds, scams, and misinformation, some information on the Net is not necessarily malicious—it's just false. If you see something on the Net that sounds not quite right, visit the **Urban Legends and Folklore** Web site and conduct a keyword search for the item. If it's an Internet classic, you'll find it here. In time, you'll learn to spot an Internet hoax a mile away.

Things to Remember

- Read the terms of all AUPs that apply to you.
- Never tell anyone your password.
- Change your passwords periodically.
- E-mail is not private, and chat room participants can be traced.
- Do not offer personal information on a site before seeing and agreeing with the site's privacy policy.
- Handle e-mail attachments with great care, and use antivirus software.
- If you are running Windows, turn off the File and Printer Sharing feature.
- Do not give out credit card account information on an insecure Web page.
- Computers in a workplace might be monitored for offensive materials.
- Just because something is easy to do doesn't make it legal.
- It is your responsibility to know the laws that pertain to your activities (both online and offline).

Important Concepts

acceptable use policy (AUP)—usage restrictions for computer accounts, Internet access accounts, and many other Internet-related services.

computer virus—potentially destructive code hidden inside of a host program and distributed to a large number of computers.

copyright infringement—the unauthorized distribution of material protected by copyright restrictions.

e-mail virus—a worm (erroneously called a virus) that is spread by e-mail attachments or scripts associated with HTML-enabled e-mail.

harassment—offensive, unwanted, and unavoidable communications or content, usually characterized by multiple or habitual incidents.

libel—damaging statements about a company or individual.

password security—your first and most powerful line of defense against hackers.

secure Web page—a Web page where it is safe to enter sensitive data such as credit card account numbers.

software piracy—the unauthorized distribution of commercial software.

terms of service (ToS)—same as an acceptable use policy.

Trojan horse—unauthorized code, often designed to enable remote control over your computer at a later date.

worm—potentially destructive code that depends on networked communications and commonly used software in order to propagate.

Where Can I Learn More?

Computer Virus Myths   `http://www.kumite.com/myths/`

Antivirus Online   `http://www.av.ibm.com/current/FrontPage/`

Widespread Virus Myths   `http://www.stiller.com/myths.htm`

Urban Legends and Folklore   `http://urbanlegends.about.com/index.htm`

File and Printer Sharing (NetBIOS) Fact and Fiction
`http://cable-dsl.home.att.net/netbios.htm`

PFIR—People for Internet Responsibility   `http://www.pfir.org/`

Electronic Frontier Foundation   `http://www.eff.org/`

Privacy Rights Clearinghouse   `http://www.privacyrights.org/`

Electronic Privacy Information Center   `http://www.epic.org/`

Center for Democracy and Technology   `http://www.cdt.org/`

First Amendment Cyber-Tribune   `http://w3.trib.com/FACT/`

Problems and Exercises

1. What is an acceptable use policy (AUP)? Find the AUP for your Internet access account, and study it carefully. Have you ever violated the terms of your AUP without realizing it at the time? Are there any restrictions that you do not understand or to which you object?

2. Explain how a computer virus, a Trojan horse, and a worm differ from each other.

3. The Melissa virus used an innovative strategy for tricking people into opening e-mail attachments. How did Melissa fool users?

4. What is an RTF file? Can an RTF file contain a macro virus? Should Microsoft make RTF the default file format for Word? Explain your answer.

5. What is `normal.dot`? Explain how `normal.dot` is used to spread macro viruses.

6. Explain how HTML-enabled e-mail clients can spread worms without the use of e-mail attachments.

7. Which is safer to use online: a check, a credit card, or a money order? Explain your answer.

8. What two things should you look for before you enter any personal information on a Web page?

9. What laws protect the privacy of American consumers? Is personal privacy protected by the U.S. Constitution?

10. According to Internet Fraud Watch, what online activity is responsible for the largest number of consumer complaints?

11. If you are thinking of participating in an online auction, what four safeguards should you look for at the auction site?

12. When can someone be sued for libel? Why is it relatively safe to criticize a politician?

13. Is it safe to criticize a person or company in a personal e-mail message to a friend? Is it safer to make the same statements in a personal telephone call? Or a written letter? How about posting the statements on a Web site if you don't give out the URL to anyone? Discuss the relative risks and worst-case scenarios in each of these cases.

14. What is the maximal penalty for making a threat of bodily harm that crosses state lines?

15. What law makes a business liable for harassment in the workplace? What steps are companies taking to protect themselves against harassment lawsuits?

16. What is the legal definition of software piracy? Do you have to profit from your activities in order to be guilty of software piracy?

17. When is it legal for a private individual to make a copy of an audio CD? Is it illegal to make copies of audio CDs by using a CD-R drive?

18. What is the Recording Industry Association of America, and what is it doing to combat the illegal distribution of MP3 files?

19. Is it illegal to download pornography? Can your employer legally override your First Amendment rights in its AUP? Can your employer legally monitor all of your online activities? Can it censor objectionable Web sites on workplace computers?

20. Why do so many virus hoaxes exist on the Net, and why don't they ever die out?

Personal Safety Online:
Above and Beyond

The No Electronic Theft Act of 1997

Software piracy is a serious threat to the software industry. Intellectual property laws never anticipated the unprecedented ease with which software can be duplicated and distributed over the Internet. New laws are often motivated by specific incidents, and, every so often, someone seems to deliberately challenge the establishment in order to force a change.

Such seems to be the case when in 1994, a 21-year-old MIT student, David LaMacchia, set up a public server on the Internet and invited people to post their favorite software for public distribution. LaMacchia made no effort to commercialize his server or benefit from its software archive financially. He merely gave people a place where they could freely upload and download all sorts of software. Much of the software that people posted was subject to copyright restrictions, and the people who traded these files were breaking the law. However, it seemed silly to go after the people who used the site without going after LaMacchia for facilitating software piracy on an international scale. The tricky part was finding a law that LaMacchia had broken. He was not guilty of software piracy himself, even though he clearly encouraged it. Moreover, it seemed that he had found a legal loophole in existing copyright law. That is, as long as he did not benefit from the activities on his server, his actions did not fall under any of the criminal statutes for copyright violations. LaMacchia's actions were thought to have cost software copyright owners more than one million dollars in losses.

Eventually, he was indicted by a grand jury for wire fraud under the wire fraud statute [18 U.S.C. Sec. 1343] enacted in 1952 to protect consumers from false advertising on radio and television. It was never intended to apply to copyright infringements, and it certainly didn't anticipate computer-mediated communications. LaMacchia filed for a dismissal of the case, and the judge agreed. Lawmakers soon thereafter went to work on new legislation to make sure something like that could never happen again. Most important, industry proponents wanted to close what had come to be called the "LaMacchia Loophole," the loophole in copyright laws that protects software distributors from prosecution for copyright infringements as long as they do not profit from their actions.

Three years after LaMacchia's case was dismissed, in December 1997, President Bill Clinton signed into law the No Electronic Theft (NET) Act. NET makes it illegal to reproduce or distribute copyrighted works, such as software programs and musical recordings, even if the defendant derives no financial gain. A person who reproduces or distributes one or more copies of a copyrighted work with a value of more than $1,000 and up to $2,500 can be charged with a misdemeanor, which can result in up to one year in prison and a fine of up to $100,000. Reproducing or distributing 10 or more copies of a copyrighted work that have a total value of more than $2,500 can be charged with a felony, punishable by up to three years in prison and a fine of up to $250,000.

The Digital Millennium Copyright Act of 1998

While software manufacturers have been struggling with the problem of software piracy over computer networks since the 1980s, the publishing and entertainment industries began to grasp the magnitude of their potential losses only after the Internet went mainstream in the 1990s. Publishers and movie studios want to capitalize on the Internet, but they also need to protect their lawful intellectual properties from unauthorized online distribution.

Although NET was a step in the right direction, copyright violations on the Internet are still notoriously difficult to enforce. If responsibility for enforcing copyright restrictions is not shared by networks and online services, copyright owners will face a major uphill battle. Who should be liable when a copyright infringement shows up on a Web site or a mailing list? Should the managers of the server be held responsible, as well as the author of the Web page or mail message? Should liability extend to the author's ISP and the network service behind the ISP? How far should liability extend, and who should police copyright infringements?

The policing question is a crucial concern for ISPs and system administrators. With countless people posting personal home pages on millions of Web servers, the task of checking all of those sites for copyright infringements would drive all commercial ISPs out of business and force universities to shut down all student Web sites. This is not a viable scenario for a technology that is transforming everything from education to economic prosperity.

Any new law designed to strengthen the enforcement of copyright restrictions on the Internet need to limit the liability of the service providers. Also, system administrators needs to assume some responsibility for Web sites that contain copyright infringements. The Digital Copyright Millennium Act (DCMA) was designed to balance the responsibility of service providers and copyright owners.

DCMA is based on a very simple idea. Each service provider must create a point of contact, an *agent*, for DCMA administration. This agent must respond to all reports of possible copyright violations involving Web sites or other digital communications that the service provider supports. Complaints can be filed by anyone, although frivolous complaints can lead to legal repercussions. Once a report has been filed, the DCMA agent must inform the party responsible for the alleged infringement that their Internet privileges will be terminated unless the matter is resolved. Notification of an alleged copyright violation by the DCMA agent amounts to a cease-and-desist order. In most cases, people violate copyright protections out of ignorance, and they are happy to remove any offending materials, once the matter is brought to their attention. However, if a dispute ensues and the case goes to court, the DCMA limits the liability of the service provider's "contributory infringement." That is, a service provider who complies with the DCMA will not be held responsible for copyright infringements by its own subscribers.

Plagiarism

Copyright violations occur when you reproduce a substantial subset of a written work verbatim. If you *paraphrase* a work, you are not guilty of a copyright violation, but you could be guilty of plagiarism. **Plagiarism** is the presentation of the ideas of a published work in one's own words but without proper attribution. Although plagiarism is not publishable by law, all educational institutions recognize it as a form of academic dishonesty and prohibit it by a code of ethics for all professional writers. For example, Mike Barnicle, a veteran columnist for the *Boston Globe*, resigned after someone noticed that he had plagiarized excerpts from the book *Mind Droppings* by George Carlin in one of his columns. College students who plagiarize published materials for course assignments are at the mercy of their professors, who are usually free to flunk them.

Note that responsibility for registering infringement complaints rests with the individual copyright owner. If a lot of revenue is at stake, the copyright owner will make an effort to police the Web for copyright violations. Companies exist that will monitor the Web on behalf of clients concerned about copyright infringements. Some corporations, such as Disney Corp., Playboy, Inc., and Coca-Cola Co., are very aggressive about protecting corporate images and trademarks. In fact, if a copyright holder makes no effort to protect its intellectual property, that holder's legal rights are weakened. This is especially true for large companies that have the resources to police their intellectual property.

If you want to incorporate copyrighted materials on a Web page, you need to know about the *Doctrine of Fair Use*, as well as when any copyright is due to expire. If you are an artist or writer with an interest in protecting your own works online, you'll want to learn how you can strengthen your legal rights in this area. The use of copyrighted materials on Web sites will be discussed in more detail in Section 4.10.

Notice and Consent Policies

The next time that you use a Web search engine, watch the banner ads that pop up each time that you conduct a search. For example, if you ask a question about cars, you'll see an ad for a car dealer. If you ask a question about the books that are in print, you'll get an ad for a bookstore. Web advertisers know that you're more likely to click an ad related to your queries than a random ad that is of no interest to you. Thus commercial search engines sell keywords to their advertisers; when you type a keyword that has been procured by an advertiser, you'll get an ad from that advertiser.

Recall that Web servers can watch you when you visit a Web site and can easily collect information about you and your interests based on your queries. They can ask you to fill out forms, as well as track the pages that you visit, the amount of time that you spend on each one, and the links that you click. All such data is potentially valuable for marketing purposes and can be sold to data brokers who specialize in online data collection.

The good news is that you don't have to avoid online services in order to preserve your privacy. Whenever you visit a Web site that is in a position to collect marketable data, look for a privacy policy concerning data collection. For example, you might see a statement like one of the following.

> "Occasionally, we share the e-mail addresses of our subscribers with providers of quality goods and services. If you would prefer not to receive such mailings, make this change to your subscription file by . . . ."

> "We consider the information regarding your membership, orders, and the products you purchase to be personal and confidential . . . . We will use the information to communicate special news, promotions, and product deals to you on a regular basis, unless you indicate that you do not wish to receive the messages . . . ."

Many e-commerce companies have adopted privacy policies based on ***notice and consent***. They post a statement that explains what data is collected and how it is used. A user then can deny or approve the service the right to resell the user's personal data. It is your responsibility to look for these policy statements and to communicate your wishes to the company and thereby stop its distribution of your personal data, if desired. If you can't find a policy statement or if the policy statement doesn't give you an opportunity to block the unapproved use of your personal data, you should assume the worst.

Note that privacy policies are always set up so that you must **opt out**, that is, explicitly deny permission to use your data. If you do nothing, they can do what they want with your data.

How Cookies Work

One of the most controversial data collection practices on the Web involves the use of cookies. A **cookie** is a file created by a site's Web server and stored on your host machine by your Web browser. It's a small file that patiently awaits your next visit to that Web site. Any Web server can check to see whether you have a cookie file and, if so, whether it has any useful information about you. For example, suppose that the last time you visited a particular site, you spent all of your time on two particular pages. A cookie can record this information so that on your next visit to that site, the server might greet you with a page display that makes it especially easy for you to navigate to those pages again.

Cookies allow Web servers to create a profile about you and your prior activities. Parts of this profile might have been collected with your assistance (for example, you have to tell it your name if you want a personal greeting). Other parts might be deduced from your past interactions with the server.

How can you tell if you've got cookies on your hard drive? Search your hard drive for a file whose filename includes the string "cookie." It might be called `cookies.txt` or `MagicCookie`. Once you've located a cookie file, open it —it's just a text file that contains separate cookies from different Web sites.

Here's an example of a short cookie file that has eight cookies from eight different Web sites. The names of the sites are given first, so you can always tell which sites dropped their cookies into the file.

.realaudio.com	TRUE	/ FALSE	946684740	uid	2062544869497233244
.timecast.com	TRUE	/ FALSE	946684740	uid	20618930869497239997
.dailybriefing.com	TRUE	/ FALSE	946684740	dbprofile	1040|fdotx
.abcnews.com	TRUE	/ FALSE	1500192813	SWID	711D5932-01DBCF9-080009DC93B5
.pathfinder.com	TRUE	/ FALSE	2051222400	PFUID	cc47f22035221ff33f41000ffff9d
.hotbot.com	TRUE	/ FALSE	937396800	ink	IU0TiDPvAC5874DFB49F09E6BCA7A
.boston.com	TRUE	/ FALSE	946684799	BGEP	206.119.237.14:24463877899644
www.geocities.com	FALSE	/ FALSE	941580297	GeoId	20413652878508297662

Cookies can make your time on the Web easier. For example, Amazon.com tracks the books that you browse when you visit its pages so that the company can offer recommendations the next time that you visit its site. The more time that you spend looking at books, the better these recommendations are likely to be. **The New York Times on the Web** is free but requires visitors to register with a name and a password. Once you've registered at the site, a cookie is installed that checks for your name and password each time that you return to the site. Thus you can enter the site automatically without having to enter your name or password, as though the site were unrestricted. This is particularly convenient for people who have a lot of passwords and have trouble remembering them.

Cookies are also used to target potential customers with banner ads. For example, if you visit ZDNet.com, the site will record any of your mouse clicks that reveal an interest in specific technologies. A resulting cookie might be used the next time that you visit ZDNet.com to show you an ad about a product that reflects your interests. For more details about how cookies and banner ads are used to create consumer profiles, read Section 9.4 and visit **Privacy.net**.

You might think that cookies provide a useful service. Maybe you want to hear about products and promotions that you might find interesting. You also might want to be reassured that all of that personal information is not being sold to information brokers and marketing companies. At the very least, you might want to be informed if a Web site is going to put a cookie on your hard drive. In an effort to respect your privacy, most Web browsers now ask their users for permission to install a site's cookie on the visitor's machine; the most recent versions of Navigator and MSIE are now "cookie-correct" in this way. Figure 2.13 shows a cookie alert box that pops up when a Web browser asks a user for this permission.

Figure 2.13:
Browser Asking
Permission for a
Cookie to Be
Installed

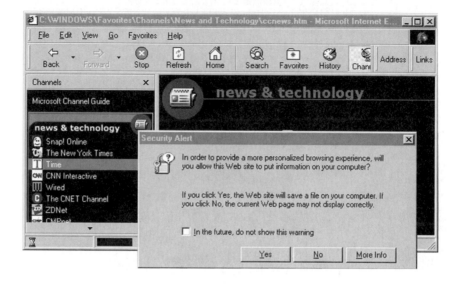

You can accept or reject the request, and your browser will proceed as instructed. You can also instruct your browser not to bother you with any more cookie requests during this visit to this host (some Web sites can create multiple cookies for each user). Each time that you restart your browser and return to the Web site in a new session, you'll have to respond to an initial cookie query all over again, but at least you can avoid some of the cookie requests during the session.

In addition, you can opt to avoid all cookie requests by reconfiguring your browser's preference settings. Figure 2.14 shows the options available to MSIE users. You can opt to accept all cookies unconditionally, reject all cookies unconditionally, or be prompted to review all cookie requests via cookie alerts.

The pros and cons of cookies are hotly debated among Netizens. Most people are more comfortable with cookies when they can exercise some control over who is allowed to create them. Exercising this control does take time, however, so some people prefer to automatically block all cookie requests in order to maintain maximal privacy while keeping their Web sessions as streamlined as possible. If you want more power over which cookies you accept and reject and you don't want to be bothered with cookie alerts, software is available for managing cookies. Cookie management is discussed in the Above and Beyond section in Chapter 9.

Privacy, Digital Records, and Commercial Interests

Some concepts are so entrenched in our culture that we rarely examine them. As long as our lungs are full of air, we don't have to think about respiration. As long as our supremacy in the food chain is secure, we don't have to think about predators.

Figure 2.14:
Browser Giving You
Control over
Cookies

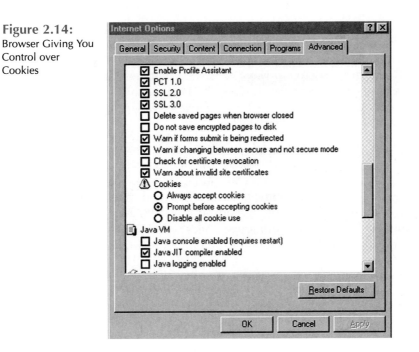

As long as life moves along in a predictable fashion, we try not to dwell on potential catastrophes. Then, when the unexpected happens, we cope first and reflect later.

The concept of privacy has been a dormant assumption in the lives of most Americans. Most people know the difference between public and private activities and keep a safe social distance from whom people they don't know or don't want to know. In addition, everyone has information that they share only with trusted friends and most don't have to elude paparazzi or worry about being the next hot item in the tabloids. So, they drop the shades at night and feel safe from the eyes of the world. As social causes go, privacy issues have yet to make much of a dent in the collective consciousness, although the Internet is beginning to sensitize people to privacy violations.

The U.S. Constitution does not protect privacy rights for U.S. citizens. Most laws related to privacy are state laws, so your rights might vary. Any federal laws concerning privacy tend to be very narrowly drawn. For example, Congress passed in 1988 a law protecting videotape rental records. In 1997, it passed a law making it illegal for Internal Revenue Service employees to view random tax returns for their entertainment. During his second term, President Bill Clinton pushed hard for a medical records privacy, in the form of a Patients Bill of Rights. The resulting Norwood-Dingell bill was pending as this book went to press. If it passes, it will be the first federal law that regulates the privacy of medical records.

Federal law also doesn't protect consumer data. However, companies that plan to tap European markets will have to comply with European privacy standards, which offer strong consumer protection. American support for European standards might force Congress to enact consumer privacy legislation, but lawmakers remain reluctant to regulate business on behalf of consumers. The only consumer privacy law in the United States at this time is the Children's Online Privacy Protection Act, which applies to online data collection from children.

No legislative body in the United States studies privacy or works toward a systematic legal code for privacy rights. The privacy laws that do exist result from isolated crusades. Thus their protection is like a crazy quilt, with a patch here and a patch there. For example, the videotape rental law came into being after the U.S. Supreme Court confirmation hearings for Judge Robert Bork in 1987. An enterprising news reporter had dug up information about Judge Bork's video viewing habits. The incident scared elected officials, and they quickly crafted legislation to help prevent other such occurrences.

A lot of publicly available information has always been available for the taking, but only with some effort. Before the Internet, a court record from a divorce proceeding was public, but it was available only if you visited the courthouse at which it was stored. Copies of old newspapers usually were available on microfiche, but to view them you had to travel to the newspaper's offices or to a regional library and spend time in front of a microfiche reader. Private investigators doing background checks know their way around all of the public resources, as well as a few back-door tricks of the trade. Whatever sources they traditionally used, the job always involved some amount of footwork. Hence, obtaining information that technically was free demanded a high price in terms of time and energy.

The Internet is changing many of the hidden costs associated with free information. When a court places its records online, no one needs to travel to the courthouse to see them. Once telephone listings for the entire United States are available online, you'll be able to research 10 cities as easily as one. The Internet isn't giving people anything they couldn't get before; it simply makes many information-gathering tasks much easier. In a legal sense, nothing has changed with respect to the availability of information. However, in a practical sense, nothing will ever be the same. Not only is the work of the private investigator facilitated. People who previously never would have taken the time to learn about the resources that a public library offers are now surfing Web information resources. Amateurs are barging in where only professionals used to tread.

Computer technologies are also altering the line between transient information and archival information. Articles in newspapers and magazines used to have a limited shelf life. A 10-year-old newspaper article could easily vanish and be gone forever. Now, as more newspapers put their contents online, newspaper stories become part of the permanent record. Anyone can create a massive digital library for anything online, hook it up to a search engine, and post it on the Web—and the world has instant access to an archival resource. Items that used to fade and die natural deaths can now have the technological equivalent of eternal life.

Digital records also make it easier for people to assemble information from disparate sources. Pulling up an instant profile of someone who is active online takes less than a minute—give the name to a Web search engine and you'll be rewarded with hits from Web pages, Usenet newsgroups, and mailing list archives. All of the legwork of looking in different places and all of the brainwork of figuring out where to look in the first place has been solved by the indexing capability of a search engine that operates almost instantaneously.

When it comes to personal data, the whole is always greater than the sum of the pieces. No one piece might be particularly threatening or worrisome by itself. However, when a hundred pieces of information can be pulled together, a bigger picture begins to emerge. Big Brother didn't materialize as the result of a massive totalitarian government, but it might now emerge from what amounts to technological serendipity. Nobody planned it this way. Like so many things on the Internet, forces were simply set into motion and now the consequences require careful consideration. If you would like to see what information can be assembled about you based on 1,600 government and commercial databases, you can order a **PrivacyScan Report** for a small fee. If PrivacyScan cannot find any information on you, it waives its fee.

People are accustomed to thinking about degrees of privacy. Absolute privacy is difficult to attain, but relative privacy might be a reasonable goal. For example, most e-mail messages are read and discarded or sometimes just discarded without even being read. A message posted to a mailing list is public relative to that list but private with respect to the world at large. Even when mailing lists are archived, the business of locating and searching a mailing list archive may not be easy. Therefore, as long as the convenience factor is low, mailing list participants enjoy some degree of privacy. However, the use of computers often makes formerly difficult tasks effortless. All of those difficult-to-read mailing list archives now can be placed on Web pages, where suddenly they are fairly easy to find. Before you know it, search engines are pointing to messages sent seven years ago. Archives that were relatively private in 1990 can suddenly pop up in search engine hit lists for the entire world to see. If it's digital, the potential for public distribution is unimaginable.

You need to consider whether the Internet's benefits outweigh the possible indignities of reduced privacy. For some people, the ability to communicate freely and openly on a global scale is well worth it. For others, any loss of privacy is an unsettling prospect.

Broadband Risks and Remedies

Anyone who spends a lot of time on the Internet over a telephone line would welcome a broadband connection such as cable modem or DSL. The difference in speed is significant and very visible to a Web surfer. However, broadband connections to the Internet introduce additional, invisible, security risks that likely are not discussed in the ISP's promotional material. Cable modems are not just fast; they can also be left connected all of the time without additional charges to the user. For people tired of waiting for dial-up connections whenever they want to get online, constant connectivity might sound very convenient. However, fast Internet connections are also more attractive to computer hackers, and connections that are active 24 hours a day are very desirable as platforms for *remote-controlled operations*.

Some users don't worry about hackers and computer security. They think that hackers and other perpetrators of cyberattacks would not be interested in them. However, hackers don't always break into systems simply to, say, steal credit card account numbers. Sometimes they do so in order to acquire a base from which to conduct illegal activities. This extra level of indirection affords the hacker some protection from the law. However, it can cause the user significant grief if the FBI decides to seize the user's computer in order to secure evidence.

Distributed Denial-of-Service Attacks

In February 2000, **denial-of-service attacks**, efforts to reduce or eliminate service to a site, were aimed at large, highly visible Web sites for three days. Yahoo, amazon.com, CNN, eBay, eTrade, and ZDNet were among the sites targeted. During the attacks, each site experienced crippling numbers of packet requests for a period of about three hours. Nothing was stolen, but users were largely shut out of these sites during the attacks due to overloaded servers (hence, "denial of service"). The attacks were accomplished by hackers doing nothing more than sending unusually large numbers of packets to the targeted servers. In order to avoid detection, the packets were sent from a large number of "zombie" hosts that were called into action after the hackers installed appropriate remote control software on each zombie. The remote controls could have been installed via a Trojan horse months before the actual attack. Once enough zombies had been properly prepared to respond, one or more hackers could then mount a coordinated attack at any time by sending simultaneous commands to all the zombie computers. *Any computer with a continuous high-speed connection to the Internet is a perfect candidate to be a zombie for a distributed denial-of-service attack.*

Any computer with continuous access to the Internet is a valuable target for hackers, even if its contents are of no interest in their own right. If you have broadband Internet service, you should *not* keep your computer connected all of the time, unless you have taken special steps to secure your system. Commercial **firewall software** is designed to give you complete control over your Internet communications, and is available for home users (see Chapter 9's Above and Beyond). Figure 2.15 shows an alert box generated by the **ZoneAlarm** firewall after it blocked a host from establishing an unauthorized Internet connection with a home computer. All users with a broadband connection should install a firewall, especially if they remain connected for hours at a time.

Figure 2.15:
Firewall Alert Box

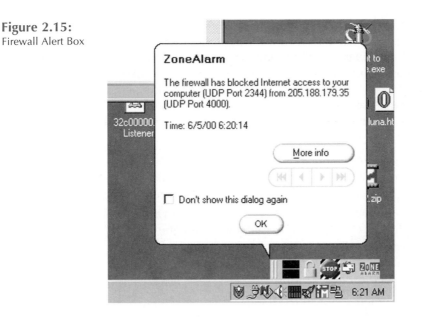

Hacking: Phone Phreaks, Hackers, and Script Kiddies

The general public has become accustomed to images of computer hackers created by Hollywood and fueled by the mainstream media. Kevin Mitnick has been portrayed as a brilliant arch villain, and 14-year-olds who leave electronic graffiti on government Web sites are often portrayed as computer geniuses. Whereas all of this might be fodder for exciting stories (remember how the media primed us for Y2K catastrophes?), the facts behind the stories are generally more mundane.

Once upon a time, students who loved computers did whatever it took to get a few hours alone with a coveted mainframe computer. Prior to 1970, most computers did not have time-sharing capabilities, so only one program could be run at a time. Thus time with the computer was highly prized. Hands-on learning began when the routine work of the day was done. This meant that the people who were most passionate about computers tended to be up late at night in order to get some time with the machine. Few schools taught computer programming, and no textbooks about computers existed. People who wanted to learn about computers had to study arcane technical manuals and pick up what they could from friends and contacts. There was no Internet to facilitate student-to-student communications, so computer geeks tended to cluster in favorable environments such as MIT and other high-powered research universities. This is how the culture of the computer hacker was born.

Circa 1970, the term "hacker" described a self-taught expert who had extensive first-hand knowledge of one or two computers. Computers at the time were rather primitive, and programmers worked with low-level programming languages designed for a specific CPU and its particular instruction set. By today's standards, these computers were ludicrously limited by their miniscule amounts of memory and sloth-like clock speeds. However, this only made it all the more important for programmers to understand how to push a given machine to the limit. Tricks and secrets were shared over late-night snacks. Hackers tended to hang with their own, united by curiosity and a passion for computers. Being a hacker back then was not glamorous. Rather, a love for computers was nothing to brag about at a time when hippies were cool, the military-industrial complex was evil, and technology was something that a lot of young people were trying to live without (albeit not very successfully).

The First Personal Computers

The first personal computers were sold as kits for home hobbyists who had a background in electronics. In March 1974, the Scelbi Computer Consulting Company of Milford, Connecticut, started advertising the *Scelbi*, a computer built around the Intel 8008 microprocessor. The Scelbi came with 1K of RAM and sold for $565. An additional 15K of memory was available for $2,760. The 8008 had a clock speed of 200 KHz.

In January 1975, *Popular Electronics* ran a cover story describing the *Altair* computer. The computer revolution was off and running. The Altair was the brainchild of a company named MITS (Micro Instrumentation Telemetry Systems), which was originally in the electronic calculator business. The Altair contained an Intel 8080 microprocessor and 256 bytes of RAM, all for just $400. It had to be assembled, however, and it came with no software, but it was a hit, in part because of the exposure it got in *Popular Electronics.*

It was a few more years before the concept of a personal computer sparked the public imagination. The political protest "Power to the People" (fade to a video clip of student demonstrators in the 1960s chanting with raised fists on high) took on a new, technological, meaning a decade later. The year 1975 saw the beginning of the end of the monopoly of IBM mainframes. Computers became available to a rising proletariat class, and computer access was no longer restricted to the ruling class of Fortune 500 data processing departments.

The Origins of Commercial Software

Two young programmers, Paul Allen and Bill Gates, wrote a version of the BASIC programming language for the Altair computer. Paul Allen was subsequently given a job as the Director of Software for MITS (in charge of a department of one). Bill Gates, who had not yet dropped out of Harvard, worked for MITS part-time before moving on to found Microsoft in 1975.

In 1975, no commercial software was available for personal computers; computer owners were expected to write their own. The advent of the personal computer and the nascent hacker culture was a marriage made in heaven. With no commercial software market in sight, the task of writing software for the first personal computers fell into the able hands of hackers. Programs were freely shared, published in photocopied newsletters (the Internet was not a public resource at that time), and subjected to endless rounds of revisions by anyone who saw a way to contribute an improvement. This was the beginning of the "open-source" software movement, which eventually produced the Linux OS. Professional programmers had "real" jobs working on "serious" computers. The evolution of the personal computer was left to a grassroots campaign consisting of students and random computer aficionados. Apple Computer grew out of this culture and maintains its countercultural David versus Goliath image even today.

The momentum of the growing personal computer industry began to bring new elements to the mix, and people began to look for ways to make money (enter Bill Gates). Hippy chic was on the wane, and maturing baby boomers decided that economic stability might not be such a bad thing after all. The hacker culture nevertheless thrived and preserved its traditional activities: tinkering, experimenting, and unconstrained inquiry. Primitive modems were added to personal computers in the 1980s, thereby prompting computer bulletin board systems (BBSs) to spring up in every U.S. major city.

BBSs were managed by a strange brew of people who probably had nothing in common beyond an interest in what could be done with computers and a healthy respect for free expression. Some BBSs were initiated with lofty public visions of community service. Others catered to kids looking for games. Many were dedicated to the distribution of pornography. Dial-up BBSs were a grassroots phenomenon whose popularity mushroomed in the early 1980s, thus giving computer buffs a pre-Internet taste of computer-mediated communication. Although the evolution of the Internet was well underway by 1980, the Internet was still largely restricted to research laboratories funded by the U.S. Department of Defense and was unknown to the general public.

Hacking Is a Felony

Under the Computer Fraud and Abuse Act, a hacker in the United States faces a maximum penalty of 10 years in jail and a fine of $250,000, or in some cases, twice the dollar loss to the victim.

Phone Phreaks When telephones were added to computers, another colorful countercultural element joined the mix. With the telephones came the **phone phreaks**. Before the advent of the Altair, technically inclined kids were playing games with the telephone company, which was, at that time, only AT&T, a powerful monopoly in the 1960s and a politically attractive target for countercultural disdain. Ripping off the telephone company was both an act of civil disobedience and a protest against the Vietnam War (for this to make sense, you probably had to be there).

Within this peculiar zeitgeist, a small but significant segment of the 1960s counter-culture used plastic toy whistles and home-made "blue boxes" to trick AT&T's switching circuits into giving away free telephone calls. It was a political statement, it was radical, and it was harmless (big, faceless corporations were thought to be invincible).

The phone phreak ethos was based on a world view that held that "the establishment" was evil, people who worked within the establishment were robotic morons, and one's ability to get around the establishment was evidence of political commitment. Today, no unpopular war exists to unite America's youth. However, we still live in a predominantly anti-intellectual culture in which bright youngsters are frequently ostracized and too often spend their adolescent years feeling exceptionally angry, alienated, and isolated (see Figure 2.16). There will always be bright teenagers who take refuge in technological, brave new worlds. They think, if you are not happy with your current world, it makes sense to position yourself on the brink of change and contribute to the next new thing, whatever that might be.

Hackers Combine the anarchistic tendencies of phone phreaks with the passionate dedication of hackers, and you have a cultural heritage in which knowledge is power, open communication is a life force, and all authority must be questioned. Today's hackers are portrayed in the media as criminals who wreak havoc for fun or terrorists who are bent on undermining national security. In fact, hackers come in various types and colors.

A black-hat hacker engages in criminal activities with no remorse or misgivings. This type of hacker will break into a computer and steal sensitive data and then often report the theft to the violated party in an extortion attempt. An example is a 19-year-old Russian who demanded $100,000 from CD Universe in exchange for 30,000 stolen customer records. A **white-hat hacker** will break into a computer only when invited to do so in order to identify security holes. Government laboratories started this tradition in the 1970s with the use of **tiger teams**. A tiger team was a group of white-hat hackers who were invited to do their worst and then discuss the outcome afterwards. This practice is a respected and effective way to strengthen system security in the never-ending struggle to stay on top of what the black-hat hackers know. Finally, there are grey-hat hackers. A **grey-hat hacker** will hack only when provoked by some "greater" social injustice. For example, a grey-hat hacker might cripple a Web server run by a hate group or an oppressive government or perform the periodic defacement of Web pages on `.gov` Web sites.

Script Kiddies During the 1990s, a new breed of troublemaker developed, the **script kiddie**. Unlike the original hackers who cultivated knowledge and worked to understand as much as they could about CPUs and OSs, script kiddies are only superficially interested in computers. They are interested primarily in determining what they can get away with and who will be impressed. Most of the so-called 14-year-old computer geniuses are only script kiddies. Someone told them where to find a piece of software that can be used to crack passwords and another piece of software

Figure 2.16:
A Hacker Explains
Why

```
                      Written on January 8, 1986
=-=-=-=-=-=-=-=-=-=-=-=-=-=-=-=-=-=-=-=-=-=-=-=-=-=-=-=-=-=-=-=-=-=-=-=-=

Another one got caught today, it's all over the papers.  "Teenager Arrested in
Computer Crime Scandal," "Hacker Arrested after Bank Tampering"...
        Damn kids.  They're all alike.

But did you, in your three-piece psychology and 1950's technobrain, ever take
a look behind the eyes of the hacker?  Did you ever wonder what
made him tick, what forces shaped him, what may have molded him?

I am a hacker, enter my world... Mine is a world that begins with school...
I'm smarter than most of the other kids, this crap they teach us bores me...
        Damn underachievers.  They're all alike.

I'm in junior high or high school.  I've listened to teachers explain for the
fifteenth time how to reduce a fraction.  I understand it.  "No, Ms. Smith, I
didn't show my work.  I did it in my head..."
        Damn kid.  Probably copied it.  They're all alike.

I made a discovery today.  I found a computer.  Wait a second, this is
cool.  It does what I want it to.  If it makes a mistake, it's because I
screwed it up.  Not because it doesn't like me...
                Or feels threatened by me...
                Or thinks I'm a smart ass...
                Or doesn't like teaching and shouldn't be here...
        Damn kid.  All he does is play games.  They're all alike.

And then it happened... a door opened to a world... rushing through the phone
line like heroin through an addict's veins, an electronic pulse is sent out, a
refuge from the day-to-day incompetencies is sought... a board is found.

"This is it... this is where I belong..."

I know everyone here... even if I've never met them, never talked to
them, may never hear from them again... I know you all...
        Damn kid.  Tying up the phone line again.  They're all alike...

You bet your ass we're all alike... we've been spoon-fed baby food at school
when we hungered for steak... the bits of meat that you did let slip through
were pre-chewed and tasteless.  We've been dominated by sadists, or ignored by
the apathetic.  The few that had something to teach found us willing pupils,
but those few are like drops of water in the desert.

This is our world now... the world of the electron and the switch, the
beauty of the baud.  We make use of a service already existing without paying
for what could be dirt-cheap if it wasn't run by profiteering gluttons, and
you call us criminals.  We explore... and you call us criminals.  We seek
after knowledge... and you call us criminals.  We exist without skin color,
without nationality, without religious bias... and you call us criminals. You
build atomic bombs, you wage wars, you murder, cheat, and lie to us and try
to make us believe it's for our own good, yet we're the criminals.

Yes, I am a criminal.  My crime is that of curiosity.  My crime is that of
judging people by what they say and think, not what they look like. My crime
is that of outsmarting you, something that you will never forgive me for.

I am a hacker, and this is my manifesto.  You may stop this
individual, but you can't stop us all... after all, we're all alike.

                    +++The Mentor+++
```

that can crash a remote host, and that's how the 14-year-olds crack passwords and crash systems.

Script kiddies can do a lot of seemingly impressive things with only a superficial knowledge of computers and no knowledge of computer programming. They share their knowledge, such as it is, much like other kids bargain for trading cards, rarely digging deep in order to understand the tools that they use. Like many adolescents, script kiddies enjoy the fact that they can create havoc for adults. They generally have no sense of the seriousness of the damage that they inflict.

How Hard Is It to Attack Another Computer on the Internet?

How difficult it is to attack another computer on the Net depends on how much security is in place on the target host. UNIX hosts are usually managed by computer professionals and are relatively difficult to disrupt. Hosts running Windows, however, often are very vulnerable, especially if OS upgrades and software patches are not being installed to address known security problems. If a computer open to attack is connected to the Net, anyone on the Internet can send it a "hostile" packet that will cause it to crash. All you need is the IP address of the target host and the right program (which is easy to find on the Web once you know what to look for). .

Anyone who knows how to download software can fire off hostile packets without understanding exactly what they are doing and why it works. The user being attacked will know only that the computer crashed for some unknown reason (not an unusual event for Windows users). A casual user has no way of knowing that the system was shot down by a sniper somewhere on the Net.

From one perspective, computers and computer networks are property, and property owners have a right to protect their possessions. Unauthorized computer access and unauthorized network utilization are the electronic versions of breaking and entering. It is a crime and is punishable by law. Another perspective is that of an explorer on a quest for knowledge. From this perspective, computers and computer networks create a virtual space that begs to be explored and investigated and a property owner who cannot protect his or her own property deserves the results because private property within this space should be protected by impenetrable boundaries. Computer security is a game of wits in which superior knowledge always wins.

Protecting Your Computer on the Internet

The difficulty of protecting your computer on the Net depends on how safe you need to be. If you cannot tolerate any risk, then you shouldn't be connected. Corporations work to reduce risk to acceptable levels by installing firewalls between in-house computers and the Internet. Home computers are generally difficult to protect because new security holes are discovered as soon as the old ones are plugged up. However, a reasonable level of security can be achieved for casual users by following these steps.

1. Install OS updates and security patches regularly.
2. Invest in the best antivirus software available and keep it up-to-date.
3. Install a firewall to monitor all Internet communications and block unauthorized contacts.
4. Disconnect your computer from the Internet whenever possible.

To maximize your own security with a minimal amount of time and effort, simply buy a second computer. Keep all of your most sensitive files on one computer that never connects to the Net, and use the other for all of your Internet activities. This won't prevent trouble on your Internet host, but it will protect your sensitive data.

If the Internet is a new frontier, the hackers are its cowboys. Some hackers are idealistic people who deeply distrust authority and are passionate defenders of freedom in cyberspace. Others are career criminals and terrorists driven by darker forces. On the one hand, anyone who gains unauthorized access to a computer is a criminal in the eyes of the law. On the other hand, Internet technology is forcing us to reexamine our legal system, our concept of ownership, and our ability to control valuable resources in a digital world. For better or for worse, hackers are forcing us to confront these uncharted territories and challenge our understanding of life in a digital world.

Above and Beyond: Problems and Exercises

A1. Explain the difference between plagiarism and copyright infringement.

A2. What is a notice and consent policy? Some Web sites manage to comply with notice and consent guidelines for consumer protection while making it very difficult for consumers to withhold consent. How do they do it?

A3. Check to see whether you have any cookies on your hard drive. If you delete your cookie file(s), how would your browsing sessions be affected? Do you frequent any Web sites at which cookies are a welcome convenience? Describe one, and explain why you like the way that cookies are used by that site. What preference settings does your browser offer for cookie management?

A4. Some information is technically free but nevertheless requires substantial time and know-how. How is the Internet changing the balance of relative privacy? Do you have to be active online in order to be affected by this change? Explain your answer.

A5. Explain how a denial-of-service attack works. Is it more important to recruit "zombies" with fast Internet connections or 24/7 availability?

A6. Explain the difference between a script kiddie and a serious hacker. Is it possible to crack a password or crash a remote host without knowing anything about computer programming? Why do you think that adult hackers like to recruit minors and encourage them to engage in hacking activities?

A7. **[Find It Online]** If you have space on a Web server through your school or a commercial ISP, who is the DMCA agent responsible for materials posted on that server. How hard was it to identify this person?

A8. **[Find It Online]** Conduct a search on the Internet for issues of the online newsletter *Phrack*. When was *Phrack* started, and how long did it run? Do you think that the authors of *Phrack* were breaking the law by distributing the information that they did? The First Amendment protects publishers from censorship by the government, but it does not protect publishers from lawsuits. Do you think anyone has a right to sue the publishers of *Phrack*? If so, on what grounds?

A9. **[Take a Stand]** The RIAA sued mp3.com after mp3.com established an online service called BeamIt. Go online to find out (1) what BeamIt was originally and (2) the current status of the RIAA's lawsuit against mp3.com. Do you think that the No Electronic Theft (NET) Act applies to BeamIt? Was the RIAA's lawsuit an unfair attack on an innovative service for legitimate CD owners? Should mp3.com be legally responsible for users who violated the ToS for BeamIt? Do you think that the Digital Millennium Copyright Act can be generalized to protect services such as BeamIt?

A10. **[Take a Stand]** Script kiddies would not be able to operate if stronger actions were taken to stop the people who make tools for hackers and distribute them freely. Pornography is not given to children even though it enjoys First Amendment protection. Why can't destructive software be treated in the same way? That it, it could be tagged with an X-rating and laws would prevent its distribution to minors. Explore this issue on the Net, and make a case for or against the concept of X-rated software.

CHAPTER 3

E-Mail Management

CHAPTER GOALS

- Become familiar with the basic operations of your mail client.
- Understand the basic differences among the SMTP, HTTP, POP, and IMAP mail protocols.
- Learn how the MIME protocol and HTML-enabled mail clients have changed e-mail.
- Find out how to augment your primary mail service with a Web-based e-mail account.
- Learn to use mail filters to save time and combat information overload.

3.1 TAKING CHARGE

E-mail is here to stay, and a lot of people have a love-hate relationship with it. E-mail has become an indispensable tool for business communication and a speedy, inexpensive alternative to *snail mail*. People of all ages use it to stay in touch with friends and relatives. Virtual communities blossom via e-mail, and virtual relationships transcend geography because of e-mail (see Chapter 7).

However, e-mail also has a dark side. As convenient as it is, it can still be time-consuming, and there is no escape from it if your workplace requires frequent e-mail contact. Indeed, e-mail has undermined the concept of "normal working hours" for those who check their workplace mail from home. A message that begs for an urgent reply might be difficult to set aside, no matter when you read it. It is downright impossible to estimate how much time will be needed to deal with a pile of new e-mail. Ten mail messages might look like something that should require no more than 15 minutes of your time, but if just one of those messages compels you to investigate a URL or compose a thoughtful reply, those 15 minutes can easily expand into

30 minutes or more. This can mean the difference between a boiling pot of water and a very hot but empty pot that is beginning to crackle because you let all of the water boil away. (I have ruined a lot of cookware because of e-mail.) It also can make you late for an appointment, a dinner date, or a class, if you were silly enough to check your e-mail just before you had to go somewhere. If you are reading e-mail a few times a day, you might have noticed how your e-mail habit can rob you of those little blocks of time that used to be used for other things (a water cooler break, a quick game of fetch with the dog, or a quiet moment of contemplation). Everyone seems to feel pressed for time these days, and e-mail might be one reason why.

If you have just started to use e-mail and you are only getting ten or twenty messages a week, you probably don't have much of an e-mail problem. The challenges mount with the amount of e-mail in your mailbox. More and more people are receiving at least a hundred messages a day, and that's when you really need to look at the amount of time you are spending with e-mail. You might not be at this level now, but there's a good chance you will join the "100 Club" sometime in the near future. Even if you are not yet flooded with e-mail, but you do need to check your e-mail once a day, you will find useful information in this chapter.

E-mail is a compelling siren that claims our time and can lure us away from lots of little things that we used to do. It can become an addiction, especially when it masquerades as a work requirement or an enjoyable social activity. The activities that we drop in order to accommodate an e-mail habit might not seem important enough to mourn. However, if a large number of these unimportant activities are abandoned with little or no thought, the long-term effects of an e-mail habit might creep up on us in unexpected ways. Many people who telecommute or who augment their normal workday with "overtime" e-mail sessions begin to resent their work. When no clean division exists between working hours and personal time, the feeling of being constantly "on call" can be very stressful for some people (not to mention their families). The ubiquitous availability of e-mail access seems like a wonderful convenience at first but can result in "e-mail burn-out" when people let the technology run them, instead of the other way around.

As compulsive behaviors go, an e-mail habit is relatively easy to modify and manage. If you want to spend less time on e-mail (or perhaps just more time on other things), it's really not that difficult. You just need to understand your options. This chapter describes time-saving software options, along with software tips to help you manage your e-mail more productively.

3.2   BASIC E-MAIL CLIENT OPERATIONS

Before learning about e-mail management strategies, you need to understand the basic functions of an e-mail client. If you have been using e-mail for a year or more, you probably know everything in this section; simply skim the next few pages to make sure. If you are new to e-mail , this is the place to start. Read this section care-fully, and do the e-mail checklist exercises to make sure that you have these opera-tions under control. Each e-mail client works a little differently, but all support the basic e-mail operations. If you aren't sure how to do something with your specific e-mail client, visit the **Checklist Solutions** on the Web or browse the resources under **Where Can I Learn More** to find tutorials and online help.

If you do consult a tutorial for your client, don't worry about all of the preference settings for now. Many advanced features are available, and you don't have to understand them all now. Your software comes preconfigured with default prefer-ence settings; these will be fine while you are learning.

3.2.1 Anatomy of an E-mail Message

An e-mail message is very similar to an office memo, sharing the following charac-teristics:

- E-mail messages are usually fairly short.
- Each message usually addresses a single topic.
- Most messages rely on plain text (no graphics or fancy fonts), although this is changing.
- Messages are usually written in an informal style.
- Some messages are replies to previous messages.
- Messages can be sent to one person or many people.
- Messages can be forwarded to many other people.
- E-mail is often timely.
- A reckless e-mail message might someday come back to haunt you.

Although these are typical features of e-mail messages, the technology can be pushed in different directions. You could send an entire book manuscript to some-one via e-mail (although there are better ways to send large documents). You can send files through e-mail that are not text files (for example, photographs). You can also have an e-mail dialog with someone about all sorts of highly personal matters, despite the fact that e-mail is neither secure nor truly private (see Chapter 11 to learn how *encryption* can make your e-mail truly private).

Each e-mail message contains two parts:

- Header
- Message body

The header contains addressing information, such as who the message is from and who the message is being sent to, the time that the message was sent, and a subject line describing the content of the message. Figure 3.1 shows a short e-mail message.

Figure 3.1:
A Typical E-Mail
Message

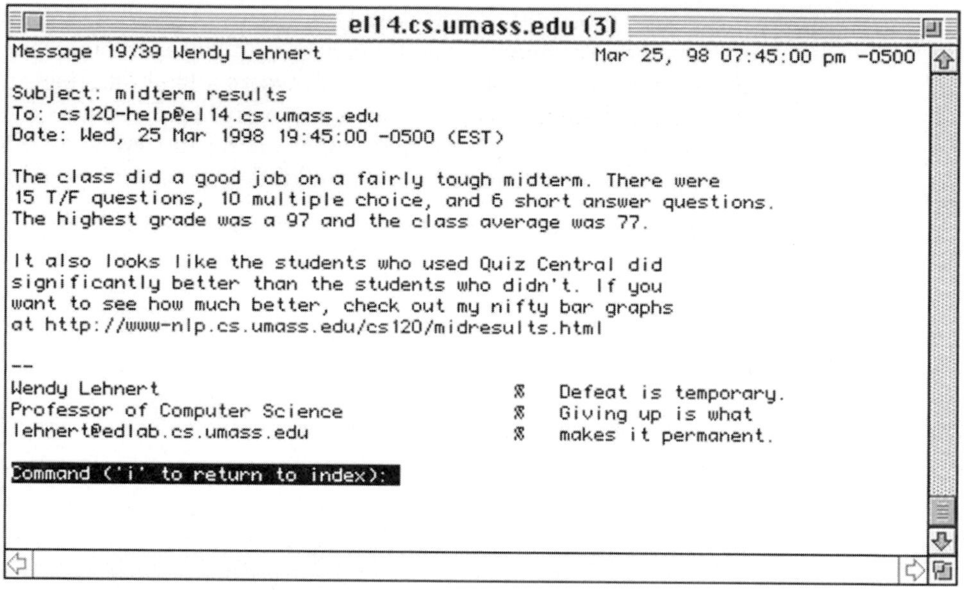

```
┌─────────────────────────────────────────────────────────────┐
│ ▣         el14.cs.umass.edu (3)                          ▣ │
│ Message 19/39 Wendy Lehnert           Mar 25, 98 07:45:00 pm -0500 ▲│
│ Subject: midterm results                                      │
│ To: cs120-help@el14.cs.umass.edu                              │
│ Date: Wed, 25 Mar 1998 19:45:00 -0500 (EST)                   │
│                                                               │
│ The class did a good job on a fairly tough midterm. There were│
│ 15 T/F questions, 10 multiple choice, and 6 short answer questions.│
│ The highest grade was a 97 and the class average was 77.      │
│                                                               │
│ It also looks like the students who used Quiz Central did     │
│ significantly better than the students who didn't. If you     │
│ want to see how much better, check out my nifty bar graphs    │
│ at http://www-nlp.cs.umass.edu/cs120/midresults.html          │
│                                                               │
│ --                                                            │
│ Wendy Lehnert                    §   Defeat is temporary.     │
│ Professor of Computer Science    §   Giving up is what        │
│ lehnert@edlab.cs.umass.edu       §   makes it permanent.      │
│                                                               │
│ Command ('i' to return to index):                             │
│                                                              ▼│
│ ◁                                                          ▷ ▣│
└─────────────────────────────────────────────────────────────┘
```

The first four lines of the message are part of the header, and the rest is the message body. When you create an e-mail message, the From: and the Date: fields of the header are always filled in automatically for you by the mail program. You complete the To: and the Subject:. You *must* complete the To: field, but you can leave the Subject: field blank. You can even leave the message body empty and still have a legitimate e-mail message. However, if you leave the To: field unfilled, your message will have no place to go.

When completing the To: field, you must specify an e-mail address. A *valid* **e-mail address** consists of a **userid** and a **host address** separated by the @ character. If the address contains any typographical errors, your message typically will be returned to you along with an error message. However, a typographical error might send your mail to a legitimate address—only not the one that you intended. In that case, no error message will alert you. If the accidental recipient does not respond, you may never know that something went wrong. So be careful when you complete the To: field.

Here are some examples of valid e-mail addresses.:

Userid	Host Address	E-mail Address
ajones	apple.orchard.com	ajones@apple.orchard.com
deadbug	antfarm.net	deadbug@antfarm.net
kgranite	context.wccm.org	kgranite@context.wccm.org

If you don't know the address of the person that you want to contact, you'll have to track it down. Many online directories can help you find e-mail addresses. You can take a guess, but only if you don't care that your mail might go to a wrong person. Some userids are not particularly formulaic. For example, if you know that Dave Brown is an AOL subscriber, you will have only the host address, aol.com. It would be impossible to guess at a userid like DRBMC986.

Shortcuts for E-Mail Addresses

If you send a lot of e-mail to the same person, most mail programs will let you refer to that person's full e-mail address by using a shortcut abbreviation, or a *nickname*. Check your mail client for an *address book feature*. When an e-mail address is very long or hard to remember, put it in your address book and assign a nickname for that entry. Then you need to remember only the nickname, and whenever you enter the nickname in a mail header, your mail client will automatically substitute the full e-mail address.

A system of first names followed by a last initial is easy to remember. If the names of two people collide by using this system, you can add another letter from their last names. Whatever system you use, use it consistently. Nicknames can save you a lot of time, but only if you can get the address you need on the first try.

Although you type in only a few header fields when you send e-mail, the header that your mail software uses is a bit more involved. Figure 3.1 showed only a short version of the full mail header. Figure 3.2 shows a full e-mail header.

Figure 3.2:
A Full E-Mail
Header

```
┌─────────────────── el14.cs.umass.edu (3) ───────────────────┐
│ Message 19/39 Wendy Lehnert              Mar 25, 98 07:45:00 pm -0500 │
│                                                               │
│ From lehnert@elux3.cs.umass.edu  Wed Mar 25 19:44:30 1998    │
│ Received: from el14.cs.umass.edu (el14.cs.umass.edu [128.119.42.24]) │
│         by elux3.cs.umass.edu (8.8.7/8.8.7) with ESMTP id TAA25614 │
│         for <cs120_hlp@elux3.cs.umass.edu>; Wed, 25 Mar 1998 19:44:29 -0500 │
│ Received: (from lehnert@localhost)                            │
│         by el14.cs.umass.edu (8.8.7/8.8.7) id TAA02485        │
│         for cs120-help; Wed, 25 Mar 1998 19:45:00 -0500 (EST) │
│ From: Wendy Lehnert <lehnert@elux3.cs.umass.edu>              │
│ Message-Id: <199803260045.TAA02485@el14.cs.umass.edu>         │
│ Subject: midterm results                                      │
│ To: cs120-help@el14.cs.umass.edu                              │
│ Date: Wed, 25 Mar 1998 19:45:00 -0500 (EST)                   │
│ X-Mailer: ELM [version 2.4ME+ PL37 (25)]                      │
│ MIME-Version: 1.0                                             │
│ Content-Type: text/plain; charset=US-ASCII                    │
│ Content-Transfer-Encoding: 7bit                               │
│ Status: RO                                                    │
│                                                               │
│ The class did a good job on a fairly tough midterm. There were │
│ 15 T/F questions, 10 multiple choice, and 6 short answer questions. │
│ The highest grade was a 97 and the class average was 77.      │
│ MORE (you've seen 30%):                                       │
└───────────────────────────────────────────────────────────────┘
```

The header in this message contains routing information and various time stamps that indicate when the message was received by different hosts along the route from your machine to the recipient's (note all of the different Received: fields). Most users don't need to see this information, so most mailers hide it. However, it should always be available on request because sometimes the full version is useful.

Each e-mail message that you receive is stored in a plain text file. The full header appears at the top of the file, and the message body follows. Your mail program is responsible for scanning this file and deciding how much of it you probably want to see. Don't confuse a mail message with the way that the mail message is being displayed. There might be more to your mail than meets the eye.

Other address fields are available to use when you send an e-mail message. The most commonly used optional field is Cc: (carbon copy). When you put an e-mail address in this field, a copy of your message is sent to that person. Some people always Cc: themselves so that they can have a copy of all of the messages that they send. This is called a self-Cc:. Some mailers give you a switch that you can set to make self-Cc: copies automatically. If a message is intended primarily for one person but also would be useful to other people, use the Cc: field for the other addresses. However, if your message is intended for more than one person, all of whom are equally important as recipients, put their addresses in the To: field.

The Bcc: field is similar to Cc: but is a *blind* carbon copy. When you include an address in this field, the message is sent to that recipient, but the recipient's address is not visible in the header received by other recipients. Blind carbon copies are used when you want to preserve someone's privacy or not broadcast that person's e-mail address.

How to Create a Distribution List

If you send mail to the same group of people regularly (for example, you all are members of the same committee), you can use the address book feature to create a *mail distribution list*. To do this, follow these steps:

1. Create a new address book entry.
2. Enter the list of e-mail addresses, separated by blanks or commas.
3. Give the list a nickname.
4. Use the nickname as you would any other address book entry.

A distribution list will save you from a lot of tedious typing and possible typographical errors.

3.2.2 What to Expect from Your Mail Client

Many different e-mail clients (also called *mailers*) are available, and their operations and features are all quite similar. Once you've seen one mail client, you'll know what to expect from another. This means that you don't have to worry too much about which mailer to adopt. Moreover, if you ever need to switch mail clients, you won't have to learn how to work with it from scratch. A few basic commands are enough to make you operational. If you're accustomed to some special features in your former mailer, you should be able to find equivalent features in your new mailer.

All mailers will enable you to do the following.

- Send a message that you have written yourself.
- Read any message that has been sent to you.
- Reply to any message that has been sent to you.
- Forward a message to a third party.
- Save or delete messages sent to you.
- Scan the Subject: and From: fields of all of your new mail.

A good e-mail client also supports other features, such as:

- The ability to sort mail and save it in different locations.
- The ability to tag unread mail messages for easy identification.
- An address book to hold frequently used e-mail addresses.
- A reply option that allows you to edit the original message.
- A customizable mail filter that sorts and routes incoming mail.
- The ability to include a *signature* automatically.

If you're working on a Windows-based personal computer or a Mac and have Internet access through an ISP or university, the Eudora mail program is a popular option. It includes many advanced features and has an intuitive interface. However, you also can manage your mail with the mail clients that are bundled with the Navigator and MSIE Web browsers.

A good mail program will give you the most commonly used commands in convenient toolbar buttons and pull-down menus. In addition, if you can't remember all of the details of your particular mailer, looking up something in the online documentation is usually easy.

Which Mailer?

If you can't spell, look for a mailer with a spelling checker. If you expect to handle a lot of e-mail, look for a mailer that offers automated filtering and routing. For some users, a single crucial feature might be enough to decide which mailer to use. For example, most modern mailers recognize URLs inside of mail message bodies. If someone sends a URL in a mail message, the mailer will recognize it as a hyperlink, underline it in the display, and make it an operational hot link that you can click if you want to visit the Web page right then. For people who get a lot of Web pointers in their mail, this might be the most wonderful feature in the world. For others, it might not matter. Only you can decide what features are important to you.

3.2.3 Viewing Your Inbox

Typically, the first thing that people do when they open their mailer is to check for new mail. New mail is stored in your inbox upon downloading. The **inbox** is very much like a mailbox, in which new mail awaits your retrieval. Many mailers take you directly to the inbox at start-up. Others might require you to load the inbox in order to see your new mail.

The inbox displays a list of each piece of mail received and not deleted, with a single descriptive line for each mail message. This line displays the Subject: and the From: fields so that you can see what each message is about and who sent it to you. Most also show the message's date of arrival. Figure 3.3 shows Navigator's mail client, with a display of the inbox headers in the upper right-hand corner.

Figure 3.3:
A Mail Inbox
Display

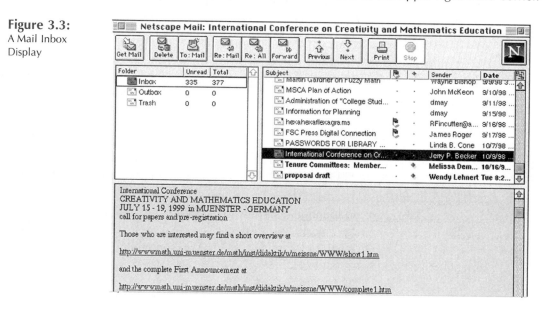

Each message in this inbox display is given a header line that indicates

- the subject header for the message,
- whether the user has marked the message for deletion,
- whether the message has been read,
- the name of the author, and
- the date received.

In most inbox displays, a message listed without an icon or marker next to it usually means that the message has been read. All of these messages in Figure 3.3 have been sorted by their dates. A preference setting can be reset if you prefer to have them sorted by another criteria, such a the senders' names, the subject headers, or the lengths of the messages. A subject header or a sender's name that is too long is *truncated* (shortened) in the display; however, you can resize these fields within the fixed dimensions of the message header display window in order to show more information. Keep this in mind when you write your own subject headers. If you give a mail message a long subject header, only the first few words may be visible in the recipient's inbox display.

Note that some of the sender entries are actual e-mail addresses, whereas others are names of people. Whenever you send mail, your From: field is filled with both your e-mail address and an **alias**, or alternative identifier, for yourself. Most mail programs give you an opportunity to enter your full name in one of your configuration or preference settings. If it does, whatever you enter becomes your e-mail alias and that alias will be added automatically to the From: field (along with your return address) whenever you send mail. Other mail programs that receive your mail often display aliases in addition to or in place of e-mail addresses. You can specify any alias that you want; most people use their real names.

Sometimes your inbox contains more messages than your screen can display in one window. In that case, you can scroll to the next block of messages and move back and forth across different segments of your inbox. Be sure to view all of the headers in your inbox so that you can see everything that's in there.

E-Mail Checklist—1

Study your mailer's documentation to be sure that you know how to do the following.

1. View your inbox and identify all your new mail.

2. Know how to distinguish read messages from unread messages.

3. Navigate multiple pages in a large inbox (both forward and backward).

3.2.4 Viewing Individual Mail Messages

When you view your inbox, you see only a short header for each mail message. To see the body of a message, click the message header to open the message. You'll then see a screen display that contains an abbreviated version of the full message header followed by the message body. A very long message body won't fit in a single screen display. However, you can navigate both forward and backward by using the vertical scroll bar on the right border of the window.

All mailers offer many options that you can set, along with many advanced commands that you might find useful. Start by learning the settings and commands that you need in order to complete the e-mail checklists in this chapter. Whenever you need to learn a new command, use your Help menu or visit the **Checklist Solutions** for various mail clients online.

E-Mail Checklist—2

Study your mail program's documentation to be sure that you know how to do the following.

1. Select a specific message in your inbox.
2. Open a single mail message in order to view its message body.
3. Page forward and backward through a long message body.
4. Exit a mail message display, and return to the inbox.
5. Display the long version of a message header.

3.2.5 Sending a New Mail Message

All mailers have a command that puts you in a mode for creating and sending a mail message. Look for a New Message command in a pull-down menu or a special "new message" icon on a toolbar. Once in that mode, you enter information in the To: field, the Subject: field, and, optionally, the Cc: field. The From: field will be filled in for you automatically. You will probably be given a window display in which all of the information can be entered by clicking the field that you want to complete. If you don't want to put something in a given field, press the Return or Enter key to leave it blank. Remember, the only field that you must complete is the To: field. Note, if you're new to sending messages, you can experiment by sending a message to yourself before sending one to someone else. Simply put your own userid in the To: field, and the mail will be sent to you.

In most mailers, a blank window is reserved for the message body. Type your message in it and edit it as needed, and then you're ready to send it. All mailers are designed to make the most basic operations highly intuitive, so editing an e-mail message isn't likely to require much beyond the most basic editing commands.

What Can You Send?

Some mailers can display text in different fonts or with special effects such as color. Outlook and Outlook Express make it easy to create messages with these features. While composing a new message, go to the Tools menu and select Rich Text (HTML) to bring up a toolbar that offers access to such text effects as boldface, colors, italics, and indented lists.

You also can create hyperlinks or insert graphics from files. Some mailers, such as Outlook and Outlook Express, can do this in a message body and even create operational hyperlinks (as shown in Figure 3.7). This makes the message body resemble a Web page. A mailer that can do this is called an **HTML-enabled mail client**. HTML-enabled mail is fun when you want to send someone a colorful greeting or a photograph. However, not everybody else has it. For various reasons, many people still use mailers that are not HTML-enabled.

Enter the text for your message body, review it to be sure that it says what you think it says, and prepare to send your message. If you have a spell checker, use it (especially if you are a poor speller). Then click the Send button.

All mailers also allow you to scrap the message if you decide you don't want to send it. You simply close the window that contains your message without saving or sending it.

Now that you've learned the basics of sending a mail message, it's time to add two more features to your repertoire. Earlier this chapter discussed the nickname feature as a shortcut device for handling long or difficult to remember e-mail addresses. Now is a good time to start an address book that you can update as needed. Set up an address book entry for someone you know that you'll be writing to often (perhaps your Internet instructor!). Then the next time that you send e-mail to this person, use that person's nickname instead of the full e-mail address. This powerful feature can save you a lot of time.

3.2.6 Signatures

Another time-saver is the **signature file** (or **sig file**). People who send a lot of e-mail have signature files that they append to the end of the message body. A sig file identifies the sender in some way. It personalizes your e-mail and saves you the tedious task of retyping the same identifying lines for each message. For business communications, it should contain your name, title, organization, mailing address, telephone number, fax number, and e-mail address. For casual e-mail, it could include a name and e-mail address, with perhaps a favorite quotation to add a little personality to an e-mail message. Figure 3.4 shows some sig files that I use.

Some mailers automatically add your sig file to the end of your message body, whereas others add it only on command. You might or might not be able to see your sig file at the end of your outgoing mail message. If you can't, that doesn't mean it isn't being included in your outgoing messages (send yourself a test message to see). Some mailers also let you set up and select from multiple sig files to convey different online personas. You might want to use a straightforward signature until you've been online for a while and have seen a lot of different signatures.

Some people will see your signature repeatedly. An unobtrusive sig file wears well after repeated exposures. Extremely lengthy signatures become annoying after a few encounters. Generally, keep your sig file to no more than four lines. By using all of the available horizontal space, you can pack a lot of information into those four lines.

Figure 3.4:
Sample Signature
Files

```
| Prof. Wendy Lehnert          Office hours: Mon. 11-12 and Wed 2:30-3:30
| lehnert@elux3.cs.umass.edu   LGRC A327 (the lowrise)
| (413) 545-3639               http://www-edlab.cs.umass.edu/cs120/
| ICQ #4909018                 http://www-nlp.cs.umass.edu/aw/home.html




| Prof. Wendy Lehnert       Get my public PGP key from:                   |
| lehnert@cs.umass.edu      http://pgp5.ai.mit.edu/pks-commands-beta.html |




--
Wendy Lehnert                      %
Professor of Computer Science      %  "640K ought to be enough for anybody."
University of Massachusetts        %
lehnert@edlab.cs.umass.edu         %                        -Bill Gates, 1981




        Wendy Lehnert, dachshund owner and member of the world famous
                      Dachshund Underground Railroad
                      ( - We Go The Extra Lengths - )
             http://www.geocities.com/Heartland/Prairie/5370/index.html
```

Message Body Do's and Don't's

Beginners often make some common mistakes regarding their e-mail. Because you're reading this book, you can avoid the most common Newbie errors.

- Avoid inserting carriage returns into your message body. If you must insert them, then limit the width of each line to no more than 72 characters—65 characters is better (see the Above and Beyond section for more details).

- Keep your sig file short and sweet. Generally, use no more than four lines for it.

- Always include a signature in the message body that contains your full name and return e-mail address.

- Reread the complete message body before sending your mail. Be sure that it says what you think it says, and correct any errors. Careless errors can be embarrassing, especially if the message goes to many people. Be extra careful when people are relying on you for accurate information.

3.2.7 Importing Text into Messages

Importing text from an existing file into an e-mail message body is often useful. If the text fragment is small, you can easily insert into your message body using copy-and-paste (but see the Above and Beyond section for a discussion of "raggy text"). Text insertion comes in handy when you want to set up stock replies to frequently encountered requests or situations. You essentially create a form letter in a file and then when you need to send it to someone, you insert it into your message body, change it here and there as needed, and you're done.

Form letters are most often needed in work environments, but you might find them useful for certain casual communication as well (see the Above and Beyond section for an example of a convenient e-mail form letter).

3.2.8 Importance of Good Writing

Practice sending e-mail to a friend until you feel comfortable and confident about your mailer. Once you have the hang of it, the mechanics of sending e-mail will be second nature and you can concentrate on content.

Be aware that on the Internet, you are what you type. A message filled with misspelled words and ungrammatical sentences does not reflect well on the sender. The quality of your writing is particularly important when you're writing to people who have no other contact with you. Some people take creative liberties with e-mail, devising their own quirky writing styles. While this might be appropriate in some contexts, it probably will not be appreciated in the business world. Think about who you're writing to, how busy that person is, how well you know that person, and the point of your message. Each message that you send takes time to read it. Try not to waste anyone's time. Think carefully about what you write. The rules of e-mail *Netiquette* are discussed in more detail in Section 3.4.

E-Mail Checklist—3

Study your mail program's documentation to be sure that you know how to do the following.

1. Set up an address book entry with a nickname for someone.
2. Begin a new message.
3. Enter information in the message header and the message body.
4. Change the message header and message body as needed.
5. Cancel a message before you send it.
6. Run the spell checker (if the mailer offers one).
7. Set up a sig file (if your mailer supports that feature).
8. Insert text from a file into a message body.
9. Send a message after you've completed the message body.

3.2.9 Replying To and Forwarding E-Mail Messages

Many e-mail conversations begin when someone replies to a message. By using the Reply command, you can conduct one-on-one discussions in a series of replies to previous messages, as well as conversations involving a large group of people.

Before replying to anyone, first be sure that you know the difference between two variations on the Reply command: the **sender-only reply** and the **group reply** (sometimes called **reply-to-all**). In the first case, your message is sent only to the original author of the current message. In the second case, your message is sent to the original author, as well as everyone included in the To: field and everyone included in the Cc: and Bcc: fields. The first type of reply is private; the second type, however, might be very public. Sometimes, you might want to use a group reply, but you'll probably more often use the sender-only reply.

One of the most helpful features of mailers is the inclusion of the original mail message in the reply message body. All the better mailers give you the option of either including the original message to which you are replying in your message body or starting from scratch with an empty message body. In addition, if you include the original message in your reply, you don't have to preserve it all. You can keep only the parts that you need in order to make your reply coherent by using your editor to delete anything that doesn't need to be seen again. This courtesy is especially important if your reply is going to many people who have already seen the original. No one wants to scroll through a long message that they've already read.

Each mailer uses a convention for distinguishing the text of an original message from the text that you add in the reply. An example is indenting of each line preceded by caret (>) character, as shown in Figure 3.5.

Figure 3.5:
An E-Mail Reply with an Indented Original Message

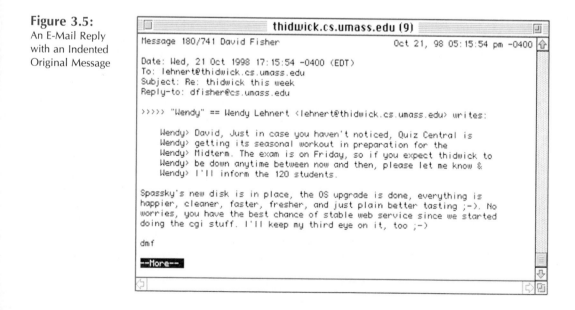

A reply to a reply shows two levels of indentation, a reply to that shows three levels, and so on. You can make a dialog more readable by using blank lines to separate different speakers. Use your editor freely.

E-Mail Reply Do's and Don't's

Here are some more mistakes that beginners make and that you'll want to avoid.

- Know the difference between the sender-only reply and the group reply. If you use the group reply for a message intended for the original sender only, you might embarrass yourself by broadcasting something unintentionally.

- If you get into a lengthy dialog with someone, take the time to replace the subject in the Subject: field with a new subject when the original no longer describes the topic of your conversation. It's easy to keep the original subject content, but after exchanged replies, your mailbox might contain many messages that have the same subject. If you ever need to return to one of these messages, you won't know where to look.

- If you find yourself responding emotionally to a piece of e-mail, cool off a bit before replying, especially if you feel angry. Although your feelings might be justified, take some time to think about what you want to say before responding.

- Be selective when you include text from the original message in your reply. Don't duplicate the original message in its entirety unless it is absolutely necessary. However, do include enough so your reply will make sense to someone who can't remember the message that preceded yours.

When you reply to a message, your mailer might or might not include your sig file automatically. It might include a preference setting to control this default. If all of your e-mail replies go to people who already know you, it makes sense to forgo a sig file; friends and colleagues don't need to see your signature repeatedly. In addition, many people who have been using e-mail since its beginning tend not to use sig files because they grew up in an e-mail culture in which they sent messages only to people whom they knew. Sig files make more sense when your mail is going to people who don't know you.

Forwarding e-mail is like replying to e-mail, except that you send the message to a third party. Most mailers will let you edit the message body when you forward a message, a useful feature when you want to insert your own comments. You can forward anything to anyone; however, be aware that you might be dealing with sensitive information or information given to you in confidence. Betraying a confidence can hurt someone who trusted you, as well as make you look untrustworthy. Just because a program makes something easy to do doesn't necessarily make doing it a good idea.

E-Mail Checklist—4

Study your mailer's documentation to be sure that you know how to do the following.

1. Send a reply only to the original author of the current message.
2. Send a group reply to everyone associated with the current message.
3. Include the text of the current message in your reply.
4. Reply by using a blank message body (no old text included).
5. Change the subject header for your reply.
6. Forward a message to a third party with or without your comments.

3.3 MIME ATTACHMENTS AND HTML-ENABLED MAILERS

Once upon a time, all mailers expected to see plain ASCII text in their message bodies, and life was simple. No one had to worry about e-mail viruses (although some bogus virus warnings tried to convince the uninitiated otherwise), and no one had to spend much time beautifying their messages because there's only so much that can be done with plain ASCII text. However, people are rarely happy with what they have, and so it was with e-mail. Why be limited to plain ASCII text? Wouldn't it be nice to be able send binary files?

For a long time, users got around the text-only message body constraint by converting binary files into *ASCII-encoded binary files* (see the Above and Beyond section). These converted files could then be inserted into plain ASCII text message bodies and sent via e-mail. Mailers needed to make no changes to handle these files, although extra work was required to encode the file before sending it and to decode after it was received. It worked well enough, but it was a little clumsy.

As more people began using e-mail, demand grew for more sophisticated e-mail programs. E-mail software programmers decided to make the software smarter about handling binary files by having it do all of the encoding and decoding automatically? The process wasn't that difficult to automate, and it would save everyone a lot of time. To do this, a new protocol was needed.

3.3.1 The MIME Protocol

To encode and unencode binary files automatically, a special mail protocol was created in 1991: the **Multi-Purpose Internet Mail Extension (MIME)**. Today, the MIME protocol is a globally recognized standard. If you have ever sent or received an e-mail attachment, you have used MIME. Thanks to MIME, modern mailers now make sending any file as a mail attachment easy to do. You either click a toolbar button for adding an attachment (often marked by a paperclip icon) or an "add attachment" command in a pull-down menu. Then you use a dialog box to navigate your way to the local file that you want to include as an attachment, select the file, and return to your message (see Figure 3.6). You can add more than one attachment to a single message, and you can include a file in any file format.

MIME is clearly an improvement over the old way of doing e-mail. New users need to be aware about possible dangers whenever they received an e-mail attachment (see Section 2.5).

Figure 3.6:
Including a File in a Message as a MIME Attachment

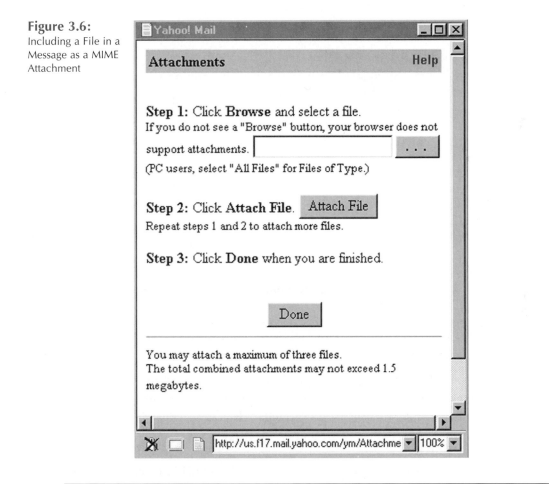

Before You Send That Attachment, Read This!

As explained in Section 2.5, people receiving e-mail attachments must protect themselves from e-mail viruses. You should never send an e-mail attachment unnecessarily. There is almost always some way around sending e-mail attachments. An attachment that is a plain text file can be inserted directly into the message body by using copy-and-paste. A Word file can be saved in RTF format and the resulting text inserted into the message body, again, by using copy-and-paste. A photograph can be posted at a Web site for public photo albums and a URL pointing to it there sent to friends instead of an attachment.

However, if you absolutely must send an attachment, be careful to include some personal information in the message body so that your recipient will know that the message really is from you (rather than some devious e-mail worm who appropriated your mailer after infecting your computer). Always identify the attachment by name, format, and file size.

3.3.2 HTML-Enabled Mailers

Soon after MIME was created, the Internet was opened up to commercial ISPs and the general public. Commercial software vendors saw an opportunity to make the Internet as user-friendly as possible, and e-mail was one popular application in which improvements could be made. The result was the HTML-enabled mailer. Suppose that you want to send a hyperlink to someone. If you send it in a plain ASCII text message body, the recipient will have to copy and paste it into a browser window. It would be better if it could simply show up in the message body as a clickable hyperlink. Then the user will need only click the link in order to be linked automatically to the referenced Web page. Embedding hyperlinks inside of the message body would be fast, convenient, and easy to understand.

The first HTML-enabled mailers were programmed to recognize URLs and render them as clickable hyperlinks, as they would be on a Web page. Navigator's mailer sent its URLs to Navigator, and MSIE's mailer sent its links to Explorer. A few independent mailers (for example, Eudora) let the user decide which browser to use in a preference setting.

Clickable hyperlinks were only the first step. If a mailer could recognize a URL, why not have it render entire Web pages like a Web browser would? Web pages are simply ASCII text files, so a Web page could be sent as an e-mail message body without any alterations to existing mail protocols. All that was needed were mailers that could make message bodies look like Web pages. Then e-mail could be as flashy and as much fun as a Web page (see Figure 3.7).

Of course, most people don't want to have to author Web pages in order to send a simple e-mail message to a friend. Sometimes, all you need is plain ASCII text. However, advertisers were quick to jump on the idea of HTML-enabled e-mail. This new form of e-mail meant the difference between sending out a black-and-white typed paragraph and sending out a slick color brochure. In addition, Web-based e-mail and free e-mail services on the Web had begun to catch on. If you're using your Web browser to read mail on the Web, why not see some mail that looks like it belongs on the Web? Of course, graphics files are still binary files. However, they

Figure 3.7:
Viewing Mail with an HTML-Enabled Mail Client

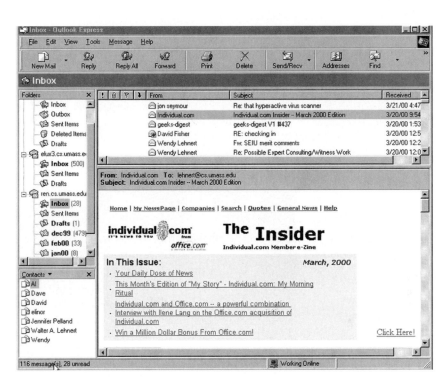

can be retrieved from a Web server by using the HTTP protocol, which is a more efficient way to moving a graphics file than e-mail (see Section 4.6).

Users who simply want to send a picture to a friend need not create an HTML file or post the picture on a Web server. They can just send the picture as a MIME attachment and trust the receiving mailer to handle the attachment appropriately. Most Web-based mail accounts (see Section 3.8) automatically display graphical attachments in a Web page display, as one would expect an HTML-enabled mail client to do (see Figure 3.8).

Use of HTML-enabled mailers does entail some risk. Some mailers run executable scripts in order to render Web pages more effectively. This enables a new breed of e-mail virus based on malicious scripts embedded in e-mail messages. The BubbleBoy virus, which surfaced in 1999, was the first scripting virus. It attacked Outlook and Outlook Express users and was more theoretical than real. BubbleBoy nonetheless demonstrated that the new breed of mailer could be tricked into running malicious code even when it was reading only a plain text message body. Microsoft solved the BubbleBoy problem by releasing a software patch for that particular type of attack. However, many users remain concerned about the possibility of new scripting viruses.

Figure 3.8:
A Web-Based Mail Client Automatically Displaying a Graphical MIME Attachment

E-mail remains the most widely used application on the net, surpassing even Web browsers in the size of its user population. Now that e-mail is a commercial concern, the widest possible population must be able to use it as easily as possible. The MIME protocol and HTML-enabled mailers were designed to enhance the e-mail experience without complicating it.

Can I Protect Myself from Malicious E-Mail Scripts?

If you use Outlook or Outlook Express and you are worried about scripting viruses, you can turn off the **Windows Scripting Host option** and you will be safe. It is also a good idea to install any security patches released by the software manufacturers of your Internet applications. Most security breaches could be avoided if everyone kept their software up-to-date in order to prevent known problems. You can visit the **Microsoft Download Center** to find all the available security patches for Microsoft products. Always go back to the original manufacturer's site for any software upgrades, updates, or patches.

3.4 ■ E-MAIL NETIQUETTE AND NETSPEAK

Practicing good e-mail etiquette, or **Netiquette,** is all about respect. Good Netiquette shows respect for people whom you don't know and might never get to know all that well despite long-standing, online conversations. It is especially important because the Internet encourages interactive communication between strangers on such a grand scale. People have never experienced such scale in other public forums, in which the reality of physical distance limits their reach and binds them to familiar communities.

Whenever you send e-mail, remember the following Netiquette guidelines.

- Keep your messages short and to the point.
- Watch your grammar and spelling.
- Be careful with humor; avoid sarcasm.
- Use uppercase words sparingly. UPPERCASE TEXT YELLS AT THE RECIPIENT.
- Never leave the Subject: field blank.
- Include your name and e-mail address in the message body (for example, in your sig file).

If you are new to e-mail, you probably have not experienced its mixed blessings. Some people deal with a hundred or more e-mail messages every day. They are understandably annoyed by any message that wastes their time, especially if the person writing the message doesn't use good Netiquette. Online conversations are not the same as face-to-face or even telephone conversations. When you talk online, no body language cues or vocal intonations are available to help the recipient interpret your message. If you are inexperienced with online dialogs, you might not realize how important and useful all of this "unspoken" communication is. For example, much well-intentioned humor falls flat on the Internet. Or worse, such humor may be completely misinterpreted and end up making someone feel hurt or angry. If you're in the habit of speaking sarcastically, temper that tendency until you have a good feel for how your written words are come across to people. What you intend is not always what others perceive.

3.4.1 Emoticons

Some people express themselves by using **emoticons**—combinations of keyboard characters that represent emotions. The most commonly seen emoticon is the **smilee**, shown as :-). A smilee might seem unnecessarily cutesy and perhaps a little annoying :-(if you aren't used to it, but they are useful :-o . A smilee explicitly tells the reader when something is being said in jest or when something shouldn't be taken seriously <grin>.

Messages with smilees are written by people who want to ensure that no one misunderstands :-{ the spirit of their words. I don't think that I've ever seen someone take offense >:-(at a statement punctuated by a smilee. It's the equivalent of a smile and a wink ;-) or a friendly laugh accompanied by a pat on the back. It works well among people who don't know each other well :-}. In general, emoticons allow people to insert some personality {ll:-) into their writing without fear =:-o of being misinterpreted.

3.4.2 Flames, Flaming, and Flame Wars

If you find yourself in an emotional exchange, it's best to cool down before responding. An angry e-mail message is called a **flame**, and people who write them are **flaming**. Flaming is not polite, and if you ever get flamed, you might feel hurt or downright abused. The Internet seems to encourage some people to indulge their pent-up rage by subjecting innocent bystanders to verbal abuse. Two people trading flames are engaged in a **flame war**. This behavior seems to be peculiar to the Internet; it probably wouldn't occur in a face-to-face interaction.

Flames can be contagious. Emotional heat has a way of generating more emotional heat, unless someone is willing to cool off and break the cycle. If a message angers you, wait a while before responding. You might have misinterpreted what was written. A flame war usually isn't worth the elevated blood pressure. Sometimes the best reply is no reply. If you care about good working relationships, you can't be too careful with your online communications. If you're angry or upset about something, deal with it face-to-face. E-mail is not a suitable medium for everything.

3.5 | SMTP AND MAIL SERVERS

The *client/server software model* is the foundation for all e-mail service. The mailer that you use to read and send e-mail is an e-mail *client* that depends on a mail *server* each time that you launch it to read mail or send mail. It might depend on two separate servers: one to send outgoing mail and one to read incoming mail. If one host machine is responsible for mail going in both directions, one piece of software will handle the outgoing mail and a different piece will handle the incoming mail. Thus e-mail involves two separate programs, depending on the direction in which the mail is headed.

Mailers are programmed for user convenience so that people can send and receive mail messages using the same software. However, the server side of the picture is always viewed from one direction or the other. When you install and configure a new mailer, you need to know the names of the servers that are responsible for outgoing mail and incoming mail. Figure 3.9 shows the preference settings for Netscape Communicator. Two mail servers are needed to set up e-mail. Your ISP can tell you the required preference settings for a new mailer. This section discusses outgoing mail. Section 3.6 deals with two models for incoming mail.

Mail is sent over the Internet by using the **Simple Mail Transfer Protocol (SMTP)**. SMTP is one of the oldest Internet protocols and is the universal standard for moving

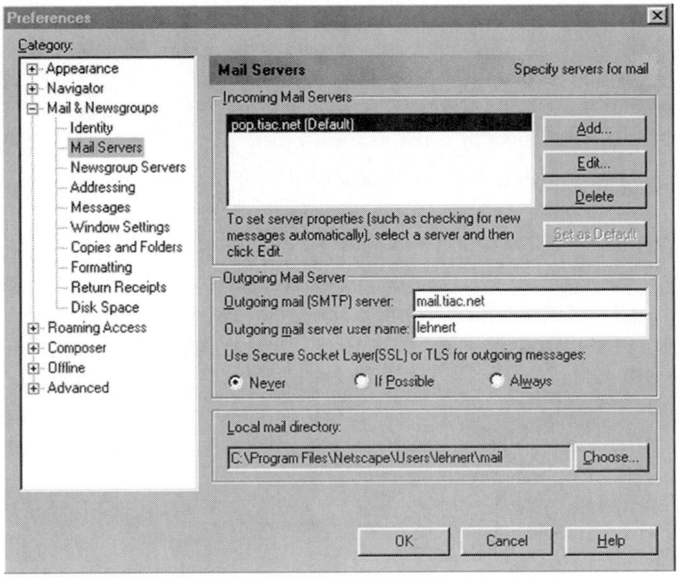

Figure 3.9:
Incoming and
Outgoing Mail
Server Information
Required by the
Mailer

mail over the Net. To send e-mail, you need to have access to an SMTP server, the e-mail address of your intended recipient, and a mailer. When you sign up for Internet access, you are given access to an SMTP server, using an account that you can activate with a userid and password. Note that some mailers allow you to access multiple mail servers for incoming mail but only one SMTP server for outgoing mail.

A mailer sending a mail message to a specified address contacts your SMTP server, which passes the DNS address to a DNS name server for verification and translation into an IP address. If an outgoing message bounces back to you with a "host unknown" error message, the DNS name server could not locate the host name in its directory of known DNS addresses. If all goes well with the DNS name server, an IP address is returned for your intended recipient, and the mail message is prepared for transport out over the Net using TCP/IP.

When mail is received at its destination, another mailer catches it and saves it in an inbox for the specified recipient. At that point, SMTP is done with the message. Another server steps in to negotiate the final delivery to the recipient's mail client. This is where things get a bit more complicated.

3.6 ▌ HTTP, POP, AND IMAP

Different kinds of mail servers are designed to deliver incoming messages to mail clients. If you are setting up a new mail account, note that not all mailers are compatible with all mail servers. If you are shopping around for a mailer, first check to find out the type of incoming mail service you have, as that will constrain your choice. Currently, the three most popular e-mail protocols (for incoming mail) are

- Hypertext Transfer Protocol (HTTP mail),
- Post Office Protocol 3 (POP mail), and
- Internet Message Access Protocol (IMAP mail).

3.6.1 Hypertext Transfer Protocol

The Hypertext Transfer Protocol (HTTP) might be familiar to you as a Web protocol because it is used to specify URLs for Web browsers. It also can be used as an e-mail protocol by Web sites that provide Web-based e-mail services (see Section 3.8). In this case, the Web browser steps in and acts as the mailer because the mail is being delivered via the Web. If you know that your mail recipient is using an HTTP mail account (for example, a Yahoo! Mail account or a Hotmail account), you can send that recipient a file for a Web page that is viewable just as if it were a Web page (see Figure 3.10). Web-based E-Mail is always HTML-enabled. However, keep in mind an important caveat.

To send a Web page via e-mail, you must reference all of the links on the page (including all links to any image files) by using *absolute URLs* (absolute URLs are

Figure 3.10:
HTML-Enabled
Web-Based E-Mail

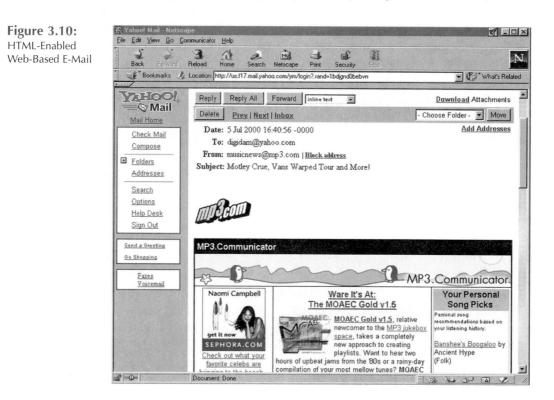

described in Section 4.5); otherwise, they will not be operational when your recipient views the page. Most Web pages usually don't reference image files by using absolute URLs. As a result, most Web pages don't travel well via e-mail.

MSIE has a feature that makes sending a Web page to an e-mail address easy (see Figure 3.11). Using this Send Page by E-mail feature works fine, except that the graphics probably won't be visible on the receiving end.

Figure 3.11:
MSIE's Send Page by E-Mail Feature

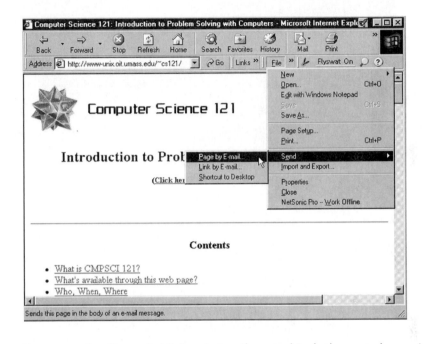

For example, Figure 3.12 is missing the graphical element shown in Figure 3.11 because the Web page was not written with e-mail forwarding in mind (see Section 3.8 for more about forwarding Web pages to e-mail accounts). If viewing the graphics is important, send the URL for the Web page instead of the actual Web page.

3.6.2 Post Office Protocol 3 and Internet Message Access Protocol

Although Web-based mail has some nice features, people who rely on e-mail for business or other crucial communications opt for either a POP or IMAP mail service. Note however, the choice might not be yours, as most ISPs offer one service or the other but not both (see Figure 3.13).

Some mailers can handle both POP and IMAP servers, but you need to know which service you want to use when you install your mailer (see Figure 3.14).

Figure 3.12:
Missing Graphic on
a Web Page for
HTTP Mail Not
Written with HTTP
Mail in Mind

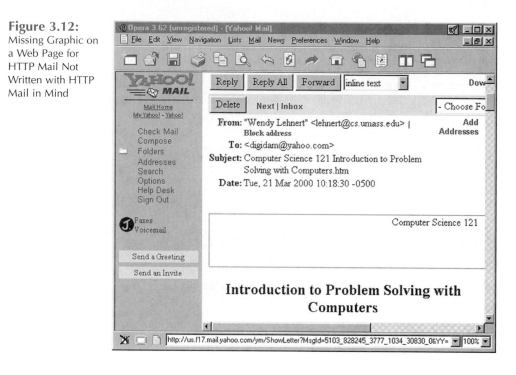

Figure 3.13:
IMAP, POP, and
SMTP Mail Servers
Move Mail Across
the Internet

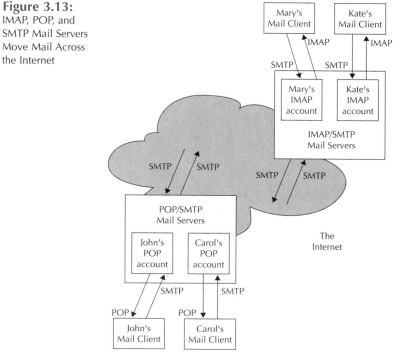

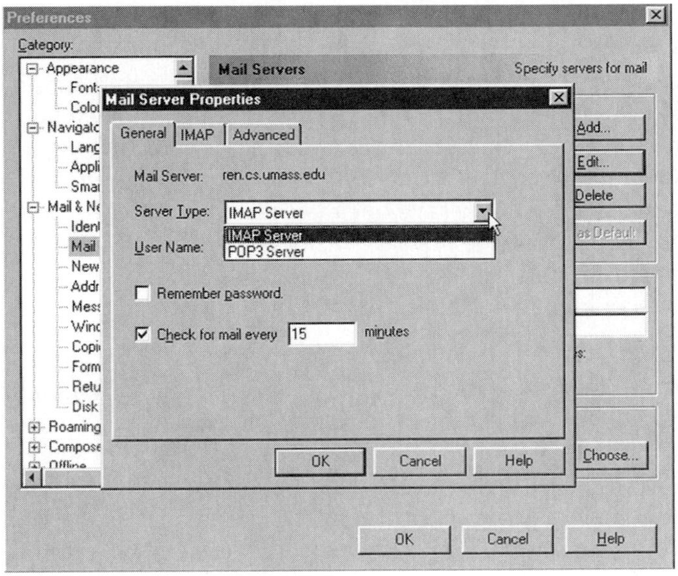

Figure 3.14:
IMAP or POP?
Netscape
Communicator
Needs to Know

Post Office Protocol 3 If you had an ISP account before 1999, you were probably using a POP mail server. Both Communicator and Internet Explorer came with POP mailers, and Eudora was a popular POP mailer for both Windows-based personal computers and Macs.

POP was designed to support offline mail management, which made great sense when people had to pay for connect time by the hour. Users are in offline mode when they work without an active Internet connection. In a POP mail service, the server is basically a drop box in which mail is temporarily stored until the client connects and asks for it. The server then forwards all of the accumulated mail to the client and clears its temporary store to make room for more mail. The user downloads the mail, disconnects from the Net, and deals with the e-mail offline. After reading the messages, the user deletes them or stores them in a local folder. The user also writes messages or replies to messages while offline and sends them all at once the next time that the user connects to the mail server. Thus the most time-consuming work is completed offline, and the Internet connection is reserved for brief mail uploads and downloads. Any mail that is saved is stored on the local host, thereby freeing up the server to accept new mail.

Anyone who has had to access their e-mail from multiple locations understands a major drawback with POP mail. Suppose that you have a computer at work and a computer at home and you want to be able to read your e-mail at both locations. Now suppose that you download 20 messages to the office machine so you can catch up on the day's mail before you go home. However, you never get around to reading the last ten before you leave the office. You'd like to read them at home later, but your home computer cannot access them because they have already been removed from the mail server by your office computer. To get at the mail from your home, you need a connection between your home computer and your office computer so that you can transfer a mail folder from your office machine to your home machine. This is cumbersome, but it can be done. Copying a mail folder enables you to read those messages, but now you have copies of the same mail messages in two places. If you want to save one message and delete the others, you have to figure out where to save the message that you want to keep (on the home machine or the office machine?). You also have to delete all the other messages twice because you have copies of everything in two places now.

This is tedious and time-consuming, not to mention risky because it's easy to make mistakes. (For example, you thought you had saved an important message on one machine, so you deleted it on the other machine, but you were confused about where it was saved, and you deleted your last copy.) POP servers can be instructed to download mail without deleting it, but having multiple copies of every message in multiple computers complicates mail management. Coordinating offline mail in multiple locations is difficult—especially for people who have high volumes of mail and urgent communication requirements. This offline model for e-mail dominated the Internet throughout the 1990s. Increasingly, however, it is being replaced by the Internet Message Access Protocol, a newer, more powerful e-mail service.

Internet Message Access Protocol An alternative to offline mail management is "online" mail management. In **online mode**, the mail client works with the mail server as if it were a program running on the server. The user manipulates mail and mail folders as if they were local, but everything stays on the server. Instead of downloading all the mail messages in a single block, the user can start by downloading just the mail headers. Some mail can be deleted on the basis of the header alone, so it might not be necessary to download all the mail messages to the local host. However, if the user wants to read a message, or search a mail folder for a keyword in the message bodies, then any or all of the mail messages can be downloaded as needed. This is how the IMAP model works. With IMAP, the client and the server work together more interactively in an effort to make mail management more flexible and negotiable.

Depending on how the client is configured, an IMAP mail program can work online, offline, or in a "disconnected" mode. In **disconnected mode**, the client connects to server, creates a local cache of selected messages, and goes offline. The user then has an opportunity to go through the mail, delete some messages, write some replies, and maybe compose some new messages. At any time the client can reconnect with the server to send off new mail or purge a message marked for deletion. When the client and server reconnect, the client automatically resynchronizes its local cache with the server. All mail folders and all mail are left on the IMAP server at all times, making it easier to work with the same mail store from different locations.

IMAP client options are more flexible than POP options because an IMAP client can work in online, offline, or disconnected modes. A POP client only works in offline mode. This can make the preference settings for an IMAP client more complicated, but it is not necessary to master all the settings in order to work with an IMAP server. If you ever need to switch from a POP server to an IMAP server, just remember that the POP server gave you a "store and forward" service. The IMAP server allows you to store messages on the server and manage mail folders on the server through your IMAP client. All of the old familiar mail operations will still be available, but you are working with messages that remain on your mail server until you explicitly (1) mark them for deletion and then (2) purge your deleted messages. You do not need to store mail on a local host, and you do not need to download all of your unread messages in order to read just one. You also don't need to worry about when you are in online mode, offline mode or disconnected mode. Just select the basic mail operations you need to perform and let the client negotiate the client/server communications. You can just concentrate on your mail, and your IMAP client will take care of everything else.

3.7   FILTERING AND ROUTING

People who receive a lot of e-mail find it useful to organize their mail in mail folders. A mail folder is like a file folder for correspondence. Storing mail messages in a system of mail folders makes it easier to find specific messages and to move large blocks of mail into long-term archives (or the trash) when the time comes to thin out the current folders. It takes some thinking and experimentation to come up with a set of folders that will work well: no two people can hope to use the exact same system. If 90% of your mail comes from the same 20 people, you might want to create a folder for each person. If you just want to separate out your personal mail from your business mail and your mailing lists, you could start out with three folders for those three categories. And if your mail is difficult to categorize, you could create a new mail folder once a month in order to store monthly archives chronologically.

Once you settle on a good system of mail folders, you might find it convenient to move mail into certain folders automatically. This can be accomplished with a mail client that supports "filtering" and "routing." E-mail **filtering** is a way of recognizing specific messages based on keywords in their subject headers, from fields, or message bodies. E-mail **routing** is a way of directing mail to a specific folder or subdirectory for later viewing. Filtering and routing are usually combined to help people manage large volumes of e-mail: messages of a certain type can be recognized by filters and then routed to a single folder. Some folders trap important messages that require daily review while others are less urgent and require attention once a week. Many people rely heavily on mail filters and cannot imagine life without them. It is about as close as most of us will ever get to having a personal secretary who faithfully sorts our mail, seven days a week, 24 hours a day.

If your mail client supports mail filters, you will probably find it easy to create any number of filter rules for your own needs. Each filter rule should try to identify mail messages that belong in a particular mail folder, filter them out of the incoming mail stream, and then route them to the appropriate folder. For example, it is usually easy to write a filter rule that routes e-mail from a mailing list to a folder for that mailing list. In Figure 3.15 we see how to create a filter rule for a Yahoo! mail account. This filter rule traps messages from a mailing list newsletter about Unix tips. It recognizes the messages to filter on the basis of the From: field and the Subject: field. We have also told the rule *not* to trap messages that contain the (fictitious) name "Joe WayBeyondMe" just in case I never understand anything written by this individual and I've given up trying to read his tips. I could create a separate filter rule to trap anything written by Joe on this mailing list so those messages could be routed to a folder for probable disposal at some later time.

Figure 3.15:
Creating Filter Rules
for a Yahoo! Mail
Account Is Easy

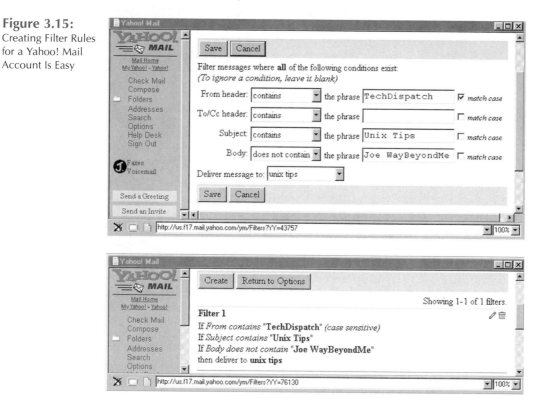

When you see how easy it is to create filter rules, you might be tempted to create filters for everything you can think to trap and route to a folder. It's fine to experiment with lots of filter rules. If one turns out to be a bad idea, you can always delete it. Just watch out for the "out of sight, out of mind" pitfall. When mail is automatically routed to a mail folder, it's very easy to forget about it—totally. So when you first start routing mail into mail folders, remind yourself to take a look at all those folders at least once a week. Then decide if and how you are going to pay attention to those folders. *If anything urgent could be routed into a folder, it's important to check the folder at least once a day.* Also pay attention to how much mail is being routed to each folder: you might have to watch your memory quota. You might also need to make sure that certain messages are *not* being picked up by filters so you will be able to see them as quickly as possible in your inbox.

Automatic mail filters can teach you a lot about how you spend your time and how you might spend your time differently. If you aren't constantly watching over your inbox for new mail, you can better control the time you spend on your mail. Set a time each day to handle work-related mail that's been routed into work folders. Then schedule a block of time once or twice a week for recreational folders. A recreational mailing list might be given one hour twice a week, after more important things have been taken care of.

When used correctly, automatic mail filters can help you stay focused and less distracted by a constant barrage of e-mail. You might even discover that you can drop an entire mailing list that doesn't really interest you that much anymore, now that you aren't seeing the messages all the time. Or you might find out that you just don't want to set aside a dedicated block of time for a specific interest – that interest was actually just an excuse for avoiding work-related messages. If you want to improve your time management, try out some automated mail filters: you might be surprised by what you learn.

3.8 | WEB-BASED MAIL ACCOUNTS

Every major portal on the Web offers free Web-based e-mail in order to maximize repeat visits to the site. These services are usually subsidized by banner ads and they give advertisers easy access to your attention at least once a day or, at worst, maybe once a week. It is usually easy to register for these services—you just have to think of a userid that no one else thought of first, and you may need another e-mail address in order to verify your identity. Some sites require additional personal information, and some don't. Once you've signed up, your account is password protected.

Cookies and Web-Based E-Mail

Some Web-based e-mail services only work when cookies are enabled in your browser. If you have disabled cookies, you might need to manually enable them each time you visit your Web-based mail account. If this becomes annoying, you can download a cookie manager and set it to enable cookies at your mail site, but no where else (see the Above and Beyond section in Chapter 2 for an introduction to cookies).

Web-based e-mail has some very nice features. Since you read it with a Web browser, it is always HTML-enabled (see Figure 3.16). It often supports filtering and routing capabilities, and when it does, the process of rule creation tends to be fast and easy. Some of the big portal-related mail services offer an instant messaging client (see Section 7.7.3) that can monitor your mail account and alert you when a new mail message arrives. Others allow you to consolidate incoming mail from multiple POP accounts so you can read all your POP mail in one place. Different services offer different features so it pays to look around and watch for new features.

Figure 3.16:
Web-Based Mail
Can Deliver Mail
Messages That Look
Like Web Pages

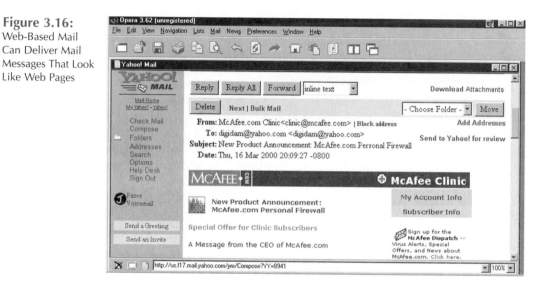

Unfortunately, the quality of service can also vary from service to service, and you might need to shop around for a service you can trust. Some of the most popular mail services struggle to keep up with a rapidly expanding subscriber population. As a result, their servers might be overloaded from time to time. Hotmail has been known to refuse to accept e-mail for hours at a time, when their system load is high. America Online (AOL) is not a free e-mail service, but it often behaves like one. When their systems are overloaded, e-mail can take just as long to be accepted by aol.com as it takes for hotmail.com. In addition, AOL has had mail server failures that have lasted longer than a day, with no e-mail going in or out of aol.com. Many Web-based mail servers are stable, but most experience periodic difficulties (see Figure 3.17). *If you have to have the most reliable mail service possible, it is best to look for a POP or IMAP mail account instead of an HTTP mail account.*

If you are experienced with e-mail, a Web-based e-mail account should be easy to handle. You might, nevertheless, run into one option that could use a little explanation. Whenever you have an HTML-enabled mail client, you need to think before you forward an HTML-enhanced mail message to a new recipient. If that recipient reads their mail with Web-based mail client, you can forward the message and it

Figure 3.17:
HTTP Servers Seem
to Experience More
Down Time Than
Do IMAP or POP
Servers

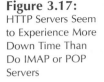

> **There was a problem accessing your mailbox.**
>
> This is most likely a temporary problem that should resolve itself within 10 minutes.
> Until the problem is resolved, you will not be able to send or receive e-mail messages.
> We are working to restore your service as soon as possible.
>
> We apologize for this inconvenience. Thank you for your patience.

will be rendered faithfully just as it appears in your own inbox. However, some people do not read their e-mail on a Web-based e-mail account. Then the question is whether or not they have an HTML-enabled client. If they have an HTML-enabled client, they will see the same message you do. But, what if your recipient does not have an HTML-enabled client? You can still send them your message as a MIME attachment, but they will have to download it and display it with a Web browser in order to see the same message you do. This might be asking a lot of the person on the receiving end. If they are pressed for time, it might be better to send a plain ASCII text version of the enhanced message (see Figure 3.19). In order to give you control over how you forward HTML-enhanced mail messages, you might see a menu like the one in Figure 3.18.

Figure 3.18:
Forward HTML-
Enhanced E-Mail
with Care

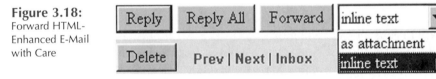

Yahoo! Mail gives us a choice whenever we forward a mail message from our Yahoo! Mail account to another party. If we select the "attachment" option, it will be easy to view the enhanced version of the message with any HTML-enabled mail client. If we select the "inline" option, our recipient will see only a plain text rendering of the original message (see Figure 3.19). This is not a good choice if any multimedia elements are crucial and should not be lost. However, it might be your best choice for users whose mail client cannot handle HTML-enhanced mail messages.

Note that there is a difference between (1) mailing a Web page that you found on the Web, as discussed in Section 3.6, and (2) forwarding an HTML-enhanced mail message that you found in your inbox. In the first case, the Web page probably won't travel well because it was never designed to be moved from its original server. Under those circumstances, it is generally best to send the URL instead of trying to forward the original Web page. However, in the second case, it is safe to assume

Figure 3.19:
An Inline Version of
the Mail Message in
Figure 3.16

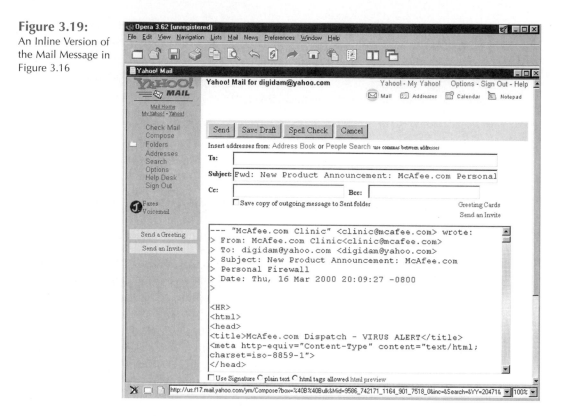

that any HTML-enhanced mail message was designed for transport across servers: if it looks good in your inbox, it will look good in any inbox. So in this case, you don't have to worry about the document per se, but you still have to think about your intended recipient: are they equipped to view this file without being inconvenienced? Note also that in this case, there is no URL to forward, so forwarding the original message is really your only option.

If you already have a POP or IMAP mail account, you might want to experiment with a few Web-based mail accounts in order to help you segregate certain kinds of e-mail for better mail handling. For example, one Web account might be reserved for commercial transactions. Then all the e-mail receipts and follow-up messages that often follow an online purchase will be found in one place and never get tangled up with other types of e-mail. Another Web account might be reserved for mailing lists and newsletters—any material that does not require immediate attention or fast responses. By reserving entire mail accounts for different types of e-mail, we are really just filtering and routing e-mail on a large scale. However, we might also succeed in segregating a large proportion of the spam that we receive (expect it to show up in the account for commercial transactions if you did not opt out of those "third-party vendor" offers. Just try not to set up too many separate Web accounts. The extra added overhead of having to visit multiple mail accounts might overwhelm any advantage associated with heavily segregated mail. If you push it too hard, excessive mail filtering might generate new problems for you. Only you can know when the cost/benefit ratio of multiple mail accounts has crossed a line (see the Above and Beyond section in Chapter 3).

Things to Remember

- Do not send files larger than 50KB in an e-mail message body.
- POP mail accounts are good for offline mail management.
- IMAP mail accounts support offline, online, and disconnected mail management.
- Free Web-based mail accounts may not be as reliable as POP or IMAP accounts.
- Don't set up a filter to route mail into a mail folder and then forget about it.
- Web-based e-mail accounts may require a cookie-enabled Web browser.

Important Concepts

e-mail client—software that can transfer e-mail messages between a local host and a local e-mail server, as well as display and compose messages on the local host.

e-mail server—software that can send e-mail messages to and receive e-mail messages from other e-mail servers, as well as hold incoming messages for local e-mail clients.

emoticons—a symbolic system for expressing simple emotions in ASCII text.

filtering—a way to recognize specific messages based on keywords in their Subject: fields, From: fields, or message bodies.

flame—an uninhibited display of anger or aggression online.

HTTP—a Web-based e-mail protocol.

IMAP—an e-mail protocol where mail is stored on a mail server.

Netiquette—standard rules of courtesy for online communication.

POP—an e-mail protocol where mail is stored on a local host.

routing—a way to direct mail to a specific folder or subdirectory for later viewing.

SMTP—the original protocol for moving e-mail over the Internet.

Where Can I Learn More?

Everything E-Mail `http://everythingemail.net/`

Harness E-Mail: How It Works `http://www.learnthenet.com/`
  `english/html/20how.htm`

> **Beginning E-Mail** `http://email.tqn.com/internet/email/`
> `msub10.htm`
>
> **E-Mail Pet Peeves** `http://www.thebee.com/bweb/iinfo43.htm`

Problems and Exercises

1. Name two header fields that are completed for you automatically when you send an e-mail message.

2. What does a signature file contain? What is a good length for a signature file?

3. What is the difference between the Cc: field and the Bcc: field?

4. Why is it a bad idea to compose long Subject: fields?

5. What are emoticons, and why are they useful?

6. Explain the difference between a group reply and a single author reply.

7. When you include the original message in an e-mail reply, should you always include the original message in its entirety? Explain your answer.

8. If you exchange a series of e-mail messages with someone by using the Reply command, what should you remember to do every so often?

9. What is an HTML-enabled mail client?

10. Your best friend has a Hotmail account, and you want her to see a really cool Web site that you just discovered. You use MSIE and know about its send Web page feature. Given the choice of sending your friend the actual Web page that you found or the URL for that Web page, which is better? Explain why.

11. When is it safe to forward an HTML-enhanced mail message to a friend? How does this differ from sending an arbitrary Web page via e-mail? Explain what happens if you use Yahoo's "inline" option for mail forwarding.

12. Explain the main difference between an IMAP mail service and a POP mail service. Which is more powerful? Which was designed to minimize connect time? Which is better for people who need to work with their mail from multiple locations? Which would you want if your hard drive were very full but you still needed to save a lot of mail?

13. What is the MIME protocol used for, and how does it save time?

14. Suppose that you have a Web-based mail account that opens and displays graphical file attachments automatically. Do you need to worry about macro viruses on this account? Explain your answer.

15. Is an HTTP mail account more like a POP mail account or an IMAP mail account? Think about where the mail messages are stored, and then explain your answer.

16. **[Find It Online]** Visit **Everything E-mail** (`http://everythingemail.net/`) and find definitions for the following Netspeak terms in its e-mail glossary: AFAIK, CMIIW, CUL, IAC, IKWUM, IMHO, OTOH, ROTFL, and TIA.

17. [**Find It Online**] Visit Joan Stark's **ASCII Art Gallery** (`http://www.geocities.com/SoHo/7373/`), and find out when typewriter art was first documented. (*Hint*: Look under the History of ASCII Art).

18. [**Hands-on**] Send yourself an e-mail message. Does your mailer default to a full-header display or a short header display? If it defaults to a short header, how many lines are in the header display? Can you find a command that will show you the full header display? How many lines are in the full header? Look at another mail message in your inbox, and check its short and long header displays. Do the short headers for these two messages have the same number of lines? Do the full headers have the same number of lines?

19. [**Hands-on**] Visit **Everything E-mail** (`http://everythingemail.net/`), and send yourself a postcard. What did you have to do to view your postcard? Several postcard services on the Web work like this. Why don't they use e-mail attachments instead?

20. [**Hands-on**] If you subscribe to a mailing list, examine some messages from the list and design a filter rule to trap all incoming mail from your list by using the filter rule options such as the ones in Figure 3.15.

E-Mail Management: Above and Beyond

Spam: Trouble in Paradise

Sooner or later, everyone who uses e-mail encounters instances of Internet abuse. It is important to understand what constitutes Internet abuse so that you don't inadvertently contribute to it yourself. It is also good to know how to respond to it when it happens to you. The most common form of Net abuse via e-mail involves unsolicited messages. These are typically commercial advertisements. However, they can also be political calls for action, religious sermons, philosophical manifestos, or the incoherent ravings of someone with a mental problem.

If you are affiliated with a commercial interest, never broadcast unsolicited product announcements or advertisements via e-mail. Unsolicited e-mail sent to a large number of people is called **spam** and is a classic form of Internet abuse. It is all right, for example, to compile a list of friends and acquaintances and then tell them that you've changed jobs and now have a new Internet address. Just don't try to sell anything at the same time. You can tell people what your new company does. You can even include a URL pointer to a corporate Web page. Just keep the chest-thumping to a minimum lest anyone think you are plugging your new employer.

Why Is It Called Spam? The term spam comes from an old Monty Python sketch. The connection to digital spam is self-evident:

Scene: A cafe. One table is occupied by a group of Vikings with horned helmets on. A man and his wife enter.

Man: You sit here, dear.

Wife: All right.

Man: (to Waitress) Morning!

Waitress: Morning!

Man: Well, what've you got?

Waitress: Well, there's egg and bacon; egg sausage and bacon; egg and spam; egg bacon and spam; egg bacon sausage and spam; spam bacon sausage and spam; spam egg spam spam bacon and spam; spam sausage spam spam bacon spam tomato and spam;

Vikings: (starting to chant) Spam spam spam spam...

Waitress: . . . spam spam spam egg and spam; spam spam spam spam spam spam baked beans spam spam spam . . .

—from *Monty Python's Previous Record*

144

If you are new to the Internet, you won't see much mail spam right away. After you've been online awhile, you will begin to see spam from time to time. How much you get depends on how visible your own e-mail address is, who has collected it, who has sold it and who has bought it.

Since the Internet is not policed by any legal authority, only customs and conventions associated with Internet abuse can be described; the abuse can't be defined in strict terms. There are clear-cut cases of Internet abuse, and there are some borderline areas that will strike some people, but not everyone, as a form of abuse. Here's an example of the latter. Suppose you send a very short message to a very large list of "acquaintances" announcing your move to a new company. The message includes a corporate URL in the message body but nothing remotely personal about you as anyone more than a corporate contact. If this goes out to people who don't recognize your name, it is probably Internet abuse. An even trickier example is the case of sig files. What if you insert a brief plug for your freelance services in your sig file just in case someone might be interested? If the sig file is no more than four lines, chances are no one will object. However, some people might consider even that to be tacky.

All of these prohibitions apply primarily to commercial interests, although politics and religion are not far behind. No one wants to get unsolicited e-mail about a favorite political cause (no matter how worthy) or one's latest transcendental experience (no matter how profound). If you study a few hundred sig files, you will find that most Netizens stick to "tag lines" (witty quotations) or opinionated proclamations of a purely technical nature. Responsible people try to err on the side of caution when it comes to Internet abuse.

If you find yourself becoming a **spam magnet**, there are a number of defensive maneuvers you can try. The simplest one involves nothing more than your Delete button. Once you learn to recognize spam on the basis of the mail header alone, just delete it when you see it and get on with your life. This is a good solution when the amount of spam you receive is not very great. When more spam starts piling up in your inbox, you will probably want to try a more sophisticated response.

Try filtering and routing all likely spam messages into a mail folder where they can sit until you get around to deleting them. If it is not reasonable for you to manually design your own spam filter rules, you might want to look into available shareware or freeware that is designed to stop spam. For more information about other things you can do, visit **CAUCE** (The Coalition Against Unsolicited Commercial E-mail) (see Figure 3.20).

If you're more worried about preventing spam than ducking it, you'll need to learn more about the various ways that spammers obtain e-mail addresses. You can start by foiling the automated address harvesters that crawl across the Web looking for e-mail addresses. Never post your address on a public Web page unless you first take steps to fool the spambots (see the Above and Beyond section in Chapter 7 and Exercise #17 in Chapter 8).

Figure 3.20:
CAUCE Is a
Clearinghouse for
Spam Resistance

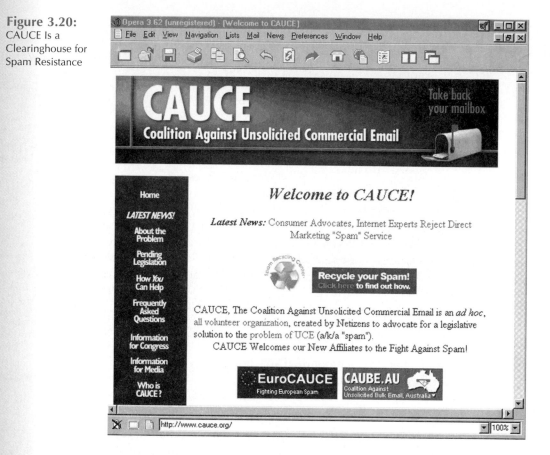

You will also need to develop some healthy cynicism about data collection and privacy policies on the Internet. Whenever you are asked to provide personal information over the Web or via e-mail, you should know what, if any, privacy policies will be applied to protect your privacy. No laws in the United States protect the privacy rights of consumers, so users must be savvy about what goes on behind the scenes. If a company offers you a free e-mail account, how much information do you have to give up in order to participate? Data resellers generate a lot of revenue by selling Internet user profiles to advertisers, marketing organizations, and scam artists. Whenever anyone on the Internet offers you a free service in exchange for information, understand that you are probably being bought and sold. If the service is worth it to you, fine. Most people just don't realize that they are really trading personal privacy for free e-mail or free space on a Web server.

How to Fight Back against Spam

If you have been defending yourself as best you can, and you are starting to get angry about the time and effort that spam demands, it is time to fight back. Just make sure you know how to go about it.

If you get spammed, don't bother going back to the offending party for retaliation. Do not try to reply to the original sender directly. An angry reply to the sender will have no effect whatsoever. It might occur to you to send hundreds of retaliatory e-mail messages to the reply address in the hope of causing disk quota overloads. Don't try it. Chances are that that account was terminated or abandoned right after the spamming event (the people who do these things are no fools) and all that e-mail could bounce right back to you. Alternatively, the account in question might have been broken into by the spammer, in which case you will only be victimizing another victim. It is also relatively easy to forge a mail header, so the information in a From: slot might be totally fictitious (in which case, your e-mail bounces back to you again). Mailing hundreds of messages to a single e-mail address is called **mail bombing**. Mail bombing is just another form of Internet abuse, no matter how justified it seems. There are legitimate things you can do in response to Internet abuse, but retaliation with more Internet abuse is not one of them.

If you are spammed, you can bring the offense to the attention of appropriate system administrators. This is easy to do, it doesn't take a lot of time, and it helps technical support people track down the mail spammer. Inspect the From: header in the offending mail message and identify the host name of the address found there. To contact the system administrators for that host, send mail to the postmaster at that address. Here's an example, a spam message that came to me a while ago:

```
Date: Sun, 8 Dec 1996 03:55:03 -0500
Subject: Search for Paradise
_____

Forwarded message:
Subj: Search for Paradise
Date: 96-12-08 03:41:25 EST
From: ChrisM 11
To: ChrisM 11


This is to inform you about the new adult game that VCS
Magazine rated "The best game of '96" and gave an
"Outstanding ****" (4 stars). "The Search for Paradise is
no doubt one of the greatest XXX Adult games available."
```

This message continued on for some time, concluding with instructions for how to order the game. This mail was sent shortly after midnight on a Sunday morning. A lot of spammers deliberately strike at that time because it gives them the greatest head start for a clean getaway. Sunday mornings are usually periods of low Internet traffic. Most recipients of this spam wouldn't see it for at least 12 hours, maybe even up to 24 hours. This delay gives the spammer time to erase his tracks.

To see the full address of the sender, examine the full message header, which in this case identifies the originating address as `ChrisM11@aol.com`. This is an AOL account. So you would send a note about this incident to `postmaster@aol.com`.

All Internet hosts have an account named "postmaster" that is read by technical support staff. The postmaster is responsible for fielding complaints about e-mail originating from the host machine.

Where's the Administrator?

If you are having trouble contacting a postmaster, you can send your complaint to the **Network Abuse Clearinghouse**. Send your complaint to (domain name)@abuse.net. Your message will be forwarded to all of the abuse contacts for that domain.

For example, gnn.com@abuse.net is converted to gnnadvisor@gnn.com and abuse@aol.net, both of which are GNN's abuse contacts. You will need to register at the site to use the service, but the service is worth it.

Sometimes mail headers are doctored so that you can't know for sure if the account the spamming came from is the actual originating account. If the spammer is very sophisticated, you're looking at a false lead. However, there is more information in the full message header that might be useful to technical support folks who want to track this down. So when you contact the postmaster, forward a copy of the spamming message along with the full mail header. This will give tech support all of the information they need to track down the offending party.

Where Do I Find the Full Header?

To track down spammers, technical support staff needs to examine full e-mail headers. All mail clients have a command that will display the full mail header of a message. In Outlook Express, go to the File menu, select Properties and then the Details tab. A text window will appear that contains the full header for the current message. If you need to forward the header to an administrator, you can copy and paste the text from that window.

Other clients might have short and long display preferences that can be changed as needed. If you are having trouble finding the full header display for your client, consult the online documentation or look for help on the Web.

Whenever I forward a mail spam to a postmaster, I include a form letter at the head of my message to explain what's going on. I keep this in a file so that I can grab it and insert it into a mail message quickly and easily whenever I need it. Here is the letter:

```
Dear Administrator,

The following message was sent to me by a mail spammer. Please
take action w.r.t. the offending account to ensure that no
additional Internet abuse can originate from this site.
```

```
Thank You,

Professor Wendy G. Lehnert
Department of Computer Science
University of Massachusetts
Amherst, MA 01003 lehnert@cs.umass.edu


==========================================================
```

Then I append the full message headers and the message body from the spamming message. You can write a similar message for these situations yourself. You don't need an official title to report instances of Internet abuse. Everyone has a right to complain about unsolicited e-mail.

When you write to a postmaster, you might either receive no reply, an autoreply form letter, or a personal reply. When I wrote to the postmaster at AOL, I got a generic autoreply message:

```
Date: Sun, 8 Dec 1996 12:33:54 -0500 (EST)
To: lehnert@thidwick.cs.umass.edu
Old-Subject: Re: Notification of Spamming Activity
Precedence: junk
X-Loop: pmd@aol.net
Reply-To: postmaster@aol.com
Subject: Postmaster Mail Receipt Notification

Dear Internet Correspondent:

Thanks for writing to us with your question, concern or com-
ment. You are receiving this automatically-generated message
to acknowledge that your mail has been received. To keep
from further consuming bandwidth and mailbox space, you will
only receive this message once a month (per account).

Our goal is to process all mail sent to postmaster@aol.com
within 24 hours of receipt, and when possible to personally
follow up on mail we've received. However, during times of
high volume, staff outages and similar situations, we may not
be able to meet this goal. We hope that you will understand
that under these conditions, replies may be delayed or omit-
ted. We will only do this when it is necessary, and your
patience and understanding is greatly appreciated. Due to the
large number of reports we receive regarding USENET abuse,
not all complaint/reports can be responded to personally.
```

This message continued with additional information for people in different situations, much like a written version of a voice-mail recording. Eventually, a human being will see my actual message, but in the meantime, I feel reassured that my complaint was sent to the right place and (I hope) that the recipient is prepared to deal with it. In any case, that's as much as I normally ever do when I get spammed. By my reporting the spamming to the appropriate authorities, actions can be taken to prevent the same person from trying it again. If this mail really did come from an AOL account and AOL can determine that the owner of the account was responsible for it, that account will be shut down and the person responsible for it will (I assume) be blacklisted from AOL.

In this particular case, the AOL postmaster followed up with a second reply a few days later:

```
X-Authentication-Warning: zipcode: pmd7 owned process doing-bs
Date: Fri, 13 Dec 1996 13:25:54 -0500 (EST)
X-Sender: pmd7@zipcode.atg.aol.com
To: Mike Truman <pmd7@aol.net>
Subject: Got the spam...

Hello,

You don't have to reply to this, but thought I'd send an E-
mail to thank you for sending the large and rather nasty junk
E-mail that was sent from our site. We've taken measures to
stop the person responsible for this from doing it again. If
in the future you receive mail of this nature just send it
directly to postmaster@aol.com and we'll take care of it.
Thanks.
Have a good one,
**********************************************************
Michael Truman pmd7@aol.net
Assistant PostMaster postmaster@aol.com
America Online, Inc.
PostMaster Services Team
**********************************************************
```

You don't always get a follow-up like this, and indeed, this is quite possibly another form letter as well. However, this type of response gives the recipients of spam the sense that someone is doing their job and that it is worthwhile to report mail spammers. At least you don't have to feel totally helpless in the face of unwanted junk mail.

Managing Multiple E-Mail Accounts

With so many personal computers in offices, homes, and hotel rooms, many people are not just wired into the Net, but wired two and three times over. As we saw in section 3.6, some mail clients make this easier than others. Not only do we have the same person trying to access the same mail account from multiple computers, but we might also have the same person trying to deal with multiple e-mail accounts (see Section 3.8) on multiple computers. These are two separate problems but they both require some careful planning on the part of the user.

It might seem that the natural solution to multiple e-mail accounts is to consolidate those accounts into one hefty inbox, and to some extent that's right. You can find mail clients that will assist in this strategy. For example, Outlook Express will allow you to set up input from multiple POP or IMAP servers (see Figure 3.21), but it won't let you mix both POP and IMAP servers on the same installation.

Figure 3.21:
Consolidating
Multiple E-Mail
Servers with
Outlook Express

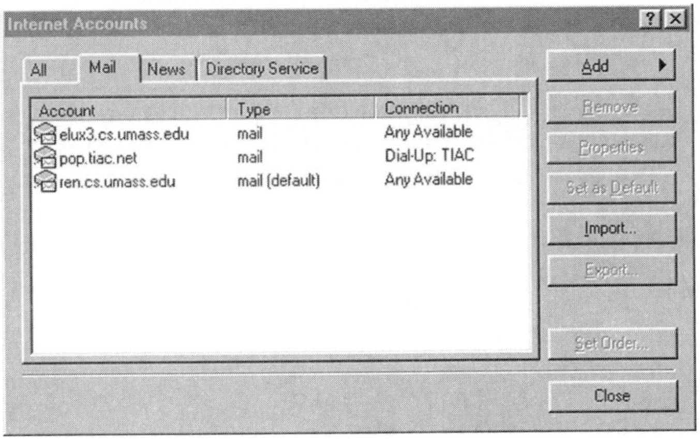

If you are consolidating multiple POP accounts, proceed with caution. POP mail accounts do not give you a lot of control over what gets downloaded—if you have 500 mail messages on the server, you basically have to download 500 messages in order to find the one or two that require an urgent response. This is about the worst e-mail nightmare anyone can imagine and perhaps the strongest argument you can muster against consolidating POP mail accounts. If you are dealing with a lot of traffic on POP mail servers, try to stay on top of it so you never have to deal with huge backlogs.

The consolidation of multiple IMAP accounts is a completely different story. On an IMAP server the user has a lot of control over what gets read, what gets ignored, and what gets set aside. If you have multiple IMAP accounts, consolidation is an excellent strategy. There will still be times when the mail piles up, but that's when you really need the sort of control that IMAP offers.

If you research available freeware and shareware on the net, you might be able to find additional mail management tools that will meet your needs. Alarm systems can be very useful when you are expecting specific mail messages and you want to grab them as quickly as possible.

It might also be possible to schedule online discussions in chat rooms in an effort to minimize redundant e-mail. Consider the teacher who fields the same questions from lots of different students via e-mail. Reading all that mail and sending the same replies out to everyone is extremely inefficient. If it is possible to consolidate all of that communication in a real-time chat room, one question can be answered for ten different people for the same amount of effort needed to answer it for one person. Sometimes you need to consolidate your mail, but with an eye toward reducing it or handling it more efficiently. With a little creativity, you might be able to find the perfect combination of e-mail and some other medium. Suppose the teacher asks her students to send in questions via e-mail prior to a scheduled chat room session. Those questions can then be answered and discussed interactively as chat topics, and the teacher will have the advantage of some advanced preparation in order to make the chat time as productive as possible.

If you find yourself drowning in e-mail, you can segregate it by categorizing it, filtering it, and routing it to different mail folders or different e-mail accounts. The ongoing segregation of your e-mail can all be automated with the right software. However, sooner or later, you actually have to look at latest arrivals and figure out what to do with them. That's when it pays to consolidate, but consolidate with as much control as possible over the client/server interactions. Watch for new ideas in the area of mail management and experiment with new tools that sound useful to you. If you've made a serious effort to get your mail routine under control, and it is still more than you can manage, look for support from a mail management consultant. If people are willing to pay personal consultants to organize their closets, we cannot be too far from personal e-mail consultants.

Conquering Raggy Text

One thing that a good mail editor should do for you is wrap text from one line to the next so that you don't need to insert your own carriage returns unless you want to start a new paragraph. Otherwise, people reading your mail might see **raggy text**—text that wraps around to the next line and then abruptly halts after an inch or two, only to continue on the next line where it wraps around again, and then halts, and so on (see Figure 3.22). Raggy text is very difficult to read and will annoy people who are trying to read your mail. You might inadvertently create raggy text if you use copy-and-paste operations to insert text from some other document into your message body. If you do see raggy text in your message body, fix it before sending it off. Or prevent it in the first place by controlling line lengths in the source document (if possible). *Lines terminated by carriage returns should not exceed 72 characters or you might subject your recipients to raggy unreadable text.*

Check your mail client to see if you can set a margin for your outgoing mail (see Figure 3.23). If your client is set to automatically wrap your lines to fill the available space, you don't really have to set the margins for 72 characters or less as long as you don't insert your own carriage returns at the end of each line. If you are prone to adding an occasional carriage return out of force of habit, then make sure your line length is limited to 72 characters or less (some people prefer 65 characters so replies and nested replies don't turn raggy).

Figure 3.22:
Hard to Read
Raggy Text

> **Subject: Martin Gardner on Fuzzy Math**
> **Date:** Wed, 9 Sep 1998 02:26:12 -0500 (CDT)
> **From:** Wayne Bishop <wbishop@calstatela.edu>
> **Reply-To:** amte@csd.uwm.edu
> **To:** Multiple recipients of list <amte@csd.uwm.edu>
>
>
> Martin Gardner, "The New New Math," _New York Review of Books_, Sept. 24, 1998,
> pp. 9-12.
>
> Gardner is the former mathematical puzzle editor of _Scientific American_ and a
> prolific writer on science and math topics. The Cover headline is "The Fuzzy New Math."
>
> The article includes a detailed criticism of the textbook _Focus on Algebra: An
> Integrated Approach_, also known as "Rainforest Algebra."
>
> An excerpt from Gardner's article:
>
> "I seldom agree with the conservative political views of Lynne Cheney, but when
> she criticized extreme aspects of the new new math on the Op-Ed page of _The
> New York Times_ on August 11, 1997, I found myself cheering."
>
> **

Uuencoded Mail

Attachments clearly make e-mail more versatile. Most people today use MIME attachments to move binary files through the mail. However, you might someday run into an old technique that people used to move binary files before the advent of MIME. UNIX users have long had access to a tool called **uuencode**, which turns a binary file into an ASCII-based version suitable for e-mail and Usenet (we will introduce Usenet in Section 7.4). Uuencoding is still around, and you will find tools for creating and reading uuencoded files in many file utilities. Uuencoded files are still used in Usenet newsgroups whenever someone wants to post a graphics file. Figure 3.24 shows an example of some uuencoded text. You can always recognize a uuencoded file by the way it begins. The string "begin 666..." followed by a lot of random characters always signals a uuencoded file.

The uuencoded part is of the sig file in Figure 3.24 is

```
"begin 666 foo B22!C86XG="!B96QI979E('EO=2!D96-O9&5D
('1H:7,A"A@ ` end"
```

FIGURE 3.23:
Avoiding Raggy
Text Using the Right
Preference Setting.

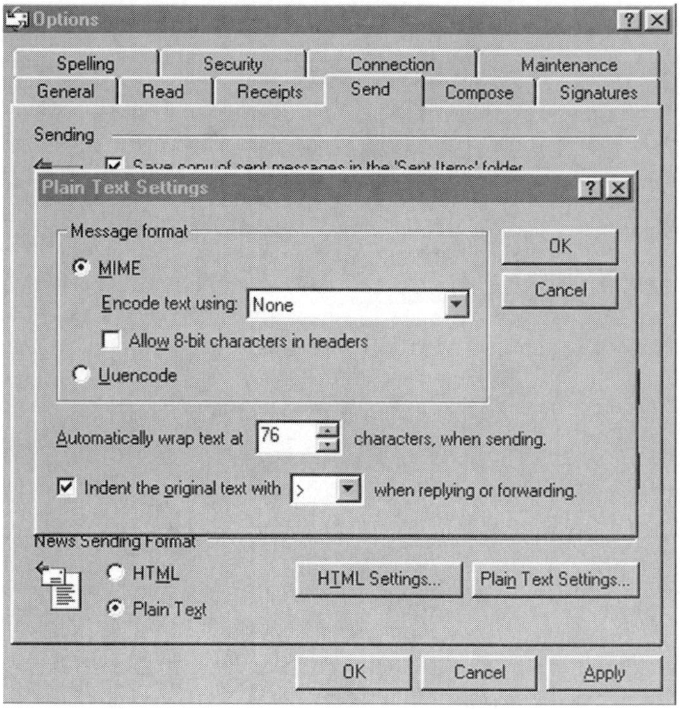

Figure 3.24:
Uuencoded Text (A
Short Sample)

```
--
XXXXXXXXXX EMT-P, K5ZC, PP-ASEL | Never ascribe to malice that which can
XXXXXXX@oac.hsc.uth.tmc.edu     | adequately be explained by stupidity.
  "begin 666 foo B22!C86XG="'B96QI979E('EO=2!D96-O9&5D('1H:7,,A"@ ` end"
              -- XXXXXXXXXXXX
```

To see what this fragment means, you have to run it through uudecode. Most uuencoded files are considerably longer than this sample one, so not much can be
expected from the small sample fragment given here. Uudecoded, it reads:

```
"I can't believe you decoded this!"
```

Typical geek humor. By the way, if you want to decode this yourself, be aware that
the string will have to be broken into three lines in order to be readable by uudecode. Reformat it to look like this:

```
"begin 666 foo

B22!C86XG="'B96QI979E('EO=2!D96-O9&5D('1H:7,,A"@ `

end"
```

Then after running this through uudecode, look for the output in a file named foo.

Above and Beyond: Problems and Exercises

A1. If you receive spam and you want to complain about that, what should you do? Why is it a bad idea to reply to the sender?

A2. Describe three ways that spammers cover their tracks so that they are hard to trace.

A3. The only way to reduce the amount of spam that you receive is to never give out your e-mail address. This is difficult, since many services on the Web require an e-mail address as part of their registration process. Describe a strategy for isolating spam so that it doesn't interfere with your daily routines.

A4. Explain what causes raggy text. How can you make sure that your e-mail messages don't look raggy to your recipients?

A5. Explain what a uuencoded file is. What protocol effectively replaced uuencoded files in e-mail communications?

A6. [**Find It Online**] Investigate **Privacy.net**'s "stealth e-mail" service (`http://www.privacy.net/email/`). Do you think that you might want to use this service yourself? Do you think this service is a good idea? Explain your answers.

A7. [**Find It Online**] Visit CAUCE (`http://www.cauce.org/`) and find out what the Electronic Mail Preference Service (e-MPS) is. Why is CAUCE opposed to e-MPS?

A8. [**Find It Online**] Visit CAUCE (`http://www.cauce.org/`) and find out how an antispam law that doesn't carry criminal penalties can still be upheld in the courts and act as an effective deterrent against spammers. (Hint: Look in the Frequently Asked Questions section.)

A9. [**Find It Online**] Visit Junkbusters (`http://www.junkbusters.com/ht/en/junkemail.html`) and find out why some people believe that the United States might already have a law that makes spam illegal. What law are they talking about, and when was it passed?

A10. [**Hands-On**] Monitor all of your e-mail (over multiple accounts if need be), and count the number of times that you are spammed during a one-week period. If you are filtering incoming e-mail to reduce your spam exposure, trap the filtered messages so that you can count them. How long have you been online? Do you think that the amount of spam that you are receiving is increasing? Decreasing? Holding steady? If you are part of a class in which everyone is collecting this data, form a task force to collect all of the data and post it on a scatter-plot graph (track the amount a spam on the y-axis and the amount of time online on the x-axis). See if any patterns to the data are evident.

CHAPTER 4

Basic Web Page Construction

CHAPTER GOALS

- Learn how basic HTML elements are used to create Web pages.
- Understand how to use HTML tags and tag attributes to control a Web page's appearance.
- Learn how to add absolute URLs, relative URLs, and named anchors to your Web pages.
- Find out how to use tables and frames as navigational aids on a Web site.
- Get the answers to all of your questions about copyright law and the Web.

4.1 ▌TAKING CHARGE

Anyone with access to the Internet can post a Web page. Moreover, it doesn't take much expertise to do so. A neophyte can put up a decent Web page in about an hour, using the right resources. More than a few college students are bringing in extra income as freelance Web page designers; some will turn this sideline into a full-time career after graduation. Professional seminars are available for people who want to stay on top of the latest developments in Web design. Beginners, however, can get started right here.

You don't need to major in computer science in order to master Web page design, although the professionals do need to know something about computer programming. Creating sophisticated Web pages is becoming more possible for nontechnical users, thanks to increasingly powerful software tools. This chapter reviews the basics of Web page construction. Chapter 5 covers more-advanced topics, including maintenance issues for large sites, strategies for managing timely information, and ways to add dynamic elements to your Web pages.

To create a Web page, you need only a text editor and a browser. However, you can make the process easier and faster with software designed to expedite Web page development. There are many Web page construction tools available, some designed specifically for beginners, and all are easy to use once you understand the basics. If you want to experiment with an HTML editor or a Web page construction tool, look for the Web Page Construction checklists throughout this chapter and do each exercise using the software of your choice. If you can't figure out how to do something, consult the online documentation for your software.

Many Web page construction tools are designed for people who want to put up a Web page as fast as possible without understanding of the machinery behind the scenes. *"So easy, a child can do it!"* So, why bother with the underlying machinery at all? Why not simply concentrate on how to use a construction tool and be done with it? It's possible to build nice-looking Web pages without any real understanding of what makes a Web page work, but you will have much more control over your Web pages if you know a few basics. Plus, it's not that hard. You do not need to learn a programming language, but you do need to learn a *document mark-up language* (which is similar to but quite a bit easier than any programming language). Then, when you want to make some simple changes to your Web page that your Web page construction software might not make easy, you can duck "behind the curtain" and do it yourself. You can still use specialized software to cut corners and save time, but you won't be limited by that software. When you take charge and learn the basics, you will truly have the best of both worlds.

4.2 WEB PAGE HTML ELEMENTS

Your Web browser is designed to display any ASCII text file that has a filename with the file extension `.htm` or `.html`, even if that file is not formatted for the Web. To experiment, find a file on your hard drive that has a `.txt` file extension (if you're on a Mac, look for a SimpleText file), and make a copy of that file, giving it a new filename that ends with `.htm`. Then, in the File menu of your browser, look for an "Open" or "Open Page" or similar command and select it. The resulting pop-up window will give you different choices, depending on your browser, but all will give you an opportunity to browse your local hard drive for a file (see Figure 4.1).

Learning how to load a local file into your browser is the first step toward becoming a Web page author. You can view any text file of your own creation with a Web browser. The file that you picked for this exercise was probably not written with Web browsing in mind, so it won't look like a page that you would want to post on the Web. However, you've already learned the first lesson of Web page design: Web browsers will display any ASCII text file, even if that file is not formatted for the Web.

Figure 4.1:
Using Your Browser to Display Local Files

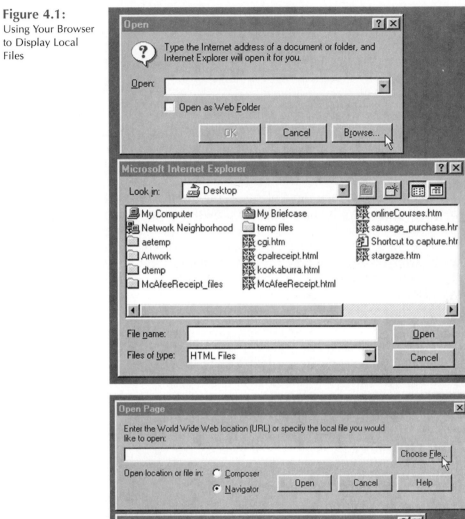

View Web Pages Offline during the Design Process

Any ASCII text file with the extension .htm or .html will be recognized as a Web page by any Web browser. You can view your own Web pages locally on your own computer as you develop them. A Web server is not needed during your design phase.

Take a minute to view your local file with your Web browser. You will see that the text has been faithfully preserved, but none of the original formatting remains. Paragraphs and line breaks are gone. If there were any titles or subtitles in the original file, they now run together with the rest of the text. You might also notice that the lines do not break in the same places as previously. This illustrates something very important about Web browsers. Web browsers rework each Web page in an effort to display it in the best way possible for each visitor. Different visitors view the same Web page using different window sizes and screen resolutions depending on the size and power of their computer monitors. Laptops, for example, have smaller screens than desktops. Web browsers must handle all of the resulting display variations.

You can watch your Web browser work for you by resizing its window. If you increase the width of your browser's window, you will see how the browser increases the width of each text line to fill as much of that horizontal space as possible. If you decrease the width of your browser's window, the text lines are shortened accordingly. This is why the original line breaks in your source file are not preserved when you view the file through your Web browser. The Web browser *dynamically reworks* the file in order to fill the display window as best it can. If you want to override the browser, you can control the display in a variety of ways. However, you first need to learn some HTML.

Web Browsers Rework Each Web Page for Each Visitor

The same Web browser will render the same page in different ways for different readers. You can see how the display for a Web page changes when you resize your browser's window. Web page authors can control how much liberty a Web browser can take with a Web page, but it is usually not a good idea to take away all of a Web browser's ability to make dynamic adjustments.

4.2.1 What Is HTML?

Hypertext Markup Language (HTML) is a *mark-up language* that gives Web page authors control over what a Web browser can and can't do when it displays a Web page. It's good to have Web browsers that can dynamically rework Web pages to better suit individual visitors. It's also important to see paragraph breaks as needed, along with other useful formatting devices.

Web page authors communicate formatting commands to Web browsers by inserting HTML *elements* inside of their Web page files. An HTML element can be used to add content to a Web page (as in the case of an image element) or to specify a style for a segment of text (as in the case of a font element). There are many HTML elements, but you don't need to learn them all before you start working on your first Web page. In fact, you can create some very nice Web pages by using only a small number of the more important HTML elements, those used to create line breaks, paragraph breaks, headings, and lists. These are covered in Section 4.3.

Text formatting is just one area of Web page design. The visual impact of a Web page comes from its graphical elements. HTML gives Web page authors a lot of control over the graphical elements of a Web page, including its background color or background pattern; the size, color, and font of the typeface used; and any images that appear on the page. The basic graphical elements of Web page design are covered in Section 4.4.

The addition of links on a Web page gives you hypertext. There are three types of links that visitors can click in order to jump to a new location. The HTML elements associated with hypertext links are covered in Section 4.5.

Two HTML elements, tables and frames, are powerful devices for controlling the layout of a Web page. Web page layouts are challenging because Web page authors must balance what they want and what they need with what the Web browser is prepared to do for individual visitors. If the Web page author is too demanding about the details of the layout, some visitors might not see the best possible layout for their displays. At the same time, there are some demands that nevertheless must be met if a complicated Web page is going to be well-organized and easy to navigate. The use of tables and frames for controlling Web page layouts is discussed in Sections 4.6 and 4.7.

Before discussing the different categories of HTML elements, the chapter presents four basic elements that should always be present on any Web page. You can add these to your experimental page by using a simple text editor in order to move yourself one step closer to being a bona-fide Web page author. Because Web browsers can display any HTML file, even if it contains no HTML elements, no HTML elements are absolutely required. Web browsers are designed to be forgiving about errors in Web page files. However, a well-designed Web page will contain these four elements because they help the Web browser interpret the file more efficiently and effectively.

All Web Pages Should Contain Four Basic HTML Elements

- HTML
- HEAD
- TITLE
- BODY

The next section shows a general Web page template that includes these four elements. All well-designed Web pages should start from this template of four elements.

4.2.2 Editing HTML Files

HTML elements can be added to a text file by using any text editor. If you use Windows, the best editor is Notepad. If you use the Mac, use SimpleText. You can use a more sophisticated editor, such as Word, but there are fewer opportunities for trouble with a simple editor. Even with Notepad, there is one potential snag. When you try to open an existing `.htm` or `.html` file by using Notepad's directory dialog box, you must change the default setting file type from Text Documents to All Files (see Figure 4.2). If you leave the file type on its default value, no HTML files will appear in the directory window.

Figure 4.2:
Adjusting Notepad
to See HTML Files

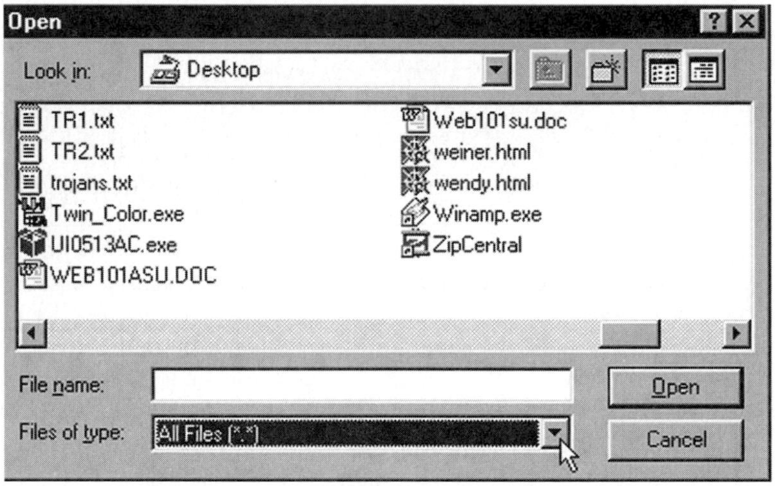

Open
Look in: Desktop
TR1.txt	Web101su.doc
TR2.txt	weiner.html
trojans.txt	wendy.html
Twin_Color.exe	Winamp.exe
UI0513AC.exe	ZipCentral
WEB101ASU.DOC	
File name:	Open
Files of type: All Files (*.*)	Cancel

Use a Simple Text Editor for Editing HTML Files

Beginners who are familiar with Word often try to create their first Web page by using Word. Unfortunately, Word can throw you off track when you try to manually edit a simple HTML file. Use Word if you must, but don't say you weren't warned.

First, be careful to save your file by using the Save As command on the File menu. Do not use the Save as HTML command in Word. Save as HTML invokes an *HTML converter* (see the Above and Beyond section), which is not what you want when you are writing HTML files.

Second, when you use the Save As command, be careful to set the Save option for Text Only with Line Breaks (*.txt). If you do not change the default save option, Word will not save your file as a plain text file. (Word defaults to a binary file format unless you override it.) Your browser will not be able to read the file.

You add an HTML element to a text file by inserting an HTML tag or pair of tags with a text editor. For example, the HTML element requires a pair of tags: `<HTML>` and `</HTML>`. The first tag marks the beginning of the HTML element, and the second marks the end of the element. In general, any HTML tag that starts with a forward slash (/) marks the end of an HTML element. HTML tags tell a Web browser how to render a Web page

HTML tags are used to divide a Web page into segments where different kinds of information belong. Some tag pairs can also be *nested* inside other tag pairs in order to produce a hierarchical structure for each Web page. Figure 4.3 shows the correct structure for all Web pages, along with its text file representation. The indentation of text in this figure is not necessary inside of a Web page file, but it is shown here to emphasize the hierarchical structure of the HTML elements. At the top level we have an HTML element. Inside the HTML element are the HEAD and BODY elements. All Web pages should contain these elements organized in exactly this fashion. The HEAD contains information that is useful behind the scenes, but which is not displayed as part of the Web page display. For example, the TITLE element controls the browser window's title bar. The title bar is not part of the page display per se, so the TITLE element belongs inside the HEAD element. If you do not insert your `<TITLE></TITLE>` tags inside the `<HEAD></HEAD>` tags, the browser will not recognize it and the title bar will not display your title.

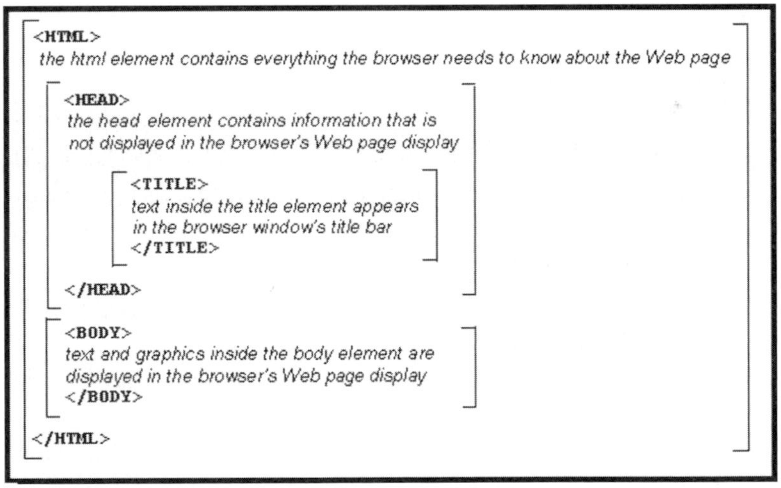

Figure 4.3:
A General HTML
Template for All
Web Pages

```
<HTML>
the html element contains everything the browser needs to know about the Web page

    <HEAD>
    the head element contains information that is
    not displayed in the browser's Web page display

        <TITLE>
        text inside the title element appears
        in the browser window's title bar
        </TITLE>

    </HEAD>

    <BODY>
    text and graphics inside the body element are
    displayed in the browser's Web page display
    </BODY>

</HTML>
```

Most HTML tags come in pairs, but a few do not (some elements, such as a line break, do not need to be terminated). The most basic HTML elements appear inside of the `BODY` portion of the Web page; this is where the visible elements of the Web page belong. Most Web page authors type their HTML tags in uppercase letters, although Web browsers don't care if the tags are in uppercase or lowercase characters. The uppercase tags stand out better for people viewing the Web page and make it easier to make sense of the Web page. Special HTML editors take this idea a little further by highlighting HTML tags in different colors and adding indentations much like those shown in Figure 4.3.

Four-Step Web Page Development Cycle

The Web page development cycle involves four-steps that you repeat until your page looks exactly the way that you want. The cycle begins with an .HTM or .HTML file.

1. Save your file with the Save command.

2. Reload the new file into your Web browser.

3. Review the new Web page to see how it looks.

4. Revise your page as needed using a text editor or an HTML editor.

Be careful to remember Steps 1 and 2, or your browser will not display your last round of revisions.

Some HTML editors can preview your Web page as you edit it so you don't have to switch back and forth between an editor and a browser. This speeds up the development cycle and makes it easier to experiment with different HTML elements while you develop your page. If you expect to do a lot of Web page development, you will come to appreciate any time-saving features that speed up the development process.

Web Page Construction Checklist #1

1. Create a plain text file on your hard drive, and view it with your Web browser.

2. Add the four basic HTML elements to your file, using a simple text editor.

3. Add some text inside of the different elements of the Web page, and view the results with your browser.

4. Resize the browser's window to see how the Web page display is dynamically adjusted.

5. Create a Web page that looks like the one in Figure 4.4 when you resize the window properly. Make sure that your page displays *The Dachshund* on the browser's title bar as shown in Figure 4.4.

4.3 BASIC WEB PAGE FORMATTING

The visible elements of a Web page generally go inside of the **BODY** of the page. This is where you can control the way that your text looks on a Web page. The next subsections explore the most useful text formatting commands by adding text to the Web page shown in Figure 4.4.

Figure 4.4:
Two Web Browsers
Displaying the
Same Local File
Differently

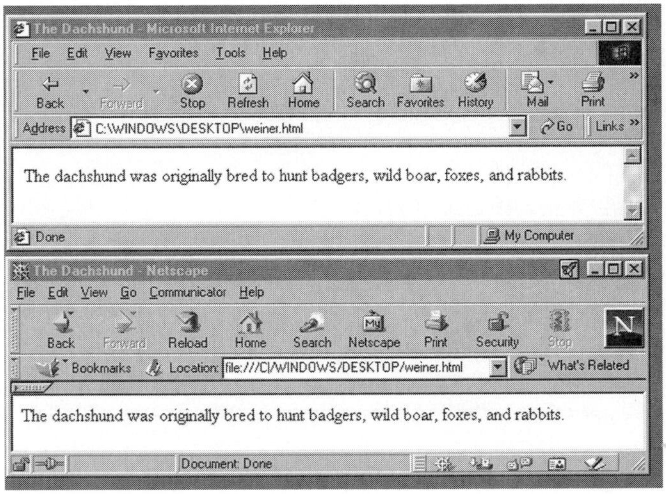

4.3.1 Adding a Heading

As with any written document, it's usually a good idea to tell the reader what the document is all about before launching into a lot of text. This can be done with a title. You've already seen how an HTML element named `TITLE` is used to put identifying information in the title bar for the browser window. However, now you want a title inside of the window, at the top of your Web page display. This can be done with a **heading element** inside of the body of the Web page. Note that heading elements should not be confused with the head element—these are completely different things.

Headings come in six sizes, ranging from `<H1>very large</H1>` to `<H6>very small</H6>` (view these with a browser to see the difference). You can insert a heading anywhere inside of the `BODY` of a Web page, and you can insert as many headings as you want. Large headings are often used for document titles, and smaller headings can be used to mark subsections of long text.

Sometimes, it is useful to fine-tune an HTML element by adding specific *attributes* to the element. For example, you might want to center a heading instead of having it left-justified. An **HTML attribute** is a property of an HTML element, consisting of an attribute name and an attribute value. In fact, many HTML elements use their own, default, attribute values if you don't specify your own. For example, the `H1` element in Figure 4.5 is left-justified because an alignment attribute was not specified inside of the `H1` tag. The default alignment for heading elements is left-justification. However, you can override the default alignment if you prefer something different. Inside the `H1` tag, you can add your own value for the alignment attribute. In Figure 4.6, we added the attribute name ALIGN with the attribute value CENTER to the H1 element, in order to produce a centered heading.

Figure 4.5:
Adding a Heading
Element

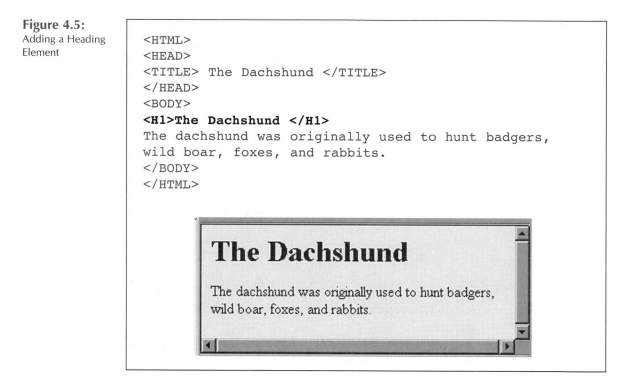

```
<HTML>
<HEAD>
<TITLE> The Dachshund </TITLE>
</HEAD>
<BODY>
<H1>The Dachshund </H1>
The dachshund was originally used to hunt badgers,
wild boar, foxes, and rabbits.
</BODY>
</HTML>
```

Much of the fine-tuning that goes into a Web page concerns setting attribute values inside of HTML elements. A good HTML reference (you can buy an HTML reference book or find free ones on the Web) will show you all of the attributes and possible attribute values that can be inserted into HTML elements. This book does not attempt to give a comprehensive introduction to all of the attributes (or all of the tags), but it does show you some of the most useful ones.

Tag Attributes and Attribute Values

When you add attributes to an HTML tag, make sure that the attribute goes inside of the angle brackets of the leading tag (the first tag if there is a start/stop pair). If an attribute falls outside of the angle brackets, it will not be recognized as an attribute.

Now that you have a title for your Web page, you can add some more text. The HTML paragraph pairs of tags, <P> and </P>, makes it possible to break up your text into blocks of text set off by blank lines. You won't get an indentation on the first line of the paragraph, but you can at least mark blocks of text when you want to signal topic shifts or break things up a little (see Figure 4.7).

Figure 4.6:
Using the Align
Attribute

```
<HTML>
<HEAD>
<TITLE>The Dachshund</TITLE>
</HEAD>
<BODY>
<H1 ALIGN=CENTER>The Dachshund </H1>
The dachshund was originally used to hunt
badgers, wild boar, foxes, and rabbits.
</BODY>
</HTML>
```

The Dachshund

The dachshund was originally used to hunt badgers,
wild boar, foxes, and rabbits.

Most Web page authors like to place each paragraph tag on its own line. This makes
the HTML document easier to read and won't change the resulting Web page display. Note that you can close paragraphs with a **</P>** tag or not—the **</P>** is
optional according to current HTML specifications.

Shooting Blanks

When you put extra whitespace characters or extra blank lines in an HTML file,
don't expect to see them on your Web page display. When a Web browser ren-
ders a Web page, it normally ignores whitespace (later in the chapter, you'll find
out how to make a browser insert whitespace characters and lines). So, feel free to
add whitespace or blank lines to make your HTML source file easier to read.

Whereas titles and paragraphs are standard fare for all writers, Web page authors
favor lists more than other authors do, and with good reason. Lists of hyperlinks are
a common fixture on many Web pages and are useful as navigational devices. For
example, a large Web site might start with a list of links that operate as a clickable
table of contents. Although you aren't ready to add any links to your Web page, next
you'll see how to set up a table of contents by using HTML list elements.

Figure 4.7:
Making Text Easier
to Read by Using
Paragraph Tags

```
<HTML>
<HEAD>
<TITLE> The Dachshund </TITLE>
</HEAD>
<BODY>
<H1 ALIGN=CENTER>The Dachshund </H1>
<P>
The dachshund was originally used to hunt
badgers, wild boar, foxes, and rabbits.
</P><P>
The name "dachshund" means "badger dog" in German, where
these dogs were first bred. Woodcuts and paintings from
the fifteenth century show badgers being hunted by dogs
with short legs, long bodies, and hound-like ears.
</P><P>
To this day, the dachshund's short muscular legs
are well suited for burrowing into tunnels and
underground lairs, although the breed has never
been active as a hunting dog in the United States.
As pets, dachshunds are lively, loyal, and assertive
watchdogs.
</P>
</BODY>
</HTML>
```

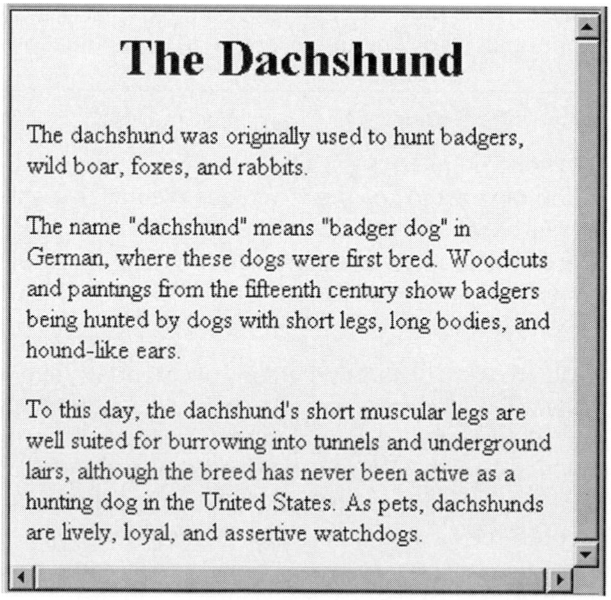

The Dachshund

The dachshund was originally used to hunt badgers, wild boar, foxes, and rabbits.

The name "dachshund" means "badger dog" in German, where these dogs were first bred. Woodcuts and paintings from the fifteenth century show badgers being hunted by dogs with short legs, long bodies, and hound-like ears.

To this day, the dachshund's short muscular legs are well suited for burrowing into tunnels and underground lairs, although the breed has never been active as a hunting dog in the United States. As pets, dachshunds are lively, loyal, and assertive watchdogs.

4.3.2 Adding a List

There are two types of lists commonly found on Web pages: the bulleted list (each list item gets a bullet before it) and the enumerated list (the list items are numbered). The tags `UL>` and `</UL>` are used to specify an *unordered list*, commonly bulleted lists. The tags `<OL>` and `</OL>` are used for an *ordered list*, commonly enumerated (numbered) lists. Figure 4.8 shows how these two types of lists differ.

Figure 4.8:
Two Types of Lists

```
<UL>
<LI>Dachshund Origins</LI>
<LI>Different Kinds of Dachshunds</LI>
<LI>The Dachshund Underground Railroad</LI>
</UL>
<OL>
<LI>Dachshund Origins</LI>
<LI>Different Kinds of Dachshunds</LI>
<LI>The Dachshund Underground Railroad</LI>
</OL>
```

- Dachshund Origins
- Different Kinds of Dachshunds
- The Dachshund Underground Railroad

1. Dachshund Origins
2. Different Kinds of Dachshunds
3. The Dachshund Underground Railroad

Each list item inside of a list must be marked with list items tags: `<LI>` and `</LI>`. Like the paragraph tag, the list item tag can be used with just the `<LI>` tag. If you leave out all of the corresponding `</LI>` tags, the Web browsers will still format the list properly. Although most of the tags that you've used so far come in pairs, a few are defined only as singletons and do not come in pairs. One very useful one is the line break tag: `<BR>`. If you place this tag at the end of a line of text, your display will insert a line break after that text. The line break works much like a paragraph tag. Unlike the paragraph break, it does not insert a blank line before the next visible page element.

Learning from Examples

You can learn more HTML elements by looking at the HTML files for existing Web pages. If you see something that you like on the Web, you can use your browser's Source command (look for this in the View menu) to view the underlying HTML file.

Copy the tags that you see in the file to duplicate text formatting or other Web page elements in your own Web pages. You can view the HTML version of any Web page in this way. Existing Web pages can be very instructive, and learning from examples is a painless way to master HTML.

4.3.3 Working with Fonts and Type Styles

If you are used to a sophisticated word processing program, you might be surprised to find that your choice of fonts is somewhat problematic in HTML. Font assignment is difficult because different computers will have different fonts available on them and there is no core set of shared fonts that you can count on. Even when the same font is available on two platforms, it might not have the same name. To make matters worse, visitors who have a preference for a specific font can configure their browsers to override the font specifications of a Web page author. Therefore, even when a specific font is available, you can't be sure that it's the font that your Web browser will use.

You can, however, specify a list of font choices in the `FACE` attribute of the `FONT` element. A browser will work through the list from left to right, selecting the first font in the list that is available on the machine on which it wants to display the page. If you use the most common fonts and include a list of the most common fonts found on each platform, then you can exert some control over the fonts seen on your Web pages.

Here are the safest choices for the font face attribute.

- For a sans serif font, choose Arial for Windows, Geneva for Macs, and Helvetica for others:

  ```
  <FONT FACE="Arial, Geneva, Helvetica">
  ```

  This is what Arial/Geneva/Helvetica looks like.

- For a serif font, choose Times New Roman for Windows and Times for Macs:

  ```
  <FONT FACE="Times New Roman, Times">
  ```

  This is what Times New Roman/Times looks like (this is the standard default font for most browsers).

- For a monospaced font, choose Courier New for Windows and Courier for Macs:

  ```
  <FONT FACE="Courier New, Courier">
  ```

  `This is what Courier New/Courier looks like.`

When using fonts, Web page authors must respect the preferences of Web users. Someone with poor vision might have a browser preference set for an easy-to-read font and that preference will override any font attributes specified by the Web page author. It is not wise to design a page that depends on specific type properties, since users can always override those properties if they have their own preferences.

Some useful text effects are nevertheless available to you:

`<B>``The boldface element darkens any text inside the tag pair.` **`</B>`**

`<STRONG>` `This is like <B> but more general. (good for text-to-voice renderings, etc.)` **`</STRONG>`**

`<I>` `The italic element italicizes any text inside the tag pair.` **`</I>`**

`<EM>` `This is like <I> but more general. (good for text-to-voice renderings, etc.)` **`</EM>`**

`<FONT COLOR="red">` `This changes the color of the text inside the tag pair.` **`</FONT>`**

`<FONT SIZE=+2>` `This changes the size of the text inside the tag pair.` **`</FONT>`**

Note that any number of these HTML elements can be combined by nesting multiple elements whenever more than one should apply. For example, you can create boldface italics by nesting a pair of `<B></B>` tags inside a pair of `<I></I>` tags (or vice-versa—it doesn't matter).

Sometimes, it's useful to add *comments* to your HTML file. Comments are visible to people viewing an HTML source file, but they do not show up as part of the Web page display. Comments can be added to the source file at any point by using the `Comment` tag, `<!--, -->`, as follows:

`<!--` `Anything inside a Comment tag is ignored by the Web browsers.` **`-->`**

Also, sometimes you'll want the Web browser to recreate some text with the spacing and line breaks exactly the way that you typed them, for example poetry and computer code, when you can't trust a browser to do the right thing with line breaks and indentations. Browsers can be told to preserve text and white space with the `PRE` (preformat) tag pair: `<PRE>` and `</PRE>`.

Troubleshooting Your Page

If your Web page won't display properly when viewed through a Web browser, there is probably an HTML error in the file. Here are the most common HTML errors.

- Check all of the HTML elements that require a pair of start/end tags, and verify that both tags are present and don't have any typographical errors.

- Be sure that all of your angle brackets really are angle brackets (not parentheses or some other kind of bracket).

- If you have quotation marks inside an HTML tag, be sure that they are closed off inside of that same tag.

If you create a large file and look at it only when you're done, locating HTML errors might be difficult. Viewing your file periodically as you create it will make it easier to track down errors.

If your Web page is just text, you probably won't have to tinker with it very much. Most of the serious Web page tinkering is associated with graphical elements and layouts for complicated pages that mix text with graphics. That's when things get a bit more challenging (and interesting).

Web Page Construction Checklist #2

1. Explain the difference between a `<P>` tag and a `<BR>` tag.

2. Which is larger, an `<H3>` heading or an `<H2>` heading?

3. Explain the difference between an `<OL>` and a `<UL>` tag. What is the `<LI>` tag used for?

4. Explain how to make a word boldface, italic, and boldface italic.

5. What tag can you use to preserve the whitespace and line breaks in a text block?

4.4   BASIC WEB PAGE GRAPHICS

A Web page without color or graphics is a rather dull. The addition of just one or two colored or graphical elements can make a big difference.

4.4.1 Using Color

The easiest way to dress up a page of text is with a background color or pattern. When you tell a Web browser to color the background of a Web page, you have a choice of 16,777,216 colors. If that seems too overwhelming, you can select from any of 216 **Web-safe colors**, colors that can be faithfully reproduced on any computer monitor regardless of OS used.

All Web browsers use a code system for describing colors in **hexadecimal notation**. Each code contains six characters from 16 the possible alphanumeric digits (0123456789ABCDEF) used to represent numbers in base 16 (hence the name, "hexadecimal"). You can find out which codes to use for various colors on **any number of Web sites** that show color wheels or charts illustrating the 216 Web-safe colors (see I-9 in the color insert).

If you want to add a background color to a Web page, include a `BGCOLOR` attribute in the `BODY` element, with a code string for the attribute value. For example:

```
<BODY BGCOLOR="#FFFFFF">
```

creates a Web page that has a white background. Always enclose the color code between a pair of double quotation marks, starting the code string with the # character.

Adding a background *pattern* is done very similarly, except that you use a `BACKGROUND` attribute and you must specify a graphics file that holds the background pattern that you want to use (see I-6 in the color insert).

4.4.2 Working with Image Files

All artwork and photographs found on the Web are stored in binary files. These files are stored on a Web server along with the HTML files that refer to them. There are many ways to obtain graphics that you can use on your Web pages, including clip art on the Web, digital cameras, scanners, and software for artists (or adventurous amateurs).

File Formats Used for Images Two file formats are used for Web page graphics: the GIF format and the JPEG (JPG) format. The **GIF (Graphics Interchange Format)** format is best for line art, cartoons, and simple images. The **JPEG (Joint Photographic Experts Group)** format is better for photographs and artwork that include many colors or special effects. Figure 4.9 shows a GIF image acquired from a book via a scanner. Be careful with images from books, magazines, and newspapers—they are usually subject to copyright restrictions (see Section 4.10). This file is named `woodcut2.gif`, and its size is 38K.

Figure 4.9:
A 38K GIF Image Acquired from a Scanner

THE BADGER-DOG AT WORK.

The scanner originally created a TIFF (Tagged Image File Format) file (another graphics format) that was 100K. Then a software tool was used to convert the TIFF file into a GIF file (see the Above and Beyond section in Chapter 5 for a description of graphics viewers and converters). The GIF image looks as good as the TIFF image, but it is considerably smaller. Keeping graphics files small is important when you are putting them on the Web. This is because smaller files mean faster Web page downloading. As a rule of thumb, try to use image files that are no larger than 40K. The GIF format is very good for the Web because it can significantly reduce the size of an image file without compromising the quality of the image.

The JPEG file format is better suited for high-resolution photographs and sophisticated artwork that contains many colors (see Figure 4.10). Software tools that convert graphics into the JPEG format typically allow users to control the amount of compression applied to the image. In this way, the user can control the trade-off between file size and image quality. Some images can be greatly compressed without visible detriment, but eventually a large amount of compression causes the quality of the image to degrade. Some amount of degradation might be worth an additional reduction in file size, but eventually the image will become unacceptable.

When large images cannot be reduced effectively via compression techniques, Web page authors have other tricks that they can use. One of these, the thumbnail preview, is described in the Above and Beyond section. But first, let's look at the HTML element that allows you to add images to Web pages.

Adding an Image   The `<IMG>` tag is used to place image files onto a Web page. An `SRC` (source) attribute inside of `IMG` is used to specify the file that contains the image. Suppose that you have a file named `dachsie.jpg`. You can add it to a Web page by using the tag `<IMG SRC="dachsie.jpg">`.

Figure 4.10:
A 107K Photograph in the JPEG Format

Image tags belong in the Web page `BODY`, and the placement of the tag within the HTML file determines where it appears on the Web page.

The `IMG` tag creates an *inline image* on the Web page. Understanding inline images will help you understand how the image will appear on the page display. An **inline image** is an image that is treated like a single, alphanumeric character like that created when you type keys on a keyboard. If you place an `IMG` tag between two sentences, it will be inserted as if it were another typed character. The main difference is its size. That is, the image that you insert is usually larger than the characters in your Web page display. This forces the Web browser to rework the text placement near the image. Figure 4.11 shows what happens when an inline image is placed in the middle of a paragraph.

Figure 4.11:
An Inline Graphic

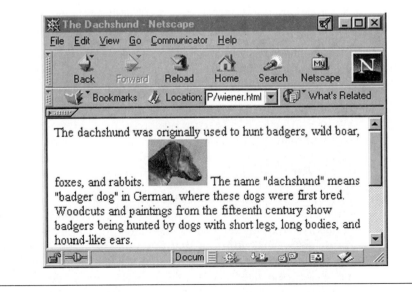

```
The dachshund was originally used to hunt badgers,
wild boar, foxes, and rabbits.

<IMG SRC="Donutprofile3.gif"
ALT="a dachshund head">

The name "dachshund" means "badger dog" in German,
where these dogs were first bred. Woodcuts and paint-
ings from the fifteenth century show badgers being
hunted by dogs with short legs, long bodies, and
hound-like ears.
```

IMG Tags and the ALT Attribute

Some people use a browser named Lynx that does not display graphical elements. **Lynx** is an older text-based browser that is still used in environments in which bandwidth is at a premium or other network limitations apply. If you usually incorporate many visual elements on your Web pages, you should also consider how your page will look in Lynx. Some larger commercial sites support an alternative set of Web pages for Lynx users. (You might have seen a mysterious link on a commercial site that says simply "text only"—that's the welcome mat for Lynx users.)

You might not want to go that far, but you should get into the habit of adding ALT attributes to all of your IMG tags. The **ALT attribute** allows you to specify a line of text that will be displayed to the Lynx user in place of the image. This at least gives the users some idea of what they are missing.

To see how your Web page looks under Lynx, go into your browser's preference (or option) settings and *turn off* all of the graphics. Then, when you view your page, you'll have an idea of how it will appear to users of Lynx. Also, be aware that the ALT attribute is not just for Lynx users. Visually impaired users can now use text-to-voice readers to render Web pages. They depend on ALT attribute values, instead of graphics, to convey important content.

The Web browser needs to make room for the oversized inline graphic, so it increases the vertical space set aside for the text line that contains the graphic. This is a reasonable interpretation of the HTML file, given no additional directives, but it is probably not the best way to combine text and graphics.

Aligning Images   A more attractive combination of text and graphics can be obtained by alternating left-justified and right-justified images, with text flowing down and alongside the images. This is done by using the ALIGN attribute in the IMG tag (see Figure 4.12).

When you include an ALIGN attribute in the <IMG> tag, any text near that image will automatically flow around the image, which is almost always what you want it to do. You can also control the vertical alignment of an image relative to its text baseline by using the ALIGN values BOTTOM, TOP, and MIDDLE.

Additional control over text behavior around an image can be achieved by inserting a CLEAR attribute inside of the <BR> tag. When a <BR> tag with CLEAR=LEFT is encountered, the browser immediately interrupts the flow of text and resumes it on the next available line that has no image set against the left margin. When CLEAR=RIGHT is used, text is resumed on the next available line that has no image set against the right margin. To drop the text to the next available line with no images on either margin, use CLEAR=CENTER.

```
<IMG SRC="Donutprofile3.gif"
  HEIGHT=54 WIDTH=70
  ALIGN=LEFT>
```

The dachshund was originally used to hunt badgers,
wild boar, foxes, and rabbits.

```
<IMG SRC="woodcut2.gif"
  HEIGHT=232 WIDTH=219
  ALIGN=RIGHT>
```

The name "dachshund" means "badger dog" in German,
where these dogs were first bred. Woodcuts and paintings from the fifteenth century show badgers being
hunted by dogs with short legs, long bodies, and
hound-like ears. To this day, the dachshund's short
muscular legs are well suited for burrowing into tunnels and underground lairs, although the breed has
never been active as a hunting dog in the United
States. As pets, dachshunds are lively, loyal, and
assertive watchdogs.

Two other important `IMG` attributes are `HEIGHT` and `WIDTH`. Each image has vertical and horizontal dimensions that should be specified in the `IMG` tag. If you tell the browser the dimensions to expect, it can work out the page layout and print the text without having to wait for each image to download. If you don't include these dimensions, the page will still display properly, but it will take longer to display. This is because the browser will have to wait for each image to download in order to find out how much space should be set aside for it. A Web page that can display its text while it waits for the images is easier on users, especially those with slow Internet connections.

Image Files and HTML Files

When you develop your Web page locally, keep your image files in the same directory as the HTML files that refer to them. All browsers look for `SRC` attribute files in a location that is *relative to* the HTML file being rendered. If both files are in the same directory, it is enough to specify the name of the image file. However, if you are comfortable working with directory paths, you can use different directories, as long as you specify the correct directory path in the `SRC` attribute. If you are not familiar with directory path notations, don't worry about it. Simply keep all of your files in the same directory.

Scaling Images Sometimes, an image is not the right size for your Web page. It might be too big, or perhaps you don't think it's big enough. In these cases, you need to **scale** the image, that is, resize it by increasing or decreasing its dimensions on the Web page. It's easy to adjust the amount of space allocated for an image by changing its `HEIGHT` and `WIDTH` attributes. If you want a larger image, increase the attributes' values. If you want a smaller image, decrease them. The woodcut image shown in Figure 4.9 was scaled from its original dimensions, 927 × 876, to a smaller size, 232 × 219, by dividing the original height and width by 4.

When you resize an image, be careful to preserve the original scale (the height:width ratio) so that the resized image is not distorted. Also, keep in mind that shrinking an image by scaling it *does not* reduce its memory or bandwidth requirements. To reduce download times, you must *compress* the image (see Figure I-2 in the color insert).

Finding an Image's Dimensions

If you have an image file, but you have no idea what its dimensions are, open it up using your Web browser. You will either see the height and width in the title bar of the browser window or be able to see both by viewing Page Info (look under the View menu). Let your browser tell you what you need to know.

Transparent GIFs   There are many tools and special effects that you can use to make your graphics more striking. Many of them do not require artistic talent. One that every Web author should know about is the effect achieved by transparent GIF images. A **transparent GIF** looks as if it was drawn directly on your Web page (see Figure 4.13). To create a transparent GIF, you designate some portion of the image as the background of the image. Then, whenever that image is placed on a Web page, the image's background region behaves as if it were transparent, inheriting the background color (or pattern) of the Web page beneath it.

Figure 4.13:
A Transparent GIF

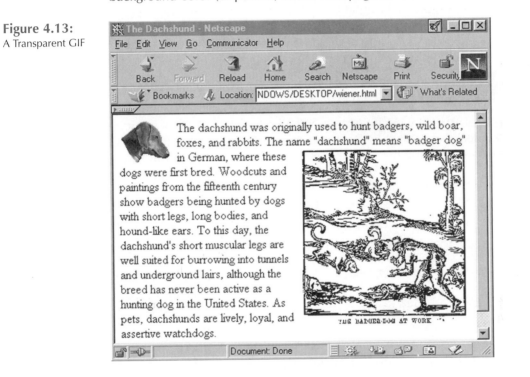

Transparent GIFs work well on images that have clearly defined backgrounds. Line art and cartoons work well. A photograph can be turned into a transparent GIF after some digital tinkering with the right graphics tools. The trick is to make the background of the image one solid color so that it will be obvious which pixels should be replaced with the background color (see Figure 4.14).

Figure 4.14:
Transforming a
Photograph into a
Transparent GIF

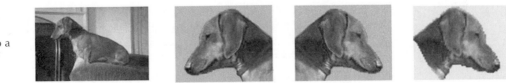

There are many good image editing tools available to help you doctor your images (see the Above and Beyond section in Chapter 5). If you want to turn a photograph into a transparent GIF, you will need to edit the background of the photograph in order to make it one uniform color (even if a photograph appears to have a uniform background color, there are almost always a few different colors dispersed throughout that region— you can see them at the pixel level when viewed with an image editor). Pick a color not found elsewhere in the picture. If the background color occurs in places other than the background, those pixels will be replaced by the Web page's background as well. Once the image has been prepared, you can convert it to a transparent GIF. Figure 4.15 shows a Web page service that will help you to convert plain GIF files into transparent GIF files, as long as you can upload the image that you want to convert onto a public Web server (see Section 4.9).

Once you have a transparent GIF, you can experiment with various background colors to find one that works well with the image.

Transparent GIFs are often used for buttons and navigational icons as well as larger pieces of artwork. A few small transparent GIFs can dress up a Web site without overpowering it. Keep them small (in terms of bytes) so that they don't slow down your Web page's downloading. Transparent GIFs can also be used in various ways to create special effects (see Figure I-7 in the color insert) and color-coordinated page layouts (see Figures I-10 and I-11 in the color insert).

Figure 4.15:
Creating a
Transparent GIF on
the Web

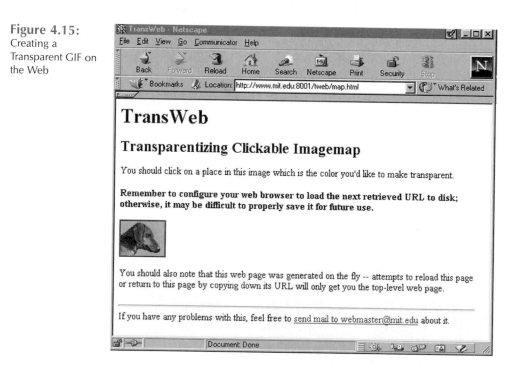

Images for Web Page Backgrounds Before leaving the topic of images, let's return to the question of how to add a background pattern to your Web page. The mechanics are simple. You need only add a `BACKGROUND` attribute to your `BODY` tag and specify the name of a graphics file, just as you do for `SRC` attribute inside of `IMG` tags. The browser that is displaying your page will place the background file in the upper left-hand corner of the Web. It will repeat the background display behind your other Web page elements in a tiling pattern from left to right and from top to bottom the number of times needed to fill the display window (see Figure 4.16).

Figure 4.16:
Web Page Tiled
Pattern Background

```
<BODY BACKGROUND="bk.jpg">

<H1 ALIGN=CENTER>The Dachshund</H1>

<B><FONT SIZE=+1>

The name "dachshund" means "badger dog" in German,
where these dogs were first bred. Woodcuts and paint-
ings from the fifteenth century show badgers being
hunted by dogs with short legs, long bodies, and
hound-like ears.

<P>

To this day, the dachshund's short muscular legs are
well suited for burrowing into tunnels and underground
lairs, although the breed has never been active as a
hunting dog in the United States. As pets, dachshunds
are lively, loyal, and assertive watchdogs.

</FONT></B>

</BODY>
```

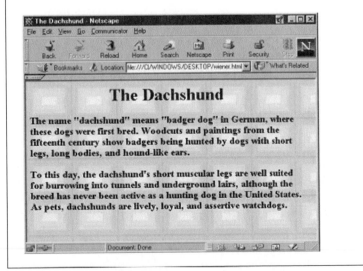

bk.jpg

Some files work better as tiles than others for patterned backgrounds. Experiment with backgrounds of your own design (see page I-6 in the color insert). Keep the files small (byte-wise) so that you don't slow down your page's downloading. If you cannot resist using a large file for your background pattern, you can add both a BGCOL-OR attribute and a BACKGROUND attribute to your BODY element. The background color will appear first while your background file is downloading. This will give a finished-looking page for visitors to view while the background is loading.

A common design mistake that many beginners make is to go overboard with background patterns. Don't use a background pattern that distracts from the content of the page or that makes it difficult to read the text on a page. Background patterns should be subtle and, well, in the background.

Large bold headings can stand out against background patterns, but you might need to beef up any regular text that is on top of the background. Boldface fonts and over-sized fonts are often needed to keep text readable against a background pattern. Also, check your color combinations so that the text contrasts well against the background. Dark text on a dark background pattern will drive away visitors.

Restraint, Restraint, Restraint

If you are new to computer graphics and are playing around with image editors and paint programs for the first time, it is tempting to pack too many visual elements onto your Web pages. It's fun to play with all of the new tools, and you naturally want to show off your new toys. The result is often a confusing hodgepodge of too many things that don't work well together. Here are some tips to follow for good Web page design.

- Design your Web page with restraint. Don't allow images, backgrounds, and special effects to fight each other.
- If you want to show off many graphics, spread your goodies over many pages. Pick one graphical theme for each page and stick to it.
- If you have a background pattern, avoid putting images on top of that background.
- If you want to include many pictures on your page, use a solid color for your background and forgo a background pattern.

Print pages look jumbled if they contain too many different fonts. Similarly, Web pages look confused if their visual elements are not carefully coordinated.

One of the better ways to add a background to a Web page is to run a border down the left side of the page that does not repeat anywhere else on the page. The spiral notebook effect in Figure 4.17 is the work of a background pattern that is 999 pixels wide and 18 pixels high. The pattern was tiled as for any Web page background.

Figure 4.17:
A Wide Background
Pattern That Results
in a Border for a
Web Page

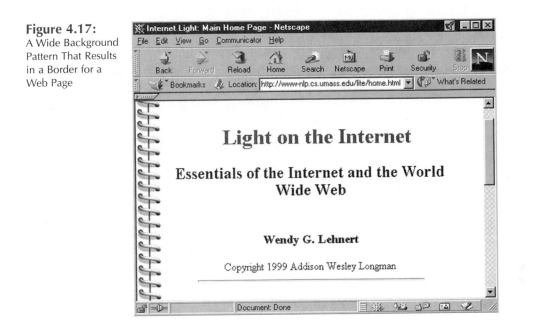

However, the image is quite wide, so you need a very large monitor to see it repeat near the right-hand side of a page display. As long as the background is displayed within a normal-sized display window, you'll see only the tiles repeating along the vertical dimension, which produces the spiral binding pattern.

Much of the fun associated with Web page design happens behind the scenes with software designed to help you produce digital images that have cool effects. Photographs can be retouched to remove imperfections, and text can be twisted and tweaked ad infinitum. In addition, massive libraries of clip art are available on the Web (at no cost!) if you absolutely must have, for example, a penguin dancing on a soccer ball. In fact, the Web offers all sorts of resource and tool archives for Web page designers that go far beyond the realm of clip art (see the Above and Beyond section in Chapter 5).

Web Page Construction Checklist #3

1. Explain how to change the background color of a Web page.
2. When should you use the JPEG file format? The GIF format?
3. What HTML element is used to insert inline graphics on a Web page?
4. How does a transparent GIF image differ from a nontransparent GIF?
5. What HTML tag and tag attribute are used to set a Web page background pattern?

4.5   THREE TYPES OF HYPERLINKS

Using only a few formatting commands, you can create a simple Web page of text. It won't be hypertext, however, until you add some hyperlinks. There are three types of HTML links (URLs), each used for a different type of situation:

- **Absolute URL**: Connects two Web servers.
- **Relative URL**: Connects one page to another page in the same Web site.
- **Named anchor**: Connects two locations on the same Web page.

If you create a Web site of any complexity, you will need all three types of links. They are not difficult to create, so there is no reason to be stingy with them. All have two components:

- Link label (the visible link on a Web page – the label can be a piece of text or an image)
- Link destination (the target destination)

Once you understand these two components, you'll be able to add any links that you need to your Web pages.

4.5.1 Absolute URLs

Suppose that you want to add a link to a page that is written by a different author and located on a different Web server. This is an **absolute URL**. It requires not only the URL of the original page but also that of the other page. To set up an absolute URL, you mark a label that will operate as the link on your Web page. The label could be a segment of text embedded in a paragraph, an item in a bulleted list, or, if you want to create a clickable image, an **IMG** element.

For example, suppose that you are creating a Web page about tree houses and you want to link to a page that contains tree house construction plans that has the following URL:

```
http://www.treehouse.com/construct/plans.html
```

This URL is the destination for the link.

A link is created by using a pair of *anchor tags (A-tag)*, **<A>** and **</A>**. The link label goes between these two tags (see Figure 4.18). This is one HTML tag pair whose closing tag (**</A>**) you don't want to forget. If you omit it, your link label will include any text and images that follow the **<A>** tag until the next **</A>** tag: if there is no **</A>** tag, the link label will extend throughout the remainder of your Web page. The destination for your link is added to the A-tag as the value of a *hypertext reference* (**HREF**) attribute inside of the A-tag.

```
<HTML>

<HEAD>

<TITLE> How to Build a Tree House </TITLE>

</HEAD>

<BODY>

<H1 ALIGN=CENTER> How to Build a Tree House </H1>

<P>

If you want to build a tree house,you need a tree, some
good lumber, and a few tools.
A <A HREF="http://www.treehouse.com/construct/plans.html">
construction plan</A> is also a good idea, but some people
think they can wing it.

<P> Make sure the tree is large enough to support the
extra weight. Sometimes a stand of two or three trees
works nicely. If you distribute the weight over two or
three trees, smaller trees can be considered.

</BODY>

</HTML>
```

The text label associated with the new hyperlink will appear on your pages as bold-faced or underscored or colored, depending on the Web browser that displays the page. Figure 4.18 shows the result.

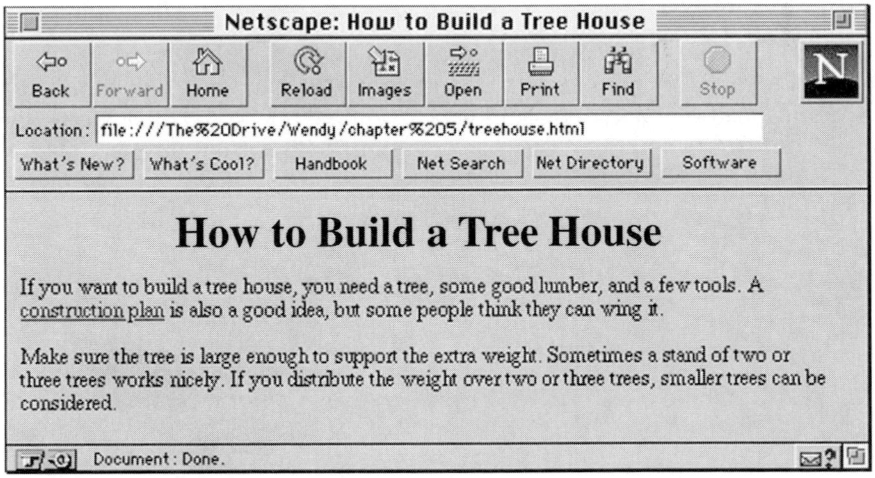

Figure 4.18:
A Web Page with
an Absolute URL

That's all there is to it. If the URL is current, and you insert it into your HTML file without typos, it should be operational. ***Always check each link that you add to a Web page to be sure that it works.*** Visitors get frustrated by nonworking links, so keep your Web page in good operating condition. To maintain your Web page properly, periodically check it to verify that all links still work. It is not enough to know that a link was working when you created it. A link that works today might not work tomorrow, if the page's author renames some files or directories. Ongoing maintenance is needed to ensure an operational Web page next week, next month, and next year. This is one of the hidden costs associated with posting pages on the Web. It's fun to create new Web pages, but most people find that maintaining them is tedious.

4.5.2 Relative URLs

When you have multiple Web pages in the same directory on your Web server, you can insert links to your own pages without specifying the full URL (although the full URL will also work). You instead can use a shortcut address that consists of only the file's name and its location *relative to the current directory*. This is a **relative URL**.

The simplest relative URL connects two pages that are in the same subdirectory. Here's what an example A-tag would look like:

```
<A HREF="booklist.html"> .... </A>
```

Relative URLs work only when the destination is on the same Web server as the page that contains the link. If you see a relative URL on someone else's Web page, you cannot simply copy that link and expect it to work on your Web page. You must convert the relative URL to an absolute URL in order to make it operational on your own Web page.

If your Web pages are stored in a different directory, you will to need to include a directory path to the filename in the relative URL. If you are familiar with directory paths, you know what to do. If you are not, avoid the added complication of trying to use them by keeping all of your Web pages in the same directory.

Use Relative URLs Whenever You Can

When you create a link to another Web page on your own site, you can use either a relative URL or an absolute URL. It's best to choose relative URLs. Doing this will make your Web pages *portable* if you need to move them from your current Web server to a different Web server. When a Web page is **portable**, you can relocate the page on a new Web server and all of its links will still be operational. People do switch Web servers for various reasons. When you move your Web pages, you want to install them on the new server with a minimal amount of work and adjustment. If your internal links are all absolute URLs, you will have to edit them to replace the old domain name with the new domain name. If the links are all relative URLs, they will work as-is on the new Web server (unless you change your directory structure).

You can't know when you might need to move your Web site to a new server, so plan for an uncertain future and opt for relative URLs whenever possible.

4.5.3 Named Anchors

The third type of hyperlink is a **named anchor**. This link points to another location in the same document. Setting up a named anchor takes a little more work than setting up absolute and relative URLs. This is because you must mark the destination location in the current document so that the Web browsers can find it. This is done with a `NAME` attribute inside of an A-tag.

Here's how it would work if the previous tree house example were longer and contained different sections in which various subtopics were discussed in some detail. Suppose that you want your page to include a bulleted list at the beginning that will be a clickable table of contents. You can do this by making each item on the list a named anchor that points to some other section in the same document. The HTML source code would look like this.

```
<HTML>
<HEAD>
<TITLE> How to Build a Tree House </TITLE>
</HEAD>
<BODY>
<H1 ALIGN=CENTER> How to Build a Tree House </H1>
<P> If you want to build a tree house,
you need:
<P>
<UL>
<LI> <A HREF="#tree">a tree</A><BR>
<LI> <A HREF="#lumber">some good lumber</A><BR>
<LI> <A HREF="#tools">a few tools</A><BR>
</UL>
<P> A construction plan is also a good idea, but some peo-
ple think they can wing it.
<H3><A NAME="tree">A Tree</A></H3>
<P> Make sure the tree is large enough to support the
extra weight. Sometimes a stand of two or three trees
works nicely. If you distribute the weight over two or
three trees, smaller trees can be considered.
    .
    .
    .
<H3><A NAME="lumber">Some Good Lumber</A></H3>
    .
    .
    .
<H3><A NAME="tools">A Few Tools</A></H3>
    .
    .
    .
</BODY>
</HTML>
```

Figure 4.19 shows the result.

Figure 4.19:
A Clickable Table of
Contents Created by
Using Named
Anchors

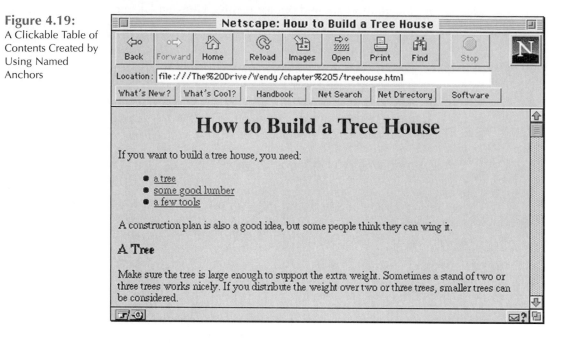

A named anchor uses the same **HREF** attribute, just like absolute and relative URLs, but instead of specifying a URL or a filename as the attribute, you specify a link name. To help Web browsers understand that this **HREF** value represents a named anchor, you must insert a pound (#) character at the beginning of the link name (as shown above). Then you need to ensure that each named anchor is anchored to a marked location somewhere in the current document. These anchors are also marked with A-tag pairs, but the anchors contain a **NAME** attribute instead of an **HREF** attribute (see Figure 4.19).

Named anchors help visitors move through a page's text in a nonlinear fashion. If you create a clickable table of contents, you should insert additional named anchors at the end of each "chapter" that will take visitors back to the table of contents; these links are often labeled "Back to Top." Good Web page design includes anticipating all of the directions that a visitor might want to go and making getting there as easy as possible.

4.5.4 Testing Your Hyperlinks

After you update your Web page, always check the new version to ensure that it properly displays and that links work. Watch out for the following scenario.

1. You view one of your Web pages and find a problem with one of the links.
2. You replace the faulty link with an updated link and save the modified file.
3. You view the new Web page to check it, but the problem is still there.

To avoid this, be sure that you're viewing the newly updated HTML file. If the Web page is being retrieved from a disk cache, you're seeing the original file instead of the updated one. Before concluding that your update isn't working, click the Reload or Refresh button to see the new file.

Web Page Construction Checklist #4

1. Explain the difference between an absolute URL and a relative URL.
2. Explain why using relative URLs is better than using absolute URLs.
3. Add an absolute URL to a Web page, and then test it.
4. Add a relative URL to a Web page, and then test it (you'll need a second Web page for this).
5. Create a named anchor, and then create a second named anchor that links to the first one.

4.6 PAGE LAYOUTS WITH TABLES

If your Web pages are mostly text and largely utilitarian, you can skip this section. However, if you want your Web pages to grab attention and show off your content in style, you'll want to use HTML's *TABLE element* to control the layout of your graphical elements.

Tables have a lot to offer; for example, you can do the following:

- Change your background colors for different areas of the same page.
- Add margins around your text so that there is more room between the text and the edge of the browser's display window.
- Create an image that has clickable regions (as in a graphical navigation menu).
- Create a two-column text display to make a Web page look more like a newsletter.
- Override a busy background pattern with regions of solid colors in order to make text segments easier to read.
- Add a three-dimensional frame around a picture to give your Web page a look of depth.
- Center an image on a Web page no matter how the browser window is resized.
- Display a table of numbers.

Tables are powerful tools because they can adjust to any browser window and give the Web page author a lot of control over the layout of different visual elements.

Creating Tables the Easy Way

Tables are simple enough to create, in theory. In practice, it's easy to mess them up. A large, complicated table involves a lot of tags and tag attributes. If you are doing all of the HTML manually, check your progress with a browser often so that you can isolate errors sooner rather than later.

To save yourself a lot of time and trouble, use a good HTML editor when you are working with tables. Although not necessary, it makes table creation much easier.

All tables contain *rows and columns.* The tag structure for tables in HTML requires a distinct row element for each row of the table. Within each row are placed distinct column elements for each column. The simplest possible table is a table that has one row and one column. If you have ever studied arrays or matrices in a mathematics class, an HTML table may look to you like an array. The basic idea is the same, but with tables, the rows and columns are not indexed, so you can't refer to them with subscripts. In HTML, each table element contains a collection of nested elements that define the structure of the table (see Figure 4.20).

Figure 4.20:
A Table with One
Row and One
Column

```
<TABLE>
  <TR>
    <TD>
      <IMG SRC="donut.jpg" ALT="a dachshund">
    </TD>
  </TR>
</TABLE>
```

The table in Figure 4.20 contains one table row, specified by the `<TR>` and `</TR>` tag pair. Within that row is one table data element (sometimes called a *cell*) specified by the `<TD>` and `</TD>` tag pair. The table data element corresponds to one column inside of the row. An image is inserted inside of the table data element. This is a very simple table that contains a single graphic. Although the nesting of table data elements inside of table row elements might seem cumbersome, it does give you a lot of flexibility. In HTML, different rows inside of a table do not have to contain the same number of columns. Examples of this very useful feature are given later in the chapter.

4.6.1   Creating Borders by Using Tables

If you insert the table in Figure 4.20 on a sample Web page, it won't appear to add anything to the image display. You can see the table better if you add a `BORDER` attribute to the `TABLE` tag. Try adding `BORDER=5` ; the result is a JPEG image framed by the containing table, as shown in Figure 4.21.

Figure 4.21:
A Table Border
Creating a Picture
Frame Effect

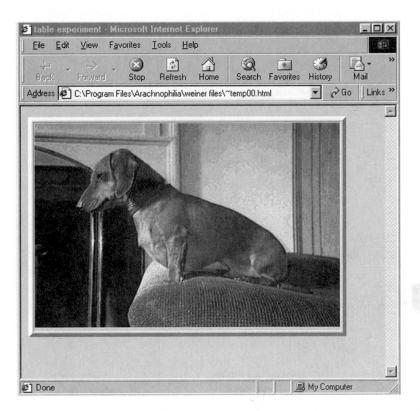

HTML tables are powerful because you can put anything inside of a table's data element, even another table. Figure 4.22 shows how to use tables to display and emphasize blocks of text. It also shows how a background pattern can run behind multiple tables, thereby giving the page a more interesting look without sacrificing the legibility of the text.

Adding attributes to your tables makes them more powerful. For example, you can control how much of the display window the table should occupy by setting WIDTH and HEIGHT attributes inside of the TABLE tag. You can give these attributes constant values if you want the dimensions to be a fixed number of pixels, or you can specify a percentage of the total width or height of the window. If you use percentage values, the table will dynamically adjust itself whenever the browser window is resized. Figure 4.23 shows the HTML for a table that will always resize itself to fill (almost) all of the available space. This was accomplished by setting the WIDTH and HEIGHT attributes to 100%.

Next, a background color (#000000 = black) was assigned to the table by using a BGCOLOR attribute. Finally, the ALIGN attribute was set to the value CENTER inside of the TD tag. The resulting display is shown in Figure 4.24.

Figure 4.22:
Making Tables Distinctive by Using Borders

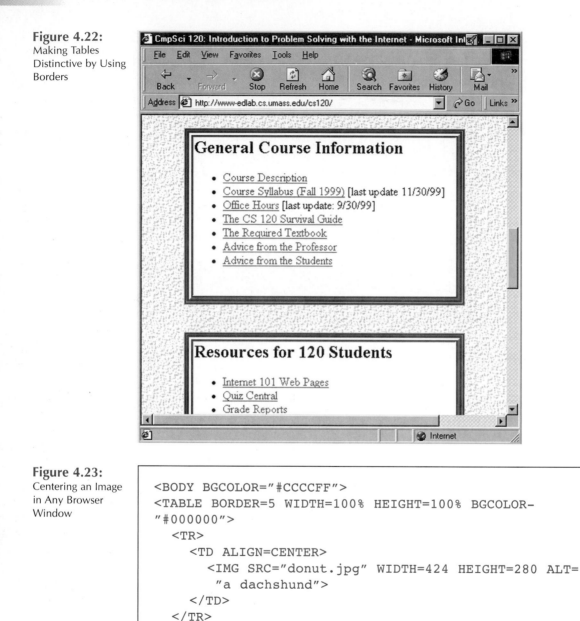

Figure 4.23:
Centering an Image in Any Browser Window

```
<BODY BGCOLOR="#CCCCFF">
<TABLE BORDER=5 WIDTH=100% HEIGHT=100% BGCOLOR-
"#000000">
  <TR>
    <TD ALIGN=CENTER>
      <IMG SRC="donut.jpg" WIDTH=424 HEIGHT=280 ALT=
      "a dachshund">
    </TD>
  </TR>
</TABLE>
```

A border and a contrasting table background in Figure 4.24 make the table element more visible. If you remove the **BORDER** and **BGCOLOR** attributes in the **TABLE** tag, you will see only the graphic, perfectly centered in the browser's window on a colored background. The image will remain centered even when you resize the window.

Low-resolution images are fine for the Web

This photograph was taken with a KODAK DC265 digital camera in high-resolution mode (1536 × 1024 pixels per picture). The camera produced a JPEG image that consumed 695KB of memory. This is a high level of resolution suitable for printing high-quality images on paper. If you are only taking pictures for the Web, you can take pictures at lower levels of resolution (1152 × 768 pixels or 768 × 512 pixels) because computer monitors display fewer pixels per inch than high-quality printers. A good printer has a resolution of 300 dpi (dots per inch), while a good computer monitor displays only 72 dpi (pixels become "dots" in the context of printer resolution). Lower-resolution settings on your camera allow you to take more pictures before you run out of memory. For example, a 32MB memory card holds about 40 high-resolution (1536 × 1024) photographs or 160 low-resolution (768 × 512) photographs.

JPEG files can be compressed

If you have a high-resolution image, you should compress it before adding it to a Web page (no one wants to wait for an 800MB image to download). If you save the image using the JPEG file format, you can specify your level of compression when you save. JPEG is a "lossy" compression technique: each time you reduce the memory requirements for the image, you will lose a little of the image's original quality. But you can control the size/quality tradeoff by deciding how much compression to use. The images above range in size from 114KB to 44KB to 27KB to 18KB (moving clockwise from the upper left-hand corner). The loss of quality is apparent at 27KB and 18KB, but this level of quality (or worse) would still be acceptable for a thumbnail sketch (the small image to the right is the 18KB version). Note that you do not reduce the download time for an image by merely reducing its WIDTH and HEIGHT attributes inside an IMG tag. Those attributes control the size of the image on your Web page, but they do not alter the size of the image with respect to its memory requirements. To make an effective thumbnail sketch, you must compress your original image file.

Different color palettes produce different images

If you are serious about photography and want to post your own photographs on the Web, you should know that the same photograph may look very different on different computers. Each computer has a fixed color palette that it uses to display color images. Color monitors work with 8-bit color displays (limited to only 256 colors), 24-bit color (about 65,000 colors), or 32-bit color (about 17 million colors). Your computer has preference settings you can adjust if you want to see some different palettes on your own computer (look under "monitor display"). In addition to differences across monitors, the computers that run Windows use a different color palette than Macintosh computers. The photographs on this page show our original photograph as it appears under four different color palettes. The one with the pink overtones was obtained by switching a monitor from an 8-bit display back up to a 24-bit display—sometimes the palette gets corrupted and odd colors appear. You can also obtain color displays like this with graphics editors that support special effects. Look for filters with names like "solarize" or "posterize" to add psychedelic effects to your photographs. Graphics editors will also let you adjust the contrast, brightness, hue, and saturation of your images. (The hue adjustment is very handy if your green iguana isn't looking very green).

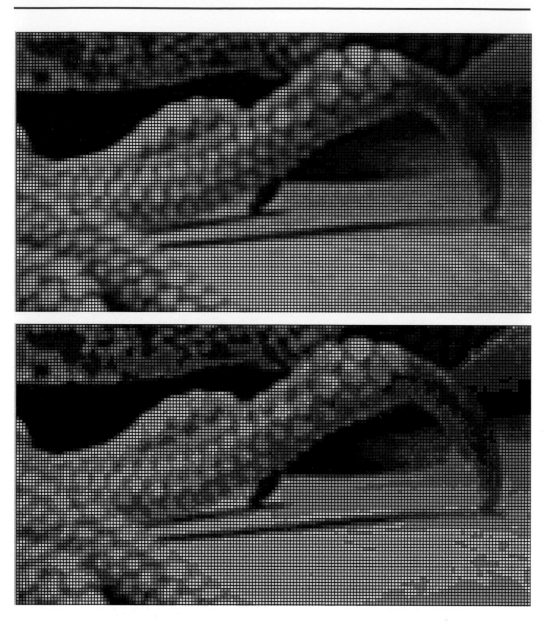

Hue adjustments may result in less detail

When you adjust the hue for a photograph you may lose subtle shadings and small details. The bottom image on this page was derived from the top image using a hue adjustment, but the loss of detail shown here is very similar to the type of loss associated with JPEG image compression. If the image you are modifying is high-resolution, this loss may not be visible on a Web page. The grid lines on these images mark individual pixels: these images have been magnified by a factor of five.

High-resolution images tolerate image manipulations well
The loss of detail that is apparent under magnification is perceived at this level as a loss of contrast. Still, the image is quite good and could perhaps be doctored to bring back some of the contrast.

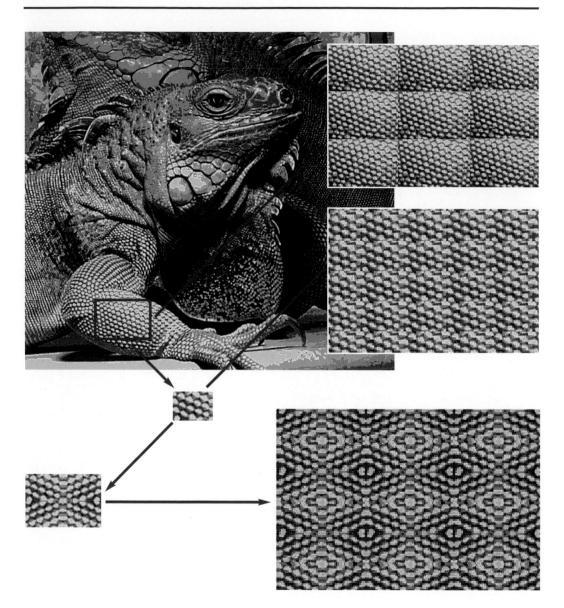

Create your own backgrounds with a photograph and an image editor

Photographs can be an excellent source of material if you want to experiment with your own Web page backgrounds. To make a uniform background, you will need a small image segment that is as uniform in color and shading as possible. Unedited excerpts from photographs usually show rectangular boundaries when they are tiled onto a background. If you want a quilt or checkerboard effect, that's great. But if you want a more subtle pattern, pick a very small area to lessen the boundary effects. Alternatively, use an image editor to create reflections of the original image and piece together a pattern of the sort seen in a kaleidoscope. This can result in some interesting and unexpected patterns like the diamond pattern above. The diamond was achieved by reflecting the original pattern once through the vertical axis, once through the horizontal axis, and once through both axes in order to piece together the larger four-part tile used above.

Transparent GIFs can be layered on top of one another to create interesting effects, such as text that appears to be a part of a background image.

1. Start by picking a background image. For best results, pick an image with an interesting pattern or texture. We've chosen a photograph of water in a swimming pool.

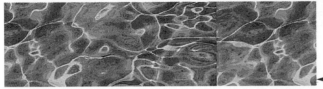

2. Next, create some text using a word processor. Pick a simple font that has a lot of thickness to it. Anything too detailed is likely to get lost in the overlay.

3. Take a screen shot of your text so you have an image file to work with. Save this as a GIF file so you can transform it into a transparent GIF. For this transparency, you want to make the letters transparent—not the background. Display this transparent GIF on a Web page over the background file and take another screen shot.

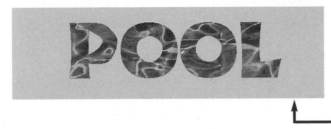

Note: If we used this version of our text for the next transparent GIF, we'd end up with an image that is invisible when we display it on top of the background image: the pattern in the letters will line up perfectly with the pattern in the background. We aren't going to all this work to create an invisible image, so we have a little more work to do.

4. Now we need to modify our patterned text using an image editor. The image seen here was obtained using special effects in Softkey's PhotoFinish 4. Experiment with lots of effects to find one you like. You want to retain enough of the pattern to keep it connected to the background, but you also want it to stand out from the background in some obvious way.

5. Once we are finished editing the text image, we save it as a GIF file and make it transparent—this time making the background transparent. Add it to a Web page with the original background file, and it's done. If you like, take another screen shot and you've got a portable image—the original background file doesn't have to dominate your Web page to obtain the special effect.

Color editors typically support a 24-bit color palette

If you want a solid background color, it is easy to try out some different ones with a good Web page construction kit. In the figure above, we see a color editor used by Arachnophilia. If you can't find the color you want in the grid of basic colors, look for a large color wheel or some other display where you can select additional colors by moving your mouse over a full spectrum.

The display on the right is a color editor used by ImageForge. It features slider controls that you can use to specify the three RGB (Red-Green-Blue) values. Each slider spans a range of integer values from 0 to 255 (8 bits of information) yielding a 24-bit color palette. Sometimes the 0 to 255 range is expressed in decimal values, and sometimes in hexadecimal values (00 to FF). Either way, there are always 256 values.

Be careful when selecting color combinations for background and text colors if the text is going to rest directly on the background. Some combinations are impossible to read and others are possible to read but may result in eye-strain. Be kind to your readers and make sure your text is legible.

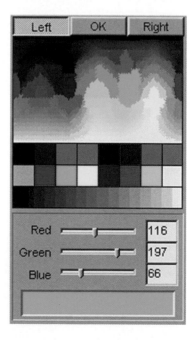

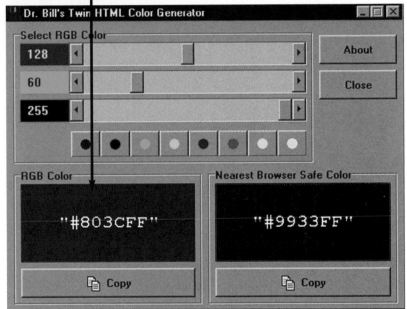

Use Web-safe colors when colors matter

Why are there 216 Web-safe colors? It all comes down to the inconsistencies and limitations of color computer monitors. A 24-bit RGB color palette resides in a three-dimensional (RGB) space that is a discrete cube (256 × 256 × 256) of possible values. Unfortunately, not all monitors display the same 24-bit palette. But all modern color monitors can display an 8-bit color mode (256 colors) consistently. So in principle, a common set of 256 colors would be Web-safe. Then why do we only have 216 Web-safe colors? If we want to represent a Web-safe palette as a discrete cube (which is convenient for color editors and other graphics software), we need to work with three dimensions that can assume no more than six possible values (6 × 6 × 6 = 216 fits inside 256, but 7 × 7 × 7 = 343 is too big). And so the values 00, 33, 66, 99, CC, and FF (equivalent to 0, 51, 102, 153, 204, and 255) were chosen for the six values of each Web-safe RGB dimension. The number 216 just happens to be the largest color cube supported by the 8-bit color mode.

Not all colors are created equal when it comes to the Web. Your monitor may be capable of handling millions of colors, but a wise Web page designer normally works with a set of just 216 Web-safe colors. The Web safe colors are platform invariant: no matter what computer you are running, or what browser you are using, a Web page made up of Web-safe colors will look the same to me as it does to you. When a Web page contains colors that are not Web-safe, a background that looks reddish-brown on one computer may look like dark brown on another computer. If these colors and color combinations matter, it is very important to avoid colors that are not Web-safe.

There are many software tools on the Internet to help you with Web page color management. Eyedropper 2.1 is a desktop tool that will show you the RGB code for any pixel on your computer monitor. Dr. Bill's Twin HTML Color Generator lets you specify a color with either RGB or hexadecimal notation, and shows you the nearest Web-safe color in an adjacent window so you can compare the two.

A screen shot utility is a must for graphics design

You can create titles for a Web page with any fully-featured word processor. For example, Microsoft Word includes a number of different fonts that can be displayed with a palette of about 150 colors over the same palette of colored backgrounds. Here we display a title in a Word document: we take a screen shot of the Word document and save the screen shot as a GIF image. Simple screen shots can be taken by pressing Alt+Prt Sc on Windows or ⌘+⇧Shift+3 on a Mac. Crop the resulting image as needed using an image editor and convert it into a GIF format using an image editor or file converter. If you are happy with the colors, you can use the image as is. Alternatively, you can add colors from a larger color palette by creating a transparent GIF. Starting with a GIF version of the screenshot, we can make the background behind our text transparent with a utility like GiFFY 2.0.Then you can use the HTML background attributes to fill in the background with the color of your choice (as seen on the next page). This approach makes it possible to change the background color of an image file with a few keystrokes in a text editor, which is very convenient if you want to experiment with lots of possible color combinations.

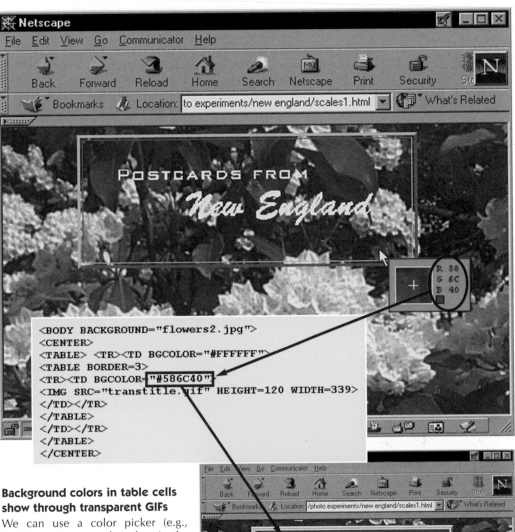

```
<BODY BACKGROUND="flowers2.jpg">
<CENTER>
<TABLE> <TR><TD BGCOLOR="#FFFFFF">
<TABLE BORDER=3>
<TR><TD BGCOLOR="#586C40">
<IMG SRC="transtitle.gif" HEIGHT=120 WIDTH=339>
</TD></TR>
</TABLE>
</TD></TR>
</TABLE>
</CENTER>
```

Background colors in table cells show through transparent GIFs

We can use a color picker (e.g., EyeDropper) to sample colors in the Web page's background as shown above. Once we have found a good color, we can use its hexadecimal code to set the background behind the transparent GIF. We place the GIF inside an HTML table and set the background of the GIF's table cell using the BGCOLOR attribute as shown above. Then we make the boundary for the table solid by embedding the first table inside a second table that has its own BGCOLOR attribute (for this example we chose white: #FFFFFF). Color pickers make it easy to coordinate graphical elements on a Web page for a professional customized look. Notice how effective a two-color theme can be (shades of green and white in this case). Background colors are most effective when they are not overdone.

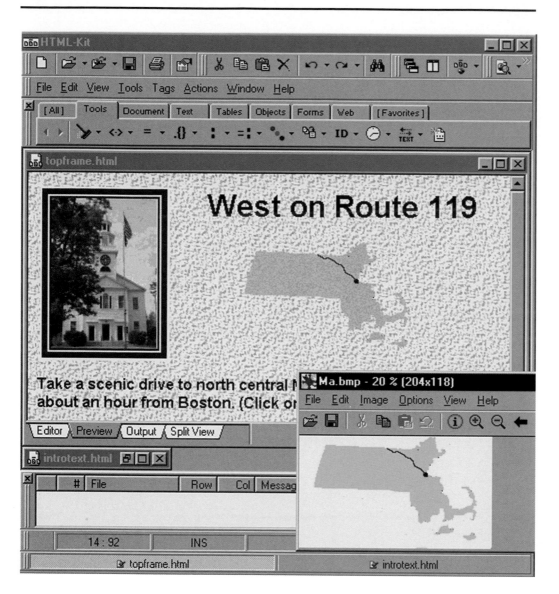

The right tools make Web construction easier

Web site construction is easy with the right tools. Here we see an HTML-Kit workspace for a Web page under construction. HTML-Kit makes it easy to move between the HTML source file (the "Editor" tab) and a browser rendering of the page under construction (the "Preview" tab). If you need to work on more than one HTML file at a time (for example, while constructing a page with multiple frames), HTML-Kit can keep multiple workspace windows active.

This Web page contains a transparent GIF (the map of Massachusetts) that needed to be resized. To find the correct HEIGHT and WIDTH attributes, we viewed the same image with IrfanView and used IrfanView's Magnify/Shrink feature to resize the image as needed. Once we find an appropriate level of shrinkage (20% of the original image), IrfanView tells us the exact pixel dimensions for our IMG attributes.

Each frame element is a separate HTML file that can be developed independently and modified as needed. For example, the design of the header element is managed with a table. This header contains one text title, two images, and one block of explanatory text. We want the header to look good no matter how wide the browser window, and we also want to minimize the amount of vertical space it consumes, so we will have space left in the browser window for the menu frame and the content frame.

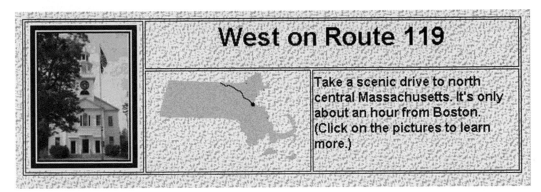

Tables can control graphical layout

When working with tables for graphical layouts, it is best to make the cell borders of the table visible as shown above. Now we can see that this component contains two rows and three columns. The first table element is the picture of the church, and it is extended across both rows by setting the ROWSPAN attribute to 2. The second data element is the title text string, and it is extended across two columns by setting the COLSPAN attribute to 2. The map image occupies a single data element within the second row and the second column, while the introductory text occupies a single data element within the second row and the third column. The data element containing the title contains an ALIGN="CENTER" attribute so the title will always be centered across whatever space is available to the right of the church image.

```
<table>
<TR>
<TD ROWSPAN=2>
<img src="church1.jpg" alt="Ashby Town Green" ALIGN=LEFT>
</TD>
<TD COLSPAN=2>
<h1 ALIGN=CENTER><font face="Helvetica">
West on Route 119</font></h1>
</TD></TR>
```
— Row 1

```
<TR>
<TD>
<img src="ma-trans.gif" alt="" HEIGHT=118 WIDTH=204>
</TD>
<TD>
<font face="Helvetica"><strong>
Take a scenic drive to north central Massachusetts. It's onl·
</strong></font>
</TD></TR>
</table>
```
— Row 2

Frames create "split-page" layouts

A standard Web page layout includes (1) a page header containing the page's title and other introductory information, (2) a navigation menu containing hyperlinks to other pages, and (3) a content component containing text or anything else appropriate for the page. The best way to manage these three components is with three separate HTML files inside three frames.

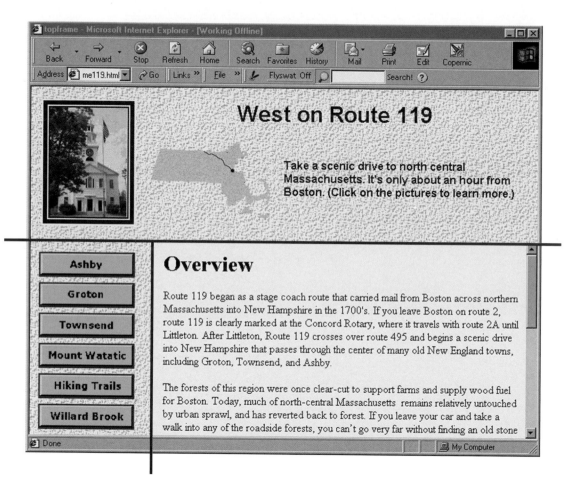

By organizing these page elements inside frames, the navigational menu can be kept constant throughout the entire Web site. An ever-present and familiar menu helps visitors move around a large site without getting lost. These menus are usually found in a left-hand frame (as in this example), or in a smaller menu bar framed at the top of each Web page. All of the content for the site appears in the content frame, which changes when the user clicks on menu items or additional hyperlinks inside the content pages. Some sites employ a secondary browser window and send all of the hyperlinks in the content pages to the secondary window by specifying a TARGET attribute in the hyperlink elements. A secondary window also helps users keep their orientation as they navigate large Web sites—although more than one secondary window can be confusing if too many browser windows are allowed to proliferate and create clutter.

Each frame contains its own HTML file

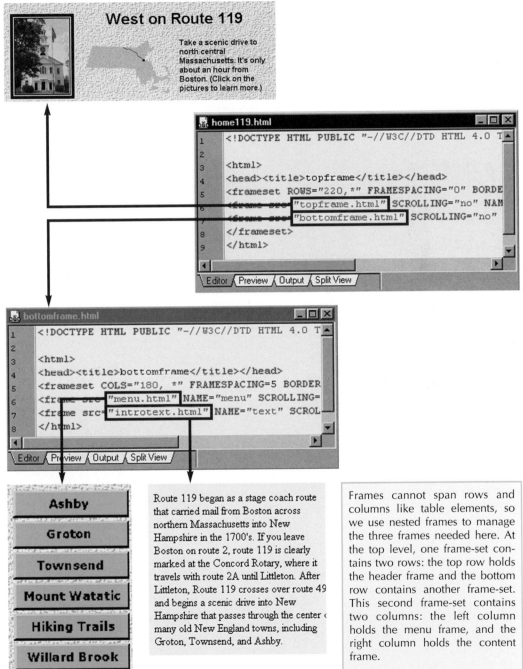

```
home119.html
1  <!DOCTYPE HTML PUBLIC "-//W3C//DTD HTML 4.0 T
2
3  <html>
4  <head><title>topframe</title></head>
5  <frameset ROWS="220,*" FRAMESPACING="0" BORDE
6  <frame src="topframe.html" SCROLLING="no" NAM
7  <frame src="bottomframe.html" SCROLLING="no"
8  </frameset>
9  </html>
Editor / Preview / Output / Split View
```

```
bottomframe.html
1  <!DOCTYPE HTML PUBLIC "-//W3C//DTD HTML 4.0 T
2
3  <html>
4  <head><title>bottomframe</title></head>
5  <frameset COLS="180, *" FRAMESPACING=5 BORDER
6  <frame src="menu.html" NAME="menu" SCROLLING=
7  <frame src="introtext.html" NAME="text" SCROL
8  </html>
Editor / Preview / Output / Split View
```

Ashby

Groton

Townsend

Mount Watatic

Hiking Trails

Willard Brook

Route 119 began as a stage coach route that carried mail from Boston across northern Massachusetts into New Hampshire in the 1700's. If you leave Boston on route 2, route 119 is clearly marked at the Concord Rotary, where it travels with route 2A until Littleton. After Littleton, Route 119 crosses over route 49 and begins a scenic drive into New Hampshire that passes through the center of many old New England towns, including Groton, Townsend, and Ashby.

Frames cannot span rows and columns like table elements, so we use nested frames to manage the three frames needed here. At the top level, one frame-set contains two rows: the top row holds the header frame and the bottom row contains another frame-set. This second frame-set contains two columns: the left column holds the menu frame, and the right column holds the content frame.

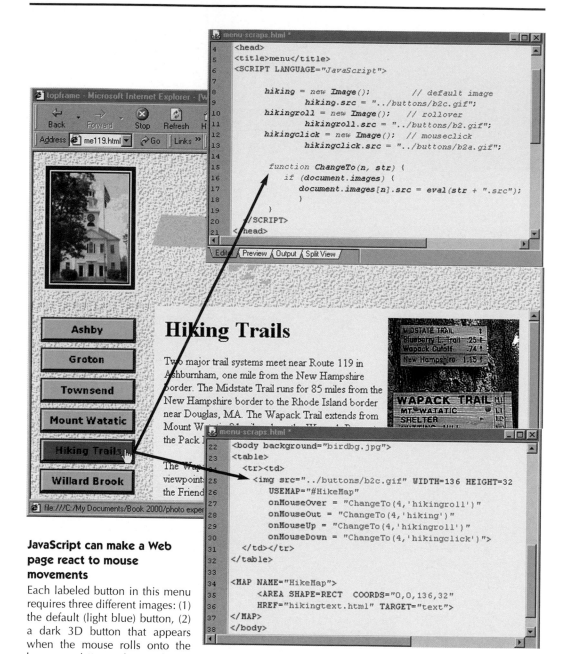

```
4   <head>
5   <title>menu</title>
6   <SCRIPT LANGUAGE="JavaScript">
7
8       hiking = new Image();          // default image
9               hiking.src = "../buttons/b2c.gif";
10      hikingroll = new Image();    // rollover
11              hikingroll.src = "../buttons/b2.gif";
12      hikingclick = new Image();   // mouseclick
13              hikingclick.src = "../buttons/b2a.gif";
14
15      function ChangeTo(n, str) {
16          if (document.images) {
17              document.images[n].src = eval(str + ".src");
18          }
19      }
20  </SCRIPT>
21  </head>
```

Edit | Preview | Output | Split View

Hiking Trails

Two major trail systems meet near Route 119 in
Ashburnham, one mile from the New Hampshire
border. The Midstate Trail runs for 85 miles from the
New Hampshire border to the Rhode Island border
near Douglas, MA. The Wapack Trail extends from
Mount W

The W
viewpoints
the Friend

```
22  <body background="birdbg.jpg">
23  <table>
24    <tr><td>
25      <img src="../buttons/b2c.gif" WIDTH=136 HEIGHT=32
26          USEMAP="#HikeMap"
27          onMouseOver = "ChangeTo(4,'hikingroll')"
28          onMouseOut = "ChangeTo(4,'hiking')"
29          onMouseUp = "ChangeTo(4,'hikingroll')"
30          onMouseDown = "ChangeTo(4,'hikingclick')">
31    </td></tr>
32  </table>
33
34  <MAP NAME="HikeMap">
35      <AREA SHAPE=RECT   COORDS="0,0,136,32"
36      HREF="hikingtext.html" TARGET="text">
37  </MAP>
38  </body>
```

JavaScript can make a Web page react to mouse movements

Each labeled button in this menu requires three different images: (1) the default (light blue) button, (2) a dark 3D button that appears when the mouse rolls onto the button, and (3) another 3D button that looks depressed when the user clicks the button. The two HTML excerpts on this page show a one-button version of the actual menu—simplified to one button in order to save space. Similar elements are needed for each menu button in the complete menu frame.

The navigational menu can be enhanced with mouse-over effects so that each menu item changes in appearance as the mouse rolls over it. This is accomplished with a JavaScript that works in conjunction with an image map for each menu button. The script replaces each menu button image when specific mouse events are detected.

Figure 4.24:
Applying a
Background to a
Table

4.6.2   Creating Margins by Using Tables

Suppose that you want to run a border down the left side of your Web page (see Figure 4.17). It's easy enough to create an image file that can be tiled into a border background. However, if you do only that, you might see text running into your border (see Figure 4.25). Borders and text should be separated.

Figure 4.25:
Borders and Text
Running Together

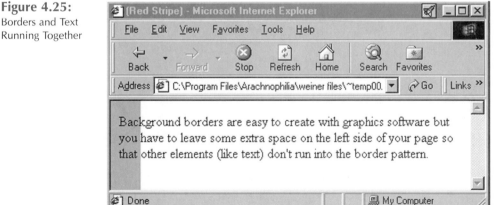

You can keep the visual elements on your page separate from a border by creating a table that has an empty column that runs the entire length of the page (see Figure 4.26).

Figure 4.26:
HTML for a Two-Column Table with an Empty Column 50 Pixels Wide

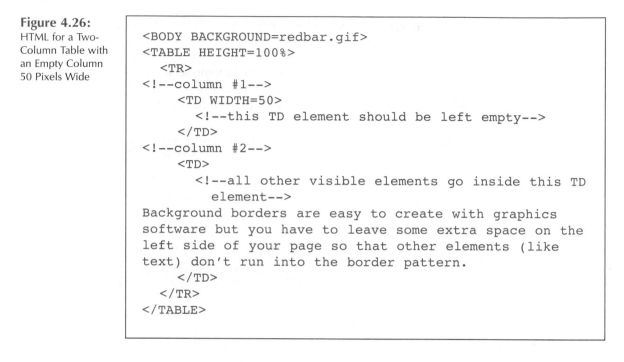

```
<BODY BACKGROUND=redbar.gif>
<TABLE HEIGHT=100%>
   <TR>
<!--column #1-->
     <TD WIDTH=50>
        <!--this TD element should be left empty-->
     </TD>
<!--column #2-->
     <TD>
        <!--all other visible elements go inside this TD
           element-->
Background borders are easy to create with graphics
software but you have to leave some extra space on the
left side of your page so that other elements (like
text) don't run into the border pattern.
     </TD>
   </TR>
</TABLE>
```

You reserve one column for the border pattern and one for all of the other visual elements of the Web page. In this way, you ensure that the two regions stay separated from each other (see Figure 4.27). If the border is to be a solid bar, you don't need a background graphic. You can simply create a table column with a fixed pixel width and a solid background color.

Figure 4.27:
An Empty Table Column Acting as a Margin Setting

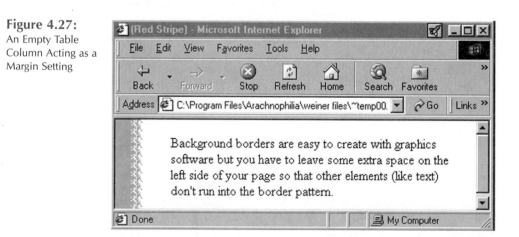

Some pages work nicely in a newsletter format with two columns of text. You can use a table to achieve this look, but you won't be able to "chain" the text across the columns (that is, text in the left column won't flow into the right column). To do this, create a two-column table and fill the columns with formatted text, as if each column were a separate Web page. Figure 4.28 shows a table that contains one row and two columns. Each column has a `WIDTH` attribute set to 40%. Additional whitespace has been placed between and around the columns by including a `CELLPADDING` attribute inside the `TABLE` tag and setting its value to 20 pixels.

Figure 4.28:
A Two-Column Table with Cell Padding

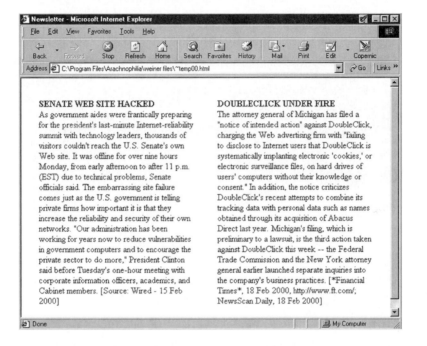

Although tables can be very effective with text, think carefully before you put a lot of text into a multicolumn format. Lynx does not support tables. In Lynx, the text will be visible, but all of the whitespace in each row will be compressed and the remaining text will be left-justified. As a result, a Web page like that shown in Figure 4.28 will be impossible to read. If your Web site is primarily text, keep it accessible to Lynx users. Either avoid tables altogether, or offer an alternative set of pages designed for Lynx.

4.6.3 Organizing Graphical Elements in Tables

As we've seen, tables are a powerful device for Web page layouts. Table cells can contain text, graphics, hyperlinks, and each cell can also have its own background pattern or background color. In this section, we will look at ways to modify the size of table cells so different cells can be different sizes. When a table's displays visual elements cells occupy differently sized regions, the predictable boundaries based on a fixed number of rows and columns are less apparent, and our Web page takes on a more fluid look.

Arranging Images Although tables can be used to break text into segments, they can also be used to format images in a picture gallery. If all of your images are the same size, a uniform table with a fixed number of rows and columns is all that you need. However, if you have images of different sizes you might need a table that has a different number of columns in each row or perhaps a different number of rows in each column. Figure 4.29 shows a layout of two rows, with one TD element in the first row and three TD elements in the second row. To make the TD element in the first row span all three columns, add a COLSPAN attribute to the TD tag and give it a value of 3.

Figure 4.29:
A Table Layout That Uses the COLSPAN Attribute

To extend a column across multiple rows, you can use a ROWSPAN attribute to a TD tag. Figure 4.30 shows a table layout with ten rows, ten columns, and COLSPAN and ROWSPAN attributes. Each rectangle is colored with a BGCOLOR attribute. COLSPAN and ROWSPAN are often used together to create Web page layouts (see Figure I-13 in the color insert).

Creating a Navigation Bar Creating a graphical navigation bar or menu is best managed by using some additional software, such as Microsoft Paint (see Figure 4.31). A special-purpose image splitting utility is needed to divide the image into rectangular sections that are then reassembled as a table. The example shown in Figure 4.31 was created by using Paint and a freeware utility called **Splitz**.

Figure 4.30:
A Table Layout That
Uses Both
COLSPAN and
ROWSPAN Attributes

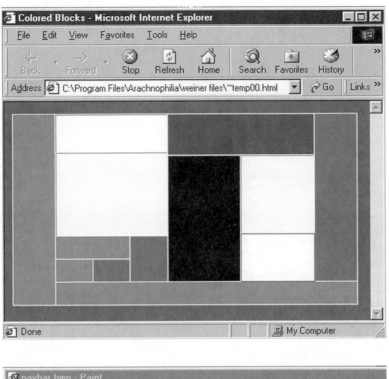

Figure 4.31:
Using Paint and
Splitz to Create a
Navigation Bar

Once you've created a graphical image to use as a navigation bar, you input that file into a tool that will divide the image into rectangular subsections that can then be reassembled back into the original image, but with different parts of the image appearing in separate cells of an HTML table. Figure 4.32 shows Splitz at work on the navigation bar created in Figure 4.31. The Splitz user specifies where the vertical and horizontal cuts should be made: In this case, it makes sense to chop up the image along the vertical boundaries separating the menu items.

Once the cuts have been made, Splitz generates separate image files for each subsection of the original image (in this example, five image files) and then creates the HTML code for a table. This code will reconstruct the original image (see Figure 4.33).

Figure 4.32:
Dividing an Image
into Subsections

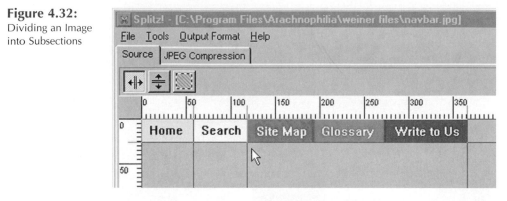

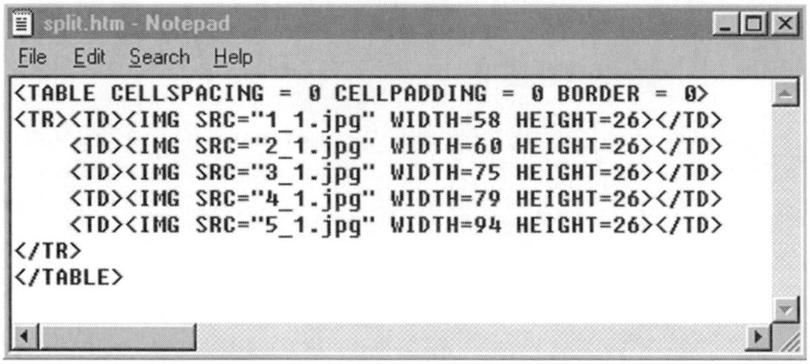

Figure 4.33:
Reassembling the
Original Image in
an HTML Table

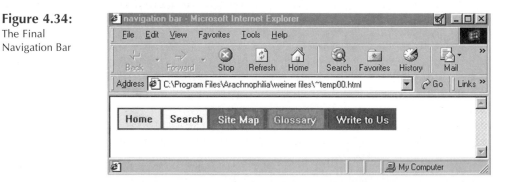

Although the table in Figure 4.33 looks like the original navigation bar, now that it has been recast as a table, you can associate different links with each table data element. Each of the five images inside of this table can now become an anchor for a link (see Figure 4.34).

Figure 4.34:
The Final
Navigation Bar

One last action removes the borders around the image elements in the navigation bar so that the final navigation bar looks exactly like the original created with Paint. If you place a BORDER attribute with a setting value of 0 inside of each IMG tag in Figure 4.33, the highlighting shown in Figure 4.34 will go away.

Web Page Construction Checklist #5

1. Use a table to add a three-dimensional frame around an image.
2. Create a 3 × 4 table—three rows and four columns—and type the name of a city inside of each table cell.
3. Add background colors to the 3 × 4 table so that each row has its own color.
4. Nest the 3 × 4 table inside of another table so that the grid is always centered after the window is resized.
5. Replace the first column of the 3 × 4 table with a solid vertical bar by using ROWSPAN.

4.7　NAVIGATION MAPS WITH FRAMES

When you build a large Web site that has many pages, you need to think carefully about navigational features. Visitors who are not familiar with your site will need signs and guideposts. Navigation bars (see Section 4.6.3) and navigation menus are useful for large Web sites, but to provide maximal ease of use to your visitors, they need to appear on each Web page. You'll make life easier on your visitors if you show them *the same* navigational options on each page. In effect, you want one part of each Web page to remain constant across your entire site. You can accomplish this by duplicating the same navigational device (for example, a menu or a map) on each page. However, this is tedious and, more important, a nonoptimal use of bandwidth. A much better solution is to use HTML *frames.*

A frame allows you to partition a Web page into multiple segments so that you can display a different HTML file within each segment. Think of each frame as a small, independent browser window. By using frames, you can set up links that alter the content of one frame without disturbing the contents of the other frames.

You have probably seen frames in action at search engine sites, Web portal sites, and other large commercial sites. Some sites run, at the top of each Web page, a horizontal frame that contains a navigational bar. Other sites run a vertical frame segment along the left side of each Web page for the same purpose. Some sites use both. Windows are resized from the lower right-hand corner, so it makes sense to place navigational tools in the upper left-hand corner where they will always be visible (or at least partially visible) no matter how the browser window is resized.

Frames are not difficult to set up, but you must design frame pages carefully so that they can be viewed without excessive scrolling by the visitor. A vertical frame with a long list of navigational choices might require some scrolling, so visitors will be able to figure out that additional elements are available. However, avoid page displays that require horizontal scrolling (people are more accustomed to layouts that scroll vertically). When you create a frame for a Web page, you can specify a *scrolling frame* or a *nonscrolling frame*. We will see how in the next section.

4.7.1 Creating a Frame

To create a frame, insert a **FRAMESET** tag immediately after the **HEAD** element on your Web page. Whenever you include a **FRAMESET** element inside the HEAD, you do not need a **BODY** element. All of the visible content will be stored in other HTML files referenced by the FRAMESET. A Web page that contains frames does not contain any visible content of its own—it can only display content found in other HTML files. **FRAMESET** divides the page display by using a **COLS** attribute, a **ROWS** attribute, or both. Each attribute takes as its value a set of percentage values separated by commas. For example,

```
<FRAMESET COLS="20%, 80%" ROWS="60%, 40%">
```

divides the Web page into four frames (see Figure 4.35). You can have as many rows and columns as you want, but most layouts require only two rows (for a horizontal navigation bar) or two columns (for a vertical navigation menu). More complicated layouts can be achieved by *nesting* frames (see Figure I-15 in the color insert).

Figure 4.35:
A Web Page with
Four Frames

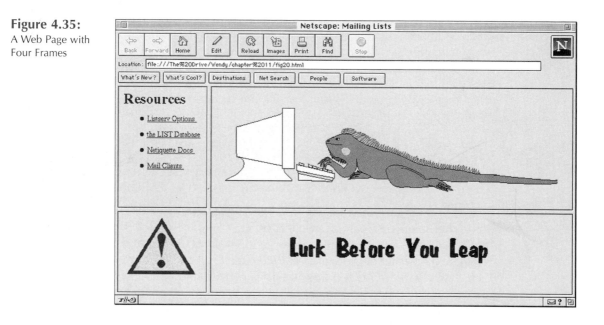

To fill each frame with visible content, use a **FRAME** tag with an **SRC** attribute. If you want the frame to be fixed, set the **SCROLLING** attribute to no. The following construction produces the Web page shown in Figure 4.36.

```
<FRAMESET COLS="70%, 30%">
<FRAME SRC="fig21c.html" SCROLLING="no">
<FRAME SRC="fig21a.html">
</FRAMESET>
```

Figure 4.36:
A Web Page with a
Scrollable Frame

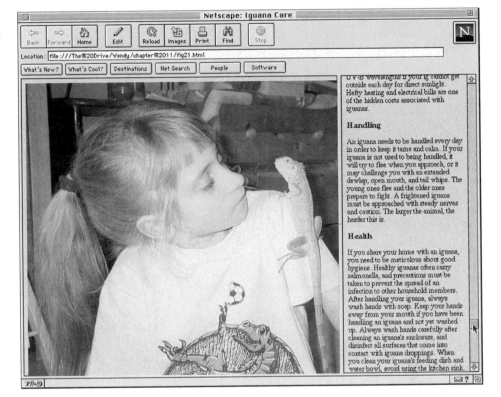

Some browsers, such as Lynx, don't support frames, and some people don't like frames even if their browsers do support them. Frames make it difficult for other Web page authors to create their own links to your Web pages, so if you want to encourage pointers to your site, think twice about using frames. Sites with a lot of dynamic information that changes every day (for example, a search engine) are better suited for frames than are sites with relatively stable information. It is easier and safer for a Web site author to edit one frame that requires frequent updates than it is to dive into a large complicated Web page in order to update different parts of that page as needed. Frames allow an author to break a Web page display up into separate modules. Then some modules can be updated regularly while others are relatively constant. Modular designs are especially valuable when a large site is maintained by more than one person: different people can concentrate on their own separate modules and not step on each others' toes when modules require updates or revisions.

If you do decide to use frames, consider placing a link on each page that will let a visitor exit the FRAMESET page and view just one HTML file directly. This will take some work, as you'll have to learn JavaScript (see Chapter 5). However, it is a good way to give your visitors the best of both worlds (frames versus no frames).

4.8   A WEB SITE CONSTRUCTION CHECKLIST

Now that you've been exposed to some of the details of HTML, step back and consider the big picture. A good Web page author must try to anticipate the needs and interests of a page's visitors as much as possible. It is easy to forget this when you're first learning HTML and are preoccupied with the practical aspects of Web page construction. Read this section now to familiarize yourself with the big picture issues. Then review it as you gain experience and begin to feel at home with Web page design.

4.8.1 The Three C's of Web Page Design

While developing your Web pages, always remember the three C's of Web page design:

- Quality *content*
- Reader *convenience*
- Artistic *composition*

Most important, be sure that you have quality content. Check your facts, cite sources when appropriate, and produce a credible document. Next, consider potential visitors. Construct your Web pages with their convenience in mind. Make it easy for them to find things, move around, and view the page as you intend it to be viewed. And keep download times to a minimum. Then, and only then, should you concentrate on artistic composition. The look and feel of your Web page will be appreciated only if the first two concerns are adequately met. Beginning Web page authors often are so enamored with the fun of digital graphics that they forget about content and convenience. It's fine to have fun, but be sure that the cosmetics aren't getting more of your attention than the content.

The following sections review some of the important points to keep in mind when designing Web pages.

4.8.2 Avoid Common Mistakes

If you spend much time on the Web, you've probably seen pages that are exemplary, as well as some that are frustrating or disappointing in some way. When you create your own pages, try to avoid the mistakes that others have made while building on the styles and organizational layouts of pages that you admire.

Hypertext should be readable as normal text and subject to all of the usual rules of good writing. In addition, links should be self-explanatory so that visitors can quickly decide which to visit.

Keep the text as concise as possible to minimize scrolling. Sometimes, it is a good idea to limit each topic to a short page that can be viewed in its entirety without any scrolling. A richly linked collection of many short pages loses the linear organization of a traditional text, but it is convenient for someone who is browsing. Your visitors control the content of a hypertext document by choosing to traverse some links but not others. An effective Web page author will create pages that read well no matter which pathways are followed.

Web page authors have less control over their creations than do authors of traditional text because visitors can move through a Web page in many ways. Well-written pages will encourage this and ensure that each pathway through a Web site remains coherent.

4.8.3 Check Pages before Installing Them

All Web pages should be written, viewed, and tested before being installed on a Web server. You can develop your Web pages on any convenient computer platform (for example, a home personal computer). After you've uploaded your pages to a Web server, check them one last time. Don't experiment with Web page development on a public server; keep your Web page experiments to yourself.

If you're serious about designing robust Web pages that will look the way that you want them to, you must install more than one Web browser on the machine on which you develop the pages. Viewing your pages with different browsers will give you a good idea about the features that are industry standards and the features that are browser-specific. If half of the population is using MSIE and you're checking your pages with Navigator only, your pages might look horrible to half of the people who access them.

A Web author's life would be easier if everyone used the same browser. A professional Web page designer checks each page on perhaps half a dozen different browsers to ensure that the page will display properly in each case. The relatively large number of browsers available to Web users creates a lot of work for serious Web page designers. You should, at least, use the two most currently popular browsers (Navigator and MSIE) to check your pages before posting them.

Remember, too, that there will always be a sizable percentage of the Internet population using a text-based browser, so it is also important to check your pages using Lynx on a UNIX platform.

4.8.4 Use Effective Web Page Titles

Keep your Web page titles short but accurate and descriptive. Search engines treat titles with more weight than they do other text elements. By selecting your titles carefully, you can enhance the visibility of your work to Web search engines and ensure that your titles appear prominently in a list of search engine hits. Web page titles also appear in bookmark files when someone saves a bookmark for your page. So, pick a title that will identify it easily in a list of bookmarks.

4.8.5 Keep Download Times Short

Before adding graphics to a Web page, always think about the download times that they involve. Visitors accessing the site through a modem might be downloading your page at a rate of only 1K to 2K per second. When conditions are unfavorable, that rate can drop to as low as 100 Bps. If you're working on an Ethernet or other fast connection to the Internet, be sure to remember all the people who connect with modems over telephone lines. People using telephone lines can't see Web pages as quickly as you can, and slow Web pages don't win friends. Avoid large graphics at the top of your main page; visitors will be forced to wait while that image downloads. Use the techniques in the Above and Beyond section to accommodate people who have slower Internet access.

4.8.6 Make Your Pages Portable

For your own convenience, always create links with *portability* in mind. For example, if you're developing pages on a Mac, the Mac, which is case-insensitive, will forgive you for typing a filename in lowercase when you really meant uppercase. However, if you move your Web pages to a UNIX host, where case sensitivity rules, those filenames will generate unknown file errors. Always enter filenames with care, and don't let a platform-specific convenience lull you into a false sense of security. You can save yourself a lot of aggravation by simply avoiding all uppercase characters in your directory names and filenames.

If you create subdirectories of Web pages, plan to use the same directory structure on your Web page server, with the same directory names and filenames. Remember, relative URLs are always better than absolute URLs for portability purposes, so never use an absolute URL unless you're connecting to an external host. For your own pages, use relative URLs and keep your directory structure stable if you're storing Web pages in multiple file directories.

4.8.7 Choose between State-of-the-Art or Maximal Access

If you're determined to learn as much about Web design as you can, you'll inevitably be tempted to use sophisticated graphics, audio, and maybe even video clips. Remember that the most sophisticated Web page displays are also the most computationally intensive. Anyone operating an older computer with limited memory and a slow telephone line is going to give up on a page designed for state-of-the-art machines. If you create computationally expensive pages, don't expect everyone to see them.

4.9   INSTALLING WEB PAGES ON A WEB SERVER

Once your Web pages are ready for public access, you are ready to install them on a Web server. This often causes beginners some difficulties. There are many ways to install (sometimes called *publish*) a Web page on a Web server, but all require some crucial information that is specific to your particular Web server and your personal computer account on that server. This section describes the general steps needed to upload files to a Web server, but we cannot tell you everything you need to know. You will need to check with your local ISP's customer support resources, your school's help desk, your instructor, or your all-knowing roommate in order to fill in the missing details.

To make your pages visible to people, you must install your HTML files on a Web server. Some commercial sites offer free Web space (usually 10MB) where you can post your pages, for example Yahoo's Geocities, Netscape's NetCenter, and Xoom.com. You need only register at the site and be willing to have a commercial banner ad to appear in the browser window each time that someone visits your site. If you pay for your Web server access by subscribing to a commercial ISP, you can publish Web pages without the ads.

To install your pages on a server, you need to upload (copy) your files onto the server and make sure that they go to the right place on the server. Some people run into trouble because they have the name of their Web server but are not clear about where their Web pages have to go on the server. This typically results in a failure to gain access to the server. Locations for files on Web servers are specified by directory paths. However, there can be more than one directory path. The path you see in a URL may not be the path that you need to use when you upload your files to the server. This can be a cause of much confusion.

Once you've uploaded your pages to the server, you are almost home free. However, there are still some snags that can get you. First, you need to know the URL that will allow you to view your pages with a Web browser. If you don't know that URL, you won't be able to tell people how to get to your site. Second, if your pages are on the server but the general public can't see them you might need to fuss with file protection codes on the Web server. This should never occur on a commercial site, but it can in educational environments where the computer administrators might not be bending over backwards to make your online activities as easy as possible (what did you expect for $20 a semester?).

4.9.1 Six Steps to Publish a Web Page

Here is a summary of the six steps to publish a Web page.

1. Acquire access to a Web server.

   This must be done before you can do anything else. You need to know your userid and password for your personal account on the Web server.

2. Find out the DNS address of your Web server.

You might be able to find your Web server's DNS address in online documentation for your computer account. Look for a *Frequently Asked Questions* document. This address might have either prefix: `ftp://` or `http://`. These represent the two different protocols that Web servers might support. If you can't find the DNS address in online documentation, visit the Help Desk for your computer account: they will be able to tell you the correct host name for your Web server.

Warning: You probably won't be able to guess the DNS address that you need. It might be the same www-address that appears in URL addresses for the server, or it might be something different. Chances are, it is something different.

3. Find out the pathname that is needed when you upload files to the server.

This step is very similar to Step 2. You may be able to find this information online, or you may need to ask the Help Desk staff.

Warning: Don't try to guess at this directory path. It is probably not the same directory path that appears in the URL for your home page.

4. Upload your Web files to the Web server.

Do this using an FTP client or a Web page construction tool such as Navigator's Composer. As long as you have the correct information from Steps 2 and 3, you should be able to complete this step. This step is discussed in more detail in Section 4.9.2.

5. Find out the URL to use to view your home page.

While working on Steps 2 and 3, ask about this URL. Anyone who knows the answer to the first two questions should be able to answer this one.

6. Fix any file protection codes that need fixing (with luck you won't need to do this).

This step applies only if you've successfully completed Steps 1 through 5 and you still cannot view your home page on the Web server. If you visit your page and the browser displays an error message that says you are not authorized to view the page (it may say something about access permission), then you need to adjust some settings on the Web server that control which files can be viewed by the public and which cannot. If you visit your page and the browser returns a 404-Not Found error message, then your Web page has not been installed correctly. To fix this problem, you'll need to repeat one of the earlier steps.

4.9.2 Uploading Your Pages

If you are using an HTML construction kit, check to see whether it has a publishing feature (conduct a search with the keyword "publish" in the online documentation). If it has one, you will be able to upload your pages using that. If you are not using a construction kit, you can upload files with either Netscape Communicator or Internet Explorer (see the tip box "How Do I Upload Files with My Browser?" in

Section 8.7 for more details). You can also upload files with an FTP client (see Sections 8.7 and 9.9). In this section, the process of uploading your pages is illustrated by using Netscape Communicator's Composer (a simple HTML construction kit); other software will operate similarly.

The Web page construction tool in Communicator is called the Composer, which is launched from the Communicator menu. Even if you created your Web pages without using Composer, you can use Composer to upload them to a Web server. Follow these steps:

1. From the File menu, select Open Page and then use the directory dialog box to locate an HTML file that you are ready to upload.
2. From the File menu, select Publish. Figure 4.37 shows the window that pops up at this time.
3. Complete all of the fields in the pop-up window.

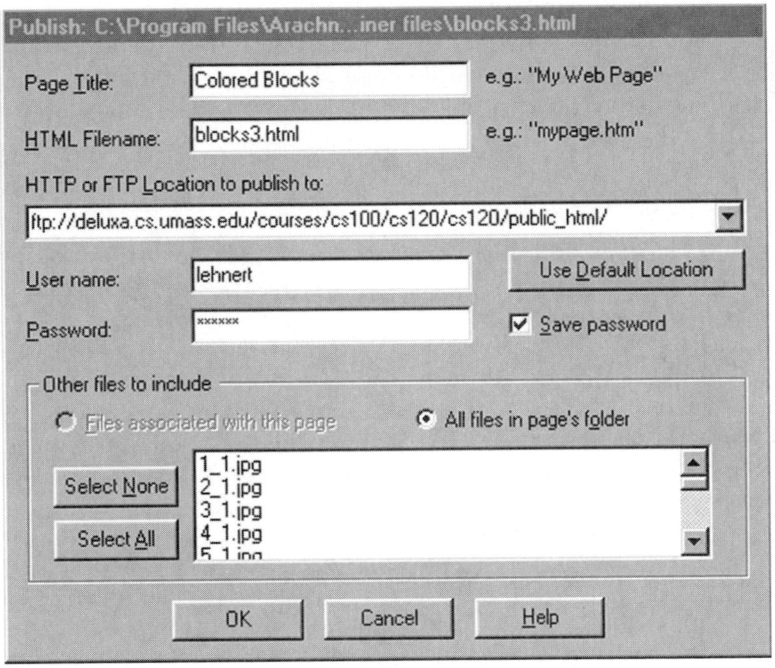

Figure 4.37:
Publishing Web Pages with Netscape's Composer

If you opened a Web page before you reached this pop-up window, the first two fields in Step 3 will be filled in for you automatically. In the third field, "HTTP or FTP Location to publish to," enter the DNS address (from Step #2) and the directory path (from Step #3). You will probably need to prefix the DNS address with `ftp://` as shown in Figure 4.37. In some cases, you can use the `http://` prefix. If one doesn't work, try the other. Once you've entered this information, it becomes a default; Composer will fill it in for you automatically next time you need to upload more Web pages. In the next two fields, your userid and password are those for your account on the Web server (from Step #1). Check the "Save password" checkbox so that these entries will be saved for you.

The Composer has a convenient feature that makes it easy to upload groups of related Web pages all at once. If there are other files in the same subdirectory as the current page, you can load all of them along with the open file. Therefore if your whole Web site is in one subdirectory, you can upload the entire site by clicking the radio button "All files in page's folder" and then clicking OK. Alternatively, you might opt for just the files that are referenced by the current page via links on the current page. In any case, it is not necessary to upload one file at a time (which becomes tedious if you have more than one or two HTML files to upload).

File Uploads Cannot Be Undone

If your directory on the Web server already contains a file with the same filename as one of the files that you are uploading, the file being uploaded *will overwrite* the file on the server. You will not see any warnings, and you will not be asked if you want to overwrite the file. It will just happen. Once the original file has been overwritten, you won't be able to recover it if you decide you've made a mistake. Once you upload a file and overwrite an existing file, you can't undo the file upload.

If you have an FTP client, for example WS_FTP for Windows or Fetch for the Mac, then you can upload your files to a Web server by using that client. You will need the same information discussed in the previous Steps 1–3, but you will be able to path your way into the correct Web page directory by clicking each subdirectory along the way. This might seem easier than typing in the complete path as shown in Figure 4.37. However, it also might be slower if any of the intermediate subdirectories contain a thousand or more directory entries (this can happen on some large Web servers that have many user accounts). Either way, you can connect to the server and upload your files.

Text, Binary, or Automated?

Some FTP clients have a setting that you need to check before each upload command. You might need to tell your FTP client the type of file being uploaded: text or binary. Or, your client might offer an automated setting that, when checked, instructs the client to figure this out based on the file extension. If you have an automated option, take it.

All FTP clients can recognize the most common file types used for Web pages. If you have to select this setting yourself, separate your text files (.htm and .html) from your binary files (.jpg and .gif) and move them into different upload groups. If you pick the wrong setting for a file, the file will be transferred to the server and no warning or error message will be seen. However, the resulting file will probably be mangled and unusable. If any of your file transfers fail to produce healthy copies of your original files, try the transfer again, paying attention to any file type settings that you might need to reset.

If you do end up with an access permission error after you've uploaded your Web pages, contact your system administrator for assistance. You can fix it yourself, but you will need a working knowledge of UNIX protection codes; most people don't want to be bothered with this. Most Web servers available for general use are programmed to save authors from having to make these protection adjustments. With a little luck, you will never have to deal with Step 6.

4.10 ▌ COPYRIGHT LAW AND THE WEB

Copyright laws protect the creative and economic interests of writers, musicians, and artists. In a free society, creative works should be freely distributed, although with some restrictions. However, no one should be allowed to steal a creative work, either by taking credit for its creation or by receiving any revenue from its sale or use.

If you've created a work and would like to distribute it over the Internet, you need to learn more about copyright law than this book can teach you. To maximize your legal protection, consult a legal advisor. Before you post anything, be sure that you understand the consequences of placing your work online. For example, if you intend to publish a written work, you should know that some print publishers won't publish a work if it has been distributed digitally. Once you've made something available online, you can't take it back.

Chances are, you aren't worried about a work of your own creation. Rather, you want to know what you can and can't do with all of the text and graphics online. Web browsers have made it easy to create personal copies of files no matter where they are located. However, you need to know the restrictions that apply to the legal use of those files, specifically the answers to the following most commonly asked questions.

- Can I incorporate files found elsewhere into my own Web pages?
- Can I alter files and make those altered files available online?
- Can I excerpt material and distribute that excerpt online?
- Can I print copies of online materials?
- Can I store on my personal computer files that I find elsewhere?
- Do I have a right to download a Web page and mail a print copy of it to a friend?

Popular software makes doing all of these things so easy that you might have assumed that to do so is legal. However, are these actions legal? Later sections answer each of these questions in detail. First, however, the next section discusses the general concept of copyright.

4.10.1 Copyright Basics

The foundation for copyright and patent law is in the U.S. Constitution (Article I, Section 8, Clause 8):

> The Congress shall have Power . . . To promote the Progress of Science and useful Arts, by securing for limited Times to Authors and Inventors the exclusive Right to their respective Writing and Discoveries.

A copyright confers certain rights and privileges to its owner. Copyrights are normally granted to the author of a written work or to an artist, musician, or other person who creates some intellectual product. These rights can be transferred to another individual or company via a written contract. For example, the author of a book typically transfers his or her copyright to a book publisher in exchange for a publishing contract. Sometimes, copyright privileges are automatically granted to an individual's employer when a work has been generated as part of the person's job.

A copyright protects not only the creator's economic interests but also the integrity of a work. It does so by authenticating its originality. No one can copyright a work that has prior copyright protection. However, someone might challenge the validity of an original copyright if that person can prove that a work was stolen, plagiarized, or adopted from an existing work and modified in minor ways (an argument most often applied to musical creations). Authors normally want to gain widespread readership, but they also want recognition for their work, as well as compensation for the sale of books, magazine articles, and other print distributions of the work.

Copyright laws convey to the copyright owner certain **intellectual property rights**— a broader category of legal protections that include the protection of patents and of trademarks. A copyright normally protects a written document, whereas a patent protects an artifact (invention). Copyrights are automatically associated with all written documents that contain original material, whereas obtaining a patent requires a complicated legal procedure.

The following subsections discuss common questions about copyrights.

Can I Go to Jail for Violating a Copyright?   Yes, but such punishment is unusual. Most copyright violations are treated as civil offenses rather than criminal offenses. In a civil court, you can be sued for damages but can't be sent to jail. Some *criminal* copyright penalties include both large fines and jail terms, but only the federal government can instigate a criminal copyright action. The next time that you play a rented videotape, read the FBI warning at the beginning of the tape for a description of criminal copyright violations.

If I Don't Make Money from a Copyright Violation, Can I Still Be Sued for Damages?
Yes. If you distribute a document online, you might undermine the potential for a profitable print distribution, which could be assessed in terms of lost income to the copyright owner. The fact that you didn't profit yourself is irrelevant.

4.10.2 What Is Protected

The following subsections cover briefly what is protected by copyright laws.

Does an Author Renounce Copyright Privileges When a Work Appears Online? No. An author can relinquish copyright privileges only by putting a work in the public domain or transferring copyright privileges to another party. For a work to be placed in the public domain, the author must include a statement that says, in effect, "I grant this to the public domain." An author can transfer copyright privileges to a third party only by contract. Copyright privileges are not surrendered in the absence of such a contract.

Are All Web Pages in the Public Domain? No. Web pages are all copyrighted and subject to copyright restrictions, unless the Web page author expressly places them in the public domain.

Are All Older Written Works in the Public Domain? How Can I Tell Whether Something Is in the Public Domain? An author is allowed to maintain copyrights on his or her works for his or her lifetime. After the death of an author, the author's heirs or publisher may renew the copyrights for another 70 years. If an author has been dead for 70 years, any materials by that author are considered to be in the public domain.

If something is in the public domain, it might be distributed freely in both electronic and print form. However, it is dangerous to assume that a work is in the public domain simply because it is popular or ubiquitous. For example, the song "Happy Birthday" is not in the public domain.

Does an Author Have to Mark a Document with a Copyright Notice For It to Be Protected? No. An explicit copyright declaration used to be required in the United States. Then the law was changed so that works created after April 1, 1989 are copyrighted and protected regardless of whether they contain a copyright notice. If you see a document that has no copyright notice, you should always assume that copyright protections apply.

Can an Author License Specific Rights to the General Public by Including a Statement Describing the Rights and Privileges Being Granted? Yes. For example, a Web page might include a statement like the following:

> Permission is granted to freely copy (unmodified) this document in electronic form or in print as long as you're not selling it. On the WWW, however, you must link here rather than put it on your own page.

Such a statement effectively allows anyone to reproduce and post an exact copy of the document online in almost any fashion. However, mirrored Web pages are explicitly prohibited.

Another commonly encountered copyright provision reads as follows:

> This work may be redistributed freely, in whole or in part, but cannot be sold or used for profit or as part of a product or service that is sold for profit.

If no such statement is included, you must assume that no such privileges apply. When a copyright provision allows for redistribution without permission, you still must identify the author, source, and publisher (if there is one) in all distributions of the original work.

4.10.3 Personal Use of Online Materials

The following subsections cover briefly what constitutes allowable personal use of online materials.

Can I Print Copies of Online Materials?   If you print one copy for your own personal use, there is no problem. If you want to print copies for friends and the material does not contain an explicit statement about allowable distributions, you should obtain permission from the author or whoever owns the copyright.

Can I Store on My Own Personal Computer Any Files That I Find Elsewhere?   Yes, provided that you don't distribute those files to others or make them publicly available. Keep in mind that the author of the work no longer controls the copy. If you want to reference the file or quote from it later, you should locate a current version, in case the author has changed it.

Can I Download a Web Page and Mail a Print Copy of It to a Friend?   This is duplication and distribution. If the Web page doesn't explicitly grant you permission to distribute it freely, you need permission from the author. In the case of a Web page, it is easier to send your friend the URL in an e-mail message. This is the correct way to share Web pages without violating the rights of Web page authors.

4.10.4 Publishing on the Web

The following subsections briefly cover questions concerning what you are allowed to do on your Web pages regarding copyright works.

If a Photograph or Cartoon Has Been Published in a Newspaper or Magazine, Can I Scan It and Put It Online?   No, not unless you track down the owner of the copyright and secure written permission to do so. The copyright owner might be the photographer or artist, a wire service (in the case of a photograph), or the publication in which the work appeared.

Photographs and drawings are protected by default copyright restrictions, like written text is. For example, Playboy Enterprises sued the Event Horizons BBS for distributing unauthorized digital copies of Playboy photographs. It received $500,000 in a settlement. Photographs and artwork often have greater revenue potential than do text documents and must therefore be handled with extreme caution.

Can I Incorporate Files Found Elsewhere on My Own Web Pages? Yes, as long as you observe some restrictions. Most important, you must not make a copy of someone else's Web page and then create a link to that copy. To reference another Web page, create a pointer to the original page. In that way, the author of the page retains control over the material. If the author wants to update, correct, or modify it in any way, you will automatically benefit from those efforts. If the author removes a page from public distribution, your pointer will become obsolete, but removing the page is the author's prerogative.

If you find some graphics on someone else's Web page and want to incorporate them into one of your own Web pages, similar restrictions apply. Because graphics files are commonly copied and redistributed across the Web without proper copyright permissions, there is an excellent chance that any graphic that you find on someone else's Web page has already been pirated and is being used illegally. This is especially true of professional photographs. A responsible Web page author will attempt to locate the rightful owner of any image and secure permission to use it. The owner of the image might want to control the context surrounding the image (for example, any captions under the image) and might therefore refuse permission or reserve the right to withdraw permission, depending on the use of the image. No fair use guidelines apply to images (see Section 4.10.5 for more information about fair use guidelines).

It may occur to you that you can add a graphical image from someone else's Web site by simply referencing the address of the image on the other site's Web server. This practice is known as "deep linking" and it has led to a number of lawsuits. The legal status of deep linking looks unfavorable—one judge has ruled it a "contributory infringement." In any case, the practice is highly controversial and should be avoided.

Some Web page authors ask that you reference their pages at some "top-level" entry point. They don't want you to set up a link to a secondary page if that page wasn't designed to be a self-contained, stand-alone page. When an author explicitly makes such a request, you should respect it. There are also practical reasons for linking to top-level entry points for large Web sites. Webmasters who maintain large Web sites occasionally rearrange its pages and rename its files. If you reference a secondary page directly, your link might become obsolete when the Webmaster reorganizes the files for that site. If you reference the main entry to a Web site and identify the links needed to get to a secondary page, your citation is more likely to require fewer updates.

Keeping Web page pointers current and operational is one of the overhead costs associated with Web page design and maintenance. Anything that you can do to avoid obsolete pointers will be greatly appreciated by your visitors.

Can I Alter Files and Make Those Altered Files Available Online?   When you alter a document that isn't yours, you must be extremely careful to acknowledge the extent of your alterations and the source of the original document. Some authors suggest that the altered file be identified as a "heavily edited modification of an original source document by so-and-so, which can be found at such-and-such a location."

If you alter someone else's file and present it as your own, you might or might not be violating copyright laws, depending on how much original material survives verbatim. However, you are probably guilty of plagiarism. Recall that plagiarism occurs when you adopt the substance of someone else's work, rewrite it in your own words, and fail to give proper credit to the original source. If you present the substance of someone else's words, be sure to identify and acknowledge the original source. In an academic environment, plagiarism is a form of academic dishonesty and grounds for serious disciplinary action.

An Exception to the Rule   There is one notable exception to this general document modification scenario. If you download the HTML version of a Web page because you like the format of the page, you may retain all of the HTML commands and substitute your own content into the HTML framework, without permission or acknowledgments. The "look and feel" of a computer screen is not protected by copyright or patent and can be freely duplicated without permission. As long as you substitute your own content, you're not violating any copyright restrictions and you're not plagiarizing any material. Indeed, this is an easy way to create a sophisticated Web page, as well as an honorable way to learn HTML.

Copyright Violations Are So Common on the Internet That No One Can Keep Track of Them. What Difference Will It Make If I Add One More Violation?   Even if you aren't sued for a copyright infringement, your actions can affect other people and might result in a loss of online resources. For example, there used to be a Dave Barry mailing list on which columns by humorist Dave Barry were posted each morning. Mr. Barry's publisher asked everyone to respect the copyright of those columns by not redistributing the columns. The Dave Barry mailing list worked for a while, until someone chose to ignore the restriction and one of the columns showed up on another mailing list. Upon finding out that the copyright restriction had been violated, the publisher shut down the mailing list. The publisher didn't sue the individual responsible for the copyright violation, but shutting down the mailing list denied thousands of people the enjoyment of reading Dave Barry online. The actions of one thoughtless individual affected thousands of other people. Old Dave Barry columns can be found online in some Web archives, but no one can any longer read new Dave Barry columns via e-mail.

4.10.5 Fair Use Guidelines

The following subsections cover briefly what is covered by fair use guidelines.

Can I Freely Distribute an Excerpt from a Larger Document Provided That I Identify It and Acknowledge the Source?   This is normally okay as long as you conform to the doctrine of fair use. The **doctrine of fair use** allows writers and scholars to refer to other works by quoting excerpts from those works. This is typically done to argue a point, to present evidence, or for the sake of illustration.

What Does the Doctrine of Fair Use Require? To quote from a copyrighted work, you must follow certain rules of thumb. Note, however, that you might see various differing guidelines for fair use. This is because there are no absolute legal guidelines, only conventions. Widely accepted conventions are safe to use, but be prepared to be flexible if people object to your use of their materials. In this spirit, following are some rules of thumb that you can use when you are working with published text.

- You may quote 300 words from a book or 150 words from a magazine or newspaper article as long as you observe the following guidelines:

   The excerpt is not a complete unit in the larger work (for example, a complete poem, a complete article, or a complete list of rules from a manual).

   The excerpt comprises less than 20% of the original work.

   The excerpt is integrated into your own writing and does not stand alone as a self-contained section or chapter opening.

   You give full credit to the author, source, and publisher.

- If you excerpt a series of quotations from a single work, the total sum of those word counts should not exceed 300 words from a book or 150 words from a magazine or newspaper article.

- If you want to quote a personal e-mail message, a Web page, or an unpublished document, you first must obtain permission from the author to do so.

When fair use guidelines do not apply, copyright permission must be secured for exact quotations from the works of others. Note that *ideas* cannot be copyrighted; it is the specific arrangement of words used to express an idea that is the object of copyright protections. You are always free to summarize or restate the content of any work in your own writings. However, a summation of someone else's work without proper acknowledgment is plagiarism. Always acknowledge a source if you are drawing detailed information from that source.

If an explicit statement prohibits the distribution of an excerpt that normally would be justified under the fair use doctrine, the doctrine can't be applied. For example, suppose that the following prohibition appears in an online document:

> No part of this electronic publication might be reproduced or retransmitted without the prior written permission of the publisher.

In this case, no excerpts can be reproduced without prior consent.

Alternatively, suppose that someone distributes a document that contains the notation "Do Not Quote." If you see that annotation, you can't distribute any excerpts. Explicit restrictions always override default conventions.

I'm Teaching a Class and want to Distribute Print Copies of an Online Document to My Students. Is This Protected by the Fair Use Doctrine?   The fair use doctrine is commonly invoked by teachers and professors who distribute copies of journal, newspaper, and magazine articles to students in classes as a part of their educational practice. The fact that these activities are nonprofit is commonly thought to protect them under the fair use doctrine. However, some recent court cases associated with the creation of "course packs" by commercial copying services suggest that the application of the fair use doctrine is far from straightforward in these situations.

If you're a teacher, you should investigate these controversies and find out what practices have been adopted by your school. For a timely discussion of this issue, see **"University Copy Centers: Do They Pass The Fair Use Test?"**. If an online document explicitly states that redistribution is permitted, there is no problem with doing so. The question is more problematic for documents that grant no explicit permission, in which case obtaining permission from the author or publisher (who might ask for a royalty) is always prudent.

Can I Excerpt Material and Distribute Those Excerpts Online?   Yes, if you adhere to fair use guidelines. To use more material than can be justified under fair use, you should obtain permission from the author or whoever owns the copyright.

4.10.6 Copyright Law in a Digital Era

When you consider the rights and restrictions that apply to online text, think about how easily a text document can be distributed in digital form. If someone posts a document to a mailing list, it might be accessible through an archive for years to come. Copies of it might be mirrored at countless Web sites and redistributed repeatedly via e-mail. If the original author wants to correct an error in the original document or revise it with important updates, recalling all of the copies of the original version will be impossible. The author no longer controls the document in the same way that a publisher can control print editions of a book.

Everyone benefits when authors retain maximal control over the digital distribution of their documents. This is the only way to minimize the propagation of misinformation or outdated information. In addition, it gives everyone access to the best-quality information online. In the interest of effective online communication, you must be sensitive to the rights of authors, no matter where a document was originally posted or how limited the potential scope of the document might be. With 150 million people online, it's impossible for anyone to predict the digital trajectory of an online document.

The body of law that establishes precedents for copyright law is always challenged when new technologies emerge. Important precedents are being established on the issue of data collections. For example, can the contents of a database be copyrighted? Can someone own the data that describes the human genome? Can someone own the DNA sequences associated with a specific gene? As soon as a technology makes it possible to ask a thorny question about new forms of intellectual property, court cases require judges and juries to attempt to sort out relevant precedents.

For example, in 1991 the U.S. Supreme Court decided that no one can copyright the information contained in a telephone directory's white pages (*Feist* v. *Rural Telephone*). According to the court, no copyright can be granted for a compilation of facts unless the compilation entails some original "selection, coordination, or arrangement" of those facts. Some databases are compiled at great expense and represent an investment that could give a company a clear commercial advantage. Exactly when do the criteria of "selection, coordination, or arrangement" apply? These legal questions are largely untested, but databases are key components of many online resources. Thus it is reasonable to assume that copyright protections apply to subject trees, clearinghouses, and file archives.

In 1993, the Clinton Administration created its Working Group on Intellectual Property Rights as part of the Information Infrastructure Task Force. Its purpose was to resolve concerns about intellectual property and the digital distribution of text, images, video recordings, and audio recordings. A proposal advocating a revision of copyright law was released in 1994, but it has met substantial resistance because it would interfere with free and open communication among the scientists and educators for whom the Internet was originally designed. As in many endeavors, there is tremendous tension between advocates for commercial profit and legislative policies designed to protect the public good.

In October 1998, the On-Line Copyright Infringement Liability Limitation Act was signed into law in an effort to strengthen intellectual property rights on the Web. This new law protects an ISP from liability for copyright infringements on the ISP's Web servers, as long as the ISP has no prior knowledge of the infringement. However, once the matter is brought to its attention (for example, if a copyright owner complains to the ISP), then the ISP must disable online access to the material in question. This means that you must use with care the clip art and the fonts that you place on your Web pages. If you're not authorized to redistribute them, your Web pages could be yanked from their server. It's too early to say what the impact of this new law will be on the Web and the ISPs who must now respond to all copyright infringement complaints. However, clearly we are past the point of "anything goes" with respect to copyright infringement on the Web.

In a digital environment, questions of ownership and control need to be carefully reexamined. When text was restricted to physical print, controlling distribution of that text was relatively easy. The advent of copying machines eroded that control and forced people to rely to a greater extent on voluntary compliance with copyright laws. Now the rapidly growing body of digital text has upset the balance yet again, forcing people to assume even greater responsibility for voluntary compliance with existing laws. During periods of swift technological change, everyone needs to stay abreast of major court decisions, new legislation, and public policy debates. These are the forces that shape new behavioral codes and social responsibilities in our increasingly technological society.

Things to Remember

- An HTML editor saves you time if you need to create many Web pages.
- You can learn HTML by examining the HTML (source) files of pages already on the Web.
- Different Web browsers can display the same Web page differently.
- Keep your image files small (30K–40K) for faster downloads.
- Use graphical elements with restraint.
- Remember that Lynx users can't see graphics or table layouts.
- Check to see that your pages look good in different-sized browser windows.
- Check all hyperlinks on your pages to make sure that they work correctly.
- Do not violate copyright laws when you add materials to your Web site.

Important Concepts

absolute URL—a hyperlink to a Web page on a different Web server.

copyright restriction—a prohibition on the duplication and distribution of intellectual property.

GIF file—an image file in a format especially well suited for line art.

Hypertext Markup Language (HTML)—the markup language used to format Web pages.

HTML tag—a marker within an HTML file that delimits an individual HTML element.

HTML tag attribute—a variable within an HTML element.

HTML source file—the text file downloaded by a Web browser and used to display a Web page.

hyperlink (link)—a clickable element on a Web page.

inline image—an image positioned inside of a text file as if it were a single, oversized character.

JPEG file—an image file in a format especially well suited for photographs.

named anchor—a hyperlink to another location on the current Web page.

relative URL—a hyperlink to a Web page on the same Web server.

Where Can I Learn More?

Learning HTML by Example `http://www.ida.net/users/pbmck/learn/00conten.htm`

HTML 4.0 Reference `http://www.htmlhelp.com/reference/html40/`

Web Monkey `http://hotwired.lycos.com/webmonkey/`

Devs.com HTML Design 1 `http://www.devs.com/zresources/`
`html.html`

Problems and Exercises

1. Which two file extensions signal a Web browser that a file is a Web page file?

2. What four HTML elements should be present in any Web page file?

3. Explain why you should always include `HEIGHT` and `WIDTH` attributes for an image file even if you don't need to scale the original image.

4. Describe in detail a Web page layout that uses a table in which the table's `WIDTH` attribute should take a percentage value. Describe in detail a layout in which that attribute should take a constant (pixel) value?

5. What HTML tag reproduces text exactly as it is typed, preserving all whitespaces and blank lines?

6. When does a Web page not need a `BODY` element?

7. Why do some people dislike frames?

8. Explain the difference between a 404-Not Found error and an access denied error.

9. **[Find It Online]** HTML contains some special characters that are often useful when the character you want to print is ignored (as with whitespace) or interpreted as part of HTML (as with left and right angle brackets). Search some online HTML documentation, and find out how to make a Web page display the following line (exactly, with all of the HTML tags showing) *without* using a `PRE` or `CODE` tag:

   `<HEAD><TITLE>My First Web Page</TITLE></HEAD>`

   Create an HTML file, and check your solution by viewing it with a Web browser. Have you been able to recreate the text exactly as it appears above?

10. **[Hands-On]** What happens if you put an `H1` tag inside of a `HEAD` element? What if you put a `TITLE` tag inside of a `BODY` element? Does it matter if you reverse the order of the `HEAD` and the `BODY` elements in an HTML file? (Try it to see for yourself.)

11. **[Hands-On]** View the following HTML with a Web browser, and describe what you see.

    ```
    This is line number 1.
    <P><P><P>
    This is line number 2.
    <P>
    This is line number 3.
    <BR><BR><BR>
    ```

```
This is line number 4.
<P>
This is line number 5
 <P> <P> <P>
This is line number 6.
```

What does this tell you about adding whitespace to your Web pages?

12. **[Hands-On]** Visit a Web page that has images, and download some image files using your browser. Point to the image that you want to keep, click the right mouse button, and click Save Image As from the pop-up menu. If you are using a Mac, hold down the Shift key when you click your mouse in order to see the same pop-up menu.

13. **[Hands-On]** Create a Web page that has images on both sides of the page, with text flowing continuously between the images. Add a sequence of left-justified images with text flowing along the right side of the images and no text or blank lines separating the images along the left side of the page.

14. **[Hands-On]** What happens if you reverse the `HEIGHT` and `WIDTH` attributes of an image on a Web page? (Try it to see for yourself.)

15. **[Hands-On]** If you have a graphics tool (the Paint program that comes with Windows will do), create an image file to add a red stripe down the left side of a Web page. Convert your file to a GIF or JPEG format, and add it to a Web page that contains some text. Use a table to create a left margin so that the text does not run into the red stripe.

16. **[Hands-On]** Use a table to create two columns of text on a Web page. Insert a quarter inch of whitespace between the two columns. Make sure that your columns are evenly spaced and will look good if the browser window is resized.

17. **[Hands-On]** Create a Web page that has an image that is perfectly centered against a black background, no matter how the browser window is resized.

18. **[Hands-On]** Create a Web page that has solid bar stripes running down both the left and right sides of the page. Make sure that the borders make appropriate adjustments when the browser window is resized.

19. **[Hands-On]** Reproduce the table layout in Figure 4.29 (you can download images from a copy of **Figure 4.29 on the Web** for this exercise). Nest one table inside of a second table in order to keep the four images grouped in a fixed configuration that stays centered in the browser window, no matter how the window is resized.

20. **[Hands-On]** Upload a Web page file to a Web server using a Web browser or an FTP client. What is the URL for your Web page? Make sure that the page is visible on the Web.

Basic Web Page Construction: Above and Beyond

Graphics and Download Times

If you're going to work with many image files on your Web pages, you should take some time to learn about file compression techniques, image resolution, image sampling, filters, and color palettes. A little knowledge about computer graphics can help you create Web-friendly image files that do not consume too much bandwidth. The good news is that images for the Web do not have to be bandwidth-intensive. Whereas at least 600 dots per inch (dpi) is needed for high-quality printing, anything more than 72 dpi is wasted on a Web page. Most people access the Web with a 56K or slower modem, so image files should be kept as small as possible. A file reduction from 30K to 20K might not seem significant, but if you have ten such images on a Web page, the difference between 300K and 200K will be significant for many visitors.

A Web page does not have to load completely within two seconds, but enough visible material should appear within that time to occupy your visitors while the rest of the page is downloading. If nothing shows up after five seconds, impatient visitors will give up and move on. This means that special attention should be paid to the top of the page to make that part of the page load as quickly as possible. If the page has large image files, try to position them lower on the page so that they can download in the background.

When a page contains both graphics and text, be careful to include `HEIGHT` and `WIDTH` attributes for all of your image files so that the text portions of the page will be visible as fast as possible. Doing this doesn't speed up download times, but it can ameliorate a long wait for the first graphic by giving people something to read while the graphics download. Avoid large files for backgrounds. If you must use one, add a `BGCOLOR` attribute to your `BODY` so that the background color will be visible while the background file is downloading.

Using Thumbnail Previews When you can't avoid a large image file and don't want to burden your visitors with long download times, let each visitor decide whether the wait is worth it. The standard way to do this is to provide a thumbnail preview. A **thumbnail preview** (also called a **thumbnail sketch**) is a smaller version of a graphic that is placed on the page; the larger version is available only on request. Visitors request the larger version by clicking the preview.

It is a good idea to include some instructions that explain this convention because some people are in the habit of clicking everything on a page just to see what happens. If you make the thumbnail's image very small, experienced Web users will probably understand what's going on, but it never hurts to explain. Figure 4.38 illustrates the HTML behind a thumbnail preview.

Figure 4.38:
Making a
Thumbnail Preview

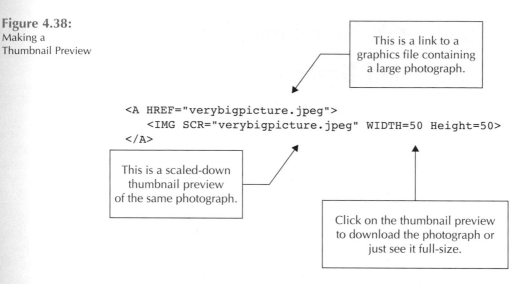

You need to use an image processing application to create a *second* image file for your thumbnail preview. If you simply shrink the original image by using smaller **HEIGHT** and **WIDTH** attributes, visitors will still be downloading the original slow file even as they are viewing a scaled down version of it. This is obviously not the intention. To reduce the size of an image file, use a graphics editor to resize the original image and then resample it. You might also want to apply more compression to your JPEG images. Many applications will give you an opportunity to compress a JPEG file when you save it.

You don't have to use thumbnail previews to give visitors control over large downloads. Any text link can be used to point to a large image. The important point is to isolate the large images from your main Web pages.

Using Interlaced GIFs   Another way to make slow downloads less annoying is to use *interlaced* GIF files. When a GIF file is **interlaced**, the browser displays the file incrementally. The first pass produces a fuzzy version of the image. The next pass looks a bit better, and eventually the complete file is displayed in full detail. The effect is typically achieved by first displaying every tenth line of pixels. On the second pass, every fifth line is shown. On the third pass, every other line is filled in, and on the fourth pass, the complete image is displayed. Incremental graphic displays can be interesting to watch and will pacify all but the most harried Web users.

Any GIF file can be *converted* to an interlaced GIF file, provided that the original file conforms with the GIF89 formatting standard. Many file utilities and GIF converters support an interlaced GIF option (see Figure 4.39). Note that if you use one file utility to interlace a GIF file and another utility to make the GIF transparent, be careful to interlace the image first and then make it transparent. Otherwise, your image might show some gray ghosts on your Web page.

Figure 4.39:
Giffy Creating
Interlaced GIFs by
Using the Program
Giffy

In addition, you can create your own incremental downloads by splitting an image into subsections and reassembling it with a table, as described in Section 4.6.3. This requires an image-splitting utility, but it is easy to do and can result in an interesting download.

Audio Files for the Web

If you are new to the Internet music scene, there's a lot to learn that isn't covered here, including the following:

- How to digitize a track from a CD with a CD ripper (this is legal if you own the CD)
- How to burn your own music CDs (this is legal if you acquire the sound tracks legally)
- How to convert audio files to different formats
- All of the features of an MP3 player
- What to look for in a portable MP3 player

However, there is a wealth of information on the Web about this and more. You can learn everything that you want to know from such sites as mp3.com (look for the Getting Started link) and mp3place.com (check out its guides section).

If you intend to put audio files on the Web, you should probably use the MP3 file format. This is the most popular format for audio files on the Net because of its relatively fast download times. Even so, it takes 20 to 30 minutes to download one popular song via a 56K modem, so MP3 sites with a lot of traffic consume a lot of bandwidth. Once you have an MP3 file in hand (see the Above and Beyond section in Chapter 4 for a discussion of the legalities concerning this), you can add it to your Web page with an A-tag and an **HREF** attribute, just as you would add a relative URL to another HTML file. Here's an example:

```
<A HREF="moo.mp3">Mad Cow Blues</A>
```

The link label appears on the Web page as it would for any hyperlink, so be careful to warn your viewers that if they click the link they will start to download a rather large file. A better hyperlink would be:

```
<A HREF="moo.mp3">Click Here to Download <I>Mad Cow Blues</I>
(3.1MB)</A>
```

After that, it's out of your hands. The file will be either downloaded to disk or opened with an MP3 player, depending on how the receiving host is configured. If the receiving host does not have an MP3 player installed, the user will not be able to hear the file.

Some sites use JavaScript programs to query the local host's browser in order to learn what plug-ins are available. If a browser can't find the one it needs, a notice to the user pops up explaining that a new plug-in is needed. This plug-in notification window is a good exercise in JavaScript programming.

Copyright Guidelines for Multimedia Projects

The doctrine of fair use was originally motivated by a desire to give educators a reasonable amount of flexibility to use copyrighted material in the classroom. Amendments to the Copyright Act of 1976 allow performances and displays of copyrighted materials for educational purposes within the context of the classroom. Therefore a play could be performed in a school auditorium without permission from the copyright holder, but the school could not broadcast that same play over closed-circuit television without permission.

More generally, materials can be copied and distributed for nonprofit purposes without the permission of a copyright owner as long as the copies fall under the provisions of fair use. Although there are guidelines for what constitutes fair use, no laws exist that cover this. As a result, the application of the fair use doctrine is a delicate matter that is periodically tested in the courts. In an effort to steer clear of lawsuits, educators and publishers have developed unofficial guidelines for fair use. The guidelines described in Section 4.10.5 are an example of such unofficial guidelines for the reproduction of text. This section discusses unofficial guidelines for multimedia content (audio clips, video clips, and animated sequences).

Computers and networking technologies have made it easy to distribute multimedia files on the Web. These materials are generally protected by copyright restrictions even if they are unpublished or do not contain a copyright notice. Therefore it is important for Web page authors to understand their liability and responsibilities with respect to multimedia materials. Acts of willful infringement can result in fines of up to $100,000. A person who unknowingly violates a copyright can still be fined as much as $20,000 for each infringement. Universities that supply Internet access to faculty and students can be held liable for copyright infringements on their network facilities, subject to certain limitations (see the Above and Beyond section in Chapter 2).

Although the law is clear about the penalties that apply to copyright violations, very little experience with the concept of fair use is available as it might be applied to multimedia creations. The courts will have to give their interpretation of the doctrine as lawsuits occur. Until then, you need to be aware of and honor the Digital Millennium Copyright Act (see the Above and Beyond section in Chapter 2) and use common sense regarding all intellectual property that does not belong to you.

Students who produce multimedia projects for a course must honor copyright restrictions for all materials that they do not own, although more latitude might apply to course projects as long as they are not performed outside of a classroom setting and cannot be copied. For example, one might assume that the doctrine of fair use allows a student to reproduce a portion of a popular song (legally acquired) within a course project that will be played for the class one time during a class period (with no tape recorders or other recording devices present). However, the student may not distribute copies of a CD that contains that same song excerpt without the explicit permission of the copyright owner. Under no circumstances should an audio file that contains the song excerpt be posted to a public Web server.

In the case of a distance learning course, such a project might be posted to a secure server for restricted (say, password-protected) distribution to all class members, as long as technological safeguards are in place to prevent anyone from copying the project in its entirety. Under no circumstances should such a project be posted to a public Web server, even if access to the project is password-protected, unless additional measures have been taken to prevent copying.

A similar set of restrictions should apply to classroom presentations by faculty. A multimedia lecture that contains materials whose use is justified by the fair use doctrine in the context of a classroom lecture should not be posted on the Web. It may be posted to a restricted access server, but only if steps have been taken to prevent copying.

If available servers do not support special features to prevent copying, password-protected access alone might be deemed acceptable as long as the work is not available on the server for more than 15 days. Limited access, technological safeguards, and time limitations all work to prevent the digital (re)distribution of multimedia materials without permission. These steps are clearly in the spirit of the fair use doctrine, even if the specific details (for example, 15 days) might not stand up in court. Questions of liability in the event of a computer break-in or negligent server security remain to be tested. In the meantime, it should be enough to act in good faith and take reasonable precautions.

In this spirit of good faith, the following section offers some guidelines for portion and aggregate limitations. **Portion limitation** is the amount of a copyrighted work that can be used without permission under the fair use doctrine. **Aggregate limitation** is the total amount of material that is permitted from a single copyrighted work. These limitations should be applied cumulatively over an entire semester or term for each student.

Fair Use Guidelines for Educational Multimedia Projects Be warned, these are only guidelines. The law does not provide hard and fast rules at this level of detail. How the courts will decide future disputes about fair use and multimedia is unknown.

- Video clips

  Up to 10% or three minutes, whichever is less, of a copyrighted video may be reproduced or incorporated as part of a multimedia project.

- Textual material

  General text: Up to 10% or 1,000 words, whichever is less, in the aggregate of a copyrighted work, may be used.

  Poems fewer than 250 words: An entire poem of this length may be reproduced, but no more than three poems by one poet or five poems by different poets from a single anthology may be used.

  Poems greater than 250 words: Excerpts no longer than 250 words may be used, but no more than three excerpts by one poet or five excerpts by different poets from a single anthology may be used.

- Music, lyrics, and music video

  Up to 10%, but no more than 30 seconds, of the music from an individual musical work may be reproduced or incorporated into a multimedia project.

- Illustrations and photographs

  Up to five images by an individual artist or photographer may be reproduced or incorporated into a multimedia project.

In all cases, proper attribution and citations must accompany the inclusion of any work by another author or artist.

Note that these fair use guidelines should be applied only to projects and presentations created for educational purposes. They do not apply to personal multimedia creations that you intend to post on the Web for public distribution. *For general Web site distributions, you should not reproduce any protected illustrations or photographs without permission, and you should not reproduce any portion of a copyrighted video or audio file without permission.*

The application of copyright law to the Internet is a legal quagmire, and many competing special interests are at stake. Ignorance of the law is never a good defense. Nor is the notion of safety in numbers (as in, "Hey, everyone else is doing it."). If you must take risks with copyright law, don't say you weren't warned.

Who Has the Final Word on Fair Use?

The fair use guidelines for general Web pages are conservative and might seem excessively restrictive, since so many Web sites violate them. Why shouldn't people be able to post 10% or 30 seconds (whichever is less) of a song track on the Web? No one should post the entire track, but how much harm is there in posting a short segment?

At some point, a judge will have to decide if a song is more like a magazine article (where portion limitations apply) or more like a photograph (where no portion limitations apply). Until then, no one can specify the correct guidelines with certainty. The U.S. Supreme Court, however, has indicated that an adverse effect on the income potential for a commercial work is the most important factor in determining fair use. So if anything on your Web site might be taking income away from the legitimate owner of a work, think before you post it. To stay on top of the most current court cases and legislation, check out *IP Worldwide: The Magazine for Law and Policy for High Technology*.

HTML Editors and Web Page Construction Tools

HTML editors are easy to use and wonderful time-savers. You can either buy a commercial package or take advantage of some excellent freeware options, such as **Arachnophilia**. Pull-down menus and toolbars give you everything that you need to point-and-click your way to a Web page.

Figure 4.40 shows how Arachnophilia gets you off the ground after you create a new HTML file and enter the title "The Dachshund." The basic HTML template is created automatically and is ready for the addition of more HTML tags and content. In Arachnophilia, a preview button displays your page inside of your favorite Web browser so that you can watch it develop as you go.

Other packages, such as the Composer, give you a *WYSIWYG (what-you-see-is-what-you-get) editor* that allows you to modify a *display version* of your page rather than the underlying HTML file. WYSIWYG editors try to distance Web page authors from the underlying HTML document as much as possible in order to simplify the design process. However, WYSIWYG editors cannot always give you a truly accurate page display (see the Above and Beyond section in Chapter 4), so people who are not afraid to see actual HTML tend to prefer a Preview button to a WYSIWYG editor.

Another good time-saver is the HTML converter. An **HTML converter** takes a text document in a non-HTML format and converts it to an HTML file. For example, Word has an HTML converter that you can use to convert Word documents into HTML files (you invoke the converter by selecting File and then Save As HTML). Whereas an HTML converter is useful for existing documents that were not originally designed as Web pages, you should never use one to build a Web page from scratch. Converters get the job done, but they do not generate good HTML (Word

Figure 4.40:
The Web Page
Editor
Arachnophilia at
Work

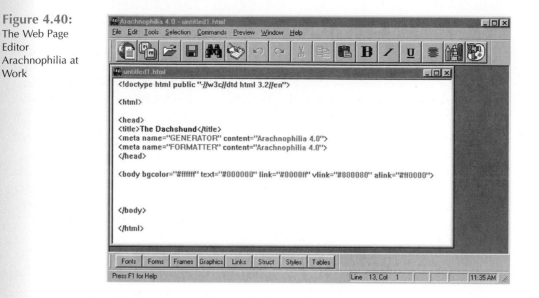

97 generates awful HTML). You still will need to redesign the original document if you want it to look like a real Web page (as opposed to a document that was merely converted from some other format).

In addition to HTML editors and converters, there are a number of graphics tools available to help you create impressive graphics effects, animated images, and dynamic displays that interact with visitors. Chapter 5 explores some of these.

How to Increase Your Web Page Hit Counts

A Web page is *visible* when people can easily find it via search engines, subject trees, clearinghouses, and links on related pages. To make your pages more visible, there are a number of things that you can do, including paying a Web site promotion service to do the same things described in this section.

With so many commercial sites competing for attention, there are plenty of sites and online newsletters that deal with the subject of online visibility. Take advantage of free tips and tools before you consider a commercial service. Then if you do decide to pay for Web site promotion, do your homework and research the available services very carefully. Some of these operations are scams, some are legitimate but no better than what you can do on your own, and some might actually be worth what they charge. Proceed with caution, and read Chapter 10 before you hand over your credit card account number.

If I Build It, Will They Come?

Unfortunately, the answer is no. You need to put some effort into making your site more visible, at least initially, until the forces of natural selection take over and propel you into the big time.

If you care about how many people are visiting your site, the first thing that you need to do is start monitoring your page hits. You won't know if your efforts are paying off if you don't have daily data about the number of hits on your page. Your Web server administrators might already be collecting hit rate statistics for all of the pages on the server or might offer an optional page counter at no charge. Check with your service provider to see if it can help you obtain page hit statistics or a hit counter. If not, you can collect your own data by adding a hit counter supported by an external server. Some good ones are listed at **SiteStruct's Counter/Tracker page.**

Alternatively, go to your favorite search engine and enter the query "hit counters." You'll receive hits on basic, free counters, as well as more-sophisticated fee-based services that compile a variety of statistics. Some services place a visible counter on your page with a link to their home pages, whereas others might require you to display an ad banner. A few offer an "invisible" counter option, if you don't want to display actual hit counts on your Web page.

All counters require you to add a small JavaScript program to the Web page that you want to track. Whenever someone visits your page, the Javascript code executes and sends information to the server that maintains the counter. The counter's server then updates a database for your site and compiles reports that you can view on the Web or receive via e-mail. Figure 4.41 shows a hit count report generated by the Hitmeter counter service.

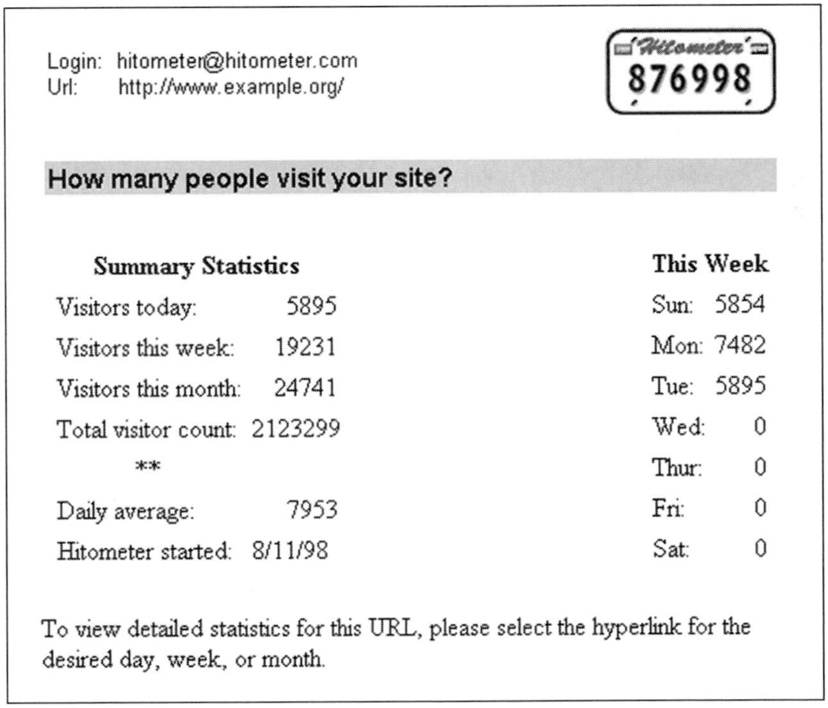

Figure 4.41:
Free Hit Counter Service Offered by Hitmeter

Login: hitometer@hitometer.com
Url: http://www.example.org/

Hitometer
876998

How many people visit your site?

Summary Statistics		This Week	
Visitors today:	5895	Sun:	5854
Visitors this week:	19231	Mon:	7482
Visitors this month:	24741	Tue:	5895
Total visitor count:	2123299	Wed:	0
**		Thur:	0
Daily average:	7953	Fri:	0
Hitometer started:	8/11/98	Sat:	0

To view detailed statistics for this URL, please select the hyperlink for the desired day, week, or month.

Once you have a counter in place, you can prepare your Web pages for maximal visibility to search engines. All HTML files can be tuned for search engines by adding **META** elements. List all of the keywords that should be associated with your page, and add them to your page inside of a **META** tag (see Figure 4.42). It is also important to write your own brief page description, and place it in a **META** tag. Most search engines will display that page description when they generate hit lists that contain your page.

Figure 4.42:
Using META Tags to Enhance Search Engine Visibility

```
<META name="Keywords" content="modem, modems,
connection, connections, troubleshoot, troubleshooting,
performance, telephone, line, lines">

<META name="Description" content="Troubleshoot your
modem connection or maximize your modem's
performance.">
```

Once your pages have been prepped for search engines, you can submit selected URLs to several. Search engines depend primarily on Web spiders (see the Above and Beyond section in Chapter 6) to build their databases. However, they also accept pages when Web authors take the time to submit a form informing the search engine of the pages. If you are satisfied to contact the top 10 or 20 search engines, you can find freeware or Web sites, such as SimpleSubmit, that will submit the necessary forms for you automatically (see Figure 4.43). If you want to contact 1,000 different search engines, you might have to resort to shareware or a commercial Web promotion service.

Don't submit a URL to a search engine unless the page is ready for prime time. If you are planning to rework your site and rename or relocate any files, wait until the site is stable before you contact any search engines.

More Visibility for Less Work

If you are creating a Web site for a small business, it makes sense to set up a hit counter and woo the search engines in a serious Web promotion campaign. However, if your page is purely recreational, you might prefer to reach out in simpler ways. For example, if your page focuses on a particular topic, join a Web ring of related sites. A **Web ring** facilitates browsing by organizing a group of Web sites on the same subject in a linked ring. VIsitors can "walk around the ring" by following the Web ring links to the next site in the ring. You can find thousands of Web rings at **WebRing**, including a ring of 62 sites about Betty Boop and 151 anti-AOL sites.

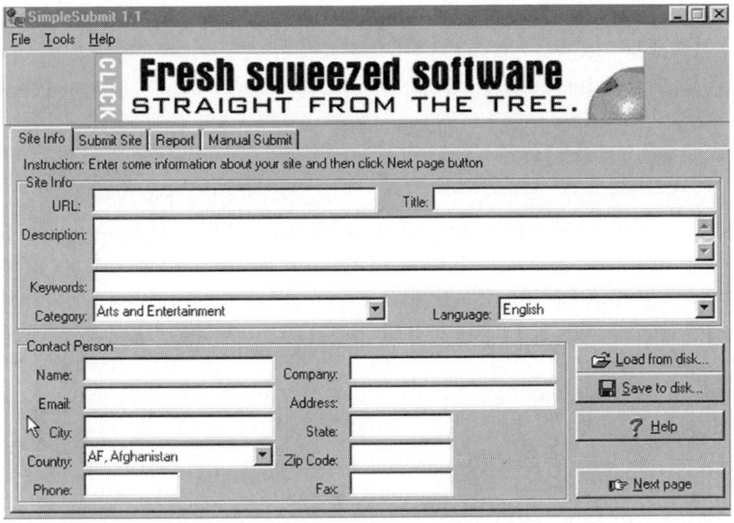

Figure 4.43:
SimpleSubmit Helping You to Contact about 30 Search Engines at Once

If you want to go the distance with Web site promotion, you'll have to pay for it, with either your dollars or your time. If you have more time than money, you can study and learn how the major search engines work and how you can optimize your META tags for each engine. Then you can create **gateway**, or **bridge**, pages that are tuned for each engine and that link back to your main site. It is not possible to optimize a Web page for all possible keywords and all possible search engines at once. However, each gateway page can be designed with optimal weighting for one keyword and one particular search engine. Then you cover all of the bases by creating multiple gateway pages and submitting the right pages to the right engines. Learning how to optimize a gateway page takes time, but you can do it. If you look hard enough, you can find all of the information that you need free.

Do It Yourself Web Site Promotion

You can learn the ins and outs of Web site promotion without spending a dime. Here are some good places to start. Subscribe to their free newsletters, and search out the free tools. Just expect to invest some time in the undertaking. The information that you need might be free, but it does cost your time and effort.

Search Engine Submission Tips `http://searchenginewatch.com/webmasters/index.html`

The Art of Business Web Site Promotion `http://deadlock.com/promote/`

Website Promotion `http://directory.netscape.com/Computers/Internet/WWW/Website_Promotion`

How to Publicize Your Web Site over the Internet `http://www.samizdat.com/public.html`

Internet Marketing Challenge!   `http://www.marketingchallenge.com/home.shtml`

BBL Internet Media   `http://bblmedia.com/`   (lots of links here; hunt for the freebies)

If you have more money than time, you likely don't want to do all of the work yourself. Shop around for a service or a high-quality software package. Visit a software clearinghouse, and conduct a search with the keyword "promotion." You'll find some of the pricier (typically over $100) shareware packages on the Net. Alternatively, use a general search engine to conduct a search on the phrase "web promotion." You'll find ASP (Application Service Provider) products and other commercial products, with some priced in excess of $1,000. Web site promotion is a big business on the Net, so decide on your price range, shop around, read a lot of reviews, search the Net for public grumbling about possible rip-off operations (see Chapter 6), and make an informed choice. You don't want to jump on the first product that you find. However, you can definitely save yourself a lot of time if you let someone else battle the details so that you can skim the surface, or at least limit your involvement in what can be a major undertaking.

Browser-Specific Extensions and Page Testing

Professional Web page designers spend a lot of time testing their pages to make sure that they look good no matter which browser (and browser version) views it under various screen resolution settings. If you're not being paid to produce a quality product, you might wish to side-step arduous Web page testing. However, it's reasonable to view your pages with a recent version of the two most popular browsers, in case something important isn't being handled by one or the other. If you don't want to install a second browser, visit **anybrowser.com** and let them generate alternate page displays for you.

There are three major reasons why some Web pages look good under one browser but not another.

1. You might be using **browser-specific extensions**. These are unofficial HTML tags and attributes that are supported by only one browser. If you are learning HTML by studying other people's Web pages online, you might unknowingly incorporate browser-specific extensions into your own pages. If a Web page has a little warning that says "This page is best viewed with Netscape Navigator," the page probably uses some features that are supported by only Navigator.

2. Your page might rely on a default value for some tag attribute, but different browsers might not use that same default.

3. Two different browsers sometimes do slightly different things with the same tags and tag attributes. Figure 4.44 shows how Navigator (a) and MSIE (b) display the same Web page.

Figure 4.44:
Two Browsers
Displaying the
Same Page
Differently

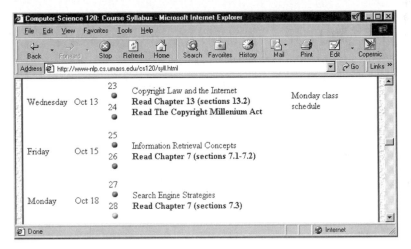

In this example, Navigator marks the boundaries around its table cells, whereas MSIE ignores them. Navigator also aligns the content in the third table column differently (and better) than does MSIE. The problems with the latter display can be fixed without adversely affecting the Navigator display (see Figure 4.45). You need only to change the table's BORDER attribute from 0 to 1, set the BORDERCOLOR to blue, and add NOWRAP attributes to the TD tags for the third table column.

If you test many Web pages, you'll begin to watch for browser idiosyncrasies. Most are easy to fix if you have an HTML reference that describes the HTML standards and browser extensions. Another way to test your Web pages is to subscribe to a Web page testing service, if you're serious about the quality of your Web pages. If the test reports are good, and they save you the time that it would take to figure

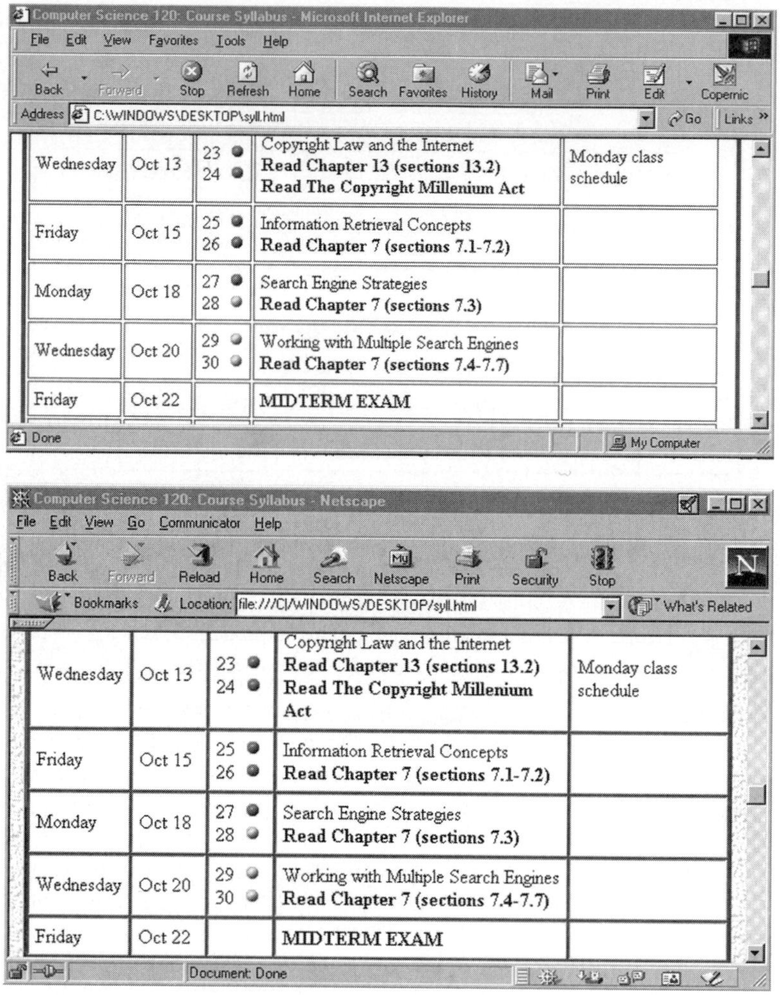

Figure 4.45:
Still Not Identical,
But Close

everything out on your own, the cost of having your Web pages checked by a professional service can be worth it. Figure 4.46 shows a summary report generated by NetMechanic, an ASP specializing in Web site support. Each report returns the results of a link checker, an HTML checker, a browser compatibility checker, a spell checker, and a load-time benchmark.

The browser compatibility test, whose results are summarized in the report illustrated in Figure 4.47, checks the page under three versions of MSIE and three versions of Navigator.

The report in Figure 4.47 shows three significant errors, one of which will affect only users of Navigator 2.0 (a very old version of Navigator). The table uses statistics on Web browser usage to estimate how many users will be affected by each

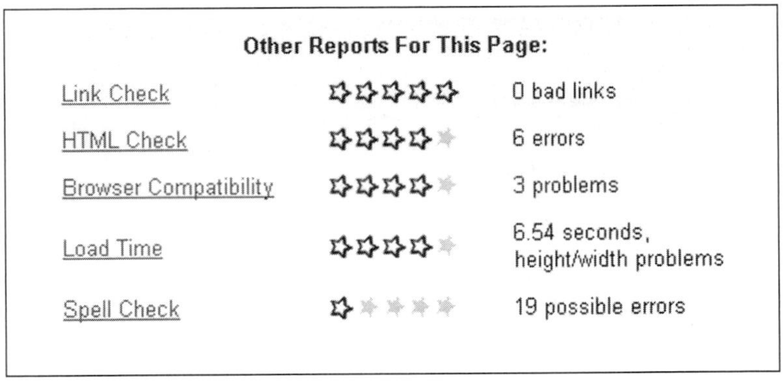

Figure 4.46:
A Web Page Report
from NetMechanic

Other Reports For This Page:

Link Check	☆☆☆☆☆	0 bad links
HTML Check	☆☆☆☆✶	6 errors
Browser Compatibility	☆☆☆☆✶	3 problems
Load Time	☆☆☆☆✶	6.54 seconds, height/width problems
Spell Check	☆✶✶✶✶	19 possible errors

Figure 4.47:
A Browser
Compatibility
Report

Tag	Attribute	Lines	Visitors Affected	Microsoft			Netscape		
				3	4	5	2	3	4
INPUT	**ALT**	46	31.00 %	N	Y	Y	N	N	N
INPUT	**BORDER**	46	72.00 %	N	N	N	Y	Y	Y
LARGE	--	36	99.00 %	N	N	N	N	N	N
TABLE	BGCOLOR	33	1.00 %	Y	Y	Y	N	Y	Y

error. You might decide not to worry about the 1% of the population still using Navigator 2.0, but you should look into the nonexistent **LARGE** tag that is sure to affect everyone. More interesting is that this report shows that the **ALT** attribute inside of an **INPUT** tag is not supported by Navigator and the **BORDER** attribute inside of an **INPUT** tag is not supported by MSIE. These differences might or might not be important enough to fix, but at least you can see all of the possible problems instead of immediately jumping into the first problem. Although the bogus **LARGE** tag is a problem for everyone, it might be benign, since all browsers are programmed to simply ignore any tags that they don't recognize.

Figure 4.48 shows two excerpts from NetMechanic's HTML checker. This part of the test analyzes the HTML file by looking for errors in HTML syntax. The test standard is the most recent version of HTML, 4.0, so any problems found with this test are errors relative to the definition of this version and are not browser-specific problems. Manually edited HTML files are much more likely to contain syntax errors. If you use an HTML editor, your pages should not contain syntax errors.

The HTML checker found six syntax errors on the test page, including the two shown in Figures 4.48(a) and (b). In this case, the order of the closing tags was reversed for a **CENTER** element that should have been nested inside of a **FORM** element. These sorts of errors are easy to make, difficult to find via manual inspection, and sometimes quite fatal for a Web page display. An HTML syntax checker can be very useful if you need to troubleshoot a Web page gone bad.

Figure 4.48:
Syntax Errors
Spotted in Lines 62
and 63

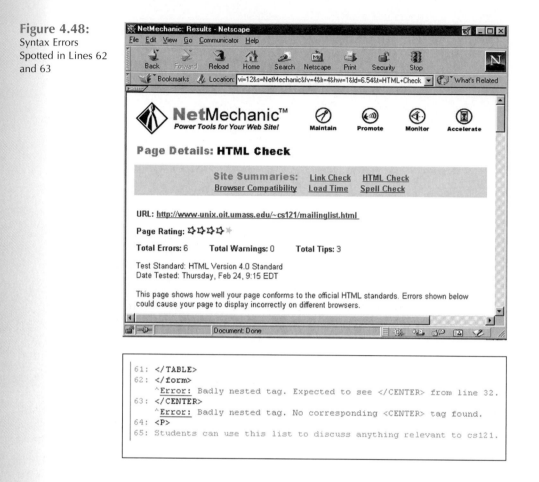

Figure 4.48:
Syntax Errors
Spotted in Lines 62
and 63

```
61: </TABLE>
62: </form>
    ^Error: Badly nested tag. Expected to see </CENTER> from line 32.
63: </CENTER>
    ^Error: Badly nested tag. No corresponding <CENTER> tag found.
64: <P>
65: Students can use this list to discuss anything relevant to cs121.
```

Most Web designers are amateurs and probably can get by without professional ASP services for their Web sites. However, it's good to know that help is nearby if you ever need to maintain a large site and you can't afford to hire your own Webmaster to do the job.

Above and Beyond: Problems and Exercises

A1. Some HTML editors are called WYSIWYG editors. What does this mean, and why is it never completely true?

A2. Explain the difference between an HTML syntax checker and a browser compatibility checker. Are all syntax errors harmful? Describe three ways in which different Web browsers can produce different displays for the same Web page.

A3. Can you reduce the time required to download an image file by scaling it down with smaller **WIDTH** and **HEIGHT** values? Explain your answer.

A4. How can the **META** tag affect the visibility of your Web pages?

A5. What is an interlaced GIF? Do interlaced GIF images download faster than noninterlaced GIFs?

A6. Explain how thumbnail previews can speed up a Web page whose images download slowly.

A7. How can you check for major browser compatibility problems without spending money on a Web page testing service?

A8. Why are **META** tags important for Web page visibility?

A9. What is a gateway page, and why is it a good idea to have more than one?

A10. How much of a copyrighted music file can you post on a public Web page without permission from the copyright owner?

A11. According to the fair use doctrine, can you record a popular song from the radio and incorporate that recording into a school project?

A12. Can a Web page author control which application is used to play an MP3 file on a Web page?

A13. **[Hands-On]** Launch Arachnophilia (or any other HTML editor of your choice), and recreate the dachshund Web page shown in Figure 4.15. You can download the graphical elements from a copy of **Figure 4.15 on the Web**. Were you able to add all of the necessary HTML elements by using pull-down menus and toolbar buttons? Did you have to tinker with the HTML tags directly in order to get the layout that you wanted?

A14. **[Hands-On]** Reproduce the table in Figure 4.30. Use ten rows and ten columns. Do this with an HTML editor so that you don't have to create all of the table elements by hand. A WYSIWYG editor is probably the best choice for this exercise.

A15. **[Hands-On]** Select a free hit count service, and install a hit counter on your home page. Keep it for at least a week. Which counter did you select? What did you learn about your site? Will you keep the counter? Why or why not?

CHAPTER 5

Advanced Web Page Construction

CHAPTER GOALS

- Explore how to use image maps and JavaScript to create livelier Web pages.
- Learn how to find JavaScript programs on the Web and install them on your Web pages.
- Find out what Java applets can do and how to add them to your Web pages.
- Discover how you can customize JavaScript programs and Java applets to meet your needs.
- Learn how data-driven Java applets make it easier to manage frequent Web page updates.
- Find out what Web site construction kits and site maintenance tools can do for you.

5.1 TAKING CHARGE

Once upon a time, it was hip to have your own personal home page on the Web. That was before everyone had one. Nowadays, it's getting harder to be hip on the Web because the eight-year-old next door has her own home page, complete with a quote of the day, a guestbook, and a voting poll. You probably have less time to work on this than the average eight-year-old, and all of the eight-year-olds on the block are trading Web page design tips with each other the way that you used to trade tips for your favorite video games. Let's face it, if you aren't a professional Web page designer (or eight years old), the deck is stacked against you. But don't despair. You can show up the most-precocious kids on the block, once you know the same tricks that they do. It's actually very easy, by adding *dynamic elements* to your Web pages.

Five years ago, it took some effort to add dynamic elements to a Web page. At the very least, you had to learn a programming language called *JavaScript*. If you wanted more than JavaScript could deliver, you had to learn another programming language: either *Perl* or *C* or a (then) relatively new language named *Java* (which is not, despite the name similarity, related to JavaScript). Today, you could learn both JavaScript and Java in order to create the Web pages of your dreams. Alternatively, you can take some shortcuts and settle for a more expedient solution. For most people, the decision is simple. It takes a lot of time and hard work to master a programming language. If you're interested in creating only two or three Web sites in the foreseeable future, and you don't intend to earn a living at designing sites, then you really don't need to know what the professional Web designers know. It's not worth the effort. You can manage quite nicely by using shortcuts.

How Much Should You Learn?

If you want to become a professional Web page designer, you should learn both JavaScript and Java (for starters). But if you've no desire to make Web page design your profession, you can still piece together impressive, highly functional Web pages by taking advantage of Web page freebies on the Net. You'll see how later in this chapter.

You won't need to devote a lot of time to study a programming language (programming skills are not acquired overnight), your Web pages will make you look like you know more than you do, and everyone will wonder how you find the time to do all of the things that you do. It's easy. But you do need to learn a little about how *JavaScript programs* and *Java applets* work. This chapter will show you that much. It does not attempt to give you a solid introduction to either JavaScript or Java. If you want to learn more about either, check out the pointers to useful resources located at the end of the chapter. If you want to go the distance, start with this chapter. However, plan to keep going with online tutorials and how-to articles that interest you.

If you want a quote of the day, a voting poll, or a guestbook on your Web pages, you can add one easily by using the appropriate JavaScript program or applet. A **JavaScript program** is a bit of code that has been written specifically to enhance a Web page. Many JavaScript programs are free and are often distributed with instructions for people who have no programming experience. Many are excellent, and most are serviceable.

An **applet** is a piece of code, written in *Java,* that can often be used by people who have no programming experience. Applets can do things that JavaScript programs can't. Some of the most stunning visual effects seen on Web pages are produced by applets. Other applets can be customized in so many ways that they come with a user's manual. Many excellent applets are available on the Web at no cost; a few of the more complicated ones can cost up to $100. You don't need to know anything about Java to install applets on your Web pages. In fact, a well-documented applet is often easier to install and customize than a well-documented JavaScript program. Many collections of free applets can be found on the Web. If you have the time, it's fun to peruse applet libraries and see what's available.

Scripts and Scripting Languages

A **script** is a small computer program written in a scripting language. A **scripting language** is usually more limited and somewhat simpler than a full-fledged programming language but it produces code that is relatively easy to read and extend.

There are many scripting languages, including JavaScript, HyperCard, AppleScript, JScript™, and VBScript™. Some are designed specifically for Web pages, whereas others (HyperCard and AppleScript) have nothing to do with the Web. JavaScript is the most popular scripting language for the Web, and it's the only one discussed in this book. From now on, the term *script* refers to a JavaScript program.

Scripts are usually acquired in one of three ways.

1. Customized for you by a Web server at an interactive Web site, where you are asked to answer a few questions before you're given your script. See **htmlGEAR** for some good examples of server-side script customization.

2. Available as software downloads. You download and install a utility, an **authoring tool** (often called a *wizard*), to your computer that helps you to customize the script. Such utilities are generally found in software archives that specialize in Web construction tools and are often free. Visit **HTML Goodies** to see some good examples of authoring tools that produce customized scripts.

3. Distributed as cut-and-paste text files that contain baseline code for a script along with instructions for simple modifications. Some of these scripts are well documented and are therefore easy for anyone to install, whereas others offer minimal assistance and are more appropriate for experienced programmers. Visit **JavaScript Search** for a large collection of cut-and-paste scripts.

This chapter shows you how to find the scripts that you want and how to add them to your Web pages.

To use these resources, you first need to know how to create a basic Web page. You also need enough understanding of HTML to make manual adjustments to a Web page when you add a script or applet. If you're familiar with the material in Chapter 4, you'll have no problem putting the material in this chapter to work. And if you enjoy working with Web pages, this chapter will open up a whole new world of Web design possibilities. It's not really difficult, if you find the right resources—and that's getting easier all of the time.

5.2   CLIENT-SIDE IMAGE MAPS

The best Web sites are easy to navigate. An eye-catching navigational menu is the hallmark of a well-designed Web site. You can create professional-looking navigation menus by adding dynamic visual elements, an excellent way to catch and hold attention. These effects are achieved by creating *hotzones* with image maps, which are described in this section. Section 5.3 shows you how to combine image maps with JavaScript to create dynamic elements.

Anyone who has spent five minutes on the Web has seen an image map in action. An **image map** makes it possible to click a **hotzone** (an arbitrary region) of an image instead of a text label or an inline image. A hotzone is just another way of inserting a hyperlink into a Web page. With hotzones you can specify more than one hyperlink per image so different parts of the image can correspond to different hyperlinks. Early image maps required a program called a **server-side image map** which was run on the Web server. Today, however, most image maps are run by Web browsers; these are called **client-side image maps**. Client-side image maps became popular in 1997 when a `MAP` tag was added to HTML 3.2. Many image maps respond to mouseovers (movement of the mouse over a region) as well as mouse clicks. However, this section begins with the simplest image maps: maps with *clickable hotzones*.

It's possible to write an image map manually. However, it's somewhat tedious and time-consuming. Each clickable region in an image map must be specified with *x–y* coordinate notation. To mark a region, you must first find the *x–y* coordinates for appropriate points on your image. Many image map utilities can be found on the Web (search any software clearinghouse with the query "image map"). A full-featured tool will support the creation of rectangular and circular hotzones, as well as hotzones defined by any *n*-sided polygon.

Hidden Hotzones

When you select an image for an image map, pick one that is intuitively obvious. Your user should be able to look at the image and immediately understand that this is a place to point and click. One can always hide a hotzone in an image where no one expects it. However, doing that will only annoy people unless the site is deliberately designed to be a puzzle of some sort.

To create an image map without using an image-mapping tool, you must first figure out the coordinates for each region, as well as the convention for representing each region. The coordinate system might be a little confusing at first because the *y*-axis is *positive* beneath the *x*-axis rather than negative (this is *not* the standard *x–y* coordinate system that you were taught in high school). In the coordinate system for an image map, the *y*-axis increases as you move down the axis (instead of up). Once you have that straight, the `AREA` tag requires just a little coordinate geometry. For example, you can represent a rectangle by specifying the upper left-hand corner and the lower right-hand corner of the rectangle.

The `ISMAP` Trick

Using Navigator or MSIE, you can view any image and see the *x–y* coordinates for any spot in the image by positioning your cursor on the spot. Follow these steps:

1. Set up an `IMG` tag with an `ISMAP` attribute, and make it a label for an A-tag, as follows:

   ```
   <A HREF="placeholder.html"><IMG SRC="test.jpg" ISMAP></A>
   ```

2. Replace `test.jpg` with the filename for the image that you want to map. Don't worry if the file `placeholder.html` doesn't exist—you have to create this hyperlink but you never need to click it for the sake of the `ISMAP` trick.

3. Display the file that contains this line, and then examine your image.

4. Place your cursor inside of the image, and look at the status message at the bottom of the browser window. At the end of the filename are two numbers separated by a comma—these are the *x–y* coordinates for the current cursor position (see Figure 5.1). (If the status message is obscured by a toolbar, enlarge the browser window.)

Figure 5.1:
Finding the *x–y*
Coordinates by
Using the `ISMAP`
Trick

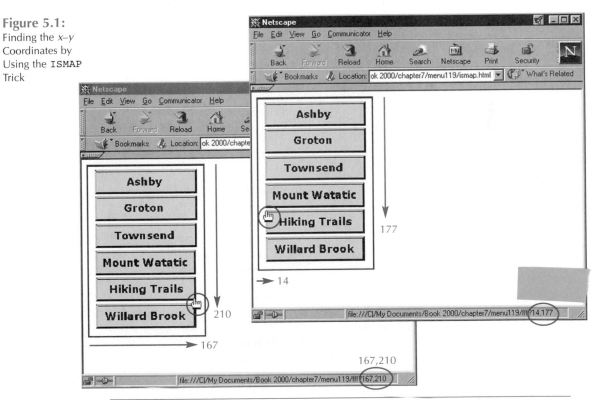

Scaling Your Image before You Map It

Before you start collecting coordinate pairs for your image, be sure that you're working with an image that is the exact size it will be on your Web page. If you have to scale your image by using `HEIGHT` and `WIDTH` attributes on your Web page, take a screen shot of the image as it appears in your browser window and work with that when the time comes to map the image. If you map an image that is larger or smaller than the one on your Web page, your hotzones will be confused and unusable because your coordinate locations won't map correctly to the coordinates of the image being displayed.

If you need only to define rectangular hotzones for your image map, you can get by with only the ISMAP trick. Suppose that you want to create an image map for the navigational menu in Figure 15.1. The image file contains six buttons, and you want a separate hotzone for each. Start by collecting the x–y coordinates for the upper left-hand corner and the lower right-hand corner of each button. Then use the **MAP tag** to create the actual image map. The `MAP` tag allows you to specify multiple hotzones within a single image and **AREA tags** are used to specify each hotzone. The `AREA` tag's attributes allow you to specify a shape, in this case, a rectangle, by using the `SHAPE` attribute and `RECT` value, like this: `SHAPE=RECT`. Then you define coordinates for that shape: `COORDS="`x_1, y_1, x_2, y_2`"` where (x_1, y_1) are the coordinates for the upper left-hand corner of the rectangular hotzone and (x_2, y_2) are the coordinates for the lower right-hand corner). You also need `HREF` attributes to specify the destination for each hotzone. The resulting image map looks like this.

```
<MAP NAME="menumap">
 <AREA SHAPE=RECT COORDS="14,5,168,42" HREF="ashby.html">
 <AREA SHAPE=RECT COORDS="15,46,171,88" HREF="groton.html">
 <AREA SHAPE=RECT COORDS="13,89,170,124" HREF="townsend.html">
 <AREA SHAPE=RECT COORDS="13,131,170,166" HREF="watatic.html">
 <AREA SHAPE=RECT COORDS="14,174,170,209" HREF="hikingtext.html">
 <AREA SHAPE=RECT COORDS="14,215,167,252" HREF="willard.html">
</MAP>
```

This `MAP` element must be added to the `BODY` of the Web page, and the attribute `USEMAP="#menumap"` must be added to the `IMG` element of the image being mapped.

Note that these coordinates don't have to line up perfectly with the buttons on the image. Users won't know or care if the hotzones are off by a few pixels.

Make Your Own Image Map

Try making your own image map with an image of your choice. Pick an image with obvious rectangular regions for hotzones (e.g., a list of link names, a column of buttons, or a navigation bar like the one shown in Section 4.6.3). Follow the instructions below, and when you get to steps 4-6, model your HTML on the "menumap" example shown above.

1. Start with an image file (GIF or JPEG—it doesn't matter which).
2. View your image with your Web browser by using the `ISMAP` trick.
3. Record the coordinate pairs for each rectangular hotzone that you want to define.
4. Create an `AREA` tag for each hotzone, and put each inside of a `MAP` tag.
5. Add the `MAP` tag to the `BODY` of the Web page.
6. Add a `USEMAP` attribute to the `IMG` tag for the image just mapped.

When an image map is used in conjunction with a navigational menu, the menu is normally displayed inside one frame and the links associated with the menu buttons load new pages into a different frame (see pages 114 and 115 in the color insert). To accomplish this, each `AREA` element needs a `TARGET` attribute. You'll see an example shortly that includes the `TARGET` attribute.

As we've just seen, it is possible to create image maps with rectangular hotzones by hand, using nothing but the ISMAP trick. But image maps are tedious to make when you create them this way. If you expect to create many image maps or if you want to work with nonrectangular hotzones, you should use a software utility called an *image mapper*. An **image mapper** generates an entire `MAP` element for you based on the information that you give it. The next section walks you through the process using a freeware image mapper called **Dr. Bill's Image Converter and Map Generator**. Once you've seen how one mapping tool works, you should be able to figure out any other mapping tool, as they're all very similar.

5.2.1 Step 1: Loading an Image File

Begin by launching the program and going to the File menu. Select the Open command (see Figure 5.2). A directory dialog window will appear in which you specify a GIF or JPEG image for your image map.

This particular tool gives you some useful options before you map the image. It allows you to convert a color image to gray scale (see Figure 5.3) and it gives you the option of shrink the image before mapping it (recall that you must always scale an image to its intended display size before mapping coordinates for an image map).

Figure 5.2:

The Image Mapper Beginning with an Image File

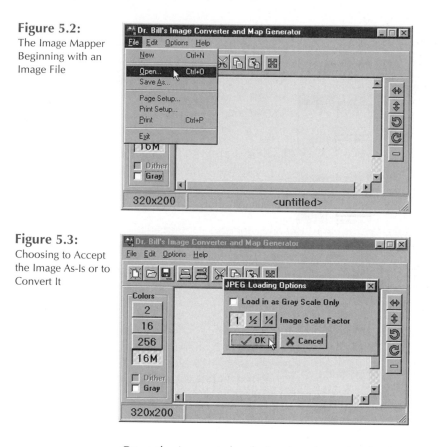

Figure 5.3:

Choosing to Accept the Image As-Is or to Convert It

Once the image is loaded, select from the Options menu the option "Edit an HTML Map File" (see Figure 5.4).

Selecting this command pops up a window that has four tabs: Overall Page Design, Map Options, Build an Image Map, and Final HTML Code (see Figure 5.5). You'll work your way across each tab, starting with the leftmost, Overall Page Design. This set of options allows you to mark a checkbox named Create a Complete HTML Page. Checking this option causes the program to generate a complete HTML page that contains the image map. If it is unchecked, the program will generate the HTML tags only for the image map, which you could grab and drop onto an existing Web page. The other settings on this tab are self-explanatory.

The Map Options tab lets you specify some general options, as well as a default URL if you want the unmarked regions of the map to link to a different location (see Figure 5.6). If you don't specify a default URL, then the user will click regions of the image that are not hotzones and nothing will happen. In this example, you'll leave it empty.

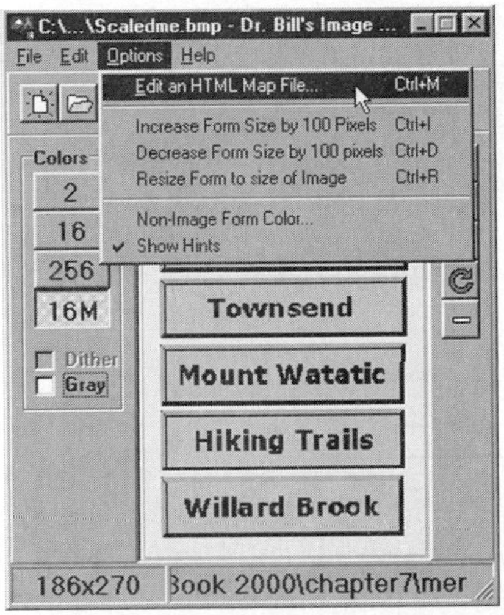

Figure 5.4:
Creating a Map

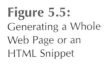

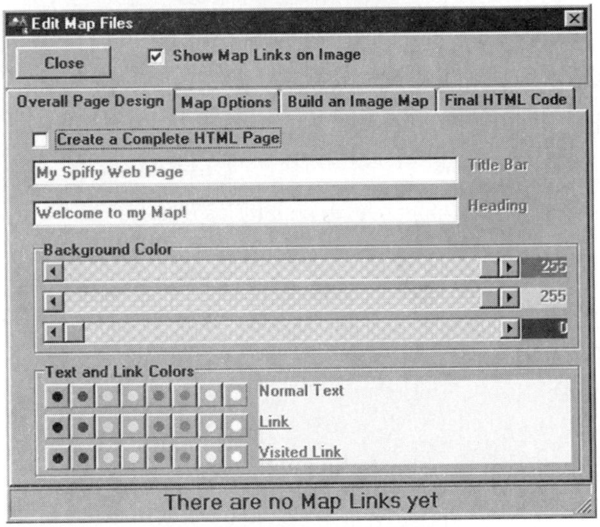

Figure 5.5:
Generating a Whole
Web Page or an
HTML Snippet

5.2.2 Step 2: Mapping the Hotzones

After all of the preliminaries have been taken care of, you can map the hotzones for the image map. The Build an Image Map tab lets you specify shapes for hotzones. You'll use rectangles for each of your menu buttons (see Figure 5.7).

After you've selected the radio button for a rectangle, you can go to the image window and mark a rectangular region on the image with your mouse. To make rectangles, click and hold the mouse button to mark the upper left-hand corner of the rectangle and then drag the mouse to the right-hand corner. Release the button, and you'll have specified a rectangle (see Figure 5.8).

Figure 5.6:
Leaving the Default
URL Empty

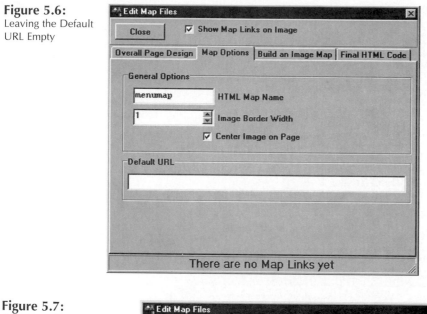

Figure 5.7:
Selecting a Shape
for the First
Hotzone

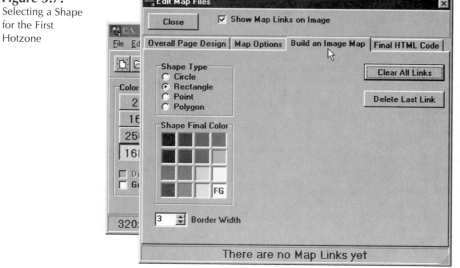

After you release the mouse, a third window pops up, in which you name a destination for the hotzone just defined. You can enter an absolute URL, a relative URL, or a keyword placeholder that you'll replace with a URL later. For this example, you chose a relative URL (see Figure 5.9).

Next, you return to the Build an Image Map tab and repeat this process for each hotzone in your image map (see Figure 5.10).

Figure 5.8:
Dragging the
Mouse to Mark a
Rectangle

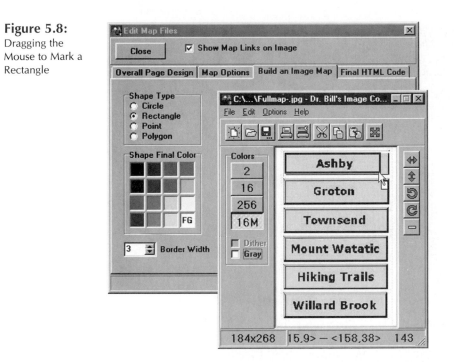

Figure 5.9:
Tagging Each
Hotzone with an
Address or a
Temporary Keyword

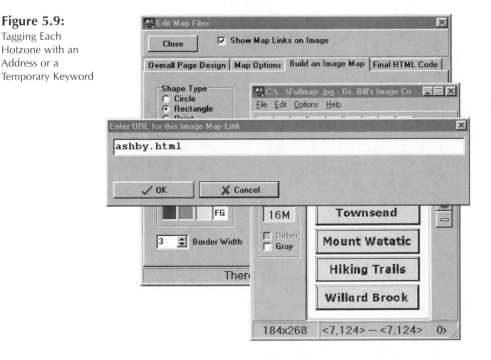

Figure 5.10:
The White Boundaries Mark All the Hotzones in the Image

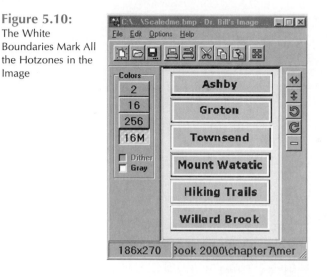

5.2.3 Step 3: Installing the Image Map

At any point, you can click the Final HTML Code tab to see what your HTML output looks like (see Figure 5.11). When you are done marking hotzones, you can save the resulting HTML to a file or copy it to the clipboard for insertion into another HTML file.

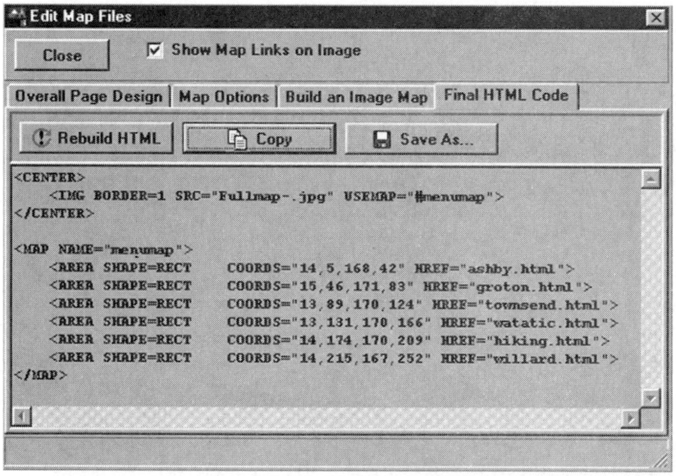

Figure 5.11:
Image Mapper's HTML Output

```
<CENTER>
    <IMG BORDER=1 SRC="Fullmap-.jpg" USEMAP="#menumap">
</CENTER>

<MAP NAME="menumap">
    <AREA SHAPE=RECT    COORDS="14,5,168,42"    HREF="ashby.html">
    <AREA SHAPE=RECT    COORDS="15,46,171,83"   HREF="groton.html">
    <AREA SHAPE=RECT    COORDS="13,89,170,124"  HREF="townsend.html">
    <AREA SHAPE=RECT    COORDS="13,131,170,166" HREF="watatic.html">
    <AREA SHAPE=RECT    COORDS="14,174,170,209" HREF="hiking.html">
    <AREA SHAPE=RECT    COORDS="14,215,167,252" HREF="willard.html">
</MAP>
```

Notice how this program insulated you from all of the details associated with the MAP and AREA tags. You don't need to know how the tag attributes are used or how the regional coordinates within the AREA tags will be interpreted. It's enough to mark your regions, specify the appropriate link locations, and save the final results for reuse later. With tools like this, you can get by without learning everything about client-side image maps.

In general, it's easier to use an HTML construction kit or a scripting tool than to create HTML tags manually. The tools can be used without your fully understanding the underlying HTML, and they are usually much faster to use than doing everything manually. Professional Web designers use tools like this to speed up their work. However, they also find it useful to make manual adjustments occasionally to the resulting constructs.

Authoring Tools Can't Automate Everything

Authoring tools can save you a lot of time. However, they are no substitute for understanding the underlying HTML constructs. Whereas you will benefit from the efficiency of an authoring tool, you still need to understand the underlying HTML in order to make small adjustments to your Web pages.

Image maps are useful in a variety of situations. You can create menu bars, point-and-click site maps, pictorial directories, and other navigational devices. An intuitively obvious image map is a welcome change from hyperlinks that depend on text anchors. However, an image map by itself is not as engaging as a visually dynamic image that changes and interacts with the user. To add dynamic elements to an image map, you need to delve into the world of JavaScript. Using JavaScript, you can design Web pages that change as the user sweeps the mouse across the page display. The whole page or just one part of the page can change. This type of dynamic display is achieved through the use of *mouseover events*, which are explored in the next section.

5.3 ⬛ JAVASCRIPT AND MOUSEOVER EVENTS

Recall that JavaScript is a programming language designed to enhance Web pages through the use of small client-side programs. Each script is attached to an HTML file and must be executed by the Web browser rendering the Web page. JavaScript enhancements can add a lot to a Web page. However, you must be careful with it because different browsers support slightly different versions of the language. It's easy to write a script that runs correctly under one, and only one, browser. If you want to learn JavaScript, you can find many excellent (and free!) tutorials on the Web or you can pick up a book on it at most bookstores. If you're new to computer programming, JavaScript is not a bad place to begin learning how to program. Look for a book aimed at beginners. You'll also find plenty of examples on the Web to spark your interest and reinforce your learning. Many people learn JavaScript by copying scripts found on the Web and adjusting them for their own Web pages. This approach is less systematic than a thorough trip through a textbook, and some aspects of the language will be difficult to grasp in the absence of good exposition and explanations. But working from examples is fun because you'll be drawn to the examples that interest you, thereby maximizing your motivation to learn the language.

Tackling Browser Compatibility Problems

Many useful scripts are designed to work with Navigator but not MSIE or vice versa. When professionals add JavaScript to a Web page, they test the page extensively not only with both browsers, but also different versions of both browsers.

To attain uniform page displays, it's often necessary to add two separate scripts to the same page: one for Navigator and one for Explorer. A test condition is then added to the Web page that asks the current browser to identify itself; once it does, the program can summon the script that works for that particular browser. Even then, you might still see some differences when the same page is viewed with different browsers because it's not always possible to reproduce exactly the same effects across the board.

Professional Web site designers spend a lot of time grappling with JavaScript compatibility problems. If you don't want to be bothered, you can test your pages by using your current browser to make sure that it works with at least one browser. Then you should insert a warning to your readers as needed for the other browser; for example, "This page is best viewed with Netscape Navigator." Users running the wrong browser won't be thrilled, but at least they will have been warned.

This section can only hope to whet your appetite by offering an example that is used extensively throughout the Web: the *dynamic mouseover*. A **mouseover** is the action of sweeping your mouse over a region on a Web page that has been programmed to respond to the mouse's presence. As soon as your mouse's pointer enters a hotzone, something happens; for example, a comment box pops up, a button changes color, or an image is transformed in some way. This makes the Web page visually interactive, which in turn makes it more fun for people to explore. Mouseovers are one of the most versatile features you can add to a Web page, since there are so many different things that you can do with them.

Before you look at the JavaScript behind the mouseovers, consider the images at work behind them. For each button on the navigational menu, you need at least two different images: a default button when no mouse activity is present and a highlighted button when the mouse is inside of the button's hotzone (see Figure 5.12). These are almost identical images, so the browser can swap them (exchange one for another) on the Web page and make it look like a single image that magically changes before one's eyes. Most browsers can swap images so smoothly that there is no flickering or other indication that one image has been exchanged for another.

Creating Your Own Button Sets

If you're making your own image files, start with one default file for the entire menu and then modify the original with a drawing program to obtain the different mouseover variations. A simple bitmap image editor such as Paint™ is all that you need to create your buttons, if you're patient and have some time.

When you modify the original, try to make as few changes as possible. You need to keep all of the buttons lined up in exactly the same locations for all your image files; otherwise, the user will see the buttons shift when the images are swapped. Rather than redraw entire buttons, keep the original button outline and text label and use a fill operation to change the background color on the button. The same operation can be used to change the color of your text if you want the mouseover to highlight text. You might need to experiment a little with your first button set. However, once you get the hang of it, you'll be able to create a set of ten buttons as easily as a set of two or three.

Figure 5.13 shows two variations of a default button: a highlighted button for mouseovers and a depressed button for mouseclicks. The difference between the two is the *shadow* that borders a button's face. To show a raised three-dimensional surface and a depressed surface, you reverse the light and dark edges surrounding the face of the image. Wider edges make the 3-D effect more prominent, and narrow edges make it more subtle.

This button set contains 13 files: one default display and two variations on the default for each of six buttons. Working with the whole menu at once makes the image layout easier (you need only to swap the same image repeatedly). However, this is not a good approach should you ever decide to modify your menu later, as any change to this button set will require you to remake all 13 files. To make revi-

Figure 5.12:
A Mouseover for a
Navigational Menu

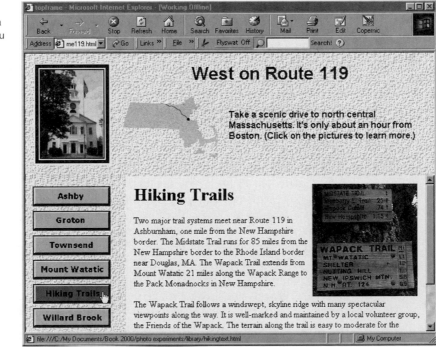

Figure 5.13:
Three Image Files
from a 13-File
Button Set

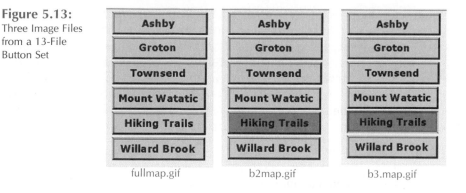

sions as painless as possible, create a separate default file for each button and display the buttons by using a table. The file swaps are a little more involved this way. However, it's not that difficult, and you'll have less work when you want to add a new button or replace an old one.

The previous section discussed how to create an image map that marks the hotzones to use for mouseovers. Now, all that you need to do is attach instructions to each hotzone, specifying what should happen when the mouse enters the region and what should happen when the mouse leaves the region. That is, you specify which image file is loaded when a *mouseover* occurs (the mouse enters a specific hotzone) and which image file is loaded when a *mouseout* occurs (the mouse leaves the hotzone). You'll also need instructions for a *MouseClick*, if you want to see a depressed button as well.

The script that accomplishes your image swaps relies on a simple procedure that allows you to load any image into any image location on the existing Web page. In this case, your Web page consists of multiple frames. However, you are concerned only with the HTML file for the menu frame; the other frame elements can be ignored. Furthermore, the menu page contains a single image location (one IMG tag for the default menu display), so it's not hard to figure out which image should be replaced. If you were using separate image files for each button, you would need to number the images so that you could keep them all straight.

Image swapping is easy to handle once you understand how JavaScript looks at an HTML file. Each IMG tag in an HTML file is considered to be a fixed object—an *instance* of an object, for those of you who know *object-oriented programming*. Once you create an object, the object itself is fixed, but its attributes can be changed by a script. An object's attributes control the appearance and behavior of the object, so changing an object's attributes can result in a completely different looking object. In particular, the SRC attribute of any IMG object can be changed, and this is all that you need to accomplish in an image swap. JavaScript also makes it easy to specify one particular IMG object when a Web page contains more than one. It counts the IMG tags as they appear and assigns each an integer based on its position in the file (the first IMG tag, the second IMG tag, and so on).

Although this example involves only one image object, you'll define your swapping function more generally so that you can use it on Web pages that have multiple images. You need to know exactly how JavaScript keeps track of multiple IMG objects by counting the IMG tags. Although humans like to count starting from 1 (1, 2, 3, and so on), JavaScript uses a counting convention that starts from 0, like this: 0, 1, 2, 3, and so on. Therefore, as far as your script is concerned, the first image in an HTML file is always image 0, the second image is image 1, the third is 2, and so on. You have only one IMG tag in your menu file, so your button menu is always image 0.

In addition to knowing how to refer to multiple images, you also need to know how to refer to the different image files in a button set. JavaScript handles this by creating *multiple instances* of image objects. Each image object is assigned a SRC attribute much like the IMG tag and SRC attribute in HTML. However, the syntax for describing an image object in a script is a little different from the syntax for images in HTML. Remember that HTML and JavaScript are two different languages, even though they both allow you to manipulate the same types of entities (such as images from files). One representational system applies to HTML, and a different representational system is used for scripts. When an HTML page contains a script, it's always inside of a SCRIPT tag. The text inside of a SCRIPT tag might look something like HTML. However, it's not! It is always a script.

The script needed to swap images consists of two parts:

1. A set of object instances that specify all of the image files in the button set
2. The procedure that actually makes the swaps

The full script for this example will need 13 image instances to cover the 13 button files. However, this example will deal with only the 3 image instances needed to handle the Hiking Trails button. If you stopped there, your menu would have only one dynamic button. However, that's enough to illustrate the script in action.

JavaScript lets you assign a name to each image object so that you can refer to them from other places in the script whenever you need them. This will make it possible to change the SRC value of the IMG object on demand. This is how you'll make the image swaps when the mouse enters or leaves a hotzone.

Figure 5.14 shows a complete script for handling mouseovers and mouseclicks. The script is found inside of the <SCRIPT></SCRIPT> pair of tags that are normally inserted inside of the HEAD element. In this case, the program creates three image objects and defines a procedure named "ChangeTo." This procedure accepts two bits of input:

1. The location (as specified by number) of an image on the current Web page
2. An instance of an image object defined inside of the script

When you execute this procedure, it loads the graphics file for the script's image object into the specified image on the Web page. In other words, it performs an image swap.

Figure 5.14:
A Script for Image Swapping a Drawing from a Three-File Button Set

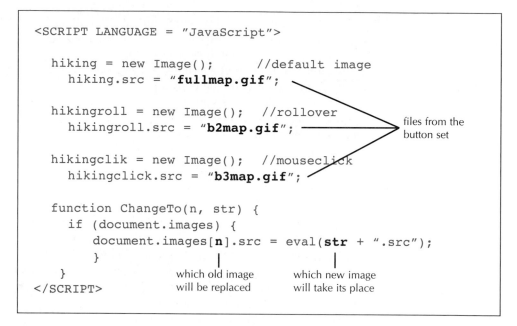

Don't get bogged down in the syntax of the script. It looks a little strange because it uses JavaScript syntax. That's alright—you don't need to reproduce this script from scratch. Just try to understand roughly what's going on. Figure 5.15 might help. It's easier to understand someone else's code than it is to write your own (unless you're a programmer, in which case the opposite is true). Understanding JavaScript at a fuzzy level is sufficient if you only want to add some scripts to your Web pages.

This script gives a procedure for swapping images. However, you haven't said when the procedure should run and with what input. Having a definition of the ChangeTo procedure is great. However, now you have to decide how to use it. Those instructions will be added to your image map. Inside each of the **AREA** tags within the **MAP** element, you'll add some new attributes named **onMouseOver** and **onMouseOut** (see Figure 5.16). The value of these attributes will be a call to the procedure ChangeTo. Each procedure call specifies which image location should be swapped (it's always the same one) and which image object should be inserted (it's always one of the three image objects named in the script).

That's all there is to it. If you can make sense of Figures 5.14–5.16, you should understand this script well enough to plug it into your Web page and adjust it to fit your own image-swapping needs. JavaScript gives your Web page the power to respond to many different types of mouse events, and image maps give you the freedom to define different behaviors for different parts of your Web page.

Figure 5.15:
JavaScript Syntax
Demystified

```
<SCRIPT LANGUAGE = "JavaScript">

  hiking = new Image();        //default image
    hiking.src = "fullmap.gif";

  hikingroll = new Image();  //rollover
    hikingroll.src = "b2map.gif";

  hikingclik = new Image();  //mouseclick
    hikingclick.src = "b3map.gif";

  function ChangeTo(n, str) {
    if (document.images) {
        document.images[n].src = eval(str + ".src");
        }
    }
</SCRIPT>
```

create an instance
of an image object
and name it
"hiking"

set the SRC attrib-
ute of the hiking
object to
"fullmap.gif"

set the SRC attribute of
the nth image object in
the Web page equal to
the value of the SRC
attribute in the image
object that was input to
this procedure

JavaScript Recognizes Many Types of Mouse Events

The example in this section uses four mouse events: `onMouseOver`,
`onMouseOut`, `onMouseUp`, and `onMouseDown` (see Figure 5.16). You can use
others, as follows, in your `AREA` tags if you want to experiment with more dynamic effects.

- `onClick` is recognized when a `mousedown` event is immediately followed by
  a `mouseup` event.
- `onDbClick` is a fast double-click.
- `onMouseMove` is recognized when the mouse moves inside of the hotzone.
- `onKeyDown` is recognized when a key on the keyboard is hit.
- `onKeyUp` is recognized when a key on the keyboard is released.
- `onKeyPress` is recognized when a key is hit and immediately released (analogous to `onclick` for the mouse).

Figure 5.16:
Calls to the Script
Inserted in the
Image Map

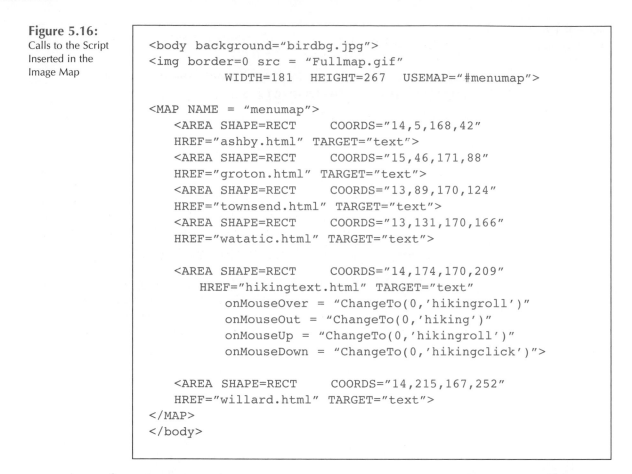

```
<body background="birdbg.jpg">
<img border=0 src = "Fullmap.gif"
           WIDTH=181   HEIGHT=267   USEMAP="#menumap">

<MAP NAME = "menumap">
   <AREA SHAPE=RECT     COORDS="14,5,168,42"
   HREF="ashby.html" TARGET="text">
   <AREA SHAPE=RECT     COORDS="15,46,171,88"
   HREF="groton.html" TARGET="text">
   <AREA SHAPE=RECT     COORDS="13,89,170,124"
   HREF="townsend.html" TARGET="text">
   <AREA SHAPE=RECT     COORDS="13,131,170,166"
   HREF="watatic.html" TARGET="text">

   <AREA SHAPE=RECT     COORDS="14,174,170,209"
      HREF="hikingtext.html" TARGET="text"
         onMouseOver = "ChangeTo(0,'hikingroll')"
         onMouseOut = "ChangeTo(0,'hiking')"
         onMouseUp = "ChangeTo(0,'hikingroll')"
         onMouseDown = "ChangeTo(0,'hikingclick')">

   <AREA SHAPE=RECT     COORDS="14,215,167,252"
   HREF="willard.html" TARGET="text">
</MAP>
</body>
```

Now You Try It

1. Review Section 5.2, and create your own image map for an image file of your choice. If you wish, you can grab **all of the graphics files for the example in 5.3** from this textbook's affiliated Web site. Set up a Web page with two frames so that you can direct the links from the image map in the first frame to the display in the second frame. Before you continue, make sure that your hotzones are working as hyperlinks.

2. Add a script for handling mouseover effects, starting with the onMouseOver event. Remember that ChangeTo takes two input arguments: the first an integer that specifies which image on the Web page will be replaced and the second the name of an image object defined inside of the script. The second argument determines which new image will be used to replace the old one. If you have only one image on your Web page, the first argument will always be 0. If you have more than one image, they are indexed by the order in which they appear in the HTML file (remember to start counting at 0 instead of 1).

Don't worry about setting up files for all of the hotzones in your image map. It's enough to see one hotzone working correctly.

Stop Here If You've Had Enough

3. If you survived part 2, add another effect for on`MouseDown` and on`MouseUp` as described in this section. Again, it's enough to see this working for only one hotzone.

    WARNING: The script in the book works correctly under MSIE but not quite perfectly under Navigator. Communicator 4.5 handles the on`MouseOver` events as intended but ignores the on`MouseDown` events. If you're running Navigator, you might have trouble with the on`MouseDown` events, depending on your version of the browser and your version of Windows (it was tested only under Win95). If you cannot get the on`MouseDown` to work with Navigator, feel free to give up and move on. Alternatively, figure out how to make it work and request extra credit from your instructor.

4. If you're artistically inclined, fire up a graphics editor and try your hand at designing your own menu buttons. The work might go very slowly at first, and you might have to redo many files until you get it right. Don't be discouraged; there's a lot to learn if you've never tried this before. The next time that you do it, the work will go faster.

Can JavaScript Spread Computer Viruses?

If you've read Chapter 2 carefully, you might be wondering if JavaScript has a dark side. After all, scripts are *executable computer programs* that are being executed on your computer whenever you visit a Web page that contains JavaScript. Computer programmers worried a lot about this when browsers first started to support JavaScript. Happily, many of those worried programmers were responsible for making JavaScript safe.

Thanks to safeguards built into JavaScript, no one has been able to embed a true virus in a script. However, it is possible to create a *malicious script*. For example, an ill-tempered programmer could a create script designed to open a thousand browser windows as soon as you visit a booby-trapped Web page. Opening this many windows would quickly crash your system.

Most programmers with any pride would opt for something subtler. If you're inclined to worry about malicious scripts, the greatest dangers lie in the realm of social engineering and ToS violations. For example, a Web page might masquerade as the Yahoo! home page and ask you to enter your Yahoo! userid and password. If you aren't on your toes (How did you get to this page? Was it via a link on an obscure Web site?), you could enter that information, a JavaScript could send it back to the counterfeit Web page, and before you know it, your Yahoo!

account has just been cracked. A really clever programmer will use the account information to log on to your Yahoo! account from the counterfeit Yahoo! page, so it will appear that nothing unusual happened. Your account would be compromised, and you'd have no clue that it had happened. This sort of trickery is a real danger with any scripting language for the Web, no matter how careful its design.

What can you do to be safe? One option is to disable all scripting languages in your browser. It's done by setting another preference. For Navigator, go to the Advanced preference settings and uncheck the checkbox for Enable JavaScript. For MSIE, go to Internet Options, select the Security tab, highlight Internet, click the Custom Level button, and then activate the Disable Active Scripting radio button. But disabling all scripting languages will cost you. You'll miss out on a lot of what the Web has to offer, including most e-commerce transactions, most user-customizable sites, and most sites that require user registrations (not to mention all of the nifty interactive visual effects).

Suppose that you don't want to do anything so drastic. You next best bet is eternal vigilance. Be on your toes when you navigate new neighborhoods, especially when you're asked to fill out any forms on the Web. You won't be 100% safe from all possible tricksters, but you'll probably be alright. Security risks associated with JavaScript do surface occasionally. However, they can be addressed only by the people who program the browsers.

For most people, the level of risk associated with JavaScript is acceptable. If you're willing to walk out of your house despite the fact that some crazy person could drive by and take a shot at you for no apparent reason, then you really shouldn't worry about JavaScript. For most people, these are reasonable risks.

As explained earlier, there is a big difference between understanding a script well enough to plug it into your own Web pages and understanding it well enough to reproduce it from scratch. In one case, you need only some vague understanding of what's happening, and in the other, you need to really understand the underlying concepts of the programming language: its syntax, strengths, and limitations. This highlights the difference between script kiddies (see the Above and Beyond section in Chapter 2) and serious programmers. The term *script kiddie* was coined by legitimate programmers to distinguish themselves from all of the so-called 12-year-old computer geniuses who appear to know what they are doing (but really don't). If you want to be a programmer, you have to learn at least a few programming languages well enough to write your own programs from scratch. Alternatively, you can settle for a more superficial level of understanding, which is all that you need to add scripts written by other people to your Web pages. Even a poorly understood script can be successfully modified to suit your needs (see Exercises 18, 19, and 20), if you're patient. There is really nothing wrong with being a script kiddie, as long as you don't confuse what you're doing with real programming. To understand JavaScript, you must look at more than one example and read more than one book about the language.

Derogatory nomenclature aside, the life of a script kiddie is not so bad. You can surf the Web looking for cool scripts and impress your friends with all of the new things that your Web page can do. If your interest in Web design is more professional than recreational, you can significantly improve your Web pages with a minimal amount of time and expense. For most people, surfing for scripts is more fun than studying a book. And if you end up wanting to read a book about JavaScript down the road, you'll be ready to dive into it with a lot of questions and curiosity.

Locating Script Libraries

To locate a script library, use any general search engine and enter the query "JavaScripts." Here is a sampling of what's out there (in no particular order). The sites marked with asterisks are especially good for beginners.

```
http://www.JavaScripts.com/
http://www.webmonkey.com/
http://www.developer.com/downloads/code/JavaScripts.html
http://www.wsabstract.com/          ***
http://www.infohiway.com/JavaScript/indexf.htm
http://www.scripts.com/JavaScript/
http://JavaScript.internet.com/          ***
http://www.thefreesite.com/freejava.htm
http://www.essex1.com/people/timothy/js-index.htm          ***
http://www.24fun.ch/
http://www.geocities.com/SiliconValley/7116/
http://www.js-planet.com/
http://www.JavaScriptsearch.com/
http://www.exeat.com/
http://www.freecode.com/
```

Keep in mind that some scripts are simpler than others. Some might be well documented, whereas others are not documented at all. As a beginner, look for simple ones that are well documented. It won't hurt to take a peek at something really complicated just for kicks, but don't expect to understand it. You should also know that there is usually more than one way to achieve your objective by JavaScript. If one approach makes no sense to you, keep looking until you find one that does. Don't forget that some approaches might work for only one browser, so pay close attention to comments about browser compatibility.

Learning to Write Your Own Scripts

You can learn JavaScript on the Web, or you learn it by studying a book. Here are a few good online tutorials to get you started.

30-step JavaScript Primer by Joe Burns
>`http://www.htmlgoodies.com/primers/`

Voodoo's Introduction to JavaScript by Stefan Koch
>`http://rummelplatz.uni-mannheim.de/~skoch/js/`
>`tutorial.htm`

Thau's JavaScript Tutorial (in 5 lessons)
>`http://hotwired.lycos.com/Webmonkey/98/03/index0a.html`

A collection of short JavaScript tutorials on specific topics
>`http://www.wsabstract.com/javaindex.shtml`

Free JavaScript Learning Center (a 14-lesson tutorial)
>`http://www.crays.com/learn/`

JavaScript for Beginners
>`http://www.builder.com/Programming/JavaScript/`

Scripts are not limited to creating cosmetic special effects. They are also useful for practical processing tasks. For example, a script can check Web form entries before form data is sent to the server. Have you ever filled out a form and skipped over a required entry? Chances are, you were then told to go back and fill in the missing entry. This correction was probably generated by a special-purpose script (a *form verification script*), but no data was yet sent out over the Net.

Scripts can also be used to place cookies on your hard drive, read cookies that are already there, and personalize your experience on the Web accordingly. Utilities that block cookies typically work by inserting a script into each Web page that you download *after* it is retrieved from a Web server and *before* it is displayed. The script inserted by the cookie blocker overrides the script inserted by the Web page author, and the cookie blocker wins.

JavaScript is a highly versatile programming language, and programmers are always exploring new applications for it. To stay up on the latest developments, subscribe to a weekly newsletter that is affiliated with one of the larger JavaScript clearinghouses (see "Where Can I Learn More?" later in the chapter).

DHTML and CCS

If you're exploring the Web for JavaScript resources, you might see references to *DHTML* scripts next to or mixed in with some JavaScript libraries. DHTML is **Dynamic HTML** and refers generally to Web content that changes each time that it's viewed. It's a mix of JavaScript and other techniques, some of which are supported only by either MSIE (Microsoft's DHTML extensions) or Navigator

(Netscape's DHTML extensions). This is one of the lingering consequences of the great "Browser Wars" circa 1997. At that time, Navigator was the best Web browser available and Microsoft was playing catch-up with Internet applications, and Microsoft tried to promote its own scripting language (JScript) that was based on, but not fully compatible with, JavaScript. JScript was released but it never became as popular as JavaScript. Locate scripts that cross the browser divide whenever you can. Sometimes, however, there won't seem to be a solution that works for both browsers.

You might also see references to CSS. **CSS** stands for **cascading style sheets**, which make it easier for Web page designers to apply a uniform look to each page in a large Web site. It supports a lot of time-saving shortcuts that are especially important for professional designers who want to minimize the number of repetitive HTML tags and attributes needed for each Web page when they develop a new Web site. CSS is less important for a small Web site. However, if you're involved with a large Web site, you'll find it to be a welcome addition to your Web pages. If you decide to use CSS, then, as with DHTML, watch out for possible browser compatibility problems.

Before you move on, one last cautionary note is in order. If you find yourself experimenting with a lot of scripts and you're interested in setting up a Web site for e-commerce, think twice about trying to create an e-commerce storefront on your own. You'll find scripts on the Web that claim to provide various storefront capabilities (site-specific search engines, password-protected Web pages, and so on), and this might tempt you to patch together something on your own. However, a virtual store is nothing to play around with if you're new to Web design. There are security issues and customer service features that require absolute reliability if you want your site to succeed. If you try to do it yourself, you'll be taking on a lot of risk that could be minimized if a professional were to handle the tricky parts for you. Free scripts on the Web are fine for some interactive enhancements and for recreational and purely informational Web pages. However, you'll need heavier machinery to handle a storefront operation. If your livelihood depends on a reliable Web site with zippy page displays, expect to pay for it. You need to research your options, determine your budget constraints, and make an informed decision about professional site support.

Playing Around Where You Won't Get Hurt

If you're not a professional programmer, you should not attempt to create an e-commerce site on your own. You might find many free scripts on the Web designed to support e-commerce operations. However, this is one time when you can expect to get what you pay for (see Section 5.7 for more information about e-commerce software support).

When real-life customers are involved and money is changing hands, you don't want to learn anything very important the hard way.

5.4 JAVA APPLETS

If you read the last section and tried your hand at installing some scripts on your Web page, you might have concluded that working with JavaScript is too time-consuming. Some people have the time and enjoy the challenge. Others can't be bothered and feel frustrated when things don't work perfectly on the first try. Either way, you'll be relieved to hear that Java applets are easier to install than scripts.

A Java applet is similar to a script in that it is a small program that is attached to a Web page and executed by the client when the Web page is retrieved from its server. However, it's different in terms of the requirements on the client side. A Java applet must be executed by a **Java Virtual Machine** (JVM), which works alongside the browser in order to execute the applet when the page containing the applet is downloaded. You might have noticed how your browser takes a long time to download certain pages the first time that you visit those pages during a browsing session. This might be because your browser is loading Java in order to execute an applet on the Web page being downloaded. When a browser loads Java, it launches the JVM, which is a substantial application in its own right. Once the JVM is running, it stays alive in the background so that you don't have to relaunch it during that session.

To write your own Java applets, you first must learn the Java programming language, which is similar to but not the same thing as JavaScript. Java is a full-featured programming language for creating not only applets for Web pages but also applications that have nothing to do with the Web. JavaScript can be used only to enhance Web pages. Because it's more powerful, Java is harder to master than JavaScript and is best approached with a good textbook in hand. And whereas JavaScript can be learned from examples, in bits and pieces, Java requires serious and more systematic study. If you've never done computer programming, it will be hard to learn Java on your own.

Java is unique among programming languages because it was designed to be *platform-independent*. The same Java program will run without adjustments on computers running the Windows, UNIX, or Macintosh OS (at least in theory). Each platform needs its own JVM; however, once the JVM has been installed, any Java program can be run on any JVM. Although the platform-independent claims about Java have not been fully realized yet (there are a few different versions of the JVM), applets benefit from the attempt. The same applet can be run on any Java-enabled browser on any OS. It might not produce perfectly identical displays or behavior on all computers, but browser compatibility is much less of a problem for applets than it is for scripts.

Can Applets Spread Computer Viruses?

As always, the question of safety should occur to you. You're downloading executable code from an unknown source. How much risk is there in this? In general, applets are safer than scripts because they are not allowed to read or write to any files (not even cookie files). Those restrictions make it impossible to embed a computer virus inside of an applet. However, applets can send information back to the server that sent the applet to you. So whenever you interact with an applet, you might be sending information back to a server, perhaps without your knowledge. If an applet asks you for personal information, the usual privacy concerns apply.

In general, applets pose less of a risk than do scripts. If you're willing to run a JavaScript-enabled browser, you should not be afraid of running a Java-enabled browser.

Although Java is harder to learn than JavaScript, applets are easier to add to a Web page than are scripts. Unlike the latter, each applet is packaged in a "locked box" that cannot be opened, inspected, or modified. You take what you get and plug it in, and it either works or it doesn't. You can't modify an applet by fussing with its code, a line here and a line there. In fact, you can't even see the source code for an applet unless the author has chosen to distribute it alongside the applet for educational purposes. However, the source code is intended for Java programmers and is not explained to nonprogrammers who view it.

Here is a sample applet to demonstrate how easy it is to install someone else's applet on your Web page. Figure 5.17 shows an applet called **Qgoo** running inside of the Opera Web browser.

When you install Qgoo on your Web page, you specify an image file for it to display. In this case, a JPEG screen shot of an HTML table, first seen in Chapter 3, was selected. If Qgoo did nothing but display the image for you, it would be a rather boring applet. But Qgoo allows you to stretch and distort the image in a variety of ways (see Figures 5.18 and 5.19).

This is basically a recreational applet that is especially entertaining when applied to photographs of faces (you can obtain some seriously disturbing facial distortions).

Figure 5.17:
Qgoo Displaying an Image

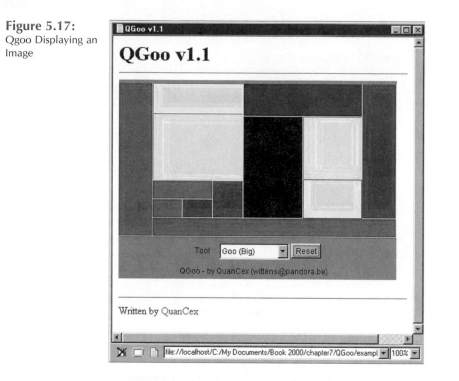

Figure 5.18:
A Single Mouse Movement Distorting One Region of the Image

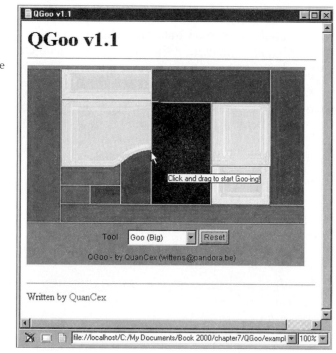

Figure 5.19:
Multiple Distortions
Producing a New
Image

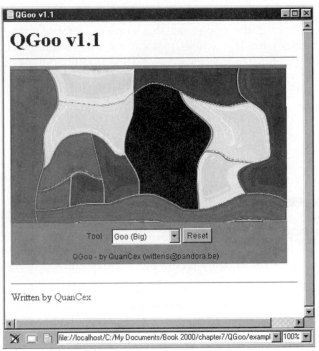

Here is the HTML file used to produce these screen shots.

```html
<html>
  <head>
    <title>QGoo v1.1</title>
  </head>
  <body>
    <h1>QGoo v1.1</h1>
    <hr>
    <applet code=QGoo.class width=500 height=330>
    alt="Your browser understands the &lt;APPLET&gt;
        tag but isn't running the applet, for some
        reason."
      <param name="image" value="blocks.jpg">
      <param name="bgcolor" value="#2498FF">
    </applet>
    <hr>
    Written by <a href="mailto:wittens@pandora.be">
        QuanCex</a><BR>
  </body>
</html>
```

This block of code was distributed with the applet exactly as shown here. The crucial element here is the applet tag that contains attributes and **PARAM** tags. The applet's attributes explain where to look for the executable code by naming a `.class` file and how much space to set aside for the applet's display.

code=QGoo.class	This is the executable file that the JVM needs to run the applet
width=500	The width of the applet display
height=330	The height of the applet display
alt="Your…"	Text to be displayed if the applet can't be executed

Only the **code** attribute is technically required. However, most applet installation instructions specify values for the **WIDTH** and **HEIGHT** attributes that should be included for the intended display. If no directory path is included as the **code** attribute value, the file named there must be in the same subdirectory as this HTML file. In this case, you must ensure that the file **QGoo.class** is in the same directory as your Web page.

The **PARAM** tags enable a user to customize the applet. For those of you who know a little programming, each **PARAM** tag corresponds to an applet input parameter. In the case of the QGoo applet, you can customize the applet by specifying the image file to display (the **PARAM** tag named "image") and the color to display in the applet's background (the **PARAM** tag named "bgcolor").

```
<param name="image" value="blocks.jpg">
<param name="bgcolor" value="#2498FF">
```

When you install an applet on a Web page, examine the **PARAM** tags to see whether you should modify any. Some parameters are self-explanatory, whereas others might require some explanation. Read any documentation for the applet and advice concerning the applet's **PARAM** tags. If you do modify a **PARAM** tag, plan to change the **VALUE** attribute value; never change the **NAME** attribute value. Whenever a filename is needed for a **PARAM** value, make sure that the file is located in the same subdirectory as the Web page (unless you include a directory path for some other location).

Sometimes an applet distributed for general use will require additional support files for its parameter values. You might need to supply your own support files, or these files might be packaged with the applet. Downloadable applets are generally stored in file archives (see Chapter 8), so you'll receive everything that you need in one download. Always look for a **readme.txt** file—it usually contains important instructions for the applet's installation. In general, expect to install your applet in seven steps (see the tip box below).

How to Install an Applet

1. Download and unpack the applet (see Chapter 8 for more about this step).
2. Read all available documentation.
3. Insert the required HTML snippet into your Web page.
4. Modify `PARAM` values as needed.
5. Upload your Web page to the server.
6. Upload the required `.class` file to the server.
7. Upload required support files to the server as needed.

Finding Applets on the Web

This book can't possibly list all of the worthwhile applet sites. However, here's a starter set. You can add to it as you discover more.

`http://javaboutique.internet.com/` (one of the major sites)

`http://freewarejava.com/` (a very large site)

`http://wsabstract.com/java/` (a very large site)

`http://www.javapoyyoured.com/` (very nice stuff; visit the showcase, and check out the newest applets)

`http://www.free-applets.com/` (a smaller site; nice if you're feeling overwhelmed by too many choices)

`http://www.echoecho.com/freeapplets.htm` (a small but select collection; visit its applets tutorial if you're having trouble adding an applet to a Web page)

`http://www.jars.com/` (not just applets; not all free, but check out WWW Tools under the JARS Categories)

`http://www.codebrain.com/java/` (beautiful applets—a must see; for example, check out the Gutenberg applet)

`http://java.sun.com/java.sun.com/applets/applets.html` (the birthplace of Java)

`http://www.developer.com/directories/pages/dir.java.html` (not only applets; time-consuming to navigate but lots of stuff)

`http://www.thefreesite.com/freejava.htm` (a great directory that describes lots of free applet sites)

Some Java applets do the same things as scripts (for example, mouseovers); others offer functionality you won't find anywhere else. Some programmers use applets to distribute their software to the public with a minimal amount of client-side effort.

The software is automatically downloaded by the Web browser, requires no installation by the client, and consumes no permanent storage on the client machine. In addition, an applet consumes no computing server resources once the download is completed. If the software needs to be updated, a new `.class` file replaces the old one on the Web server, and everyone downloading the applet automatically receives the updated code. Java applets are an example of Web-based client/server computing that allow programmers to distribute their software to remote hosts with minimal overhead (no download sites, no upgrade announcements, no version control problems), while maintaining maximal control over the code.

5.5 | DATA-DRIVEN WEB PAGES

It's a rare Web page that never needs to be updated. When a Web page needs to be updated regularly, you can design it as a *data-driven Web page*, or more properly, a *data-driven display within a Web page*. Applets can be especially useful in these situations because an applet can be designed to accept data entries that are applet-independent. This will all become clearer when you see an example of a data-driven display. As the last section explained, applets can be designed to accept as a **PARAM** value either an entire file or a single data item such as a hexadecimal color code. This makes it possible to design an applet that receives data from its **PARAM** values, taken either from the values themselves or from data files specified in the values.

Here is an example of a data-driven display, the **Hollywood Text applet** written by Bill Giel. This applet is well documented and illustrates very nicely the concept of a customizable data-driven display. Once installed, this applet displays an unlimited amount of text in a fixed amount of space by allowing the user to click through successive screen displays (see Figure 5.20).

Web pages that contain announcements require periodic updates. This is often handled by directly updating the underlying HTML file. A much cleaner design adds a text-driven display to the Web page. The display engine remains the same and requires no modification; only the text driving the display needs to be updated. This is what makes it a data-driven display. Figure 5.21 shows a customization of the same applet shown in Figure 5.20. A border for the text display has been added, as well as text, added by changing the applet's **PARAM** values.

Here's what you must do to customize the Hollywood Text applet. First, you need to supply your own text data. This applet reads input text from a plain ASCII text file, so you can use any text editor to create your input text. The applet also recognizes a simple system of four formatting tags so that you have some control over the final text display. The input file used for the displays in Figure 5.21 is shown in Figure 5.22.

Figure 5.20:
Hollywood Text: A
Text-Driven "Click
Through" Applet

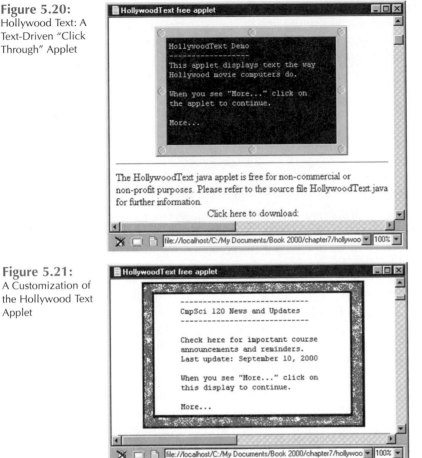

Figure 5.21:
A Customization of
the Hollywood Text
Applet

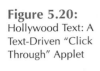

Figure 5.22:
A Simple Text File
That Drives the
Display

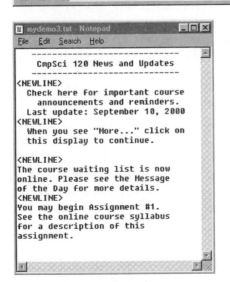

Once the applet has been installed, this text file is the only file that you need to modify each time that you want to update the page display. Replace the old text in this file with new text, and the Web page is updated. Bingo! You're done.

The input text is given to the applet through a **PARAM** value, in this case, named **SCRIPT**. However, the Hollywood Text applet has a long list of **PARAM** settings that you can use to modify the applet's appearance if you don't want it to look like the default applet in Figure 5.20. Always look for a documentation file that should come with any applet that you want to install. If the applet can be customized by using **PARAM** values, the documentation should describe how each value affects the applet. Figure 5.23 shows part of the documentation that accompanies the Hollywood Text applet. If you understand how each **PARAM** value for this applet can be adjusted, you can give the applet a unique appearance.

The most important visual component for this applet is the graphics file for the **BGIMAGE** parameter. This is where you can insert your own border and background color for the applet. For those of you involved with MP3 player software, you'll recognize this as the *skin* for the applet. A display has a skin when the background color or pattern for that display can be easily replaced by the user. The term became popular with MP3 players (the virtual kind) and now generally refers to any display that can be easily customized by the user. The Hollywood Text applet comes with one skin (shown in Figure 5.20). However, you can design your own by using a paint program or photo editor if you want to create a unique look for your personal version of the applet. You can make the display larger by controlling the **HEIGHT** and **WIDTH** attribute values, and you can control the location of the text within the display with **PARAM** values such as **INITX**, **INITY**, and **MAXY** (remember that *y*-values *increase* as you move *down* the *y*-axis).

Other **PARAM** values for this applet control the appearance of the text. Although the figures in this book can't show it, this is a dynamic text display when it runs on a Web page. The text appears in real time, one character at a time, along with soft clicking sounds that reminds one of a teletype or a typewriter (if you are old enough to know what those things are). The text for each screen display does not appear all at once. It unfolds slowly, thereby making it more fun to read (unless perhaps the display is slow enough to be annoying). If needed, you can control the speed of the text display with the **CPAUSE**, **LPAUSE**, and **SPAUSE PARAM** settings (although the applet author's default settings look pretty good).

You might need to spend an hour or so tweaking the applet's appearance. However, once you have a display that you like, it's easy to update the text display as needed. The only file that requires updating is the text file for the **SCRIPT** parameter . You can always test the appearance of a new **SCRIPT** file locally before you upload anything to your server. With a little experience, you can probably learn to write perfect **SCRIPT** files on the first try, thereby making it easy to update your Web pages as often as needed.

Figure 5.23:
Lots of PARAM values for Lots of Customization

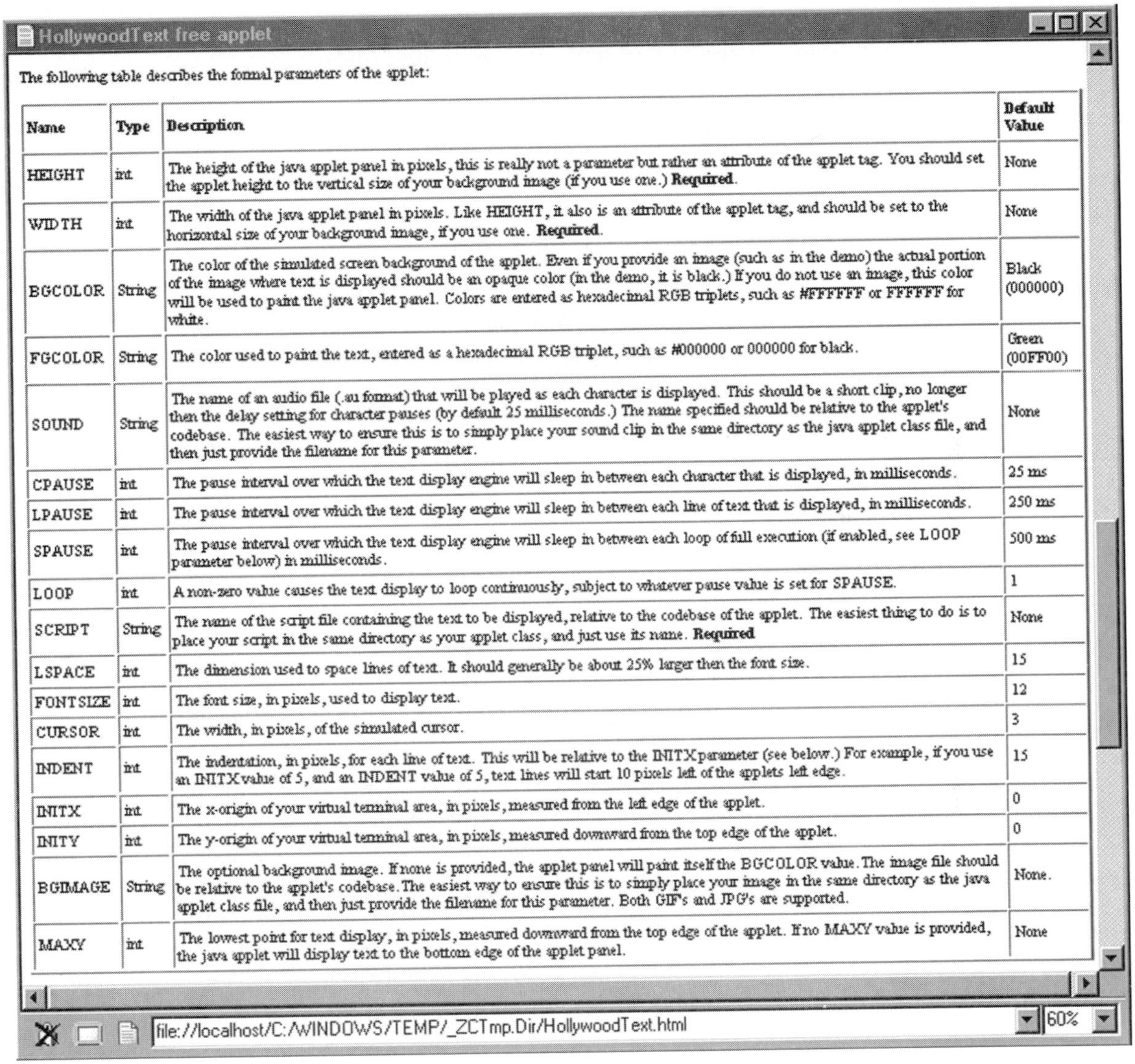

		HollywoodText free applet	

The following table describes the formal parameters of the applet:

Name	Type	Description	Default Value
HEIGHT	int	The height of the java applet panel in pixels, this is really not a parameter but rather an attribute of the applet tag. You should set the applet height to the vertical size of your background image (if you use one.) **Required**.	None
WIDTH	int	The width of the java applet panel in pixels. Like HEIGHT, it also is an attribute of the applet tag, and should be set to the horizontal size of your background image, if you use one. **Required**.	None
BGCOLOR	String	The color of the simulated screen background of the applet. Even if you provide an image (such as in the demo) the actual portion of the image where text is displayed should be an opaque color (in the demo, it is black.) If you do not use an image, this color will be used to paint the java applet panel. Colors are entered as hexadecimal RGB triplets, such as #FFFFFF or FFFFFF for white.	Black (000000)
FGCOLOR	String	The color used to paint the text, entered as a hexadecimal RGB triplet, such as #000000 or 000000 for black.	Green (00FF00)
SOUND	String	The name of an audio file (.au format) that will be played as each character is displayed. This should be a short clip, no longer then the delay setting for character pauses (by default 25 milliseconds.) The name specified should be relative to the applet's codebase. The easiest way to ensure this is to simply place your sound clip in the same directory as the java applet class file, and then just provide the filename for this parameter.	None
CPAUSE	int	The pause interval over which the text display engine will sleep in between each character that is displayed, in milliseconds.	25 ms
LPAUSE	int	The pause interval over which the text display engine will sleep in between each line of text that is displayed, in milliseconds.	250 ms
SPAUSE	int	The pause interval over which the text display engine will sleep in between each loop of full execution (if enabled, see LOOP parameter below) in milliseconds.	500 ms
LOOP	int	A non-zero value causes the text display to loop continuously, subject to whatever pause value is set for SPAUSE.	1
SCRIPT	String	The name of the script file containing the text to be displayed, relative to the codebase of the applet. The easiest thing to do is to place your script in the same directory as your applet class, and just use its name. **Required**	None
LSPACE	int	The dimension used to space lines of text. It should generally be about 25% larger then the font size.	15
FONTSIZE	int	The font size, in pixels, used to display text.	12
CURSOR	int	The width, in pixels, of the simulated cursor.	3
INDENT	int	The indentation, in pixels, for each line of text. This will be relative to the INITX parameter (see below.) For example, if you use an INITX value of 5, and an INDENT value of 5, text lines will start 10 pixels left of the applets left edge.	15
INITX	int	The x-origin of your virtual terminal area, in pixels, measured from the left edge of the applet.	0
INITY	int	The y-origin of your virtual terminal area, in pixels, measured downward from the top edge of the applet.	0
BGIMAGE	String	The optional background image. If none is provided, the applet panel will paint itself the BGCOLOR value. The image file should be relative to the applet's codebase. The easiest way to ensure this is to simply place your image in the same directory as the java applet class file, and then just provide the filename for this parameter. Both GIF's and JPG's are supported.	None.
MAXY	int	The lowest point for text display, in pixels, measured downward from the top edge of the applet. If no MAXY value is provided, the java applet will display text to the bottom edge of the applet panel.	None

file://localhost/C:/WINDOWS/TEMP/_ZCTmp.Dir/HollywoodText.html   60%

To add the applet to a Web page, you insert an APPLET tag. Some Applet tags have parameters, and some need only the CODE, HEIGHT, and WIDTH attributes. The Hollywood Text applet is very customizable, so you'll see many PARAM tags inside of the APPLET tags.

```
<applet code="HollywoodText.class" width="350" height="230">
   <param name="cabbase" value="HollywoodText.cab">
   <param name="bgcolor" value="#FFFFFF">
   <param name="fgcolor" value="#000000">
   <param name="sound" value="blip.au">
   <param name="cpause" value="25">
   <param name="lpause" value="250">
   <param name="spause" value="500">
   <param name="loop" value="0">
   <param name="script" value="mydemo3.txt">
   <param name="lspace" value="15">
   <param name="fontsize" value="12">
   <param name="cursor" value="3">
   <param name="indent" value="40">
   <param name="initx" value="20">
   <param name="inity" value="20">
   <param name="bgimage" value="fuzz4.jpg">
   <param name="maxy" value="200">
</APPLET>
```

This is the HTML insert for the applet as seen in Figure 5.21. This is a fairly unusual applet installation; most applets require only one or no **PARAM** tags.

Data-driven Web page displays are one of the tricks that professionals use to minimize the amount of effort needed for ongoing Web page maintenance. An applet such as Hollywood Text is very powerful because it gives you many customization options. The same applet could be used on different Web pages and look very different on each. If you don't like the real-time typing effect, you can turn off the **SOUND** parameter, set the **TIMING** parameters to 0, and the text will pop up instantaneously. If you don't want a border around the text, don't use the **BGIMAGE** file; you can specify a background color for the applet's display instead.

If you want more control over your text than this applet provides, look for another that gives you more features. Check out the Gutenberg Applet at **CodeBrain.com** for what might be the ultimate text-driven display applet—it's amazing! If you don't like something about one applet, or if you've simply outgrown an applet that met your needs last year but no longer does, shop around for another.

Data-driven displays are not limited to text. You can find data-driven applets for charts, graphs, and multimedia displays. You can use applets to set up slide shows for any number of graphics files. You can also install interactive applets that accept data from the user for data-driven displays that are controlled by the user (for example, a body fat calculator or a movie finder, if you've the right data files to support one). Once you become comfortable with applet installations, you'll be able to take your Web pages to a whole new level of sophistication.

As a source of applets, programmers are always posting new ones on the Web. You might be able to convince someone to write one for you (computer science students sometimes like to try out their new-found programming "muscles" on other people's problems, just for the experience). If you really like what you can do with other people's applets, you might want to learn Java so that you can write your own. The sky's the limit when you can write your own. However, don't underestimate what you can do as a nonprogrammer. Applets give the nonprogrammer a lot of the freedom and creativity that used to require programming expertise or a development budget plush enough to buy that expertise. It's no longer possible to look at a Web page and ascertain the technical expertise of the person who wrote it. Some very sophisticated pages can now be pulled together by nontechnical users, thanks to applets and the generosity of the people who distribute their applets at no cost. All you have to do is read and honor the licensing agreements for the applets that you want to use.

5.6 ▌ WEB SITE MAINTENANCE TOOLS

As your Web sites become more sophisticated, they will probably also become larger and more difficult to maintain. Although ongoing maintenance is a relatively tedious task, it's absolutely necessary if you want to maintain a reliable site that is useful to users. Fortunately, there are two types of utilities that can assist you with your Web site maintenance tasks:

- Link checkers, which automate the testing of a site's hyperlinks
- Site mappers, which automate the creation of accurate site maps for your site

If your site is small and manageable without these tools, you can skip this section. But if you have a reasonably large site and you've been struggling without either of these tools, then read this section.

5.6.1 Link Checkers

Hyperlinks to external URLs can become obsolete. Checking and correcting obsolete links requires ongoing attention. If you have only five to ten links, you can check them manually every week or two and thereby stay on top of your site. However, if you have more than ten links, this routine becomes very old, very fast. If you forgo the routine, your site will suffer and your users will feel neglected or annoyed. That's when you could lose them. If your site is compelling and entertaining enough, your users will forgive you. However, most of us shouldn't risk this. It's important to keep your hyperlinks operational and current.

An **automated link checker** is a utility that takes much of the drudgery out of ongoing link maintenance. If you have a moderately large Web site with more than a hundred links and you care about your users, you absolutely must use a link checker. There are two ways to go. You can subscribe to an ASP (Application Service Provider) service that will produce link reports for you on a weekly or monthly basis. You won't have to remember to check your links; the service will remember for you. All you need to do is to read the reports and fix stale links. These services are very good. However, you pay for them as long as you use them, which could be indefinitely.

If you want to put a cap on this maintenance expense, consider your second option: Install your own link checker so that you can run the tests yourself. Many link checkers are available on the Web. A few are distributed at no cost, whereas others are free during a trial examination period. The most sophisticated products (**Watchfire's Linkbot Pro 5.0** retails for $395) are for professional site administrators and offer sophisticated features for comprehensive site administration. Figure 5.24 shows in action a more moderately priced ($39.95) link checker named **LinkRunner**.

Figure 5.24:
LinkRunner after Having Tested 1,684 Hyperlinks in 115 Files

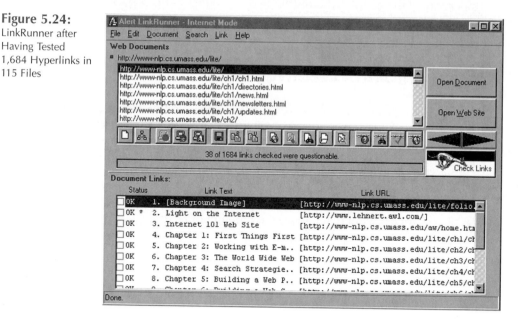

You will not be able to automate every aspect of hyperlink maintenance. All that the link checker can do is bring problems to your attention. A good link checker will produce a report summarizing all possible problems found on your site (see Figure 5.25). For each link that is flagged as questionable or broken, you have to decide what to do about it. You might need to find a new URL for the original resource, or you might need to remove the reference altogether. In either case, some updating of the Web page will be needed and only you can decide what to do for each link that requires attention.

Figure 5.25:
A LinkRunner
Problem Report in
HTML Format

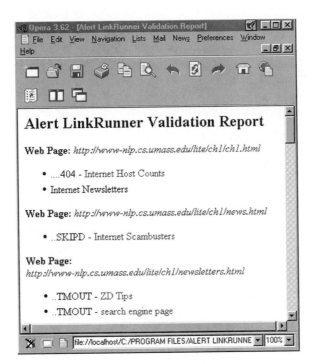

A good link checker should be easy to use with a minimal amount of study and preparation. All you need to specify is the location of the Web site to be checked. This can be done by specifying a directory location on the Web server or by listing specific URLs individually. Then the link checker collects all of the hyperlinks in the target documents and sends out requests to all of the servers that are hosting targeted links. If a server replies with a valid Web page, the link to that server passes the test. If an error message is returned, the link is added to the list of problem links. A good link checker will associate an error code with each problem link (see Figure 5.26).

You might have to pay for a good link checker. However, the investment is worthwhile if you want to keep your Web pages healthy and up-to-date. Some failures are transient and will disappear if you wait 24 hours. Others are more serious. By minimizing the amount of time that you must spend on routine maintenance, you'll have more time and energy for creative enhancements and major overhauls. Link maintenance is not as gratifying as the discovery of a cool applet. However, a site whose links are always operational will be appreciated and is likely to win a loyal following.

5.6.2 Site Mappers

If you have a reasonably large site, another maintenance tool to consider is a site map utility. Site maps are very useful to first-time visitors and should be carefully

Figure 5.26:
Error Codes Describing the Different Ways That a Link Can Fail

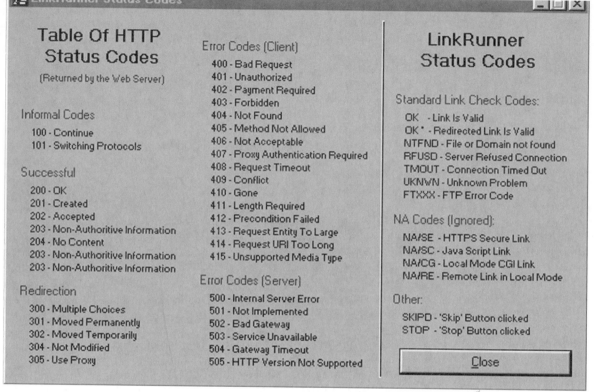

updated each time that you reorganize your site. The best way to maintain a site map that stays in sync with your site is to use a site map utility. As with link checkers, you can find freebies on the Web. However, you'll probably find it easier to work with a utility that you have purchased.

If you want state-of-the-art, you can spend thousands of dollars. For example, Inxight's hyperbolic tree utility, **Site Lens**, retailed for $5,000 at the time of this writing. Site Lens creates a graphical display of your site that morphs into a new display each time that the user clicks a link. Site Lens is a proprietary applet distributed without source code. It analyzes your site and creates a site map automatically. See the Above and Beyond section in Chapter 6 for some figures of Site Lens in action (where it is a feature of **AltaVista Discovery**), and visit the demo at **Inxight** to see it in action.

On the other end of the spectrum is a freeware program named **Joust Outliner**. Joust Outliner creates an expandable hierarchy of your site, with folders that expand or contract like the directory displays in Windows Explorer or a Mac's list view in the View menu. A highly customizable script distributed with documented source code,

Joust Outliner is data-driven and requires you to manually format the tree entries in a text file. Figure 5.27 shows a Joust Outliner site map.

Figure 5.27:
The Joust Outliner
Customizable Site
Map Utility at Work

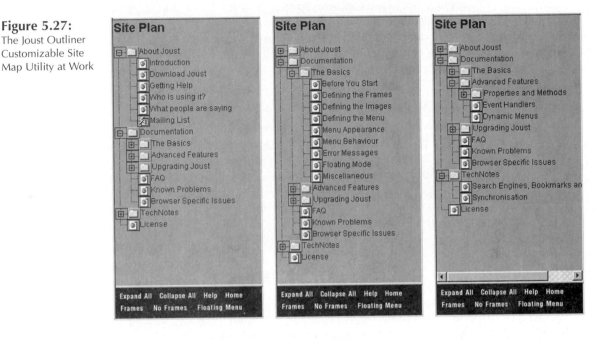

You can visit the Joust Outliner home page to play with the same site map. If you want to try Joust Outliner, expect to spend some time at it. The documentation is excellent; however, the data file that you create for your site must follow a special format. Read all of the instructions, and follow them carefully. Start with only two or three Web pages, and create a working map for them before attempting a complete site map. *Note*: This should not be your first JavaScript installation. If you're new to JavaScript , try something simpler such as an image map.

5.7 ▌ SITE CONSTRUCTION KITS

Web site construction is a labor-intensive undertaking. If you're creating a recreational site, you can afford to learn what you want when you want and experiment with the tools and utilities that interest you. One class of utilities worth investigating are Web site construction kits. These are not generic HTML editors or template collections, but rather packages designed to help you customize sophisticated sites, such as a *turnkey e-store*, an informational site with daily news items, or a Web site limited to paid subscribers. These usages are big business, and different products target professional users, amateur users, or in some cases both. Sophisticated construction utilities such as **Adobe GoLive** and **Macromedia Dreamweaver** are favored by the pros and are priced at $200 and up. Some construction kits are aimed at professionals who want to target a specialty market. For example, **Elemental Software's eStore Builder** lists for $599 and is designed for Java programmers. If you earn a living designing Web pages, it makes sense to invest in a high-end development tool that will save you time and pay for itself in the long run. If you are contemplating a high-end development tool, read some reviews to see if it is the right product for you. You can get in over your head if you don't do your research.

If you don't plan to devote your life to Web page design, but you've gone beyond basic HTML and would like to explore the next level, you might want to look into a mid-level site construction kit. **HotMetal Pro 6.0** ($129) is a good example of a tool that attempts to serve both neophytes and professionals. A Site Maker wizard, learning tools, and reference materials are valuable additions for less-experienced Web designers who want to strengthen their skills. At the same time, its more sophisticated features will serve more demanding users who are ready to explore cutting-edge Web technologies.

Allaire's Homepage 4.5 and **Luckman's WebEdit Pro 3.1** are similarly priced construction kits aimed at people who are well beyond their first Web page but not yet ready for a high-powered professional package.

If you're looking for an e-store development kit for nontechnical users, you can spend some really big bucks. **Allaire's Spectra** development kit, which includes shopping carts, credit card account authorization software, and user profiling capabilities, retails for over $7,000. Products such as this make sense for established retail operations ("mortar stores") that want to join the online revolution and become "click-and-mortar" operations. For existing retail operations, it makes sense to invest a few thousand dollars and roll out a professional Web presence without any glitches. In fact, if you're a really successful retailer, you can probably step up to the $15,000 to $200,000 range and let a professional Web designer take the whole problem off your hands. Click-and-mortar conversions are a fast-paced niche market. It pays to research the options before you embrace the first solution that you find. If you have this kind of money to kick around, don't expect to find adequate advice in any book, this one included. It might be best to hire an independent design consultant who can analyze your existing operation, assist you in formulating a business plan for online sales, and make development recommendations based on your specific business needs.

Perhaps you don't have a thriving business and a budget for design consultants. Instead, suppose that you're thinking about starting a small e-commerce business for as little money as possible. If that's the case, you're not alone and you have many possibilities. Some will cost you nothing more than your current Internet access costs. Many Web hosting services are trying to attract small businesses to the Web by offering e-commerce service options. They will set up all of the software that you need (virtual shopping cards, secure credit card transactions, status reports for current orders, and so on), register a domain name for you, submit your site to the major search engines—or perhaps include your site in a virtual shopping mall—and help you to acquire a merchant's bank account so that you can process credit card orders. If your inventory is limited and fairly simple, these services might be all that you need. The costs are minimal, and the set-up process is simple (see Figure 5.28). However, you must research your options online for current information about hosting services. The information in Figure 5.28 was accurate in 1999 but has undoubtedly changed since. Some of these hosting services might no longer be in operation, and newer ones will have probably materialized by the time that you read this.

Figure 5.28:
Some Online
Storefront Services

	Bigstep	**iCat Web Store**	**Merchandizer**	**Yahoo! Store**
setup fee	no charge	no charge	$149	no charge
setup time	1 hour	1 hour	1 day	1 hour
monthly fee	no charge	10 items/$9.95 50 items/$49.95 100 items/$99.95	100 items/$79.95	50 items/$100
merchant account	no setup charge $14.95/month $.15/transaction	$195 setup charge $15/month $.35/transaction	no setup charge $9.50/month 2.3% of price + $.25/transaction	$250 setup charge $45/month $.30/transaction
include their logo?	yes	yes	no	sometimes
add existing pages?	no	no	yes	if you use "RTML"
is there a virtual mall?	no yes	no	yes	

If you've ever used a free Web hosting service and created a home page using one of their tools (for example, Tripod's **Homepage Studio** or **Yahoo!'s PageBuilder**), you'll find it easy to create an e-commerce business by using one of the online storefront services. No software downloads are needed—it's all done with forms and a Web browser.

If these costs are still too much for you, you might consider basing your business at **eBay** or another auction site. If you have only a few items to sell, you can put them up for bid and move your merchandise that way.

You can also opt for a free e-commerce service, if you can find one. However, be warned that a free hosting service could disappear in the near future. Early experiments with free e-commerce support indicate that the participating sites are less likely to be maintained and managed by their owners. E-commerce support that cost nothing are more likely to be abandoned and left unattended than those that require ongoing fees. This is clearly bad for the advertisers who subsidize the real costs of these sites. Too many abandoned storefronts will doom any virtual mall and the hosting service behind it. So, if you intend to stay in business for more than a few weeks or months, you might want to avoid no-cost operations, unless they guarantee responsible store management throughout. Your success depends on the hosting service's success, so pick the service carefully.

No matter how you set up your first online retail operation, remember that there is more to your business than your Web site. Real merchandise must be shipped by using real carriers; customer service requires a personal touch. A person answering a telephone 40 hours a week can be as important as a spiffy Web site. Don't forget to cover the nitty-gritty operations while you're thinking about your online presence.

Things to Remember

- An applet is a small Java program that is downloaded with a Web page and executed by a Java-enabled browser on the client's host.
- A script is a small computer program that is downloaded with a Web page and executed by a script-enabled browser on the client's host.
- You don't need to know how to program in order to install an applet or a script on your Web page.
- Applets and scripts usually have their own licensing agreements; know your legal obligations before you add them to your Web pages.
- Mouseover effects are achieved by using image maps and JavaScript.
- JavaScript is used for all types of behind-the-scenes Web functionality.

Important Concepts

applet—a small Java program that is attached to a Web page.

construction kit—a program that helps you to build Web pages or sites.

data-driven applet—a customizable applet that displays data.

image map—a means to create hyperlinks inside of graphical elements.

Java—a programming language that has powerful Web applications.

JavaScript—a scripting language designed for the Web.

script—a small program written in a scripting language.

site maintenance—the process of keeping a Web site timely and healthy.

Where Can I Learn More?

JavaScript Tutorials `http://webdesign.about.com/msubjscriptinfo.htm`

JavaScript Hoaxes and Bombs `http://antivirus.about.com/library/weekly/aa081299.htm`

Using Java Applets (without programming)
`http://java.about.com/library/weekly/aa032499.htm`

Java Tutorials `http://java.about.com/compute/java/`
`msubmenu4.htm`

Problems and Exercises

1. Server-side image maps are slower than client-side image maps. Can you explain why? Which type of image map requires less bandwidth?

2. Where are scripts inserted in an HTML file? What tags are needed to create an image map? Which tag attributes are necessary when you create an image map?

3. How are scripting languages different from other programming languages? Is JavaScript the only scripting language for the Web?

4. Do image maps have browser incompatibility problems? When do you need to worry about browser incompatibilities?

5. List ten mouse events that JavaScript recognizes.

6. Explain how much testing is (ideally) required when you add a new script to a Web page. How do professional programmers deal with the legacy of the "Browser Wars" when they use JavaScript?

7. What are malicious scripts, and how can you protect yourself from them? Explain how JavaScript can be abused to create dangerous Web sites. Can these problems be fixed? Can you ever be 100% safe? Explain your answers.

8. If you're running software to block cookies, what might happen if you disable JavaScript in your Web browser?

9. Which Web page enhancement is more prone to browser compatibility problems: a script or an applet? Explain your answer.

10. Compare and contrast scripts with applets. Describe one way that they are similar and three ways that they are different.

11. Should a programmer who wants to distribute a program without making the code public write a script or an applet? Explain your answer.

12. What is a data-driven applet? When should you think about adding a data-driven applet to your Web page?

13. What is a link checker, and who needs to use one?

14. What is a site mapper, and when would you want to use one?

15. Suppose that you want to create an image viewer for some large photograph files. The overall page design will rely on frames. One frame, the control frame, holds a display of from 10 to 20 thumbnail sketches. When the user clicks a thumbnail, the full-sized version of that same image appears in a second frame (the viewer frame). Each time that the user clicks a different thumbnail in the control frame, a new image appears in the viewer frame. Does this page require JavaScript? Explain how you would build this Web page.

16. **[Hands-On]** Obtain a client-side image mapping utility (for example, you can download **Dr. Bill's program** for Windows), and create a simple map for an image of your choice. Include one circular region and one rectangular region. How long did it take you to create a working image map? Suppose that you want to enlarge your hotzones after you have generated your image map. Will it be easier to make that adjustment by hand or to use the utility to remap the image?

17. **[Hands-On]** Create a client-side image map that has a triangular hotzone. If you have a mapping utility that doesn't support polygonal regions, you can manually write an **AREA** tag for your triangle. Use **SHAPE="POLY"** and study an HTML 3.2 (or higher) reference on the Web to learn how to use the **COORDS** attribute for a triangle.

18. **[Hands-On]** Take two images with the same dimensions, and create a Web page that uses a mouseover script to swap the images when the user passes the mouse over them. Adapt the script described in Section 5.3 to accomplish this.

19. **[Hands-On]** Use a paint program to create a simple rectangular navigation bar that contains three navigational options. Create an image map for it, either by hand or by using a mapping tool. Then add mouseovers for each bar segment so that the text in the active segment becomes underlined when the user moves the mouse over the hotzone. You'll need to modify your original navigation bar image three times to handle three different image swaps. Adapt the script described in Section 5.3 to accomplish this.

20. **[Hands-On]** A **slide show** is a Web page that displays a different image each time that you click a button. Sometimes, it will pick a random image each time that you click. If the number of available images is small, you'll eventually see the same images again. The script described in Section 5.3 can be adapted to display random images. All you need is a bit of code that can give you a random integer within some legal range (you need the same number of indices as you have images). The following function, **ChoosePic**, can be used to display one of ten possible random images, based on source files for ten image objects defined in a script. The ten image objects must be named **ran0, ran1, . . . , ran9**, and you must set the file values for each of their **SRC** attributes (for example, you'll need statements such as **ran0.src = "horse.jpg";**).

```
function ChoosePic(n) {
  if (document.images) {
  var picnum = Math.floor((10 * Math.random( )));
  document.images[n].src = eval("ran" + picnum + ".src");
  }
  }
```

21. Use **ChoosePic** to create a Web page that displays random images. Start with a Web page that displays a single image and then add a script so that each time someone clicks the image, a new image replaces the old. You'll need an image

map that has only one region. You can call `ChoosePic` by inserting the statement inside of the **AREA** component of your **MAP** element:

```
onClick = "ChoosePic(0)"
```

This is very similar to a navigation bar that has mouseovers. However, the image map is simpler and the mouse event is a button click instead of a rollover.

22. **[Hands-On]** Download from the following site the **Hollywood Text applet** described in Section 5.5, and install your own customized version of this applet on a Web page of your own:

    ```
    http://www.free-applets.com/HollywoodText/
    HollywoodText.html
    ```

    Use a paint program to create a background file (the border for the display), and write your own text file for the applet. Watch and report how much time that you spend on various parts of this project. How long to download and unpack the applet? To read the `HollywoodText.html` file? To create (and perfect) a background file? To create (and perfect) a text file for the script **PARAM**? Did you find the documentation adequate? If not, what parts of the applet gave you trouble?

23. **[Hands-On]** Find your own pie chart applet at an applet archive, or download the pie chart applet at the following site, and customize it for a Web page display:

    ```
    http://home.att.net/~eugenia_kuznetsova/java/piechart/
    ```

    Pick a data set that interests you, or make one up. How much time did it take you from start to finish? Discuss your experience with the applet. Did you find it easy or difficult to create the display that you wanted? Would it be difficult to update this display regularly? Could anybody do it, with a little instruction?

24. **[Hands-On]** Download the **Joust Outliner script** (`http://www.alchemy-computing.co.uk/joust`), and create a site map for a Web site of your choice. Note that you can use the absolute URLs for the framed pages even if you install the site map frames on a different Web server. (This can be a controversial practice. Don't misrepresent someone else's Web pages as your own.) *Note*: This is an ambitious exercise in configurable JavaScript. Consider trying this as part of a group of your classmates.

25. **[Hands-On]** IMINT.COM (`http://www.imint.com/`) specializes in applets for Web site navigation. They have hundreds of tree applets, expanding button applets, sliding button applets, and more. Explore the demonstration center (`http://www.imint.net/demos/index.html`) to see what the site offers, and then visit the "Free stuff" link (`http://www.imint.net/info/freestuff.htm`) to see what's available at no charge. Then do the following:

    a. Select one of the free navigation applets, and install it on a test page with just a few links to other pages.

b. Read about the site's free indexing system (`http://www.imint.net/gen5/g5_0.htm`), and use it to generate an index for a reasonably large Web site (perhaps a Web site for a course that you're taking).

c. Use the site index generated in (b) to drive the applet that you installed in (a). How much time did each exercise take? Describe any parts that gave you trouble. Would you be able to bring up a second navigational system for a new Web site in less time? What are the advantages of using an indexing tool in conjunction with a navigational applet?

26. **[Find It Online]** Research a few low-cost e-commerce hosting operations on the Web, and update the information in Figure 5.28 in Section 5.7. Can you find any free services available at this time? (Don't count the bank charges associated with a merchant's account.)

Advanced Web Page Construction: Above and Beyond

Image Processing Utilities

If you become more interested in dynamic Web page design, you'll probably find yourself getting more involved with graphical displays. You might want to design your own navigational menus, complete with mouseover and mouse-click variants. You might want to install applets that can be easily customized with your own images, background patterns, or skins. You might want to customize table borders to give your site a unique and consistent look throughout. All of these enhancements require that you be at least somewhat familiar with image processing utilities. Further, as you add more graphics to your Web pages, you must work that much harder to keep your download times as short as possible. If your page is viable over broadband connections only, you'll lose 95% of your potential audience.

This section describes some indispensable graphics tools that belong in any Web page designer's toolbox. The specific software tools mentioned here are illustrations only; they are not meant to be product endorsements or "winners" for each category. If you want to build your own software toolbox, read some software reviews on the Web and decide which packages are best for you. If you're not sure how to download and install the software that you find on the Web, read Chapter 8 and you'll be set.

Image Viewers When you double-click a GIF or JPEG image file, your computer probably launches your default Web browser to view that image. This is fine; however, it's like using a sledgehammer to swat a housefly. To review a collection of images without having to click your way through the Open command, forget the browser and install an image viewer. Image viewers are not only faster to launch than Web browsers; they also support features that are very welcome when you work with many image files. For example, you should be able to click through all of the image files in the current directory by hitting a single key. You might also be able to do some basic image editing operations such as cropping or saving the image in a different image format. One especially speedy viewer is IrfanView, which is free if you use it for noncommercial purposes (see Figure 5.29).

Image Converters If you're working with different image editing tools and utilities, you'll eventually need an image converter. An **image converter** allows you to convert an image in one format into a different format. Although the Web demands GIF and JPEG images, many of the most popular graphics programs work only with `.bmp`, `.tif` (`.tiff`), or `.pct` (`.pict`) images. Some allow you to save files in various formats. However, the available options are not always the ones that you need. This is when you need an image converter. You might find it necessary to obtain a conversion utility that does nothing but convert images. Alternatively, you

Figure 5.29:
IrfanView's Many
Good Features

might be able to use another utility that offers enough conversion support for your needs. For example, IrfanView can convert all of the most commonly encountered file types (see Figure 5.30).

Although photographs are usually stored as JPEG files and artwork is usually stored in the GIF format, nothing prevents you from converting a JPEG to a GIF or vice versa. Both formats use compression algorithms to reduce the amount of memory needed to store the image, although somewhat differently. The GIF format works better with images that contain only a few colors, whereas the JPEG format is better for images that contain many different colors. The JPEG format is *lossy*, which makes it very useful for the Web. A **lossy** image format uses a compression technique to trade image quality for greater memory savings. Different images can withstand different amounts of compression without sacrificing too much degradation in quality. Figure 5.31 shows how a 38K JPEG photograph (upper left) can be saved at varying degrees of file compression and image degradation. You can compress this particular file to a 10K file (upper right) without serious degradation. However, rapid deterioration is evident at 5K (lower left) and 4K (lower right).

If you need to work with many graphics and also need to minimize your download times as much as possible, look for articles on the Web that describe compression techniques and compression utilities. There's a lot that can be done with filters and other features to minimize the size of your graphics files. For example, blurring a photograph can often reduce its memory requirements without causing discernible harm to the image. There's a lot to learn here, and you can find useful resources on the Web.

Figure 5.30:
The Many Different File Formats That IrfanView Can Read and Save

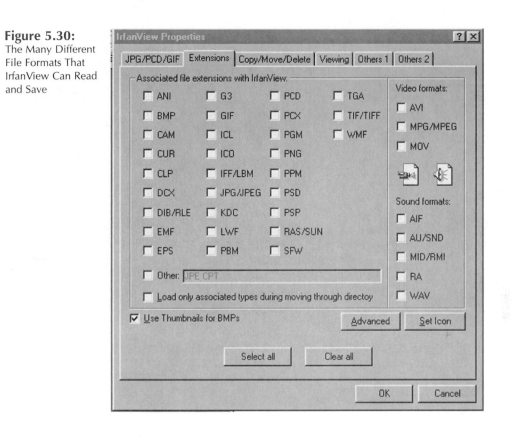

Color Samplers HTML standards have made it possible for the same Web page to look (mostly) identical when displayed by different Web browsers on different computer platforms. One area that requires special attention is the role of color in Web page displays. Although many computer monitors can display millions of colors, there is no guarantee that different monitors will produce the exact same colors. For example, Mac computers produce different color displays than do Windows-based personal computers. To address this problem, all Web browsers recognize a collection of 216 Web-safe colors. This guarantees that everyone viewing your page sees the same colors. If you care about the colors on your Web page, it's best to work with the Web-safe colors. Otherwise, those maroon and white school colors might look brown and white to people using different platforms or different color monitors. The full palette of 216 Web-safe colors is printed on the back cover of this book; you can find Web sites with similar displays.

What if you want to find the closest Web-safe color to replace a random color taken from a larger color palette? You can try to find the best match based on your manual inspection of the Web-safe color palette, or you can look for a utility that will convert any color to its closest Web-safe cousin. An example of such a utility is **Dr. Bill's Twin HTML Color Generator** (see Figure 5.32).

Figure 5.31:
Trading Image
Quality for Memory
Savings by Using
JPEG Image
Compression

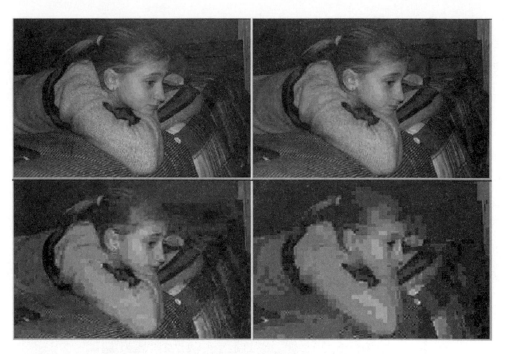

Figure 5.32:
Look for Web-Safe
Colors When You
Try to Match a
Color

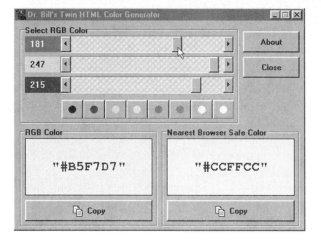

Sometimes, you see a color in a photograph or other image and want to use that color on your Web page. For example, a colored border around a photograph looks best when it matches an important color in the photograph. You can always determine the hexadecimal code for any color on your computer screen if you have a color sampler. For example, using **EyeDropper** you position your cursor on top of a color on your screen and EyeDropper displays the hexadecimal code for that color in a small pop-up window (see Figure 5.33).

Figure 5.33:
EyeDropper 2.0
Showing the
Hexadecimal Code
for Any Pixel on
Your Monitor's
Display

You need a color sampler that displays hexadecimal color codes. Some give you only the RGB codes. If you use those, you'll need another utility to convert the RGB code into the hexadecimal code.

RGB and Hexadecimal Color Codes

The hexadecimal color code and RGB (red-green-blue) color code are two different notations for describing the same color palettes. The RGB code is based on three-color dimensions: red, green, and blue. These are the colors given off by the phosphorous coating inside of an RGB color monitor in order to create colored pixels on the monitor. Each dimension can have any value of between 0 and 255 inclusive; a value from each of the three spectra specifies a unique color for that pixel. For example, the RGB value (0,0,255) is royal blue and the value (0,192,192) is a dark turquoise blue. All RGB decimal numbers can also be described as hexadecimals (base 16 instead of base 10). For example, (0,0,255) in decimal notation becomes (0,0,FF) in hexadecimal notation and (0,192,92) becomes (0,C0,C0).

To minimize keystrokes, you can run hexadecimal RGB values together into one six-digit string, adding leading zeros as needed to fill up the full six digits; for example, (0,0,FF) is written as 0000FF. Given one notation, you can always convert to the other. However, because HTML requires hexadecimal notation, it's more convenient to work with software that gives you the hexadecimal color codes directly.

Special-Effects Utilities Any experienced Web page designer will have a big bag of tricks when it comes to special effects. If you've been trying to create graphics for your Web pages from scratch by using generic tools such as Paint, you need to explore the world of special-effects Web utilities. There are many utilities created specifically for the design of Web graphics, including image mappers (as described in Section 5.2), transparency utilities (as described in Section 4.4.4), thumbnail sketch generators, texture utilities, tiling utilities, and GIF animation tools (see Figure 5.34).

Figure 5.34:
Graphics Effects Are
Easy to Create with
the Right Tools

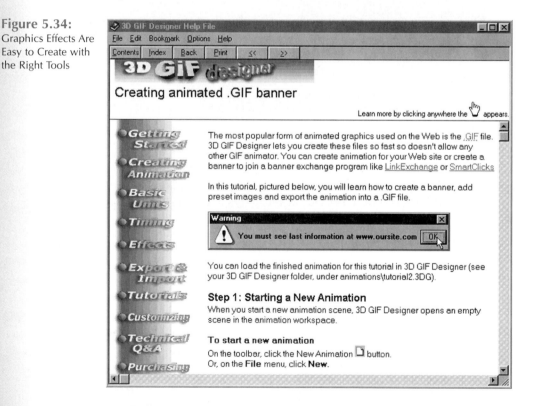

Applets, too, can create special effects and animations for Web pages (as discussed in Sections 5.4 and 5.5), and new effects are being created all of the time. Many of these are distributed at no cost for noncommercial use, so there is no limit to what you can try. For example, the **Magic Buttons applet** gives you hundreds of special effects for your navigational buttons: you just have to check out all the options and make a selection (see Figure 5.35).

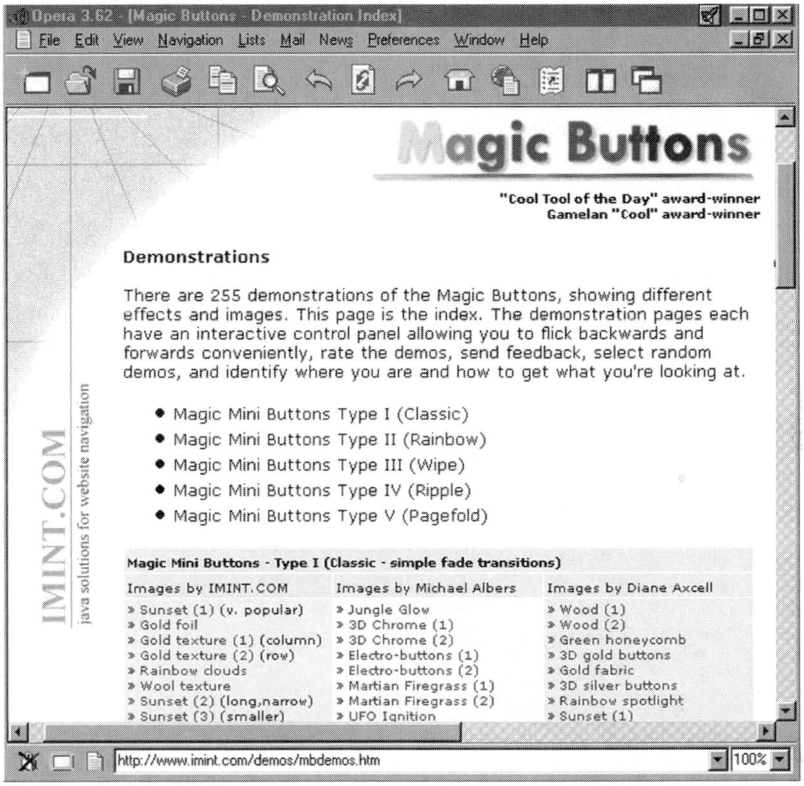

Figure 5.35:
Scoping Out All of the Possibilities is the Hardest Part

It might take time to review all of the options available in some of these tools. However, it's fun to see what's possible. In addition, finding the right effect can inspire you to make your Web pages look more professional.

CGI Scripts

The client/server software model allows Web programmers to decide where real-time computations are best carried out: on the client or on the server. Most tasks can be accomplished on either (at least in theory), so the deciding factors are generally bandwidth constraints and CPU loads. If a program is small and requires little CPU power, it should probably be sent to the client as an applet (for example, QGoo). But if a program is too big to download fairly quickly, it should be run from the server (for example, a big search engine). In some cases, the nature of the computation decides the question. For example, password protection for a Web page can be accomplished with either client-side or server-side programs. However, a server-side solution is usually more secure than an applet for this task. It's fine to use a password validator applet for general information or recreational pages. However, pages that contain sensitive information should always be protected by a password validation script located on the server.

When a program on a Web server interacts with Web pages in real-time, the Web page passes information to the program through a standard interface called the **Common Gateway Interface** (**CGI**). These programs are called **CGI scripts**. A CGI script can be written in any programming language, but probably most common is *Perl* (see Figure 5.36). You don't need to know anything more about CGI or Perl unless you want to write a CGI script yourself.

CGI scripts were around before Java or JavaScript. They were the original solution when Web page designers wanted interactive Web pages. If a designer, before 1997, needed to add a form to a Web page, the data in that form could be handled only by a CGI script. The first image maps, too, were based on CGI scripts. The early browsers weren't capable of doing anything other than process URL requests; the servers had to do everything else.

Figure 5.36
An Excerpt from a
CGI Script Written
in Perl

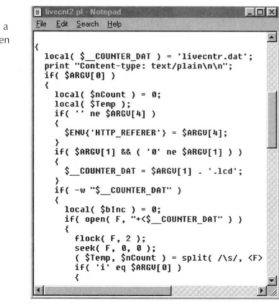

```perl
{
  local( $__COUNTER_DAT ) = 'livecntr.dat';
  print "Content-type: text/plain\n\n";
  if( $ARGV[0] )
  {
    local( $nCount ) = 0;
    local( $Temp );
    if( '' ne $ARGV[4] )
    {
      $ENV{'HTTP_REFERER'} = $ARGV[4];
    }
    if( $ARGV[1] && ( '0' ne $ARGV[1] ) )
    {
      $__COUNTER_DAT = $ARGV[1] . '.lcd';
    }
    if( -w "$__COUNTER_DAT" )
    {
      local( $bInc ) = 0;
      if( open( F, "+<$__COUNTER_DAT" ) )
      {
        flock( F, 2 );
        seek( F, 0, 0 );
        ( $Temp, $nCount ) = split( /\s/, <F>
        if( 'i' eq $ARGV[0] )
        {
```

Although scripting languages and applets have replaced many CGI scripts, there will always be a need for server-side programs. Consider, for example, a simple hit counter for a Web page (see Figure 5.37), as discussed in the Above and Beyond section in Chapter 4. Now you can think about them from the client/server perspective. Each time that someone downloads a Web page, the request for that page is sent to a Web server. This makes that server a logical place on which to maintain a hit counter. The server can update a counter each time that a request comes in for a particular page and can keep a separate counter for each page that it hosts. Most Web server software packages can be configured to maintain these statistics as a matter of course. However, if you want to log additional data (for example, the time of each hit or the address of the host making the request), you need to enlist the help of other software.

Figure 5.37:
A Web Page Hit Counter

Visitors since March 1, 1998:
016023

A script can collect much data each time that a JavaScript-enabled browser loads a Web page. If the script then sends that data to a server where it can be stored, you have the basis for a sophisticated hit counter or tracking service. Note that JavaScript can be used to send data to any server on the Web; it doesn't have to go back to the Web page server that houses the Web page being tracked. This makes it possible for third-party sites to offer hit count services based on a simple script installation (for example, the Hitmeter service described in the Above and Beyond section in Chapter 4).

In the simplest case, the script contacts the third-party server each time that a JavaScript-enabled browser downloads your page. Then a CGI script updates the hit counter on that server and downloads the current value of the hit counter to display on your page. More-sophisticated tracking services operate essentially in the same way, except that they store more information in their data files (and might not give you a hit counter that you can display on your Web page). Visit **Extreme Tracking** to see an example of an extensive tracking service. Figures 5.38(a) and (b) show two of the reports that it generates. All of the information that it collects is based on information that browsers are prepared to relinquish when queried by a script. Any Web page can gather this information from you if your browser is JavaScript-enabled.

The most extensive third-party tracking services (and other ASPs) are usually commercial services that you can purchase for weekly or monthly subscription fees. But if you've more time than money, you might be able to duplicate these commercial services with the right CGI script and do it all at no cost. There is a caveat, however. Because CGI scripts are executed on a Web server, you need access to a Web server that permits CGI scripts. Many servers, for example free Web servers such as Yahoo/Geocities, either don't permit CGI scripts or permit them only with the approval of the server's administrator. University servers, too, might not permit CGI scripts (it might depend on who you are and who you know). Commercial ISPs might permit CGI scripts, although possibly conditionally and on a case-by-case basis. If you find yourself balked in your efforts to use CGI, don't take it personally. System administrators are generally nervous about giving people the power to install random code on their servers. A hacker might find a security hole or otherwise misuse these privileges.

Figure 5.38(a):
Two Reports from
the Extreme
Tracking Service

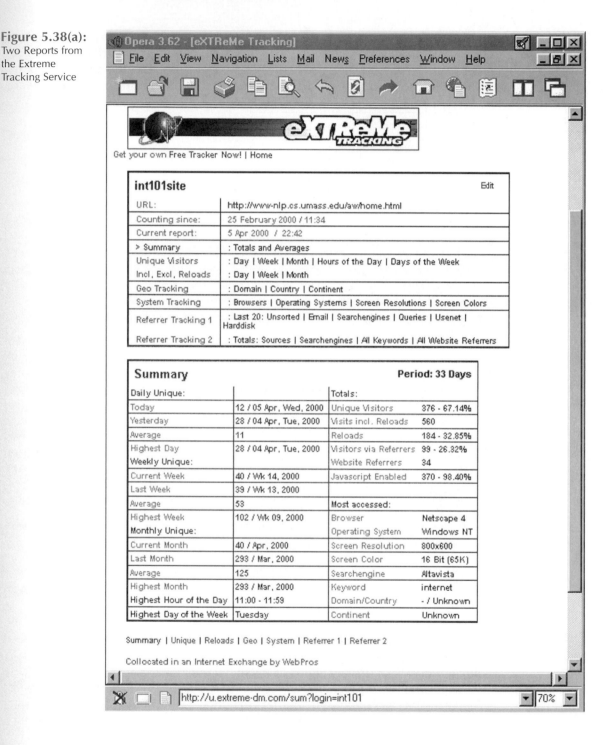

Figure 5.38(b)

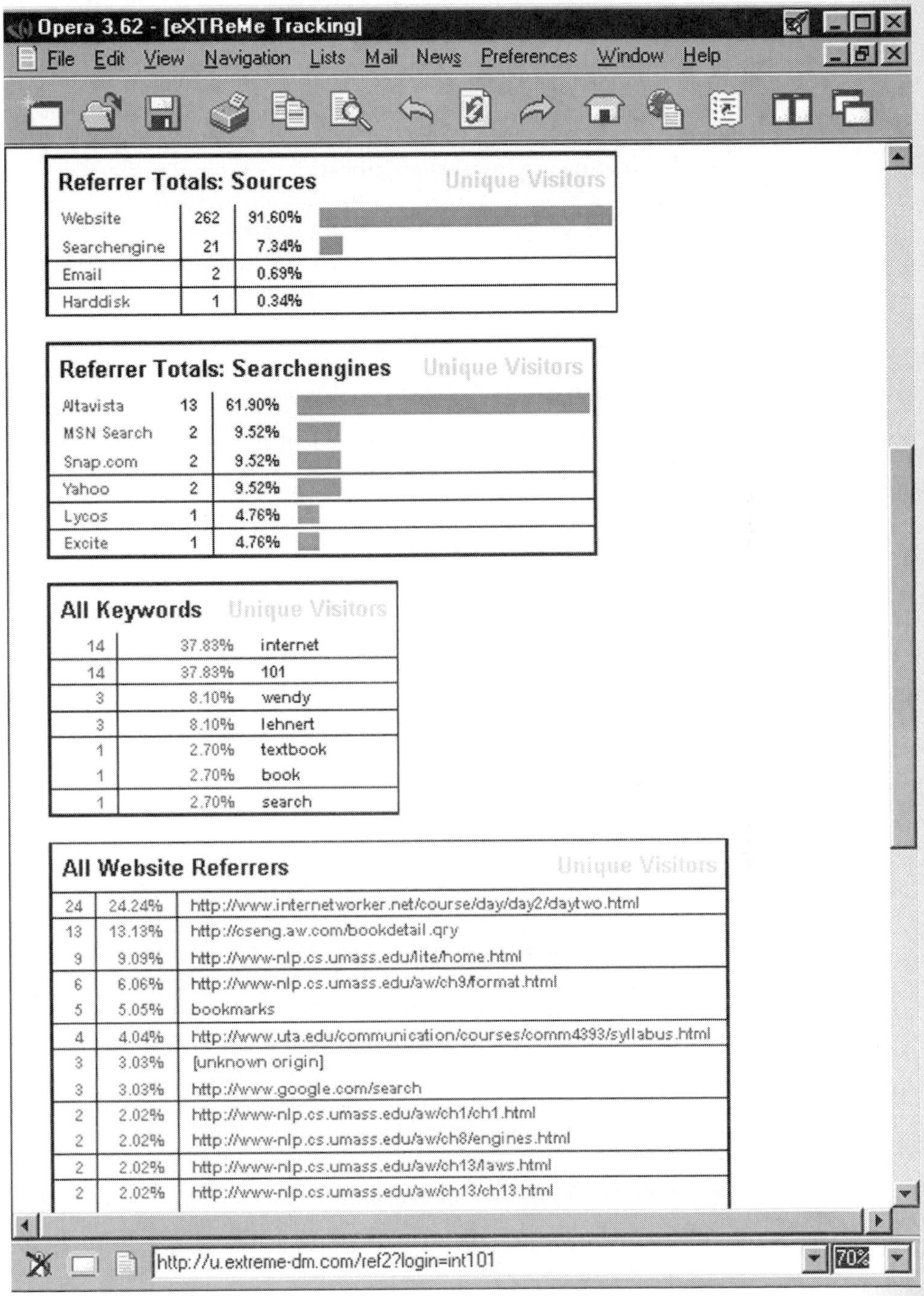

Opera 3.62 - [eXTReMe Tracking]

File Edit View Navigation Lists Mail News Preferences Window Help

Referrer Totals: Sources   Unique Visitors

Website	262	91.60%	
Searchengine	21	7.34%	
Email	2	0.69%	
Harddisk	1	0.34%	

Referrer Totals: Searchengines   Unique Visitors

Altavista	13	61.90%	
MSN Search	2	9.52%	
Snap.com	2	9.52%	
Yahoo	2	9.52%	
Lycos	1	4.76%	
Excite	1	4.76%	

All Keywords   Unique Visitors

14	37.83%	internet
14	37.83%	101
3	8.10%	wendy
3	8.10%	lehnert
1	2.70%	textbook
1	2.70%	book
1	2.70%	search

All Website Referrers   Unique Visitors

24	24.24%	http://www.internetworker.net/course/day/day2/daytwo.html
13	13.13%	http://cseng.aw.com/bookdetail.qry
9	9.09%	http://www-nlp.cs.umass.edu/lite/home.html
6	6.06%	http://www-nlp.cs.umass.edu/aw/ch9/format.html
5	5.05%	bookmarks
4	4.04%	http://www.uta.edu/communication/courses/comm4393/syllabus.html
3	3.03%	[unknown origin]
3	3.03%	http://www.google.com/search
2	2.02%	http://www-nlp.cs.umass.edu/aw/ch1/ch1.html
2	2.02%	http://www-nlp.cs.umass.edu/aw/ch8/engines.html
2	2.02%	http://www-nlp.cs.umass.edu/aw/ch13/laws.html
2	2.02%	http://www-nlp.cs.umass.edu/aw/ch13/ch13.html

http://u.extreme-dm.com/ref2?login=int101   70%

If you clear the permission hurdle, you still have to grapple with the more substantial problem of finding a CGI script that you can handle. Many are available on the Web. However, most are documented by programmers for other programmers. CGI was originally designed by programmers for programmers; no one ever expected the general public to take an interest in it. So, nonprogrammers likely will have trouble understanding the installation procedure. Of course, that won't stop some from trying, and there are a few CGI scripts that have excellent documentation. If you want to try CGI scripts, pick your first one carefully. You need one that is documented for the nonprogrammer, the person who has no knowledge of OSs and no familiarity with command mode interfaces (such as UNIX). You're entering geek territory here, and you need a very friendly road map.

Experimenting with CGI Scripts

If you want to experiment with CGI scripts, you'll need the following:

1. Permission to install CGI scripts on your Web server
2. Some information about your Web server (talk to technical support):
   a. The OS on which it runs
   b. The location of its Perl interpreter (assuming that the script that you are using is a Perl script)
   c. The directory path to the location where CGI programs must be stored
3. An FTP client for uploading files and perhaps a Telnet client to set file permission codes
4. A script with very detailed installation instructions, for your first try (see LiveCounter below)
5. Time and patience, as you might need to do some troubleshooting before your script will work

The best CGI script distribution that I've seen for nontechnical users is a Web page hit counter called **LiveCounter**. This program is distributed at no cost for noncommercial use; you must register in order to receive the URL for the download site. When you visit that site, you'll find very detailed instructions for installing the program. Most of the explanations and troubleshooting tips will apply to any CGI script installation, so the instructions really are a CGI script installation tutorial. Even if you aren't interested in Web page counters, you should consider installing this CGI script for the sake of learning how to work with CGI scripts. If you start there, you might learn enough to tackle other CGI installations that are not as well documented.

The LiveCounter installation consists of five files (see Figure 5.39):

- A .class file (for an applet)
- Three .pl files (.pl is the Perl program file extension; these comprise the actual CGI script)

Figure 5.39:
The Five Files of
LiveCounter

Name	Size	Type
lcdgts_a.gif	1KB	GIF Image
livecnt1.pl	3KB	PL File
livecnt2.pl	3KB	PL File
livecntr.pl	20KB	PL File
LiveCounter.class	11KB	CLASS File

5 object(s)   35.0KB

- A GIF file that contains images of the digits for the counter display

All of the files must be uploaded to your Web server. The Perl files go into a different directory than do the `.class` and GIF files. The LiveCounter installation notes include detailed step-by-step instructions and lots of useful information. You must follow the instructions very carefully and not be discouraged if things don't work correctly on the first try. It will probably take at least an hour to install and troubleshoot LiveCounter, not counting the time that it takes to contact your Web server's technical support personnel to get answers to any specific questions that you might have.

If all that you want is a hit counter, it's easier to sign up for a free third-party hit counter. So don't go the CGI script route unless you have a general interest in CGI scripts, you want more control over the appearance of your counter, or you want to avoid all commercial trademarks, ad banners, and pointers to external sites.

What Else Is There Other Than Hit Counters?

In addition to used for hit counters, CGI scripts are the best way to:

- Add a site-specific search engine to a Web site
- Password-protect restricted Web pages
- Provide any interaction that requires the secure long-term storage of user information

In general, whenever a Web page contains a form or needs to collect information from a user, a CGI script will be involved. Applets that collect information are often only the front end of a larger client/server combo that includes a CGI script on the back end.

The LiveCounter script described in this section is a good one to start with, even if you don't care about counters, because it is so thoroughly documented. Most CGI scripts on the Web come with minimal documentation. They assume that anyone considering their use already knows how to install one. So, if you think that you're ready to get off the porch and bark with the big dogs, here are some good places to look for CGI scripts.

Matt's Script Archive `(http://www.worldwidemart.com/scripts)`
WebReference.com `(http://www.webreference.com)`
WebReview.com `(http://webreview.com)`
Perl.com `(http://www.perl.com)`
CGI101.com `(http://www.cgi101.com/class)`
HTML Writers Guild `(http://www.hwg.com)`
FreeCode `(http://www.freecode.com)`

Web page hit counters are so popular that most Web servers come with their own hit counter already installed and ready to use. If a CGI script is already in place, you'll still have to follow a set of customization instructions in order to take advantage of that script. However, you won't need to go through a complete CGI script installation. Some commercial ISPs offer additional CGI script-based features, such as site-specific search engines and chat room support. As amateur Web page designers become more sophisticated, expect to see more CGI scripts available on more Web servers. If you see a CGI script that interests you, ask your technical support personnel about it before you attempt your own installation. If the script has broad appeal, technical support might decide to install it themselves and make it available to everyone on their servers.

How Far Can You Go without Programming?

How far can you go without knowing how to program? This is an interesting question, the answer to which changes often. In general, you can expect to do increasingly more each year, especially if you have money to spend on the right productivity tools. Programmers are always creating utilities to make their own work go faster. Low-level programming languages gave way to high-level programming languages; visual programming languages make it even easier to write code for some types of programs. With each new innovation in programming languages, the time between hatching an idea for a program and creating the actual working code shrinks a little more. Not only can experienced programmers write programs faster, but the amount of expertise needed to write certain types of computer programs is diminishing as well. Some programs now can be written by people who have no background in programming at all. However, they do need powerful tools.

The Web and all of its economic potential has intensified the push for powerful Web design tools aimed at the widest possible market. Even without specialized tools, nonprogrammers can dress up a Web page with countless scripts and applets written by others. If you know where to go for scripts and applets, you can pull together a very sophisticated-looking Web site at no cost and with minimal experience. Many enterprising freelance Web page designers have figured this out and have dived into Web page design without having any experience in computer programming or computer science.

All Productivity Tools Have Some Limitations

An **Integrated Development Environment** (**IDE**) is a program that helps programmers produce working computer code. A good IDE can reduce development times significantly by making it easy to review, modify, and test computer programs under development. When a graphical user interface (GUI) is needed, **Rapid Application Development (RAD)** editors can dramatically reduce the programming time needed to design the GUI. Most Java IDEs contain a RAD editor to facilitate applet design because applets always contain at least a simple GUI component. RAD editors have evolved so that almost anyone can learn to generate a GUI for an applet, without knowing anything about Java. As a result, scripting utilities are now aimed at nonprogrammers who want to write their own applets. As long as the applet (or script) does not require any unusual behind-the-scenes computation, these utilities will do the job.

There are still plenty of programming jobs that require an experienced programmer—programmers cannot be replaced by GUI development tools. However, you don't need to study Java if all that you want to do is create your own GUI for a reasonably routine applet.

Suppose that you want to hang out a shingle and design Web sites for other people. How far can you go without knowing how to program? The easiest Web sites are static sites that won't need to be updated. A basic knowledge of HTML will suffice to design such a site. Add a slick dynamic navigational script, and the site will have a cool, professional look.

Slightly more challenging is an informational site that requires frequent updates. If the updates are small and can be segregated from the rest of the site, you can find text display applets that will do the job. All of the changes can be made to a plain text file that is input to the applet through a `PARAM` tag. You upload a new text file to the Web server, and the Web site is automatically updated. Other applets, such as the pie chart applet, can also support isolated updates but will require changes to HTML files. However, most people can learn how to update `PARAM` tags for a simple applet; no programming is needed if you can find the right applet.

What if the updates are more extensive and you can't find the right applets for the job? You might be able to handle such a situation by using the right tools. Database-driven Web sites have created a market niche for software support utilities. A number of commercial options facilitate the design of Web sites that require extensive and frequent updates. Some of these assume that the Web page designer has no programming experience, and some don't. If you can find the right tool, you might be able to penetrate this potential market. However, it will take some time to learn how. Some tools are generic utilities with broad applicability, whereas others address very specific types of sites. For example, a utility might be limited to sites for real-estate operations and another to producing online e-commerce storefronts. Tools of this complexity usually have a rather steep learning curve and are rarely available at no cost. However, they generally give you a sophisticated Web site without your needing to know how to program.

The most technically challenging Web sites require server-side computations. For example, a full-featured site-specific search engine for a large Web site is best managed on the server side because there is simply too much code for an applet download (although you'll nonetheless find applets for site-specific search engines). Currently, it's very difficult to add server-side functionality to a Web site without some computer programming experience. Even if you want to use code written by someone else, Perl or C programs often require complicated installation procedures that are not user friendly. Perhaps new tools will appear in the next few years to make such installations easier. However, currently, the available software is complicated, expensive, and a big stretch for a nonprogrammer.

Of the Web sites that require server-side computational support, the most difficult ones to get right are those that handle e-commerce. Credit card account information must be encrypted and, ideally, stored on a separate host that is not a Web server. A database of orders and order status should be available to customers, although only through password-protected gateways. Security on the Web server must be handled correctly (but often isn't). Even professional programmers make mistakes with sites of this complexity. Under no circumstances should anyone without a background in computer programming be paid, encouraged, or allowed to design an e-commerce site. If you're tempted to jump in despite this warning, then consider your legal liability. Are you prepared to handle a lawsuit if something goes wrong? That's the bottom line when it comes to e-commerce. This is serious stuff. The following table summarizes the expertise, tools and money needed to create different types of Web sites.

Type of Site	Can a Non-Techie Do a Good Job?	What Tools are Needed?	What Will It Cost?
Informational sites without updates	Yes	Scripts and applets	Free*
Informational sites with limited updates	Yes	Scripts and applets	Free*
Informational sites with substantial updates	Maybe	Specialized software for database-driven sites	$30–$500
Sites requiring routine server-side computations	No	Some programming experience	$100–$1,000
Sites requiring customized server-side computations	No	Substantial programming experience	$1,000 and up
E-commerce sites and/or traffic-based fees	No	A reputable professional service	Monthly and/or traffic-based fees

*Be careful here—some applets are free for noncommercial use but require a fee for use in commercial sites. Always read the licensing agreement.

To summarize, nonprogrammers can exploit available scripts and applets that are freely available in order to attain a certain level of sophistication on their Web pages. However, there are limitations. If you cross the line into heavily database-driven sites or sites that require computation on the server-side, it becomes much more difficult, if not impossible, for a nonprogrammer to succeed. Under no circumstances should an amateur attempt to put up an e-commerce site without professional support. Potential complications are substantial, and mistakes could destroy the business.

New creative utilities are constantly expanding the reach of nonprogrammers in the area of Web site design. This is an exciting area to watch, and it's impossible to predict where it will be in five years. To give you an idea of what's possible now, consider a modestly priced shareware utility called Balitools. Balitools is an applet design tool for people who know HTML but don't necessarily know Java. Java programmers can also use utilities like this to speed up the process of applet construction.

Balitools relies on an HTML-like mark-up language called **JavaText Markup Language** (JTML). JTML is not an industry standard—it was invented by the makers of Balitools—so you won't be able to learn it from a book (unless someone writes a book about Balitools). But if you download Balitools, you'll find a nicely designed tutorial to get you off the ground, some sample projects to show you what's possible using the tool, and a user's manual that covers the details. The Balitools IDE makes it easy to add JTML tags to a document that is under development (see Figure 5.40).

As you add more JTML tags to your project file, you can view the resulting applet with your Web browser. This makes it easy to make incremental adjustments as you add new visual elements to the display. Notice how the WYSIWYG display in Figure 5.40 changes after a few more JTML tags are added to the .bali file (see Figure 5.41).

Learning JTML is easier than learning Java (see Figure 5.42), and JTML makes it easy to add GUI elements to an applet. Such JTML tags such as **PARAMETER** and **CALCULATE** support behind-the-scene calculations so that your applet can return results and display user data.

If you want to create your own applets, but you aren't ready for a course in Java, Balitools might be a good intermediate step. If you go on to learn Java, you'll be at home with the idea of an IDE and will find it easier to use the RAD editor in a full-fledged Java IDE. You won't be learning Java; however, you might be more motivated to learn it when you encounter the limitations of JTML. If you don't feel limited by JTML, that's fine, too.

Balitools is not the only GUI development environment designed for nonprogrammers. If you're interested in finding an alternative, search the Web for similar products, reviews, and prices. You can expect to see many new products along these lines over the next few years.

Figure 5.40:
Inserting JTML Tags
into a .bali File by
Using the Balitools
IDE

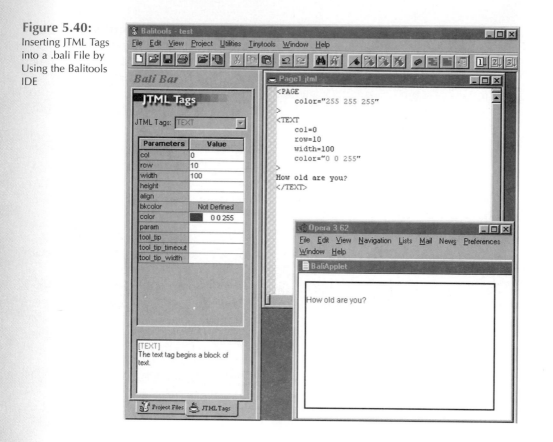

Above and Beyond: Problems and Exercises

A1. What does it mean when a file format is "lossy"? Which image format for the Web is lossy?

A2. If you're looking for special graphics effects that you can add to your Web page, should you search a JavaScript archive or an applet archive? Explain your answer.

A3. Why can't a Web page hit counter be implemented by using JavaScript and cookies?

A4. Suppose that you want to create a virtual community in which people can post information about themselves that will be available only to other registered members of the community. You want to protect the privacy of this information with a strict AUP and appropriate software safeguards. Should you look for an applet or a CGI script to support this undertaking? Explain your answer.

A5. Can CGI scripts be installed on any Web server? Explain your answer.

Figure 5.41:
Incremental Code
Development by
Using a Good IDE

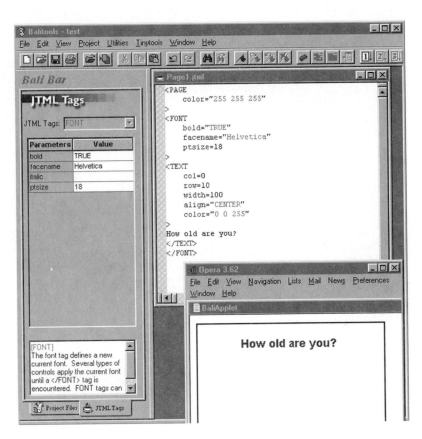

A6. You can find both CGI scripts and applets that implement site-specific search engines for Web sites. Explain the pros and cons of each. Is it better to use a CGI script? Explain your answer. (*Hint*: Why do all of the big search engines use CGI scripts?)

A7. If you don't have a technical background, what type of Web site should be created by a professional or hosting service? Explain.

A8. Do you still need programmers if you have utilities such as Balitools? Explain.

A9. [**Hands-On**] If you use Windows, download and install the "test drive" version of **Balitools** from `http://www.balitools.com`. Then run the tutorial to get a feel for the Balitools IDE and JTML. How long did it take you to complete the tutorial? What JTML tags are used in the tutorial? Explain how the PARAM tag is used in the tutorial. Did you have to consult the PDF file user's manual in order to clear up any confusion? (*Note*: If you're having trouble running the tutorial, go into the preferences setting and make MSIE the default browser for Balitools. Other browsers, such as Navigator and Opera, might have problems with the Balitools tutorial.)

Figure 5.42:
JTML Makes It Easy to Add Sophisticated and Dynamic Features to Web Pages

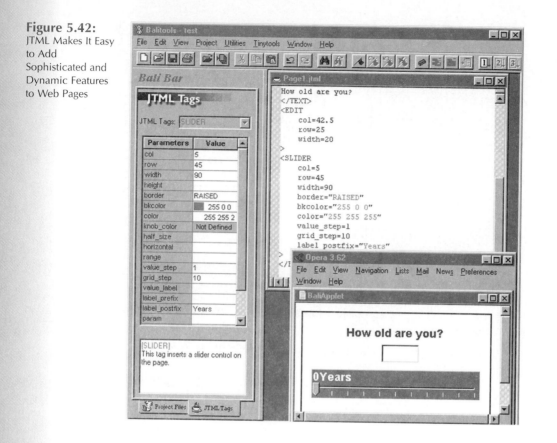

A10. **[Find It Online]** VBScripts are written by using the VB scripting language. Investigate VBScripts on the Web, and find out if they are client-side programs or server-side programs. Can a VBScript be viewed on any platform by using any browser? If not, what restrictions apply?

CHAPTER 6

Find What You Want– Fast!

CHAPTER GOALS

- Find out how to analyze your information needs in order to select appropriate tools for the job.
- Learn how to search subject trees and clearinghouses for useful information and resources.
- Discover how to use successive query refinement when you visit a general search engine.
- Explore how and when to select a new search mode.
- Find out about advanced search features and specialized search engines.
- Understand how intelligent agents and search bots can help you to manage information needs.
- Find out how to assess the credibility of information on the Web.

6.1 ▌ TAKING CHARGE

The Web opened the Internet to the public, generated a great deal of excitement, and created teenage Web surfers. However, for people trying to integrate the Web into their work routines and professional activities, the Web is sometimes more monstrous than magical. High expectations for the Web quickly deflate in the face of disappointment, often supplanted by frustration and disdain. User-friendly software is supposed to be easy to use, so when it fails to deliver, users tend to blame the software. In fact, some effort is needed on the human side of the equation; otherwise, even the most impressive software is likely to disappoint. Computers may be powerful, but they can't read minds.

Anyone who has used a search engine knows the frustration of trying "to drink from a fire hose." It might be mildly amusing to see that the search engine offers 800,000 documents on the Web that seem to relate to your query. However, most people don't have time to look at more than 20 to 30 document summaries and perhaps four or five actual documents. So, the trick to effective Web searching is to make the first ten documents in the search engine's **hit list**, the ones you want to see.

If you expect to get what you want with your first query, you'll almost certainly be disappointed. You need to take time to think about your search; you'll be rewarded accordingly. An initial search that might bring in 800,000 documents can often be reduced to a few dozen excellent documents, and in only a few minutes. This chapter shows you how to analyze your information needs, create queries, and select appropriate search strategies.

Your ability to find what you need—fast—has little to do with mastering advanced search techniques or being privy to insider search engine tips. Rather, the key is *advance preparation*: some familiarity with the available resources and a thoughtful analysis of your information needs. The most popular search engines overhaul their user interfaces—their "look and feel"—at least once a year in an effort to look current and stay competitive. However, the underlying technology that makes them work remains relatively stable. When you first begin to work with search engines, it pays to consult their online documentation, located under the Help or Search Tips link. Once you're more experienced, the shifting interfaces won't confuse you because you'll know that the underlying mechanism hasn't changed. You can stay up to date on search engines by visiting **Search Engine Watch** (see Figure 6.1), which offers timely articles, reviews, and performance evaluations.

Each time you begin a Web search, first decide which of the following three types of question that you have.

- Voyager

    A **Voyager question** is an open-ended, exploratory question. You use it when you're curious about something and simply want to see what's out there on the Web. You might have some general expectations about the subject, but otherwise you're largely ignorant and willing to be educated. This type of question derives its name from the Voyager space probe. (If the topic of interest were the solar system, you would send out the Voyager space probe to collect as much data as possible, just to see what would come back.) Voyager questions tend to cover a lot of ground and require time for exploration.

- Deep Thought

    A **Deep Thought question** is also open-ended but is more focused and goal-oriented than a Voyager question. It might have many possible answers. This type of question derives its name from the *Hitchhiker's Guide to the Galaxy*, by Douglas Adams. In that book, a computer named Deep Thought sets out to learn the meaning of life. This is a good example of an open-ended question with a specific goal. The search for an answer could go on for quite a while

Figure 6.1:
Search Engine
Watch Home Page

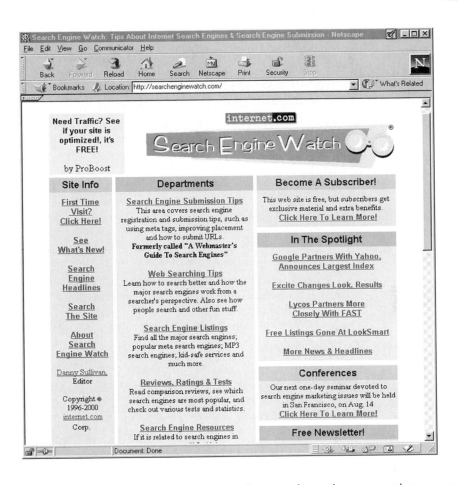

because it's difficult for you to know when you have the answer that you seek. Most people quit when they're too tired to continue or, in the case of Deep Thought the computer, after 7.5 million years. Whenever you want to collect multiple hypotheses, opinions, or perspectives on an issue, you ask a Deep Thought question, which is often philosophical, political, or academic in nature.

- Joe Friday

    A **Joe Friday question** is very specific and characterized by the expectation that there will be a simple, straightforward answer. This type of question derives its name from the 1950s television show "Dragnet." In that weekly show, actor Jack Webb played a police detective named Joe Friday—a dry, businesslike soul who was famous for the line, "The facts, ma'am. Just the facts." With a Joe Friday question, you'll know the answer when you see it and there will be no point in looking further. Questions that ask about names, dates, locations, and other verifiable facts are examples of Joe Friday questions. Once you know how to handle them, most Joe Friday questions can be answered on the Net in a minute or two.

As you explore the various search strategies available on the Web, it will become clear that each of these three question types is best handled by a specific type of Internet resource.

- Voyager and Deep Thought questions require input from multiple documents. Once you've found the right resource, browsing is an integral part of the exploratory process.

- Joe Friday questions require facts. Facts are facts; their context does not require extensive examination.

Four types of Web resources are available to help you to find the answers to questions.

1. Subject tree

   A **subject tree** is a hierarchically organized category of topics with lists of Web sites and online documents relevant to each topic. By navigating the hierarchy, you can find information sources for questions about specific topics. Subject trees are also called **directories** and **topic hierarchies**.

2. Clearinghouse

   A **clearinghouse** is a collection of Web sites and online documents about a specific topic. The topic might be broad, in which case the clearinghouse might be either divided into subtopics or organized hierarchically, like a subject tree. However, a clearinghouse is always more narrow in its focus than a subject tree. A clearinghouse supplies links to the sites or documents.

3. General search engine

   A **general search engine** is a search engine that indexes a large collection of Web pages that users retrieve by entering keyword queries. A general search engine relies on an automated *Web spider* (see the Above and Beyond section) to create a database of documents. They are not restricted to specific topics, and they index more Web resources than do subject trees. It might be difficult, however, to find in a search engine's database the resources that are relevant to a specific question. These databases are very big, and relevant resources can be buried deep in the hit list.

4. Specialized search engine

   A **specialized search engine** is like a general search engine, except that it is limited to Web pages that feature a specific topic. The topic might be broad, as in a clearinghouse, and many specialized search engines use a clearinghouse as a starting point. However, a specialized search engine takes the clearinghouse concept a step further by gathering all of the relevant documents known to the clearinghouse and indexing them for the user; the clearinghouse, as mentioned previously, only supplies links to the documents. It is harder to create a specialized search engine than a general search engine. While a general search engine relies on an automated Web spider to create its database, a specialized search engine relies on a handpicked collection of documents that a person has selected as relevant to the topic.

Different Resources for Different Question Types

Once you know the type of question that you want to ask, you can select an appropriate resource on the Web.

Type of Question	Resource
Voyager	Subject tree or clearinghouse
Deep Thought	Subject tree or specialized search engine
Joe Friday	Subject tree or general search engine

Note that many Joe Friday questions turn out to be Deep Thought questions, once you've dredged up some information. This happens typically with historical events, in which opinions and facts often intertwine. For example, suppose that you thought that there was a straightforward answer to the question "Who invented the telescope?" or "When was the first English dictionary published?" Dig a little deeper, however, and you'll find yourself in Deep Thought territory. When this happens, simply keep going until you're satisfied that you've gathered all of the data that you want.

Not So Fast

With Voyager and Deep Thought questions, don't expect to find all of the information that you need at one site. Depending on the topic, you might need hours, or sometimes days, of careful exploration before you'll be satisfied. With a Joe Friday question, answers come faster. However, don't always stop at the first one that arrives. If you're not confident about the credibility of a source (see Section 6.9), check a second, and maybe even a third, site to make sure that you're getting reliable information.

Note that general search engines are recommended for only one of the three question types: the Joe Friday. This does not mean that they're not useful for the other two types of question. On the contrary, a general search engine can be used to locate clearinghouses or specialized search engines that are on target for Voyager and Deep Thought questions. Some questions must be answered in stages. To learn who invented the telescope, for example, you might start with a general search engine, because you think that you have a Joe Friday question. However, when conflicting answers begin to arrive, you can shift into Deep Thought mode and look for a specialized search engine on inventions or inventors in order to get a fuller picture.

Many questions are best tackled by asking more questions. As you acquire more experience with more Web resources, you will become more systematic about the process of question answering. Each time one question leads you to another question, identify the new question type and go to a resource that's right for that question.

6.2 │ MORE ABOUT SUBJECT TREES AND CLEARINGHOUSES

A subject tree is actually a browsing aid. It requires some exploration and yet is designed to get you where you need to go as fast as possible. **Yahoo!** is the Web's oldest, largest, and most popular subject tree. However, other trees include **About** and the **Open Directory Project**. These three are discussed in more detail in the following sections.

6.2.1 Yahoo!

When you browse a subject tree, you start from the *root* of the tree and *branch* out to more-specific topics, at each decision point selecting appropriate options. For example, suppose that you want to send a letter to Elton John and you need his fan mail e-mail address. You can use Yahoo! to conduct a search. On the Yahoo! home page (see Figure 6.2), you need to find a branch of the tree that will head you in the right direction; in this case, that branch is the Entertainment branch:

Entertainment → **Music** → **Artists** → **By Genre** → **Rock and Pop** → **John Elton**

The Elton John page contains a number of fan-related links (*leaves*) that you can explore to find an official or unofficial address to which you can send fan e-mail (see Figure 6.3).

A good subject tree will make getting where you want to go easy. Yahoo!'s subject tree, growing since its inception in 1994, now organizes over 500,000 documents. Note, however, that this is nowhere near as many as those that the largest general search engines handle. Each document is added to Yahoo! by people who check the document for its content and proper position in the tree structure. This keeps the documents well organized; however, it does not mean that every document has been subjected to quality control for content. It is relatively easy to glance at a document to see what it's about. Editorial control requires knowledgeable reviewers and is far more time-consuming.

Although a lot of effort goes into maintaining a subject tree's organization, subject trees are not immune to organizational problems. It is difficult to design a comprehensive hierarchy in a way that seems intuitive to everyone who uses it. Different subject trees use different categories and subtree structures. Although there's no one best hierarchy, some subject trees might be easier to navigate than others.

Figure 6.2:
Yahoo!'s Subject
Tree

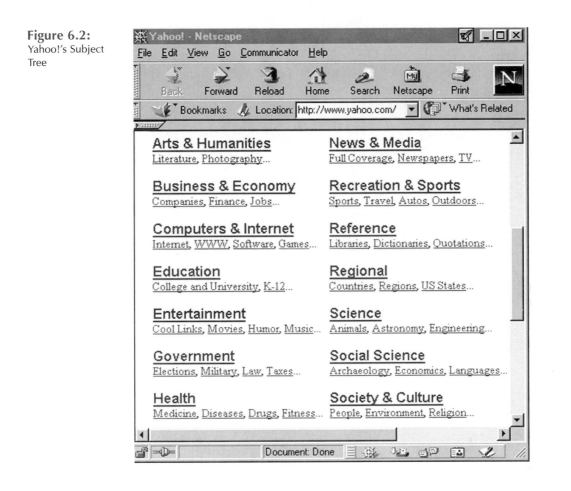

Another difficulty with subject trees is that it's often impossible to store everything that is relevant to a single topic under a single location in the tree. For example, if you're interested in weaving, should you look under keywords "art," "textiles," or "crafts"? Depending on exactly what you want to know, you might find relevant documents under all of these. This makes it difficult to know when you've exhausted the possibilities in a subject tree. Happily, the larger subject trees are equipped with search engines to help you cover all of the bases. When you use a search engine for a subject tree, you're conducting a site search. A **site search** is a search whose hits are restricted to Web pages within the current Web site.

Subject Trees with Search Engines versus Search Engines with Subject Trees

A subject tree that has a search engine (for example, Yahoo!) allows you to conduct a search that is restricted to the subject tree's subtrees and documents

Figure 6.3:
Some "Leaves" on the Elton John Branch at Yahoo!

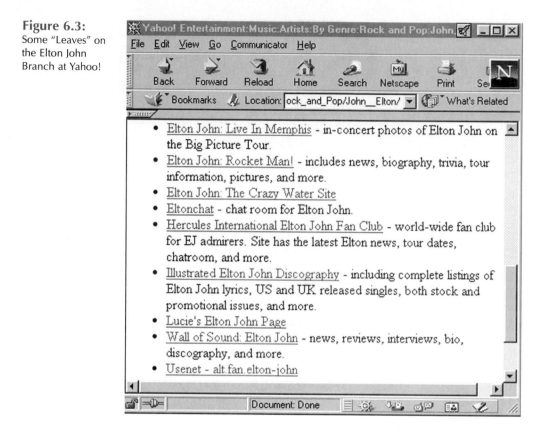

indexed by the subject tree. The main attraction is the subject tree; the search engine is there only to enhance the subject tree. Sometimes a search engine for a subject tree will give you the choice of searching the tree or searching the Web. If you choose to search the Web, you'll leave the subject tree and move to a general search engine.

By contrast, the reverse configuration, a search engine that has a subject tree, is a completely different animal. Examples of this type of configuration are AltaVista, GoTo.com, and Excite. A search engine that has a subject tree returns hits from a large database of documents that includes, but is not restricted to, the documents in its subject tree. In this case, the search engine is the main attraction and the subject tree is an added feature.

A subject tree with a search engine lets you see how many branches might hold documents relevant to your topic. For example, suppose that you want to assemble a long list of different types of clocks. This is a Deep Thought question (it has a focus but it's open-ended). A subject tree is a good place to start. However, you'll definitely want to query the search engine for the subject tree.

Keywords for Site Searches

When you conduct a site search at a subject tree, you're searching for categories in the subject tree as well as for documents. For a Voyager or Deep Thought question, the category hits are more important than the document hits because they show you all of the perspectives that you should consider before you start digging into specific documents.

To yield a good list of category hits, follow these tips:

- Use only one keyword instead of a list of keywords.
- Choose a keyword that is simple and obvious.
- If you can think of different keywords, investigate them one at a time.

Some keywords will open worlds of information, and others will return nothing. You might need to try a few keywords before you find the right one to the tree.

Yahoo! always shows categories and documents. Each Yahoo! **category** is a location in the tree at which you can examine subcategories or jump directly into relevant documents. Documents are always represented by URLs for Web pages (which are not part of the Yahoo! Web site).

When you query Yahoo!'s search engine, the results come back in two parts: category matches and site matches. As an example, go to Yahoo! and enter the query "clocks" (see Figure 6.4).

First shown are category matches. A **category match** shows all of the places in the subject tree where you can examine a branch that has something to do with clocks. In this example, you get back a list of all of the category titles that contain the keyword "clocks." There are 17 different branches on the Yahoo! tree that have something to do with clocks (see Figure 6.5).

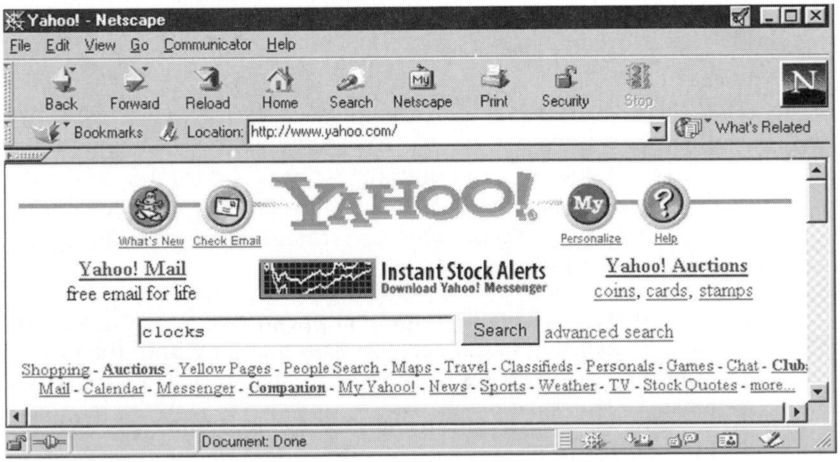

Figure 6.4:
Using Yahoo!'s Search Engine to Search for the Keyword "clocks"

Figure 6.5:
Yahoo!'s
17 Subtrees
About Clocks

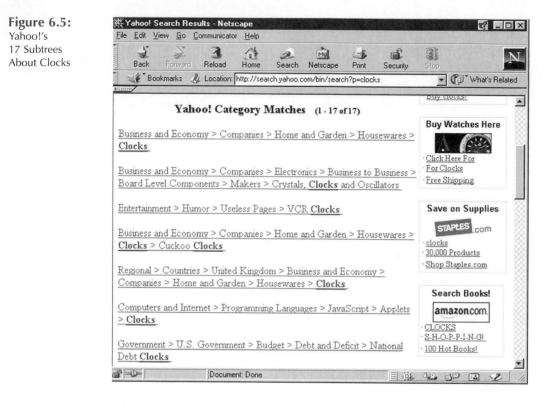

After the category matches are the site matches. At Yahoo!, a **site match** is a list of relevant documents found inside of Yahoo!'s subject tree. To avoid confusion about Yahoo!'s use of the term *site match* and the more general notion of hits returned by a site search, this book refers to Yahoo!'s site matches as *document matches* or *document hits*. This will distinguish them from Yahoo!'s category matches without confounding the idea of a site match with a site hit.

Examine the category matches for the keyword "clocks." Notice that the categories for clocks include one for clocks as housewares, one for businesses that manufacture computer clocks, one devoted to humor about VCR clocks, and one about national debt clocks. Click the housewares/clocks category (see Figure 6.6), and take a closer look. Notice that now there are four subcategories about clocks that might be of interest: Antique@, Cuckoo Clocks(10), Repair(9), and Watches@. Because we are dealing with a subject hierarchy, each of these subcategories corresponds to a branch within the tree structure of the hierarchy, and occupied a fixed position within the larger hierarchy

Two of these categories list a number in parentheses, and two are followed by an @ character. Each numbered category is a branch within the current subtree, and the number tells you how many document hits are stored within that particular branch of the tree. The @ character tags cross-listed categories that are found somewhere

Figure 6.6:
Four More
Subcategories

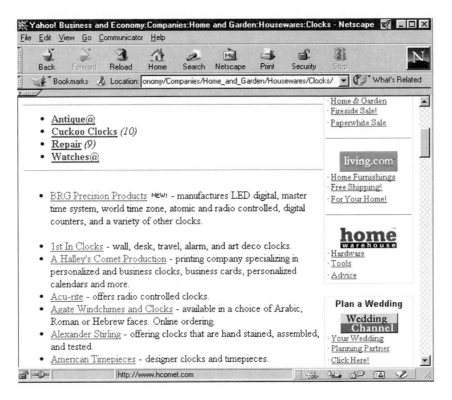

outside of the current subtree. Those categories are listed here because they are strongly associated with the current category. Both the subtree categories and the cross-listed categories give you opportunities to explore relevant parts of the subject tree. You might not have found the subtree about watches in your initial keyword search for clocks. However, the cross-listing reminds you that watches are a type of clock; you might want to explore that category, also.

Follow-Up on a Site Search in a Subject Tree with Some Browsing

Subject trees are designed to facilitate browsing. Use a site search at a subject tree to find relevant locations within the tree. The resulting category matches are all possible starting points for browsing expeditions. Don't rush into the document hits before you've scoped out all of the category matches. You can miss a lot of information if you narrow your search too quickly.

A large subject tree is a great way to explore open-ended questions because someone else has already figured out what categories relate to a concept and what associations should be made between categories that reside in different parts of the tree. In the clock example, you probably don't need to examine documents as much as you need to explore the category matches to see how many different kinds of clocks you can find.

Subject Tree Exercise #1: Clocks

Do the following to become familiar with Yahoo!:

1. Search **Yahoo!** and create a list of different types of clocks. Do this search for 15 minutes.
2. How many clocks did you list?
3. Do you think that you've exhausted all that Yahoo! has to offer for this exercise?

Although hierarchical organizations are powerful devices for information retrieval, don't let the logic of categories and subcategories lull you into mindlessness. You might still need to think about search strategies for subject trees. Recall the Deep Thought computer in *The Hitchhiker's Guide to the Galaxy*. When asked to explain the meaning of life, Deep Thought worked for 7.5 million years and produced the answer "42." Douglas Adams has many fans, and they have naturally pondered this answer in an effort to understand its deeper meaning. Some have set out to answer such questions as, "What role does the number 42 play in the lives of all dogs?" Subject Tree Exercise #2 asks you to work on that question by using Yahoo!. It is a Deep Thought question (that is, there may not be only one "correct" answer).

Subject Tree Exercise #2: The Role of the Number 42 in the Lives of All Dogs

At this point, it will be instructive to go to the Web and try your hand at this problem before you discuss it further. Visit **Yahoo!** and see if you can find out what role the number 42 plays in the lives of all dogs. Can you find the answer? Take some time to try it before you read any further in this book.

From the question, "What role does the number 42 play in the lives of all dogs?", you might be hard-pressed to find some useful keywords. Specific numbers tend to be bad keywords (many search engines ignore numbers). If you conduct a keyword search at Yahoo! on the keyword "dogs," you'll get 334 category matches and 6,519 documents (site matches). A keyword search on "42" yields 2 category matches (!) and 197 site matches. None of the category matches look promising, and no one wants to wade through long lists of site matches. If you search with the query "dogs 42," you'll find 2 site searches (see Figure 6.7). However, neither looks like it has anything to say about the role of the number 42 in the lives of dogs.

What can you do? You could try to guess at some plausible answers and work backward from those. However, this could take a long time. Maybe you need to think more about the query. Perhaps you were a little too quick to jump on what seemed to be the obvious keywords. Maybe you can think of other keywords that will take you where you want to go by using *associative thinking*.

Figure 6.7:
Yahoo!'s Two Site
Matches for the
Query "dogs 42"

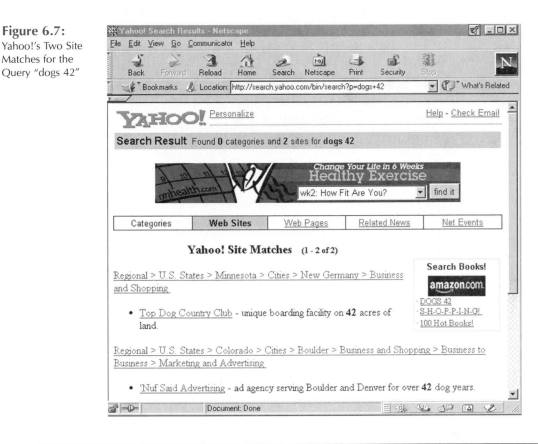

Associative Thinking

When you think about keywords and categories, sometimes you really have to
think. Don't just fixate on the immediate question. Ask yourself:

- Who would care about the answer to this question?
- What sort of people might be talking about this topic?
- Are any organizations responsible for posting the information that I want?

Try to associate a query with people or organizations; those connections might be
the breakthrough that you need. This type of thinking is called **associative thinking**, and it can be a powerful search strategy.

Let's consider the larger context in which this question was originally posed. Where
did it come from? What motivated it? If you can answer these additional questions,
you'll have some new leads that you can use at Yahoo!. The only people who would
ever ask this peculiar question are Douglas Adams fans. So search Yahoo! to learn
what is available using the query "Douglas Adams." Yahoo! has a category devoted

to Douglas Adams, as well as 35 site hits that mention his name. Once you've made the Douglas Adams connection, you're just a couple of links away from the answer. See if you can find it.

Yahoo!, the largest subject tree on the Web, offers a hierarchy that contains over 500,000 documents and 25,000 categories. On the Web since its beginning, Yahoo! is a major Web portal and has a loyal following. This is a tough act to follow. However, that doesn't mean there aren't other good general subject trees. The following two sections discuss two of these: About and Open Directory Project.

6.2.2 About

If you need solid reliable information on a serious topic, check out **About** (originally called the Mining Company). It is a subject tree that supports over 700 major topic sites, each with its own hierarchical subject tree and each managed by an expert in that subject (see Figure 6.8). About displays category matches and document hits, although the document hits at About are always Web pages written by About **guides**—topic experts who work for About and write overviews about their topics.

About does not index as many Web pages as Yahoo! does. However, all of the pages that it does index have been written or reviewed by an expert in the field who polices Web page content for reliability and accuracy. The About enterprise is very similar to an encyclopedia in its scope and operation. As such, it's a good subject tree for introductory articles and short tutorials. Articles at About can be trusted to contain good solid information.

6.2.3 Open Directory Project

Another subject tree with a strong following is run by Lycos.com: the Open Directory Project. Lycos was one of the first search engines with a subject tree. Now, in an aggressive quest to outperform Yahoo!, it's concentrating on its **Open Directory Project**. This subject tree emphasizes practical know-how more than academic expertise, as its home page illustrates (see Figure 6.9), so it might not actually be competing with Yahoo! head-on. The **Open Directory Project** uses a system of category matches and document hits like Yahoo! does, including the @ tag for cross-listed categories.

To expand its Web coverage, the Open Directory Project uses 22,000 volunteers who act as editors in specific content areas—the directory contains over 230,000 categories. Time will tell if a system of volunteers can maintain the quality control that Lycos cultivated in its early years (under the name "Lycos Guides") with paid staffers. In any event, the Open Directory Project is a resource worth bookmarking.

Some of your questions will be general and easily satisfied, whereas others might be more sophisticated and harder to answer. As your information needs shift from casual questions to more demanding questions, you'll need to find new Web resources. This is where clearinghouses come into play.

Figure 6.8:
About: A Subject Tree Managed by Experts in 700 Topic Areas

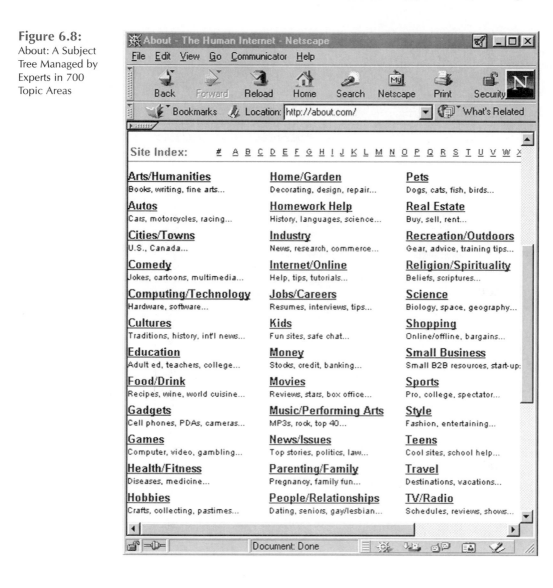

6.2.4 Clearinghouses

Recall that a clearinghouse is a large collection of resources or documents about a topic. On the Internet, some publicly available clearinghouses were created and are maintained by researchers subsidized by federal funding. Others are compiled by commercial interests and might be available only to paid subscribers. A few are compiled by librarians, teachers, or other individuals. Some clearinghouses focus on documents available online, whereas others index documents that are available only in printed form.

Figure 6.9:
Open Directory
Project Home Page

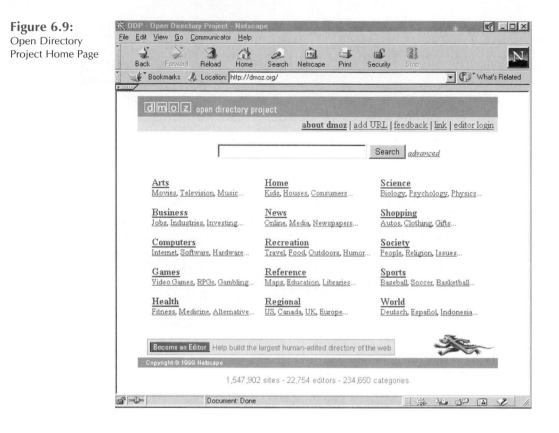

Always be on the lookout for clearinghouses that address your interests. Each is organized in its own way and supports its own search tools, so you need to learn about them one by one. Some are slick professional sites, whereas others are minimal lists of plain text and hyperlinks. Figure 6.10 shows the home page for the **Environmental Law Net**, a clearinghouse devoted to environmental laws, regulations, enforcement, and pending court cases.

A relevant clearinghouse is a powerful research tool because it is both comprehensive in scope and maintains high standards for document quality. When you use a good clearinghouse, 90% of the hard work has already been done for you. All you need to do is work your way through the offerings to locate the specific information that you want. Figure 6.11 shows one of the specialized resources available at the Environmental Law Net clearinghouse, a comprehensive list of cases in the state courts of the United States.

There are thousands of online clearinghouses. To conduct some in-depth research, always first check to see if a relevant clearinghouse can help you. Go to any general subject tree for the Web, and conduct a keyword search that includes the word "clearinghouse." For example, **FAST Search** returned over 10,000 documents that contain the word "clearinghouse" in their Web page titles.

Figure 6.10:
The Environmental
Law Net
Clearinghouse
Home Page

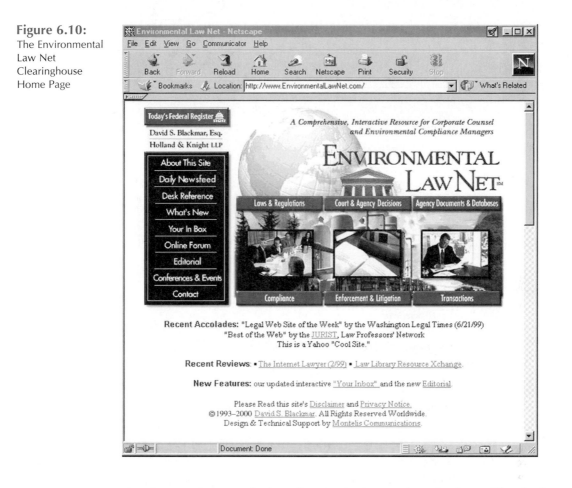

Another good way to find quality clearinghouses is at the **Argus Clearinghouse** (see Figure 6.12). Argus is a *clearinghouse of clearinghouses*, complete with its own search engine and rating system (see Figure 6.13).

You might also find some comprehensive resource pages that haven't been identified with the keyword "clearinghouse." To locate them, think of organizations that might be involved with the topic. Who cares about these issues? Is there a nonprofit group or coalition that might track relevant resources? If you can find such an organization, you might be able to benefit from the work of a professional Internet researcher who has spent a lot more time than you can tracking down relevant resources.

Argus Clearinghouse is a good source for clearinghouses and is unique in its efforts to evaluate available clearinghouses, but many excellent clearinghouses are not listed at Argus. If Argus doesn't have what you want, there are other clearinghouses you can try.

Ready Reference Using the Internet

`http://www.winsor.edu/library/rref.htm`

BIOTN (see the alphabetized subject index)

`http://vweb.sau.edu/bestinfo/alpha.htm`

NetGuide

`http://www.netguide.com/Browse/`

Figure 6.11:
A Comprehensive List of Court Cases Offered by the Environmental Law Net Clearinghouse

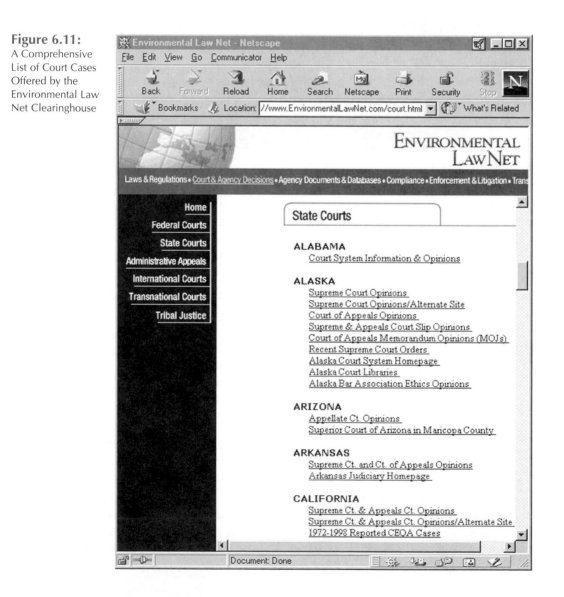

Figure 6.12:
The Argus
Clearinghouse
Home Page

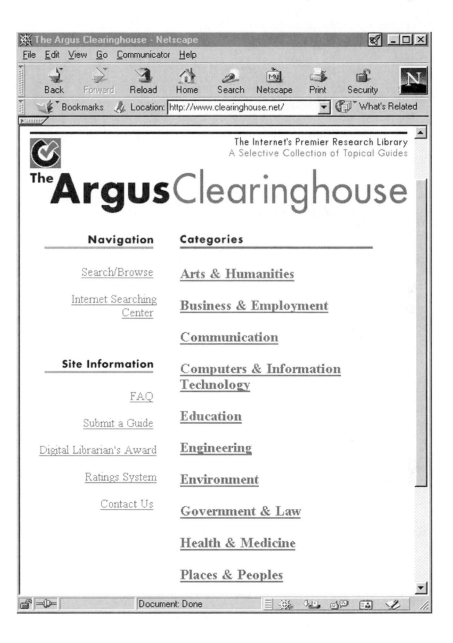

High-quality clearinghouses can also be found in archive collections of Web site reviews. Many mailing lists review Web sites of all kinds and maintain searchable archives on the Web. Some specialize in educational or academic sites, and others focus on popular, often quirky, sites. If you can't find what you want anywhere else, check out the following archives.

Netsurfer Science (all science)

http://www.netsurf.com/nss/search.html

Netsurfer Digest   (all sorts of things)

http://www.netsurf.com/nsd/search.html

Scout Report Signpost (academic/educational)

http://www.signpost.org/signpost/

Figure 6.13:
A Clearinghouse
Rating Summary

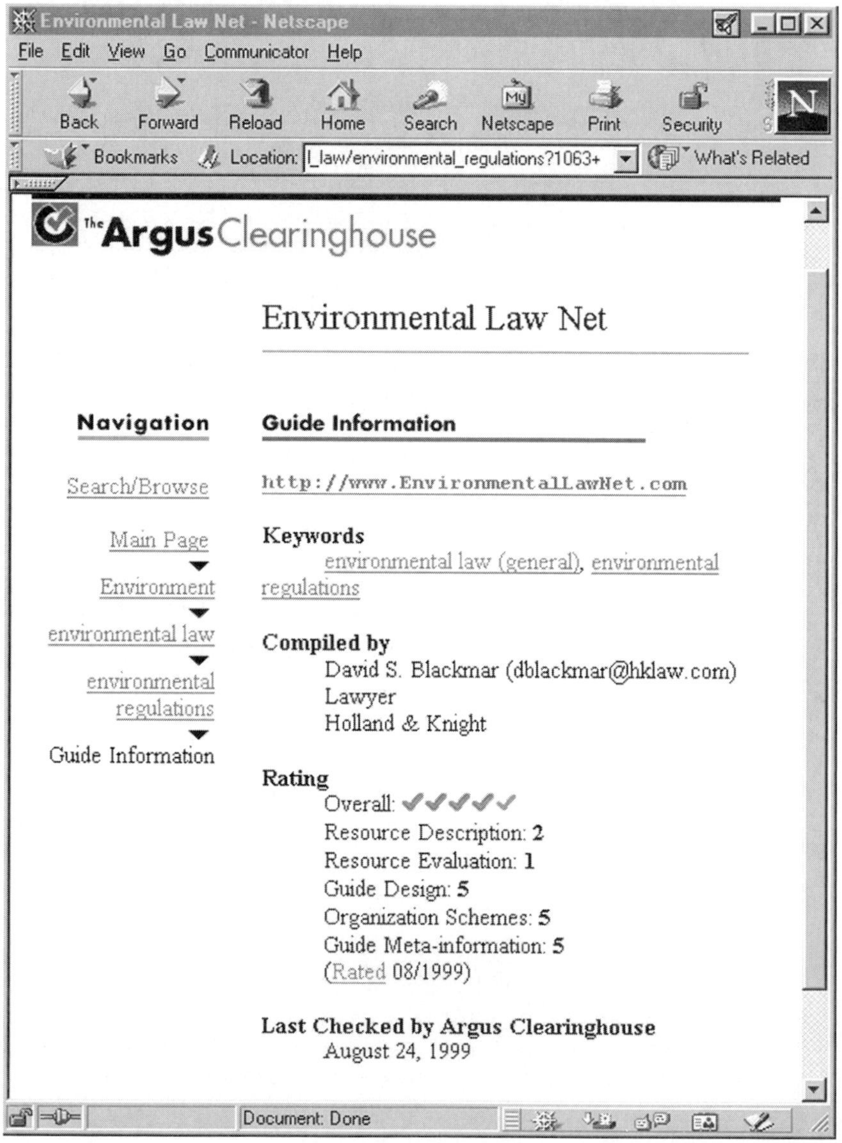

Always investigate pointers to clearinghouses that might be useful to you. Someone else has already created a comprehensive bookmark file for a particular topic, so you don't have to do it yourself. Clearinghouses are great bookmark entries because they give you fast access to many links via a single URL. If your primary activities on the Web tend to focus in one direction, you might want to set your default home page to an appropriate clearinghouse page so you can hit the ground running each time you get on online.

6.3 GENERAL SEARCH ENGINES AND META SEARCH ENGINES

A great deal could be said about search engines. You could talk about concepts in *information retrieval* (see the Above and Beyond section) and explore the manner in which search engines compile databases of documents and then index those documents for retrieval. You could delve into the tricky business of ranking documents so that the best ones appear at the top of the hit list. If you're interested in what goes on behind the scenes, the Above and Beyond section offers an introduction to search engine technologies.

For now, concentrate on purely practical advice. For example, use general search engines only for Joe Friday questions. Such engines work hard to be all things to all people, and they sometimes succeed. However, sometimes a general search engine is not the best place to start a search.

6.3.1 Some Ground Rules

Before you start, here are some ground rules

Ask Some Key Questions about Any New Search Engine before You Begin a Search
Suppose you're visiting a particular search engine for the first time. Before initiating a search, you should review the information at any link called Search Tips or Help (see Figure 6.14) to learn how the engine operates and what it offers. Here are some of the features that various search engines provide.

- Return only pages that contain all of the keywords in your query.
- Return pages that contain some but not all of your keywords.
- Automatically look for morphological variations on your keywords. For example, you enter the keyword "book" and the search engine looks for both "book" and "books."
- Look for variations on a word if you enter a keyword with the wildcard (*) character, as in "book*."
- Automatically add synonyms to your query. For example, you enter the keyword "law" and the search engine looks for "legislation."

You need to know what a search engine is doing with your queries; otherwise, you'll be unable to tune your queries effectively.

Never Look beyond the First 20 to 30 Hits for Any Given Query Most search engines are proud to announce how many hits were found, as if you should be impressed to know that the document that you really want might (or might not) be somewhere in a list of, say, 1,200,000 hits. In fact, a good query will display the hits that you most want at the top of the hit list. A bad query is not worth more than a quick glance at the top ten hits. If the top ten hits are off-base, don't waste time looking any further in the hit list. If the top ten hits are pretty good, you might want to look at the next ten or twenty, but no more. If you want to see additional hits, enter a different query.

Experiment with Different Keywords in Different Queries Conducting a keyword search is like learning a musical instrument. The more that you work at it, the better the results. Each search has its own learning curve: some queries are easier to fine tune than others. Start out with a fast query based on the best keywords that you can think of. Examine the hits that come back, and then adjust your original query, broadening it (to bring in more hits) or narrowing it (to bring in fewer hits).

Each new query should benefit from the feedback resulting from the preceding queries through a process of *successive query refinement* (this is described in detail later in the chapter).

Don't Expect the First Query That You Try to Be Your Last No matter how experienced you become with keyword searches, the process will always require adjustment and refinement. Even the experts try one or two preliminary queries before they expect anything very useful to materialize. Don't waste time trying to perfect your first-pass queries; let the search engine's feedback help you out.

Figure 6.14:
Google's Clickable Help Page Makes It Easy to Learn the Ropes

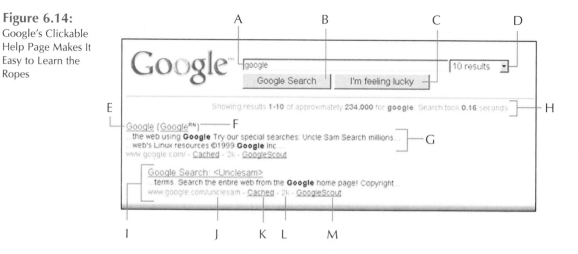

6.3.2 Getting Started

Now that you understand the basic process of working with search engines and search queries, it's time to start experimenting with queries. For a Joe Friday query about a mainstream topic (that is, something that many people might want to know about), **AskJeeves** is a good place to start; it's one of the simplest search engines available.

For example, suppose that you want to know who invented the telescope. You type the question that you want answered and then see what is returned. Unlike other search engines, AskJeeves doesn't return hits. Instead, it shows you a set of questions for which it already has answers. Some of these questions will be on target; others will not. However, at least one of them likely is relevant and will give you the information that you want. Figure 6.15 shows how AskJeeves responds to the query, "Who invented the telescope?".

AskJeeves has a database of over 7 million hand-crafted questions and answers. When it analyzes a query, it tries to match the query to one of its question/answer (Q/A) entries. The matching process is not perfect, so AskJeeves takes a few of the best matches it finds and returns each of those for your inspection. For the telescope question, you can see that the keyword "telescope" figured heavily in the matching process and took you in some directions that you don't want to go.

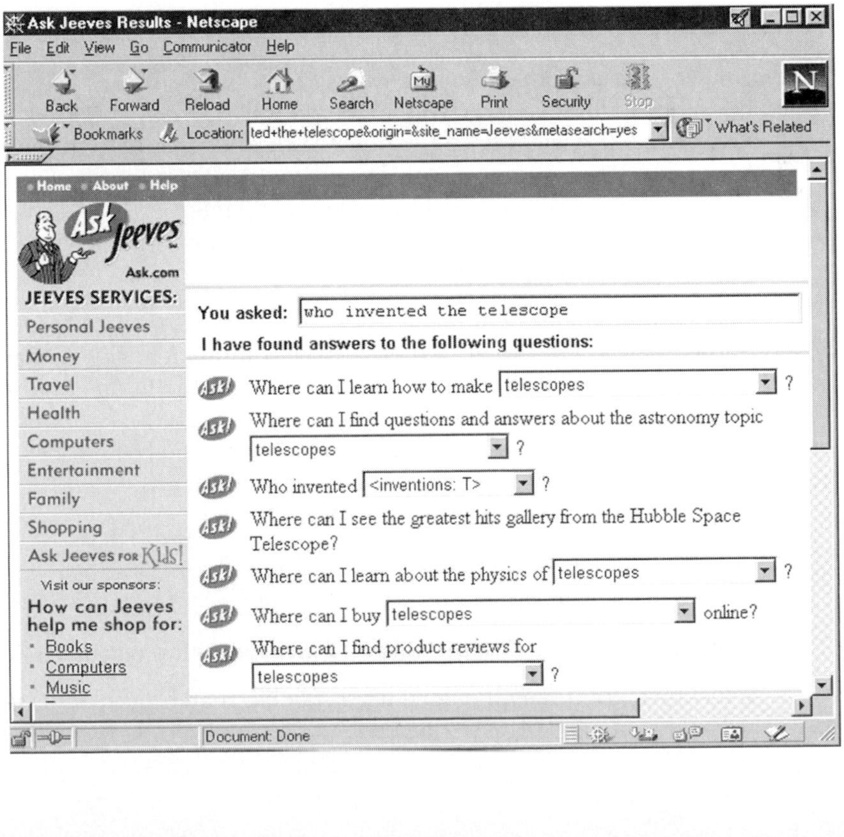

Figure 6.15:
AskJeeves's Attempt to Match Each Query to a Question/Answer Database

Not All Keywords Are Equal

When you create a query for a search engine, concentrate on using *nouns*. Search engines don't understand English, even if they encourage users to post a query "in plain English." They extract some keywords from each query and ignore other words, for example prepositions and articles. Word proximity is usually taken into consideration, so don't enter your keywords in a random order. If a noun phrase is important, enter those words in sequence, even if you aren't asking for exact phrase matching. It is not easy to anticipate all the ways an author might reference your topic, but descriptive nouns may be more reliable indices than descriptive verbs. If you have an important verb in your query, try replacing it with an analogous noun, even if the query ends up sounding less like real English.

Search Engine Exercise #1: Who Invented the Telescope?

1. In **AskJeeves**, enter the query "Who invented the telescope" (do not include the quotes). See if you can find an answer based on Q/A hits that AskJeeves knows how to answer.
2. Which hits look promising enough to examine?
3. Do any hits take you to the answer that you desire?

AskJeeves is a wonderful search engine for beginners. It's easy to see whether the questions returned are relevant to the query and there are no hit lists to ponder and investigate. If AskJeeves can connect your query to the right answer, you're done. Many questions, however, AskJeeves cannot answer easily. For example, suppose that you need a ranked list of California's 20 largest cities. Although the information seems mainstream, AskJeeves has (at this writing) trouble producing a document that contains this information.

Most search engines will have trouble producing a list of California cities ranked by population. You might be able to find alphabetically ranked lists of cities in California, along with their populations, from which you could derive the list that you want. However, this takes time and you might make a mistake. Sometimes a hit is painfully close but not good enough (you might find a ranked list of the ten largest cities but not the 20 largest). When your queries come up dry, you have two choices:

1. Try different search engines.
2. Try different queries.

Strategies for (1) are discussed next. Those for (2) are discussed in Section 6.4.

Selecting a good search engine for a specific search problem is perhaps one of the most difficult challenges. None cover the entire Web, so experimenting with at least three or four of the better-known ones is a good idea. The document that you need might be available at, for example, AltaVista but not Hotbot. In addition, you can't know whether your document is simply hard to find or not on the Web at all.

Search Engine Exercise #2: Find a Ranked List of California's 20 Largest Cities

Before you read further, try to find a list of California's 20 largest cities. Enter the keywords "California cities populations" at two or three of your favorite search engines and observe what is returned. If you have no favorite search engines (yet), pick from this list:

AltaVista	http://www.altavista.com/
FAST Search	http://www.alltheweb.com/
Google	http://www.google.com/
NorthernLight	http://www.northernlight.com/

Meta Search Engines Tapping into multiple search engines is repetitive and tedious, as well as largely mechanical. But there's good news. For every repetitive and mechanical computer activity, someone has probably written software to automate it for you. The automated answer for multiple Web searches is the meta search engine. A **meta search engine** is an engine that sends a query to several different search engines and then returns some number of the top hits found by each. With a meta search engine, you type in your query once, hit Enter, and then sift through the hits that are returned.

The Web Offers Many Good Meta Search Engines

Here are some good meta search engines to bookmark:

DogPile	http://www.dogpile.com/
InFind	http://www.infind.com/
MetaCrawler	http://www.metacrawler.com/index_metafind.html
C4	http://www.c4.com/index.html?cyber411=1
Highway 61	http://www.highway61.com/

Many meta search engines are publicly available on the Web. The better ones are careful not to swamp you with too many hits or with duplicate copies of the same hits. A meta search engine collects the top hits from each of the other search engines that it polls and decides how to present them to you. It might attempt to interleave them in a single ranked hit list, or it might let you view them in blocks, one engine at a time. Using a meta search engine leverages your time and reduces your effort, thereby enabling you to streamline your Web searches.

AskJeeves offers the results of a meta search engine in case its database of known questions misses the mark. It lists the top hits for each search engines used; short titles are available on pull-down menus (see Figure 6.16):

Figure 6.16:
AskJeeves Falls Back on a Meta Search Engine (Just in Case)

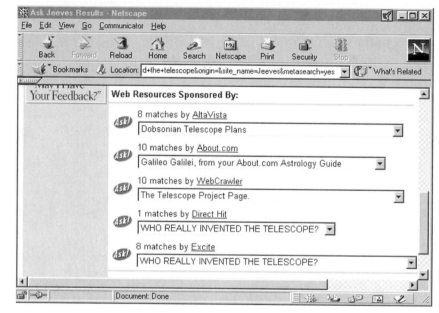

Although the meta search engine at AskJeeves is often helpful, it consults only five other search engines. Thus it might not be as comprehensive as you want. Most meta search engines tap the resources of at least six search engines, and some analyze hits from more than a dozen. Whereas all search engines rank the hits, displaying the best candidate hits first, with a meta search engine, the ranking problem is more challenging. This is because multiple hit lists must be merged and possibly re-ranked in order to create a single hit list. If this **merge-and-rank problem** is not handled well, the advantages of having broader Web page coverage can be lost by an inability to recognize the best hits. Some meta search engines avoid the problem by simply showing you the tops hits from each search engine, making no attempt to merge them in a single hit list. While not an optimal solution, this might be better than your having to look at the results of an ineffective merge-and-rank strategy. Experiment with a few meta search engines to find one or two that you like.

If you give a good query to a good meta search engine, you'll probably find what you're seeking. However, you might have to examine a few documents on the hit list. For example, suppose that you use a meta search engine named **InFind** to track down the list of California cities (see Figure 6.17).

The results are grouped in different ways. For example, hits in one group contain the phrase "California Cities" in their Web page titles. Hits in another are only for

Figure 6.17:
Fast Results by
InFind Based on Six
Search Engines

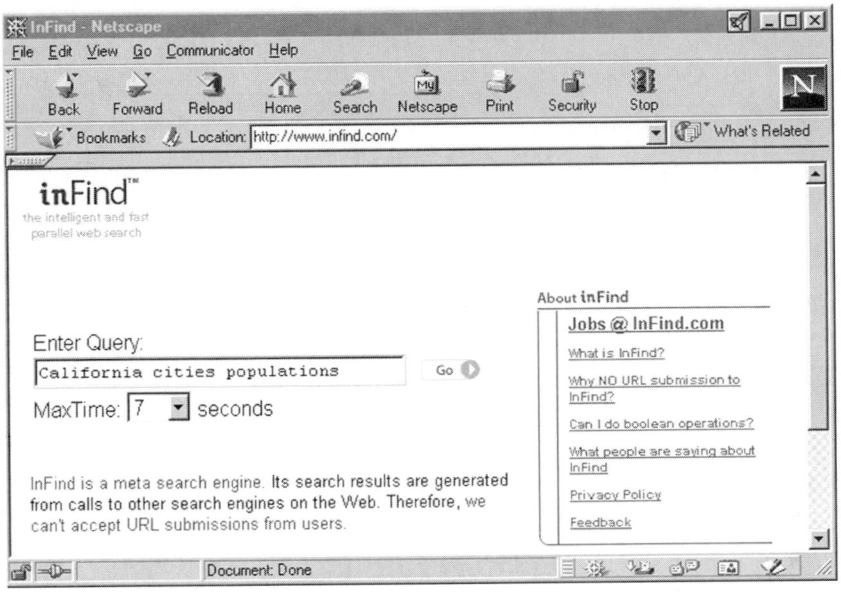

documents from California state government agencies. Once you figure out the basis on which each group is organized, you might be able to focus on the more likely groups for a closer examination. Although InFind does not offer page descriptions of the Web page titles, these groups can be very informative. In this case, you might expect to find good hits among the state government pages. Some of the choices are shown in Figure 6.18. Can you find the right link?

Meta Search Engine Exercise #1: Find a Ranked List of California's 20 Largest Cities

1. Use **InFind** and the keywords "California cities populations" to try to obtain a ranked list of California's 20 largest cities.

2. Examine the hits that come back to find a list of the top 20 cities.

Your hit list probably won't look exactly like that shown in Figure 6.18. Hit lists, like the Web, shift and change with time.

InFind's hit categories are very useful. However, once you've found one that you like, you might need to visit a number of its hits in order to see which are helpful. Web page titles don't always tell you everything that you need to know. A meta search engine that could merge all of its hits in a single list, with the best hits at the top, would be even better. Can it be done?

Figure 6.18:
One of These Links
Is the Right One

Back | Forward | Reload | Home | Search | Netscape | Print | Security | Stop

Bookmarks | Location: .exe?query=California+cities+populations&time=7&x=41&y=4 | What's Related

California City

- "California City Realtors, Patricia Gordon services California City , CA - "
- A California City, California Real Estate For Sale
- CALIFORNIA - City Resource Sites for planning weddings, meetings and special events
- CALIFORNIA CITY AND COUNTY SALES AND USE TAX RATES January 1999 - Table of Content
- California City Internet Services
- California City Today
- Foster City , California - City information: moving, apartments, relocation, real estate, ...
- Green Power Network - Santa Monica Becomes First California City to Okay Green Power Purchase
- Northern California City Guide
- San Francisco, California - City Information
- Santa Monica Real Estate - City Information Santa Monica - California City Information The ...
- Worldwide Soaring Turnpoint Exchange: California City, California

California Cities

- California Cities Ranked by Total Population January 1
- California Cities Ranked by Total Population January 1
- California Cities and Towns Listed by Name - V
- California Cities, Cities in California, Cities in the State of California, State of ...
- California Cities, Cities in California, State of California Cities, California Counties, ...
- Get population data on California cities
- Northern California Cities & Towns

Ca Site

- 96 E-1 Population Estimates for Cities and Counties
- CA Home Page: Your Government-Local Governments
- California Department of Insurance
- City of Delano
- Corona Economic Development - Press Release of March 24, 1997
- Los Angeles County
- Reports and Research Papers

Meta Search Engine Exercise #2: Find the ABCDE Rule for Skin Cancer

1. Visit each meta search engine mentioned in this section, and find the five signs of skin cancer (also called the *ABCDE rule* for skin cancer). Don't settle for the similar ABCD rule—make sure to find the ABCDE rule.

2. Which meta search engine was able to deliver this information to you most efficiently? Explain your answer.

One meta search engine, **Copernic 2000**, comes very close to solving the merge-and-rank problem. However, it's not available on the Web. You need to download it and run it on your local machine (not all of the search engines that it polls—only the meta search engine part!).

Copernic 2000 works with 16 search engines. It requires a minute or two to collect its results, depending on the speed of your Net connection. However, you can watch its progress with each search engine while you wait (see Figure 6.19).

Figure 6.19:
If You Like Progress Bars, You'll Love This Window

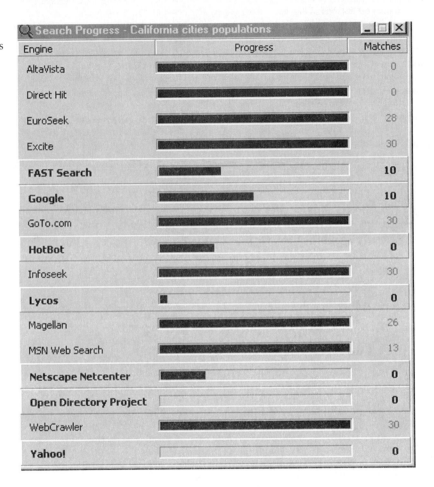

Once all of the results are in, Copernic merges the results in a single hit list, with a short description for each (see Figure 6.20).

If you've experienced the merge-and-rank problem, you'll appreciate what you see in Figure 6.20. The first two hits, Historical Census Populations, point to the same document. They weren't merged because they are *mirror documents*—the same document is posted on two separate Web servers. This document points to a file that contains a long list of California cities with their populations from the 1990 census. However, the file is formatted for Microsoft Excel™. If you don't have Excel on your computer, and you want to view this file, you'll need to download an Excel viewer.

Figure 6.20:
Merged-and-Ranked Hits Produced by Copernic 2000

☐	☑	Title	Address	Score ▽	Engines
✿	☐	**Historical Census Populations of Places...**	http://www.dof.ca.gov/html/D.../histtext.htm	▨	Excite, FAST Searc...
		California State Department of Finance Demographic Research Unit 915 L Street Sacramento, CA 95814 (916) 322-4651 State of...			
☐	☐	Historical Census Populations of Places, Tow...	http://goto.com/d/sr;$sessionid$2LOKREIAB...	▨	GoTo.com
		California State Department of Finance Demographic Research Unit 915 L Street Sacramento, CA 95814 (916) 322-4651 State of...			
✿	☐	**California's Population**	http://www.mathstories.../california_pop.htm	▨	Excite, Magellan
		Sheet # 76/California's Population Show your work California's population on January 1, 1998 was 33,252,000. Ten Largest Cities...			
✿	☐	**Reports and Research Papers**	http://www.dof.ca.gov/html/D.../repndat.htm	▨	Excite, Magellan, W...
		Reports and Research Papers California Demographic Research Unit Reports E-1 City/County Population Estimates with Annual Pe...			
✿	☐	**Yahoo! Regional>U.S. States>Californi...**	http://sg.yaho.../Departments_and_Programs	▨	HotBot, MSN Web S...
		Help - More Yahoos Home > Regional > U.S. States > California > Cities > San Diego > Education > College and University > Publi...			
✿	☐	**Relocating to California - Anaheim, Los...**	http://relocating.to/relocating-to-california.htm	▨	EuroSeek
		Relocating To California? You can save with Cybernet!			
✿	☐	**22-0455 COMMUNICATING EFFECTIVEL...**	http://www.commandcollege.c.../22-0455.htm	▨	FAST Search
		California Law Enforcement Command College 22-0455 COMMUNICATING EFFECTIVELY WITH NON-ENGLISH SPEAKING CUSTOME...			

In this file, the city list is ordered alphabetically, so you could to go through it by hand to find the top 20 cities manually. This is not a problem if you use Excel, however, because Excel will reorder the list for you based on the population entries (see Figure 6.21).

Figure 6.21:
The Top 20 Cities Shown in an Excel Document

	A	B	C	D
1	**Historical US Census Populations of**			
2	**Places, Towns, and Cities in California,**			
3	**1850-1990**			
4				
5				
6	**Incorporated**	**County**	**Place/Town/City**	**1990**
7				
8	1850	Los Angeles	Los Angeles	3,485,398
9	1850	San Diego	San Diego	1,110,549
10	1850	Santa Clara	San Jose	782,248
11	1850	San Francisco	San Francisco	723,959
12	1897	Los Angeles	Long Beach	429,433
13	1852	Alameda	Oakland	372,242
14	1850	Sacramento	Sacramento	369,365
15	1885	Fresno	Fresno	354,202
16	1886	Orange	Santa Ana	293,742
17	1878	Orange	Anaheim	266,406
18	1883	Riverside	Riverside	226,505
19	1850	San Joaquin	Stockton	210,943
20	1909	Orange	Huntington Beach	181,519
21	1906	Los Angeles	Glendale	180,038
22	1898	Kern	Bakersfield	174,820
23	1956	Alameda	Fremont	173,339
24	1884	Stanislaus	Modesto	164,730
25	1869	San Bernardino	San Bernardino	164,164
26	1956	Orange	Garden Grove	143,050
27	1903	Ventura	Oxnard	142,216

However, suppose that you don't have Excel and you don't want to pick through the list by hand to find the top 20 cities. Check to see whether any of the other hits have what you need. The third hit, California's Population, is an elementary school worksheet that lists the ten largest cities in California along with their population figures. This is close. However, you still need ten more cities.

The next hit, Reports and Research Papers, doesn't sound promising. However, take a look at it because it is ranked immediately under two other documents that come very close to what you want. If you visit this hit, you'll find (not surprisingly) a long list of reports and research papers (see Figure 6.22).

Figure 6.22:
One Link Away from the Jackpot

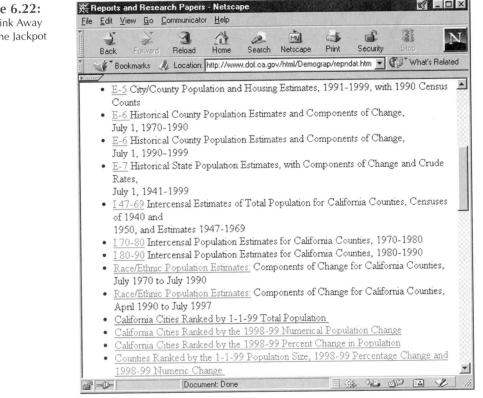

With a little persistence, you can locate the document that has exactly what you want (see Figure 6.23).

Searching and Browsing Go Together

The information that you need might be one or two links away from an item on a search engine's hit list. If you see a document that's not exactly on target, check to see whether it contains any links that look promising.

Also, it's important that you stay on track and not get distracted by interesting but irrelevant hyperlinks. Carefully focused browsing just can get you where you need to go when you're hot on the trail of an elusive Web page.

Figure 6.23:
The Jackpot

California Cities Ranked by Total Population January 1, 1999

RANK	CITY	COUNTY	POPULATION
1	LOS ANGELES	LOS ANGELES	3,781,500
2	SAN DIEGO	SAN DIEGO	1,254,300
3	SAN JOSE	SANTA CLARA	909,100
4	SAN FRANCISCO	SAN FRANCISCO	790,500
5	LONG BEACH	LOS ANGELES	452,900
6	FRESNO	FRESNO	415,400
7	OAKLAND	ALAMEDA	399,900
8	SACRAMENTO	SACRAMENTO	396,200
9	SANTA ANA	ORANGE	315,000
10	ANAHEIM	ORANGE	306,300
11	RIVERSIDE	RIVERSIDE	254,300
12	STOCKTON	SAN JOAQUIN	243,700
13	BAKERSFIELD	KERN	230,800
14	FREMONT	ALAMEDA	203,600
15	GLENDALE	LOS ANGELES	199,200
16	HUNTINGTON BEACH	ORANGE	196,700
17	SAN BERNARDINO	SAN BERNARDINO	185,000
18	MODESTO	STANISLAUS	184,600
19	CHULA VISTA	SAN DIEGO	166,900
20	OXNARD	VENTURA	158,300

If you had tried Copernic first, you could have found what you needed within 5 minutes. If you do a lot of searching and find yourself struggling with many queries, you might want to experiment with Copernic 2000. It offers a freeware version, which is what we used for this example, as well as two enhanced (but not free) versions that contain additional features. In addition, other meta search engines are available that you can download and evaluate, for example **WebFerret**, another popular choice similar to Copernic.

6.4 ▮ SUCCESSIVE QUERY REFINEMENT

Remember, don't expect to get the best hits on the first try. No matter how skilled you become with Internet searches, each new search problem will require some experimentation. Through a process of systematic trial and error, you'll modify and tune your queries to get increasingly better hits. The process of moving from an initial experimental query to a final successful query is called **successive query refinement** (see Figure 6.24).

Figure 6.24:
Successive Query
Refinement

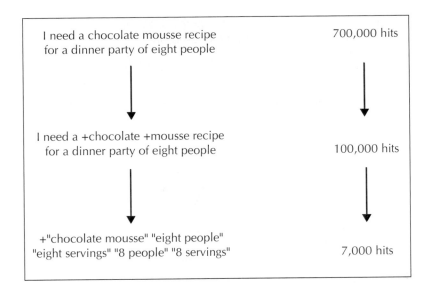

I need a chocolate mousse recipe
for a dinner party of eight people   700,000 hits

I need a +chocolate +mousse recipe
for a dinner party of eight people   100,000 hits

+"chocolate mousse" "eight people"
"eight servings" "8 people" "8 servings"   7,000 hits

With experience, you can become skilled at successive query refinement. However, it helps to know your tools and how to use them.

6.4.1 Fuzzy Queries

The most popular search engines offer a simple query option where you are encouraged to type full sentences or questions that describe your information needs. Such a query is called a **fuzzy query**. A fuzzy query requires only plain English. However, don't confuse fuzzy query processing with human sentence comprehension. Remember, search engines don't understand English (or any other human language). You can enter ungrammatical sentences, incomplete sentence fragments, disjoint phrases, or nonsense words—the search engine won't know the difference. It sees only a collection of keywords.

A fuzzy query is often a good starting point for a search session because it gives you a sense of how large your overall search space will be. A fuzzy query with a large number of keywords will normally return many hits, possibly more than 100,000 if the database is very large. This isn't very helpful, except to indicate that your query is pulling in a large number of documents. If a fuzzy query returns a small number of hits (fewer than 1,000), you know that you're dealing with a relatively small and specialized collection of documents.

The 1,000 Document Limit

Although a search engine might tell you that it has found thousands of hits for your query, no search engine is prepared to deliver more than the top 1,000 hits on the ranked hit list.

You can usually improve the hits at the top of the document by marking keywords in the query as follows:

- *Required keyword*: Mark with a + before the keyword.

  When a keyword has been marked as *required*, the resulting hit list will contain only documents that contain the required keyword.

- *Prohibited keyword:* Mark with an - before the keyword.

  When a keyword has been marked as prohibited, the resulting hit list will contain no documents that contain that keyword.

Most search engines that offer a fuzzy query option let you mark keywords in this way. When a search engine sees these tags, it reduces its hit list by deleting all documents that contain any prohibited keywords, as well as all documents that fail to contain all of the required keywords. As an example, here is a fuzzy query designed to find a recipe:

```
I need a chocolate mousse recipe for a dinner party of
eight people
```

The surviving keywords (those that aren't ignored) are likely to be "chocolate," "mousse," "recipe," "dinner," "party," and "eight." AltaVista returns about 83,325 hits in response to this fuzzy query. By marking keywords as required and prohibited, you could produce a better query:

```
I need a +chocolate +mousse recipe for a dinner party of
eight people
```

AltaVista returns about 20,524 hits for this query. That's still too many. However, revising the query in this way shows that over 75% of the hits from the original query must have been totally irrelevant, so the results of the second query are actually a big improvement.

The query could still return a recipe for a vanilla mousse cake with chocolate frosting. You can eliminate false hits of this sort by using another query feature: exact phrase matching. To do this, enclose important keywords, in this case, "chocolate mousse," within *double quotation marks* (instead of using two separate keywords "chocolate"' and "mousse," which might appear in two different parts of the document), as follows:

```
I need a "chocolate mousse" recipe for a dinner party of
eight people
```

Exact phrase matching means that the entire quoted phrase is treated as a single keyword and that documents that contain that exact phrase will be ranked more highly than documents that don't. Most search engines recognize double-quoted phrases in a query as a signal to perform exact phrase matching. Exact phrase matching can be very useful in fuzzy queries, where both phrases and single words can be marked with + or −.

Search Tips for the Most Popular Search Engines

It takes time to visit each search engine and peruse all of their online documentation. To obtain a quick overview of engine-specific search tips conveniently bundled in one place, go to **FindSpot**, select Search Tools from the main menu, and then click the search engine of your choice (see Figure 6.25). A display will appear that shows important search tips, example queries, and a search box in which you can submit a query to the search engine directly from the FindSpot Web page. This is a great way to get started with a new search engine. Another good place to go for search engine tips and tricks is **The Spider's Apprentice**.

Figure 6.25:
FindSpot Helping You Learn How to Use Search Engines

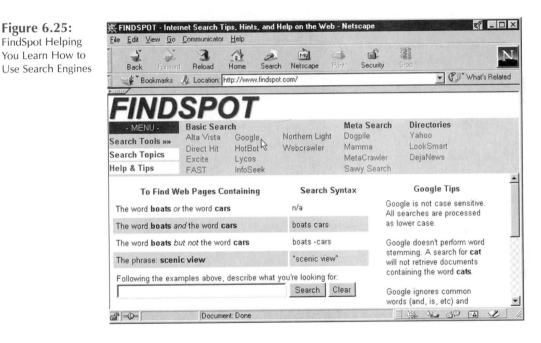

Once you understand how fuzzy queries are handled, you can create queries by starting with an English sentence and then modifying it as needed. For example, the keywords "dinner" and "party" are not likely to get you any closer to chocolate mousse recipes. In fact, including them is probably counterproductive because they might lead to a narrative in which someone goes to a dinner party and eats chocolate mousse. However, you might be able to zero in on recipes by adding a new required keyword, "servings," as follows:

```
+"chocolate mousse" +servings
```

AltaVista returns 1,057 hits for this query. Notice that you did not choose the word "recipe" even though you are looking for recipes. You chose instead a word that you expect to see in a recipe. Successive query refinement can begin with an

English sentence, but it often pays to move away from the words in that sentence in order to better anticipate the words that you expect to see in your target documents.

How Numbers Are Handled

Most search engines don't index specific numbers. Instead, they replace numbers with a generic number marker so that numbers will match numbers (just not necessarily the same number). To match a phrase that contains a specific number, check to see whether your search engine includes specific numbers in its document indexes by trying a test query with a required number in it and observing what is returned.

When working with a new query, start with a simple fuzzy query to see how many hits come back. Then narrow your query by marking required and prohibited keywords where possible. Sometimes a quick inspection of highly ranked hits will suggest helpful prohibited keywords that can narrow your query. Continue to refine your query in this way until it results in a manageable number of hits. With good document rankings, you don't need to narrow the query to a very small hit list. A hit list of 1,000 documents with 20 good hits at the top is usually a signal to stop searching. Never judge a search result without a quick look at the top ten hits.

6.4.2 Using Term Counts

HotBot and AltaVista's Simple Search option show you term counts for each word in your query. A **term count** is a statistic that tells you how many times a keyword (term) has been seen throughout the entire document database. This figure is not the same as the number of documents that contain the keyword. Some documents contain the keyword more than once. When a term count is calculated, each instance of the keyword is counted in those cases.

Knowing how often a keyword is used can be helpful. If a query brings in too few hits, you can check term counts to see whether a required keyword was excessively restrictive. Here are two tips to increase or decrease your hit count by using term counts.

1. To increase your hit count, examine your required keywords and remove the required tag from the keyword that has the smallest term count. Required keywords that occur with low frequency are very beneficial when they are on target.

2. To decrease your hit count, add some required or prohibited keywords. Sometimes the inclusion of one additional required keyword will reduce your hits dramatically, even for a fuzzy query.

For example, the following query includes the new required keyphrase, "Julia Child," and produces exactly nine hits on AltaVista, including some that are right on target (see Figure 6.26):

```
+"chocolate mousse" +"Julia Child" +servings
```

Figure 6.26:
A Successful Query
Bringing Good Hits
to the Top of the
Hit List

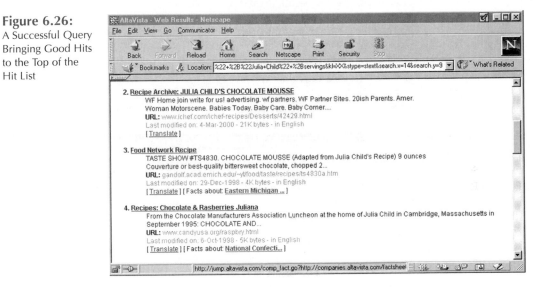

Note that it didn't take a very complicated query to reach these relevant documents. It required only that you refine the query with a highly restrictive required keyphrase (Julia Child). In fact, AltaVista indexes 17,170 documents that contain the keyphrase "Julia Child," 24,196 documents that contain the keyphrase "chocolate mousse," and 339,637 that contain the keyword "servings." So, none of the terms is very restrictive by itself. When combined, however, they result in a very small intersection of documents that contain all three (see Figure 6.27). Always consider keywords in the context of the full query in order to assess their effectiveness in successive query refinement.

Figure 6.27:
An Intersection of
Required Keywords

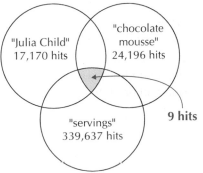

Where Can I Enter a Fuzzy Query

Most search engines offer fuzzy queries as their first search option, often called the Simple Search option. If you are allowed to enter an English sentence or question, that's the fuzzy query, or Simple Search, option (see Figure 6.28). Don't expect to find an input box labeled "fuzzy."

In addition, any search option that allows required (+) keywords and/or prohibited (-) keywords is a fuzzy query option. Most search engines support fuzzy queries although the interface may not make this obvious. For example, to enter a fuzzy query for HotBot, change the default query option "all of the words" to "any of the words."

Figure 6.28:
The Simple Search
Option at AltaVista

alta^vista: SEARCH | Search Live! Shopping Raging Bull Free Internet Access Email |

Find: | +"chocolate mousse" +"Julia Child" +servings | Search   Language: | any language ▾ |
    • Help   • Family Filter is **off**   • Language Settings   **Advanced Web Search**

6.4.3 Boolean Queries

In general, if you're looking for a very specific type of document, a particular news item that you can date, or an item associated with a specific person (who is not a major news figure), then a *Boolean query* is probably the way to go. A **Boolean query** is a query that consists of keywords, like a fuzzy query, but with **logical operators** (AND, OR, NOT) inserted between the keywords to specify *combinations* of required and prohibited keywords in a logical fashion:

X AND Y	will return only documents that contain both X and Y.
X OR Y	will return only documents that contain either X or Y.
X AND NOT Y	will return only documents that contain X and do not contain Y.

The logical operators AND, OR, and NOT are always recognized by search engines that accept Boolean queries. However, you need to make sure that the search engine is expecting a Boolean query. Before trying a Boolean query, look for a Boolean search mode. (For example, at HotBot, it's in the search mode pull-down menu, and at AltaVista, it's in an advanced search option (see Figure 6.29).

Some search engines have only one input window in which you enter your query; others have two or three. Many such windows come with one or more pull-down menus from which you can set a variety of query preferences, called **query modes** or **search options**. Consult the search engine's online documentation to learn more about these modes or options. At the very least, be sure to scan the entries in all of the pull-down menus, as they will show you the most important preference settings.

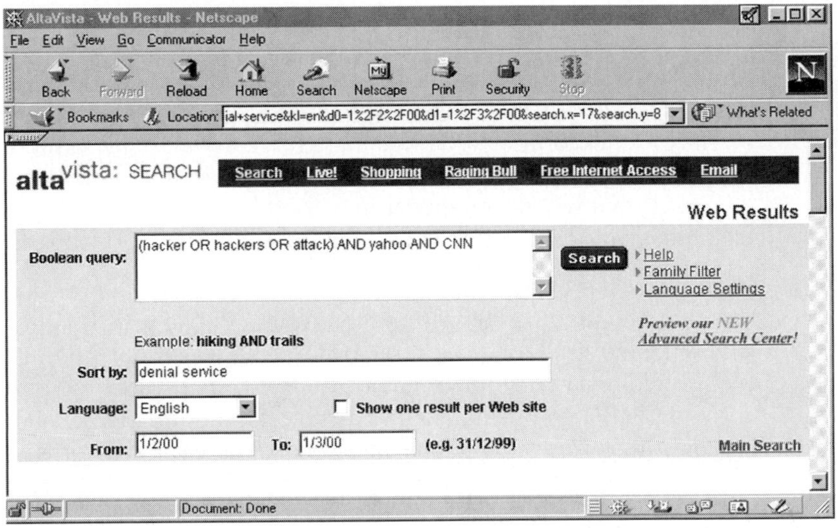

Figure 6.29:
An Advanced
Search Query at
AltaVista

Although an unfamiliar interface might make everything look initially strange and confusing, there are only a few standard options that you'll see repeatedly. When you're getting to know a new search engine, watch for the following standard features that an engine might offer.

- If there are two separate query windows, one is probably for fuzzy queries and the other is probably for Boolean queries.
- The first query window that you see is normally the fuzzy query option.
- A window for fuzzy queries will encourage you to use plain English.
- A Boolean query window is often called an Advanced Search option.
- If there's only one query window, check to see whether a pull-down menu controls the query options.
- A pull-down menu might be offered that displays the preferences for your hit lists. You can usually select from two or three levels of detail for each hit.
- You can usually control the number of hits returned per Web page.

Search engines aren't very helpful regarding mistakes in a query. If a query comes back with no hits, you either asked for something that's not in the database or you're in the wrong query mode. If a Boolean query returns an outrageous number of hits, the search engine probably processed it as a fuzzy query. Be aware that a Boolean query in a search window for fuzzy queries will be interpreted as a fuzzy query and all of the Boolean logical operators will be ignored.

Boolean queries are not difficult to master. Nor are they always needed.

When to Try a Boolean Query

The success of a Boolean query depends on how reliably you can predict the presence or absence of specific keywords in your target documents. If you can identify a collection of keywords that you're certain will be present in all of the good hits, a Boolean query can be very effective. If you can identify one or more keywords that will never appear in a good hit (but which might pop up in lot of false hits), you can narrow your query by using the NOT operator.

When Boolean queries fail, it might be due to a logical error in the construction of the query or to some bad assumptions about the keywords being used. You can minimize the risk of logical errors by keeping your Boolean queries relatively simple (or taking a course in formal logic). It is considerably more difficult to make sure that you aren't making a bad assumption about your keywords. If your hit list strikes you as surprising in any way, reconsider your keywords.

If you know that all of your target documents will contain one keyword or combination of keywords, list them in a Boolean query by using the AND operator—these are the required keywords. The more unusual the required keywords, the better. The AltaVista query in Figure 6.29 shows a query that you hope will find articles that describe the denial-of-service attacks against a number of popular Web sites (including Yahoo! and CNN) in February 2000. The result will be documents that contain the keywords "yahoo" and "CNN," as well as at least one of the three keywords "hacker," "hackers," or "attack." Another restriction limits us to documents created between February 1, 2000 and March 1, 2000. Documents that contain the keywords "denial" and "service" will be ranked more highly in the hit list.

If you can find an unusual keyword that is associated with many false hits (documents you don't want to see), you can filter out those documents by using the AND NOT operator. For example, to find documents about browser cookies while avoiding recipes for edible cookies, you might try a Boolean query with the keyword "cookie" and "recipe":

```
cookies AND NOT recipe
```

6.5   ADVANCED SEARCH OPTIONS

Occasionally, you'll find a question that can benefit from advanced search features. Most search engines offer at least a few advanced features; they'll be under a link named Advanced Search. Hotbot's advanced options are on its home page. However, most search engines take you to a different page for the advanced search options. Each search engine offers a different collection of advanced features, so it's important to read the available documentation before trying out any advanced features for the first time (see Figure 6.30).

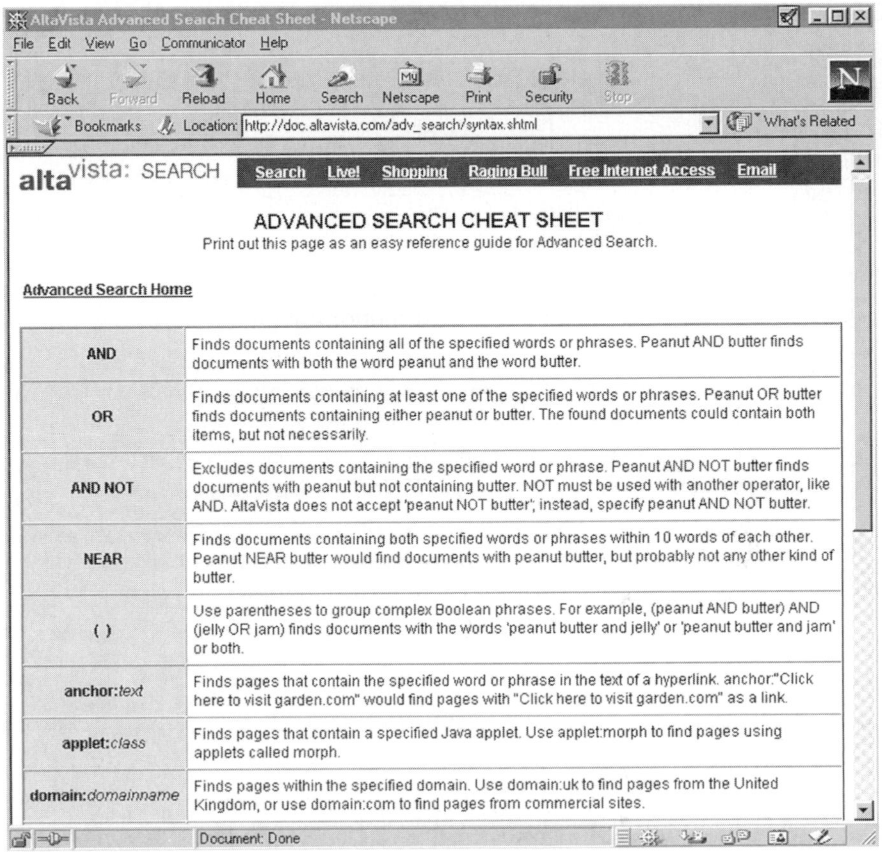

Figure 6.30:
Always Read the
Online
Documentation for
Advanced Search
Features

Many search engines let you specify documents dated within a specific time period (a very useful feature if you're looking for current news updates). With AltaVista, you can even control the document ranking criteria. The online documentation for these features is usually well written and easy to understand. Even if you think that you're experienced because you've worked with advanced features at other search engines, take the time to check out the documentation for any new engine with which you aren't familiar. You might find a surprise or two that can have a major impact on your query results.

Some search engines will let you mark keywords with special tags in order to narrow your search in various ways. AltaVista's keyword tags can be very useful if you're trying to narrow a search on a specific topic. For example, a **title:** tag provides for a particular keyword to appear in the title of a Web page (see Figure 6.31). Thus the query

```
title:cookies AND browser AND NOT recipe
```

will return only those documents that contain the keyword "cookies" in the document title.

Figure 6.31: AltaVista's Keyword Tags

anchor:_text_	Finds pages that contain the specified word or phrase in the text of a hyperlink. anchor:"Click here to visit garden.com" would find pages with "Click here to visit garden.com" as a link.
applet:_class_	Finds pages that contain a specified Java applet. Use applet:morph to find pages using applets called morph.
domain:_domainname_	Finds pages within the specified domain. Use domain:uk to find pages from the United Kingdom, or use domain:com to find pages from commercial sites.
host:_hostname_	Finds pages on a specific computer. The search host:www.shopping.com would find pages on the Shopping.com computer, and host:dilbert.unitedmedia.com would find pages on the computer called dilbert at unitedmedia.com.
image:_filename_	Finds pages with images having a specific filename. Use image:beaches to find pages with images called beaches.
link:_URLtext_	Finds pages with a link to a page with the specified URL text. Use link:www.myway.com to find all pages linking to myway.com.
text:_text_	Finds pages that contain the specified text in any part of the page other than an image tag, link, or URL. The search text:graduation would find all pages with the term graduation in them.
title:_text_	Finds pages that contain the specified word or phrase in the page title (which appears in the title bar of most browsers). The search title:sunset would find pages with sunset in the title.
url:_text_	Finds pages with a specific word or phrase in the URL. Use url:myway.com to find all pages on all servers that have the word myway in the host name, path, or filename--the complete URL, in other words.

If you find a large Web site that you want to search but there's no search engine for a site search, try a **host:** tag to simulate a site search of your own. A host: tag restricts your search to only one Web server. Unfortunately, you can't be sure that every Web page on the site has been indexed by the search engine that you're using, so the **host:** tag is no substitute for a comprehensive site search facility. If you really need a site search facility for a site that doesn't support one, you might be able to create your own client-side site search engine database (see the Above and Beyond section).

Advanced search features are very effective when you need to zero in on something very specific, such as the answer to a Joe Friday question. With some experience and a little luck, you should be able to pull in shorter hit lists, whose hits are all on target. You might miss some relevant hits, but when you're dealing with a Joe Friday question, you might not mind if a few good ones get away from you.

6.6 ■ SPECIALIZED SEARCH ENGINES

If you can find a comprehensive clearinghouse for a specific topic, you can handle all of your information needs for that topic through the clearinghouse. However, how do you know if a clearinghouse's coverage is comprehensive? Some clearinghouses are not actively maintained and might therefore be missing recently created resources. Others might point to a large number of resources but were never intended to be all-encompassing. How can you know exactly what a clearinghouse does and does not cover? This is a major problem with clearinghouses, no matter how much effort might have gone into them. If you're relying completely on clearinghouses for information on a broad topic, then you have reason to worry about what might be missing.

As an alternative to clearinghouses, specialized search engines focus on a particular topic and therefore offer maximal coverage. The Web offers many specialized search engines. If you find yourself conducting frequent searches on a particular topic, you should look for a specialized search engine in that one area. To find specialized search engines, try a search engine that specializes in this type of search engine. The best one is probably **Invisible Web** (see Figure 6.32).

When you conduct a keyword search at Invisible Web, use general rather than specific keywords. You're looking for large searchable sites on a particular topic, so enter a single keyword that best describes your topic. For example, if you enter the keyword "freeware," Invisible Web will find 14 searchable freeware sites (see Figure 6.33).

Figure 6.32:
Invisible Web: A
Search Engine for
Search Engines

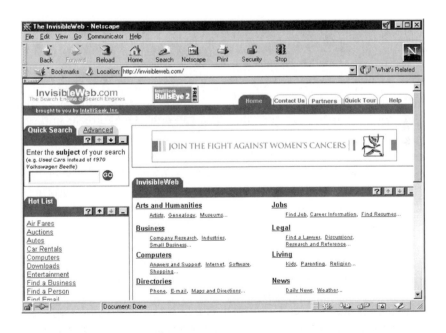

Many sites that Invisible Web indexes are searchable archives for online publications, public mailing lists, or other large document collections in a specific area. These resources are valuable for Deep Thought questions, when you need to get beyond the introductory articles and dig deep for everything that you can find.

Figure 6.33:
Searchable
Freeware Sites
Found by Invisible
Web

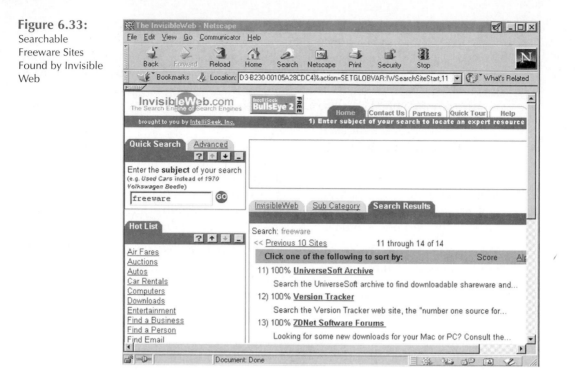

There are other ways to find specialized search engines for topic-specific searches. Visit **CNet's Search.com**, where you'll find another search engine for search engines. Scroll to the bottom of the page, and click the link named Find a Search. You'll reach a page on which you can enter keywords to find searchable resources for specific topics. You may not get as many hits here as at Invisible Web, but you might find some different ones.

Another place to find both specialized search engines and clearinghouses is **Search Engine Guide**. This site is actually a clearinghouse for resources related to search engines (see Figure 6.34). If you want to stay on top of current developments in the world of search engines, check out its links for newsletters, search engine stories in the news, and the top ten spotlight for the latest and greatest search utilities and services.

Searchable sites on specialized topics are valuable. However, a searchable site is always limited to a site-specific search. Sometimes, you might want a specialized search engine that can find items at numerous other sites. This is easy to do at Yahoo! and several other Internet portal sites. Recall that Yahoo!'s search engine is restricted to Yahoo!'s subject tree. To look in a specific direction, you can narrow the scope of Yahoo!'s site search by identifying one branch of the subject tree to which you want to restrict your search.

Figure 6.34:
A Search Engine
Technology
Clearinghouse

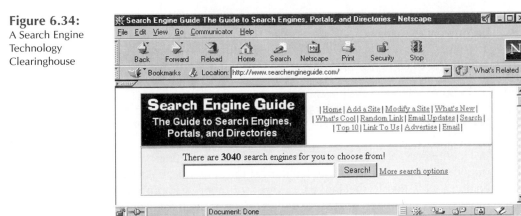

Specialized Searches at Yahoo!

If you've found a useful subtree of Yahoo!'s directory structure, you can conduct keyword searches restricted to that branch. Look for a pull-down menu to the right of Yahoo!'s Search button (see Figure 6.35). Click the "just this category" button before you click the Search button.

Figure 6.35:
Conducting a
Specialized Search
at Yahoo!

This Yahoo! feature makes it easy to conduct incremental searches. For example, you could start at the Yahoo! home page and enter the keyword "software" as a preliminary foray into the subject tree. Yahoo! will return 1,975 category matches, the second one of which is directly under the Computers and Internet subtree: **Computers and Internet > Software**. If you restrict the site search to this branch of Yahoo! and enter the keyword "freeware," you'll find 200 document hits. Had you relied on the subject tree alone, you would have had trouble assembling these 200 hits in any other way because they would have been found in different areas of the subtree. Note that if you drop to the **Computers and Internet > Software > Freeware** subtree, a search on "freeware" produces only eight site matches.

For an incremental search to work, you don't want to go too far out onto any one branch; otherwise, you reduce the number of potential hits. Stay higher in the tree structure, and work with general keywords (as always, with Yahoo!). When you see, for example, 1,975 potential subtrees from which you could choose for your search, look for those near the top of the tree (**Computers and Internet > Software** is only three levels down from Yahoo!'s top level).

Once you become adept at locating topic-specific resources on the Web, you might never want to work with a general search engine again. As the large search engines—and their users—struggle with the inherent difficulties of working with hundreds of millions of documents, specialized search engines could be the way of the future.

6.7   SEARCH BOTS AND INTELLIGENT AGENTS

In recent years, another type of specialized search engine has surfaced in response to commercial interests and e-commerce: the search bot. A **search bot** is a search engine that is highly specialized, covers a number of appropriate sites on different servers, and organizes a database of timely information for users to query and examine. Examples of search bots are all of the comparison shopping sites, at which you can look for the lowest price for a particular retail item (see Chapter 10). Search bots continually monitor multiple Web sites in order to pull in the most current information in a specific area of interest. They are not limited to formal databases or information that must be formatted in some uniform fashion. Some can consolidate information extracted from free-form text and don't require any special preparations by contributing Web sites. In this respect, the search bots are similar to general search engines. However, specialized search bots preside over somewhat larger categories of information needs. For a searchable clearinghouse of search bots, visit **BotSpot**, which includes shopping bots, stock bots, sports bots, government bots, and software bots (see Figure 6.36).

You might already be using the services of server-side search bots if you've customized a Web portal site that reflects your interests. For example, weatherbots retrieve weather forecasts for a specific region and stock bots display customized ticker tapes for stock prices. Amazon.com uses a book bot to alert customers about new publications by specific authors, and eBay uses bid bots to inform people of new bids on specific auction items. As the Web continues to grow, it makes sense to turn to specialized search bots for timely, high-quality information.

Most search bots are server-side services. However, some include client-side operations, such as the newsbots, which track unfolding news stories (see the Above and Beyond section in Chapter 5). Many client-side meta search engines offer search bot services in order to track prespecified areas of interest (for example, Copernic, **WebFerret**, and **BullsEye 2**). However, these "premium" features are rarely included in freeware or evaluation releases.

An **intelligent agent** is very similar to a search bot. However, an intelligent agent operates autonomously and is finely tuned to the individual needs of a specific user. The two terms are sometimes used interchangeably, but intelligent agents tend to incorporate more-sophisticated techniques and, as such, represent a lively research area in computer science. Some notable intelligent agents are listed at BotSpot under the categories Software Bots and Knowledge Bots.

Figure 6.36:
Finding a Bot at
BotSpot

Search bots and intelligent agents are examples of a fast-moving and exciting area of information retrieval research, one that promises greater productivity in an era of a never-ending information explosion. If you're spending too much time trying to stay on top of everything on the Web, visit BotSpot and look for a search bot to help you cope. You might be surprised to see how many search bots are available to lend a hand (and at no cost!).

6.8   PULL AND PUSH TECHNOLOGIES

As the Internet becomes more commercialized, content providers are working to find the right balance between pull technology and push technology. **Pull technology** is a distribution technique whereby information is sent to a user on demand. **Push technology** is a distribution technique whereby information is sent to the user without the user's prior permission. A Web browser is an example of a pull technology because you direct the browser to Web locations in order to *pull* requested Web pages to your local host, on demand. E-mail is an example of a push technology because e-mail messages are sent —*pushed*—to you whether or not you want them (this is considered push technology even though you need to launch an e-mail client to see them). When information comes to you automatically and periodically over some indefinite period of time, that's a push delivery mechanism. When information comes to you in response to a specific request and the response has a clear conclusion after which no additional responses are expected, that's a pull delivery mechanism.

With pull technologies, information consumers have more control over the inflow of information. With push technologies, information providers have more control over the distribution of their information. The client/server model accommodates both types of technologies, and Internet users can decide for themselves which they prefer.

Although the term *push technology* sounds vaguely obnoxious, push technologies can operate in unobtrusive ways, much like e-mail. You don't need to bother with it unless you want to, and you can always choose to ignore it. Suppose that you want a local weather forecast each morning. A push technology can have one waiting for you on your computer's desktop at 6:00 A.M. each morning. Maybe you like to track the current prices of six stocks in which you've invested. A push technology can run a little ticker tape on your computer's desktop with only those six stocks on it. Or maybe you've heard about a book that's will be published soon and you want to be told as soon as it starts to ship. A push technology can send you an e-mail message announcing its availability.

Push technologies often address ongoing information needs for periodic updates and revisions. One of the most popular applications for push technologies is news tracking. Most people like to stay on top of the news each day. This need traditionally has been filled by newspapers, news magazines, local and national news programs on television, and radio broadcasts. It didn't take long for Web portal sites to discover, however, that users like to customize their Web sites with a selection of news updates taken from different categories. Some people like to see sports scores, and others don't. Different people have different interests, and those differences become apparent when you give people the opportunity to customize personal online news deliveries. Portal customization is big business, and news filters are a big part of that.

If you're a news hound, you've probably gloried in the number of online news sources available to you and then despaired at the amount of time required to take it all in. To address this problem, a new software niche has materialized around the business of customized news delivery. A variety of desktop newsstands are available as freeware for wired news hounds of varying tastes and appetites. For example, **EntryPoint** (a direct descendent of the original **PointCast** news service) is a freeware download that places a toolbar on your desktop and offers a standard set of features for customized news updates (see Figure 6.37).

Once customized, the toolbar will deliver local weather, selected stock quotes, and news headlines on demand. Users can customize their news preferences from a number of popular sources (see Figure 6.38). The toolbar can be launched, reposi-

Figure 6.37:
EntryPoint Toolbar

tioned, saved to the task bar, or shut down at any time, thereby making it a polite example of push technology. Even the scrolling news headlines on the toolbar can be halted if the constant parade of text is too distracting.

They can also review current stories by reading headline or lead sentences, as shown in Figure 6.39.

Figure 6.38:
Customizing Your Personal News Service

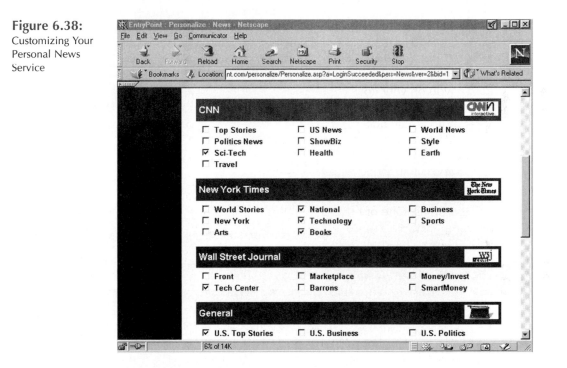

The full text for any available story is only a click away with a Web browser. For most people, EntryPoint's news coverage is welcome and sufficient, offering significant timesaving (once the initial novelty wears off and using the toolbar becomes just another part of the daily routine).

For the really serious news junkie, other applications offer a greater range of publications, content filters, and special features. For example, **newZPrint** is another freeware download that offers dozens of publications, including international newspapers (see Figure 6.40).

newZPrint also offers extensive customization options for each publication, as shown in Figure 6.41.

Figure 6.39:
Scanning Breaking
News as It Happens

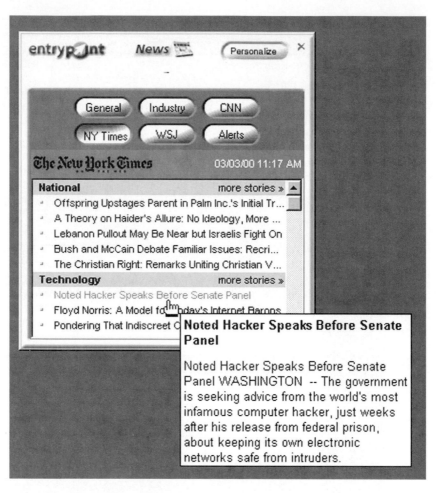

newZPrint doesn't provide real-time downloads over an open Internet connection, as does EntryPoint, so it's not as nimble as EntryPoint. In all other respects, however, newZPrint is EntryPoint on steroids. It downloads articles on demand and can be programmed to download your selections daily at a fixed time. You can send your daily news to a printer, which will render it in newsletter format (this is very nice if you have time to read during your morning commute). newZPrint even displays articles on your computer in a newspaper-like graphical display (see Figure 6.42) that might be a welcome change from your Web browser if you spend a lot of time on the Web every day.

Given these examples of push technology, you might be thinking that these news services are more like news filters than actual searches. For a search to take place, a specific query must be processed, right? Well, maybe. The line between a filter and a query is a matter of degree. If EntryPoint knows that you're interested in technology articles and not sports, you'll see only technology articles—it will filter out

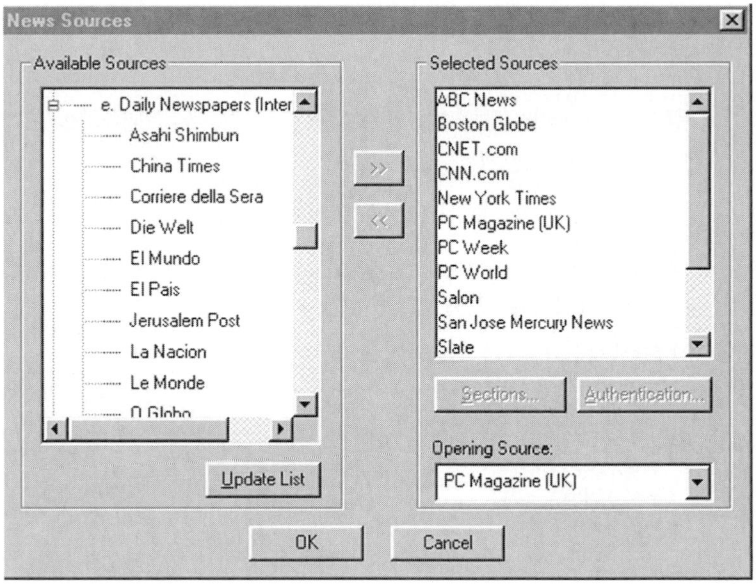

Figure 6.40:
Extensive
Publication Options
with newZPrint

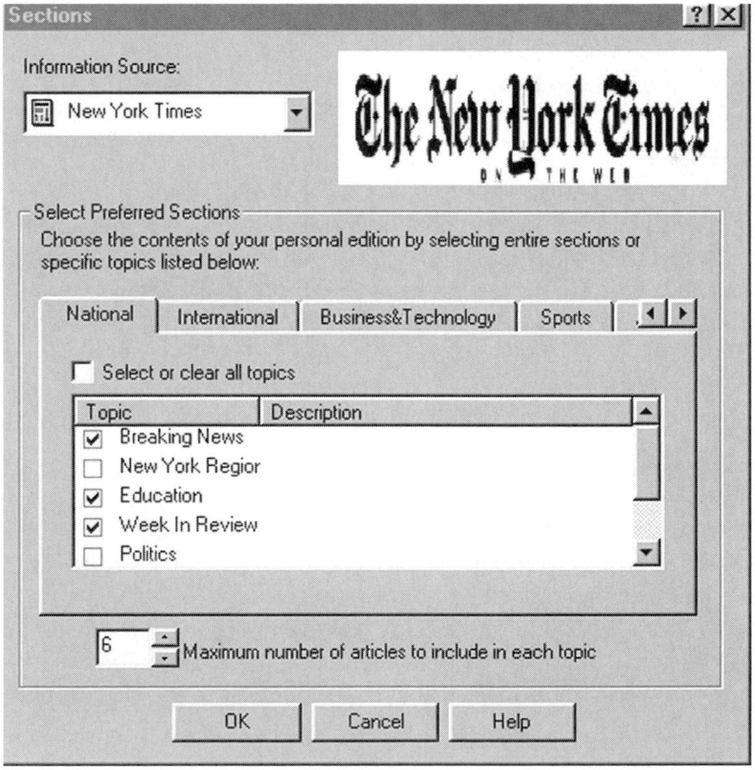

Figure 6.41:
Tuning Each News
Source

Figure 6.42:
Over the Net and to
the Printer

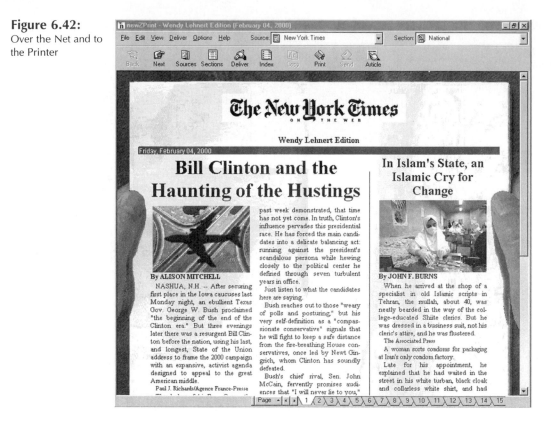

the sports offerings. However, what if EntryPoint could use a set of your keywords and send you articles that contain those keywords, as well as alert you with a sound or a pop-up window whenever a new article that meets your search criteria arrives on its server? This is beginning to feel more like a search. In fact, you have merely applied a *keyword filter* instead of a *general topic filter*. EntryPoint does offer a very primitive keyword filter option that can be used to track articles on a small number of topics (see Figure 6.43). If this feature appeals to you, then investigate the world of search bots for more-sophisticated newsbot services (see Section 6.7).

Although these two examples of push technologies are news-oriented, the world of intelligent push technology goes beyond news delivery services. For example, some client-side meta search engines allow you to set up tracking schedules for specific search queries. You can program the engine to process the query as often as you wish, for example once an hour or once a day. The results are then compiled and a summary report generated to inform you of any new results. If you want to stay on top of new developments in a given area, the right query and a tracking facility will help relevant documents find you, so that you don't have to find them.

Figure 6.43:
Keyword Filters for
Breaking News
Stories

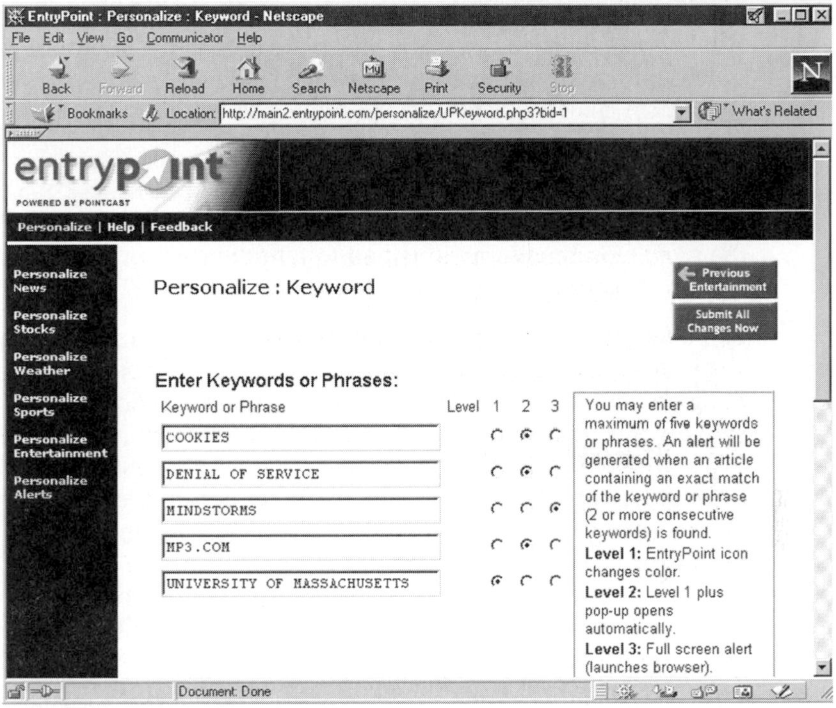

If the push/pull distinction is beginning to feel a bit muddy, try to keep some simple criteria in mind. The difference has less to do with the underlying technology than the delivery mechanism. Remember, when information comes to you automatically and periodically over some indefinite period of time, that's a push delivery mechanism. When information comes to you in response to a specific request and the response has a clear conclusion after which no additional responses are expected, that's a pull delivery mechanism. Also remember that these concepts make sense only in the context of software. Everything is a pull technology at the level of your computer's on/off button because you must turn on your computer in order for anything to happen. Similarly, you have to launch a software application in order for it to push information at you. At those levels, even push technologies must be pulled. So, start with a computer that's turned on and software that's up and running. That should make it easier to keep the push and pull distinction clean and clear.

6.9 | ASSESSING CREDIBILITY ON THE WEB

To use the Internet as a source for legitimate research, you need to develop a critical eye for high-quality information. If you aren't careful with your use of online resources, you might get, and pass on, misinformation—and damage your own credibility in the process. Many information sources on the Web are legitimate and can be trusted. However, many others are unreliable. You must learn to evaluate all online information before you reference it or use it for your own purposes.

Your evaluation should focus on the Web page content. Don't be influenced by a page's look and feel. Beautiful graphics and careful text formatting means that the author cares about the page's attractiveness. However, that doesn't guarantee the information's credibility. If the graphics don't contribute to the information on the page, you might find it helpful to turn them off in order to concentrate on the written content.

The Internet is a **content-neutral medium**. That is, it distributes falsehoods and fantasies as easily as facts and truth. It encourages people to produce pages on anything and everything, and the line between fact and fiction can be twisted in many subtle ways. A delusional author might report wishful thinking or hallucinogenic experiences as fact. If the departure from reality is subtle and believable, assessing credibility with absolute certainty could be impossible. Conspiracy theories thrive on the Internet because conspiracy buffs can easily hook up with one another and find strength in numbers. Always use common sense when assessing information credibility on the Web. If the topic that you're researching involves conspiracy theories or controversial political scandals, everything that you find should be treated with extreme caution.

A good content evaluation can be completed with the help of a *credibility checklist*. Many checklist criteria apply to the evaluation of traditional print documents; others are specific to Web documents. Several useful checklists for Web page assessment are available on the Web. The following sections discuss some of the most common criteria that can be used to assess Web page credibility.

6.9.1 Author Credibility

A page is useless for research purposes if it fails to clearly identify its author, as well as offer additional information about the author either in the current document or via hyperlinks to other documents. The author's institutional affiliation and job title should be available, as well as a telephone number and complete mailing address. Look for a short professional biography on an associated Web page.

An author's e-mail address that ends in `.gov` or `.edu` is evidence of a legitimate institutional affiliation. However, remember that college students and staff members have `.edu` addresses, as well as faculty. The author should make it clear whether he or she is the original author of the material in question. Look for a copyright statement. If there is some doubt about that statement or there is no statement, contact the author to double-check the material's originality. A legitimate author is normally happy to verify authorship.

Try to verify that the author is who he or she claims to be. If someone is identified as a biology professor at Home State University, go to the home page for the university and look for a list of the faculty in the biology department or in a general university directory. Most universities and colleges maintain a faculty/staff directory on the Web. Corporate environments might or might not have online employee directories. However, a telephone call to corporate headquarters will tell you if someone is employed by the company.

Author credibility is normally not a concern if the work has been published by a respected journal or magazine or if you've located a published citation to the work in question in such a journal or magazine. You can double-check anything that someone claims to have published by going to the publication's home page and locating a table of contents that contains the article in question. It is increasingly common for magazines and journals to maintain Web sites, where you can see at least a table of contents, if not an entire article. Checking this will protect you from a fraudulent publication claim.

After you've verified the author's identity, investigate whether the author is qualified to write on the topic. A university professor might not be an expert in an area unrelated to his or her professional specialty. The title "professor" does not automatically confer expertise in all areas, so always do a background check on the author. Look for additional evidence of scholarly activities in that area. The existence of only a single, isolated paper is more questionable than are a dozen papers in the same area. If the author has published other papers in the area but the article in question has not been published, a certain amount of credibility can be assumed from the other publications.

When the author is a writer for a news organization, it's best to verify reported facts independently. If the article mentions a published source for its information, go to that original source document and check it yourself. If no additional sources are cited, look for independent corroborating reports.

6.9.2 Accurate Writing and Documentation

If an article is poorly written and has grammatical errors and misspellings, it might be sloppy with regard to content as well. Serious writing takes time and effort. If you sense that the article was written casually and quickly, it's probably not a good source. In addition, check whether the author references other sources. Are the citations complete? If they are hyperlinks to other online sources, are the links operational and up-to-date? An accurate information source will include correct attributions where needed and disclaimers when information or conclusions are questionable.

If the resource has been published, is the online version identical to the printed version or is it a shorter version? Some magazines post partial versions of their printed articles. The Web site should state clearly whether the article is complete or partial.

6.9.3 Objectivity

If an article's author is affiliated with a commercial entity, try to separate informational content from advertising. This is not always easy. Some pages are carefully designed to make it clear where promotion stops and objective information starts. If no effort has been made to do this and the article is unpublished, you should be concerned about its objectivity.

Scientists working in private industry publish their legitimate research in order to establish credibility within the scientific establishment. Scientific papers are subjected to a process of peer review in order to maintain quality control within the sciences. Evaluating the objectivity of writers outside of the scientific establishment is difficult. However, articles in respected publications are good indicators of objective writing.

Many authors provide information online as a public service. Sometimes authors and their work are supported by or are otherwise affiliated with nonprofit organizations; objectivity can be a problem if these organizations have their own political agendas. If you cite information distributed by an advocacy group, do your own fact checking with independent sources and try to corroborate the information.

6.9.4 Stability of Web Pages

The Web is a dynamic medium, with new information popping up every day. Pages also disappear every day. You can't know whether a page will still be on the Web next year or even next month. This is a problem for people doing scholarly research. However, here are some guidelines that can help you to assess a page's stability.

- Does the page include a date? When was it last revised?
- Is it part of a larger site that has other dated materials?
- Do other Web sites reference the work at this address?
- Is the page part of an institutional resource?

A heavily referenced work might appear at multiple Web sites. If you reference an online source, always reference the *original* URL rather than a copy at a mirror site. The original site usually will be associated with the author or the author's home institution, and it is presumably the most stable site.

No matter how hard you try to select stable Web pages, it's impossible to know how long a Web page will either be available or be available at its current URL. Sometimes, a Web site designer rearranges a Web site, especially if it's growing. This means that old URLs might become obsolete but that the pages are still available, under new URLs. One study found that the lifetime of the average URL is only 75 days. Presumably, this figure is low because a large number of experimental pages created by newcomers to the Web have since ceased to exist, along with Web pages that have moved to new URLs. Regardless, this is a sobering statistic.

6.9.5 Fraudulent Web Pages

Constructing a Web site in another person's name in order to misrepresent that individual is easy. Although it's unlikely that the academic community would do this, bogus Web sites for political candidates were found during both the 1996 and 2000 presidential campaigns. Bogus home pages often are created as parodies of the real thing. If you find material on a page that is blatantly offbeat, contradictory, or surprising in any way, consider the possibility that the page is a maliciously crafted Web page.

Things to Remember

- Use different resources to find different kinds of information.
- Subject trees and clearinghouses are good sources for answers to open-ended questions.
- General search engines are good sources for answers to Joe Friday questions.
- Use successive query refinement to develop effective search engine queries.
- Think carefully about your keywords—look for associative connections to people and organizations.
- Use Boolean queries when you have unusual keywords or combinations of keywords.

Important Concepts

Boolean query—a query format based on logical operators.

clearinghouse—an exhaustive collection of online resources for a specific topic.

intelligent agent—a computer program that searches the Web in order to collect and assemble information from multiple online resources.

query—a list of keywords given to a search engine.

search bot—a computer program that continuously monitors multiple Web sites for information updates.

search engine—a query-driven interface to a document database indexed for keyword retrieval.

subject tree—a hierarchically arranged collection of topic categories and Web page resources.

Where Can I Learn More?

Search Engine Watch `http://searchenginewatch.com/`

Invisible Web—Hidden Searchable Databases `http://websearch.`
`about.com/internet/websearch/msubmenu120.htm`

Tool Kit for the Expert Web Searcher `http://www.lita.org/`
`committe/toptech/toolkit.htm`

BotSpot   `http://www.botspot.com/`

Evaluating Web Resources   `http://www2.widener.edu/`
`Wolfgram-Memorial-Library/webeval.htm`

A Short Introduction to Information Retrieval
`http://www.birkhauser.com/hypermedia/cyb4.html`

Problems and Exercises

1. Describe and contrast three general types of questions. Why is it useful to categorize your information needs before you conduct a search on the Web? Which question type is best served by general search engines?

2. How does a clearinghouse differ from a subject tree?

3. Organize your list of clocks from Subject Tree Exercise #1 in a hierarchical tree. Don't look at Yahoo!'s hierarchy or try to reconstruct its hierarchy—work out your own. Was it easy to build a tree structure for your list, or did you need to start over a few times? Was this a straightforward exercise or a difficult one? Explain your answers.

4. Explain the difference between a category match and a document match at Yahoo!.

5. Suppose that you've tried several queries at one general search engine and you're not receiving any good hits. What two options do you have at this point?

6. How does a meta search engine differ from a search engine?

7. Describe the merge-and-rank problem of a meta search engine. What can a meta search engine do to avoid dealing with this problem?

8. What will happen if you enter a Boolean query in a fuzzy query input box? If you enter a fuzzy query in the place for Boolean queries?

9. What term tag can you use at AltaVista in order to conduct a search that is limited to one specific Web server? Is this technique equivalent to using a site search facility on the same server (assuming that one is available)? Explain your answer.

10. If an article on the Web has an `.edu` address, is it necessarily more trustworthy than an article at a `.com` address? Explain your answer.

11. What is a content-neutral medium? Can you think of three communications media that are content-neutral?

12. **[Find It Online]** Which accesses a larger database of documents, the search engine at **Yahoo!** or the search engine at **Excite**? Explain your answer. (For the purposes of this question, ignore the fact that Yahoo!'s search pages give you the option of conducting a general search of the Web if you're not satisfied with the hits returned by Yahoo!.)

13. **[Find It Online]** The connection between dogs and the number 42 was discussed at some length in Section 6.2.1. Go to **Yahoo!**, and track down the answer to the question, "What role does the number 42 play in the lives of all dogs?"

14. **[Find It Online]** Visit **FindSpot** (`http://www.findspot.com/`), and read the search tips for AltaVista and Google. Explain how each handles the query

    ```
    dogs —cats collies +basenjis
    ```

    If these two search engines accessed the same document database and indexed those documents in the same way, which engine would return more hits for this query? Explain your answer.

15. **[Find It Online]** Compare and contrast the **Argus Clearinghouse** (`http://www.clearinghouse.net/`) with Invisible Web (`http://invisibleweb.com/`). What do they have in common? How do they differ? Illustrate your points by visiting Argus and conducting a search on the keyword "environment." How many resources does Argus return? Visit Invisible Web, and conduct the same search. How many resources does Invisible Web return? Does it return any of the same resources as Argus?

16. **[Find It Online]** Find the exact date of the denial-of-service attacks on Yahoo! and CNN. The attacks happened sometime between February 1, 2000 and March 1, 2000. First, use the advanced search option at **AltaVista** (`http://www.altavista.com/`). Then do the search again by using an advanced site search at **CNN** (`http://search.cnn.com/`). Which resource made it easier to find the answers? Describe your experience with this exercise at both sites.

17. **[Find It Online]** Suppose that you want to track down all of the Web pages that you can find that reference Wendy Lehnert. To ensure that you don't miss anything, look for all of the possible name variations: Wendy Lehnert, W. Lehnert, Wendy G. Lehnert, W. G. Lehnert, and Wendy Grace Lehnert. Create a Boolean query that will cover all of these variations as simply as possible. (*Hint*: Find a search engine that supports the NEAR logical operator and read the documentation for the use of NEAR. Formulate a Boolean query that uses NEAR for this exercise.) What query did you use?

18. **[Find It Online]** Experiment with Boolean queries to find informational pages about browser cookies. Keep a log of all queries that you try. Don't stop until the top ten hits on your hit list are all general pages about browser cookies; eliminate all false hits associated with recipes, food retailers, and so on. How many queries did you use to find your answers? Which search engine did you use? Did you use any additional advanced search features in addition to a Boolean query? Describe the reasoning that led you to a good hit list. Hand in a copy of your final hit list (use copy-and-paste) with your other answers.

19. **[Find It Online]** Who was the first famous woman mathematician? For what was she famous?

20. **[Find It Online]** Who was the first U.S. president to be born in a hospital?

21. **[Find It Online]** The green iguana is said to have a third eye. Investigate this. How is the third eye used? How does it work? Is it unique to green iguanas?

22. **[Find It Online]** Suppose you hear a song on the radio that you want to track down. You never caught the name of it on the radio, and the only part of the lyrics that you can remember is one line from the refrain ". . . thinking about eternity. . ." Find out the name of the song, the artist who sings it, and the name of a CD that contains the song.

23. **[Find It Online]** Find a searchable Web site (one that has its own site search facility) devoted to the subject of tigers. How did you find it? How hard was it to find the site? List the URL for the site that you found.

24. **[Find It Online]** Sometimes, blonde hair acquires a greenish tint after swimming in chlorinated water. Find out everything that you can about this problem: what causes it, how to fix it, and how to prevent it. Look for different explanations and solutions. For each piece of information that you find, rate its credibility on a scale of 1 to 10. Explain the reasoning behind your ratings.

25. **[Find It Online]** Chapter 5 explained how to add a link to a Web page for an audio clip. If the user clicks the link, the audio clip plays. Find out how to add an audio clip to a Web page so that the music starts playing as soon as the Web page is displayed. What is the solution? How did you find this information?

26. **[Find It Online]** A lot of people know about MP3 files. However, few know about MIDI files. Find out how MIDI files differ from MP3 files. When would it make sense to put a MIDI file instead of an MP3 file on a Web page?

27. **[Find It Online]** Have any U.S. presidents remained unmarried? If so, which ones? How did you find your information?

28. **[Find It Online]** There are three general modes for making digital television work interactively: single mode, simultaneous mode, and pause mode. Describe these three modes, and identify any companies that have developed working technologies along these lines.

29. **[Find It Online]** David Kline estimates that 75% of all corporate wealth is in intellectual property or patents. Who is David Kline? How many U.S. patents were granted to Internet companies in 1995? In 1998? Can business models and processes be patented? Back up your answers with specific sources and details.

30. **[Find It Online]** Can a U.S. public high school legally suspend or otherwise punish one of its students for publishing a satirical or unofficial home page for the school? Assume that the page is produced without the use of school resources. Argue yes or no by citing specific lawsuits concerning censorship by high schools. How did you find your information?

Find What You Want–Fast!: Above and Beyond

Information Retrieval Concepts

Information retrieval (**IR**) is the branch of computer science that deals with finding information in large text databases. IR existed as an academic endeavor for decades, but general interest in it has increased since the birth of the Web. A Web search engine is an IR system dressed up with a user-friendly interface. Beneath the interface is a computer program that has no understanding of human language and no ability to comprehend your information needs. IR systems work by using the keywords in your input query to attempt to locate documents that contain those same keywords.

A search engine query can be a single keyword, a grammatical sentence, or a group of words tossed together in random order. For most search engines, the grammatical construction of a query is irrelevant. The most important information lies in the specific keywords of the query. Keywords index the document database. It's your job to distinguish between effective and ineffective indexes when you compose a query. Generally, you can't know beforehand which queries are best, so experimentation and feedback are the keys to a successful query. There is a method to the madness, but you'll still need to feel your way through the process each time.

Fast response times from query engines are possible because all of the documents in a search engine's database have been indexed. Document indexing is managed behind the scenes by processes that have nothing to do with you or your search engine interactions. It goes on continually as new URLs are added to the database. The better engines work to eliminate obsolete URLs from their databases as quickly as possible. So, any Web database that you tap into today isn't likely to be the same that you'll tap into tomorrow. It won't be terribly different. However, it will be different.

The Web is one big, massive, moving target, so humans can't hope to examine each new Web page in order to identify good indexes for that page. Web search engines must create and update their document databases automatically, by using Web spiders. A **Web spider** is a computer program that examines Web pages, collecting URLs from the old Web pages that lead to new Web pages, examining those new Web pages for more URLs, which in turn lead to more Web pages, and so on. The Web spider is responsible only for finding new Web pages. As it traverses hyperlinks from page to page, it keeps a list of all of the pages that it has visited. This list of URLs for each page is returned to the search engine, with any URLs for Web pages not known to the search engine's database added to the document database. Each new page must be processed for its keyword before the page's URL is added to the database. Different indexing methods are used to index the document. The large search engines run Web spiders constantly in an effort to index as much of the Web as possible.

The entire process of collecting new Web pages, indexing them, and adding them to a document database is totally automated. Human intervention at any step along the way would only slow down the process. A Web spider can't pass judgment on the quality of a document, but it can process documents faster than people can. When we tackle the Web, we are dealing with *terabytes* of text (1 **terabyte** = 1,024 gigabytes). Web spiders are the only way we can hope to stay on top of this much text.

Search Engine Indexing Methods Some search engines explain their text indexing methods online. Specific online newsletters and subscription services are dedicated to tracking this information and summarizing it for conscientious Webmasters who want to make their Web pages as visible as possible. Indexing for any specific search engine cannot be described in detail here. Rather, this section describes the most commonly encountered methods so that you'll get some idea of how it's done.

Because search engines evolve, a change in indexing methods can result in a skewed database in which older documents are indexed with one method and newer documents with another. Online documentation sometimes describes only the most current indexing method. This makes it difficult to know whether a search engine's database has been indexed consistently throughout.

For retrieval purposes, the most important question is whether a database is indexing most of its documents with *selective text indexing* or with *full text indexing*. The answer to this question has important implications for query design and search engine selection.

SELECTIVE TEXT INDEXING Indexing that does not treat all text as equal is called **selective text indexing**. The title of a document is very important, as is the document's first paragraph and its hyperlinks. Thus a good set of indexes can be created on the basis of only those components; the rest of the document can be ignored. Each word in the title is added to the database and associated with its parent URL. Similarly, each of the first, say, 100 to 200 words might be added to the database, along with each word that is part of a hyperlink. When the same word is found in a few thousand other Web page titles, all of those URLs are also indexed under that one word. Thus a single word can index hundreds or thousands of Web pages.

Additional database entries are added in order to capture word adjacencies, which are needed to match exact phrases. The database is probably also organized in a way that makes it easy to find frequency counts for each URL index. The **frequency count** for a single word is the number of times that that word appears in a document. These frequencies are often helpful in ranking retrieved documents.

Different search engines might invoke different text selection methods. For example, one might index words found in bulleted lists or in text headers. Web pages make it easy for a computer to identify selected text because selected text can be found by looking for specific HTML tags. If you know exactly how a given search engine looks for its document indexes, you can design your Web pages with special attention to the text elements used to index the document. Professional Web page designers try to consider this to make their pages more visible to the most popular search engines (see How to Increase Your Web Page Hit Counts in the Above and Beyond section in Chapter 4).

FULL TEXT INDEXING   Indexing that allows no text to go to waste—all text in a document is scanned for indexing terms—is **full text indexing**. It takes more time to index a document in this manner, and the resulting database will be much larger than one that uses selective text indexing. Until 1995, the computational load associated with full text indexing was too demanding for most search engines. Since then, the most powerful host machines have had enough memory and speed to make compiling a full text document database viable.

Although a full text database is thought to be more powerful than a selective text database, it seldom abandons the utility of selected text. Even in a full text database, some terms are still identifiable as selected text. Thus a full text database doesn't necessarily treat all words as equals. Terms from the title or the first 50 words of the document can be tagged as such and weighted more heavily. Some search engines also allow you to conduct your search on a selective subset of all of the available text so that you can decide whether it's better to conduct your search on the full text database or a selective text subset. At times, it's advantageous to work with the smaller set of indexes associated with selected text.

Search engines that use full-text indexing typically stop indexing very large documents after a certain point. If a Web page is larger than 50K, anything after the first 50K is probably never indexed. This can be a problem for some huge archive files that contain hundreds of archived articles.

Some Words Are Ignored   All search engines have a list of words that they ignore. For example, articles, conjunctions, and prepositions appear in too many documents to be of any use as document indexes. Also, some nouns (for example, "people" and "Internet") are ignored because they appear in too many documents.

AltaVista shows you term counts for each keyword in your query so that you can see how often each appears in AltaVista's full-text database. It also shows you which keywords were ignored when its database was constructed (it marks them "ignored"). If a preposition or some other word is crucial for your query and your search engine is ignoring it, try to reword your query without the prepositional or other ignored words.

Document Rankings   In the world of IR, few things are black and white. Documents can be strongly connected to a query or only mildly connected to it. A document that contains all of the keywords in a query clears the qualifying hurdles with room to spare. However, what about a document that contains only one query keyword? Should a hit for it be returned? What if a document contains multiple instances of the query's keywords? Does a higher frequency count make a document a stronger hit?

Term counts and term frequency counts can reflect an intuitive sense of strong hits and weak hits. However, it's difficult to know how all of the hits should be ranked. Is a keyword that appears in a document's title better than the same keyword seen a hundred times in the document body? Although it might be impossible to answer this, some judgment calls must be made one way or another. As a rule, no one wants to look past the first 20 to 30 items in a hit list no matter how long the list. So some method of ranking relevant documents is needed to put the best possible candidates at the top of the list. If a Web search engine does everything else right, but gets its document rankings wrong, it will be useless.

Sometimes a search engine returns a highly ranked document that makes no sense and you can't understand why it was picked up. When this happens, the search engine might have been responding to **hidden text** on the Web page, text that is not displayed by Web browsers but that is used by search engines. This happens when a Web page designer has specified a list of keywords (using the META tag) that is included for search engine indexing purposes only (see How to Increase Your Web Page Hit Counts in the Above and Beyond section in Chapter 4).

Intelligent Concept Extraction   Some search engines offer a fuzzy query option that tries to identify underlying concepts in your query. For example, the phrase "senior citizens" refers to a concept that is semantically close to other words and phrases such as "retired people," "grandparents," and "the elderly." Most search engines require you to think of all of these variations and add them to your query in order to get full coverage from the query. A few search engines, however, perform **intelligent concept extraction**, a method of searching that automatically augments your query with synonyms and related terms.

Intelligent concept extraction attempts to rewrite the original query in words that capture its underlying concepts. This is a great feature for those who can't think of all of the different ways that a concept might be expressed (or don't want to bother doing so). If, however, you have a very specific need and you don't want to see any variations on your terms, you should avoid any search engines that use intelligent concept extraction. When a search engine supports intelligent concept extraction, it is probably not a feature that can be turned off.

If you're not finding enough hits, you might try intelligent concept extraction to see whether a broader interpretation of your needs can locate more documents. Documents will still be ranked with exact matches first, so you should easily see any documents that contain your specific keywords. In addition, you might be surprised how many more relevant documents you can find when you make appropriate keyword substitutions.

Excite and Magellan are two search engines that utilize intelligent concept extraction. This feature will probably become more common as search engines try to be more helpful and intelligent. AltaVista uses a form of it to map fuzzy queries into a large database of predefined questions and answers, called **shortcut answers**. If it can map your query to a good shortcut answer, you can bypass the entire process of successive query refinement. The developers of the AskJeeves search engine pioneered this mapping technique when they incorporated millions of shortcut answers in its query processing.

Relevance Feedback Rarely can you create the perfect query on the first try. Most people who work extensively with search engines try some exploratory queries before they settle on the query that they really want to use. Successive query refinement is one way to explore a search space and zero in on a good query. It requires you to generate a sequence of queries that are increasingly focused. Sometimes this works well, and sometimes it doesn't. So, IR researchers have tried to automate much of the effort associated with successive query refinement. The most successful strategy for this *automated query refinement* is called relevance feedback.

Relevance feedback is the process of identifying reliably useful keywords on the basis of good representative documents. It is a form of successive query refinement in which the search engine tries to meet you halfway. In classic relevance feedback, the user issues an initial query and then reviews the resulting hits. If a hit is on target, the user flags it as a good hit; otherwise, the user doesn't flag it. Once a few good hits have been flagged, the relevance feedback engine goes to work and examines the affected documents in an effort to identify words or phrases that best characterize those hits. If it finds the same word or phrase in all of the good hits, that word or phrase becomes a useful keyword or keywords.

The beauty of relevance feedback is in the use of only a few good example documents. Once you've identified such documents, you automatically generate keywords that should lead to more good documents. You don't have to think about the keywords to use or how to construct a good query because that is done automatically. Relevance feedback can be a very effective and painless way to home in on the documents that you want.

Many search engines support a simple form of relevance feedback. When you see a document that is close to the type of document that you want, look for a link named "More Like This" or "Similar Pages." Clicking this link triggers the relevance feedback feature, which will take you from that document to similar documents. If one of the similar documents is also on target, you can ask for more documents like that it. Each time that you select a document and ask for more like it, the search engine uses that document as a source of additional relevance feedback. If you select a chain of documents linked by relevance feedback, the search engine uses all of the documents in that chain each time that it searches for additional similar documents. You never see the enhanced queries generated by relevance feedback, so the entire process seems vaguely magical.

Suppose that you have a Web page that you want to use for a relevance feedback search, but you can't view it with a search engine that supports relevance feedback? Not to worry—you can hand any URL to the server-side **Extractor utility** (see Figure 6.44). Extractor analyzes the Web page and extracts a list of keywords that can then be passed on to **MetaCrawler**, a meta search engine.

Figure 6.44:
Relevance
Feedback Any
Place, Any Time

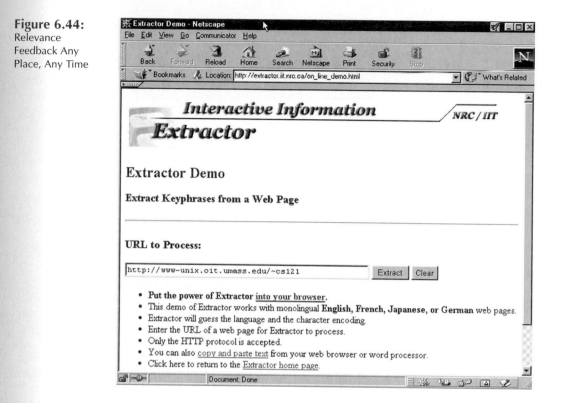

The extractor supports several interesting features, including a tool that will generate a summary of your Web page as a bulleted list of the (you hope) most important statements found on the Web page. To complete a relevance feedback search, click the link named Find More Like This (see Figure 6.45).

One of most potentially useful Extractor features is a copy-and-paste feature, which lets you feed any amount of online text to Extractor. If you follow the "copy and paste text" link in Figure 6.44, you'll be able to paste text excerpts in an input box for processing by Extractor. You can enter text from a personal document, an excerpt from a Web page, or text that has been scanned from a book and turned into a text file via optical character recognition. According to the utility's online documentation, the best results will be obtained if you enter between 1,000 and 10,000 words of nonfiction prose.

Relevance feedback works better for some documents than others. If you have a great Web page and you're having no luck finding other related pages by using relevance feedback, you can try **Alexa**. Alexa is a program that is built into Navigator (click the What's Related button next to the URL window). However, you can also run it as a browser add-on (see Chapter 9). It links sites on the Web to other, related sites, just as relevance feedback does. However, its associations are made by people instead of search engines; thus the associations tend to be very good.

Figure 6.45:
Extractor Calls on
MetaCrawler to
Conduct the Actual
Search

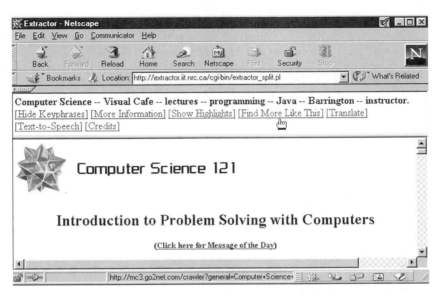

However, because they are generated manually, Alexa's database does not include all Web pages and it therefore might have no pages to suggest. Alexa tends to work well with high-visibility mainstream sites. If that's the kind of page that you have, Alexa will give you better quality control than will relevance feedback.

Search Engine Web Coverage

Many people think that the most popular search engines index all or most of the Web pages on the Web. Search engine documentation tends to reinforce this belief. However, it's far from true. In February 2000, a **joint study published by Inktomi and the NEC Research Institute** estimated the Web's size at one billion pages. At the same time, the largest search engine was indexing only 300 million documents. Some search engine databases are expanding rapidly. However, the Web is expanding as well, so it might be a while before any single search engine can claim to have indexed all of the Web. Most users have no idea that when they use these search engines, they are missing most of the Web.

Which documents are visible to search engines? In general, a search engine won't immediately find newly created Web pages. However, this lapse doesn't account for so much of the Web's not being indexed. A search engine can also miss isolated "islands" of Web pages, pages that are not referenced by any hyperlinks outside of the island. A Web page that is not referenced by any other Web pages is a good candidate for exclusion. However, one can hope that the best resources have many links pointing to them, so perhaps the search engines are picking up the best of the Web.

What the search engines don't reveal is that some of them *deliberately ignore portions of the Web in order to maximize their overall coverage.* The larger the Web site, the more of it that is likely to be missing from a general search engine's document database. To illustrate this situation, consider the Web site for my first Internet textbook, *Internet 101*, published in 1998 (`http://www-nlp.cs.umass.edu/aw/home.html`). This Web site had been up continuously for about two years at the time of this writing, and it contained 209 separate Web pages. Using the advanced search features at four popular search engines, you can see how varied the coverage is for this one, relatively small, Web site (see Figure 6.46).

Figure 6.46:
Search Engines Index Only a Fraction of Most Web Sites

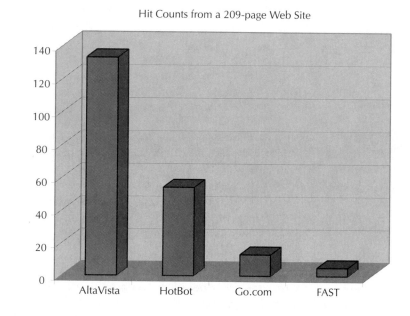

There is no rhyme or reason regarding which URLs make it into a search engine database. **FAST Search**, which claimed to have the largest document database at the time of this writing, indexed the smallest number of pages on this one particular site (5 pages out of a possible 209). Since most pages are collected automatically, which URLs are included is determined in a largely random fashion. As mentioned earlier in the chapter, the only practical way for a search engine to keep up with the Web is through the use of spiders and Web crawlers. When these methods fail to keep up with everything on the Web, it is difficult to know what is being missed.

If searching the content of a large Web site is important to you, you're better off using a site search facility, even if the site search features aren't as sophisticated as you might like. At least you'll know that all of the pages have been indexed for the site search. But, what if you depend on the content of a large Web site and the site doesn't offer its own search engine for site-specific searches? As time goes on, this should become a rarity. Until then, if you're running Windows you can construct your own client-side document database for a specific Web site. This database might require quite a few megabytes of memory and a few hours of dedicated CPU time, so it has to be worth that to you. However, doing this is actually very easy, if you use the right freeware. AltaVista supports a freeware desktop utility called **AltaVista Discovery** that enables you to do this. You can select any home page on the Web and have Discovery to index the site associated with that page. Thus you can conduct truly comprehensive site searches by using the AltaVista search engine.

The Internet 101 Web site has its own site search facility, so, in this case, you wouldn't need to create your own site search facility by using Discovery. However, the site-search at Internet 101 does not support Boolean queries. If Boolean queries are important to you for this site, then you could have Discovery take over for you.

Take AltaVista Home with You

Using Discovery's My Sites feature, I was able to index the 209-page Internet 101 Web site in about 15 minutes using a 233 MHz Pentium with 64MB of RAM and a 56K modem connection. I also indexed all of the Word and text documents on a 3GB hard drive (that took about 2 hours); Discovery consumed about 25MB of my hard drive in the process (this is no toy for children). Discovery enables you to search files on your own hard drive by using the same search features available at AltaVista (including Boolean queries). I now can conduct Boolean queries on all of those files (which includes all of the chapters for this book), and the results come back fast.

Discovery does not process queries offline—the search engine is still a server-side operation. However, you can maintain your own document databases for AltaVista locally. Simply ensure that you have the space for it and the CPU time for periodic updates as needed. I would want a larger hard drive and a faster CPU before I'd try this on any 10,000-page Web sites.

Discovery offers other interesting features, in particular, its Hyperbolic Tree feature (courtesy of **Inxight**) for interactive, graphical site maps. Once you've added a Web site to your My Sites folder, you can view it through what amounts to a fish-eye lens (if your browser is Java-enabled). This is a little difficult to describe without a demo. However, Figure 6.47 shows the start screen for the Internet 101 Web site.

Click the Chapter 5 Directory link to get a different view of the tree, with a focus that puts the link just clicked closer to the center of the site map (see Figure 6.48). When there are many links, link names can get a little crowded, so mouseover displays are available for when you want to see the link names better. Double-clicking a page title takes you to the page itself.

To see a live hyperbolic tree on the Web, visit the **Universal Library** and check out its **hyperbolic tree demo**. Perhaps more Webmasters will be adding dynamic site maps like this to their own sites. Although Discovery lets you create these for client-side viewing, the service does not extend to Web servers at no cost. Perhaps a freeware version will be available someday. Then hyperbolic trees will be all over the Web.

Figure 6.47:
A Hyperbolic Tree
Site Map

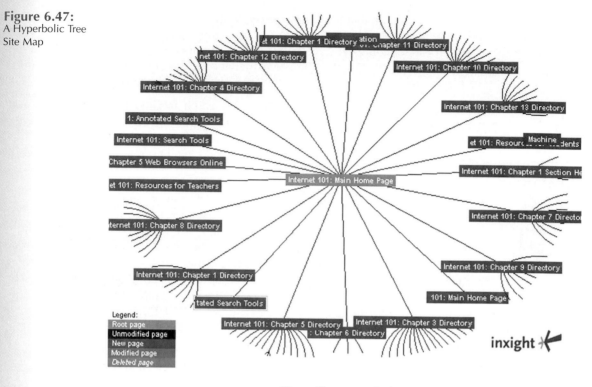

Sitemap Viewer created using
Hyperbolic Tree™ for Java from Inxight Software

Above and Beyond: Problems and Exercises

A1. Explain the difference between a term count and a term frequency count.

A2. What is relevance feedback, and when is it useful?

A3. Does relevance feedback work better with fiction or with nonfiction? Explain your answer.

A4. What is intelligent concept extraction, and when should you avoid using it?

A5. If a search engine indexes some pages on a particular Web site, can you assume that all of the pages from that site have been indexed by the same search engine? Explain your answer.

A6. Can AltaVista Discovery index documents other than Web pages? Explain your answer.

A7. Explain how Alexa works. How does Alexa differ from a search engine that uses relevance feedback?

Figure 6.48:
The View Changes
as You Explore and
Move About

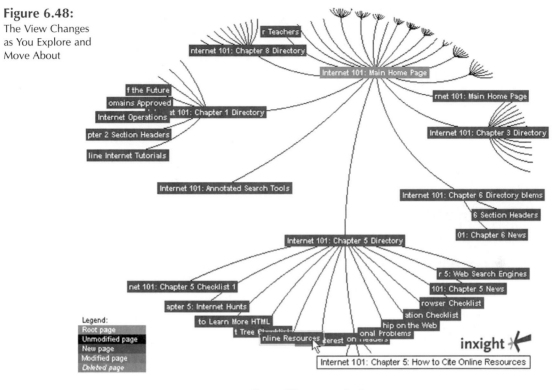

Sitemap Viewer created using
Hyperbolic Tree™ for Java from Inxight Software

A8. To conduct an exact phrase search for an entire sentence, would you expect better success at a search engine that uses full text indexing or one that uses selective text indexing? Explain your answer.

A9. [**Find It Online**] Explain the difference between full text indexing and selective text indexing. Which one does AltaVista use? Which one does Yahoo!'s search engine use? If you aren't sure, pick a lengthy document in Yahoo!'s database, extract an exact phrase from a paragraph somewhere inside of the document, and query Yahoo! with that exact phrase to determine whether it can retrieve the document for you. Try this a few times to see if your results are consistent. Does Yahoo! use full text indexing for both its category searches and its document searches? Explain your answer.

A10. [**Find It Online**] Do any general search engines index the entire Web? If not, what percentage of the Web do the largest search engines cover? Don't settle for what this book says—the numbers reported here are out-of-date. Get the most current information available.

CHAPTER 7

Joining a Virtual Community

CHAPTER GOALS

- Learn how to find and participate in mailing lists.
- Discover how easy it is to start your own Web-based discussion group.
- Discover the convenient features of Usenet gateways on the Web.
- Learn how to find Usenet newsgroups and FAQ files and to search Usenet archives.
- Find out how to use a news reader to monitor your favorite newsgroups.
- Learn about Internet relay chat, Web-based chat, and instant messaging.

7.1 TAKING CHARGE

Human beings are highly social and drawn to communication media. The siren song of newer and better communication options is a powerful life force on the Internet. Throughout the 1980s, long before e-commerce and before the point-and-click Web captivated millions of new Internet users, thousands of Internet pioneers were using the Net to communicate with each other. Before the network of networks, the Internet, separate networks served their own communities of scientists, computer programmers, and academics. These networks included the Advanced Research Project Agency network (ARPANET; sponsored by the U.S. Department of Defense), CSnet (sponsored by the National Science Foundation to expand access for computer scientists), and BITNET, derived from *Because It's Time* (created by the City University of New York).

Computer scientists first used computer networks in the 1970s to transfer files and enable remote access to powerful computers. At that time, no one anticipated affordable personal computers, today's Internet, or the wide variety of users who would come to rely on these technologies. No one thought about networked computers as a communication medium because no one thought about the possibility of computers in every home. The world of today was unimaginable even a scant 20 years ago. Before 1999, fewer than half of all U.S. households contained a home computer. In 2000, half of all U.S. households had active Internet access. We had crossed an important threshold in the widespread use of the Internet.

Today, e-mail is the most widely used Internet application, surpassing even Web browsers as the most popular Internet application. The U.S. government anticipates a steady decline in the volume of first-class mail in coming years because of e-mail. However, e-mail could be only the tip of the iceberg when it comes to Internet-based communication. Other applications include telephony and personal rich media.

- **Telephony** is the science of translating sound into electrical signals, transmitting them over a distance, and then translating them back to sound. In 1999, telephony over the Internet resulted in 2.5 billion telephone calls using the *voice-over-Internet-protocol* (VoIP).

- **Personal rich media** is the use of high-bandwidth applications to enhance personal communications over the Internet. Examples are video-enhanced e-mail and Web sites devoted to family photo albums. People have begun to trade photographs and home movies over the Internet. Soon, Web sites will be available on which people can post their digital home movies. One study predicts that text-based e-mail will be archaic by 2005 because of the expected popularity of video e-mail and personal rich media sites. Why send your loved ones a letter when you can send a movie? Even in the workplace, a video clip of a talking head might someday replace the text-based office memo.

People on the Internet today explore these new technologies often in the context of the *virtual community.*

7.1.1 Virtual Communities

A **virtual community** is a group of people, usually brought together by some shared interest, who establish ongoing group communications online. New digital communication technologies are often tested by virtual communities, whose participants look for new and better ways to communicate online.

Some people are reluctant to participate in virtual communities because of privacy concerns. If you join, for example, a support group for incest survivors or AIDS patients, you need to know how private your sensitive communications really are. Some virtual communities are more private than others, but none can guarantee absolute privacy. If a law enforcement agency wants to see all of your communications to some virtual community and the hosting service has an archive containing those communications, you should assume that the hosting service, when asked to surrender the archive, will cooperate. Further, an archive could be posted on public Web pages possibly 10, 20, or even 50 years later. Someone active in the community might someday become famous or notorious, thereby making the archive of great public interest. In addition, these communications eventually could be deemed significant for historical reasons. Graduate students in 2100 will undoubtedly study archives from 2000 for information about cultural beliefs, social mores, linguistic usage, and who knows what else.

However, you need not wait a hundred years to see such archives readily available to the general public. Although unlikely, a virtual community participant easily can create a personal archive of all of the community's posted messages and install it as a searchable Web site. In addition, the Web server that hosts the community dialogs could have poorly maintained security, thereby conceivably enabling a hacker to break into a Web server and publicize messages from a supposedly protected archive, just for the kicks. Although unlikely, illegal, and not easy, this is possible. Some small level of risk is always associated with all online communications.

Anonymous Remailers To maximize your privacy while participating in a virtual community, use an anonymous remailer. An **anonymous remailer** is an e-mail account (owned and operated outside of the United States, if you want to be safe from subpoenas) that safeguards your real identity. It is rather like a Swiss bank account for online communications. It is the only safeguard that can really protect you from the unpredictability of other community members, investigations by law enforcement agencies, data collection on behalf of corporate interests, and the vulnerability of poorly secured servers.

Some anonymous remailers are free; others charge for the service. One commercial service, **Freedom by Zero-Knowledge Systems, Inc.**, offers an anonymous remailer that has additional anonymity safeguards—its technology makes connecting customer identities with active users impossible. It also offers privacy tools for your browser in one convenient software download.

If you're concerned about your privacy in virtual communities, but not ready for an anonymous remailer, you should at least understand how visible your various communications are, to corporate data collection operations, your boss (or prospective boss, the next time that you apply for a job), and the person whom you just started dating (who is an average Internet user), among others. Throughout this chapter, a privacy assessment for each virtual community is described along with the steps that you can take to protect your privacy. These assessments are not based on empirical data; they merely reflect technological facts. No one can know that an online communication is absolutely secure in the sense that no one outside of its intended virtual community will ever see such communication. However, this chapter does consider the privacy of your communications, as well as the security of your identity in connection with specific communications. In all cases, you do have some control over your level of risk. This chapter explains what safeguards you can take to minimize that risk.

Until recently, personal communications were dominated by parties who knew each other: friends, relatives, colleagues, and acquaintances. With the advent of the Internet, strangers increasingly are exchanging e-mail messages, responding to public queries, and chatting with one another. Social ties on the Internet are not restricted to people who were first drawn together in real life, and social contacts are not constrained by geographical proximity, economic class, age, educational levels, or social graces. This is liberating for many people, yet it carries risks. As has often been said, "On the Internet, no one knows you're a dog." In this chapter, you'll learn how virtual communities use various Internet applications to coalesce and persevere.

7.2 MAILING LISTS

A **mailing list** is a forum in which people use e-mail messages to share information with each other. Some mailing lists are small and used by only a handful of people, whereas others have thousands of **subscribers**, as participants are called. Some have restricted membership, whereas others are open to anyone.

Mailing lists are extremely cost-effective from the perspective of an Internet host. A list on an Internet host imposes a negligible computing load on the host machine. Most lists are maintained by servers that also carry on many other computing tasks. Smaller mailing lists can be maintained easily as background jobs that run when nothing else is competing for CPU time. In addition, mailing lists normally use plain ASCII text, so they don't consume a great deal of bandwidth. Further, automated list management minimizes the need for human supervision in the list's daily operation. Thus maintaining a successful mailing list requires only minimal computer time, minimal network bandwidth, and relatively minimal human intervention.

Lists are either moderated or unmoderated. In a **moderated mailing list**, the list owner posts all of the messages to the list. Sometimes, the owner will welcome suggested posts from readers, while then reserving the right to not post them (much like letters to the editor in a newspaper). Many moderated lists don't accept subscriber posts at all. In that case, the list is really a broadcast medium. That is, the list owner is responsible for all of the messages that go out to the list, and everyone else merely "listens." A mailing list with thousands of subscribers is usually a moderated mailing list.

AWAD

A good example of a moderated mailing list is A.Word.A.Day (AWAD). Subscribers to this list receive one message from the list each day. The message contains an interesting word, its dictionary definition, and a quotation that uses the word.

Subscribing to AWAD is a painless way to expand your vocabulary and test your command of the English language. As of March 2000, AWAD subscribers consisted of 275,000 people in more than 184 countries. For more information about AWAD, see `http://www.wordsmith.org/awad/`.

An unmoderated mailing list is called an interactive mailing list. An **interactive mailing list** is a list on which anyone can post a message at any time without prior approval and subscribers can interact with each other through the list. This type of mailing list provides a good forum for meeting people who share similar interests, especially when those interests are atypical. Many online relationships begin with an interactive mailing list. However, the vast majority of mailing list subscribers tend to **lurk**—read posts to the list without ever posting their own. A vocal minority usually is responsible for most of the talking—one estimate is that only 10% of the subscribers on an interactive mailing list ever post a message. If you like to keep a low profile, you'll feel at home lurking on a mailing list.

Mailing List Privacy

The amount of privacy associated with a mailing list generally depends on whether an archive of all of the mail messages is maintained and, if so, how visible it is. If a *public* archive is maintained, your privacy is at risk. Keep the following points in mind.

- To keep your identity safe, use an anonymous remailer.
- To keep your messages safe from all future access, the mailing list must not be archived.
- If an archive is kept but is not publicly available, your messages will still be available to law enforcement agencies.
- If a searchable mail archive is on the Web, anyone can easily find your messages if they know which mailing list to search. It might also be possible to find portions of the archive by using a general search engine.

If you're thinking of joining a mailing list and you're concerned about your privacy, contact the list owner and ask whether an archive is kept. If one is, then ask for details about its visibility. Some searchable archives are not on the Web but can be accessed via *listserv commands* (see Section 7.2.1). Most people don't know (or want to know) how to search listserv archives online. However, downloading a listserv archive is possible, as is searching it locally by using standard file utilities.

List owners are usually sensitive to the privacy concerns of their subscribers and often explain their privacy policies in the list's welcome message. On a privacy scale of 1 to 10, with 10 the best, *mail-based mailing lists* rate about an 8 (read about *Web-based mailing lists* in Section 7.3). If the list owner is doing everything possible to protect the privacy of all list subscribers and you take advantage of your browser's privacy-related preference settings, then your privacy is largely in the hands of other list members. This might or might not be much of a risk, depending on the nature of the list. Privacy risks that apply to all mailing lists are discussed in more detail at the end of Section 7.3.

7.2.1 Subscribing to Mailing Lists

Before you can receive messages from a mailing list, you must *subscribe* to the list. Most lists are maintained automatically by server software. A list manager oversees the list and intervenes as needed when list participants get out of hand. However, a computer program typically handles the normal operations of accepting new subscribers and removing people who want to leave the list. Different mailing list software packages have different command conventions for doing this. The most important function of such software is to update subscriptions. Other commands are available for users who want additional information about the mailing list. You need to read the welcome message for each mailing list that you're interested in to acquaint yourself with the list's operation and capabilities, since they aren't all the same.

Some mailing lists offer you two delivery options: the regular list subscription and a digest. A **digest subscription** is a collection of some number of messages from the list that are bundled into a single e-mail message before being sent to you. A digest might be delivered whenever a certain number of messages have been collected, a certain amount of memory has been filled up, or a fixed period of time has elapsed. If you're active on the mailing list and want to see responses to your messages as soon as possible, a digest will delay the delivery of messages to your inbox. However, if a mailing list is kicking out a hundred messages a day, a digest delivery can save your inbox from being flooded. If you don't need the fastest possible mail delivery, a digest is usually a welcome solution to the problem of coping with high-traffic mailing lists.

Two Important Addresses for Interactive Mailing Lists Regardless of the software that manages a list, two e-mail addresses are always associated with each *interactive* mailing list: the list command address and the list distribution address. The **list command address** is the address of the computer that runs the list; you use it when you want to contact that computer, for example to subscribe to or unsubscribe from the list. The **list distribution address** is the address to which you post a message to everyone on the list.

The classic blooper of a mailing list newbie is ignorance of or confusion about these two addresses. They often send the wrong kind of e-mail message to the wrong address.

Embarrassing Newbie Bloopers

If you remember only one thing about mailing lists, remember that there are two addresses for each interactive mailing list. Be clear about when each is used.

Once you've subscribed to a mailing list, you'll receive a welcome message that contains important information, including

- the list command address,
- the list distribution address, and
- instructions on how to subscribe to and unsubscribe from the list.

Always save the welcome message for each mailing list to which you subscribe.

By using the correct address for the situation, you can avoid embarrassing yourself before hundreds, possibly thousands, of list subscribers worldwide. The only people who are allowed to post messages to an interactive mailing list are list subscribers. No one else can send mail to a distribution address and have it distributed to a mailing list. This means you don't have to worry about accidentally sending an e-mail message out to a mailing list by accident. Even if you manage (by some improbable sequences of typos) to send a message to a valid distribution address, the list server won't accept the message if you aren't on the membership list.

Note that a *moderated* mailing list has no list distribution address, so with this type of list you need not worry about differentiating between two addresses.

Subscribe and Unsubscribe Commands More than 100,000 mailing lists are maintained by listserv software, probably the most widely used software for maintaining mailing lists. Here's a brief look at the Subscribe and Unsubscribe commands used by mailing lists that listservs maintain.

TO SUBSCRIBE TO A LIST You subscribe by sending a *Subscribe command* in an e-mail message to the *listserv address* with a message body of the form

    subscribe <*name-of-list*> <*your-first-name*> <*your-last-name*>

You make appropriate substitutions for the items in italics. Listservs are not case-sensitive, but do enter your name in mixed case when you subscribe to the mailing list, for the sake of human readers.

Sending a Subscribe command automatically subscribes you to the list. Usually, you'll receive in return an autoreply—an acknowledgment or welcome message—within minutes. However, if the mailing list server is not online 24 hours a day, a reply might take as long as a day or so.

TO UNSUBSCRIBE FROM A LIST To unsubscribe from a list, send an Unsubscribe command in an e-mail message to the appropriate listserv address with a message body of the form

    unsubscribe <*name-of-list*>

Remember, to *unsubscribe* from a list, send the Unsubscribe command to the *list command address.* Do not send it to the list distribution address—everyone on the list will see it! This is very annoying for list subscribers, and it won't get you off the list.

AN EXAMPLE Suppose that I want to subscribe to an interactive list for discussion related to golden retrievers. The name of the list is "golden," and the list command address is `listserv@hobbes.ucsd.edu`. To subscribe to this list, I would send to the list command address an e-mail message that contains the following Subscribe command in the message body:

```
subscribe golden Wendy Lehnert
```

To post a message to this list, I would send the message to the list distribution address:

```
golden@hobbes.ucsd.edu
```

Only "golden" list subscribers can post messages to the list, and only "golden" list subscribers can receive the messages as they are posted.

When I'm ready to unsubscribe from the list, I will send an Unsubscribe command to the list command address, `listserv@hobbes.ucsd.edu`:

```
unsubscribe golden
```

How Many Messages Will You Get?

It's difficult to estimate how much traffic you'll receive. Some lists are highly active, whereas others are barely alive. A popular list will fill your mailbox with lots of reading material each day. A highly active list will generate 50 to100 messages a day. Most mailing lists are not this lively, but be prepared for heavy traffic if the list's welcome message mentions a digest option.

It's fine to try out a list for a short time to discover whether you like or need it. You can always subscribe to a list for a few days or weeks, never post a message, and then unsubscribe; no one will care. Just remember to save the welcome message so that you'll know how to unsubscribe.

Multiple Accounts and Mailing Lists

When you subscribe to a mailing list, the list records your e-mail address and expects to see that address whenever you interact with the list. If you have access to multiple host machines, you won't be able to post a message to a list to which you've subscribed if you send the message from a different host than the one used when you subscribed. Don't expect a mailing list to recognize you if you try to contact it from different host machines.

You must also issue your Unsubscribe command from the same machine you used when you subscribed. If you close a computer account on one machine or want to shift your daily operations from one machine to another, be sure that you first unsubscribe from all active mailing lists on the old machine. Then (re)subscribe to all of them from the new host machine.

Whenever you interact with a computer program, be careful to type your commands correctly. No human will see your listserv commands; the commands will be either accepted and processed or rejected with an error message. Note also that the listserv won't see a command typed in the Subject: field instead of the message body. It can't process a Subscribe or Unsubscribe command if you mangle the command syntax; for example, if you list your name first followed by the name of the list. Computers are very good at arithmetic, but they're not very smart when it comes to figuring out what you want if you mess up command syntax. Remember that you're dealing with a computer program and that computer programs tend to be rather unforgiving.

7.2.2 Some Great Mailing Lists

Many good mailing lists can help you master the Internet and keep you up-to-date on Internet-related news. Here are four that will keep you well informed without overwhelming your mailbox.

- **Internet Tourbus** is a weekly (more or less) newsletter that profiles specific Internet resources and offers Internet news of general interest. Written with light humor and a personal touch, the Tourbus is a friendly addition to your mailbox. To subscribe, send an e-mail message to

  `hop-on@tourbus.com`

  and then reply to the confirmation message.

- **Net Surfers Digest** is a monthly newsletter with profiles of interesting Web sites and short articles that address timely Internet news. To subscribe, use your Web browser to visit the following site and look for a subscription page:

  `http://www.netsurf.com/nsd/index.html`

- **Scout Report** is a weekly newsletter that describes new and newly discovered Web sites of interest to educators and researchers. For information on subscribing (this is not a subscription command), send an e-mail message to

  `listserv@cs.wisc.edu`

  and in the body of the message type the command

  `info scout-report`

- **Red Rock Eaters News Service** distributes items written by technologists who discuss policy, politics, and sociological issues related to the Internet. Expect five to ten messages each week. To subscribe, send an e-mail message to

  `requests@lists.gseis.ucla.edu`

  and in the **Subject:** field type the command

  `subscribe rre`

7.2.3 Mailing List Netiquette

When you participate in a mailing list, remember that each message that you post goes out to many people whom you don't know. They might not share your values, your beliefs, your sense of humor, or your neophyte sense of accomplishment. The Internet is a global communication vehicle; you never know who's out there reading what you type. Its population is not homogeneous, consisting of people from one country or one socioeconomic class. It is truly a global medium. Never forget how far-reaching your communications can be. Some lists are friendly and forgiving about minor transgressions in Netiquette. Others are policed by individuals who take a hard line on what is appropriate.

With a few rules of Netiquette in hand, you can safely explore a mailing list that interests you. If you're worried about preserving your privacy, you can conceal your identity on the list of current subscribers (which is sometimes available to the general public). Then no one will know that you're there, unless you post a message to the list.

Watch and Learn

When you first subscribe to a new mailing list, lurk before you leap. Don't feel compelled to jump in the first day you're on a new list. Read messages for a while before you post any of your own. By lurking, you can learn how the list is used, what topics are appropriate, and what might provoke angry reactions from other list members. Watch and learn before you say something that you might regret.

Many conversational threads (specific discussions involving two or more people) start on a mailing list and then shift to a private conversation via personal e-mail. For example, when you first introduce yourself as a new list member, a few friendly souls probably will reply to you and say something to make you feel welcome. Sometimes, these replies are posted to everyone on the list; sometimes, they are sent as private e-mail. If you decide to pursue a conversation with one other person, continue it privately unless you think that you're saying something that might be of general interest to the entire list. This is a good way to make new online friends if you're looking for "pen pals." Many private e-mail relationships are spawned by brief exchanges on a mailing list.

Always include your full e-mail address *in the message body* of each of your posts. Some list subscribers might be working with a mailer that does not display your return address in the message header. You want to make it easy for people to reply to you privately.

It is good Netiquette to give people your real name when you post messages to a mailing list. In some cases, fictitious personas have operated as mailing list participants. It's easy for someone to misrepresent oneself online and get away with it. Most people frown on this, considering it highly unethical. At the very least, deliberate misrepresentation is disrespectful of those who are honest about their identities.

Some people talk publicly on a mailing list, and others interact only privately. If you subscribe to a list on which you see many people posting questions, but not many people posting answers, it might be that replies are being sent privately. There's no way of knowing how responsive list members are in their private communications until you post a question yourself.

If you're considering posting a message to a mailing list and are uncertain about its relevance to the list, it's best to err on the side of caution and not post it. Many beginners pass along information that is off-topic but believed to be of general interest. If you find yourself thinking, "Surely everybody would want to know about this even though it's not relevant to the list," please resist the impulse to post. List administrators can impose whatever behavioral codes they see fit, and they can always enforce these codes by removing violators from the list.

Here are some Netiquette guidelines to remember when posting a message to a mailing list.

- Keep it short.
- Be sure that your topic is relevant to the list.
- Send personal messages to individuals, not to the whole list.
- Clearly separate facts and opinions.
- Try to avoid insulting anyone.
- Include your full (real) name in your signature.
- Include your full e-mail address in your signature.
- Do not include mail attachments.
- Do not use an autoreply if you're active on any mailing lists.

And when you move or change your ISP, always remember to unsubscribe from all mailing lists before canceling the account.

7.2.4 Netspeak

When a dialog gets rolling and the content is humorous, you'll likely notice lots of Netspeak (mysterious acronyms) laced throughout messages. Some Netspeak conveys emotional undertone. For example, you might see a cryptic LOL or ROFL in response to something, punctuated with the smilee emoticon. LOL stands for "I laughed out loud." ROFL means "I'm rolling on the floor laughing."

Other abbreviations are used to soften statements that everyone might not agree with. IMO means "in my opinion." Even more cautious is IMHO: "in my humble opinion." Using Netspeak in this way makes it clear that the message poster is not trying to assume authority and does not want to offend someone whose opinions might differ.

Commonly encountered Netspeak acronyms include the following:

LOL	Laughing out loud
ROFL	Rolling on the floor laughing
OOH	On the other hand
FWIW	For what it's worth
BTW	By the way

IRL	In real life
IMO	In my opinion
IMHO	In my humble opinion
FYI	For your information
TIA	Thanks in advance
RTFM	Read the f- - -ing manual

If you feel that your words might be misinterpreted, try to be sensitive to the ambiguities of written dialog and use emoticons and Netspeak where appropriate. Online communication is different from verbal communication, to which you're accustomed. It might look easy enough, but it takes some time to catch on.

7.3   WEB-BASED DISCUSSION GROUPS

With the commercialization of the Internet and the intense competition among big-ticket Web sites, professional Webmasters are charged with the task of not only attracting first-time visitors, but also making those visitors want to return, often. Freebies, discounts, and contests are all traditional marketing devices that are also used by Web sites to create customer loyalty. The one new device that is unique to the Web is the *Web-based discussion group* (also called a *message board*).

It didn't take long for someone to coin a new marketing dictum for the Internet: "If you let 'em talk, they will come." And so the Web-based discussion group was born. The historical roots of the Web-based discussion group are in the 1980s BBS movement (see the Above and Beyond section in Chapter 2) as well as *Usenet* (see Section 7.4). People have always been attracted to the Internet equivalent of the office water cooler. With the advent of the Web and the widespread use of Java-enabled browsers, new opportunities for ongoing discussion groups emerged. Today, two types of Web-based discussion groups are available:

1. Site-specific discussion groups (discussed here and in Section 7.3.1)

2. Web-based mailing lists (discussed in Section 7.3.2)

Examples of site-specific discussions include

- product feedback message boards,
- voting polls,
- opinion surveys,
- topical discussion threads, and
- product support message boards (see Figure 7.1).

Although anyone is free to jump in and sound off in any of these interactive scenarios, each is created by a Webmaster, who lays down the discussion topic and the

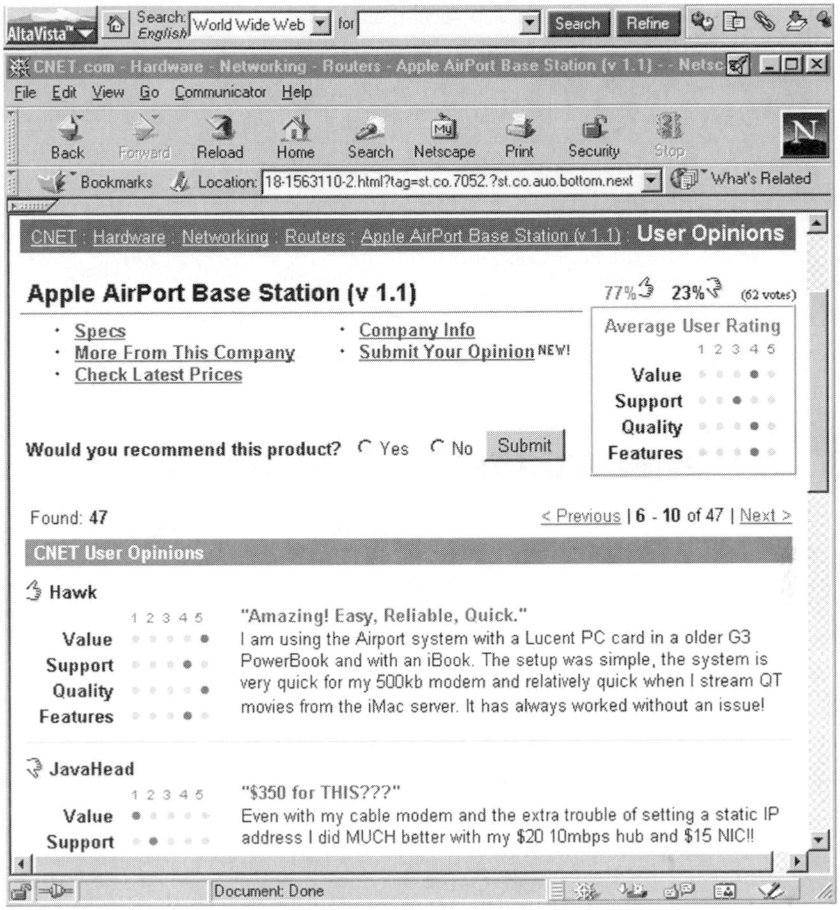

Figure 7.1:
CNet's Product
Review Message
Board

rules of conduct. Web portal sites experiment with all sorts of site-specific discussions. There's plenty of opportunity if you want to register a complaint or post a good word about anything that sparks your interest.

Most site-specific discussions are related to the Web site's content. A commercial site that promotes a product might have a discussion board on which users can look for advice and ask each other questions regarding the product. A recreational site might have a discussion board on which visitors can share tips and offer help to newcomers.

7.3.1 Yahoo! Message Boards

Yahoo! supports many **discussion groups** in which you can view or participate in a wide range of discussion topics (see Figure 7.2).

Figure 7.2:
Yahoo! Runs Many
Message Boards

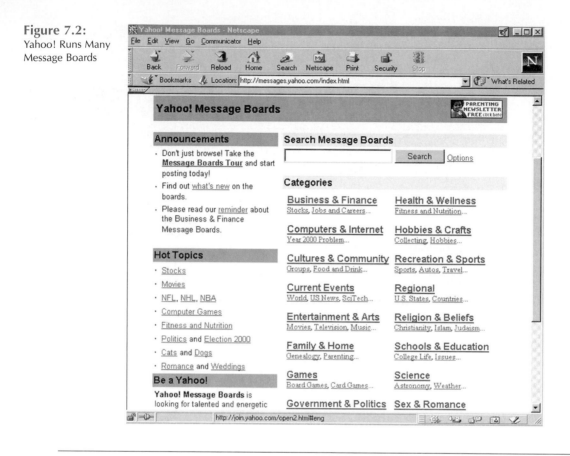

Truth, Lies, and Misinformation

When looking for information from a message board, be careful. People who post to a message board might misrepresent themselves and/or their institutional affiliation and might post false information, either deliberately or out of ignorance. Always verify important information with at least one independent source before acting on it.

Be especially careful about anyone who offers you technical, medical, or legal advice, regarding for example investments, computer troubleshooting, personal health, medical treatment, or possible litigation. Suggestions posted to discussion groups might be informed and on target, or they might be completely off base. Be wary about what you read on a message board.

You can browse the discussion groups at Yahoo! or use a keyword search, very much like when using the Yahoo! subject tree. Each discussion group tracks separate threads for which participants can respond to a single question or discuss an issue at length. Figure 7.3 shows a list of recent threads in a computer hardware discussion group at Yahoo!. The numbers in the Msgs column indicate how many messages have been posted to each thread.

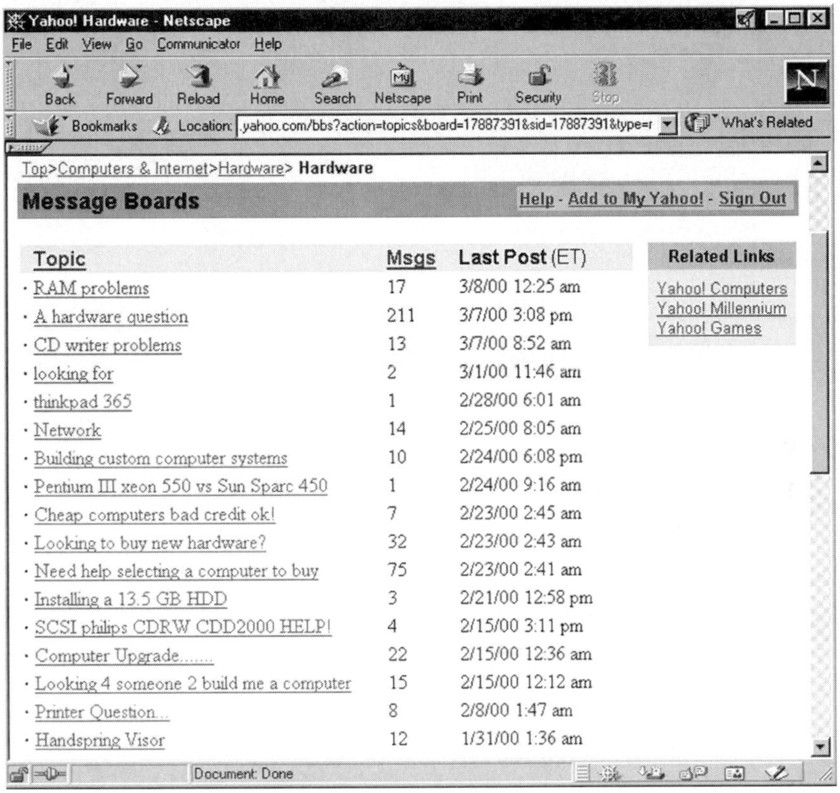

Figure 7.3:
Discussion Threads
at a Yahoo!
Message Board

Clicking a topic link opens the corresponding thread and allows you to navigate the individual messages within that thread (see Figure 7.4).

Before you post your own message or reply to someone else's post for any Web-based discussion group, always read its ToS or AUP. First Amendment protections might be (and usually are) curtailed on commercially sponsored message boards. Many message boards, in an effort to be "family friendly," place restrictions regarding what is considered to be acceptable language and content. If you violate the ToS or AUP, your posting privileges might be terminated; other site-related privileges might be revoked as well (see Figure 7.5).

Some Web-based discussion groups offer a tracking service to their members. You tell the tracking service which thread you want to track, and it notifies you via e-mail (or possibly an instant messaging service; see later in the chapter) whenever a new message is posted to that thread. You can usually request that a copy of all new messages be forwarded to your e-mail account as well. This is a wonderful time-saver.

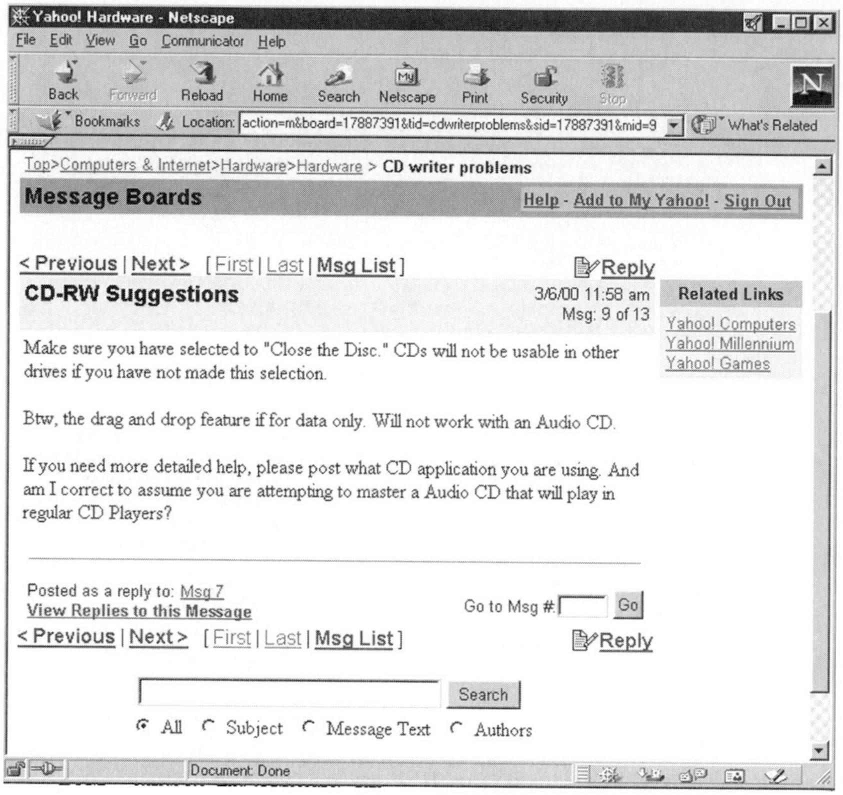

Figure 7.4:
One Message Inside
of a Thread at
Yahoo!

When you participate in a Web-based discussion group, you do *not* need to identify yourself. In particular, if you're concerned about privacy, you are advised *not* to use your real name. Most people use a temporary **handle** (alias) or, in the case of Yahoo!, their Yahoo! logon id. If you want to pursue a one-on-one conversation with one or two discussion participants, then initiate an e-mail correspondence and take the discussion off the Web. You might feel more comfortable revealing your true identity in an e-mail dialog, where your messages are relatively private (but see Section 2.7).

Do not confuse the use of a handle with true anonymity. Internet service providers protect the privacy of their customers, to a point (read their privacy policies for details). They generally draw the line when they are served with a court order or a subpoena. Recall from Chapter 2 that if asked to reveal the subscriber's identity in order to cooperate with law enforcement agencies, most service providers will surrender any identifying information that you have revealed to them.

7.3.2 Creating Your Own Discussion Group

If you want to run your own discussion group, you can create either a message board on a personal Web site by using an applet (see Chapter 5) or a *Web-based*

Figure 7.5:
Rules of Conduct
for Yahoo!'s
Message Boards

How to Write a Message

- **DO include the details.** Good posts include not only your opinion, but *why* you feel that way. Be objective and truthful.

- **DO stay on topic and keep it short.** Comments that are not specific to the topic you're posting about are annoying to other users and violate our Terms of Service. The recommended length is 250 to 500 words.

- **DO have fun.** Your opinion is worth something! Let the rest of the Web know what you have to share.

- **DON'T assume that you are completely anonymous and cannot be identified by your posts.** Never assume people are who they say they are, know what they say they know, or are affiliated with whom they say they are affiliated. Yahoo! takes user privacy very seriously and will take reasonable measures to respect your privacy. However, under special circumstances, such as to comply with subpoenas and other legal obligations, Yahoo! may provide personally identifiable information which may include IP addresses.

- **DON'T disregard the rules.** When you post a message, you agree to abide by our Terms of Service. Messages that harass, abuse or threaten; have obscene or otherwise objectionable content; have spam, commercial or advertising content or links may be removed and may result in the loss of your Yahoo! ID (including email). Never assume that you are completely anonymous and cannot be identified by your posts.

- **DON'T reveal anything you wouldn't want the world to know.** Be smart and use normal precautions when posting. Don't post real names, addresses and phone numbers unless you want them to be available publicly.

mailing list. Web-based mailing lists are very easy to maintain and are your best choice if you want to set up something fast. Before you start your own mailing list, however, check to see whether an existing mailing list already meets your needs (see Section 7.5). Attracting participants could be difficult if they are already using an existing discussion group.

Web-based mailing lists are easy to create, maintain, and join. Unlike site-specific discussions, which are generally open to anyone, a Web-based mailing list, like other mailing lists, is available only to subscribers, who can view mailing list messages from an e-mail account, a Web browser, or both.

Some mailing list host services charge a fee for their services; others are offered at no charge. The free mailing list services include the following, which you can search for mailing lists on a specific topic:

eGroups.com	`http://www.egroups.com/index.html`
globeclubs	`http://globeclubs.theglobe.com/`
Topical	`http://www.topica.com/`

Before setting up your own mailing list, subscribe to a few mailing lists maintained by some different hosting services in order to see which service you like best. You won't see the lists from a list manager's point of view, but you can at least see how the lists look from a subscriber's viewpoint (see Figure 7.6).

Figure 7.6:
Mailing List Hosting
Service Called
eGroups

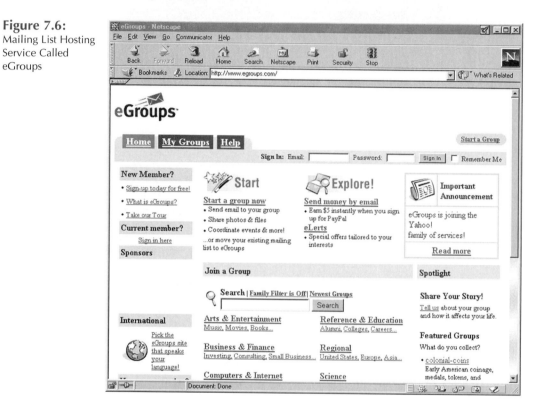

When you subscribe to a Web-based mailing list, you'll be asked to set your *delivery preferences.* You can change these preferences at any time if you want to experiment with other options. You either can have list messages sent to your e-mail account or can view the messages on the Web (see Figure 7.7).You might also be able to set preferences that determine how visible you are on the list. Such privacy safeguards can be important if you want to join, for example, a mailing list that addresses a serious medical condition or other personal problems. Most people don't want to join a Web-based mailing list if it means sacrificing personal privacy regarding sensitive topics.

Most Web-based mailing lists are open to the public; some restrict membership according to rules that the list manager deems appropriate. For example, a mailing list for a specific college course might be limited to students registered for that course. As with other types of mailing lists, you usually must be a member of the list in order to post or view messages.

Figure 7.7:
Choice of Delivery
Options Offered by
Web-Based Mailing
Lists

```
eGroups : BCs4me Subscribe - Netscape
File  Edit  View  Go  Communicator  Help

  Back   Forward  Reload   Home   Search  Netscape  Print  Security   Stop

  Bookmarks   Location: http://www.egroups.com/subscribe/BCs4me?referer=1            What's Related
```

eGroups

Home **My Groups** **Help**

Start a Group

Welcome lehnert@cs.umass.edu | My Profile | Sign Out

BCs4me
Main Page : Subscribe

Search | Family Filter is Off
All eGroups ▾ [   ] Go

Main Page	**Membership Options**
▷ Subscribe	**Message Delivery:** ○ Send email messages to **lehnert@cs.umass.edu**
Messages	○ Send a daily digest of messages (many e-mails in one message) to
Members	**lehnert@cs.umass.edu**
Files	⊙ Don't send me email, I'll read the messages at the Web site
Calendar	**Member Profile:** ☑ Display my profile to members of this group
Polls	**Status:** Click the Join button to gain full access as a member of this group.
Links	
Database	Join

Document: Done

Web-Based Discussion Group Privacy

Similar to mailing lists, the amount of privacy associated with a Web-based discussion group depends on whether the Web site maintains a searchable archive of messages on the Web.

- To keep your identity safe, use an anonymous remailer.
- If you rely on privacy preference settings at the Web site to conceal your identity, your identity will still be available to law enforcement agencies.
- If a searchable archive is on the Web and the discussion group is open to the public, anyone can find your messages very easily as long as they know which discussion group to search. Otherwise, your messages are safe.
- If a searchable archive is on the Web but the discussion group is not open to the public, your messages are safe unless someone infiltrates the group, copies the archive, and "liberates" all the archived messages for public access.

7.4 USENET NEWSGROUPS

In the musical, *Guys and Dolls,* the character Nathan Detroit runs "the oldest established permanent floating crap game in New York." Players come and players go, but the game goes on forever. The same can be said of *Usenet (the User's Network) newsgroups*, except that people participate in one long never-ending conversation.

In fact, at any one time more than 50,000 simultaneous conversations are occurring under the Usenet umbrella.

Anyone can drop in to listen, ask a question, disagree with a claim, or offer advice. Some people stay for only a minute or so; others are active, daily, for months or even years. Some newsgroups attract serious people who share technical information and help each other solve perplexing problems. Some exist purely for entertainment, and others are national BBSs of want ads (a long-standing precursor of the eBay auction site). Some are available to users worldwide, and others are restricted to a particular geographical region. And, similar to mailing lists, newsgroups can be either moderated or unmoderated and all are associated with a specific topic.

Created in 1979 by graduate students at the University of North Carolina and Duke University who wanted to talk to each other, Usenet today serves millions worldwide. It resembles the thousands of BBSs that served regional users via direct dial-up access in the 1980s, except that its scope is as global as the Internet's. Because Usenet taps such a large user population, its newsgroups can address very narrow interests and still attract a healthy number of participants. For people with esoteric interests or who are geographically isolated, Usenet is a world of virtual communities that could not exist in any other way.

The term *newsgroup* is somewhat misleading, since most newsgroups are not news-related. They are really discussion groups, much like a mailing list. However, they are organized in a *large hierarchy* and distributed by *special news servers* that support a specific Usenet protocol called Network News Transport Protocol (NNTP). A message that is posted to a Usenet newsgroup is called an **article**. Each article contains a header like an e-mail header. To read and post Usenet articles, you need access to a *Usenet news server* (ISPs normally include Usenet access in their services) and a special client program called a *news reader*. Many browsers, such as Navigator or MSIE, include their own news readers (see Figure 7.8). If you decide to spend a lot of time working with Usenet, you might want to shop around for a news reader that supports special features. However, when you're getting started any news reader is fine.

Explore Usenet with Your Web Browser

You can visit Usenet without a news reader if you know where to go on the Web. For example, at **Deja.com** look for a link to DISCUSSIONS (see Figure 7.9).

This will take you to a Usenet gateway, where you can browse the Usenet hierarchy or conduct keyword searches (see Figure 7.10). **Novell** maintains another good Usenet gateway.

7.4.1 How Newsgroups are Organized

As mentioned earlier, Usenet newsgroups are organized *hierarchically*, with a small number of names that are used to identify broad categories at the highest level (see

Figure 7.8:
Launch
Communicator's
News Reader from
a Pull-down Menu

Figure 7.9:
Deja.com Delivers
Usenet on the Web

Figure 7.10). Newsgroup names start with the broadest category on the left and move through successive subcategories from left to right (unlike host names, which start with a specific host name on the left and end in a general domain name). There are 103 top-level Usenet categories, but most of the traffic occurs in the following "Big Eight":

biz	Business
comp	Computers
sci	Scientific
misc	Miscellaneous
soc	Social issues
talk	Debates and lengthy conversations

news	News and topical subjects
rec	Hobbies and recreational

Figure 7.10:
Discover Usenet by
Browsing the
Hierarchy of
Newsgroups

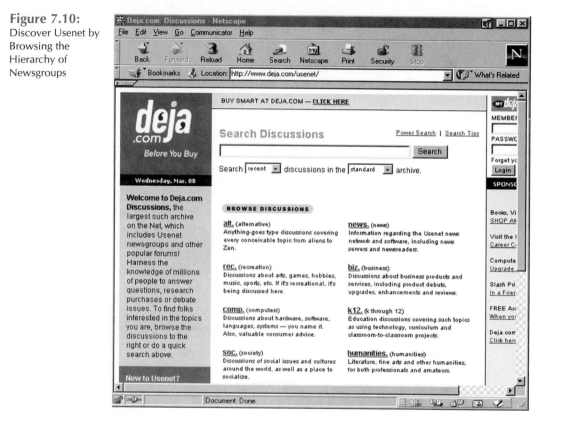

Another major newsgroup category is *alt.* This is an alternative topic hierarchy; alt newsgroups are discussed shortly.

Newsgroup names are (sometimes) self-explanatory and designed to differentiate closely related groups. A newsgroup's name might be enough to tell you what the newsgroup is about. Here are some examples of Usenet newsgroups:

```
alt.adoption.searching
alt.esperanto.beginner
sci.optics
sci.techniques.mag-resonance
comp.infosystems.www.browsers.misc
misc.health.alternative.diabetes
misc.forsale.computers.mac-specific.cards.misc
```

In many newsgroups, you can get answers to all of your questions about Usenet. These newsgroups are essentially online documentation for Usenet:

`alt.newbie` (to post a Usenet article as an experiment)

`news.announce.newusers` (moderated; informational posts for new users)

`news.groups.questions` (to ask where to post specific questions)

`news.newusers.questions` (to ask questions about the Internet)

You'll find many useful articles posted for the edification of new users on the newsgroup news.announce.newusers (see Figure 7.11). Here are some of the article titles:

What Is Usenet?

What Is Usenet? A Second Opinion.

Answers to Frequently Asked Questions about Usenet

A Primer on How to Work with the Usenet Community

How to Find the Right Place to Post

Rules for Posting to Usenet

Hints for Writing Styles for Usenet

Emily Postnews Answers Your Questions on Netiquette

How to Advertise on Usenet

Figure 7.11:
Viewing an Article from news. announce.newusers

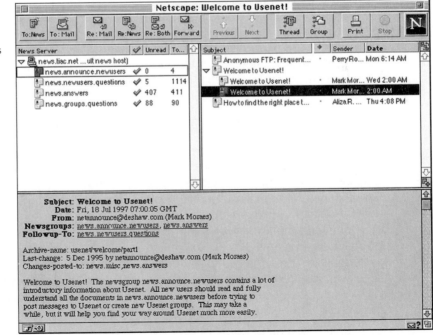

Like everything else on the Internet, Usenet newsgroups are constantly evolving. New groups emerge when enough interest in a topic materializes. Old groups can die if interest in their topics wanes. Don't expect any published list of Usenet newsgroups to be up-to-date.

7.4.2 How to Create a Newsgroup

Despite the large number of newsgroups, newsgroup creation is no small undertaking. To create a new newsgroup, you must deal with some significant bureaucratic requirements. The process requires submitting a public Request For Discussion (RFD) and a Call For Votes (CFV). Votes are collected from interested Usenet users via e-mail according to a strict voting procedure. If the vote passes, then a waiting period must be met before the new group can finally be created. The entire process takes many months and consumes a lot of time and effort. To get an idea of how much work goes into creating a new newsgroup, take a look at the sample RFDs and CFVs that are posted at the newsgroup news.groups.

The alt newsgroups are a special category. Anyone can create an alt newsgroup, without filing RFDs and CFVs. They are an "underground" region of Usenet, where the normal Usenet rules don't apply. Because anyone can create an alt newsgroup, spurious ones are created every day for the sake of sending a silly newsgroup name out to all Usenet servers. These bogus newsgroups rarely receive any posts. They only clutter up the servers until system administrators remove them.

Once in a while, a silly alt newsgroup will actually draw enough of an audience to keep it going. For example, someone was probably kidding when they created alt.tv.dinosaurs.barney.die.die.die, but that newsgroup became moderately active thanks to the popularity of its title and a healthy amount of antagonism toward Barney the dinosaur (a popular children's toy and television show). A few silly newsgroups acquire a faithful cult-like following, thereby lending credence to the idea that the alt groups represent a countercultural version of Usenet.

7.4.3 Usenet Netiquette and Advertising

Most Netiquette rules that apply to mailing lists apply to Usenet newsgroups—perhaps more so because newsgroups reach more readers than mailing lists do. Usenet users number in the millions worldwide, and any one newsgroup can easily be read by thousands. Newsgroups are very public, and their readership is very fluid. Articles are not visible indefinitely, but they can remain available on Usenet servers for as long as a month. Anyone can read articles, and no one can limit a newsgroup's readership, unless the limitation applies to a regional network. Many Usenet newsgroups are also archived for public access, so articles posted years ago might still be available. Never forget that Usenet communications are very visible and very public. It's not the place to joke about shooting the U.S. President, unless you want to be interviewed by the Secret Service.

The Usenet community tolerates commercial advertisements, but only in newsgroups that welcome commercial posts. These newsgroups can be identified easily by the inclusion in the newsgroup's name of keywords such as "marketplace," "forsale," "wanted," or "biz." Never post a commercial advertisement to a newsgroup unless you're certain doing so is appropriate. Inappropriate Usenet posts are a form of Internet abuse.

Great care is taken to ensure that each newsgroup is well-delineated regarding content. If someone, in good faith, posts an inappropriate query to a newsgroup, other Usenet participants might be able to suggest a better newsgroup for the query. Usenet regulars are generally intolerant of discussions that stray too far off topic. However, it's generally obvious when someone is honestly trying to locate an appropriate Usenet forum. Abusive Usenet posts tend to be inflammatory, insulting, or patently offensive—Usenet abuse is rarely subtle. If someone abuses a newsgroup or engages in inappropriate behavior on a newsgroup, other users are likely to assume the role of vigilante, taking steps to censure the behavior. Public admonitions from random individuals sometimes suffice. However, when abusive behavior persists, complaints to an appropriate network administrator can result in a suspension or termination of the account from which the abuse originated.

Get Out Your Asbestos Underwear

Usenet is a perfect medium for people who want to flame—it attracts a lot of cranks, adolescent malcontents, and uninhibited characters with overactive spleens. A perfectly innocent Usenet article can sometimes trigger a vicious attack. If the sender of the original article decides to fight fire with fire, a flame war can erupt.

Each newsgroup has its own culture and behavioral codes. Some seem to condone flame wars, whereas others try to maintain a standard for courteous and civilized communication. If you ever get flamed, don't bother to respond. Flames on Usenet that are ignored will usually die out quickly.

7.4.4 How Usenet News Servers Work

Usenet articles are continuously cycled through each news server. The oldest are deleted to make room for new ones, so an article that you saw yesterday might not be on the server today. The life cycle of an article depends on the server. If server space is tight, articles will be deleted quickly, within two or three days. On a server with more memory, they might linger for a week or two. Space limitations also mean that most news servers carry only a subset of available newsgroups because they don't have enough room for all of them. According to one estimate, one day's worth of Usenet traffic for all newsgroups requires more than 800 MB of storage, so memory capacity tends to be a limiting factor.

Whereas some newsgroups might be omitted from a server because of space limitations, others might be left out because of administrative policies applicable to a server. A corporate news server might not carry recreational newsgroups on the grounds that there's no legitimate need for them in the workplace. If you access Usenet through an ISP or a university and you can't find a newsgroup that you want, ask technical support if it can add it to the server for you. Most system administrators are happy to honor a request for a specific newsgroup, unless the newsgroup violates an AUP.

Watch Your Step

You might have heard conflicting claims about how much pornography is on the Internet. Some people say that the concerns about pornography are overblown; others say the Internet is a cesspool and unfit for children. Pornography *is* available on the Net, but you must know where to look for it. Newsgroups devoted to pornographic images are in the alt.binaries subhierarchy.

If you're interested in exploring pornography, be sure to review Chapter 2 so that you'll know how to avoid illegal activities. For example, it's a felony in the United States to distribute or own images depicting child pornography. Such activities undoubtedly occur at times in some of the alt.binaries newsgroups. Be aware that the FBI monitors Usenet newsgroups that are known magnets for criminal activities. If you visit such newsgroups, you could get caught in a law enforcement sting operation.

Usenet communications rely on the text-based Network News Transport Protocol (NNTP). This protocol does not accept binary files. However, users on some newsgroups can post graphics files or executable programs. This is done by posting a uuencoded version of the file or by using a MIME attachment in the same way that uuencode and MIME are used to send binary files via e-mail. To exchange binary files via a Usenet newsgroup, you'll need a news reader, which can handle these ASCII-encoded file formats.

7.4.5 Usenet FAQ Files

The Usenet phenomenon of frequently asked questions led to the *FAQ (frequently asked questions) file*, called FAQ or FAQs for short. A FAQ consists of a list of frequently asked questions and answers to those questions. The FAQ is made publicly available so that anyone new to the newsgroup can find it easily. All newbies to a newsgroup should read the FAQ before posting questions to the newsgroup so as to avoid posting questions that have been asked, and answered, many times before. A good FAQ contains the institutional memory of an entire newsgroup; some Usenet FAQs are large enough to be books. The use of FAQs has since spread to other Internet venues. Many mailing lists now have their own FAQ files, as does much popular software and many organizations and informational Web sites.

Usenet FAQs, because they are viewed by so many people, typically contain highly reliable information. The newsgroup, motivated by self-interest and self-preservation, ensures that information found in its FAQ is likely to be as safe as anything you'll find on the Internet. The most knowledgeable people associated with each newsgroup review the newsgroup's FAQ and revise it periodically. These documents perform an important service for their affiliated communities, so their content is subject to continual scrutiny. However, anyone can call a file a FAQ file, so be careful to ascertain the origin of a FAQ file on which you intend to rely. Look for the real thing on Usenet or in Usenet FAQ archives in order to make sure that you're viewing a genuine Usenet FAQ.

Usenet FAQ Archives

Some Web sites maintain an archive of all available Usenet FAQs. These files are an excellent source of highly reliable information because they have been subjected to the scrutiny of people who are seriously involved in the subject matter. FAQ files are public documents, and the authors of FAQ files will be taken to task if they post incorrect information or controversial claims. These documents are not subjected to uniform editorial standards, but they come as close as you can get in a grass-roots educational system. Some FAQs have been subjected to highly rigorous standards, depending on who is responsible for them.

To obtain a FAQ for a specific newsgroup, check out these sites:

Landfield's Internet FAQ Archives
(`http://www.landfield.com/faqs/`)

The Madhippy Usenet FAQ Archive
(`http://www.madhippy.com/faqs/index.html`)

Utrecht FAQ Search (`http://www.cs.ruu.nl/cgi-bin/faqwais`)

MIT FAQ Archive   (`ftp://rtfm.mit.edu/pub/`)

The FAQ tradition on Usenet is so well established that you can find writing guides for FAQ authors on the Internet. A well-designed FAQ is formatted with all of the questions answered in the FAQ listed at the beginning of the file so that users can quickly determine whether their particular questions are addressed. Some FAQs are very lengthy and are organized into installments that resemble book chapters. It takes considerable work to produce a good FAQ. The people who write them rarely do so because it's part of their job description. FAQs exemplify the gift economy of the Internet at its best.

Keep in mind that copyright restrictions apply to FAQs even if the file contains no explicit copyright statement. Here is a general notice posted at MIT's FAQ archive that describes usage guidelines for readers of its FAQ.

COPYRIGHT NOTICE

Nearly all of the files contained in this directory are copyrighted by their respective maintainers. (Even files without explicit copyright notices are copyrighted under the international Berne Convention, in effect in most countries.) Some of the files, although certainly not all, prohibit redistribution for any commercial purposes without prior approval; other kinds of restrictions might also be imposed by the maintainers.

Approval for use when there are restrictions imposed must be obtained from the maintainers of each file, *NOT* from the maintainers of this archive. If you have any doubts about whether you might redistribute a particular file for some particular purpose, contact its author.

Making a copy for your own personal reading is implicitly allowed.

If you're new to a newsgroup and are thinking of asking a question, make sure you check the FAQ file before you post. If you ask a question that can be answered by consulting the FAQ, your lack of Netiquette will be obvious to many Usenet regulars. You might get reprimanded by someone who is tired of newbies who don't bother to read the FAQ file. Reading the FAQ file is the first rule of Usenet Netiquette. In addition, the same rules that apply to mailing lists apply to Usenet, with an exception. Usenet readers generally understand the wisdom of one's not signing Usenet posts with one's real name (see below). In addition, real e-mail addresses are often doctored to fool spambots (see the Above and Beyond section in Chapter 7).

You might also see more flames and less common courtesy on Usenet, depending on which newsgroups you frequent. The easy in-and-out nature of newsgroups make Usenet communities less stable and less personal than mailing lists. This difference, along with the fact that people cannot be removed from Usenet newsgroups, might account for there being more abusive behavior on Usenet than on mailing lists.

Usenet Newsgroup Privacy

To keep your identity safe, you must use an anonymous remailer. Someone can find your messages very easily by using a *searchable Usenet archive* such as Deja.com, which is where most people go to search Usenet. That person doesn't even have to know which newsgroups to search. If you use your real name or e-mail address when you post to Usenet, you're creating a public, and persistent, record for the world to see.

Many people think that they are protecting themselves if they include *X-No-Archive: Yes* in their Usenet posts. The Above and Beyond section in Chapter 7 explains this feature. Although this will keep your Usenet posts out of the **Deja.com** archive, other Usenet archives don't necessarily honor X-No-Archive.

7.5   READING USENET WITH A NEWS READER

You can read and post your own Usenet messages from Deja.com (posting privileges require registration). News readers, however, offer additional features to facilitate the monitoring of the constant flow of articles in a selection of newsgroups. For example, they can organize articles in threads so that you can more easily follow an ongoing conversation. This is especially useful on highly popular newsgroups on which dozens of threads might be active at any time. To keep the available article list easier to manage, articles that you have been read are tagged and then hidden from view. (You can retrieve read articles if you want to see all of the available articles.)

Some news readers also support the concept of a **kill file**, a list of users whose posts you don't want to see. Using a kill file is like applying an e-mail filter to block e-mail from specified individuals. Because people cannot be banned from Usenet, use of a kill file enables users to deal more effectively with abusive behavior on Usenet. Whereas a mailing list owner can remove a subscriber from the mailing list for refusing to abide by the owner's guidelines for the list, no one can be banned from a specific Usenet newsgroup at the level of the news servers. This is not a problem if an individual can be rendered "invisible" by a news reader. These are some of the reasons why Usenet regulars prefer to use a Usenet news reader instead of a Usenet gateway on the Web.

How to Configure Your Browser's News Reader

All news readers receive their newsgroups through a local news server. Your service provider is responsible for maintaining a news server that you can access. Most ISPs and universities do this. You're responsible for configuring your news reader to find the news server.

To use Usenet with your Web browser's news reader, you need to configure your browser with the name of your news server so that it will know where to access Usenet. You need to obtain the name of your local news server from your service provider; check its online documentation or ask its technical support.

If you use Netscape Navigator:

1. From the Edit menu, select Preferences and then expand Mail & Newsgroups.
2. Under Mail & Newsgroups, select Newsgroup Servers and then click Add.
3. In the text box marked Server, enter the host address of your news server.
4. Close all of the windows by clicking OK.

Once you're configured, you launch the news reader by selecting Newsgroups from the Communicator menu.

If you use Internet Explorer, you can access Usenet through Outlook Express:

1. From the Outlook Express Tools menu, select Accounts.

2. Click the News tab, the Add button, and then the News option. The Internet Connection Wizard launches and asks you some questions.

3. In response to the Wizard, enter your name as you want it to appear on your Usenet posts, your e-mail address, and the name of a news (NNTP) server.

4. A pop-up screen appears and asks if you want to download newsgroups from the news server that you have selected. Click Yes.

Once your browser's news reader is configured and you have downloaded the list of available newsgroups, your news server and any subscribed newsgroups will appear in your folders window along with your e-mail servers.

If your service provider does not support a news server, go to **Dark Demon** for a list of publicly available news servers (start with list 1 for the servers with the largest number of newsgroups).

Each news server subscribes to a subset of all of the available newsgroups and stores all of the new messages posted to those newsgroups. Monitoring all of the articles coming into a newsgroup in order to censor specific Usenet posts isn't easy. The decision to add or drop a specific newsgroup is up to the news server's administrators. If you access Usenet through an ISP, the ISP reserves the right to select the subset of Usenet that it feels is appropriate for its customers. Private companies can practice censorship with impunity. In any case, news server memory limitations typically determine how many newsgroups are available on that server. Someone somewhere has to decide what to carry and what to omit; otherwise, nothing will be available.

An article posted to a Usenet newsgroup is first posted to the local news server. Therefore you can usually see your own articles fairly quickly. However, everyone else is not necessarily seeing them that quickly on their own news servers. The news server sends an article that it receives to one or more of its *nearest neighbors*—other news servers nearby on the Internet. As soon as the nearest neighbors receive the article, they post it for their users and then pass it on to all of their nearest neighbors. In this way, articles are distributed across thousands of news servers, moving from neighbor to neighbor much like gossip moving through the grapevine. Eventually, all of the news servers (or more precisely, those that handle the newsgroup to which you posted a message) pick up the new article and make it visible to everyone who reads that newsgroup.

Usenet operates automatically, with software continually running on each news server to keep the newsgroups up-to-date. The same software runs at each site but with different settings for the newsgroups being supported and different expiration policies on those groups. When a new news server is added to Usenet, it's given a feed from a nearby neighbor, as long as it agrees to act as a feed when one of its neighbors comes online and requests a Usenet feed.

No one can know exactly when an article will be visible to specific readers. If articles expire quickly on your own news server, your post might be dropped from your own server before it becomes visible to servers far away. Usenet articles ripple outward from each author, and different servers feel the ripples at different times. Don't be surprised if you see a new reply to one of your own Usenet posts a month after you first posted the article. It can sometimes take that long for everyone to see it.

7.5.1 The Three Levels of Usenet

Different news readers will use different display interfaces, but all support the same basic operations for reading and posting newsgroup articles. In particular, they all must show you Usenet at three levels:

1. The Group Selection Level: This is where you view a list of available newsgroups.
2. The Article Selection Level: This is where you view a list of article headers inside of a given newsgroup.
3. The Article Level: This is where you view a specific article inside of a given newsgroup.

Most *graphical* news readers are designed to show three levels of Usenet at once, in three different windows. In the first window, you navigate the Usenet newsgroups by displaying a set of newsgroups at the Group Selection Level. You choose a newsgroup at this level by clicking it. The next window—the Article Selection Level—displays all of the articles available in that newsgroup. There, you can view the titles and authors of specific articles. Each time that you select a different newsgroup at the Group Selection Level, a new set of articles will be loaded into the Article Selection Level. The third window displays a single Usenet article, its complete header and message body—this is the Article Level. Figure 7.12 shows these three levels of Usenet as they are displayed in Navigator's news reader. The display shows the selection of news.groups.questions at the Group Selection Level and an article written by Mike Betts at the Article Selection Level. The bottom window displays the selected article, which looks very much like an e-mail message.

What If Your Group Selection Level Is Empty?

If you have never used your news reader, your Group Selection Level might not contain any newsgroups. Pick a newsgroup that you want to visit (see the last section on how to find newsgroups), and look for a Load Newsgroup or similar command. In Navigator's news reader, click Add Newsgroup in the File menu. A dialog box will pop up in which you enter the name of a specific newsgroup. Each newsgroup that you will add will appear at the Group Selection Level. You can add as many newsgroups as you want.

Figure 7.12:
The Group
Selection, Article
Selection, and
Article Levels

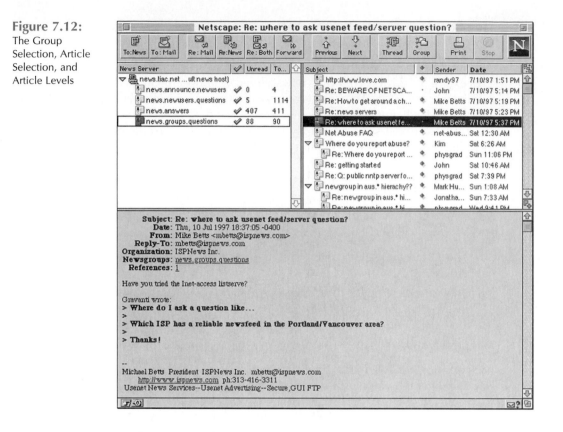

At the Group Selection Level, watch for two numbers next to each newsgroup. The larger number indicates how many articles you've downloaded from that newsgroup. The smaller number represents how many of those articles you've read. Some news readers give you a preference that you can set for the number of articles that you want to download at one time for each newsgroup. A good initial default value for this preference setting is 500. To update your Article Selection Level or load more articles than your download limit allows, look for a Load Messages or similar command. In Navigator's news reader, click Get More Messages in the File menu. See Figure 7.13.

Most modern news readers are threaded news readers. A **threaded news reader** is a news reader that collects all of the replies to a given article and displays them in a group, thereby enabling you to easily follow all of the replies to an initial article. The posting of a reply to a Usenet article begins a thread. If someone replies to that reply, the thread lengthens, becoming a chain of three related articles. There's no limit to how long a thread can be or how many threads can be attached to an initial article. Multiple threads can be attached to articles that are already part of a thread. This gives Usenet discussions a hierarchical structure that can be opened and closed, like the collapsible folders in a hierarchical directory display (for example, the List view in Windows Explorer or the Macintosh Finder).

Figure 7.13:
Navigator's File
Menu (for the News
Reader)

File	
New Web Browser	⌘N
New Mail Message	⌘M
New News Message	
Open News Host...	
Close	⌘W
Save As...	
Remove News Host	
Add Newsgroup	
Get More Messages	
Page Setup...	
Print...	⌘P
Quit	⌘Q

In threaded news readers, look for a Threaded View (or Thread Level) option. When you enter a Threaded View and expand a thread, you can see the headers for all of the thread's articles. In Navigator's news reader, a button in the upper right-hand corner of the Article Selection Level lets you toggle between a threaded display and an *unthreaded display*. The threaded display is better for browsing. Figure 7.14 shows a threaded display from rec.pets.herp.

The unthreaded display shows you all of the articles listed in chronological order, if that is useful to you. Figure 7.15 shows the same newsgroup in an unthreaded display.

Find the article with the `Subject:` field "Mud Dogs ???" in both displays. The threaded display shows that the original Mud Dogs post gathered a thread of four articles over a three-day period. In the unthreaded view, you can see the initial post, but you have to scroll through three days of rec.pets.herp articles in order to find the four replies. The threaded view is much more convenient if you want to read the thread about Mud Dogs.

What's Wrong with the Display?

The first time that you run your graphical news reader, you might find that no newsgroup names appear in the Group Selection Level and no article headers appear in the Article Selection Level. Try resizing the text display fields for these windows. The display windows for your group names and article headers might be too small. By dragging the text field boundaries, you should be able to make text appear on any line that contains a newsgroup icon.

Figure 7.14:
Navigator's
Threaded Display at
the Article Selection
Level

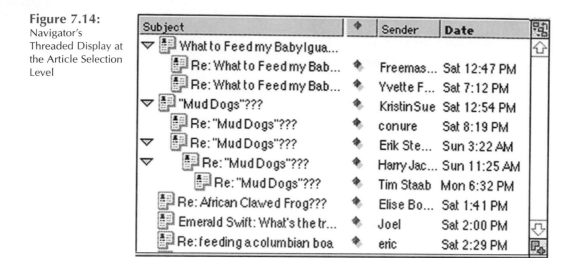

Figure 7.15:
Navigator's
Unthreaded Display
at the Article
Selection Level

Different news readers will display Usenet a little differently. However, you can always expect to find the three levels described previously. By contrast, a text-based news reader such as tin (which runs under UNIX) can show only one level at a time, although all three levels are there. Here is what the Article Selection Level looks like from inside of tin.

```
alt.folklore.urban 140T 473A 0K 0H R)              h=help
 1 +  4    Do CD-ROMs or LPs (remember them?) flow?     Leo G. Simonetta
 2 +  5    Haggis(was:tartan something...                phill malloch
 3 +       Pizza ejaculation                             Widow
 4 +       Do the French really like Jerry Lewis         James K. Lynch
 5 +  2    QWERTY Myth Refuses to Die                    Steve Hutton
 6 + 14    Songs to play during the Apocalypse           Mike Czaplinski
 7 +  2    Gorilla Suit Mischief                         Loren Skaggs
 8 +       Smilies (emoticons)                           mig@satlink.com
 9 +       "Darwin" award winner                         Patrick Fine
10 +       102-year-old dies at birthday party           Patrick Fine
11 +  8    Water being scooped up from lake              Mr. Looney
12 +  3    Two engineer-related stories                  Simon Slavin
13 + 29    Year 2000-leap year (was: 2000 and the comp)  Paul J. Ready
14 + 20    Food stereotype origins?                      Heather Aston
15 +  7    True Story-Body in the Basement               Susan Mudgett
16 +  5    Greetings from Sunny Aukland, California!      mig@satlink.com
```

```
<n>=set current to n, TAB=next unread, /=search pattern, K)ill/select,
a)uthor search, c)atchup, j=line down, k=line up, K=mark read, l)ist
thread, |=pipe, m)ail, o=print, q)uit, r=toggle all/unread, s)ave,
t)ag, w=post
```

This display summarizes the first 16 articles found in the newsgroup alt.folklore.urban, a popular newsgroup dedicated to the origins of pop culture myths. tin is a threaded news reader, so you can see which articles head threads of related articles. A number that follows the + sign indicates how many articles are included in the thread. The longest thread in this display contains 29 articles (headed by article 13).

To see who has contributed to a specific thread, you select an article at the Article Selection Level and issue a List Thread command. The Thread Level looks like this.

```
Thread (Do CD-ROMs or LPs (remember them?) flow?     h=help

0  +  [  20]  Leo G. Simonetta (lsimonetta@gsu.edu)
1  +  [  35]  Leo G. Simonetta (lsimonetta@gsu.edu)
2  +  [  10]  Andrew C Taubman (andrew_taubman@novell.com)
3  +  [  15]  Lon Stowell (lstowell@pyrtech.mis.pyramid.com)
4  +  [  19]  RMSpence (ROT13:Enaql.Fcrapr@zfsp.anfn.tbi)
```

From here, you can select the third response in the thread and hit the Return or Enter key to open it. Then go to the Article Level, where you'll see the following.

```
Tue, 06 might 1997 14:00:20    alt.folklore.urban    Thread    1 of   140
Lines 15        Re: Do CD-ROMs or LPs (remember them?) flow?
Response    3 of    4
lstowell@pyrtech.mis.pyramid.com   Lon Stowell at Pyramid Technology
Corporation

In article <336AC794.6DBB@gsu.edu>,
Leo G. Simonetta <lsimonetta@gsu.edu> wrote:

>According to the Kodak Website that talks about the lifespan of CDs,
>given reasonable care (keeping out of heat and light) the expected
>lifespan of CDs is a minimum of 50 years.  It does not go into any
>detail about what degrades over time - I thought it was delamination
>but there was no mention of it at this Website or any of the other
>two Websites I found using WebCrawler.

  Can't think of anything that would be susceptible to delamination.
  Ordinary CDs are stamped from a master, then the reflective layer
  is applied, then they are usually just lacquered, with the label
  being printed over that lacquer. The reflective layer is extremely
  thin, usually a deposited layer.

<n>=set current to n, TAB=next unread, /=search pattern, K)ill/select,
a)uthor search, B)ody search, c)atchup, f)ollowup, K=mark read,
|=pipe, m)ail, o=print, q)uit, r)eply mail, s)ave, t)ag, w=post

—More—(99%) [1597/1598]
```

Graphical news readers are easier to navigate than are text-based news readers. To switch levels in a graphical news reader, you simply click the appropriate window. To switch levels in a text-based news reader, you have to type the appropriate command. In either case, all news readers work with the same three levels of Usenet. The interfaces might be different, but if you know what to expect from Usenet, you'll be able to navigate your news reader easily.

7.5.2 Posting and Saving Messages

You can reply to an article on a newsgroup either publicly by posting your own article to the newsgroup or privately by sending the author a message via e-mail. Most news readers offer both options. In the text-based tin news reader, discussed briefly in the previous section, a public response on Usenet is called a *follow-up* and a private e-mail response is called a *reply*. In a graphical news reader, the commands for posting Usenet follow-ups and e-mail replies are more intuitive. Figure 7.16 shows the Navigator news reader toolbar, which contains Follow-up and Reply commands (among others). Watch for a Quote command or Quote option that loads the current article into the message body for your follow-ups and replies.

Figure 7.16:
Navigator's News
Reader Toolbar

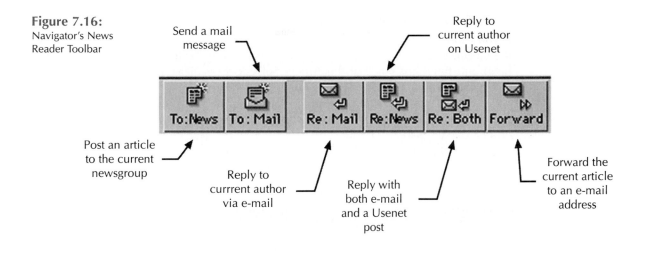

Send a mail
message

Reply to
current author
on Usenet

Post an article
to the current
newsgroup

Reply to
currrent author
via e-mail

Reply with
both e-mail
and a Usenet
post

Forward the
current article
to an e-mail
address

To save a copy of an article or a thread, select it and then forward it to your e-mail
inbox. Alternatively, you can save it directly to a file by using the Save As command
in the File menu. Remember, if you see a Usenet post that you want to save, do so
right away because it might be gone tomorrow.

News Reader Checklist #1

Study the documentation for your news reader and make sure that you know how
to do the following.

1. Start your news reader
2. Scroll through the newsgroups at the Group Selection Level
3. Open a specific newsgroup at the Group Selection Level
4. Post a new article to a newsgroup
5. Scroll through the articles at the Article Selection Level
6. See which articles at the Article Selection Level have threads
7. Open an article or a thread at the Article Selection Level
8. Forward a Usenet post to your e-mail inbox
9. Send an e-mail reply to an article's author
10. Post a follow-up article in response to a specific article
11. Delete an article that you wrote without sending it
12. Exit your news reader

7.5.3 Keeping Track of Messages

If you monitor several newsgroups regularly, you'll want to control the displays at the Group Selection and Article Selection Levels in order to keep track of what you have and have not read. At the Article Selection Level, your display can include either all of the articles currently available on your news server or only those that you haven't read. In Navigator's news reader, the unread articles are marked with a small diamond. From the View → Messages menu (see Figure 7.17), you'll see a choice of two display options: "All" and "Unread." The View All Messages option shows all the articles currently available on the server, and the View Unread Messages option shows only those articles on the server that you have never opened at the Article Level.

Figure 7.17:
Showing All
Messages or Only
Unread Messages

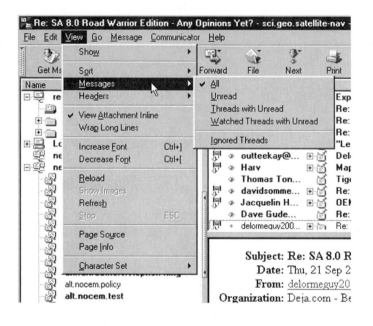

Your reading a Usenet article does not make the article go away. However, it will disappear from your Article Selection Level if you have selected the View Unread Messages option. You can read any article as many times as you want by viewing the View All Messages display. To override the read marker for a specific article, click the diamond—or the alternative dot (.)—in the View All Messages display and manually mark an article as read or unread.

7.5.4 Subscribing and Unsubscribing

Most news readers have some commands that involve the term *subscribe*. This term is a little misleading, however, because you don't have to be a subscriber to read or post to a newsgroup. Newsgroups don't have subscribers in the sense that mailing lists do. Being subscribed to a newsgroup means only that you want to see that newsgroup listed each time that you open up your Group Selection Level. In Figure

7.12, a check mark appears next to each subscribed-to newsgroup at the Group Selection Level. Here are some maneuvering tips.

- To see all of your subscribed-to newsgroups, select the Show Subscribed Newsgroups command from the Options menu (see Figure 7.18).

- To see only the subscribed newsgroups that contain articles that you haven't read yet, select the Show Active Newsgroups command.

- To manually subscribe or unsubscribe to a newsgroup, click the checkmark next to the group. By unsubscribing from a group and issuing the Show Subscribed Newsgroups command, you ensure that the newsgroup just dropped no longer appears in the list.

Figure 7.18:
Navigator's Options Menu (for Its News Reader)

Options
General Preferences...
Mail and News Preferences...
Network Preferences...
Security Preferences...
✓**Show Subscribed Newsgroups**
Show Active Newsgroups
Show All Newsgroups
Show New Newsgroups
✓**Show All Messages**
Show Only Unread Messages
Show All Headers
✓**Add from Newest Messages**
Add from Oldest Messages
Document Encoding ▶
Save Options

You can add newsgroups to the Group Selection Level either individually or as a group. To add them individually, use the Load Newsgroup (or Add Newsgroup) command. To add multiple newsgroups at one time, use the Show All Newsgroups command to see a list of all of the newsgroups available on your news server. Navigate this list (it will appear in a hierarchical system of files and folders), and mark the newsgroups to which you want to subscribe. This works if you know exactly what you want and where to find it, but the Usenet newsgroup hierarchy is not organized for systematic browsing. If you're serious about finding relevant newsgroups, visit the Web and spend some time with a newsgroup search engine.

The News Reader Is Taking Forever—What Is It Doing?

The first time that you issue the Show All Newsgroups command, your news server will download entries for all of its newsgroups. Sometimes, this download is done automatically the first time that you run your news reader. The more comprehensive news servers support at least 30,000 newsgroups, so this might take a few minutes. Fortunately, it takes this long only the first time.

Thereafter, the news reader will need to download only new newsgroups that have appeared since the last update of your newsgroup list. Either this is done automatically each time that you connect, or you might have a Show New Newsgroups command that shows all of the new newsgroups that have been added to your news server since your last newsgroup update. This list can be entertaining, but you probably won't find any groups you care about this way.

7.5.5 Adding Signature Files

Most news readers support a handy convenience: signature files (see Chapter 3). If this feature is available, your news reader will automatically append a signature file of your choice at the end of your Usenet posts. You can use the same signature as for your e-mail messages or create a different one for Usenet. As with mailing list signatures, try not to exceed the standard four-line limit.

7.5.6 Cross-Posting Queries and Messages

Sometimes, you might want to post a query or an announcement to more than one newsgroup. If the same article can go out to multiple newsgroups, you should *cross-post* the article by using the *cross-posting header.* In this way, only one copy of your article is stored on each news server, instead of separate copies for each newsgroup.

Cross-posting is more efficient for you and the Internet, as well as for many of the Usenet users who read your article. When an article is cross-posted to different newsgroups, any follow-up posts are automatically cross-posted as well. This means that a single thread can include participants from any of the cross-posted groups and that all articles in the thread will be visible to everyone in the cross-posted newsgroups. If you post a follow-up in response to a cross-posted article, your follow-up will also be cross-posted to the same newsgroups, unless you make changes to the header generated by your news reader. Many Usenet readers monitor multiple newsgroups that are closely related, so cross-posting saves them time.

Cross-posting is very convenient and appropriate when more than one newsgroup is relevant for the article's subject. However, be careful not to cross-post to inappropriate newsgroups. You can inconvenience a large number of Usenet readers with an irrelevant article, which, if it sparks a discussion, can turn into an irrelevant thread. Think carefully before you post anything to Usenet, and think twice as carefully before you cross-post anything.

An article cross-posted to several newsgroups that you have read from one news-group will be marked as read in all of the other cross-posted newsgroups. This saves you from seeing the same article more than once.

Offline News Readers

If you spend a lot of time in Usenet on a dial-up Internet connection, you can minimize your connect time by using an offline news reader that allows you to read Usenet articles and write your own Usenet posts offline. (This resembles how Eudora allows you to manage your e-mail offline.)

Be careful when you select an offline news reader. Some mangle their article headers and cause substantial problems for news servers. For more information about offline news readers, consult the FAQ file for alt.usenet.offline-readers.

7.5.7 Killing Articles

No one can be barred from a newsgroup for issuing abusive posts, but many news readers can automatically kill articles from a specific user. An article killed by a news reader is automatically marked as read so that it's never seen at the Article Selection Level. Recall that a kill file is a list of users whose posts you don't want to see. You can't control someone's behavior on a Usenet newsgroup, but making that person "invisible" is probably the next best thing. Kill files can be used to fight spam and other forms of Internet abuse in the same way that e-mail filters can save you from seeing a lot of garbage. Some news readers don't support kill files. If you want this feature, investigate the more powerful news readers that provide it.

7.5.8 Experiment before Your First Post

As mentioned earlier in the chapter, when you discover a newsgroup that interests you, plan to lurk for a week or two before you post a message. If you want to ask a question, do so only after you've searched the FAQ for an answer. When you're ready to post your first Usenet article, first try an *experimental post* to ensure that you have all of the software commands under control. However, posting test mes-sages to a regular newsgroup is a violation of Netiquette and might attract some harsh words. The newsgroups misc.test and alt.test are provided for newcomers who want to experiment with their news readers. Use these newsgroups whenever you need to try out a new news reader or to check how a new signature file looks.

You can browse Usenet much like you can browse the Web. Some newsgroups are very entertaining, and others might contain interesting exchanges about your favorite hobby or sport. If you monitor an informative newsgroup over a period of time, you can acquire a specialized education for a specific area of interest.

News Reader Checklist #2

If you have not yet posted a test message to misc.test or alt.test, do it now. Then study the documentation for your news reader to ensure that you know how to do the following.

1. Toggle through different displays at the Group Selection Level
2. Subscribe and unsubscribe to specific newsgroups
3. Set up a signature file for your news reader
4. Cross-post an article
5. Toggle through different displays at the Article Selection Level
6. Unmark a read article so that it's treated as unread
7. Make posts from one person invisible (if your news reader has a kill feature)

7.5.9 Usenet News Readers versus Usenet on the Web

News readers offer useful features that are not available if you view Usenet on the Web at sites such as Deja.com. If your Internet connection is slow, you might find that a news reader is considerably faster than your Web browser, primarily because Usenet is a text-based medium; no graphics consume precious bandwidth. Nevertheless, Web-based gateways to Usenet do have two advantages that you won't find in a news reader.

1. Web gateways make it easy to find newsgroups with full-text keyword searches (see Section 7.6).
2. If you register at Deja.com, you can ask for e-mail notifications when new articles are added to a thread that interests you. This tracking service is an excellent feature for people who are pressed for time but want to get specific information as fast as possible. You can post a query to a Usenet newsgroup, request tracking for any responses to your query, and then check your mailbox to see whether anyone has posted a follow-up to the newsgroup.

Many people prefer Usenet newsgroups to mailing lists because they employ a *pull technology* (see Chapter 6). Once you've mastered a news reader and located the right newsgroups, you can drop in to browse or post only as needed. You can ignore Usenet for several months and when you return, you won't have to deal with months of old messages – the news server will have already cycled through the oldest messages and replaced them with new ones. And if you have a one-time interest in a specific topic, Usenet is an excellent medium for a "hit-and-run" query: Once you get your information, you can disappear and never return.

7.6 ■ LOCATING MAILING LISTS AND NEWSGROUPS

To locate mailing lists on a particular topic, you need to visit *searchable directories*. No searchable directory is comprehensive, so you'll probably want to check out several. Here are some to try.

- For listserv mailing lists, visit the **CataList** site, which includes **a searchable catalog of listserv lists**. The site shows which lists have more than 1,000 subscribers and which lists have more than 10,000 subscribers, so you can determine a list's popularity by its size. You can also conduct keyword searches for specific lists. CataList is part of the official listserv software site.

- For a keyword search for mailing lists, visit the search engine at **Liszt**. Liszt maintains a larger database than does CataList because it contains other types of mailing lists (majordomo, listproc, smartlist, and so on) as well as listserv lists. It also lets you browse mailing list descriptions indexed by broad subject areas. These are fun to explore if you're casting about for new interests.

- To find Web-based mailing lists, you have to visit individual hosting sites. All support search engines or directories so that you can locate the lists that interest you (see Figure 7.19). Be prepared for some lists that have only a few subscribers. These hosting services have made it very easy for anyone to create a Web-based mailing list, many of which have not been promoted or made very visible. A mailing list that does not have enough subscribers might not be worth your time.

Locating Usenet newsgroups is easier than locating mailing lists because all of Usenet is in one place. Finding appropriate newsgroups is relatively straightforward, as they are catalogued and indexed by Usenet databases. Most of these databases are comprehensive, so if a database is up-to-date, you don't have to worry about what it might be missing. Many Web sites offer good search engines for Usenet databases. Use a few good keywords, and you'll be rewarded with descriptions of potentially relevant newsgroups.

News readers are not very helpful when it comes to locating specific newsgroups, unless you already know the name of the desired newsgroup. Many sites on the Web are designed to help you locate Usenet newsgroups and Usenet FAQs. Therefore, when you want to find a newsgroup, visit a newsgroup search engine on the Web *before* you fire up your news reader.

Search or Browse? Which Is Better?

Although all Usenet newsgroups are organized in a hierarchical structure, this doesn't mean that finding newsgroups by browsing the Usenet hierarchy is easy. The Usenet hierarchy was not designed with browsers in mind. It's fun to browse the hierarchy if you have some time to kill, but whenever you need to locate specific newsgroups, go to a newsgroup search engine.

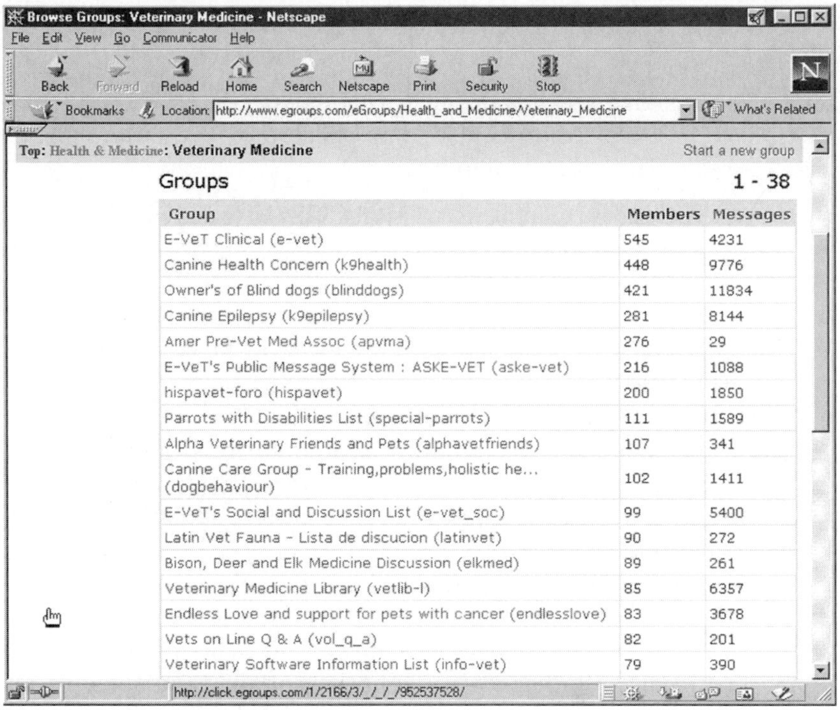

Figure 7.19:
The Most Popular
Veterinary Lists at
eGroups

Suppose that you're considering purchasing an iguana as a pet and you want to see what wisdom Usenet has to offer on the subject of iguanas as pets. Start by visiting a Web-based search engine for all of the current Usenet newsgroups; **Novell** has a good one that's also very easy to use. It refers to Usenet newsgroups as "Novell Forums." In the text box labeled Find on Novel Forums, change the pull-down menu from Forum Titles to Messages. This will return messages from different newsgroups which contain your keywords. Try a single keyword or at most two (see Figure 7.20).

A search using the keyword "iguana" yields approximately a hundred messages, many of which have nothing to do with lizards. But you do see some posts to rec.pets.herp that appear to be on target (see Figure 7.21).

Having located the name of a promising newsgroup, you can either go directly to the newsgroup to review the types of articles posted or visit its FAQ. To visit the newsgroup, you can either launch a news reader (as described in Section 7.5) or browse it from a Web-based gateway to Usenet, such as Novell. For example, to visit the newsgroup rec.pets.herp at Novell, select one of the messages posted to that newsgroup and click its title (see Figure 7.22).

Figure 7.20:

Searching for
Newsgroups at
Novell

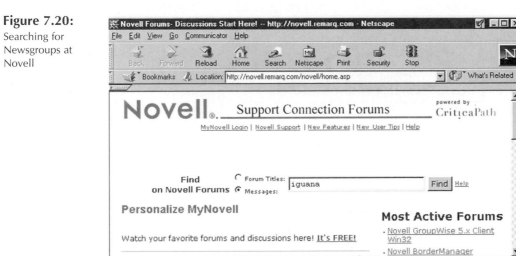

Figure 7.21:

Many Newsgroups
with Messages That
Contain the Word
"Iguana"

Figure 7.22:
Reaching a
Newsgroup by
Selecting One of Its
Articles

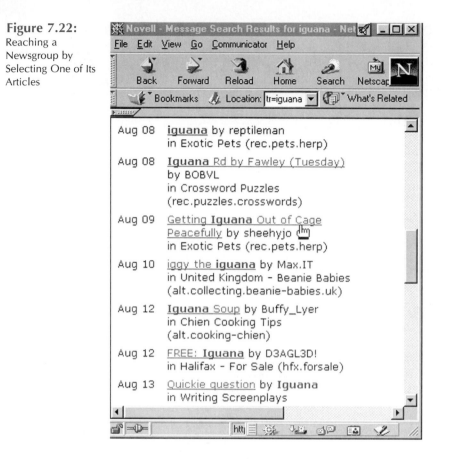

Inside of the message header is a See Also link, more specifically for this example, See Also: Exotic Pets (see Figure 7.23). Note that Novel renames the Usenet news-groups in an effort to be user-friendly. In this case, rec.pets.herp is renamed to Exotic Pets.

Clicking "Exotic Pets" in Figure 7.23 will take you to the Article Selection Level for rec.pets.herp, on which you'll see the most recently posted articles (see Figure 7.24). Click an article's title to see all of the articles for the current thread (includ-ing any replies that might have been posted) on a single Web page.

Remember that each Web-based gateway to Usenet is organized a little differently. The Novell example shows how that site works. Another site might use a different pathway of links to the Article Selection Level for a particular newsgroup. As long as you know what to expect (most important, different newsgroups with an Article Selection Level for each one), you should be able to navigate your way around any Web-based gateway to Usenet.

Figure 7.23:
Novell's See Also
Link Points to a
Newsgroup

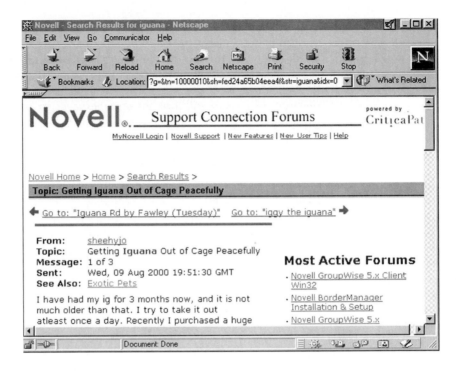

Figure 7.24:
Novell's Article
Selection Level

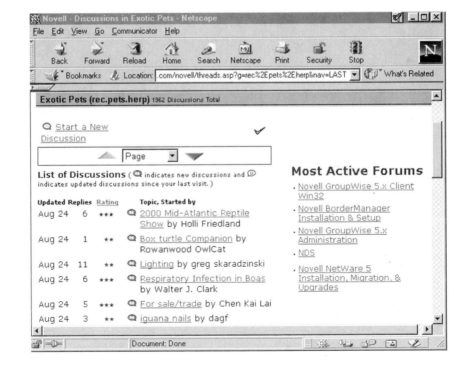

To locate a Usenet article that is no longer in circulation on the news servers, try **Deja.com**. This site offers *retired* Usenet articles, those that are no longer available on any news servers, in a searchable full-text database. It also lets you enter topical keywords in a search mode designed to help you locate relevant newsgroups. Starting from the Deja.com home page, click Search Discussions, enter a keyword, and then click Search. Deja.com will look for any messages in its archive that contain your keyword and show you all of the newsgroups for which hits were found (see Figure 7.25).

For example, enter the keyword "twins." You'll receive a list of those newsgroups that produced hits, including one about baseball and one about multiple births.

The search engine has no way of knowing if you mean sibling twins or the baseball team, the Minnesota Twins. It doesn't realize that this keyword is ambiguous. So it faithfully returns all of the hits it finds for all possible word senses. For a ranked list of newsgroups based on the number of hits found in each newsgroup, use the Deja.com's **Interest Finder** feature (`http://www.dejanews.com/home_if.shtml`).

7.7 INTERNET RELAY CHAT, WEB-BASED CHAT, AND INSTANT MESSAGING

Internet relay chat (IRC), Web-based chat, and instant messaging (IM) are three popular online communications features offered by many large Web portals in an effort to draw people to their sites. They differ from e-mail and Usenet in that they offer *real-time communication*, with response times limited only by participants' typing speed.

Online chat is not as fast as spoken conversation, but it is certainly a step in that direction and can be quite useful if you need a fast response. Occasionally, a story surfaces about someone who communicated an urgent medical emergency to an online chat partner. The partner then notified appropriate authorities, who were able to intervene quickly. If you think that you're having a heart attack while online, you're better off being in a chat room than exchanging messages in a Usenet newsgroup (although a call to 911 is still your best option).

IRC and IM are two separate Internet applications, although they share some features that make them look very similar. Newbies tend to know about IM (especially if they're teenagers), whereas it takes an old-timer (someone who was online before 1996) to know about IRC.

7.7.1 Internet Relay Chat

IRC (Internet relay chat) predates the Web and relies on a system of IRC servers that share common chat channels, much like the Usenet news servers that share common newsgroups. Users can connect to a local IRC server with an IRC client and

Figure 7.25: Deja.com Helping You to Find Newsgroups

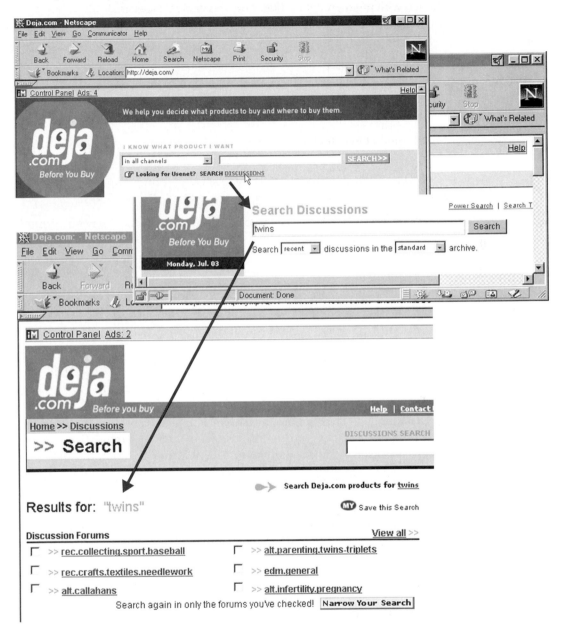

tune into any of the available channels. IRC servers are open to the Internet public, unlike the Usenet news servers that each restrict news access to some fixed set of Internet domains. It is also structured differently from Usenet. Unlike Usenet, which has only one Usenet network that all of the Usenet servers share, different IRC networks each operate its own set of chat channels. The Net offers many free IRC clients, which generally are well documented for newbies.

To try out IRC, download an IRC client and then review the basic commands before you go online. Working with IRC initially might look difficult, but you need only a few commands in order to start chatting. Your IRC client might give you a choice of servers when you first connect: you can pick any of them.

Some Different IRC Networks

Search the Web using the keyword "IRC" to find IRC tutorials and IRC-related Web sites. Then visit some IRC networks to discover whether any interest you.

Here are a few IRC networks to get you started. It doesn't matter which you visit first. *Note*: All IRC clients are compatible with all IRC networks.

   Efnet `http://www.irchelp.org/irchelp/networks/servers/`
   `efnet.html` (the best-known and largest IRC network)

   Undernet `http://servers.undernet.org/` (designed to fix problems at EFnet)

   DALnet `http://www.dal.net/home.html` (designed to fix problems at Undernet)

   IRCnet `http://www.irchelp.org/irchelp/networks/servers/`
   `ircnet.html` (the oldest IRC network; has many European channels)

   Pomme.AppleSlice.Net `http://irc.appleslice.net/` (a small family-friendly network that welcomes visitors of all ages)

Once online, you'll see a list of available channels, with some channels listing their current topics of discussion. The names of the channels are relatively stable, but the topics can change daily or hourly. In a very active channel, the discussion might look confusing because many different discussions probably are going on at once. Any number of people can join a discussion, and some like to monitor multiple chat channels at the same time.

If you want a private conversation with a friend, you can create your own channel and set it up so that others can join by invitation only. This is a great way to save on long-distance telephone calls. IRC is popular among teenagers as a place to meet new people and forge virtual relationships.

Children and Chat

Adult chat channels are not for minors. Unless the chat room is policed, participants are free to indulge in adult conversation, including X-rated language and explicit (albeit text-based) sexual encounters. In addition, IRC attracts pedophiles looking for children to befriend and pursue.

Children should be allowed to participate only in *family-friendly* chat rooms that are policed by adults to keep the content clean and the language proper. ***Any child who goes online should know not to reveal identifying information such as last name, address, telephone number, school attended, and home town.*** When an online relationship crosses over into real-world contact, criminal intent can accompany the seemingly sincere chat buddy. Some children who have revealed personal information during chat sessions have been subsequently abducted, assaulted, and even, in some cases, murdered. Such tragic events have always been a nightmare for concerned parents.

Parents teach their children not to talk to strangers and not to wander off too far from home. They must apply analogous precautions to online encounters. Internet chat with a friend or relative is one thing, but when a child or teenager starts chatting with strangers, serious risks apply.

IRC Privacy

To keep your identity safe, you must use an anonymous remailer. Although IRC channels don't maintain public archives, nothing will prevent someone from creating a searchable archive for IRC, much like the Deja.com archive for Usenet. In fact, **ChatScan** is proposing to do that for both IRC and some large number of Web-based chat rooms. Its intent is to help people locate ongoing conversations in real time, so it will likely maintain more of an IRC "snapshot" than a cumulative archive. Nevertheless, the technology to create large IRC archives is available if someone decides to create one. Extensive IRC chat logs could easily be created by law enforcement agencies during an investigation.

7.7.2 Web-Based Chat

If you have a Java-enabled Web browser, you can participate in thousands of Web-based chat sessions. Often called "live chats" or "chat rooms," these watering holes might or might not have supervisors (most do not) and might or might not focus on a particular topic. Some Web-based chat sessions are scheduled in advance and feature a special guest (see Figure 7.26). Others are always available for anyone who wants to drop in.

No single directory is available of all of the Web-based chat rooms or special events. Individual sites that support many chat activities will have their own directories and might also maintain an archive of chat sessions with public persons such as celebrities, authors, and athletes. Online chat can be fun, but if you're serious about getting answers to specific questions, you'll get better results from an active message board or a Usenet newsgroup.

Figure 7.26:
A Few Live Chat Events Scheduled at `talkcity.com`

Tuesday, March 14 - 6:30PM PT
gazoontite.com presents ...
Managing Pet Allergies with Anton Dotson MD,
and Kathryn Schrader, DVM

Wednesday, March 15 - 5:00PM PT
Chat with Mike Keenan
Stanley Cup-winning coach Mike Keenan shares
NHL insights.

Wednesday, March 15 - 5:00PM PT
Chat with a Columnist
Chat with a columnist attending the Erma
Bombeck Conference.

The Chat Rooms Are Always Empty—What's Wrong?

With so many sites setting up chat rooms for alien abductions, Zen Buddhism, and everything in between, you have to expect that the supply might outstrip the demand. If the chat rooms that interest you are deserted, try some different sites. If you're looking to socialize, you have to find the right watering holes.

Web-based chat is very popular because it requires no software downloads and installations; anyone can jump in anytime. It's so easy a child can do it—and many do. Sites also exist where you can set up your own private chat room for personal conversations.

Locating Chat Rooms

The Web offers many chat directories and chat-related sites. Here are a few popular ones.

Yahoo! Chat `http://chat.yahoo.com` (live chat events, a large number of public chat rooms, and voice chat)

Talk City `http://www.talkcity.com/` (live chat events, public chat rooms, and user-created chat rooms)

The Globe `http://www.theglobe.com/` (public chat rooms, private chat rooms, and chat rooms that support HTML so that you can post small images)

Web-based chat is so popular that some people are setting up chat capabilities on their personal Web page (see Chapter 5). Some of the IRC networks offer Web-based access to their servers so that newcomers can check out the action without downloading an IRC client. In addition, a few commercial Web sites have started to experiment with live chat for real-time customer service and online help. For example, at **Harris Interactive**, you can click the Live Support icon to talk to technical support in a chat session. They'll help you find Harris polls on specific topics (see Figure 7.27). (Be prepared to answer a few personal questions for them in return. After all, Harris *is* a marketing research firm.)

Figure 7.27:
Harris Interactive Offers Chat-Based Support

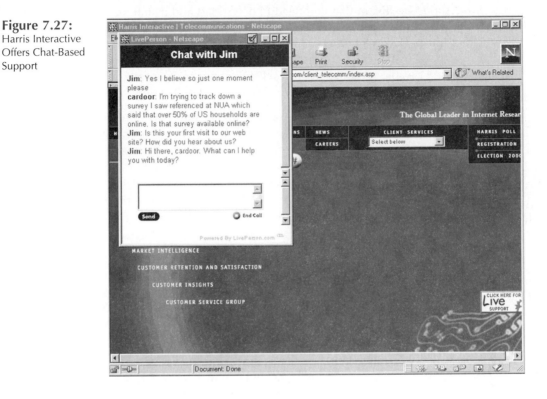

Web-Based Chat Privacy

To keep your identity safe, you must use an anonymous remailer. Most Web-based chat rooms ask you to use a handle. Many people therefore think that their identities are secure. However, many Web sites keep a log of all chat room conversations, along with records that make it possible to trace the handles that people use, either via e-mail addresses or IP addresses.

So-called "private" chat rooms offer no additional privacy as far as these monitoring activities are concerned. Chat rooms are sometimes monitored by the FBI, looking for pedophiles and child pornography operations; the SEC, looking for fraudulent stock market manipulations; and large corporations, looking for libelous statements (see Section 2.10) or the unlawful distribution of proprietary information. See also IRC Privacy in the last section.

7.7.3 Instant Messaging

IM (instant messaging) is another variation on real-time chat that combines elements of both IRC and Web-based chat. It also offers some features not found elsewhere and is user-friendly for newcomers who have little or no experience on the Net.

IM is similar to IRC in that you need to download and install an IM client. It differs from IRC in that each IM network is compatible with only its own proprietary IM client (that's how the owners of the most popular IM clients want it). For example, if you have installed AOL's Instant Messenger (AIM), which has 45 million users, you won't be able to talk to people on ICQ's network of 50 million users (ICQ stands for "I Seek You"). To access ICQ, you have to install its client software.

No industry standards exist yet to enable interconnected communications across different IM networks, and commercial competition among the IM networks does not encourage such a cooperative effort. As a result, you need to consider your client options very carefully. Find out which are being used by the people to whom you want to talk. If everyone you know is using AIM, then that's the client you want. (By the way, you do not need to be an AOL subscriber in order to download and use AIM.) If you're lucky, you will need only one client.

AOL: The Leader in IM

Smaller IM communities are pushing for industry standards so that users with different IM clients can communicate with each other. AOL, which owns both AIM and ICQ, is resisting. In 1999, releases of Microsoft Network (MSN) Messenger were compatible with AIM, thereby enabling MSN users to communicate with AIM users (much to AOL's displeasure).

AOL tries to keep its IM community to itself, and Microsoft keeps finding loopholes in AOL's software. If AOL wants to keep its users safely segregated from other IM communities, it needs to maintain secure IM servers.

All IM clients give you access to many public chat rooms; however, those are not their most popular feature. They also support private chat between pairs of people, and this is where most IM communication happens. Chat rooms filled with many strangers tend to be chaotic, in which little serious conversation can occur (see Figure 7.28). Silliness is the norm, and thoughtful communication is difficult to sustain. People who are experienced with online chat tend to split off from the crowd for more manageable pairwise conversations. The original IRC servers supported private conversations for this reason, so there's nothing new about IM—it's basically an old idea repackaged for a point-and-click audience.

Any two people who have registered with the same IM network can page each other and set up a private chat session, for example, to exchange pleasantries, communicate details of travel arrangements, or negotiate a restaurant for dinner. IM paging is faster than e-mail but does require that both parties be online.

Figure 7.28:
Silliness as the
Norm in Many Chat
Rooms

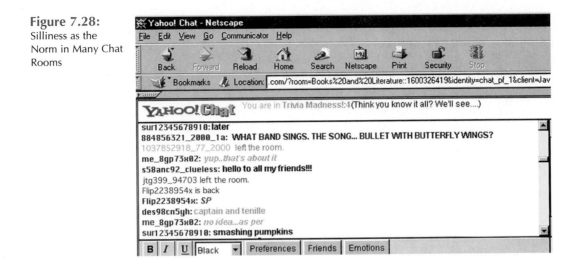

How to Start a Private Conversation

In AIM, send the other party an *instant message* that includes an invitation to talk. The other person can use the same window in which the invitation appears to reply (new text can be added to the window in the frame on the bottom), and you can hold a conversation there.

In ICQ, when you send an invitation to chat a special chat window will open up in which you can converse. Each client works a little differently but they all do more or less the same things.

If you visit a chat room and meet someone who looks friendly, you might initiate a private conversation with that person. Even in this more workable environment, however, conversations via keyboard are a little awkward. People can't type as fast as they can talk, so these real-time interactions favor short statements, telegraphic writing, and rapid responses. Worse, you can't see what your partner is typing until that person hits the Return or Enter key, so there are periodic pauses when nothing is happening on the screen and you're probably both typing something just to keep the conversation going. This can result in questions and answers that are interleaved and mixed up—much like having different conversational threads ongoing with the same person (something that doesn't happen with other communication media). Figure 7.29 shows an IM conversation with AIM in which some questions and answers show up out of order, even though both parties are trying to be polite and respond to all questions.

Figure 7.29:
Even a Two-Person
Conversation Can
Spawn Multiple
Threads

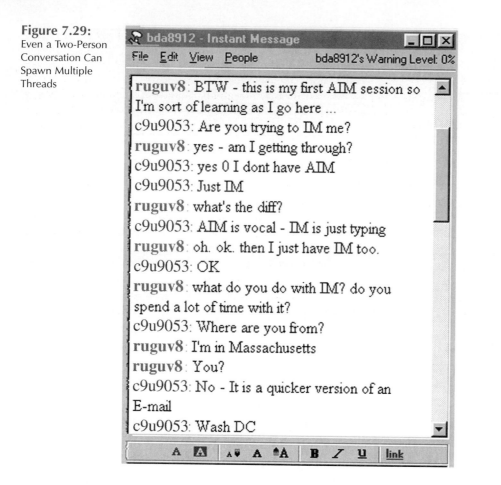

Getting Started with Live Chat

Here are some tips for engaging in live chats:

- Begin by using one of the simpler chat clients, such as AIM.
- Try talking in an IM window instead of a chat room—it's less confusing.
- Keep your questions and answers short. Don't try to say too much at once.
- To keep the conversation going, ask lots of questions.
- Don't be offended if your partner decides to leave abruptly (life is short).
- Learn how to insert emoticons to make up for the absence of vocal intonations and body language.

If you want, you can turn your computer into a telephone. Simply install a microphone and use voice chat. Many software packages now enable free long-distance telephone calls over the Internet by using either voice-enabled chat servers or special *telephony servers*. The jump from real-time chat to voice chat is not technically difficult. Once you have the IM software in place, you use a microphone instead of a keyboard and modify the chat software to handle audio files as well as text files. You'll have a plausible imitation of a telephone (although bandwidth bottlenecks and Net congestion can cause noticeable breaks and lags). Telephony is discussed in more detail in the following Above and Beyond.

If you find yourself spending a lot of time with real-time chat and IM, consider investigating some of the more sophisticated chat clients such as ICQ. ICQ is a full-featured client that offers a vast selection of online communities and many nice extras. For example, to contact people who are not currently online, you can drop a note into their message boxes for them to see when they come online. This resembles sending e-mail, except that you don't need to start a mail client and you don't need an e-mail address. ICQ also supports two chat modes for those who want to experiment with different options. In **IRC-mode chat**, no text appears until the user hits the Return or Enter key. In **split-mode chat**, each letter appears as it's typed. When two people chat using split-mode chat, the online conversations are more like real conversations.

IM Clients

AIM is the leading IM client. ICQ is also very popular, although it's somewhat more complicated and less easy to use. AIM is a better choice for beginners.

AIM	`http://www.aol.com/`
ICQ	`http://www.icq.com/`

Although AIM and ICQ are the two largest IM clients, others are available, including all of the following freeware clients.

Infoseek PeopleLink	`http://www.peoplelink.com/`
Yahoo! Messenger	`http://pager.yahoo.com`
PowWow	`http://www.tribal.com`
iChat	`http://www.ichat.com`

ICQ is a good place to hook up with people who share very specific interests. For example, if you want to learn about Internet telephony and voice chat, you can join a chat group devoted to that topic and be informed whenever another member of that group is online. You can also register your own interests in terms of a fixed set of categories so that others with similar interests can find you, even if they don't know you (see Figure 7.30).

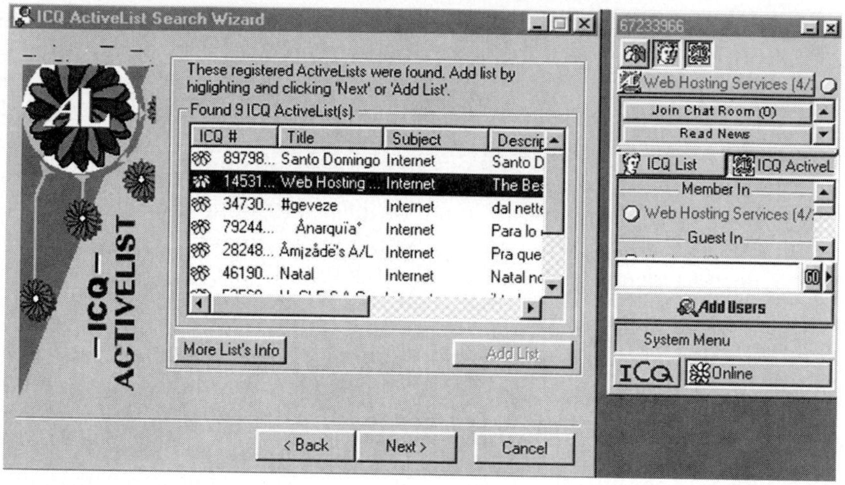

Figure 7.30:
ICQ ActiveLists
Help People Meet
People

If you're concerned about your privacy, do not reveal personal information when you set up a chat client or register at Web-based chat sites. Chat rooms are the venue of choice for pedophiles, stalkers, and other potentially dangerous individuals. The anonymity and fast-paced atmosphere of a chat room gives some people license to indulge aspects of their personality that normally might be suppressed. Always consider your personal safety.

IM clients are designed to track people online. If you're running AIM and other people running AIM add you to their "Buddy List," they will be informed each time that you connect to the Net and each time that you disconnect. They can also know when you're online but idle. This might not strike you as a serious invasion of privacy, especially if the person tracking you is a close friend. But it's not wise to have your movements watched by strangers, especially if you reveal patterns and routines that might tell someone when you're normally at home and when you aren't. If someone learns something about your lifestyle, where you live, and when your home is empty, you've set yourself up for a possible attack or burglary. When it comes to online chat with strangers, expect the worst and proceed with caution.

Administrators for chat networks understand the potential risks of their enterprises, and try to give users appropriate tools for personal safety (see Figure 7.31). Unfortunately, few newbies take the time to learn much about the software that they use and most service providers don't assume responsibility for the education of their accountholders.

For example, not all AOL subscribers realize that their online comings and goings can be tracked by anyone who knows their AOL userid, which happens to be the same userid used for AOL's e-mail addresses. To disable this rather controversial feature, you need to change the AIM access setting from its default option (which makes you visible to everyone) to a more secure option (which makes you visible to no one or only to people whom you select). First launch AIM, and then, from the File menu, select My Options, Edit Preferences, and the Control tab (see Figure 7.32).

System security is another risky aspect of IM clients. If you have AIM installed on your computer and some malicious individual tampers with the settings, they might open the door for unlimited file transfers onto your machine. Even worse is leaving

Figure 7.31:
Personal Privacy
Options for AIM

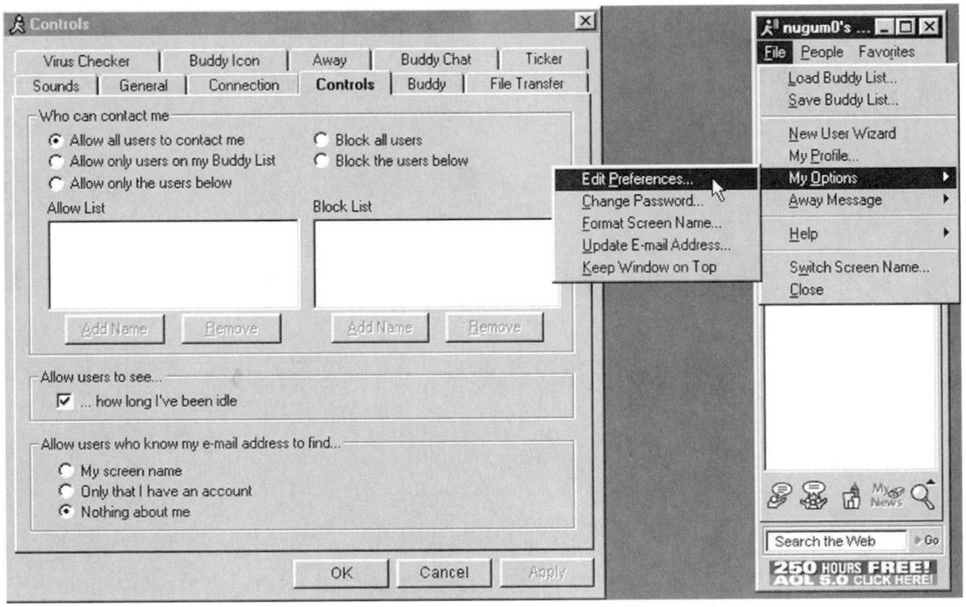

Figure 7.32:
Setting AIM Privacy
Options

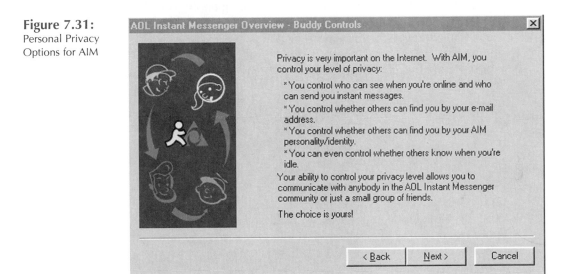

a computer online and unattended with an IM client running. This is like leaving your front door wide open and then going away for a week. As mentioned earlier in the book, it's never a good idea to keep a live Internet connection unattended for long periods of time.

Some people who get involved with online chat become addicted to it. They spend so much time chatting with people that it interferes with more important activities and responsibilities. Psychologists are studying this phenomenon in an effort to understand who is at risk and to devise the means to spot and help addicts (see Section 7.8). If you think that you might be becoming addicted, don't wait for the self-help books on Internet addiction to appear. You can visit alt.irc.recovery on Usenet and determine whether the technology that got you into trouble can help you get out of it.

IM Privacy

To keep your identity safe, you must use an anonymous remailer. Your privacy can be safeguarded with the right security and preference settings. Always hide your e-mail address and your IP address.

A poorly configured IM client represents a serious security risk, which can, in turn, result in a major invasion of your privacy. For example, some IM clients support file sharing, which is a very powerful feature. However, it can also open your entire hard drive to total strangers, if you don't carefully manage your preference settings. Whenever you install a new IM client, take some time to learn about your preferences before you go live.

7.8 ■ THE PSYCHOLOGY OF CHAT ROOMS

People, when online, often behave differently than they do in real life. Shy, introverted people become uninhibited and gregarious. People who are courteous and polite become hostile and abusive. Men pretend to be women, and women pretend to be men. Nowhere are these transformations more common than in chat rooms. Interestingly, chat rooms are also the most popular online activity for people who are pathologically dependent on the Internet.

When Does the Internet Become a Problem?

In one study, a group of Internet addicts were asked with which Internet applications they spent the most time. The results reveal that the most compelling applications involve interactive communication in real-time—chat and fantasy chat. The least compelling applications involved no human interactions—the Web and FTP. Here are the results of the study.

Feature	Percent of Time Spent
Chat	35%
MUDs (real-time chat in a fantasy game)	28%
Newsgroups	15%
E-mail	13%
Web	7%
Other (for example, gopher and FTP)	2%

Real-time interactive communication, along with online anonymity, is a powerful combination. Anonymity gives people license to experiment with different online personalities, fantasy lifestyles, and erotic relationships. When this freedom allows people to release repressed rage, to fantasize a life better than the one that they have, or simply to take a mental vacation from the daily grind, the Internet can become an irresistible and sometimes uncontrollable habit.

Even psychologically stable individuals can regress into anti-social behavior on the Internet. People who are perfectly reasonable in real life have been known to launch flame wars. Both men and women who would never be sexually aggressive in any other setting find it easy (and fun) to "hit" on people online. Online communities invite people to indulge themselves in behavior that would be censured in the real world. When people interact online, the experience may feel more like a video game than a conversation with a real person. It is easy to forget that real people are behind the words that appear on a computer monitor— responses are disembodied, and real people begin to resemble characters in a video game. It follows that if the people you meet online aren't real people, then no serious consequences will result from your actions (unless perhaps your actions violate an AUP).

Some chat rooms try to impose a social order by adopting strict AUPs. Others seem to condone an "anything goes" attitude whereby people can indulge themselves in impulsive or anti-social behaviors without fear. An opportunity to play out fantasies and escape real life might be one component of a compulsive Internet personality.

At the same time, the Internet encourages emotional bonding and emotionally intimate relationships that are free from the traditional requirements of shared experiences. Two people can enter into a purely verbal relationship unencumbered by the complications of physical chemistry, body language, and the slower rituals of socialization in real life.

A relationship based on nothing but an exchange of words is a peculiar animal. Emotionally rich fantasies about the other person can be encouraged and nurtured even as deep personal truths are revealed and souls are bared. Participants in long-time cyber-relationships often fear the possibility of a face-to-face meeting, especially if they have shared their innermost beliefs, desires, hopes, and dreams. People instinctively seem to understand how much interpersonal give-and-take is missing from a relationship made of nothing but words. The eyes see no face, and the ears hear no voice. No gestures are seen, no facial expressions are read, no intonations are interpreted, and no eye contact is made. Any or all of these missing components can contradict an ideal person constructed from words and expectations. A simple exchange of photographs could easily jar some ideal mental image, however vague, that can exist only in the mind's eye.

The computer keyboard fosters a paradoxical type of intimacy. People can dive into an exchange of personal information about themselves on a first meeting and feel perfectly comfortable revealing all sorts of things, with the exception of a real name. Many people find it easy to open up and reveal intimate details about themselves as long as these online revelations are safely separated from real life. However, the level of trust in an online relationship is very delicate and could be threatened by a partner who wants to cross the line to a real-life meeting. Even when no lies have been told and no facts have been twisted, the difference between an online relationship and a real-life relationship might be far too threatening to contemplate.

Some Fantasy Games Are Not Cool, Even in a Chat Room

Any online talk about murder or mayhem might prompt someone to save the transcript to a file and report it to both system administrators and the police. An ISP can consult its log files to determine who was in which chat rooms when and then release all such information to law enforcement authorities. If a transcript of an online chat session is deemed admissible as evidence in a court of law, someone's "harmless" fantasy game could result in a prison sentence or a fine. The "fantasy defense" has not yet been tested in court, but it looks weak.

In addition, the FBI has conducted a number of successful chat room sting operations in order to catch pedophiles trying to contact minors or to trade child pornography.

If you want to joke around about sex with children, doing away with your spouse, or pulling off a Rambo-style massacre at the local post office, don't do it with strangers in a public chat room. You could get more of a reaction than you expected.

People who insist on anonymity behind a pseudonym or a P. O. box number are often viewed with suspicion. Anonymous letters to the editor are tolerated for the sake of free expression, but in most contexts, anonymity is perceived as a dark, vaguely threatening shadow of a person with something to hide. People withholding their true identities tilt the playing field in their direction. They know who you are, but you can't know who they are. From the perspective of the mystery person, there might be something thrilling about the act of secrecy. For example, before the advent of caller ID for telephone calls, mischievous children delighted in making prank telephone calls. Even children know that some things you can do only when your identity is safely hidden.

In a chat room setting, anonymity is not only accepted but expected. People are allowed and encouraged to identify themselves by online handles. This acceptance of anonymity suggests that some rules of social conduct might be suspended. For many people, this freedom can translate into regressive behavior or dishonesty. For people with serious psychological problems, however, the absence of social censure in a chat room can open doors that might be better left closed. It's doubtful that chat rooms transform normal, well-adjusted people into pedophiles or misogynists, but they certainly can bring any such nascent tendencies to the surface. A sociopath would be hard-pressed to come up with a more comfortable place to hang out than an Internet chat room.

On the brighter side, some online communities offer heart-felt support and understanding to participants. Online friendships quickly blossom among people who share a passion for some common interest. For members of groups that are organized around personal problems or health concerns, daily conversation and member updates provide a foundation of support that is difficult to obtain elsewhere. A sensitive health problem might be easier to discuss online than face-to-face, and a good online support group will be a source of caring conversation and constant encouragement. More serious communications seem to thrive on e-mail-based mailing lists, where there's a stronger sense of a stable and controlled community. Newcomers are always welcome, but disruptive behavior won't be tolerated by the list owner.

Online communication provides a safe haven for the expression of inner thoughts and suppressed emotions. The resulting sense of freedom can manifest itself irresponsibly or lead to a genuine sense of community. To witness a virtual community rally on behalf of a community member, subscribe to a mailing list for dog owners and watch what happens when someone reports the passing of a beloved canine companion. (Search for "Rainbow Bridge" on the Web to get a sense of the emotional intensity associated with these communications. Rainbow Bridge is a description of "dog heaven" which is frequently passed along to members of mailing lists for dog owners to console fellow members at times of bereavement. Variations on Rainbow Bridge have been written for other pets as well, including goldfish.) The Internet can be a gentle, compassionate place or one in which idiocy reigns supreme. In this respect, life online is not so very different from life in the real world.

Things to Remember

- When you join a new mailing list, lurk for a while before you post.
- Find out if a mailing list is archived for public consumption before you post sensitive information to the list.
- Before you post a question to a Usenet newsgroup, check to see if you can find the answer in its FAQ file.

- Search for newsgroups on the Web, but use a threaded news reader if you want to track Usenet posts and threads regularly.
- Alwa   a handle when you sign on for any type of online chat session.
- Be ca   iving out personal information when you talk to strangers during chat se
- Locate and understand all available privacy settings before you use an IM client.
- Never post sensitive information to a newsgroup or a chat room unless you're comfortable with the possibility of its being archived and released for public consumption.
- If you do something illegal in a chat room, your identity can be traced.

Important Concepts

instant messaging—a private communication channel between people who use the same IM client software; typically used by people who know each other and want to stay in close touch.

mailing list—a discussion forum in which subscribers post messages via e-mail.

news reader—client software for reading and posting messages to Usenet newsgroups.

real-time chat—a public communication channel whereby people gather in a chat room to exchange typed messages in real time.

Usenet newsgroup—a discussion forum within the Usenet hierarchy in which anyone can drop in to ask questions or post messages.

Web-based message board—a discussion forum on the Web that normally requires you to register with the Web site if you want to post messages.

Where Can I Learn More?

E-Mail Discussion Groups/Lists/ Resources
   http://www.webcom.com/impulse/list.html
news.newusers.questions
   http://www.geocities.com/ResearchTriangle/8211/
IRC Networks and Server Lists
   http://www.irchelp.org/irchelp/networks/
Essays: Virtual Communities   http://netculture.about.com/library/
   weekly/msub16.htm

Problems and Exercises

1. Compare and contrast a site-specific discussion group on the Web with a Web-based chat room. Give at least one difference and two similarities.

2. Compare and contrast e-mail-based mailing lists with Usenet newsgroups. Which is a pull technology, and which is a push technology? Which is better if you want to create your own archive of all of the messages during a two-month period? Which is better if you want only to see some messages once in a while, when you have the time?

3. What is a mailing list digest? How is it useful?

4. Explain the difference between a mailing list's distribution address and its list command address.

5. Are some newsgroups easier to create than others? Explain.

6. Name and describe the three levels of Usenet that all news readers display.

7. What is the difference between a follow-up to a Usenet article and a reply to a Usenet article?

8. If you post an article to a Usenet newsgroup, how long will it take for it to appear on all of the news servers? How long will it be visible on each server? Will it be visible eventually on all news servers? Explain your answer.

9. Which of the following are organized into one comprehensive directory?

    a. All of the e-mail-based mailing lists

    b. All of the Web-based mailing lists

    c. All of the Usenet newsgroups

    d. All of the IRC channels

    e. All of the Web-based chat rooms

    f. All of the live chat events on the Web

    g. All IM users

10. In each of the following pairs of activities, name the activity that is easier. If you're not sure what is meant by "easier," ask yourself which activity would take less time.

    a. Starting your own e-mail-based mailing list or starting your own Web-based mailing list

    b. Starting your own private Web-based chat room or starting your own IRC network

    c. Contacting people who use three different IM servers or contacting people who are subscribed to three different e-mail-based mailing lists (assume that you're subscribed to the mailing lists)

    d. Finding a high-traffic Usenet newsgroup on a specific topic or finding a high-traffic mailing list on the same topic

11. What is cross-posting on Usenet and how is it useful?

12. Is it better to search for newsgroups by using a news reader or a Web browser? Explain your answer.

13. Suppose that you want to track a current thread on a Usenet newsgroup and you want to receive e-mail alerts whenever a new article is posted to the thread. How can you set this up?

14. If a chat room's AUP prohibits foul language and cybersex, does that mean a monitor will be present to police the chat room? What can happen to you if you violate the AUP?

15. Are conversations in a private chat room really private? Explain your answer.

16. Compare and contrast IRC with Web-based chat. Give at least four differences and two similarities.

17. In general, where does more Net abuse occur: on Usenet newsgroups or on mailing lists? Explain your answer.

18. Can people with different IM clients talk to each other? Can people with different IRC clients talk to each other? Can people with different Web browsers talk to each other if they use the same Web-page chat site? Which of these scenarios benefits from an industry standard to ensure software compatibility?

19. ICQ supports both IRC-mode chat and split-mode chat. Decide which of these two modes consumes more bandwidth. Explain your reasoning.

20. The file transfer feature in AIM is convenient when friends want to exchange photographs or audio files. Users can set preference settings for this feature to allow incoming file transfers by (1) anyone, (2) anyone on a specified Buddy List, (3) people specifically listed in the preference settings, or (4) no one. Which options seem reasonable to you? Are you completely safe if you select (4)? Can you imagine scenarios in which (1) would make sense? Do you think (2) or (3) could be regrettable choices? Explain your answers.

Joining a Virtual Community: Above and Beyond

Censorship on the Internet

If your goal is to reach as many people as possible as cheaply as possible, Usenet probably looks like a gift from God. However, it might become tedious to send out the same ad to 30,000 newsgroups manually. So thoughtful programmers have written spambots, which conveniently automate the process. A **spambot** is a program that enables you to post a message to thousands of Usenet newsgroups in only a few seconds. Of course, this is Internet abuse (spamming), so you'll want to cover your tracks. A few states are experimenting with statutes intended to make spamming illegal, but this is still very murky legal territory.

Famous Moments in the History of Spam

In 1994, two attorneys, Laurence A. Canter and Martha S. Siegal, became infamous for hawking their immigration green card services on more than 7,000 newsgroups. Although Usenet spamming was not unusual, the popular press picked up on this incident, probably because the perpetrators were attorneys who openly identified themselves and publicly argued that their activities were perfectly legal. Both claimed that the Internet had outgrown its insular academic origins and was now open territory for commercial advertisements.

Given the absence of laws and regulations regarding the Internet, Netizens were naive to think that voluntary Netiquette would be an adequate mechanism for regulating behavior on the Internet. This affront to the Net culture symbolized a turning point for the Internet. Some people even predicted its imminent death. Others decided to fight fire with fire (see later in the chapter).

Usenet articles have an interesting property that makes them very different from e-mail messages. Unlike with e-mail, a message that has been posted (to a newsgroup) can be canceled via a Cancel command. The Cancel command originally was intended to be used only by the author of an article, in the event that the author noticed an egregious error or a disastrous typographical error after the article was posted. A news server won't honor a Cancel command unless it's convinced that it comes from the same person who posted the article. A Cancel command that is accepted is distributed to all of the other news servers until the article has been removed from all of Usenet.

However, with a little trickery, a person can fool a news server into thinking that someone is the original author of an article when they aren't. This means that anyone can, in principle, cancel someone's Usenet article. Unauthorized Usenet can-

445

cellations normally represent a serious breach of Netiquette and are dealt with very harshly by system administrators.

Censorship or Self-Preservation?

In 1995, members of the Church of Scientology canceled Usenet articles posted by people who were critical of Scientology. The Scientologists argued that their actions were justified because the canceled posts contained copyrighted material used without permission.

Are copyright violations a valid reason for unauthorized cancellations? Who has the right to evaluate a possible copyright violation? Many people felt that the Church was practicing censorship. Censorship is a very real danger on Usenet, and you don't have to be in a position of authority to act as a censor.

Cancelbots and NoCeM

Third-party article cancellations are not strictly a "bug" in news reader software. Third-party cancellations are also a "feature" because they offer a technical solution to spam. Someone so inclined can monitor a newsgroup for spam and issue an unauthorized cancellation to kill any offending articles from all of Usenet. Although this is a controversial practice, most Usenet users approve of this solution. Worries about censorship and freedom of speech tend to fade when one is confronted with too many unwanted advertisements and diatribes about gun control or abortion.

Cancelbots Programs called **cancelbots** have been designed to detect spam, not on the basis of content, but on the basis of multiple postings. If the same article has been cross-posted too many times (posts to 15 or more newsgroups is often used as the trigger number), a cancelbot will recognize it as spam and issue a Cancel command.

One famous cancelbot operated anonymously for a time under the name "Cancelmoose." Cancelmoose acted with the utmost sensitivity for the rights of all Internet users. Whenever a spam was canceled, Cancelmoose issued a notice explaining the action and included full copies of the spam message. In this way, users could not claim that *their right to see spam* had been violated.

Now the spam was neatly bundled inside of identifiable notices from Cancelmoose. If you had a kill file, you could add Cancelmoose to your kill file and never see spam again. In addition, local administrators have the option of overriding Cancelmoose and refusing to allow cancellations originating from Cancelmoose. In that way, each news server could make its own policy decision with respect to Cancelmoose's actions and support Cancelmoose, or not. The war between the spambots and cancelbots is one arena in which the culture of the Internet has taken matters into its own technological hands.

NoCeM   The most recent solution to the spam problem on Usenet is a piece of software called **NoCeM** (pronounced "No See 'Em"). At this time, NoCeM is available only for UNIX news readers; however, it might become an option for other platforms if it catches on in the UNIX community. (A similar NoCeM system is under development for mailing lists.)

Here's how it works. A user who sees spam on Usenet posts, on a special newsgroup called alt.nocem.misc, a notice that describes the offending article. When a NoCeM-enabled news reader starts up, it checks alt.nocem.misc for spam notices and kills any targeted articles for which it's authorized to do so. Authorization is needed lest random censors place notices on alt.nocem.misc in an effort to kill articles that they don't like.

To authorize a NoCeM action, each NoCeM user first must create a file of authorized signatures that represent individuals whom the user trusts to issue spam notifications. The NoCeM software acts only on notices posted with authorized signatures. These signatures are encoded by using the encrypting software PGP (Pretty Good Privacy) (see Chapter 11) in order to prevent forgeries. Thus if you have one trusted individual monitoring each newsgroup for spam, then you simply collect the signatures for the spam monitors who handle the newsgroups that you read. This takes some extra effort by users, who must collect the signatures, and certainly on the part of the monitors, who must post notices to alt.nocem.misc. However, if the system were used by everyone who read Usenet, the audience for spam would be reduced to zero, as would the incentive to post spam on Usenet. NoCeM clients could also operate at the level of a local news server, thereby saving everyone on that server from having to manage NoCeM signatures on their own.

If automated cancelbots could be trusted to identify spam on the basis of frequency counts and if news servers implemented NoCeM software at the server level, then individual users would benefit from the actions of the NoCeM system without any extra overhead or inconvenience. Perhaps these technological solutions can eliminate spam from the Internet without any legal intervention.

Privacy Safeguards

The Usenet community was struggling with questions of online privacy long before the Web was born, and some of its solutions work for the Web as well. In general, you should assume that anything that you put online will always be online, so think before you post. This is true for Web pages as well as Usenet articles and archived e-mail messages. In particular, be careful where you post your e-mail address, lest it be picked up by an address harvester. An **address harvester** is a program that searches the Web and Usenet for e-mail addresses. Once yours has been harvested, you can become a spam magnet. The more visible your e-mail address, the more spam that you'll likely get. Spambots were first active on Usenet, so Usenet message authors were the first to figure out how to fool them.

Spoofing Your E-Mail Address to Fool Spambots The trick to fooling spambots is to post your e-mail address in a way that makes your correct e-mail address obvious to a human being but useless to spambots. Address harvesters are designed to collect addresses without human intervention. No person ever reviews the list of addresses that an address harvester generates in order to remove or correct invalid addresses. Some lists contain millions of addresses—if a person had to review each entry, the cost of doing business would be prohibitive. Therefore it's easy to trick the address harvester into accepting an address that won't work.

Suppose that your real e-mail address is

```
bob544@ucs.madison.edu
```

You could use a variation on your real address when you put your address on the Web, Usenet, or a mailing list. The following examples are some possibilities, all involving adding extra, irrelevant, characters. People who understand the trick will know to delete the extra characters in order to arrive at your valid e-mail address.

```
bob544NOSPAM@ucs.madison.edu
bob544@SPAM-ME-NOTucs.madison.edu
bob544SPAMMERS-DIE@ucs.madison.edu
bob544REMOVE-THIS@ucs.madison.edu
```

To ensure that your e-mail recipients can figure out what they are to do, you can explain what to do, near the address, like this:

```
bob544NOSPAM@ucs.madison.edu
```
(to mail me, remove **NOSPAM** from the address above)

By doing this, everyone but the spammers win. The spambot is not smart enough to read the instructions, but people are (you hope). You'll see this trick used often on Usenet, where the user population is relatively savvy about online privacy. It's less common on the Web, so explanations are probably needed more often on a Web page.

Note that you cannot use this trick with mailto: links in an HTML page. If you alter an e-mail address inside a mailto: link, people will end up trying to send mail to an invalid address when they click on the link. But there is a different trick that can be applied to mailto: links if you want to protect your e-mail address on a Web page (see Exercise #7 in Chapter 8).

Using X-No-Archive: Keep Your Articles Out of the Deja.com Archive Another insiders trick is available if you want to post articles to Usenet but not have them archived by Deja.com. Before you post an article to a Usenet newsgroup, add an extra header line before the `Subject:` field:

```
X-No-Archive: Yes
```

Some news readers make doing this easier than others. If you're having trouble figuring out how to add this extra header line, consult **Windows-Help.NET** for instructions. If you still can't do this, you can add this line as the first line of message body. In the article's body, it will be a little more distracting, but the archiving software will still recognize it.

Anonymizers If you want to interact with people on the Internet, but require absolute anonymity, don't trust your ISP to keep your identity safe. Services called **anonymizers** will "launder" your identity for you, thereby making it impossible for anyone to find out who you are. Anonymizers can protect you when you surf the Web and can give you anonymous e-mail service. Anonymizer products and services vary and might become more popular as Internet users become more aware of privacy risks online. For more information, do an online search using the keyword "anonymizer."

Using TRUSTe to Achieve Privacy If you're concerned about personal privacy, locate privacy policies each time that you interact with a Web site that is new to you, use a cookie manager to disable profiling software (see Chapter 9), and take steps to minimize spam. However, if you want to take these steps, but you don't want to spend a lot of time at it, be on the lookout for shortcuts.

One helpful shortcut is to click the **TRUSTe privacy icon** (see Figure 7.33), which connects you with a site's privacy policy. Many consumers are reassured to see the TRUSTe icon and assume that when a site has TRUSTe certification, their privacy is adequately protected. However, you should always review a site's privacy policy, even if the TRUSTe icon is present. Some privacy advocates fear that the TRUSTe "stamp of approval" does not represent a sufficiently stringent standard for consumer privacy.

Figure 7.33:
The TRUSTe Icon That Connects You to a Web Site's Privacy Policy

Privacy awareness and safeguards will grow as people better understand the potentially intrusive capabilities of the Internet. To stay current about available options and developments, visit **EPIC** (the Electronic Privacy Information Center), a clearinghouse for all Internet-related privacy concerns.

Internet Telephony

Since shortly after the Big Bang, teenagers and college students have considered the telephone one of life's non-negotiable necessities. Their enthusiasm for telephone conversation is matched only by the parental fear of telephone bills. The advent of *Internet telephony* (IP telephony) is one of those rare events that both teenagers and parents can appreciate. For the price of a monthly ISP contract, one now can place long-distance telephone calls over the Internet. All that is needed is a computer, an Internet connection, the right software, and a $20 headset.

Most IP telephony connections are from computer to computer, but placing a call from a computer to a regular telephone is also possible. In 1999, many new products and services appeared that were designed to exploit the inevitable convergence of computers and telephones, including Internet call waiting, Internet fax, multimedia conferencing, and "remote voice" applications whereby telecommuters can access the corporate telephone system over the Internet. In addition, the most popular IM chat clients have added a voice chat feature to their software. A few companies have also started to experiment with visual chat (you need a digital camera connected to your computer if you want people to see you).

Half-Duplex and Full-Duplex Voice Chat

Some voice chat clients support half-duplex chat, whereas others support full-duplex chat. With a half-duplex system, you can either talk or listen—you can't do both at the same time. With a full-duplex system, you can talk and listen at the same time. Full-duplex is more natural, but might stress your Net connection if there are bottlenecks. Experiment with both kinds to find the one that's best for you.

If your bandwidth limitations get in the way of decent voice chat, try *online voice mail* instead. Leaving a recorded message is not quite the same thing as having an interactive telephone call, but it won't stress a slow Net connection in the way that voice chat can.

If you want to make telephone calls over the Internet and you're already using an IM client, you might be closer to telephony than you thought. The IM clients that support chat are very easy to use: You plug in your headphones, look for a Voice Chat command on the client, and start talking. The only catch is that the person to whom you want to talk must be running the same IM client, be set up for chat, and have a set of headphones. Instant messages work well for scheduling online telephone calls, since a little advance planning is usually needed to get everyone online and running the same IM client at the same time.

Some system security issues must be considered if you expect to use voice chat a lot. Avoid opening a voice chat channel with a stranger. That person, if malicious, could take advantage of some OS security holes (a problem most often with Windows) and do something nasty to your computer. You can minimize this risk not only by talking only to trusted friends, but also by using a client that lets you *hide your IP address* (see Figure 7.34). If you must use a client that won't let you hide your IP address, consider using voice mail (the audio version of an instant message)

Figure 7.34:
Yahoo!'s IM Client
Can Hide Your IP
Address

┌─ When I use Yahoo! Messenger ──────────────────────┐
│ ☑ Stand by and wait until I connect to the internet.   │
│   │
│ ☐ Keep Yahoo! Messenger on top of all other applications. │
│   │
│ ☑ Do not reveal my IP Address to other Messenger users.   │
│   │
│ ☐ Always open browser in a new window.   │
└───┘

as an alternative to voice chat. Leaving voice mail messages is safer than opening a voice chat connection, and voice mail is sometimes a good alternative to a telephone call if you don't have much to say.

As wonderful as voice chat is, the quality of the transmission likely will not be as good as on a regular telephone. Internet telephones can sound tinny or like a walkie-talkie, and voices might sound slightly clipped. Different services offer a variety of sound quality; if the first service that you try sounds unacceptable, experiment with others. The quality should improve as the technology matures.

You'll likely want to call some people who are either not on the Internet or not up-to-speed with the world of chat clients. To talk to these people, you'll need to use an *Internet-to-telephone connection*. This type of connection works by routing your call to a gateway that connects the Internet to the telephone network. If you can find a gateway link that is reachable with a local telephone call, then you cover the long-distance part of the call on the Internet (that part is free) and you have to pay only for the local charges for the distance between the gateway and the destination phone. Internet-to-telephone services will charge you for access to their gateways, but they can give you substantial savings over most long distance telephone charges. The most popular Internet-to-telephone service at the time of this writing is **Internet Phone**.

To obtain free Internet-to-telephone service, try **Dialpad** (see Figure 7.35). This service also uses gateways, but they cover that expense with targeted advertising. If you're willing to give up some personal information and be subjected to banner ads, you can connect to any telephone in the United States (including Hawaii and Alaska) from your home computer at no charge.

More Internet telephony and new video conferencing applications will materialize in coming years. The market for such products is immense, broadband support is on the rise, and regulatory agencies are not inclined to put up hurdles. Watch this area closely for more convergence, more services, and more choices. Whenever the big boys with deep pockets enter into a winner-take-all competition, the consumer usually wins. It happened with Web browsers. It happened with ISPs. Now it's happening with Internet telephony. Enjoy.

Figure 7.35:
Dialpad Gives You
Free Internet-to-
Telephone Service

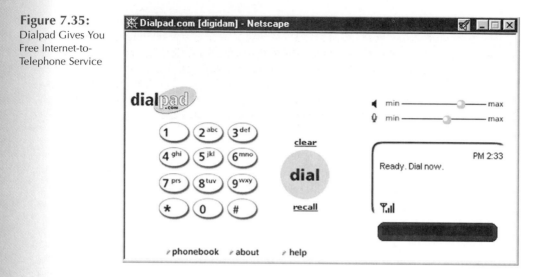

Protecting Children

Children who use the Internet need to be protected from adult content and other objectionable materials. They need protection not only from pornography sites (although they are certainly something to worry about), but also the sites for hate groups, those that glorify violence, and those filled with disturbing images of all kinds. Some steps have been taken to make the Web a safer place for children, but parental guidance will always be needed.

In 1998, almost 16 million of America's 69.6 million children under age 18 were online, almost twice the number of children (9.8 million) reported to be online in 1997. With half of all U.S. households online in 2000, the number of children online could exceed 30 million by the end of that year. Schools with Internet access are usually careful to enforce restrictive AUPs and install Web filters to protect their students. Exposure to inappropriate material online is more likely to happen in the home, where Internet access might be handled more casually.

Child Safety on the Web Many parents rely on *Web browser content filters* to protect their children from unacceptable Webfare. Commercial software packages designed to block out objectionable Web pages do a good job, but they are far from perfect. They often block sites that should not be blocked, and they can miss some sites that most parents would want blocked. However, who can say for sure which materials are objectionable for all families? This is the problem. Some parents are more protective than others. It's difficult to tune software filters according to everyone's needs. However, Web filters, although not perfect, are a step in the right direction for protecting children from unacceptable Web content.

In addition to the usual concerns about inappropriate content, many adults are offended by commercial sites that exploit children in various ways. Before 1998, many sites were designed specifically for children, who were prompted by marketers to give up all sorts of personal information in order to play a game or participate in a contest. The Children's Online Privacy Protection Act was signed into law in 1998 in an effort to stem commercial exploitation of children. This law requires commercial sites aimed at children under 13 to obtain verifiable parental consent before a child can send private information over the Web. The law has had the intended effect, although unfortunately, teenagers are not covered. Additional legislation will be required to protect them.

Parents concerned about personal privacy must discuss the do's and don'ts of Web questionnaires with all children in the household. A child who is inclined to answer online surveys can be an unwitting threat to family privacy and must be taught to resist the temptation to offer personal or family information online.

Making the Web Safe for Children

Parental guidance is made easier if a few rules are established and followed. Here are some suggested rules for making the Web safe for children.

- Set up a Web portal for family use, and use a child-friendly preference setting for all Web searches.
- Install a Web filter, if you can find one that satisfies your personal requirements.
- Instruct children never to submit a form on the Web without first obtaining their parents' permission.
- Keep the computer in a visible, central location where parents can easily see what is on the screen.
- Don't set up a computer with a Net connection in a child's room.

Child Safety in Chat Rooms Web browsing is only one online activity for which children must be supervised. Rules for online chat must also be specified. Because there are so many Web-based chat rooms, children can easily stumble into the wrong ones if no rules are in place. *Parents must see for themselves what goes on in order to decide what to allow.*

The simplest solution is to prohibit all online chat. This might be a reasonable rule, since chat has little educational value. However, some children have friends who want to talk online. A blanket prohibition then becomes harder to enforce.

Making Chat Safe for Children

Here are some suggestions for making online chat safe for children.

- Use IM software, and set its privacy options for maximal safety.
- Make the IM client visible only to people on your Buddy List.
- Accept instant messages only from people on your Buddy List.

- Require that children ask for permission before adding someone to their Buddy Lists.
- Require that children not enter public chat rooms that have not been preapproved by a parent.
- Require that children not accept invitations to private chat rooms from people not on their Buddy Lists.
- Capture log sessions of all online children's chat sessions for periodic review.
- Tell children that a record of all online chat sessions is being made.

Adopting any or all of these suggestions is a parental decision. Each family must work out its own solutions. However, regardless of the policies that are adopted, parents should supervise their children's behavior in case the temptations to engage in chat or to visit unacceptable Web sites is more than they can handle.

Ideally, restrictions on Internet access will be established when the child is very young, when a child doesn't mind having a parent sitting next to him or her during a chat session. As the child gets older, it should be easier for the parent to step back and offer some privacy. The privacy question is more delicate for teenagers—a family must negotiate a proper balance between safety and privacy. If good habits have been already established, parents will find it easier to trust their teenagers to exercise good judgment. However, parents should not hesitate to monitor online sessions if they have any reason to be concerned about online activities.

Above and Beyond: Problems and Exercises

A1. What is a spambot, and what is an address harvester? How do they work together?

A2. What is a cancelbot? How do cancelbots recognize spam on Usenet?

A3. Explain why the cancelbot approach works well for Usenet servers but wouldn't work for e-mail servers.

A4. Explain how Usenet message authors foil spambots. Does this technique work on Web pages?

A5. Explain the difference between half-duplex chat and full-duplex chat.

A6. You want to save money on long distance telephone calls. Should you look into an IM client with a voice chat feature or a telephony client such as Dialpad? How do these options differ? Defend your answer by comparing and contrasting the two options.

A7. How does the Children's Online Privacy Protection Act protect children on the Internet? What group of children is protected?

A8. **[Find It Online]** Consult the **Cancel Messages FAQ** to find out what "CancelBunny" is. Then, using Usenet find out if CancelBunny is still active. What are the general issues associated with CancelBunny?

A9. **[Find It Online]** Visit **Deja.com**, and search its Usenet archives for articles in which people have posted bogus e-mail addresses in order to fool spambots. List five such e-mail addresses. (*Hint*: Conduct an author search with the keyword "spam.")

A10. **[Find It Online]** Read "The Truth about TRUSTe and Your Privacy" at

`http://www.e-commercealert.com/article47.html`

and explain how the TRUSTe icon at a Web site might be misleading consumers. Who created TRUSTe in the first place? Has TRUSTe ever revoked its seal from a Web site in response to a privacy violation?

A11. **[Find It Online]** Visit **Wired News** (`http://www.wired.com`), and search for an article about TRUSTe's investigation of RealNetworks's data collection practices. What was the outcome of the investigation? What other major Web sites has TRUSTe investigated? What fundamental limitation applies to the TRUSTe seal of approval?

A12. **[Find It Online]** Visit **Wired News** (`http://www.wired.com`), and search for articles about privacy issues raised by Toysmart.com. Is anyone protecting consumer privacy when an e-commerce company files for bankruptcy and sells its assets? Is it legal for an e-commerce company to toss its privacy policy aside under extraordinary circumstances or at times of severe financial pressure? Explain your answers.

CHAPTER 8

Software on the Internet

CHAPTER GOALS

- Know what to expect when you download software from the Internet
- Understand how your anti-virus software is configured and how to ensure that all new files are scanned
- Become familiar with five different downloading scenarios
- Know which file utility to use when you need to open a file archive
- Find out how to locate reputable software on the Internet
- Discover where to go to find many software reviews
- Learn how to navigate FTP servers and download files from FTP servers
- Find out how to keep your computer in good working order as you add software to your system
- Learn the proper procedure for removing unwanted software from your system

8.1 | TAKING CHARGE

Many people think of their computers primarily as a piece of equipment on which to run a word processor, launch a browser, and read e-mail. That's all that many people do with their computers most of the time. How you use your computer can result from a conscious decision or simply mindless habit. However, if you understand your options and have made a thoughtful decision about how to spend your computer time, no one can tell you that you aren't using your computer to full advantage. If you've not investigated your computer's full potential, you can't say that you've made an informed decision. The power of your computer lies in the software that it can run. Most people don't need to know about most software. Everyone, however, should know about the software that can make their lives more productive, informed, and enjoyable.

Internet access makes investigating your computer's full potential easy. On the Net, you can find thousands of software-related recommendations, reviews, documentation, tutorials, and discussion groups, not to mention software itself. Once you find out how easy it is to move software from the Internet onto your own computer, you might never shop a retail software store again. Software from a retail store is more expensive to produce and distribute than is software distributed over the Net. As a result, the same software is often available through both distribution channels, with the retail version being more expensive. For that extra money, you get your software on a CD-ROM and some printed documentation that you hope you won't have to read. In addition, the software on the CD-ROM might not be the latest version available. However, you can check the manufacturer's Web site for the latest software updates, since most manufacturers that distribute software on CD-ROMs have Web sites via which the same software is distributed.

At the manufacturer's Web site, you likely can download the complete software package—or at least a limited edition version for a free-trial examination. In the latter case, you can try out the software on your own computer for 30 days at no charge, during which time you can decide if it's what you want. By doing the same with any competing offerings from other manufacturers, you can do some serious comparison-shopping. Once you've tried all of the free samples, you can decide which one is right for you and purchase a software license online.

Software distribution Web sites encourage ongoing communication between manufacturers and customers and offer streamlined customer support. For any bugs in the software, you might be able to find manufacturer's software patches that you can install to fix them. New software releases or updates might become available to registered users over the Web, often before the shrink-wrapped versions make it into the retail stores. If you are uncomfortable not having a printed user's manual, be aware that online documentation and help files usually are at least as good as the printed versions. In addition, a searchable help facility is typically easier to work with than the index in a large user's manual and corrections and additions are easier to accomplish on a Web site than in a printed user's manual. The manufacturer might also support an online technical support discussion group in which users can discuss any problems they're having with the software with each other as well as the company's technical support personnel. Another welcome feature is technical support via e-mail, for users who don't like to be put on hold when they telephone for help.

Special Edition Distributions

Software manufacturers often offer a free special edition or limited edition of their software so that you can try it out. These distributions don't contain all of the features of the complete edition, but they are good for review purposes. You then can elect to stay with the special or limited edition or purchase a complete edition.

When you purchase a software license for software obtained from the Web, you might be given a special URL from which you download the registered version of the software. Alternatively, if you have a free-trial version, you might be given a registration key that will unlock the registered version, which is already on your computer, hiding inside of the free-trial version. Commercial software that is distributed as a free-trial version along with a (usually superior) paid version is called **shareware**. Some shareware is programmed to shut itself down when the trial examination period expires. Other shareware shows you a reminder window each time that you launch the software during the examination period, reminding you to register (see Figure 8.1). This type of shareware is sometimes called **nagware**.

Figure 8.1:
A Reminder That Might Pop Up Each Time That You Launch the Shareware

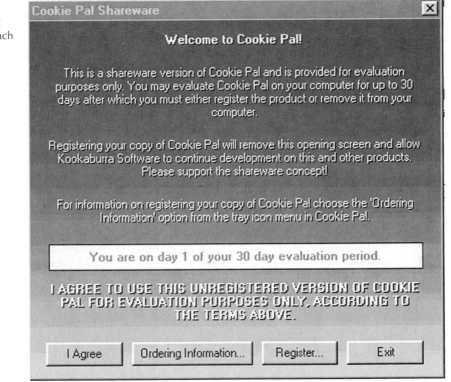

A manufacturer that withholds features from its free-trial version hopes that you'll like what you see well enough to pay for the registered version. A free-trial version purposely "crippled" by having some features omitted is still usable. In fact, it might be missing only one key feature, which is either a big time-saver or some obviously desirable feature that the manufacturer expects everyone to want. Alternatively, in the free-trial version you might have to endure banner ads from commercial sponsors. When you purchase the registered version, the banner ads go away.

Manufacturers that rely on "nag screens" hope that you'll buy the full version if you're reminded often enough (at every possible opportunity). Some nagware allows you to continue using the software after the free-trial expiration date has passed, although they keep reminding you that you've passed the deadline and you really should pay for the software. You can ignore these reminders, but sooner or later, guilt might set in or you might simply get tired of seeing the nag screen, so you eventually give in and buy the shareware. Shareware that *self-destructs* (refuses to launch) when the free-trial period is over is perhaps more effective at making people pay for the software. Making shareware self-destructive is not unreasonable from the manufacturer's point of view—it is simply protecting its inventory from shoplifters. How many retailers are willing to let you take an item home for 30 days at no charge so that you can make sure whether you like it and want to keep it? Some people, however, might feel offended by this approach's heavy-handedness.

Newbies are often surprised to discover how much software is given away over the Web at no charge. It might be natural to assume that such software, called **freeware**, must not be very good simply because it's free. This is not necessarily true. Some freeware is as good as any commercial counterpart. It could be distributed at no charge for many different reasons. For example, a manufacturer might want to increase traffic on its official Web site, so it offers a modest piece of freeware as an incentive to visit. Sometimes, however, the software is not modest. For example, during the Browser Wars of the mid-1990s, Microsoft and Netscape offered their browsers at no charge, for noncommercial use, in bids to establish market dominance. This strategy worked so well that many Internet users don't realize that other browsers are available, including at least one excellent product, Opera, that will actually cost you money (see section 9.8). Some users with considerable experience with Web browsers are willing to pay for a Web browser for the sake of having a superior product. A company needs deep pockets in order to be able to afford to give away an important product just to establish a dominant market position.

Other reasons for giving away software include the case in which a freelance programmer who is in the process of reworking a piece of software wants to obtain feedback and suggestions from as many users as possible during its development (or **beta**) phase. Or, a novice programmer might find it gratifying to see other people using his or her creation, even if no money is involved.

Some programmers distribute freeware as an act of guerilla warfare against "old-order" economic forces. For example, the authors of the Napster and Wrapster programs, which facilitate MP3 distribution over the Net, claim that their file-sharing technology is protected by the Audio Home Recording Act of 1992 and does not harm commercial sales of CDs. Recall from Chapter 2 that the trade association Recording Industry Association of America (RIAA) filed lawsuits against MP3-related Web sites to stop illegal MP3 file distributions. Napster and Wrapster consider these lawsuits as doomed efforts by the RIAA to control the distribution channels for commercial music. In situations such as this, the expression "computer revolution" is more than a metaphor for social upheaval. Entire industries can rise and fall when new technologies become freely available over the Internet.

Finally, there's long-standing support within the academic community for open source software. **Open source software** is software whose code is willingly shared publicly so that other programmers can offer their own improvements. This is done in a communal effort to create superior software. Linux is an example of open source software that has gained considerable momentum in recent years as an alternative OS to Windows. Although it is not (yet) as easy to use as Windows, Linux does have one advantage that makes it the OS of choice for programmers: Almost all of the application software developed for Linux is open source. If you value excellence in software design, open-source software often rivals the best software produced by leading software companies. In open-source software, user-friendly interfaces are typically not a priority (open source interfaces traditionally were written by programmers for other programmers), so it might not be easy to use. However, more consumer-oriented open source products are becoming available that are aimed at the general public. For example, Netscape Navigator did not begin as open source, but it became so in 1998 in an effort to compete more effectively in the Browser Wars.

By taking advantage of what the Web offers, you can explore an exciting world of commercial software, shareware, and freeware on your home computer. The right software makes a significant difference between a computer that works really well for you and one that isn't doing everything that it could. The Web makes it easy and fun to explore the possibilities. If you own your own computer and you haven't been sampling software on the Web, you're missing out on a big part of what it has to offer. This chapter covers everything that you need to know about software downloads and safe installation practices. If you're new to software downloads, you'll be surprised how easy it is. More experienced readers might want to skim this chapter for tips and tricks that can make the experience smoother and faster.

8.2 TROUBLE-FREE DOWNLOADS

Programmers have made the process of downloading software easy. Most software available on the Internet can be found on the Web, in which case your browser can usually handle the download for you. For large amounts of downloading, you might find it useful to have a *download manager* or an *FTP client*. These optional tools of the trade are discussed shortly.

You need to ensure that the software that you download from the Internet doesn't contain malicious code and has not been tampered with by anyone along the way. You do this by going to *trusted sources* for software (see Figure 8.2). Generally, when you download commercial software, you should go to the source—the original software manufacturer—if only to ensure that you download the most recent version. Using the source minimizes, but does not eliminate, the possibility of downloading an infected file. You still must take care to protect your computer from viruses no matter from which site you download.

Figure 8.2:
Tucows: A Popular Software Clearinghouse

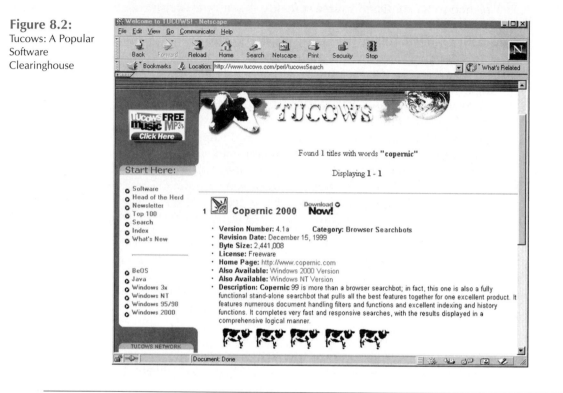

Picking a Reputable Site from Which to Download Software

To download an *executable file* (software) from the Internet, go to either the Web site of a reputable commercial software manufacturer or a large, well-known software clearinghouse. Never download an executable file from someone's personal home page, a link in an e-mail message, a link in a newsgroup article, or a link in a chat room, chat channel, or IM (instant messaging) session.

Selecting the Right Software File for Your Computer

Generally, different OSs cannot run the same computer programs. Each requires its own set of executable code. Much software is available for Windows-based personal computers or for the Macintosh but not for both. If the software that you want is not available for your OS, you'll need to search for something similar that will work on that OS. Popular software is often available for different OSs, so make sure that you download the version that's correct for your OS (see Figure

8.3). If you download the wrong version, you won't be able to install or run it on your computer. Most Web sites make it easy for you to pick the right version.

Figure 8.3:
Selecting the Right Software for Your Computer

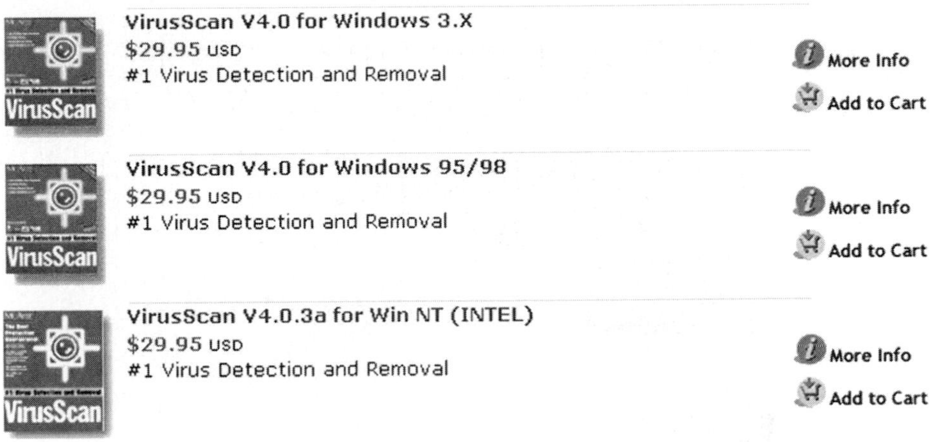

VirusScan V4.0 for Windows 3.X
$29.95 USD
#1 Virus Detection and Removal

i More Info
Add to Cart

VirusScan V4.0 for Windows 95/98
$29.95 USD
#1 Virus Detection and Removal

i More Info
Add to Cart

VirusScan V4.0.3a for Win NT (INTEL)
$29.95 USD
#1 Virus Detection and Removal

i More Info
Add to Cart

All software downloads on the Web are available via clickable hyperlinks. A link can point to a software file as easily as to an HTML file. The browser decides what to do with a link that points to a given file type; if it doesn't know, it'll ask you (see Figure 8.4). Browsers recognize file types by their file extensions. The most commonly used extensions for Windows software are `.exe` and `.zip` and for Macintosh software `.bin` and `.sit` Appendix D contains a longer list of file extensions associated with software files.

Saving Executable Files Safely

When your browser encounters a file that is not an HTML file or an image file, it checks a list of known file extensions to determine whether it knows how to open the file by using software already available on your computer. This is a good idea for data files such as PDF and MP3 but not for executable files.

All executable files should be scanned for viruses before you execute them. Your browser might be configured to notify you when executable files are encountered and let you decide how to handle the file (see Figure 8.4). Always elect to save it to a file. In this way, you'll be able to scan the file for viruses before you execute it.

In addition, if when you're downloading an executable file type you are offered a check box that says, "Always ask before opening this type of file" (see Figure 8.4), ensure that the box is checked. By doing this, you ensure that you always see your browser's current preference setting regarding executable files that are downloaded. You want to be sure that the browser is not set to automatically execute the file before you've scanned it, since preference settings can be reset without

Figure 8.4:
The Safest Option:
Save It to Disk

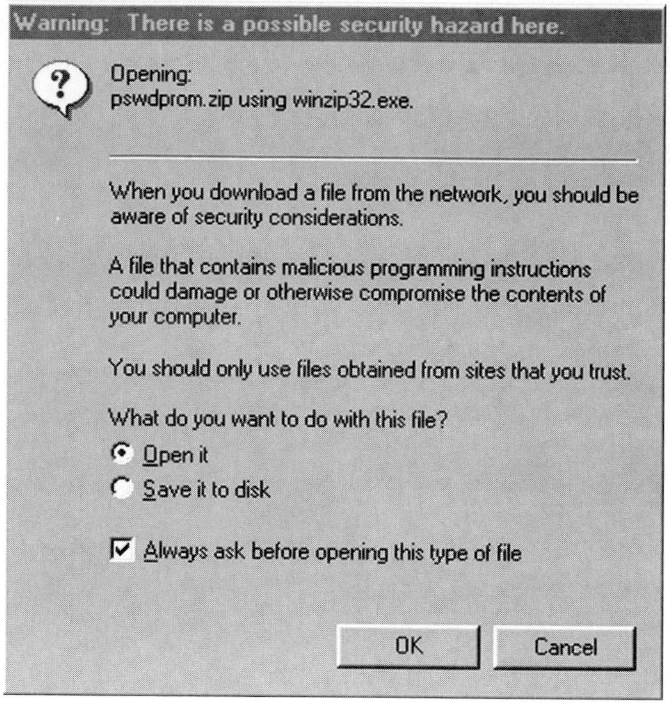

your knowledge (especially if other people have access to your computer). This will safeguard against hackers, malicious code, and default preference settings.

Sometimes, you might be given a choice between saving the program to a file and *running it from its current location* (see Figure 8.5). Again, the safest option is to save the program to disk. By the way, you can't really run the program from its current location, which is on the server. Rather, you really download it to a *temporary file* in your *browser's cache*, from which it will be executed. If you know and trust the file in question (because you've downloaded and scanned it before), choosing to run the program from its current location will save you from having to delete the executable later. However, most of the time, you shouldn't trust the file. By saving it to disk, you ensure that your anti-virus software has a chance to scan it for viruses before anything gets executed.

Whenever you elect to save an executable file to disk, you're prompted for the location in which to save it (see Figure 8.6). Either accept the default location suggested by your browser, or select any other location on your hard drive (or floppy or zip drive, as you wish). It doesn't matter where you put the file as long as you know where it is for later execution.

Figure 8.5:
The Safest Option:
"Save this program
to disk"

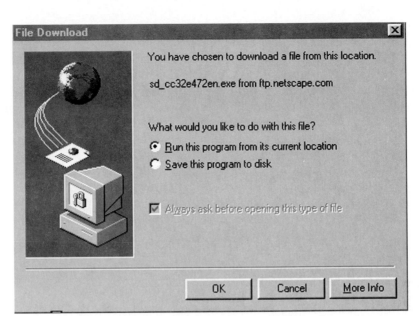

Figure 8.6:
Pay Attention to
This Window

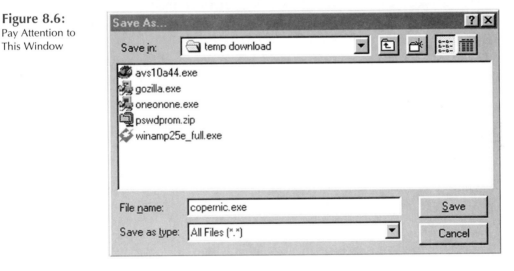

Putting All of Your File Downloads in a Downloads Folder

Your browser will suggest a location for your file downloads based on its preference settings. You can override this default location. To help you to remember
where you put downloaded software so that you can find it for later execution,
always put your downloads in the same place, in a folder expressly set up to hold
downloaded software.

Once you have selected a location for your download, the download will begin. Your browser will show you how the download is progressing by displaying a status bar. Figure 8.7 shows how Navigator tracks its file downloads. MSIE has a *download manager* that enables multiple downloads to be started and tracked simultaneously. Although it's useful to see these progress reports for large downloads, you don't need to drop everything to watch the download. You can run other applications, including your browser, while the download continues in the background. *Note*: Don't terminate your Internet connection until the download is completed.

Figure 8.7:
Navigator's
Download Progress
Report

Saving Location	⏤ ⊡ ✕
Location:	ftp://zdftp.zdne...ols/copernic.exe
Saving	C:\WINDOWS\DESKT...oad\copernic.exe
Status:	520K of 2383K (at 2.9K/sec)
Time Left:	00:10:48
▌▌▌▌▌▌▌▌	21%
	Cancel

After the download, scan the file for viruses. Assuming that you have anti-virus software on your computer, make sure that you understand how it operates. Some anti-virus utilities can be configured to automatically scan all new files as soon as they are on your hard drive; others must be manually invoked. Figure 8.8 shows how McAfee's VirusScan software can be invoked to check all of the files currently found in a folder on the Windows desktop, including the most recent download, `copernic.exe`.

Scanning for Viruses after a Download

As soon as the file has been downloaded, scan it for viruses. Remember, do not run a downloaded executable file until you have scanned it with anti-virus software. Your anti-virus software might be configured to launch automatically whenever a new file is copied to your hard drive, or you might have to start the software yourself. Either way, do not do anything an executable file until it passes a virus scan.

Also remember to keep your anti-virus software up-to-date. If you don't update your virus data files once a week as a matter of routine, at least update them each time that you download new software. Anti-virus software that doesn't know about the latest viruses can't protect your computer.

Figure 8.8:
Scan the Download
for Viruses Before
You Open It

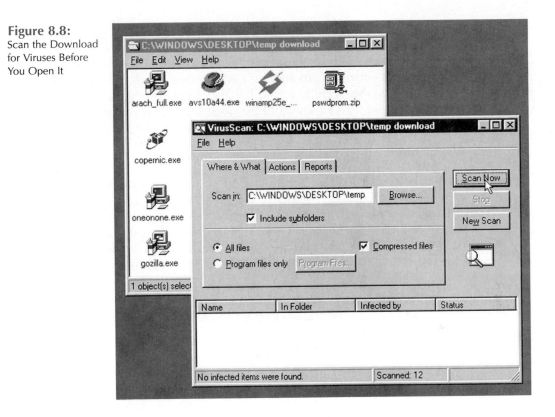

Recall that you cannot catch a computer virus simply by downloading an executable file, *even if that file is infected.* You must *execute* an executable file in order
to activate a virus. Anti-virus software that automatically intercepts and scans all
new files that arrive onto your hard drive will protect you in case you forget to scan
the file yourself. Remember to ensure that the software is running in the background
whenever you download executables from the Internet. Once the download has
been scanned and deemed safe to open, you can install your software.

8.3 ANTI-VIRUS PROTECTION

Computer viruses are a fact of life. Recall from Chapter 2 that viruses are spread via
executable files, documents that contain macros, and in scripts read by script-
enabled e-mail clients (see Sections 2.4 and 2.5). Because software consists of executable files, viruses are a possibility in downloaded software. If you don't have
anti-virus software on a Windows computer, don't download software from the
Internet. On a Macintosh computer, you're much less likely to pick up a virus from
downloaded software, so you might be able to forgo anti-virus software if you're

careful to pick popular downloads from reputable software sites. (Make sure, though, that you know how to work with e-mail attachments!) Most viruses are designed to attack Windows-based personal computers, rather than Macs, primarily because 90% of personal computers run Windows. If someone wants to create a virus that will bring the world to a halt, it makes sense to target the Windows OS. However, recall from Chapter 2 that macro viruses are platform-independent—they will infect a Mac as readily as a Windows-based personal computer. Thus anti-virus software for a Mac is a good idea for anyone who exchanges Word or Excel documents with other user people.

Suppose that you want to minimize the risk of contracting a virus and that you have anti-virus software on your computer. You need to explore its configuration to understand how it works. Some anti-virus software must be run manually on individual files or file folders whenever you want to scan for viruses. Others can be set to run in the background, where they'll intercept all incoming files and scan them automatically. An automatic scanner that runs in the background is especially convenient for people who download a lot of software.

Make Sure Your Anti-Virus Software Is Running in the Background

Even if you have anti-virus software running in the background, always double-check to ensure that it *is* running before you begin a software download and installation. Although background scanning is wonderful so that you don't have to run manual scans yourself, the software must be active in order to protect you. It's easy to forget about a background scanner. The software won't tell you when a scan turns up nothing; it will make its presence known only when it detects a virus. Although this is generally what you want, don't forget about it altogether.

You also need to ensure that your anti-virus preference settings are set to check *all* incoming files, not only executable files (see Figure 8.9). This will protect you against *macro viruses.* Note that some scanners can be configured to open *file archives* and scan their contents as well; others can't scan an archive unless you open the archive. However, all scanners will check any files being copied onto your hard drive, including files extracted from a file archive (as well as files created by a software installer). Thus, even if you don't trigger a virus warning when you download a software file archive, you can trigger a warning when files are being extracted from an archive. One way or another, your anti-virus software can protect you when you download file archives (as long as you have it turned on).

Consider also having your anti-virus software configured to test as many incoming files as possible. The CPU load is negligible, and you need to worry about macro viruses in data files as well as executable files.

Most anti-virus software allows you to scan specific files or folders on demand. (McAfee's ActiveShield is an exception. To scan a specific folder by using ActiveShield, you must go to the Web-based McAfee Clinic site and request a scan

Figure 8.9:
Checking Your Anti-Virus Software's
Preference Settings

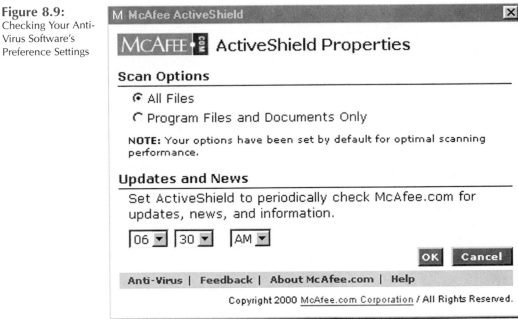

using MSIE and an active Internet connection.) If possible in this case, configure your file archive utility to launch your anti-virus software from inside of the archive program. Figure 8.10 shows how to tell the archive utility **ZipCentral** where to find anti-virus software.

Figure 8.10:
ZipCentral
Preference Setting
for Anti-Virus
Software

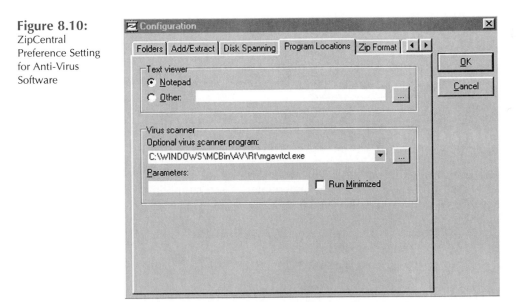

Figure 8.11 shows how to launch anti-virus software from inside of ZipCentral.

When you do this, you can scan some or all of the files inside of the archive on demand, before they are extracted from the archive. This isn't necessary if your scanner is running in the background, ready to pounce on any infected files as soon as they are extracted from the archive. However, some people find it reassuring to scan file archives manually before they proceed with an installation. A manual file scan always reports its results, regardless of whether a virus is found. It never hurts to run both an automatic scan and a manual scan on the same files.

Figure 8.11:
Scanning a File inside of a File Archive before Extracting It

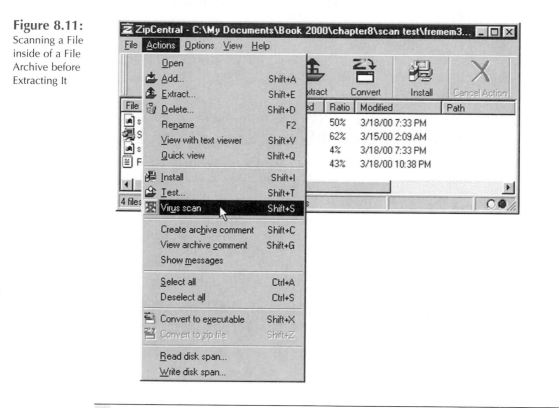

8.4 ■ INSTALLATION TIPS

Software installations are usually simple, but if you're inexperienced and don't know what to expect you might encounter a few stumbling blocks. This section describes the five standard installation scenarios that you are likely to encounter so that you can easily install software from the Internet.

1. Executable installers (most commonly used for large commercial programs)
2. Ready-to-go executables (most commonly used for small noncommercial programs)

3. Zipped file archives (most commonly used for small noncommercial programs)

4. Self-extracting archives (similar to a zipped archive but requires no extra software)

5. ActiveX installers (not seen often, as they require MSIE on a Windows system)

Note that although the file extensions for Windows differ from those for the Mac, the general installation steps given in the following sections are the same for either OS. The Web site from which you obtain your download will not explain which installation scenario applies. However, with a little experience you'll recognize the different installation scenarios and the usual procedures associated with them.

8.4.1 Executable Installers

If your download is a `.exe` file (or a `.sea` file for a Mac), you've probably downloaded an installer. An **installer** is a set-up utility that is used whenever a computer program requires multiple files in order to operate. If the file's icon includes an arrow pointing downward or a picture of a box and a floppy disk in front of a computer (see Figure 8.12), then the file is an installer. An installer might include one file that contains the executable code, additional data files (for example, help files), and some graphics files (for animations or ad banners). To install these manually, you'd need to follow detailed instructions on where to save all of the different files and probably would have to edit at least a few of them as well. Manual installations are time-consuming and error-prone; bundling complex software inside of an installer that can do all of the busywork for you is a much better arrangement. An installer needs to be executed only once. Once its job is done, you can discard it, or perhaps save it, should you ever need to reinstall the software.

Figure 8.12:
An Icon That
Identifies an
Installer

Some people like to save installers (in a specific folder for easy locating) so that they can recreate their computing environment when they upgrade to a new computer. If you have plenty of space on your hard drive, consider doing this. Zip disks and super drive disks are also useful for saving installers if you don't want your hard drive filled with nonessential files.

Figure 8.13 shows the first screen of an installer for a Windows program named Go!Zilla. If you download a lot of software, you'll see the same installer utilities used for different downloads. Each installation will look a little different, but all will ask the same types of questions and do the same types of actions.

Close All Other Applications before You Run an Installer

In some cases, new software will not run properly if you install it while other programs are running on your machine. Most installers will remind you to shut down other programs before proceeding with an installation. In many cases, an installer cannot execute properly while anti-virus software is running in the background. You can safely turn off the anti-virus software during a software installation, as long as you remember to turn it on afterwards. (Of course, you scanned the installer earlier, right after you downloaded it, right?)

Figure 8.13:
Read and Follow
the Installer's
Instructions

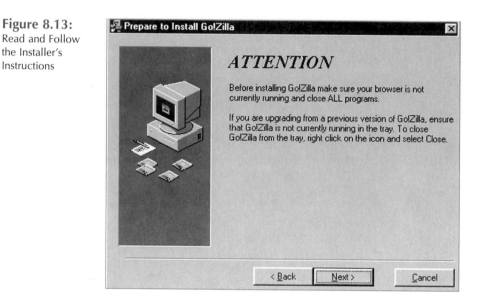

Sometimes a program is simple enough to require only one program file: in this case, no installer is needed. In this case, the file that you download is the actual computer program and you'll launch the program when you double-click the file's name. This is a **ready-to-go executable** and is less common than an installer download.

If you aren't sure which kind of download that you have, simply double-click the file's name and see what happens. If it's the actual program, and you decide to keep it, move it to an appropriate directory for long-term storage. No other installation is needed.

When to Turn Off Your Anti-Virus Software

Sometimes an installer will ask you to turn off your anti-virus software before you begin the installation. This might sound suspicious, but it is a legitimate requirement; however, proceed with caution. If the downloaded software is a popular brand and you obtained it from a well-known site, you can turn off your anti-virus software and continue the installation. (Be sure to turn it back on as soon as the installation is over.) As a precaution, you can run a complete scan of your entire hard drive right after the installation.

However, if the downloaded software is obscure or seems suspicious in any way (for example, it's not available in any of the big software archives), reconsider installing it. Turning off your anti-virus software does involve some risk, even if you do a full disk scan afterwards. A malicious installer could construct an infected executable, launch it, and delete it, before you've a chance to detect it. This is not a standard virus delivery method, but it is possible.

Most installers will ask you a few questions so that you can control certain aspects of the installation. The first is likely to concern where you want to put the executable program file(s). The installer will make a suggestion about this location, but you can override it if you prefer to store the program in a different location (see Figure 8.14). Remember that Windows shortcuts and Mac aliases enable you to access the same program from many locations on your computer, so the location of the program files might not be important. If you don't care, then take the installer's suggestion.

Select a Location on Your Hard Drive for Your New Program

If you like to categorize your computer programs and store them according to your own system, you can tell the installer where to put a new program. Otherwise, the installer will use a default location (which is fine). If you aren't sure what to do, go with the installer's suggestion.

Although it doesn't really matter where you put a program, once you've installed it, don't move any of its files. Program files often need to know the location of other support files, and these locations are recorded at the time of installation. If you move any program files around, their old locations cease to be valid, and the entire program may fail to execute correctly the next time you try to run it. If you ever need to move a program to another directory, uninstall the software (see Section 8.8) and then reinstall it at the new location.

When to Leave the Installer's Settings Alone

The installer might ask other questions about this installation before installing the program (see Figure 8.15). The more complicated the program, the more questions that might be asked. For example, you might be asked if you want a standard installation or a custom installation. The standard installation will be the installer's default setting, but you can opt for a custom installation if you understand the software well enough to take more control over the installation process (custom installations always involve more decisions).

An installer generally explains why its needs the input, but sometimes you might not be certain how to respond. In this case, you can read any help files that the installer offers to try to make sense of the question or you can accept the installer's suggested default setting (the default setting is almost always the right one anyway).

Figure 8.14:
Telling the Installer Where to Save a Program

Figure 8.15:
Some Installers Ask a Lot of Questions

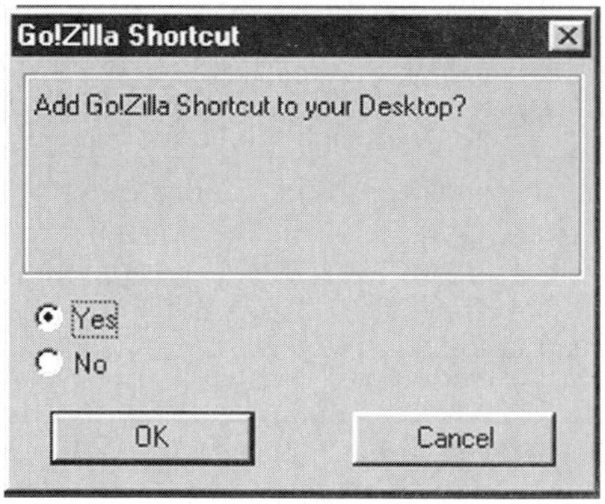

Installers usually display a copy of the software's licensing agreement and will not complete the installation if you don't agree to the terms of the license. By clicking the "I agree" option, you enter into a legally binding contract. Always read a contract before you sign it. These agreements are sometimes long and tedious, but you still should read them, as they are legitimate contracts, even though you aren't signing your name to a piece of paper.

You might also find, buried inside of these agreements, important information about known software incompatibilities (see Figure 8.16). When you add new software to your computer, you should learn everything that you can about the new software. Computer programs often depend on *shared resources* in order to operate properly. Because of this, various computer programs can interact with each other in unexpected ways, *even if they aren't running at the same time.* You might find that your system starts crashing a lot after you've installed a new program, even if the new program isn't running at the time of the crash. This problem is discussed in Section 8.8. Meanwhile, remember to read all information that your installer offers.

Figure 8.16:
Installers Might
Have Important
Information for You

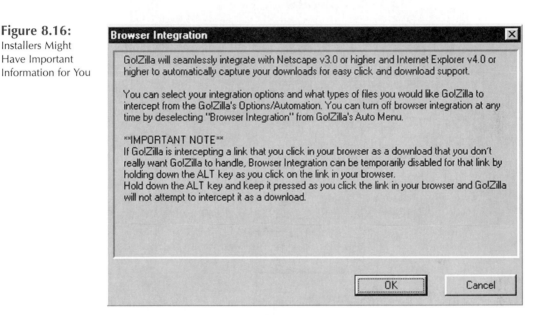

> **Browser Integration**   ☒
>
> Go!Zilla will seamlessly integrate with Netscape v3.0 or higher and Internet Explorer v4.0 or higher to automatically capture your downloads for easy click and download support.
>
> You can select your integration options and what types of files you would like Go!Zilla to intercept from the Go!Zilla's Options/Automation. You can turn off browser integration at any time by deselecting "Browser Integration" from Go!Zilla's Auto Menu.
>
> **IMPORTANT NOTE**
> If Go!Zilla is intercepting a link that you click in your browser as a download that you don't really want Go!Zilla to handle, Browser Integration can be temporarily disabled for that link by holding down the ALT key as you click on the link in your browser.
> Hold down the ALT key and keep it pressed as you click the link in your browser and Go!Zilla will not attempt to intercept it as a download.
>
> [OK]   [Cancel]

Read Everything the Installer Has to Say

Most installations are short and sweet. However, if an installer gives you something to read, it's wise to read it. (See Figure 8.16.)

Software downloads often come with a README file (see Figure 8.17). The **README file**, typically written by the software's author or manufacturer, is a text file that contains information, usually late-breaking, that the user needs and that is not included in the software's official documentation. Read these files, as they can contain important information about problems with the program or ways to avoid known bugs. If you have a problem with a particular program, always check the README file before contacting the manufacturer's technical support for assistance. You can solve many problems by consulting the README file.

Figure 8.17:
README Files
Contain Timely
Documentation

Always Read the README File

README files are a software tradition. When the author (or manufacturer) of a computer program discovers a problem with the program, the user can be alerted about the problem via the README file. In this way, anyone who purchases the most recent version of the software will be up-to-date on all of the known bugs and possible fixes. Of course, this works only when the user downloading the software reads the README file.

The last screen that the installer displays informs you that the installation is complete. An installer might automatically put a shortcut to its program on your desktop (this practice is more common on Windows-based personal computers than on Macs). You can delete the shortcut if you don't want it. In addition, it might automatically add its program name to your Start Menu (another Windows tradition). You can remove this as well if you don't want it (see Section 8.8). Both practices are designed to make it easy for you to find the program when you want to launch it. If you delete these conveniences, you can still run the program, as long as you know where it's located on your hard drive (remember when the installer asked you where to save your program?). If you can't remember where the installer put it, do a search for a file with the name of the program or possibly any file with a suitably recent creation date.

8.4.2 Ready-to-Go Executables

If a computer program is simple enough, it won't need auxiliary files—the entire program can be stored in a single file and will not require a complicated installation process. It's *ready-to-go* as soon as it arrives. In this case, you might be downloading an executable file that is the actual program you're looking for—this is a **ready-to-go executable**. In this case, you need only to decide where you want to store the program file for safekeeping. It won't matter where you put it. Unlike with an executable installer, you can move it at any time if you decide to rearrange your directories. Note that more complicated programs cannot be moved around as easily (see Section 8.8).

A ready-to-go executable won't have a README file, so be sure to check the programmer's Web site for recent news and announcements. If you need help operating the software or setting its user preferences, check the program for a Help menu. If the program lacks much documentation bundled with it, check the programmer's Web site for additional documentation. You might find all sorts of useful resources on the site, such as a user's manual, the most recent README file, and other timely communications from the programmer. Programmers who distribute their programs over the Web are relying more on the Web as their primary means of communication with their user populations.

A ready-to-go executable is usually an `.exe` file for a Windows-based personal computer or a `.bin` file for the Mac. Sometimes, it is *compressed* for faster downloads, in which case you might see a `.zip` extension for a Windows-based machine or a `.sit` extension for the Mac. Sometimes, you might see an ASCII-encoded executable (`.uue` for Windows or `.hqx` for the Mac). These formats are much less common now that the Web is the major vehicle for online software distribution. If you're having difficulty with a file that won't open when you double-click its name, see Section 8.5 for a discussion of useful file utilities.

8.4.3 Zipped File Archives

A **zipped file archive** is a file that contains other files. It's like a file folder. You can open the archive to see what's inside, if you have the right file utility (see Section 8.5). Otherwise, you can't do anything with a zipped file archive. File archives have a `.zip` file extension under Windows or a `.sit` on a Mac. If your system has the appropriate file utility application associated with the archive's file extension, you should be able to open the archive by double-clicking the file's name. Once you've opened the archive, look for a README file (see Figure 8.18). If there is one, open it, as it will typically explain the contents of the archive and tell you what to do next. Some archive files contain a ready-to-go executable along with documentation files and data files needed to run the program. Others contain an installer.

For Freemem Professional, `setup.exe` is an installer file. The README file explains what you need to know before you run this installer (see Figure 8.19). Each program's README file will contain different instructions, so look for the README file and read it carefully before proceeding with the installation.

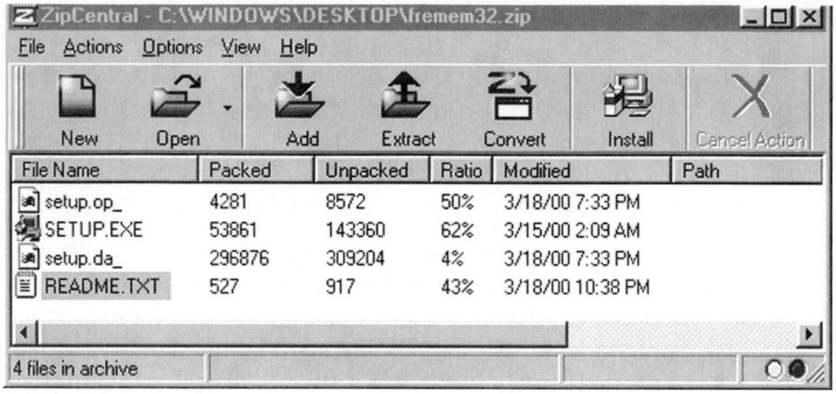

Figure 8.18:
Freemem
Professional Is
Distributed in a File
Archive Named
`fremem32.zip`

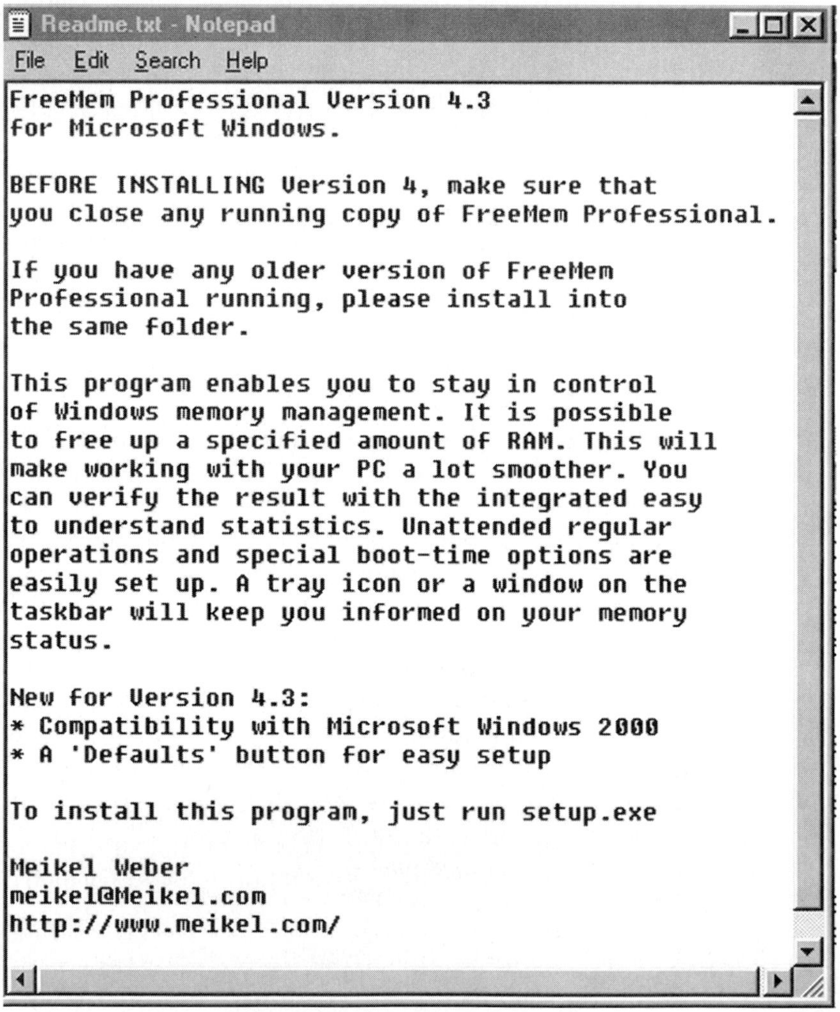

Figure 8.19:
This README File
Explains How to
Install Freemem
Professional

```
FreeMem Professional Version 4.3
for Microsoft Windows.

BEFORE INSTALLING Version 4, make sure that
you close any running copy of FreeMem Professional.

If you have any older version of FreeMem
Professional running, please install into
the same folder.

This program enables you to stay in control
of Windows memory management. It is possible
to free up a specified amount of RAM. This will
make working with your PC a lot smoother. You
can verify the result with the integrated easy
to understand statistics. Unattended regular
operations and special boot-time options are
easily set up. A tray icon or a window on the
taskbar will keep you informed on your memory
status.

New for Version 4.3:
* Compatibility with Microsoft Windows 2000
* A 'Defaults' button for easy setup

To install this program, just run setup.exe

Meikel Weber
meikel@Meikel.com
http://www.meikel.com/
```

8.4.4 Self-Extracting Archives

Some downloads are self-extracting archives. A **self-extracting archive** is an archive file, similar to the zipped archives discussed in the previous section, but no special file utility is needed to open it. It has an `.exe` extension under Windows or a `.sea` extension on a Mac. Because `.exe` extensions are also used for executable installers and ready-to-go executables, it's difficult to know when an `.exe` file is a self-extracting archive.

When you double-click a self-extracting archive, it expands its archive and creates a second `.exe` file, which is usually the executable program. Additional files might be created when you expand the archive, so watch for documentation files (look for a README file). The FTP program WS_FTP 95 is an example of an `.exe` download that uses a self-extracting archive.

A self-extracting archive places its archive files in the current subdirectory (the same directory that contains the self-extracting archive file) or creates a new subdirectory for the expanded archive. It won't hide the archive in some other directory far from the original download. You can expand the original self-extracting archive as often as needed. The archive is not altered or exhausted when you expand it.

8.4.5 ActiveX Installers

Another installation scenario relies on a technology called ActiveX™. **ActiveX** is a Microsoft product and is distributed with MSIE (versions 3.0 and higher). If you're not running MSIE on a Windows system, you cannot install software that uses an ActiveX installer. For example, ActiveX software does not run on Macs.

ActiveX installations are designed to make the software download process as simple as possible. With an ActiveX installation, you need only click a link on a Web page and you're done. The installation process is fully automated, and you won't be asked where to put any files, or any other questions. McAfee's Clinic (see Figure 8.20) is an example of a software installation that relies on ActiveX.

ActiveX programs can create or remove files on your hard drive and run executable files on your computer. Web programming languages (for example, JavaScript and Java) impose some restrictions on what their programs can do, for the sake of preserving your system security. ActiveX has no such restrictions. You must be very careful with ActiveX installations; you must trust the site that offers an ActiveX installer. If a deceptive Web site tricks you into running a malicious ActiveX installer, you conceivably could lose every file on your hard drive. Moreover, the script could be programmed to execute at some future date, thereby making it impossible to connect the destructive executable with its source on the Web. It could search for personal information in the data files of applications such as Quicken and send those files out on the Internet to someone unknown to you and without your permission. It could hunt down your e-mail address and ship it off to countless spamming operations. It could steal your credit card account number (if you store that on your computer without first encrypting it). It could steal passwords to restricted Web sites (if

Figure 8.20:
McAfee's Clinic
Uses an ActiveX
Installer

you store them on your computer without first encrypting them). Because the destructive potential of malicious ActiveX scripts is so great, special safeguards are used when ActiveX scripts are built into Web pages.

Microsoft understands the risks inherent in ActiveX. It attempts to protect users from malicious ActiveX downloads by using a mechanism called *Authenticode* that enables a system developer (such as Microsoft) to place a *digital signature* on any original ActiveX utilities. In this case, the digital signature identifies the person or organization behind the software. Your browser will check this signature before continuing with the download. Then if your browser does not recognize a digital signature as the mark of a trusted software source, it will inform you of the situation and ask if you still want to run the software anyway. Chapter 11 discusses the technology of digital signatures and their application to software downloads in. For now, it's enough to understand that your browser might issue a warning (see Figure 8.21) if it sees a digital signature it doesn't recognize.

ActiveX Programs Download and Install in One Step

You cannot scan an ActiveX installer for viruses. This is because an ActiveX installer executes automatically after downloading. ActiveX installers are very risky because you must take someone else's word that the executable is safe to execute.

Ensure that your browser is configured to check digital certificates when it downloads a file that contains a digital certificate. If you have not disabled any of your original security settings, you should be alright.

For more information about ActiveX security issues, visit

```
http://www.microsoft.com/security/new.asp
```

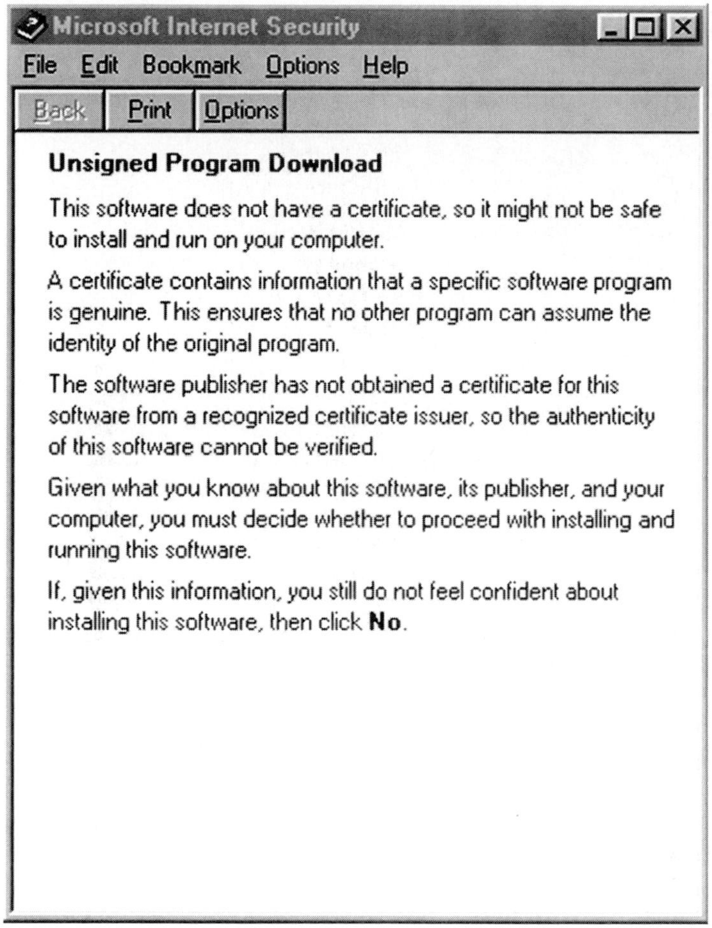

Figure 8.21:
Digital Signatures
Can Protect
Consumers from
Malicious ActiveX
Installations

> Microsoft Internet Security

File   Edit   Bookmark   Options   Help

| Back | Print | Options |

Unsigned Program Download

This software does not have a certificate, so it might not be safe
to install and run on your computer.

A certificate contains information that a specific software program
is genuine. This ensures that no other program can assume the
identity of the original program.

The software publisher has not obtained a certificate for this
software from a recognized certificate issuer, so the authenticity
of this software cannot be verified.

Given what you know about this software, its publisher, and your
computer, you must decide whether to proceed with installing and
running this software.

If, given this information, you still do not feel confident about
installing this software, then click **No**.

A signature verification failure might or might not mean that the software in question is risky. If you trust the source (and you're confident that the download site is what it says it is), you can opt to continue with the download. To be as safe as possible, reject any software that cannot be authenticated with a digital signature. Figure 8.22 warns about a program file that does not contain an Authenticode signature—its authorship can't be verified. The URL suggests that the files come from Microsoft's Web site, but the Microsoft Web page might have been hacked and the download might not be Microsoft's. In this case, you can be safe by contacting the distributor (in this case Microsoft) before accepting the download to ascertain its authenticity.

Critics of the Authenticode system point out that a verified signature is only as good as the source of the signature. If you trust the source to distribute software that does what it says it does and nothing more, then a digital signature will give you peace

Figure 8.22:
This Program File
Was Never Signed:
You Can't Be Sure
Where It Came
From

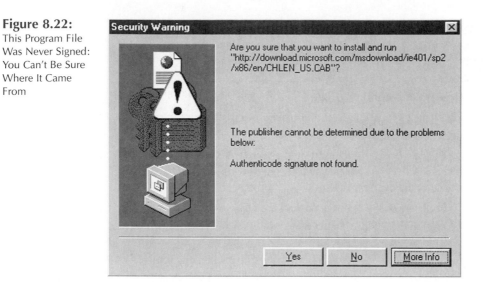

of mind. However, some software manufacturers might embed functionality in their software that they consider to be benign but that you might disagree with (if you knew what it was doing). For example, in 1999 millions of people downloaded the popular freeware version of RealPlayer 7.0, a streaming audio player. Apparently few people who installed RealPlayer questioned what *Comet Cursor* was, although it was listed as a feature in two of three download options (see Figure 8.23). Even if users had taken the time to track down the **Comet Systems site**, they still would not have discovered the true purpose of this cursor tracking application. *It was tracking user browsing behavior and sending this information to Comet Systems for inclusion in a Web-tracking database.* Comet Systems neglected to inform its consumers about this aspect of the Comet Cursor until a news reporter broke the story, raised questions about online privacy, and forced Comet Systems to explain what it was doing. In this case, a digital signature check for RealPlayer would have made no difference because RealPlayer and Comet Systems distributed software without fully disclosing exactly what it was doing. Is it conceivable that RealPlayer didn't fully understand the actual capabilities of the Comet Cursor? Would you trust them more, or less, if the company claimed ignorance?

Trusting your system security to a commercial software manufacturer is a risky business, no matter how much you might like its product. Even Microsoft has been sabotaged and by its own programmers (to find out more, do a Web search with the query "Microsoft security risk FrontPage 98 extensions"). Malicious programmers can make mischief anywhere.

If you're worried about the security risks inherent in ActiveX, don't use MSIE as your Web browser and avoid all software that depends on ActiveX. Alternatively, trade in

Figure 8.23:
The Comet Cursor
Was Bundled with
the RealPlayer
Audio Application

Select your Free RealPlayer 7 Basic
Based on your connection speed, we have selected a download size for you. To change your selection, check the button next to the one you want.

Features Include:	Complete (7.4 MB)	Standard (7.0 MB)	Minimal (3.4 MB)
Plays all Real content	✓	✓	✓
NEW! Take5 showcase	✓	✓	✓
NEW! Over 100 Radio Stations	✓	✓	✓
Support for MP3	✓	✓	✓
AutoUpdate	✓	✓	✓
Built-in Help	✓	✓	
RealJukebox Basic	✓	✓	
Comet Cursor	✓	✓	
Additional Playback Formats	All	Some	
Est. download time (56k)	18 min.	17 min.	8 min.
Make Your Selection	C	⊙	C

Download FREE RealPlayer 7 Basic beta

your Windows-based personal computer for a Mac. If you aren't sure how much you should worry about all of this, remember that whereas many things are possible on the Internet, relatively few worst-case scenarios actually materialize. Moreover, the chances of the worst case happening to you probably are fewer than the chances of your being struck by lightning. However, here are some simple common sense precautions you can take (which could save you from total disaster if you should happen to be very unlucky).

1. Periodically back up your hard drive or the most important files on your hard drive (catastrophic hardware failures can happen without warning).

2. Encrypt your most sensitive data files or store them offline (on floppy or zip disks).

3. Don't download software from obscure Web sites.

In the future, you'll see more variations on software installations, including ASP services, that minimize the need for full application downloads. Although using utilities such as ActiveX involves security risks, these same tools can be used to good advantage. The benefits easily outweigh the risks.

8.5 | FILE DOWNLOAD UTILITIES

If you expect to download a lot of software from the Internet, you'll eventually need a **file archive utility** to open a zipped file archive. Three of those most widely used are described here.

- **WinZip** (Windows shareware)

  `http://www.winzip.com/tucows/`

  For Windows, the most popular archive utility is the shareware WinZip. You can try it at no charge for 21 days. If after that you elect to keep it, then you need to register for it for $29. WinZip has won numerous software awards, including ZDNet's "Download of the Millennium."

  Don't confuse WinZip with WinZip Self-Extractor, which sells for $49. You don't need Self-Extractor unless you want to distribute your own software over the Internet. The WinZip Web site contains excellent documentation, including detailed instructions on how to configure WinZip to launch your anti-virus software (conduct a site search using the keyword "virus").

- **ZipCentral** (Windows freeware)

  `http://zipcentral.iscool.net/`

  Although it's hard to beat WinZip, the freeware ZipCentral comes very close. ZipCentral's home page is sometimes hard to access (it's free Web space from **Xoom.com**), and you might need MSIE to view it correctly. However, don't let the problems with the Web site scare you away. ZipCentral is robust, easy-to-use, and filled with all of the most important features found in WinZip. For your $29, you won't get the same level of technical support as with WinZip, but you probably won't need it because of its ease of use. Note: If you're having trouble configuring ZipCentral to launch your anti-virus software, visit the **WinZip Web site** and follow their instructions for anti-virus software integration. The instructions that work for WinZip also apply to ZipCentral.

- **Stuffit Expander** (Macintosh freeware)

  `http://www.aladdinsys.com/expander/expander_mac_login.html`

  Stuffit Expander is freeware and a must-have utility for all Mac owners. Don't confuse it with Stuffit Deluxe, which sells for $79.95, or Stuffit Lite, which sells for $30. You don't need Stuffit Deluxe or Stuffit Lite unless you want to distribute your own software over the Internet.

You'll need one of these file utilities to unpack software from the Internet. Download one from the Net, and you'll be able to handle any file types for software that you encounter on the Net. Note that you would be in trouble if you needed a file utility to unpack a newly downloaded file utility. Happily, the people who distribute file utilities understand this, so they are careful to give you installers or ready-to-go executables for their software.

Another class of file download utilities that can improve the quality of computing life is the download manager. This is especially true if your Internet connection tends to die in the middle of long downloads. A **download manager** is a utility that specializes in managing file downloads and offers many features not found in Web browsers. A Web browser can handle file downloads in a basic way, without enhancements or nonessential features. However, a download manager handles file downloads with style and can make a big difference if you're experiencing download difficulties with Web-based browsers. Chapter 9 discusses download managers in more detail.

8.6 ■ SOFTWARE CLEARINGHOUSES

The Web makes it easy to find and obtain software—you need only to know where to look. The software clearinghouse is perfect as a source of downloadable software. Just as it pays to try out a few different search engines before you decide on your favorites, it makes sense to visit various software clearinghouses in order to find those that are best for you. Each has its own combination of features and its own mix of software titles.

Many software clearinghouses index large collections of downloadable software in searchable subject trees. Most include a brief description of each software item, and some include software ratings, download counts, and e-mail newsletters to keep you on top of the best new software. Some are one component in a larger Web portal, whereas others are dedicated sites that concentrate only on software. Some specialize in programs for a particular population (for example, Web designers), whereas others focus on a specific software genre (for example, Java applets). Some are easier to navigate than others, and some have larger software collections than others.

If you have some time on your hands, visit different software clearinghouses to see what they offer. Even if two clearinghouses cover much the same software, you might like the reviews at one site better or you might enjoy a special feature that one site offers.

8.6.1 Some Popular Software Sites

- **Tucows** (`http://www.tucows.com`)

  Tucows offers a massive collection of software, as well as many special features, including the famous 5-cow rating system. Check out the editorials (follow the News link from its home page) and the How-To Tutorials under HTML Stuff. Tucows has many mirror sites. If it asks you to pick a region, try one close to home—some mirror sites will be faster than others. At times, Tucows might seem difficult to navigate, but persist. Although it includes Mac products, it offers better coverage for Windows products.

- **DOWNLOAD.COM** (http://download.cnet.com)

  DOWNLOAD.COM is CNet's download site (CNet is a Web portal for technical people). Navigate it with keyword searches. Pull-down menus let you filter your search results for a specific OS, general software category, and license type (for example, freeware). Also, take a look at its list of software-related newsletters. This is an excellent site for both Windows and Mac products.

- **ZDNet Downloads** (http://www.zdnet.com/downloads/)

  ZDNet is a Web portal for software junkies. Once you get hooked on software downloads, you might want to make this page your default home page. You can filter your searches for Windows-based personal computers, Macs, Palm Pilots, or CE laptops. If you set the filter for "all ZDNet," your keyword search will return not only hits for software downloads, but also hits for product reviews, tips and help articles, technical news, commentary, and more. Each hit list is displayed separately, so you can scan it or ignore it, as you wish. The different hit lists make this a great browsing site.

- **MACDOWNLOAD.COM** (http://www.zdnet.com/mac/download.html)

  This is the Mac side of the ZDNet portal. It's a great place for Mac software.

- **Dave Central Software Archive** (http://www.davecentral.com)

  This large site has personality, as well as some nice features. It offers only Windows products. Check out the free animated GIF of the day and the free font of the day.

- **SHAREWARE.COM** (http://shareware.cnet.com/)

  This is CNet's meta search engine for software. Use the pull-down menu to filter your search results for a specific platform.

If you think it's fun to browse software clearinghouses, you'll want to start your own collection of favorite software sites. The ones listed here will get you started. There are hundreds of others on the Web. Some are listed in the next two sections.

8.6.2 Windows Software Sites

Here's a list of Windows-based product sites to explore:

```
http://www.getyoursfree.com/
http://www.mysharewarepage.com/webtools.htm
http://www.completelyfreesoftware.com/
http://www.nonags.com/
http://www.Slaughterhouse.com/pick.html
http://www.completelyfreesoftware.com/index_all.html
http://www.32bit.com/
http://www.freewareweb.com/
http://www.thefreesite.com/
```

```
http://www.rocketdownload.com
http://www.hotfiles.com/
http://www.winmag.com
http://softsite.com/
http://happypuppy.com/
http://newapps.internet.com/categories.html
http://www.galttech.com/sharware.shtml
http://cws.internet.com/
http://www.netigen.com/freeware.html
```

8.6.3 Macintosh Software Sites

If you're a Mac user in search of software sites, you might be feeling outnumbered by the endless parade of sites for Windows products. There are not only fewer software sites for the Mac, but also less software. However, that is not necessarily bad. Most Mac owners pride themselves on the fact that their computers are only a means to an end (as opposed to a time-consuming bottomless pit of problems and headaches). Who needs 50 different screen shot utilities anyway? The important thing is to have two or three that do it well. And if there are only two or three to choose from, think of the time that you save when deciding which to use. You can research your options, make a decision, install what you need, and get back to the rest of your life much faster than your Windows user counterpart.

Here are some sites that you can explore for some great Mac software:

```
http://www.macresource.com/mrp/software.shtml
http://www.macorchard.com/
http://www.chezmark.com/
http://www.macupdate.com/
http://hyperarchive.lcs.mit.edu/HyperArchive/
http://asu.info.apple.com/
http://www.versiontracker.com/
http://www.tidbits.com/iskm/iskm-soft.html
http://www.macupdate.com/
http://Macs.Bon.Net/MacFreeware_Os_1024x768.html
```

Mac Users Only

Still feeling neglected? Check out the **ULTIMATE Macintosh**. Then drop by `http://www.maccentral.com/`, pick a story that looks interesting, read it, and scroll all of the way down to check out what other readers have to say about it. You'll be quickly reassured that the Mac user community is alive and well and at least a few jumps ahead of the competition.

8.7   FTP SOFTWARE ARCHIVES

Programmers were sharing software and maintaining software archives on the Internet long before the Web came along. How did they do it? With a device called file transfer protocol, or FTP (see the Above and Beyond section in Chapter 1). Programmers have been visiting FTP sites to find software files since the early days of the original ARPANET. FTP sites are still around, and you need to visit one some-day, for example to find MP3 files.

An address on an FTP server looks like an address on a Web server, except that the `ftp://` prefix is used instead of the Web server's `http://` prefix. To reach an address on an FTP server, you can use an FTP client or your Web browser. Either way, FTP servers are easy to handle once you know what to expect.

Project Gutenberg is an example of an archive that is stored on FTP servers. The archive is an online library of books that can be freely distributed on the Internet because their copyrights have expired and they are in the public domain. To find a specific novel at Project Gutenberg, start at its Web site (see Figure 8.24), where you can conduct a search for a specific author or title.

As an example, look for *My Antonia* by Willa Cather. This search produces one hit, with all of the information that you need to retrieve the book from the archive (see

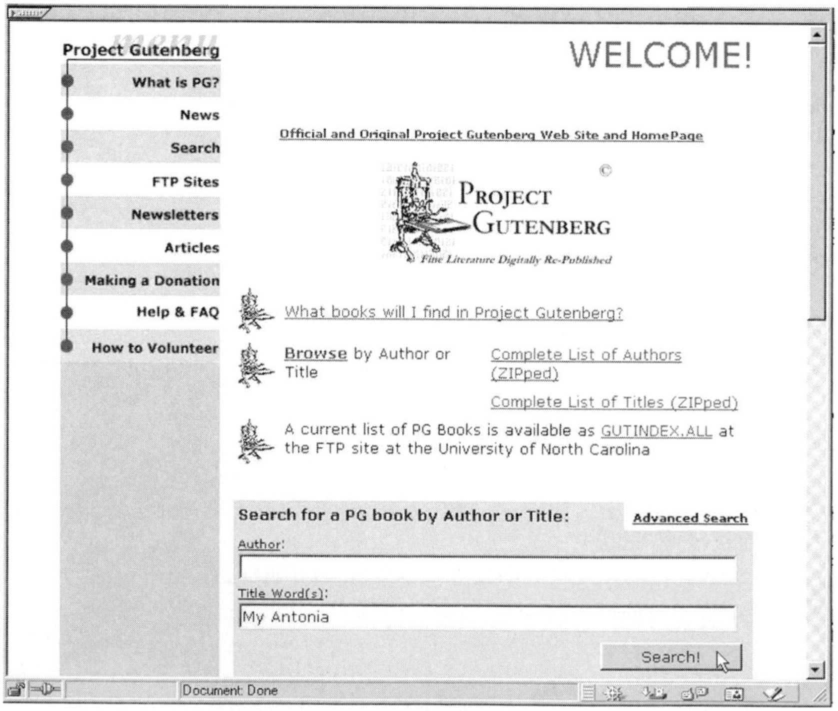

Figure 8.24:
Project Gutenberg: Classic Books That You Can Download for Free

Figure 8.25). The Web page shown in the figure is a gateway to the FTP server, where the book is actually stored. If you roll your mouse over the links for `myant10.txt` and `myant10.zip`, you'll see that the underlying hyperlinks are FTP addresses instead of HTTP addresses. Because this gateway has been designed to make file downloads easy for all visitors, you could download directly from one of these two links to get a copy of *My Antonia* (use the Save Link As command on your browser's pop-up menu). However, you want to find out how to download these files directly from the FTP server, so point your Web browser to the FTP server and find the book that way.

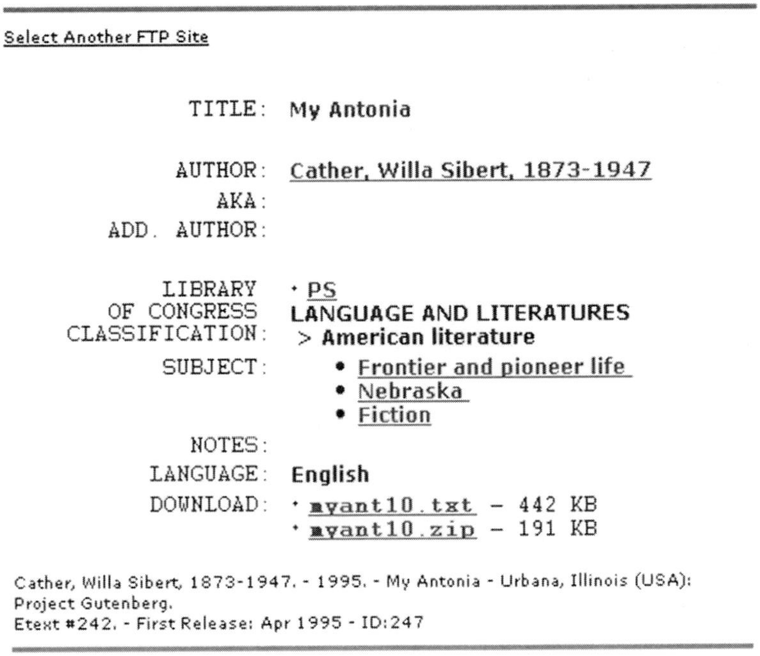

Figure 8.25:
Accessing *My Antonia* Online at Project Gutenberg

Select Another FTP Site

TITLE:	**My Antonia**
AUTHOR:	Cather, Willa Sibert, 1873-1947
AKA:	
ADD. AUTHOR:	
LIBRARY OF CONGRESS CLASSIFICATION:	• PS **LANGUAGE AND LITERATURES** > American literature
SUBJECT:	• Frontier and pioneer life • Nebraska • Fiction
NOTES:	
LANGUAGE:	**English**
DOWNLOAD:	• myant10.txt – 442 KB • myant10.zip – 191 KB

Cather, Willa Sibert, 1873-1947. - 1995. - My Antonia - Urbana, Illinois (USA): Project Gutenberg.
Etext #242. - First Release: Apr 1995 - ID:247

Before you leave this page, you should make a note of some crucial information. According to the Web page, *My Antonia* was first added to the archive in 1995 and is stored as Etext #242. This information might be important later when you're connected to the server.

Note that this FTP example may seem somewhat artificial: the Project Gutenberg Web site is set up to deliver files from the Web, so why are we looking at the FTP server fo Project Gutenberg? When a Web link for a software download works, you don't need to inerteract with any underlying FTP servers. But sometimes these Web page links don't work. That's when it's sometimes necessary to bypass a Web page like this and go directly to the FTP server on your own. If a link on a Web gateway doesn't work, you're stuck unless you know how to go to the FTP server and get it yourself. Whenever there's more than one way to skin a cat, it's often a good idea to learn at least two of them.

From the Project Gutenberg Web site, click FTP Sites in the navigational menu to reveal a choice of possible FTP servers from which you can fetch the file (see Figure 8.26). All of these servers house the same files stored in the same directory hierarchy. Multiple FTP servers that store identical copies of a single archive are called **mirror sites**. You should always pick a mirror site that is geographically close to you to minimize traffic load.

Figure 8.26:
Always Pick a
Server Near You

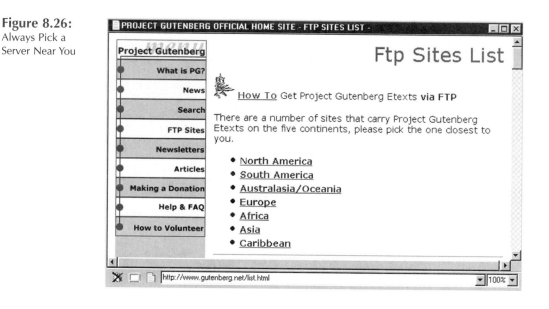

Select a mirror site and visit it by clicking a hyperlink or by entering the FTP address in the place where you usually enter URLs. Either way, you'll end up at the top-level directory for the FTP server (see Figure 8.27).

The figure shows the main file directory at the FTP server as if it were simply another Web page. Note, however, that this Web page looks more like a file directory than the typical Web page. You'll see no graphics and little or no text, but rather many directory names and filenames. If you know where you're going, this is all that you need. This is where that information you collected earlier—Etext #242—comes in handy.

I Think I Need a Map

If you're exploring a new FTP server and aren't sure where to go, watch for files named `index`, `welcome`, or `readme`, as well as subdirectories named `pub` (for "public"). A welcome message printed by the server at the top-level directory might say something useful to aid your navigation. You might also see directory-specific welcome messages whenever you enter a new subdirectory.

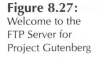

Figure 8.27:
Welcome to the
FTP Server for
Project Gutenberg

Directory of /pub/etext/gutenberg - Netscape

File Edit View Go Communicator Help

Back Forward Reload Home Search Netscape Print Security Stop

Bookmarks Location: ftp://uiarchive.cso.uiuc.edu/pub/etext/gutenberg/   What's Related

Current directory is /pub/etext/gutenberg

```
---> You are user 83 out of 200 allowed in your usage class. <--

*** All transfers are logged with your host name and email address.
*** If you don't like this policy, disconnect now!

                        UIArchive.uiuc.edu
                   - Local access to global services -

Check out the <a href=http://uiarchive.uiuc.edu/>web search engines.</a>

We welcome your comments and suggestions. Please mail any input
to ftpadmin@uiuc.edu.
```

```
Up to higher level directory
00
GUTENBRG.gif
GUTINDEX.00
GUTINDEX.96
GUTINDEX.97
GUTINDEX.98
GUTINDEX.99
GUTINDEX.ALL
NEWUSER.GUT
etext00
etext90
```

Document: Done

When you visit an FTP site for the first time, always read everything available that could help you navigate the site, but don't be surprised if the server is less than helpful. FTP servers assume that you know where you need to go. They aren't there to help you figure out where everything is.

In the Project Gutenberg example, recall that you're looking for a file that was added to the archive in 1995 under the name `Etext242`. You are also looking for the filenames `myant10.txt` and `myant10.zip`. Is that information enough to get you where you want to go? Scroll down to see some directories that appear to be indexed by years (see Figure 8.28). Click `etext95` to learn whether you'll have any luck there. You'll reach another directory that looks like the top-level directory but with different directory entries (see Figure 8.28). At first glance, the entries in this directory don't look promising. However, if you scroll down a bit, you see that this is a very large directory and that the files are alphabetically organized. Scroll down further, and you'll find `myant10.txt` and `myant10.zip`.

Figure 8.28:
Navigating Project
Gutenberg's FTP
Directory

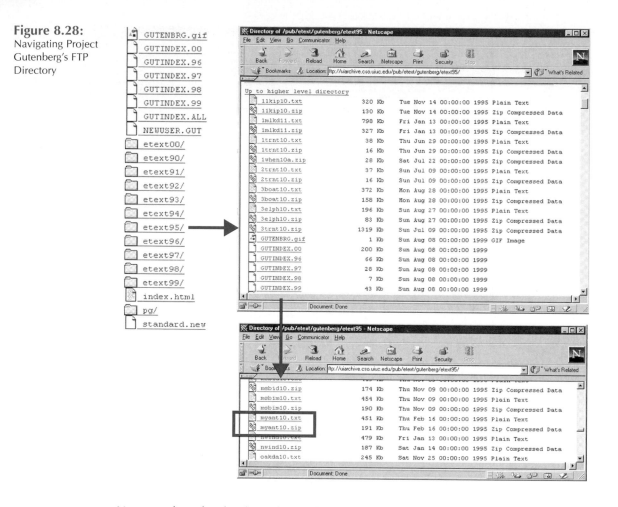

You can download either of two files: a .txt file that has not been compressed or a .zip file that you'll need to unpack.: they both contain the full text for *My Antonia*. If you select the zipped option, it will download faster. However, if you don't have a file utility that handles .zip files or if the zipped archive doesn't unpack correctly, you can opt for the .txt file.

If you select `myant10.zip`, the 192 KB archive file takes about one minute to download using a 56K modem and unpacks into a 452 KB text file. When you view the file, you are told, among other things, who digitized the original text and what equipment was used (see Figure 8.29).

Notice that the address in Navigator's `Location:` field in Figure 8.29 differs from that shown in Figure 8.27. If you ever get lost in an FTP directory, look at the current address in your browser's address box. It will show you the path of all of the subdirectories that you followed from the main directory. Each time that you click a subdi-

Figure 8.29:
Project Gutenberg's
Preamble for *My Antonia*

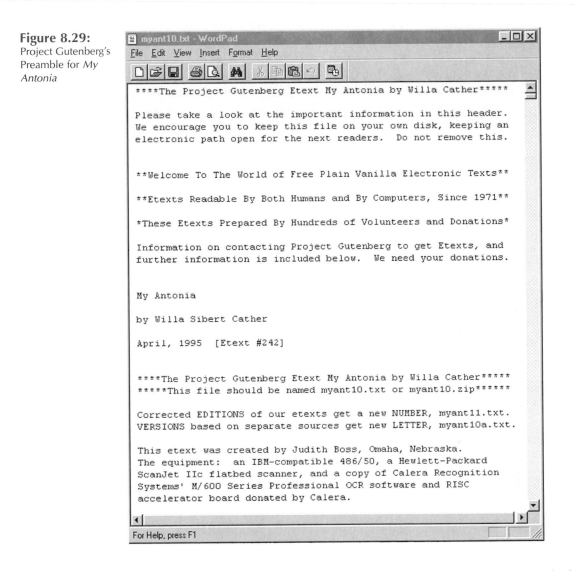

```
myant10.txt - WordPad                                    _ □ ×
File  Edit  View  Insert  Format  Help

****The Project Gutenberg Etext My Antonia by Willa Cather*****

Please take a look at the important information in this header.
We encourage you to keep this file on your own disk, keeping an
electronic path open for the next readers.  Do not remove this.


**Welcome To The World of Free Plain Vanilla Electronic Texts**

**Etexts Readable By Both Humans and By Computers, Since 1971**

*These Etexts Prepared By Hundreds of Volunteers and Donations*

Information on contacting Project Gutenberg to get Etexts, and
further information is included below.  We need your donations.


My Antonia

by Willa Sibert Cather

April, 1995  [Etext #242]


****The Project Gutenberg Etext My Antonia by Willa Cather*****
*****This file should be named myant10.txt or myant10.zip******

Corrected EDITIONS of our etexts get a new NUMBER, myant11.txt.
VERSIONS based on separate sources get new LETTER, myant10a.txt.

This etext was created by Judith Boss, Omaha, Nebraska.
The equipment:  an IBM-compatible 486/50, a Hewlett-Packard
ScanJet IIc flatbed scanner, and a copy of Calera Recognition
Systems' M/600 Series Professional OCR software and RISC
accelerator board donated by Calera.

For Help, press F1
```

rectory hyperlink, you move down one level in the directory hierarchy in the browser's display window and the name of that directory is added to the directory path. You can always return to the main directory, either by clicking the Back command button repeatedly or in a single step by using your history list. All of the usual Web browser commands and features work here just as they do with any other Web pages.

Navigational Hyperlinks in FTP Directories

In Figure 8.27, "Up to higher level directory" is a link to the next highest level in the directory tree. Sometimes, instead, you'll see only a cryptic hyperlink, containing two periods (. .). This, too, will take you up to the next level in the directory tree. The two periods are from a directory navigation command for UNIX; the original FTP users were expected to recognize this as a familiar signpost.

Today, some FTP sites (such as that shown in Figure 8.27) have taken steps to make their navigational links more intelligible for a broader audience. However, if you visit many FTP directories, you'll likely see the two periods at times.

FTP sites were never designed for easy browsing the way the Web was. A savvy FTP visitor already knows what to look for and where to find it before connecting to the server. An FTP server might contain many publicly available files but typically offers only minimal documentation. Don't expect to find more than an initial README file for new users. If you don't know exactly what you're looking for and you just want to look around, feel free to explore. However, don't expect it to be the same as browsing the Web.

This Is a Busy Signal . . . Please Try Again Later

Sometimes, you'll click a file's name in an FTP directory and your browser won't be able to download the file. You might be told something such as: "Alert!: Unable to access document." This can happen with a heavily used server during peak periods; it doesn't necessarily mean that the file is permanently unavailable. Try again later. You might be able to get it when the server is less busy.

When you visit an FTP site, you're an invited guest on someone else's property. FTP sites are maintained as a community courtesy. Visitors should understand that anonymous FTP is a privilege, not a right. If a site's administrators must field too many questions and complaints from inexperienced users, they might decide that the overhead is too great to continue the service. Any FTP server can be shut down at any time for any reason. Remember this, and honor any directives or requests made of you when you visit an FTP server.

FTP Netiquette and Commonsense

Here are some tips to keep in mind when using FTP servers.

- Try to visit FTP servers during off hours. Late evenings and early mornings are the best times.
- Always read the welcome and README files for important information.
- Don't contact the technical support staff for an FTP server unless you have first asked your local technical support staff for help and they advise you to contact staff at the FTP site.
- If mirror sites are available, use the one that is closest to you.
- Anonymous FTP access is a privilege, not a right. Be a courteous guest.

As the Project Gutenberg example demonstrated, a Web site can be set up as an interface to an FTP site or as multiple FTP mirror sites. For each file on the FTP server, a Web page can offer comments and useful information, in contrast to the FTP directory, which shows only a filename. Web servers are much friendlier places to visit, but FTP servers win hands down when it comes to speedy searching. If you know the name of the file that you want, it's much faster to search an index of all of the filenames on public FTP servers than it is to search a full-text index for HTML files all over the Web. Programmers previously used a search engine called *Archie* to search FTP servers worldwide. Today, you can find Archie-style search engines on the Web (see the tip box).

Searching for Files on FTP Servers

Visit **FAST FTP Search** if you know the file's name and you want to find it on an FTP server. If you know part of the name, but not the exact name, look at all of the available search options. Try a few searches (see exercises 19 and 20) to see how fast it is to search FTP space.

As explained, Web browsers can download files from both Web servers and FTP servers. Some also allow you to *upload* a file to an FTP server (Navigator and MSIE both support file uploads). People often find it useful to upload files when they collaborate on major projects with coworkers. For example, each chapter of this book was uploaded to an FTP server so that everyone involved in the book's production could work with those files as needed. This type of file sharing is accomplished with *full-privileged FTP sessions*, which are described shortly.

Uploading Files by Using a Browser

If you don't expect to do a lot of file transfers, try using your browser for uploads. To contact an FTP server, enter an FTP address in the `Location:` or address field of your browser (wherever you normally enter URLs). Note, you generally need an account on the FTP server in order to upload files to the server, so the address must contain both your userid for the account as well as the server's DNS address. For example, if your userid is psmith and your FTP server is `atlantic.ecc.unm.edu`, then you would enter the following address:

`ftp://psmith@atlantic.ecc.unm.edu`

Your browser will prompt you for your password, and then connect you to the server.

Once you are connected, your current working directory on the FTP server will be displayed in the browser window. You navigate the directories on the FTP server by clicking directory icons, and you move files between the server and your local host by dragging icons on your desktop. Treat the browser window like any other directory window on your desktop, and copy files from one location to the other by using drag-and-drop.

Many, easy to use graphical *FTP clients* are available for both the Mac and Windows OSs. If you need to do a lot of file transfers, you'll appreciate some of the special features that FTP clients offer and Web browsers do not. These features include the following:

- Simultaneous displays of local and remote directories
- Sorting options for directory displays
- Support for multiple FTP sessions running in parallel
- Support for multiple file transfers
- Resumable file transfers in case a transfer is interrupted
- A timer so that you can schedule large jobs to download while you're in meetings or when it's late at night or a weekend day
- Intuitive drag-and-drop file transfers
- An address book for automated logons on different servers
- File caching to speed up transfers from pokey servers
- File search facilities

When you use an FTP client to visit an FTP server, you start by specifying the DNS or IP address of the host machine that you want to contact. If you don't know which FTP server to visit, your FTP client can't help you.

Figure 8.30 shows the opening window from an FTP client named LeechFTP. You enter the DNS address of the server that you want to visit in the `Host or URL:` field. In this example, you are initiating an anonymous FTP connection, so the `Username:` field is completed with "anonymous" (the default value) and your complete e-mail address is masked (shown as a series of asterisks) and entered as the password. If you leave the `Remote Directory:` field blank, you'll go straight to the main directory. However, if you know your way around and want to go to a specific subdirectory, you can enter the appropriate directory path in this field. Finally, click OK. LeechFTP then will attempt to make the connection.

If you have a personal account on an FTP server, you can initiate a *full-privilege FTP session* in order to move files to and from the server. To create a full privilege session, you use your userid in the `User ID:` window and your private password for the `Password:` entry.

When to Use Full-Privilege FTP

If you want to set up a Web site, you might need to use full-privilege FTP. You'll be given a personal account on a Web server in which you can store your HTML files, but you might want to develop your Web pages on your home computer. Then, when you've completed your pages, you'll move your HTML files from your home computer to the Web server by using FTP. Uploading files to a remote host is easy with a full-privilege FTP session.

Figure 8.30:
Connecting to an
FTP Server by Using
LeechFTP

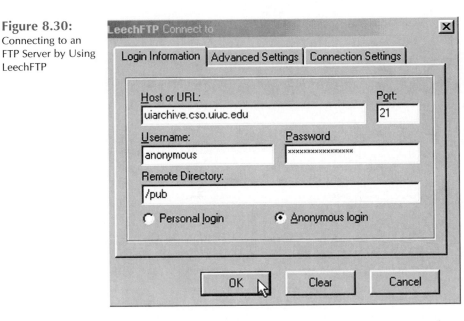

Figure 8.31 shows LeechFTP in action once the FTP connection has been established. Two directories are displayed: one for the local host (on the left) and one for the remote FTP server (on the right). Both can be navigated by using scrolling and point-and-click operations. To download a file, select the file's name on the remote server and click the download icon in the toolbar. The file will be copied to the current directory (the one in the display) on the local host. To upload a file, select the file's name on the local host and click the upload icon in the toolbar. The file will be copied to the current directory (the one in the display) on the remote host. LeechFTP also supports drag-and-drop operations so that you can move files and folders across the Internet in the same way that you move files and folders on your desktop.

Graphical FTP clients have many convenient features to make FTP fast and painless. For example, most FTP clients create a separate window for any welcome messages issued by the remote server, so you can easily refer back to those messages as needed. If you need to move a lot of files at once (for example, an entire Web site), an FTP client will let you queue up entire subdirectories so that you don't have to move each file individually. Some clients will let you view files on an FTP server without downloading them, and a few will let you edit text files remotely, provided that you're running a full-privilege FTP session. Remote editing is convenient when you're maintaining a Web site and need to make a few small corrections or updates to a Web page.

FTP servers are often used when a group of people is working on a joint project and group members need to share files. A project directory is created on a password-protected FTP server so that project files will be available only to group members.

Figure 8.31:
Point-and-Click File
Transfers with
LeechFTP

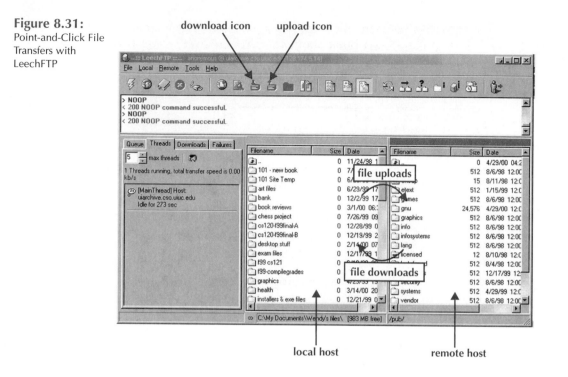

They then can download and upload files to the FTP server via full-privilege FTP sessions. This is the easiest way to share files within a geographically dispersed workforce, especially when many files are involved or the files are very big. E-mail attachments can be used in these situations if needed, but this tends to be cumbersome when too many files, too many group members, or too many file updates are involved.

8.8   MANAGING YOUR SOFTWARE

Now that you're ready to download tons of software from the Internet, you need to learn how to manage it all. How do you safely remove certain software from your computer? How can you determine if a new software addition is causing your machine to crash? What does it mean when two pieces of software conflict with each other? If your computer suddenly starts to freeze up repeatedly, how do you return it to a stable state?

Mac users might be tempted to skip most of this section because Macs tend to be more stable and less temperamental than a Windows-based machine. However, some standard maintenance routines apply to both Macs and Windows-based machines. This section focuses on those.

You need to know more about caring for your computer than this section can cover. Consider purchasing a book about your particular OS (especially since the user's manual that came with your computer is not always as comprehensive or as easy to understand as you might like or need).

8.8.1 Three Rules for All Computer Users

Here are three rules that all computer users should keep in mind, regardless of OS used.

Restart Your Computer as Needed to Recover RAM and Speed Up Processing Each time that you launch an application, your computer sets aside some amount of RAM for that application. When you exit that application, you might expect that the same amount of RAM will be freed. However, this likely will not happen; your computer will not be able to recover all of the RAM. This happens when poorly designed software "leaks" memory. The RAM that is leaked—that is, not freed up for use by other programs—is no longer available to other applications, long after the leaky application has been shut down. ***The only way to recover "leaked" RAM is to restart your system.***

How often should you restart? That is hard to predict because it depends on several factors:

- How much RAM your computer has
- How many applications you've run during a computer session
- How well behaved the applications that you have run are regarding memory leaks

Some people must restart their computers (usually Windows-based) at least once a day. Others can go for a week or more (these are usually Macs). If your computer becomes unusually sluggish or unable to open new applications, it's time to restart. Your OS probably includes a *RAM manager* that tries to free up as much RAM as possible whenever the supply looks dangerously low. You might find it instructive to watch your available RAM each time you launch a new application or exit a running application (see Figure 8.32). A RAM monitor (part of your OS) will show you how much RAM has been allocated to existing applications and how much RAM is available to launch additional applications.

With Windows, you can also monitor your *system resources* (in the Control Panel, click System and then the Performance tab). System resources generally start high (around 90%) and drop as you start up applications. Eventually, system resources could get too low. If they drop below 40%, your system is being stressed. You might or might not be able to recover system resources by exiting active applications. If resources fall to 30%, it's time to restart.

Optimize Your Hard Drive With hard drives now measured in gigabytes, one can easily forget that they still can get crowded (eventually). When you save a file to your hard drive, a fixed amount of space is allocated for that file. When you remove a

Figure 8.32:
A RAM Manager
Monitoring
Available RAM

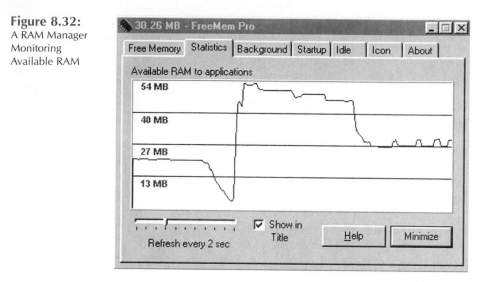

file from your hard drive, all of the space allocated to that file becomes available for new files. The OS can retrieve a file faster if the file has been allocated a big block of *contiguous (uninterrupted) space.* When your hard drive is new and mostly empty, allocating contiguous space when a file is saved is easy. However, after you've saved and deleted a few hundred, or a few thousand, files, your OS will begin to have difficulty finding contiguous space for very large files. When contiguous space is not available, your system will use smaller blocks of space and spread the file across these smaller blocks. This produces a **fragmented file**, a file that does not occupy contiguous space. You'll not have a problem working with a fragmented file, but when you want to retrieve the file from the hard drive your OS will need *more time* to piece it together, thereby slowing down the file's loading. When your hard drive has many fragmented files, the drive is called a **fragmented hard drive**. If your hard drive is badly fragmented, your computer will get sluggish. This happens over a long period of time, so you likely won't notice any sudden changes in response. You might not even realize that your computer is not as snappy as it once was. This is why you need to run a disk optimizer on your hard drive every so often. A **disk optimizer** (sometimes called a *disk defragmenter*) is a utility that analyzes your hard drive and reorganizes the files stored there in order to eliminate fragmented files. If your hard drive is very large and contains many files, it might take an hour or more to defragment it. Some books recommend that you defragment (*defrag*, for short) your hard drive once a month. How often you do so depends on how much you use your computer and the size of your hard drive. At the very least, you should defragment once or twice a year.

Don't Overload Your Computer with Too Many Running Applications RAM limitations will determine how many applications you can run at one time. Too many applications and too little RAM will lead to system crashes and freezes. If you absolutely must run your word processor, Web browser, speech recognition software, and photo editor all at the same time, and your system is crashing every two hours, you probably need to increase your RAM. Remember that lots of little applications add up to consume RAM. Included here are all of those background utilities that are automatically launched at start-up time, such as anti-virus, fax, or instant messenger software, and any other programs that are in constant use on your computer.

Computers are like people: Some are healthy, and some are barely alive. A computer that freezes and crashes six times a day is not healthy. If you have a sick computer, you must identify the source of the trouble. Sometimes the hardware is fine but too many demands are being made of it. But sometimes the problems are all in the software.

Is It a Hardware Problem or a Software Problem?

Here are some points to keep in mind when you're trying to determine if your computer problem results from hardware or from software.

1. Faulty hardware is usually apparent from the start. If your computer was fine for the first month or two after you bought it and now it's crashing or freezing, you probably don't have a hardware problem (this assumes that you used it a lot during that month or two). However, if you think that you have a hardware problem, dig up your warranty and call the manufacturer or dealer.

2. An overloaded computer is easy to spot. Watch your RAM monitor to see if you're approaching or exceeding a RAM limitation (see Figure 8.32). If you find yourself struggling with too little RAM, either shut down any open applications that you can live without or install more RAM.

3. Software accounts for all other problems. You might need to update a device driver. You might need to reinstall a corrupt program file. You might be dealing with buggy software.

A computer's health is a lot like a person's health. It's usually easier to prevent problems than to fix them. Just as you need the right tools to protect your computer from viruses, you need the right tools to protect it from software conflicts and other problems. However, if you never add new software to your computer, you can skip the rest of this section.

The more software that you install, the more that you need to practice routine system maintenance. You'll never know before installation how a new program will interact with your computer. If all goes well, no problems result. However, in rare cases, a new software installation can interfere with older software and really mess up your computer. It might never happen if you use only the most popular software (there's safety in numbers). But it's always good to be prepared. The next subsection discusses various maintenance tools that you can use to keep your computer operating at peak performance.

How to Correctly Remove Software

Sometimes, you'll want to remove a program, perhaps to free space on your hard drive or to clear it of clutter. You must be careful when removing program files. If a program consisted of only one executable file, you could delete that file and be done with it. However, that's not how it works.

Computer programs typically involve many files—sometimes dozens or hundreds. To complicate things, those files are stored in different places on your hard drive, often in places you don't know about. You can't expect to find and eliminate all of them manually: you don't know what files to look for or where to find them. A superior program always comes with an uninstaller in case you need to remove the program. An **uninstaller** is a utility designed to unload, safely and completely, all files associated with the program. Look for uninstallers when you select your software downloads, and always use an uninstaller when you want to remove a program from your hard drive.

Remember, once you have installed a piece of software, don't move any of its associated files from their original locations. If one file of the program can't find another file of the program because it's been moved from its original position, then the program might fail to launch or it might launch but later crash. If you ever reorganize your directories, *don't touch your software directories*. If you absolutely must reorganize your software directories, first uninstall any affected software (by using the uninstaller) and then reinstall it in its new location. As a rule, you should leave software files where the installer put them.

8.8.2 Maintenance Tools

Various commercial software maintenance packages are available. If you want to explore the world of shareware and freeware, you should seriously consider investing in one or more. You don't need a technical background to use them—in fact, the best tool suites make it easy for even nontechnical people to keep their computer in good health. A good set of maintenance tools will include the following:

- A disk scanner (e.g., ScanDisk) and disk optimizer (e.g., Disk Defragmenter) to keep your hard drive healthy
- A general uninstaller utility (e.g., McAfee's Uninstaller) that tracks all of your software installations so that you can undo them as needed
- A tool for making a *rescue floppy* to restore your system if needed
- A crash guard utility that intercepts system crashes and restores your system without restarting
- A registry scanner (for Windows), a system utility that helps keep Windows stable
- Anti-virus software

Note: Don't purchase each of these separately. Look for *system utility suites* in which all have been bundled.

Should you run out and buy a $100 utility suite before you download any software? No, that's not necessary. In fact, some of these utilities might be part of your OS, for example a disk scanner, disk optimizer, and a tool for making a rescue floppy. You might also have received in your initial software setup some form of anti-virus software (at least a 30-day free-trial version of one). You probably don't need to go beyond these unless you plan to download software regularly. Everything else you can live without as long as your system is stable, you don't make many changes to your software library, and you're happy with your computer the way that it is. However, if you later decide to explore other utilities, revisit this issue and think about whether your preventive maintenance routines are adequate. If a little preventative action can save you from system freezes and crashes, it's worth the extra effort.

8.9   FINDING GOOD SOFTWARE REVIEWS

If you're serious about making informed software decisions, start with what reviewers have to say about the products in which you are interested. Don't sweat the little choices, such as which free applet to download. However, do some homework before you purchase a big-ticket item. As mentioned previously in the chapter, when you shop for your software on the Net, you can try a free-trial version before you buy. However, you probably don't want to test drive every car on the lot. By seeing what the reviewers have to say, you should be able to limit your choices, or in some cases, learn about other solutions to your problems that might take you in a different direction altogether. Software reviews can be educational, and sometimes entertaining, and they almost always will save you time. You can also find out what other people think of specific software by visiting newsgroups or mailing lists. Those are good places to ask specific questions. However, if you're exploring an area in which you have little or no experience, a good software review is usually the best place to start.

As you might expect, the Net offers plenty of software reviews, in newsletters, in "zines," and at some software clearinghouses, as well at sites that specialize in the software industry or that focus on particular professions. For example, in the latter case, sites for teachers might review educational software; sites for artists might review photo editors and drawing programs; and sites for interior designers might review software for house layouts. As you browse the Web, note any sites that you see that run software reviews.

Not all software is reviewed, for example many applets and JavaScript programs because they are so numerous. Undoubtedly, many good freeware and shareware programs never get enough attention to earn a review. If you enjoy searching software archives and looking for undiscovered gems, you don't have to restrict yourself to reviewers' recommendations. If you want to save time, read a review or two and go from there. Your main concern should be getting what you need and getting on with your life. If you restrict yourself to only software that has been reviewed, you're much less likely to be victimized by malicious code (see the Above and Beyond section in Chapter 8).

Here are some sites on which you can find reviews for mainstream software.

- Software reviews for all OSs

    The Cool Tool Network `http://www.cooltool.com/search.cgi`

    ZDNet Reviews `http://www.zdnet.com/products/`

- Software reviews for Windows

    Stroud's CWSA Apps `http://cws.internet.com/`

    Win Planet Reviews `http://www.winplanet.com/winplanet/subjects/`

    Digital Duck `http://www.digitalduck.com/`

    Netigen Web `http://www.netigen.com/reviews.html`

    PCToday.com Supersite `http://www.pctoday.com/mini/smartcomputing/editorial/reviews.asp?rid=396&guid=wlvapo30`

    PCWORLD.COM Reviews `http://www.pcworld.com/top400/0,1375,software,00.html`

- Software reviews for the Macintosh

    MacReview Zone `http://www.macreviewzone.com/`

    MacDirectory `http://www.pacifeeder.com/macintosh/software.htm`

    Macs Only `http://www.macsonly.com/`

    MacHome Journal Online Reviews `http://database.machome.com/Reviews/reviews.lasso`

If you think that a software purchase from your friendly local software retail store is safer than one purchased from the Net, remember that no computer is ever free from some risk. Software obtained over the Internet is no riskier than shrink-wrapped software from a "brick-and-mortar" retail store as long as you remember to take these reasonable precautions.

- Scan all new files with anti-virus software, and keep your anti-virus software up-to-date.

- Don't download executable files from obscure Web sites.

- Don't accept a file if your browser warns you about an Authenticode signature failure.

If you're still concerned, purchase only mainstream items. Alternatively, take advantage of software reviews, Web search engines, and Usenet newsgroups to find out everything anybody ever said about the software that you're considering. If there's a problem with it, you're bound to hear about it. Remember, you're plugged into the world's largest grapevine. Listen to the buzz, use your common sense, and see how long it takes to fill that 40 GB hard drive. This is one place where you can have lots of fun with your computer.

Things to Remember

- Scan all executable downloads after you complete the download and before you execute them.
- `.exe` and `.zip` are standard file formats for Windows downloads.
- `.hqx`, `.sit`, and `.bin` are standard file formats for Mac downloads.
- Turn off any other applications that are running before you begin a software installation.
- You might be instructed to turn off your anti-virus software during a software installation. This is sometimes a legitimate installation requirement. Just remember to turn it back on as soon as the installation is completed.
- Software installers might ask you many questions. If you don't understand one, take the default setting that the installer offers and continue with the installation.
- An installer file can be deleted after the installation is complete.
- Read all of the informational screens displayed by an installer, along with any README files.
- If you download a lot of software, invest in some good system utilities.

Important Concepts

anonymous FTP—a method to access an FTP server. This method does not require you to have an account on the server. Public FTP servers allow anonymous FTP logons, but restricted (private) FTP servers require a userid and a valid password.

anti-virus software—a program that checks a file to see whether it is infected with a computer virus. Running anti-virus software is an important precaution to take before installing any software.

file archive—a single file that contains multiple files and that can be unpacked (unzipped) to produce the multiple files. Software files are often packed in a file archive for easy downloading.

freeware—software that is distributed free of charge.

File Transfer Protocol (**FTP**)—the protocol that governs a means of moving files over the Internet.

FTP client—software designed to access FTP servers and facilitate FTP file transfers.

FTP server—a server that acts as a distribution site for files, for example, a software archive. On many FTP servers, anyone is allowed to download files (via anonymous FTP), but only privileged users with accounts on the server are allowed to upload files (privileged ftp).

shareware—software that can be installed and evaluated for some fixed free-trial period at no charge but that requires the user to pay a registration fee when the free-trial period ends if the user wants to continue using the software.

software download—the process of transferring a software file or software archive from a remote host to the local host.

software installation—the process of setting up data files, executable files, and other support files needed to run a piece of software on a computer.

special edition software (a.k.a. **limited edition software**)—an incomplete version of a commercial software package distributed at no charge in order to attract customers who, the manufacturer hopes, will want to upgrade to and pay for the full version.

Where Can I Learn More?

The Beginner's Guide to Downloading
`http://www.download.com/pc/ed/review/0,357,`
`0-1600-1,00.html`

Downloading Files: Frequently Asked Questions `http://www.`
`pcshareware.com/download.htm`

The PC Magazine Utility Guide (for Windows)
`http://www.zdnet.com/pcmag/stories/reviews/`
`0,6755,2547327,00.html`

Rebuilding the Desktop! (for the Mac)
`http://www.macinstruct.com/tutorials/troubleshooting/`
`desk/index.html`

Stroud's CWSApps: FTP Clients `http://cws.internet.com/ftp.html`

Problems and Exercises

1. Explain how a special edition or demo software distribution differs from freeware.

2. Why is it less expensive for a software manufacturer to distribute software over the Internet than through traditional retail stores? What are the pros and cons of these two distribution systems for the consumer? For the manufacturer?

3. Suppose that you download an executable file that contains a virus. Can you catch the virus by simply downloading the file? Explain your answer.

4. What is an installer, and when does it make sense to package a computer program inside of an installer? How often do you need to run the same installer? Why might you want to save an installer after you have used it? Explain why and when some software downloads contain digital signatures. Is the use of digital signatures a foolproof system? Explain your answer.

5. Suppose that you have a friend who has read that surfing the Web can be dangerous. She says that according to an article she saw, a person can wipe out his or her entire hard drive by clicking the wrong link. Is this true? Describe the circumstances that would have to be in place for something like this to happen. What can you do to make sure that it never happens to you?

6. WinZip is the most popular file archive utility for Windows. Suppose that you install this utility but when you try to run your anti-virus software from inside of it, the "Run anti-virus software" command is grayed out. What is wrong, and how can you fix it?

7. Name three things that an FTP client can do that a Web browser can't.

8. What is a fragmented hard drive? How does a hard drive become fragmented? Can it be fixed? Explain your answer.

9. What is an uninstaller, and why do you need to use them?

10. **[Find It Online]** Visit the **Tucows clearinghouse** to find a *color picker utility* (similar to **EyeDropper** or **ColorFinder**) that gives you the closest Web-safe color when you select a color on your desktop. Find one utility for the Mac and another for Windows-based machines. For each, list the utility's name, its home page URL, and its price. Don't download any software to complete this exercise—only read the software descriptions at Tucows.

11. **[Find It Online]** Search some software clearinghouses to locate programs that generate *fractal images*. How many programs can you find? For each, list its name and the OS for which it was designed. Which is the most popular freeware fractal designer? Which is the most popular shareware fractal designer? (*Hint*: Go to **CNet's download site**, conduct a keyword search on "fractal," and sort the results by clicking "Downloads" in the Re-sort bar at the top of the results list.)

12. **[Find It Online]** Find out how many Web browsers are available for Win95/98 by visiting **Dave's Central**, a software clearinghouse at `http://www.dave-central.com/` and going from the index category "Web Surfing" to "Browsers."

13. **[Find It Online]** Use your favorite Web browser to visit the **Electronic Frontier Foundation** at `ftp://ftp.eff.org/`. Path down to `pub/Net_culture/ Folklore/Dead_Media_Project`. Somewhere in this subdirectory, you can find out what a "chirographer" is. (This shouldn't take you more than one minute.)

14. **[Find It Online]** The Opera Web browser is available for both Windows-based personal computers and Macs and costs $39 as of this writing. Read some software reviews for Opera, and then explain why you think that many people choose to pay for Opera instead of opting for one of the two better-known freebies (Explorer and Navigator).

15. **[Hands-On: For Windows Users Only]** The Above and Beyond section in Chapter 5 described a graphics utility called Eyedropper. You can find this utility at **inetia.com** (`http://eyedropper.inetia.com/HTML/eng/ default.asp`), which distributes Eyedropper as a zipped file archive. Visit this site, and download the latest version of EyeDropper. Scan the software for viruses, and then install it. Did you have any difficulties with the installation? How many files are inside of the zipped archive? What are their names? Use the program to find the hexadecimal color codes for the Vizija logo at the bottom of the download page. This logo contains a blue color and a brown color:

How long did it take you to complete this exercise?

16. **[Hands-On: For Mac Users Only]** The EyeDropper program described in the Above and Beyond section in Chapter 5 does not run on a Mac, but similar programs are available for Mac users. Go to **Tucows** (`http://www.tucows. com`), and conduct a search by using the keyword "ColorFinder"—this will take you to a freeware color sampler utility for the Mac. This file is an `.hqx` file, which can be opened with Stuffit Expander. Scan the software for viruses, and then install it. Did you have any difficulties with the installation? How many files are inside of the file archive? What are their names? Use the program to find the hexadecimal color codes for the bird at the top of `http:// www-edlab.cs.umass.edu/cs120/`. The bird has a yellow beak and orange feet:

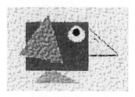

How long did it take you to complete this exercise?

17. **[Hands-On: For Windows Users Only]** Go to

    ```
    http://pluto.spaceports.com/~mobysw/en/
    mailto-encrypter.html
    ```

    and download MailTo-Encrypter 1.1. What does this program do? Who should use it? Scan the software for viruses, and then install it. Is this download an installer or a ready-to-go executable? How does MailTo-Encrypter encrypt the address `lehnert@cs.umass.edu`?

18. **[Hands-On: For Both Windows and Mac Users]** A **virtual postcard** is a GIF or JPEG image that you send to a recipient as an e-mail attachment. If your recipient has an HTML-enabled e-mail client (most people do), the image file will appear instead of a text-based message body. Some "postcard" applications give you a graphical background for your message; others give you a choice of fonts for the message. Either way, your postcard will stand out in any HTML-enabled inbox and get attention. Search the software clearinghouses for a freeware utility that creates virtual postcards on your platform. (*Hint*: Search by using the keyword "postcard" or "postcards.") What utility did you find? List the name of the utility, its home page URL, and the name of the download file. Download and install the utility, and then send yourself a postcard to see how it looks in your mailbox. How much memory does the attachment consume?

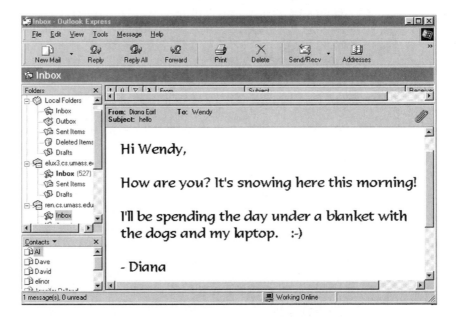

19. **[Hands-On: For Windows Users Only]** Use your Web browser to visit **FAST FTP Search** at `http://ftpsearch.unit.no/ftpsearch`. This is a search engine for FTP sites. To receive any hits, you need to match your query against

a filename or a directory name on some FTP server on the Net. Try conducting a search for the virus test file `eicar.com` (see Section 2.4 for a description of this file). You should get about a dozen hits on various FTP servers. Which server is closest to you? (Use the sort options to rank the hits.) Try downloading the file from one of the servers to see whether your anti-virus software will catch it. If it doesn't, your anti-virus software isn't turned on and running in the background. If you aren't running it in the background, can you scan the `eicar.com` file manually after it has been downloaded? (If you can't get an alert on this file one way or the other, your computer is a target for computer viruses.)

20. **[Hands-On: For Both Windows and Mac Users]** Visit **Project Gutenberg** at `http://www.gutenberg.net/`, and download a copy of *The Lumley Autograph*, by Susan F. Cooper. When was this document captured and by whom? How large is the zipped archive file? How large is the plain-text file?

21. **[Hands-On: For Both Windows and Mac Users]** Suppose that you want to get an FTP client for your computer but you aren't sure which one. Find three popular FTP clients (for your platform) and at least two software reviews for each. For each, list its home page URL, the URLs for its software reviews, and its price. What special features distinguish these three clients? Is there a consensus among the reviewers about which is the best choice? Which one would you choose? Why?

22. **[Hands-On: For Both Windows and Mac Users]** Recall that a RAM manager is a utility that monitors your available RAM and tries to free up as much RAM as possible whenever the supply looks dangerously low. Search the Web for software reviews of popular RAM managers for your OS. For each utility that you find, list its name, home page URL, price, and important features, as well as the URLs of any software reviews that you found.

Software on the Internet: Above and Beyond

Software Licenses

Whenever you obtain new software, it's your responsibility to know what the licensing agreement says. Reading this agreement isn't much fun, and if you routinely ignore it, you're not alone. The language is stiff, the restrictions predictable, and the disclaimers unsettling. How many products are accompanied by contractual agreements in which the manufacturer disavows all responsibility for any catastrophic consequences associated with the use of its product? Still, these much-maligned and traditionally ignored documents are the only weapons that stand between software manufacturers and financial ruin.

Software piracy is the bane of commercial software, and software licenses are notoriously difficult to enforce. If you install a piece of software on two computers when the license restricts you to one, the police are not likely show up at your door with a search warrant. However, using a CD-burner to create a few hundred pirated copies of the same software is different. You likely think that you understand what lines can and can't be crossed, so you ignore software licenses, use good common-sense, and avoid anything that looks risky.

Software licenses can test the ethics of even the straightest arrows among us. Consider the following scenarios.

> **The Desktop–Laptop Dilemma**   The license says that you're allowed to install the software on one computer at one time. You can't install it on two computers simultaneously. You have a desktop computer that you use most of the time and a laptop that you use when you travel. You want to use the same software on both machines. However, to comply with the licensing agreement, you would have to uninstall and install the software each time that you travel. This seems crazy, especially since you don't intend to use both installations simultaneously. You think that simultaneous usage must be what the license is trying to prohibit. Do you have the right to take liberties with the license's restrictions, as long as you adhere to their intent?

> **The Seven-Year-Old Software Pirate**   Your seven-year old daughter spent the day at a friend's house playing a computer game. She comes home with the CD-ROM for the game and asks you to install it for her so that she can play it at home. You know this can't be legal, but your daughter wants it *now*, and she's not going to be happy if you tell her she has to wait until you can purchase a copy of the software. The whole issue is further complicated by the fact that all of her friends routinely share their computer games with one another and you're the only parent who is uneasy about

the practice. Do you have the right to install the "bootlegged" software now, as long as you intend to purchase your own copy at the next possible opportunity? What if your daughter loses interest in the game and forgets all about it after two days? Do you handle this situation differently if the software costs $5, or $50? Should the price of the software enter into your reasoning?

The Garage Sale Software Deal   You've been browsing a garage sale (or a flea market or eBay) and discover that someone is offering a popular piece of commercial software at a bargain price. It's used software, but it comes with all of the original documentation and packaging. Is it legal to resell commercial software like this? What if the current owner has burned a backup CD of the original CD and is still using it? How can you know if the person is breaking the licensing agreement by selling the software? Can you be liable for entering into an illegal transaction if you don't know that it's illegal?

Many computer owners face such ethical and legal conundrums. In many cases, software manufacturers have acknowledged the difficulty of some licensing restrictions. For example, some licensing agreements have clarified the use of the software for desktops/laptops, loosening the restrictions to accommodate consumers who need to travel and take the software with them. However, other dilemmas remain. In particular, software CDs are frequently passed from person to person on eBay, resold as "almost new" each time they change hands. If the software's original packaging and registration forms are passed along with each sale, this is perfectly legal (assuming no backup CDs are being retained for continued use). Of course, there is no way of knowing if backup CDs are being burned by each buyer/seller as the software makes the rounds. Software piracy is a serious and pervasive problem for software manufacturers. One way to solve the problem is for manufacturers to remove all unreasonable/unenforceable restrictions and give the end user the right to use and redistribute software freely. Although this strategy might sound radical and incapable of supporting the people who write software for a living, it's an alternative model for commercial software and one that actually is being used by advocates for *open source software*, which is discussed later in this Above and Beyond.

Used Software: When Can You Sell It? When Can You Buy It?

Used software can be legally resold as long as the seller *does not retain a copy of the software and includes all of the original documentation*. Stores that buy and sell used software are generally adept at spotting pirated software, so anything that you buy in a store is probably being transferred legally. There is a large secondary market for computer games, and a somewhat less robust market for business software. If you find software at a flea market, look for CDs (or floppies) with the manufacturer's label and complete documentation. Handwritten labels on CDs are a sure sign of pirated software, as are CDs without documentation.

A typical freeware license includes some standard legal disclaimers and a few restrictions on secondary distributions. For example, passing on the program to friends might be alright but only if the executable is bundled with a README document or if specific comments are left intact in a source code file. If you're new to the world of freeware and shareware, you'll be pleased to know that not all licensing agreements are written by lawyers. Some are written by normal people (in many cases, the programmer who wrote the software) who have no training in legalese. These agreements are often written with humor, humility, and honest originality. Reading one of these better ones just might be the highpoint of your day. For example, some freeware licenses add a quirky twist to the usual conditions and restrictions. Many programmers just want to hear from their users, so they ask only for a quick e-mail message in return for their software. Enough people are doing this so that the practice now has a name: **postcardware**. If you look at enough freeware licenses, you might see variations on the postcard idea. For example, Jilles Groenendijk, the author of PhonConv, requests an item or postcard related to Garfield (a cartoon character) in return for his software.

In addition, check out the truly unique "careware" licensing agreement for Arachnophilia. Paul Lutus, the author of Arachnophilia, explains that his licensing agreement is wholly negotiable—he'll take anything but money in exchange for Arachnophilia. Everyone is free to suggest their own terms, but Mr. Lutus is hoping for "the really remarkable transactions, which you recognize instinctively when you see them." Here is Paul's description of his careware licensing agreement:

For example, here is a payment I will accept for a copy of Arachnophilia—

> To own Arachnophilia, I ask that you stop whining about how hard your life is, at least for a while. When Americans whine, nearly everybody else in the world laughs. You have so much, and yet you manage to:
>
> - Overlook great examples of beauty around us,
> - Miss our most important opportunities,
> - Manage to make ourselves miserable by expecting something even better to come along.
>
> Every time you whine about how tough you have it, apart from the fact that you look ridiculous, you make it harder for people around us to appreciate how much you have. You encourage people to overlook the things you do have, the gifts of man and nature. You provide a context to dismiss everything as not good enough, to be miserable in the midst of plenty.
>
> Don't get the wrong impression—many things are unjust, things that should be struggled against until they are made right. My complaint is with people who can't find even one thing to take joy in, to appreciate. These people not only make themselves miserable, but they infect others with the attitude that the world should right itself, by itself, before they will take simple pleasure in anything.

> So here is my deal: stop whining for an hour, a day, a week, your choice, and you'll have earned your copy of Arachnophilia. Say encouraging words to young people, make them feel welcome on the planet Earth (many do not). Show by example that you don't need all you have in order to be happy and productive.

Computer programmers who write their own software licenses often produce traditional-sounding legalistic licenses. However, sometimes they write something unexpected. When you download freeware and shareware from the Net, be sure to read the licensing agreements so you won't miss any idiosyncratic licenses.

Open Source Software

Although the media tend to focus on all of the wealth, millionaires, and IPOs that have resulted from the Internet, the Internet has also inspired new models of personal freedom and community that are equally deserving of attention. Prime examples are freeware and the **open source software** movement. The concept of free software seems surprising to many people because they think of software as a commercial product, a means by which revenue and profit are generated. However, if you give your software away at no cost, it's hard to view it as a traditional product anymore. It becomes a means to a different end.

Proponents of free software usually explain this concept of software in terms of two ultimate goals: total personal freedom (for the end users) and an open, cooperative development community (for the programmers). For them, the term *free* really means *nonproprietary*. In the world of software, anyone can develop nonproprietary software in a commercial setting and still charge users who use it. That is consistent with the open source concept of free software. The big catch is that you can't stop other people from giving away that software at no cost. That makes software different from other commodities.

The open source software idea has some obvious advantages. A programmer who releases open source software must release not only the actual executable program files but also all of the source code files that make the software work. This enables other programmers—thousands worldwide—to see how your software works. If the software is good, some might like it enough to fix it up a little—correct a bug or add a feature that they think people should have. The original author then has the option of accepting those fixes and enhancements, changing the original source code, and releasing a new version of the program. If a hundred programmers suggest changes to the software, many improvements can be made before the next release, possibly a lot more than could have been accomplished by a small number of in-house programmers (who might not have much personal interest in it). People who volunteer their services on a software project are probably maximally interested and maximally motivated to work with the software. If they are also competent programmers, the benefits of their involvement can be significant.

From a programmer's perspective, free (that is, nonproprietary) software represents personal freedom and cooperative communities. Open source software allows anyone to join a community of people drawn together by their common interest in a particular piece of software. Technical problems can be identified, discussed, and solved within this cooperative working group; communication within them is greatly enhanced by the Internet. Files can be shared, ideas can be discussed, and anyone can listen in. It helps to have a strong supervisor—someone who can make the call on which changes to accept and which to reject. However, that's as much control as anyone can hope to have in an open source software project. A project volunteer who disagrees with a supervisory decision is free to use the code as the basis of an alternative open source project. However, most disagreements in the open source world are discussed and resolved within one working community, so defections and splinter groups are not as common as one might expect. If someone has a bad idea, others will explain why it's bad. If someone has a good idea, others will support it. When enough people debating a design decision bring intelligence and experience to the table, and set aside economic self-interest, good decisions tend to result.

This process of software design through a cooperative community of qualified volunteers works well. People unqualified to contribute tend to watch and learn and stay out of the way. There is no input from marketing because there is no marketing department, and there's no input from some executive in the "corner office" because there is no corner office. The open source system optimizes intellectual competence. Rapid communication via the Internet speeds key discussions. Programmers are free to discuss any aspect of the project with other programmers, and no restrictions apply regarding what someone can do with the software. This is the sense in which open source software is free. Many believe it's the best way to design large, complicated computer systems.

Some Popular Open Source Software Projects

Here are some of the popular open source projects underway now:

- Apache, the world's most popular Web server
- Netscape Navigator, the second most popular Web browser
- Gimp, a digital imaging program similar to Adobe's Photoshop
- Linux, an alternative OS
- Perl, a popular programming language used for CGI scripts and other programs
- Samba, an implementation of the file-sharing protocol used by Microsoft Windows products

---

It might be wonderful to be free, but you might wonder how open source programmers are expected to put bread on the table. Do they need day jobs to subsidize their contributions to open source software? Richard M. Stallman, the President of the Free Software Association and a leader in the open source software movement, claims that better working communities for programmers and total freedom for end users are not incompatible with the notion of commercial software as a product that generates revenue and profits. This perspective requires a conceptual shift from a marketplace built on suspicion and mistrust (you pay first and then you receive your goods) to an economic system in which people treat each other with trust and goodwill (you receive your goods first and then you pay). If this sounds idealistic, consider that Mr. Stallman has been living off the proceeds of freeware and goodwill for more than 15 years. He fervently believes that if people are given the opportunity to do the right thing—in this case, to pay for their freeware with a voluntary donation—they will do it. A college student strapped for cash might not get around to it for a few years, but eventually, people who are financially able to pay for something that is of value to them, will pay. This is not a novel idea. Many charitable organizations rely on goodwill and the passage of time. If it works for college alumni donations, why not for software? A system of voluntary payments can create some challenging cash-flow problems, but for someone who can wait out economic downturns and the occasional slow year, it just might work.

Not convinced? You don't think there's enough goodwill out there to keep afloat an economy based on "pay if you want to pay"? It's too early to tell, but some strong evidence suggests that some people will act altruistically, even when no one is holding a gun to their heads. Consider *InfoWorld*'s Best Technical Support Award for 1997. This award is usually given to the software vendor that receives the most votes from *InfoWorld* readers. Although software support might not be one of the computer industry's more shining achievements, at least a few companies always manage to do it well and their grateful users do speak up to cast nominations and votes for the *InfoWorld* award. In 1997, the Best Technical Support Award went to the Linux user community. The Linux OS, as open source software, doesn't come with commercial technical support. Users who have questions and problems must rely on the kindness of strangers in newsgroups and chat rooms for help. This altruistic system for customer support apparently works quite well. While perhaps difficult to believe, in the Linux community free support from other users is apparently as good as, if not better than, paid commercial support that accompanies paid-for software.

One can also look to Microsoft for additional evidence that Open Source software deserves to be taken seriously. Consider the following excerpts from "the Halloween Documents" (internal Microsoft memos leaked to the public in 1998).

> OSS [Open Source software] poses a direct, short-term revenue and platform threat to Microsoft, particularly in server space. Additionally, the intrinsic parallelism and free idea exchange in OSS has benefits that are not replicable with our current licensing model and therefore present a long term developer mindshare threat.

> Linux has been deployed in mission critical, commercial environments with an excellent pool of public testimonials. . . . Linux outperforms many other UNIXes . . . Linux is on track to eventually own the x86 UNIX market . . .

Linux and other OSS advocates are making a progressively more credible argument that OSS software is at least as robust—if not more—than commercial alternatives. The Internet provides an ideal, high-visibility showcase for the OSS world.

The ability of the OSS process to collect and harness the collective IQ of thousands of individuals across the Internet is simply amazing. More importantly, OSS evangelization scales with the size of the Internet much faster than our own evangelization efforts appear to scale.

Open source software probably won't make anyone a billionaire, but it's a surprising and noteworthy phenomenon brought about by the Internet and the programmers who use it. The next time that someone claims that the Internet is all about greed and opportunism, tell that person about open source software.

Trojan Horses

Suppose that you check your e-mail inbox and find an e-mail message from someone at `microsoft.com`. The message body is as follows.

As a user of the Microsoft Internet Explorer, Microsoft Corporation provides you with this upgrade for your web browser. It will fix some bugs found in your Internet Explorer. To install the upgrade, please save the attached file (ie0199.exe) in some folder and run it.

What do you do? If you have to think about this for more than one second, read on.

Messages like this were widely distributed in 1999. The attached file contained a Trojan horse. Recall from Section 2.4 that a Trojan horse is a piece of code that does something surreptitiously. A program that contains a Trojan might or might not do what it says it does. However, all Trojan horses are designed to accomplish something that no user would approve of, if its true purpose were known. In the case here, the executable makes several changes to the local host and attempts to contact other systems over the Net. Although this particular Trojan horse was aimed at Windows users, a Trojan horse can target any platform.

As explained in Chapter 2, a Trojan horse can be programmed to do anything. It can delete files, modify files, transmit files to a remote host over the Net, install "zombie" code for denial of service attacks, install viruses, or install other Trojan horses. It can create a log of every keystroke typed into your computer—including on all of those supposedly secure forms used for credit card transactions—and mail the log to a third party on the other side of the world whenever you connect to the Net. You would never know that anything was amiss until unauthorized charges started showing up on credit card account statements. Even then, you'd find it difficult to learn how the card number had been stolen. The effects of a Trojan horse might not be noticed for many months. This makes it difficult to halt the spread of the Trojan horse through the use of anti-virus software, although much of this software can identify many known Trojan horses.

Users must be *tricked* into installing a Trojan horse on their systems. Any guise will work against a user who is not alert. In the example given earlier in the section, a user must know that it's easy to forge e-mail headers and that Microsoft (or any other legitimate software distributor) would never send patches or update files to users via e-mail.

An intruder can try to gain access to your system through intimidation, fear, guise, or enticement. Here are some examples.

- Someone could call you on the telephone, pretending to be a system administrator for your ISP and telling you how important it is to run a program that is going to be sent to you.

- A friend of yours might send you a greeting with an executable attachment that appears to be an animated cartoon but that is actually a Trojan horse (unknown to your friend).

- A friend might send you a game via e-mail, but the game contains a Trojan horse (unknown to your friend). Indeed, your friend might have not sent the e-mail, since a Trojan horse can scan your e-mail client's address book to find names and addresses that you'll recognize. It would expect you to be less cautious when presented with a familiar name on an e-mail message.

Users can also be tricked into opening a file that is disguised as a *non*executable data file. In 1999, the ExploreZip Trojan horse spread across the Internet via e-mail messages from *known* correspondents. The message body said the following.

> I received your email and I shall send you a reply ASAP.
> Till then, take a look at the attached zipped docs.

If the attached file was displayed by the e-mail client as a file icon, it presented itself as a WinZip file. However, if the reader double-clicked the file, expecting to launch WinZip, WinZip was not what executed. The download, which was named `zipped_files.exe`, executed and displayed an error message that looked like a WinZip error in an effort to convince the user that nothing was amiss except for this unreadable file archive. For more information about the ExploreZip Trojan, see Exercise #2 at the end of this section.

Trojan horses don't have to travel via e-mail. They can also come with random Web pages. In particular, if you frequent pages devoted to games or pornography, watch for suspicious downloads.

"Honey , Do We Know Anyone in Moldova?"

On February 4, 1997, the National Fraud Information Center posted a warning about a Web site that was responsible for unexpected and expensive telephone bills for a number of Web surfers using dial-up Internet connections. Surfers who visited a particular pornographic Web site (`www.sexygirls.com`) were shown a few teaser pictures and then told that they needed to download a special program to view the archived images. The special program was a standard image viewer—with an entire communications suite hidden deep inside. The program disconnected the user from the ISP, shut off the volume on the modem, and dialed a number in Moldova—a small, former republic of the Soviet Union. From that time, all Internet access was provided through the Moldova number, thereby resulting in huge international long distance telephone charges.

The peculiarities of this Web site attracted the interest of law enforcement agencies. The FTC halted its operation (along with that of a similar site, `erotic2000.com`) on February 19, 1997. By the time that the Moldova "hijackers" were exposed, hundreds of thousands of dollars on long distance telephone calls to Moldova had been charged to a large number of unsuspecting Internet surfers.

Trojan horses have been used in denial-of-service (DoS) attacks such as the one that hit a number of major Web sites (including CNN and Yahoo!) in February 2000. A DoS Trojan horse can be quietly installed on thousands of Internet hosts, which are then set to act as "zombie" servers, awaiting commands from anyone on the Net. The code for setting up DoS attacks is freely available on the Web. A Trojan horse in action can be difficult to detect and, under normal circumstances, virtually impossible to trace. The alleged perpetrator behind these attacks on CNN and Yahoo! was a 15-year-old boy whose only slip-up was a chat room brag.

If you're alert to the dangers, you can minimize the likelihood of a Trojan horse attack on your computer as follows.

- Never open or execute an unsolicited file received via e-mail.
- Never download executables from obscure Web sites.
- Scan all downloads for viruses (and Trojans) before executing.
- Always check the file extension of any file that you download, as a deceptive file icon can hide the actual file type.
- If you share your computer with others, especially children, negotiate a policy for file downloads that everyone can live with.
- Read the **CERT advisories** before installing any new executables.

E. T. Applications: A Different Type of Trojan Horse A more subtle type of Trojan horse that's sometimes deliberately added to an otherwise legitimate software download. This type is added by the software manufacturer. These Trojan horses monitor your online activities, collect data, and then send a report to a remote host as soon as you connect to the Internet. The data presumably is used for marketing purposes, but no one can know exactly what is going on because these activities are never documented.

Data collection Trojan horses are sometimes called **E. T. applications** because they do what Steven Spielberg's E. T. did in the movie, "E. T.": They phone home. E. T.

applications don't do anything malicious, but they are deceptive and they violate consumer privacy. Known E. T. downloads on the Net include Comet Cursor (described in Section 8.4.5), zBubbles (an online shopping advisor), PKZip (a shareware file utility), and CuteFTP (an FTP client).

Most people don't know about E. T. applications. Those who do are usually outraged when they discover that one has been "watching" them. A class action suit for $500 million has been filed on behalf of one million RealJukebox users against RealNetworks for an E. T. application that was first included in a RealJukebox download in 1998. If you're concerned about E. T. applications, consider installing a *firewall* so that you can be informed whenever a program on your computer attempts to send data out over the Net (see the Above and Beyond section in Chapter 9) for more about firewalls).

Trojan horse attacks are difficult to undo. Unlike viruses, which are relatively predictable, it can be very difficult to know exactly what a Trojan horse has done. If you're hit by a widespread Trojan horse, your anti-virus software vendor might be able to tell you how to remove it and restore your system. A less well-known Trojan horse that has not been encountered by many people is much harder to pin down. In the worst case scenario, you'll have to reformat your hard drive, reinstall all of your software from the original media, and restore your data files from backups. Knowing that this is a possibility should give you additional reason to backup your most valuable files regularly.

Above and Beyond: Problems and Exercises

A1. Under what conditions is it legal to resell used commercial software? When you buy used software, what two signs are tip-offs that the software is pirated?

A2. When Richard Stallman talks about "free" software, he is not necessarily talking about freeware. Explain what he means.

A3. Suppose that you rely on open source software and you run into a problem that you can't handle. Where can you go for help?

A4. What is an E. T. application? Give three examples of such applications.

A5. **[Find It Online]** Visit `http://counter.li.org/`, and find out how many Linux users have registered at that site. Then visit the link "My guess at the number of Linux users," and explain why it's so difficult to know how many people use Linux.

A6. **[Find It Online]** A detailed definition of open source software is presented at `http://www.perens.com/OSD.html`. Review this document in order to answer the following questions.

> (a) How does open source software differ from software in the public domain?

(b) Can a program be distributed under both an open source license and a commercial license?

(c) If anyone can modify and redistribute open source software, how can you know what version you're getting?

(d) Can someone make a trivial modification to an open source program and then market the slightly modified program under a commercial license?

A7. [Find It Online] Search the Net, and find out what UCITA is. Then read "Why You Must Fight UCITA" by Richard Stallman at `http://www.gnu.org/philosophy/ucita.html`. Explain briefly what UCITA is and why it's a threat to the open source software movement.

A8. [Find It Online] Peruse the Halloween documents at `http://www.opensource.org/halloween/` to find out what Microsoft was saying about open source software in general and Linux in particular in 1998. Then answer the following questions.

(a) When were the Halloween documents written?

(b) Who published the Halloween documents, and how were they obtained?

(c) What two claims did Microsoft publicly advance to counter the general public's interest in Linux? (Hint: See Halloween V for an interview with Microsoft spokesperson, Ed Muth.)

(d) What does FUD mean, and what companies are in a position to exploit FUD?

A9. [Find It Online] What did the WinZip Trojan horse do when it was executed? (*Hint*: Search CERT `http://www.cert.org` for the answer.)

A10. [Find It Online] If you download a program from a respected software clearinghouse, are you safe from Trojan horses? (For the answer, see `http://www.cert.org/advisories/CA-99-02-Trojan-Horses.html`.)

CHAPTER 9

Power Tools for the Internet

CHAPTER GOALS

- Gain familiarity with the world of browser enhancements and accessories
- Learn the difference between a plug-in, an add-on, and a helper application
- Find out how to locate and install browser accessories
- Learn how Web accelerators work and when they work best
- Understand how ad filters protect your privacy
- Discover how download managers can save you time
- Find out how password managers can help you to stay secure online
- Learn about desktop portals in general and special portals that facilitate online searches
- Decide if you should try out a new browser (maybe one you've never heard of)
- Find out how FTP clients can simplify file transfers online
- Decide whether any of the productivity tools described in this chapter are right for you

---

9.1 TAKING CHARGE

Without software, your computer is nothing but a bare foundation, waiting for the contractors to arrive. It's up to you to design a building for that foundation, and you should construct one that fits your needs. Your computer likely came with preinstalled software: an OS and a bundle of selected applications. The bundled software probably contained a Web browser and maybe some office applications, included to "get you off the ground." Now it's up to you to customize your computer with a personal selection of software that truly meets your computing needs. Chapter 8 covered the mechanics of locating, downloading, and installing software from the

Internet. Chapter 9 describes some important classes of software that are especially useful when you work online. It doesn't attempt to review useful computer applications in general, but rather covers only Internet applications.

Browsers have evolved over the years to address many standard online activities. In addition to their browsing capabilities, many browsers have integrated e-mail clients, news readers, and search facilities. Browser manufacturers try to anticipate your general needs in order to simplify the process of going online. Most computer users would prefer to have all of their software needs covered by a convenient bundle of applications that comes preinstalled.

There's nothing wrong with convenience. However, these mass-marketed software bundles are designed to address the needs of the masses. As you become more familiar with your own computing needs, you'll want to customize a computing environment that is more in tune with your personal work routines. Some of the utilities described in this chapter will be useful to you, and some will not. Only you can decide what you need in order to work more productively online.

Before you start, a word of caution. In an ideal world, all programmers know their craft perfectly, all software is written perfectly, and all software installations proceed perfectly. Unfortunately, we live in a world in which few programmers are perfect, many are under pressure to meet deadlines, and almost all are forced to cut corners at times. As a result, as discussed in Chapter 8 different programs can sometimes collide, with unpredictable results. If you install only a handful of programs on your computer, you'll probably experience no difficulties. However, if you install dozens, you'll likely have at least one software conflict on your system. The only way to avoid software conflicts is never to add any new software to your computer. If you're unwilling to be that cautious, your next best move is to be a "defensive driver." A good defensive driver watches for the unexpected and expects the worst case scenarios at all times. Let's start by understanding how software conflicts occur.

Software conflicts occur when two programs both rely on a single *shared resource* and one program modifies the resource in some way that affects the other program. A program might expect a specific version of a shared resource, or it might expect to see certain settings within that shared resource. When you install software, the installation process sometimes updates a shared resource's files or modifies its settings. If the updates or modifications are not what some other program expects, a software conflict could result. Perhaps you've seen one piece of software reset your screen resolution or the number of colors that your monitor can display. If the program does not restore the original settings when it exits, the next program that you run might have trouble with the new settings.

Software Conflicts

Software conflicts can be minor, in which case you might never notice a problem. However, some are serious and will interfere with your computer's ability to run certain applications, or, in some cases, interfere with the stability of your OS.

It's notoriously difficult to identify and resolve software conflicts. Known conflicts are sometimes documented in a README file, but many are not. You might know only that your computer is freezing up more often than it used to and you have no idea why. When it comes to software conflicts, the best that you can do is to be prepared for the worst. This turns out to be straightforward, if you have the right software utilities on hand.

You can't avoid software conflicts altogether, since you never know before you install one program how it will affect or interrelate with other programs on your computer. However, you can undo them if you were careful to leave a trail of bread crumbs behind you. If a new program causes substantial problems, you'll want to restore your system to its state before the program was installed. This is easy if you *backed up* the most important system files immediately before you installed the program that's giving you trouble. A good *backup and recovery utility* will make periodic system backups fairly painless. You need only the time and patience to make sure that the backups get done. As long as you have a healthy back-up version of your system, you can uninstall any recent software additions and restore your system to its previous state.

Restoring a Messed-Up Computer

To ensure that you can fix your computer in case of a serious software conflict, here are some tips to follow.

1. Invest in a good backup and recovery utility *before* you need to restore your system.
2. Perform a complete system backup *before* each new software installation.
3. After installing a new piece of software, assess the stability of your system *before* installing any additional software. Do not confound a troubled system with even more trouble.

A *system backup* is not the same as a *full backup* of your complete hard drive. A system backup copies only those resource files that are most likely to be modified during a software installation. On a Mac, these are the files in the system's extension folder. In Windows, these most often are the files that have the extensions `.ini` and `.dll`.

Although you can purchase a backup and recovery utility by itself, consider getting a suite of system utilities that also includes other useful tools, as mentioned in Chapter 8. Good utility suites are a little pricey ($40 to $100), but they offer a lot of software. For example, Norton SystemWorks for Windows includes the following:

- A registry editor that makes system backups a one-step process
- A registry tracker that keeps a log of all registry changes (another useful way to back up files before a software installation)

■ A rescue disk utility for making a rescue floppy disk to use if your computer fails to start

■ A speed disk utility for disk optimization (see Chapter 8)

■ WinDoctor for diagnosing and fixing common problems with Windows

■ Anti-virus software

In addition, SystemWorks's user's manual is a good guide to preventative maintenance. Reading it will teach you a lot about your computer (see Figure 9.1).

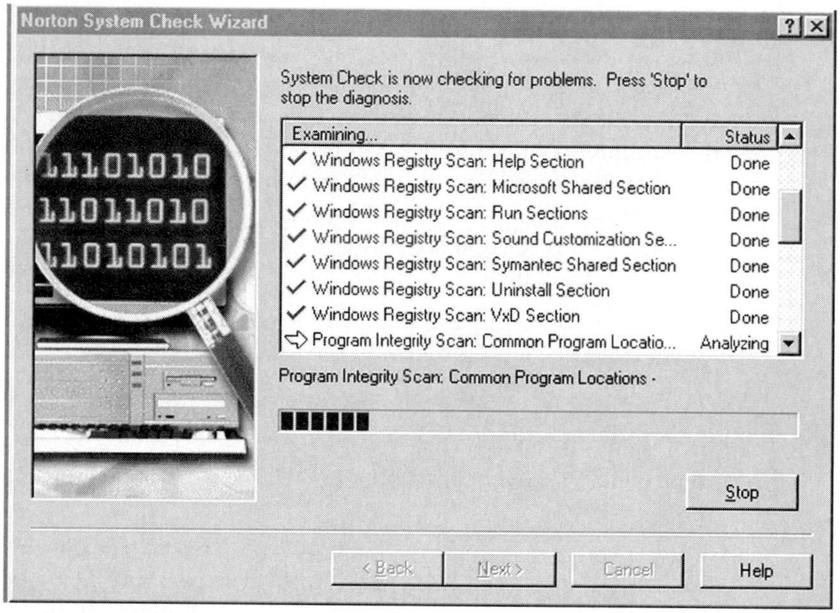

Figure 9.1:
Preventative
Maintenance
Means Checking for
Problems

![Norton System Check Wizard dialog box showing System Check examining various Windows Registry Scan items with Done status]

Recommended Utility Suites

■ Norton SystemWorks 2000 (Professional Edition) (Windows)

■ Ontrack SystemSuite 2000 (Windows)

■ Norton Utilities 5.0.2 (Macintosh)

■ TechTool Pro 2.5.3 (Macintosh)

Do you absolutely need one of these suites before you install more software on your computer? No, because not everyone needs system utilities. If you generally avoid installing new software, are happy with what you've got, and intend to keep your computer and software selection just as it is, then you can live without a utility suite. However, you would be wise to make yourself a rescue disk in case you ever need to start your computer from a floppy. You can do that without purchasing any additional system utilities. (Macs can be started from a rescue CD-ROM that comes with the computer.) If you never pull your car out of the driveway, the chances of a bad accident are virtually zero, so you can let your insurance lapse and probably get away with it. Utility suites are more valuable when you do a lot of software installs and uninstalls. Good system utilities can enable you to be a diligent defensive driver on a crowded freeway during rush hour (see Figure 9.2).

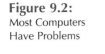

Figure 9.2:
Most Computers
Have Problems

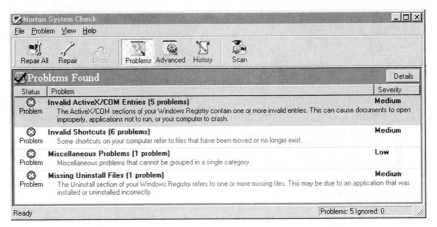

9.2 | APPLICATIONS: HELPERS, PLUG-INS, AND ADD-ONS

An **application** is a program that you run on your computer. You can obtain applications from retail software stores or the Internet (see Chapter 8). The applications that you choose to install are what make your computer unique and personal (hence the term *personal computer*). A Web browser is simply another application that possibly includes other applications. For example, recall from Chapter 5 that MSIE and Navigator include a JVM (Java Virtual Machine) so that you can run the Java applets on Web pages that contain applets. By contrast, a browser named Opera does not include a JVM, so you must add it yourself.

Just as you can customize your computer to reflect your needs and computing activities, you can customize your browser to reflect your Web browsing needs and activities. When you do this, you tell your browser how you want it to handle different types of files found on the Web. For example, if you never want to hear `.wav` audio files, you won't care if your browser can't handle them. However, if `.wav` files are important to you, you might want your browser to use a specific `.wav` player whenever it encounters a `.wav` file on a Web page.

Your browser is actually one application that uses other applications to view the Web. To view the Web in a certain way, you can configure your browser to use the applications that you want to use. Helper applications and plug-ins are two ways to enhance the viewing capabilities of your browser. In both cases, you are telling your browser that certain file types should be handled in a certain way. You browser needs to know which file types require special handling and which application is needed for which file types.

A **helper application** can be any application on your computer. When your browser encounters a file that requires a helper application, it looks for the helper application, launches that application, and then loads the file into the application. If your browser didn't know about the helper application, you would have to download the file from the Web, save it to some location on your hard drive, launch the appropriate application yourself, and open the downloaded file from inside of the desired application. When you configure your browser to use a helper application, your browser does all of this for you automatically. You can always know when your browser is calling on a helper application because a new application window will appear on your desktop.

When you install a **plug-in application**, you extend the capabilities of your browser to handle a file type that it wasn't originally designed to handle. To understand how plug-ins are different from helper applications, consider an analogy with medical problems. Sometimes you have an injury that can be handled only by a doctor, so you call your doctor; you don't enroll in medical school in order to solve the problem yourself. In other situations, you might decide that it makes sense to handle a recurring injury by yourself. So, you read a book on home remedies or you take a first-aid course. When you take the time to acquire the expertise that you need, you extend your own capabilities. Helper applications are like doctors: you call a doctor when you need one and you entrust your medical problem to the doctor. Plug-in applications are more like a do-it-yourself solution. When you configure your browser to use a plug-in, any file requiring that plug-in will be displayed inside the browser window, with the plug-in application working as if it were a part of your browser. For example, Macromedia Director is an application that produces computer animations for the Web. To view these animations, you need a plug-in called Shockwave. If your browser has this plug-in, you can view Web pages that contain this particular type of animation. If your browser does not have this plug-in, you are out of luck when it comes to certain Web pages. Plug-ins are usually easy to set up because the download and installation processes are normally *scripted*, that is, automated for you.

Adobe's Acrobat Reader (Reader) is an example of an application that can be added to your browser as either a helper application or a plug-in—*but not both!* You need Reader in order to read multimedia files in PDF format. If you seldom encounter PDF files on the Web, you can always install Acrobat Reader as a regular application, save to disk any PDF files that you happen to encounter on the Web, and launch Acrobat Reader manually to open those files. But if you encounter PDF files regularly, you'll save a lot of time if you add Acrobat Reader to your browser as a helper application or a plug-in.

Since helper applications are not scripted to set up appropriate file associations for you, it's helpful to have detailed instructions when you need to set up a helper application. Sometimes the installation instructions for a helper application are simple. In other cases, they are more involved. Figure 9.3 shows the procedure for setting up Acrobat Reader as a helper application for MSIE. Don't worry if you don't understand the procedure. It's included here only to make a point: Helper applications are usually more difficult to install than plug-in applications.

Figure 9.3:
Setting Up a Helper Application Can Be Complicated

```
To configure Internet Explorer to use Acrobat as a helper application:

    1. Exit Internet Explorer.
    2. Choose Start > Find > Files Or Folders.
    3. Type "pdf*.ocx," choose your local hard drive from the Look In
       pop-up menu, and then click Find Now. Make a note of the
       pathname to each Pdf*.ocx file on your system.
    4. Choose Start > Run.
    5. Type "regsvr32 -u X:\[path]\pdf*.ocx" in the Open text box,
       where "X" is the drive and "[path]" is the path to a Pdf*.ocx
       file. For example:

            regsvr32 -u C:\Acrobat3\Exchange\ActiveX\pdf42.ocx

    6. Click OK.
    7. Repeat steps 4-6 for every Pdf*.ocx file installed on your
       system.
    8. Delete the Pdf*.ocx and Pdf.tlb files from the
       Acrobat3\Exchange\ActiveX and Acrobat3\Reader\ActiveX
       directories or from the Reader\ActiveX directory. You must
       delete all the Pdf*.ocx files; if you rename or move the files,
       Internet Explorer can still use them.
    9. If Netscape Navigator is installed, locate the Nppdf32.dll file
       in the Netscape\Navigator\Program\Plugins directory or the
       Netscape\Communicator\Program\Plugins directory, and then move
       or rename the file. (Internet Explorer and AOL can use the
       Nppdf32.dll file if it cannot locate a Pdf.ocx file.)
   10. Restart Windows.
   11. Start Internet Explorer; the browser will start an Acrobat
       viewer in a separate window to display PDF files. If you're
       using Internet Explorer 3.0x or earlier, continue with steps
       12-20.
   12. Choose View > Options, then select Programs.
   13. Click File Types.
   14. Select Adobe Acrobat Document in the Registered File Types
       scroll box, then click Edit. If Adobe Acrobat Document is not
       listed, select New Type.
   15. Type "Adobe Acrobat Document" in the Description text box.
   16. Type "application/pdf" in the Content Type (MIME) text box.
   17. Type "pdf" in the Default Extension for Content text box.
   18. Select Open from the list of Actions and then click Edit. If
       Open is not listed, click New.
   19. Click Browse, locate and then select the Acrobat Reader 3.0x
       or Acrobat Exchange 3.0x application file, then click Select.
   20. Select Use DDE, then click OK to close each dialog box.

To reestablish the original Internet Explorer settings, reinstall
    Acrobat Reader 3.0x or Acrobat Exchange 3.0x.
```

Acrobat Reader requires a very complicated helper installation and the procedure in Figure 9.3 should be attempted only by people who have a technical background, and a taste for danger (running the `regsvr32` program is a high-risk activity because you are making changes to your system registry, which is a bit like performing brain surgery on your computer). Software manufacturers that want to encourage the use of their software in conjunction with Web browsers are wise to release a *plug-in* so that users don't have to go through intimidating and potentially dangerous helper application installations like the one shown in Figure 9.3.

Play It Safe

If you need a plug-in for a specific application and none is available, search the Web for installation instructions that will enable you to set up the application as a helper application. Make sure that the instructions are intended for the browser and OS that you use. Be careful if the only instructions that you find are confusing in any way or look like those in Figure 9.3. In that case, it is much safer to simply save files to your hard drive and launch the required application independently to open those files. This is not a slick solution, but it's preferable to restoring or reinstalling your system if something goes seriously wrong with a tricky helper application installation.

Be selective with the plug-ins that you add to your browser; you need only those that enhance your experience on the Web. It's fun to see what's available (see, for example, Figure 9.4). However, don't set up all the available plug-ins, just in case you might need one of them in the future. Add plug-ins only when you feel you really need them.

A plug-in added to your browser becomes a part of your browser. It increases your browser's memory requirements and adds to the amount of time needed to launch your browser. It therefore makes sense to use plug-ins only for file types that are frequently encountered and use helper applications for those encountered less often. Figure 9.5 shows some of the more popular helper applications and plug-ins that you might find useful.

You can add plug-ins to your browser as you need them. A good time to decide if you want to add a plug-in is when your browser tells you it doesn't know how to handle a particular file. Navigator and MSIE make locating plug-ins on demand easy by offering *plug-in finder features*. As soon as you encounter a Web page that requires a plug-in that your browser does not have, the plug-in finder figures out which one you need and offers it to you on the spot (see Figure 9.6).

To see which plug-ins have been added to Navigator, check the About Plug-ins feature in the Help menu (see Figure 9.7).

Figure 9.4:
Navigator's Official
Directory of Plug-
Ins for Navigator

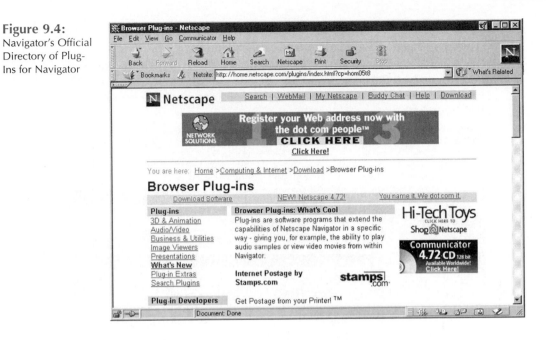

Figure 9.5:
Some Popular
Browser Helper
Applications and
Plug-Ins

Adobe Acrobat Reader 4.0	View, navigate, and print PDF files.
QuickTime 4	Displays QuickTime files and other video and audio file formats.
PowerPoint Viewer / Excel Viewer / Word 97 Viewer	View and print Microsoft Office documents without installing the Office suite.
RealPlayer G2	Plays various formats of audio and video formats, notably .au files. Widely used for streaming audio files.
Shockwave and Flash	Plug-ins for animation and documents produced with Macromedia Director or Flash. Very popular at game sites.
Windows Media Player	Displays popular streaming and local audio and video formats, including ASF, WAV, AVI, MPEG, QuickTime, and more.

Finding Plug-Ins

Navigator and MSIE help you out with the plug-in finder feature when you visit a Web page that needs a plug-in that your browser doesn't have. However, if you want to browse the possibilities yourself, here are some useful plug-in directories.

Official Netscape Plug-In Directory `http://home.netscape.com/plugins/index.html`

Windows Plug-Ins `http://winfiles.cnet.com/apps/98/plugins.html`

Plug-In Plaza `http://browserwatch.internet.com/plug-in.html`
ZDNet > Help & How-To > Internet > Plug-Ins
  `http://www.zdnet.com/zdhelp/filters/subfilter/`
  `0,7212,6003243,00.html`

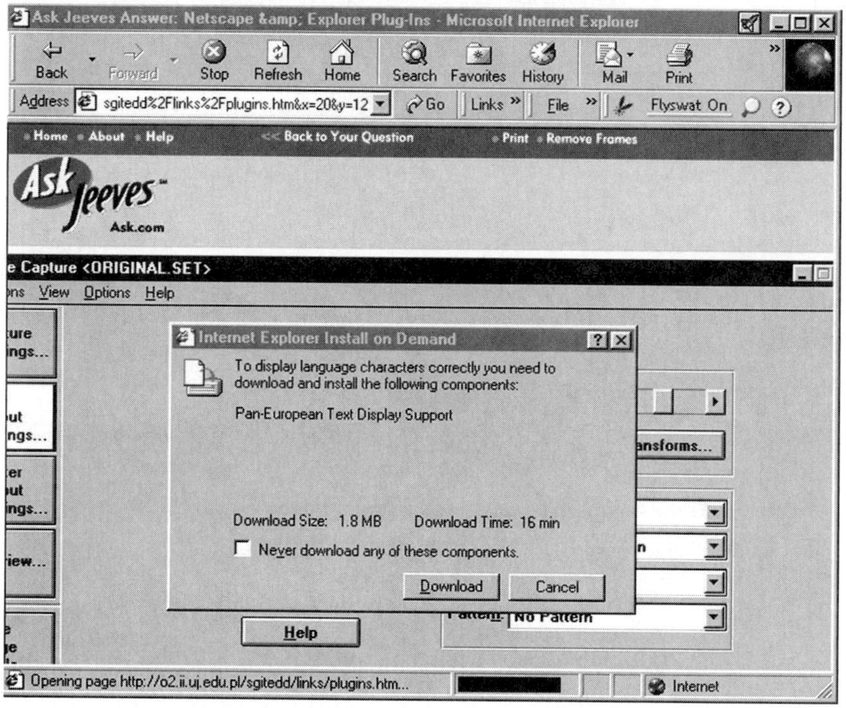

Figure 9.6:
Using the Plug-In
Finder to Install
Your Plug-Ins When
You Need Them

Browser viewing capabilities can be enhanced by helper applications and plug-ins. A third class of browser accessories are available only as browser add-ons. A **browser add-on** is an application that works in conjunction with your Web browser to enhance or compliment your browser in some specific way. Browser add-ons can be called from your browser, either automatically or manually by your clicking a toolbar icon. Some add-ons can be launched independently.

If you are having trouble keeping plug-ins, helper applications, and add-ons straight, see Figure 9.8. But don't despair if you find documentation on the Web that is still confusing to you. Unfortunately, these terms are used a little differently by different browser manufacturers. Figure 9.8 reflects the usage typically seen in conjunction with Navigator. For MSIE, you're more likely to see the terms *add-on* and *viewer*. The concepts are the same—only the jargon shifts around a bit. A **viewer** (MSIE jargon) is an independent application that makes it possible to view a specif-

Figure 9.7:
Checking Your
Personal Plug-In
Library in Navigator

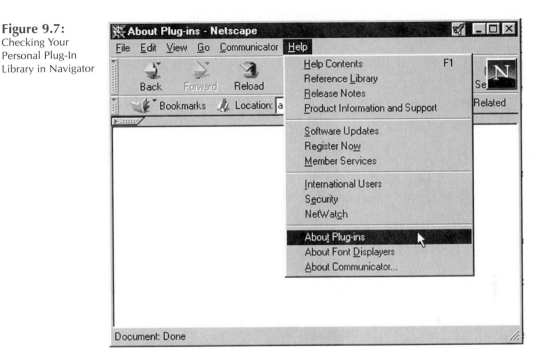

ic file format. It is one type of the helper applications in Figure 9.8. You can find viewers for office applications such as Word and PowerPoint, as well as image viewers and PDF viewers. An **add-on** in MSIE is any program that generally extends the capabilities of the browser (spanning all three categories in Figure 9.8). This book emphasizes Navigator terminology and definitions because they provide more distinctions (although the line between add-ons and helper applications is admittedly fuzzy at times).

An example of a browser add-on is the Alexa search facility (see Section 5.10.1). Netscape distributes this add-on with Navigator (versions 4.06 and above) as part of its Smart Browsing services. An Alexa installer can be downloaded for MSIE (versions 4.0 and above). This add-on is launched when the user clicks a What's Related icon on the toolbar (see the upper right-hand corner in Figure 9.9).

Other add-ons might be launched automatically. For example, if you click a link for a file that your browser does not know how to display, your browser can automatically launch a download manager (see Section 9.5).

You download and install an add-on like any other program. Most browser add-ons have their own executable installers (see Section 8.4). However, these installers may change preference settings for your browser. So if you're taking the add-on only on the test drive, make sure that you do a system backup before you install the plug-in (see Section 9.1).

Figure 9.8:
Keeping It All
Straight

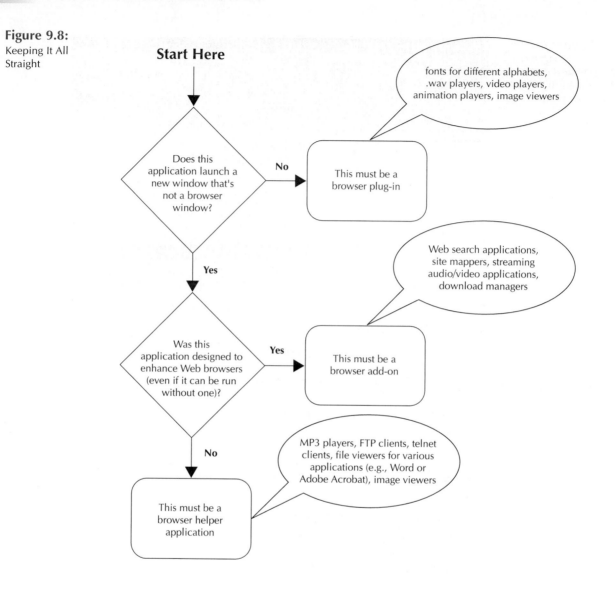

Sometimes an Internet application will be available as an add-on for only some browsers. For example, the meta search engine Copernic 2000 (see Section 5.3) can be installed as an add-on for MSIE but not for Navigator (see Figure 9.10). However, you can still use it with Navigator. If Navigator is your default browser, you simply launch Copernic as an independent application. Then Copernic will launch Navigator when you click on any link in a Copernic hit list. The only difference is that MSIE gives you a toolbar icon for launching Copernic (if you install Copernic as an add-on to MSIE). If you aren't using MSIE, you must launch Copernic from the Start Menu or a desktop shortcut, like any other application.

Figure 9.9:
Navigator Users
Launch Alexa from
a Toolbar

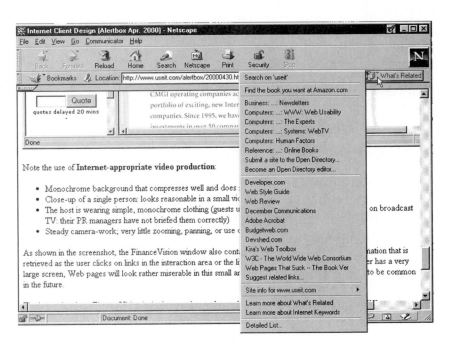

Figure 9.10:
Some Add-Ons
Give You Different
Integration Options

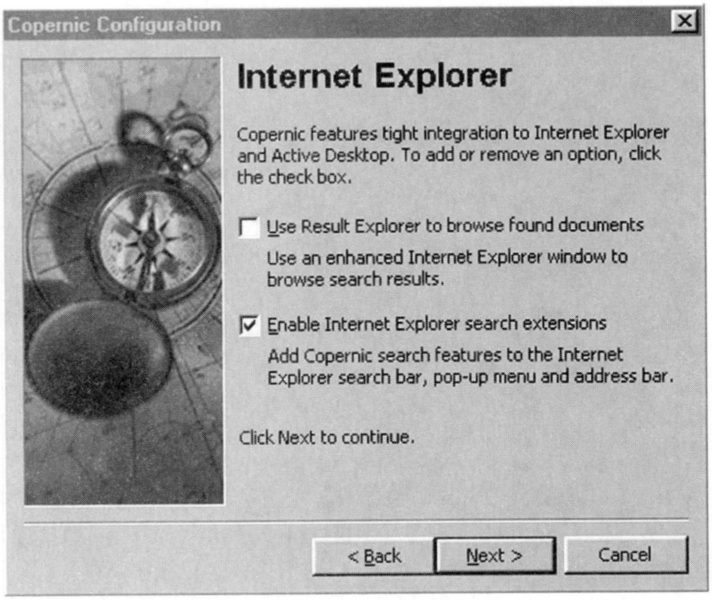

Many of the software enhancements described in this chapter are available as browser add-ons. Once you get used to having these enhancements on hand, it's hard to return to life with an unenhanced browser. Because this chapter is devoted to software applications, please remember that we will be looking at specific applications for the sake of providing some concrete examples. In each software category are many contenders for "Best of Breed," and our software selections do not constitute product endorsements. For software recommendations, check the Web (see Section 8.9).

9.3 WEB ACCELERATORS

If you connect to the Internet over a broadband connection, you probably have all of the Web acceleration that anyone could need. However, if you connect over a modem and a telephone line, this section is for you. A Web accelerator can't do anything about the speed of your Internet connection, but it can speed up your browser's page displays by making the best of the connection that you have.

Web Acceleration without a Web Accelerator

Sometimes, you can speed up your browsing session by doing nothing more than opening a second browser window. Both Navigator and MSIE let you work with multiple open browser windows. This enables you to read a page in one window while another page is loading in a separate window (this is useful when you're waiting for a search engine to produce a hit list). Then, if you have a number of useful links on a Web page in one window (such as a hit list or a page in a subject tree), you can use the second window to navigate to other sites without disturbing the first window.

Some good shortcuts are available for working with multiple browser windows.

- To open a second window, in MSIE type Ctrl-N and on a Mac, Command+L.
- To open a second window and load a page from a link at the same time, right-click a link and select Open in New Window from the pop-up menu. (On a Mac that has a one-button mouse, press and hold the mouse button over the link; don't release it right away. Wait half a second, and the menu will pop up.)
- If you already have a second browser window open and you want to send a link from the first window to the second, drag the link from the first window to the second.

To help you to understand how Web accelerators work, let's start by looking at how a Web browser works. A Web browser downloads pages from the Web on demand. You click a link, and your browser retrieves the Web page connected to the link. If you never visited the same page more than once, each click would result in a file download over the Internet. However, most people make return visits to at least some of the Web pages that they viewed earlier. If a Web page hasn't changed since the last visit, it's a waste of time and bandwidth to download the same page each time that you want to see it again. To avoid downloading the same files repeatedly, modern browsers maintain a *memory cache* for page downloads. You might have noticed that your browser can bring up a familiar page faster than a new page. This is because the page was stored in the browser's cache. The page that the browser saves in the memory cache might be saved in a RAM cache, which allows for very fast retrieval, or saved in a hard drive cache. Then the page can be retrieved from one cache or the other instead of the Internet. The browser's hard drive cache is permanent and remains after you exit your browser or shut down your computer. However, caches have size limits. The default is usually around 5MB, but you can change this amount in your browser's preference settings. When the cache gets full, the oldest pages are removed to make room for new ones.

If a Web page contains graphics or other multimedia content, those multimedia files are also stored in the cache. A **memory-intensive Web page**—that is, a page that contains a lot of graphics or only one very large graphic—is much faster to retrieve from the cache than to download over a slow Internet connection. These are the pages for which the timesaving is most apparent.

Although the use of the cache can save time and bandwidth when you revisit a Web page, browsers do have to be smart about Web pages that have changed since the last download. Sometimes, a Web page designer/programmer will help by inserting some additional instructions for the browser. For example, Web pages with *dynamic (changing) content*, such as sports scores, might contain JavaScript commands that tell browsers how often the browser should reload the page from the Internet in order for the page's information to stay current. In such cases, the browser should download a new copy from the Internet as instructed. If a Web page provides no specific instructions, the browser will work from its preference settings for the management of the cache (see Figure 9.11).

The smarter a browser can be about its cache management, the greater the benefits to the user. This is where Web accelerators come in. A **Web accelerator** removes cache management from the browser and gives the user more power over how the cache is to be handled. For example, **NetSonic Pro** gives users four different ways to use the browser's cache, each offering a slightly different way to handle Web page updates (see Figure 9.12).

The biggest timesaving, however, comes from *prefetching* options. This is where bandwidth can be traded for time. By using prefetching, Web accelerators can realize significant increases in speed. To understand how prefetching works, consider the pattern of bandwidth consumption during a typical browsing session. Sometimes, Web pages are being downloaded, and sometimes, nothing is happening. A user must wait during downloads, and the Internet connection waits the rest of the time (for example, when the user is reading a Web page or using the telephone). When pages are downloaded on demand, not a lot of bandwidth is being used between downloads. Prefetching lets your browser anticipate and act on likely file downloads while you are doing other things. When it works, the next Web

Figure 9.11:
Navigator's Cache
Options

RAM Cache

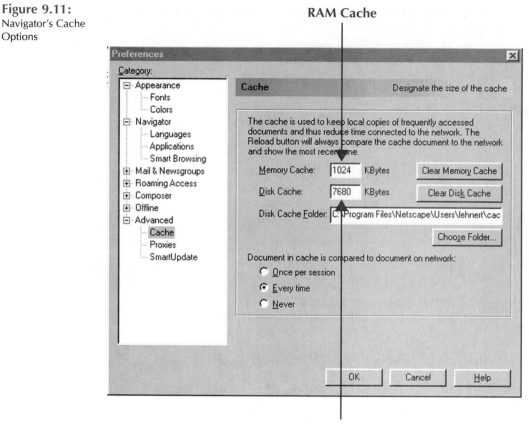

Hard Drive Cache

page you want to see will already be in the local cache, even before you knew you wanted it. The general trick is to anticipate the user's next mouse click.

The browser knows that the next mouse click will be either a link on the current Web page or the Back button, in which case the page is already in cache. So while the user is figuring out what to do next, the Web accelerator can simply gather all of the pages represented by links on the current page and start downloading each just in case the user might want it. This is one option offered by most Web accelerators.

A more restrained strategy is for the accelerator to remember which links have already been visited (assuming that the page was viewed at least once before the current viewing) and start downloading each corresponding page. Of course, any pages that can be retrieved from the cache will not require a download, so the restrained prefetch strategy is most effective on familiar pages that have a lot of dynamic content. NetSonic Pro offers both (pre-load all links vs. pre-load visited links only) of these basic options (see Figure 9.13).

Figure 9.12:
NetSonic Pro's
Cache Options

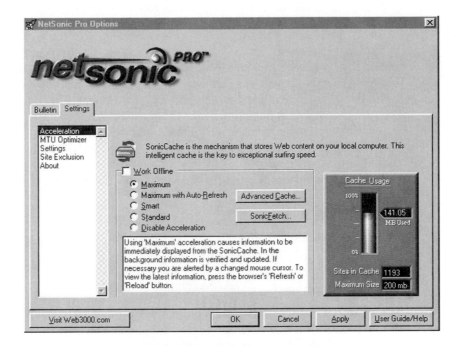

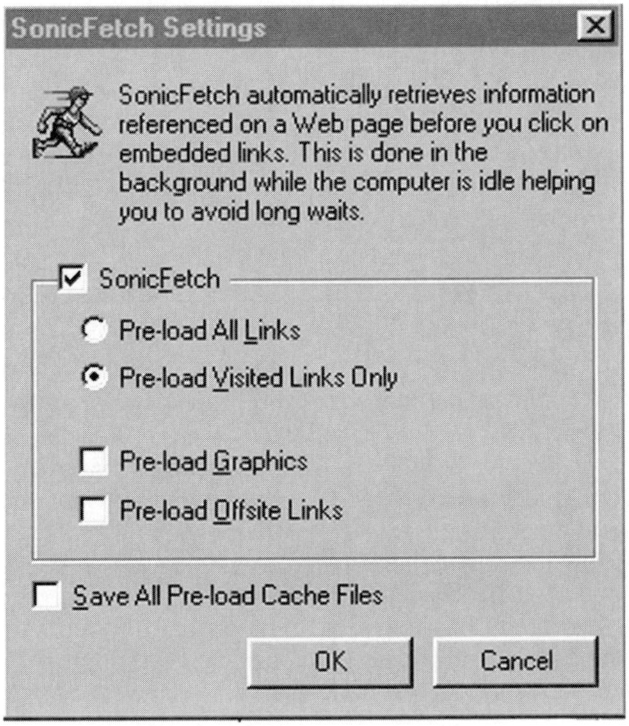

Figure 9.13:
NetSonic Pro's
Prefetch Options

The prefetch feature of Web accelerators is somewhat controversial because of its potential bandwidth impact. If you're the only person in the world who is using a Web accelerator, you could maximize the prefetch option and download every linked page on every Web page that you visit, and your impact on the Internet would be negligible. However, imagine what would happen if all of the subscribers of a given ISP used a maximal prefetch option each time that they fired up their accelerated browsers. The bandwidth demand would be quite significant, and service to everyone who uses that ISP would suffer. If the ISP's connection to the Internet was saturated with a constant stream of download requests, everyone using that ISP would feel a slow-down, and that slow-down could end up negating any speed-up effects that you might have experienced if bandwidth bottlenecks were not an issue.

Be Kind to Your Neighbors

If you decide to try a Web accelerator, don't use the maximal prefetch options. A less aggressive setting will probably give you a significant speed increase while having much less impact on bandwidth demands.

Some people claim to see a dramatic speed-up when they use a Web accelerator, whereas others say that they don't see much difference. Results will vary depending on the computer. NetSonic Pro recommends using a very large cache limit (for example, 200MB). If you don't have that amount of available space on your hard drive, you should not expect to get the best possible acceleration.

Another way to speed up downloads is by minimizing the amount of content downloaded for each Web page. The next section explores *ad filters*, add-ons that remove bandwidth-consuming graphics from Web pages. If you don't care about what gets left out, a stripped-down version of the Web might be your best solution to speeding up your browser.

9.4 AD FILTERS

Most people who talk about filters for Web browsers are referring to software that tries to censor entire Web pages in order to make the Web safe for children. That's not what this section is about. Here we discuss filters that specifically target commercial advertisements on Web pages. An **ad filter** is software that works to remove ad banners and other advertisements from your Web page displays. Some ad filters can be configured to remove ads, freeze animated GIFs, and censor objectionable images (as specified by the user) from Web pages. Some people use ad filters because they get tired of seeing advertisements on the Web pages that they view. Others use them to speed up their Web page displays (another form of Web acceleration). Figures 9.14 shows a commercial Web page with ad filtering.

Figure 9.14:
With the Ad Filter
Turned On

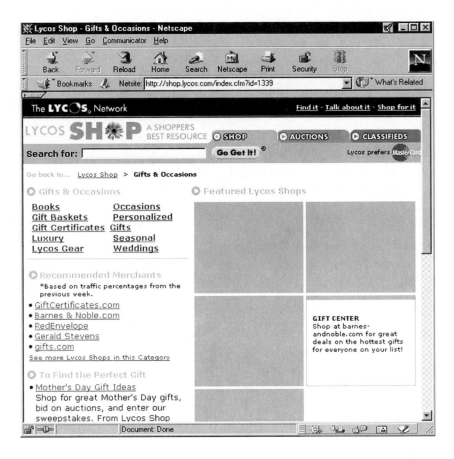

Figure 9.15 shows the same Web page as in Figure 9.14 but without ad filtering.

On most Web pages, an ad filter can be counted on to find banner ads, as seen in Figure 9.16. The filter then pulls out the ads from the page display, as shown in Figure 9.17.

One of the most popular ad filters is WebWasher, which is distributed by Siemens Corporation as freeware for noncommercial use. WebWasher identifies and removes banner ads, pop-up ads, and animated graphics. Individuals can install **WebWasher** to filter out ads on Web pages. Many companies "wash" the Web pages coming onto their computers in order to keep employees more focused and less distracted. Thus a network administrator for a business can install WebWasher on a *proxy server* in order to filter out content for everyone on the company's LAN (local area network). One could argue that this is a form of censorship. However, companies can censor anything that they want within the confines of their workplaces. By limiting the download of unwanted material to a business, WebWasher has been shown to reduce bandwidth consumption in a workplace network by as much as 45%.

Figure 9.15:
With the Ad Filter
Turned Off

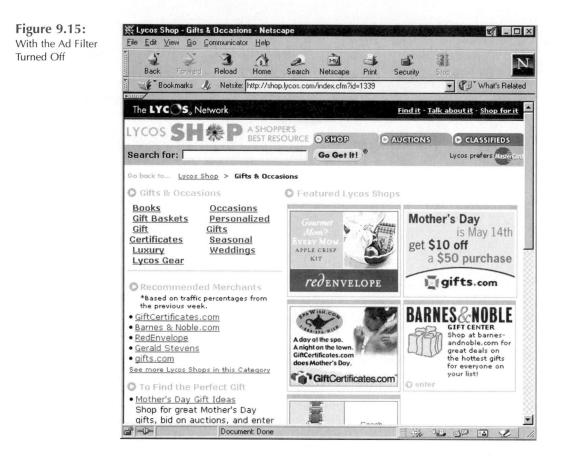

Figure 9.16:
A Banner Ad before
Filtering

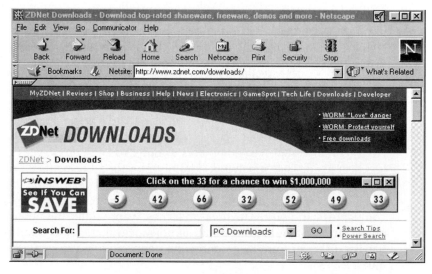

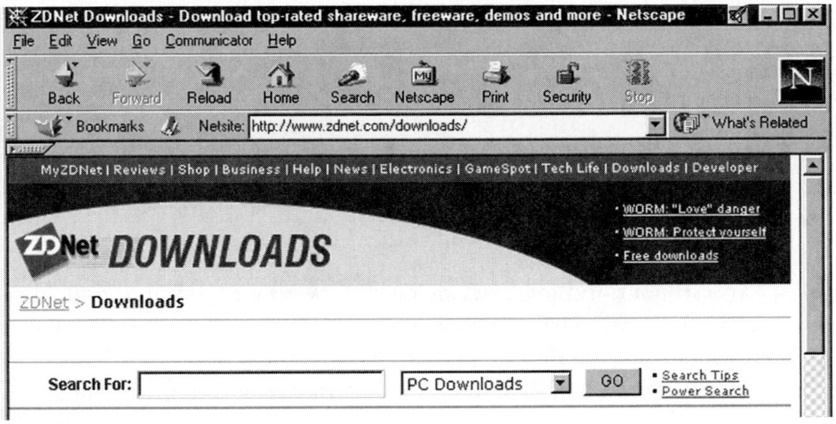

Figure 9.17:
A Banner Ad after
Filtering

What Is a Proxy Server?

A **proxy server** is a piece of software that retrieves documents on demand. When a Web browser is instructed to go through a proxy server, every document moves through the server before it's delivered to the browser. A server programmed to filter ads from Web pages removes all ads before passing the pages to a browser.

A proxy server can be located on a local host or on a remote host (for example, it could be an ISP server or it could be a firewall if you're working in a business environment). Proxy servers can also be used for purposes other than ad filtering. For example, sometimes Web pages are cached on a proxy server so that everyone in a LAN can benefit from a large cache of shared pages (this works much like your browser's personal cache). If you install software that uses a proxy, you (or your software's installer) will have to reset your browser's preferences so that your browser will know to go through the proxy server. Instructions for setting proxy preferences are given in Appendix E.

Some ISPs offer filtered proxy servers to their subscribers as a featured service so that individual members don't have to do their own filtering via browser ad-ons. When an ISP applies a content filter to all of the Web pages moving through one of its servers, its subscribers can download Web pages through the filtered server and receive "prewashed" Web pages. The ISPs who offer ad filtering usually do so at no extra charge to their subscribers.

Can Advertisers and Consumers Both Win?

We believe that giving users greater control over what advertisements they are subjected to is a win-win situation; users self-select ads they are interested in and bandwidth isn't wasted on unwanted data. Advertisers will likely have a greater success rate with the advertisements that are actually viewed. If Web sites find

that this jeopardizes their revenue stream, maybe they'll be challenged to come up with a more effective business model that is less burdensome in terms of information overload and bandwidth consumption for the user."
—Mark Ginsburg, Director of the BAB Project
at University of California at Berkeley

Are Banner Ads Really So Terrible?

You might not think that ads on the Internet are all that bad. You live with ads on television and radio, in newspapers and magazines, on billboards, buses, telephone poles, and basketball courts. Why should the Internet be any different? Well, the Internet is different. The cost of Internet advertising is minimal and does not reflect in any way the actual resources consumed. Ads on the Web consume shared resources, and everyone who uses the Internet is affected by those costs.

Each ad posted on a Web page and downloaded by a Web browser consumes bandwidth, and bandwidth is a limited resource. If too many ads consume too much bandwidth, download times increase for everyone and Internet usage patterns can be affected. For example, visit **ZDNet.com** over a telephone line connection and try to browse the site. Chances are, you'll find yourself waiting a long time for the pages to download. A recent visit to ZDNet using a 56K modem and an ad filter trapped roughly 60 ads per minute. As a result, this site is nearly impossible to browse without a broadband connection.

Companies that advertise on the Web tend to view their ad banners and pop-up windows as an essential part of their e-commerce business model. As a result, commercial advertisers are not exactly pleased with the idea of ad filters. The widespread adaptation of this technology would strike at the very heart of their enterprise and threaten their ability to recover advertising costs (however minimal). Moreover, if the advertisers were to fall, presumably Web sites subsidized by advertisers would follow, and the commercialization of the Web could be dealt quite a blow. However, this is hypothetical and far from inevitable. Even the advertisers realize that technical options such as ad filters are better for them than would be government regulations or laws designed to restrict commercial advertising on the Web.

What Is an Ad Server?

An **ad server** is a special-purpose Web server that feeds ads to Web sites. At the time of this writing, the leading ad server was delivering over one billion ads per day. Other ad servers are responsible for another one or two billion ads per week. These numbers will only grow as time goes on.

Whereas advertisers can only speculate about their future on the Web, network administrators must cope with the effects of too many ad banners and pop-up windows right now. They must absorb the financial costs that unwanted advertisements bring to their networks. These ads, which are disseminated over the whole Internet at no cost to the advertisers, consume bandwidth and impair the performance of the Internet for everyone (business people, researchers, and educators, as well as students). Consumers should have a right to opt out of the advertising stream and commercial advertisers should not assume that it's their right to profit from resources for which they don't pay.

Some Popular Ad Filtering Software

Here are some of the more popular ad filtering programs available on the Web.

Site Name	Type of Software	URL
WebWasher (Windows)	Freeware	`http://www.siemens.de/servers/wwash/wwash_us.htm`
Internet Junkbusters (Windows)	Freeware	`http://www.junkbusters.com/`
AdSubtract SE (Windows)	Freeware	`http://www.adsubtract.com/`
AdSubtract Pro (Windows) (formerly interMute)	Shareware	`http://www.adsubtract.com/se/upgrade.html`
WebFree (Mac)	Shareware	`http://www.falken.net/webfree/`

Some cookie managers also offer excellent ad filtering capabilities (see the following Above and Beyond).

One last aspect about banner ads must be mentioned. Some ad servers collect personal data from browsers that merely display a banner ad. The user need not click the ad nor do anything else, other than download the Web page that contains the banner ad. The data collection is done by making adjustments to the URL for the banner ad each time that a Web page that contains the ad is generated. For example, suppose that you visit **lycos.com** and conduct a search by using the keyword "prozac." When Lycos returns the list of hits for this query, you'll see a URL for a DoubleClick ad banner that includes the keyword "prozac."

The Referring URL (this is the URL for the hit list returned by Lycos):

```
http://www.lycos.com/srch/?lpv=1&loc=searchhp&query
=prozac&x=31&y=8
```

The Banner Ad URL (this is the URL for a banner ad that appears on the hit list page):

```
http://ln.doubleclick.net/jump/ly.ln/r;kw=prozac;pos=1;
sz=468x60;tile=1;ratio=1_2;! … (etc.) …
```

These unusual-looking URLs not only return files from Web servers; they also execute CGI scripts on their respective servers (see Section 5.8.2). The script triggered by the referring URL sends a search query to the Lycos search engine. Then when the search engine returns its hits, the script on the Lycos server creates a Web page designed to display those hits. This hit list page also contains the URL for the DoubleClick banner ad. The banner ad URL triggers another CGI script, one on a DoubleClick server. This script returns the banner ad that you see on the search engine hits page. You have no way of knowing for sure what else the DoubleClick script does, but you can see from the banner ad URL, as shown above, that the keyword "prozac" is being passed to the script. If DoubleClick has sold this particular keyword to one of its advertisers, that advertiser's banner ad will be delivered by the DoubleClick ad server. A DoubleClick script could also easily store this keyword in a database of Lycos search engine queries if DoubleClick wanted to keep track of all queries sent to the Lycos search engine.

Collecting keyword queries such as those for "prozac" is not a problem if that's all the script does. But if the user sending this query to Lycos has ever accepted a cookie from DoubleClick (see Sections 2.15.4 and 9.10.1), then the DoubleClick server will be able to associate this query with a unique DoubleClick ID number stored in the cookie. This enables DoubleClick to group a number of different queries under a common ID number. If the cookie is programmed to persist for years, a large number of keywords could be collected, saved, and associated with the same DoubleClick ID number. In addition, any other search engines that display ad banners from DoubleClick will send their query keywords back to the same DoubleClick script. Then those queries will be associated with the same unique DoubleClick ID number (see Figure 9.18). In this way, DoubleClick can amass personal information from Web pages that collect names, addresses, e-mail addresses, and other personal information that a user types onto forms. In addition, all of the information collected could be grouped under the same unique ID number. If you visit enough Web sites that display banner ads from DoubleClick, DoubleClick can accumulate a lot of valuable information about you and your interests.

A collection of data about a single user is called a **user profile**. DoubleClick says that extensive user profiles are good for users because accurate profiles make it possible for DoubleClick to send banner ads that better target the needs and interests of individual users. Privacy advocates are worried about user profiles being sold to third parties and consolidated with other database profiles in an effort to build even larger profiles. In addition, any identifying information that makes its way into these profiles can be used to associate the profile with more than a cookie's ID number. A user profile that can be connected to a person or even only an e-mail address is a valuable commodity. The following Above and Beyond explains how ad servers

Figure 9.18:
An Ad Server Can
Consolidate Data
Collected from a
Single Host
Machine

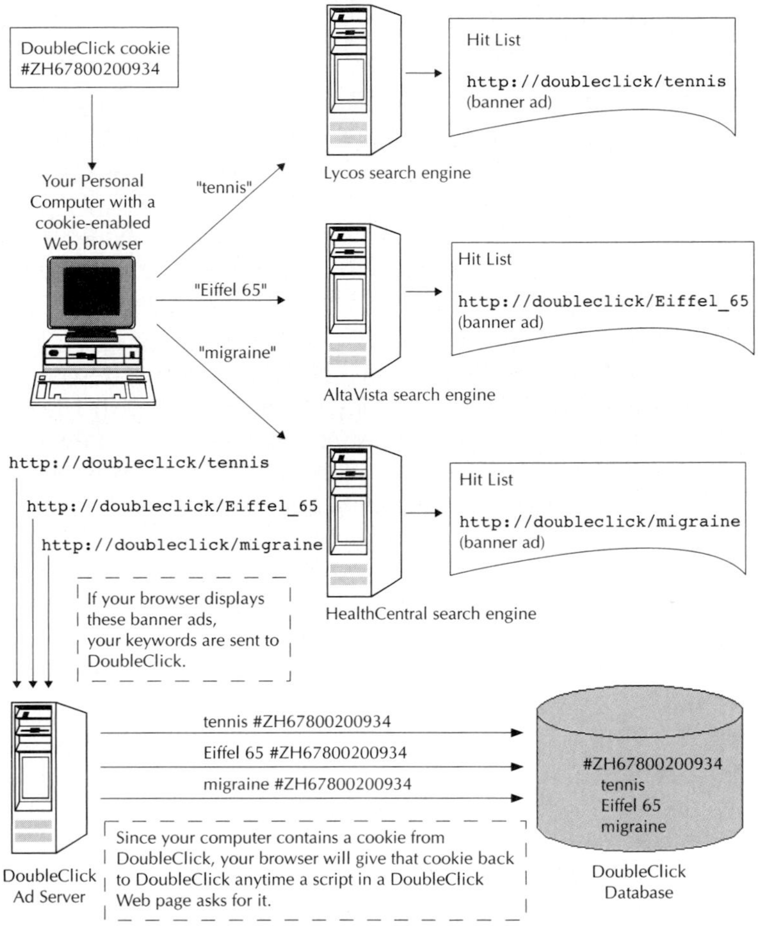

DoubleClick cookie
#ZH67800200934

Your Personal
Computer with a
cookie-enabled
Web browser

"tennis"

"Eiffel 65"

"migraine"

Hit List

`http://doubleclick/tennis`
(banner ad)

Lycos search engine

Hit List

`http://doubleclick/Eiffel_65`
(banner ad)

AltaVista search engine

Hit List

`http://doubleclick/migraine`
(banner ad)

HealthCentral search engine

`http://doubleclick/tennis`

`http://doubleclick/Eiffel_65`

`http://doubleclick/migraine`

If your browser displays
these banner ads,
your keywords are sent to
DoubleClick.

tennis #ZH67800200934

Eiffel 65 #ZH67800200934

migraine #ZH67800200934

#ZH67800200934
tennis
Eiffel 65
migraine

DoubleClick
Ad Server

Since your computer contains a cookie from
DoubleClick, your browser will give that cookie back
to DoubleClick anytime a script in a DoubleClick
Web page asks for it.

DoubleClick
Database

connect user profiles to e-mail addresses, even when you've done everything that
you can to safeguard your address.

From the online instructions for setting up an ad filter on your home computer, you
might think that filters are more trouble than they're worth. For example, the
Junkbuster's FAQ tends to scare people because it's so thorough (it does an excellent
job of covering all possible troublespots). Some filters are easier to set up than
others. The Junkbuster filter can be fully customized to suit anyone, but this makes
it more complicated than some simpler filters. Don't try Junkbuster unless you're
patient and willing to spend some time on it. To keep things simple, try **WebWasher**.
It's easy to set up, although you'll still have to change some browser proxy settings
yourself. For the easiest installation, try **AdSubtract SE**. It resets your browser's proxy
settings automatically each time that it's launched (and resets them again when you
exit AdSubtract). This is as easy as it gets. If you're working on a Mac, WebFree is
very easy both to customize and to install.

9.5 ■ DOWNLOAD MANAGERS

If you've ever had trouble downloading a file with your Web browser, you'll want to know about download managers. Browsers are prepared to download files, but they can complete the job only if there are no interruptions, no lost Internet connections, and no difficulties on the server's side. A large download over a telephone line and modem can take an hour or two and is nothing that you want to have to repeat. If you do a lot of downloading, for either software or MP3 files, you'll appreciate the special features that a good download manager offers.

Large downloads don't always make it to your host machine in one piece. They can fail for many reasons. The host might crash during the download or get disconnected from the Internet before the download is completed. The server that is sending the file might crash, get disconnected, or experience bandwidth bottlenecks due to high traffic demands. A problem with an Internet gateway along the way can cause a disruption. If you're downloading a file by using only your browser and trouble happens, you don't have a lot of choices: You can either restart the download from scratch, or you can give up. A download manager can offer you other options. For example, when you use a download manager, the server usually will let you resume your original download where you left off. This is just what you want when the download is 98% complete and your telephone connection drops out.

A full-featured download manager offers many options. An example is Go!Zilla for Windows (there are many other comparable download managers). Figure 9.19 shows Go!Zilla in the middle of a 2MB download. Notice from the top window that the file is downloading at a rate of 3.3K per second, and that the download can be resumed if it is interrupted. Not all servers can resume an interrupted download, so it's always best to work with a site whose servers can. The download is 39% complete and is expected to take another 5 minutes. Notice also the location and name of the file being downloaded and where it's being placed on the local host. The current server connection was established on the first try and Go!Zilla was prepared to try a total of 99 times if need be in order to make that connection ("Attempt 1 of 99" in Figure 9.19). This doesn't look very different from what your Web browser does, apart from a few nice graphical effects (a dynamic bandwidth chart as well as an artistic progress bar) and the convenience of being able to see where the file will be stored on the local host. However, there's more.

Notice that to the right of the bandwidth chart is a small speed control slider. When the slider is positioned up all of the way, Go!Zilla is working at maximal speed. This is fine if you're not trying to do anything else with your computer during the download and you want the download to finish as quickly as possible. However, if you're trying to surf the Web or run other programs while your download shuffles along in the background, you can adjust the speed control slider for a slower download. Slower downloads devote fewer system resources to the downloading process, freeing up resources for other applications so they can run faster.

Figure 9.19:
Go!Zilla during a
File Download

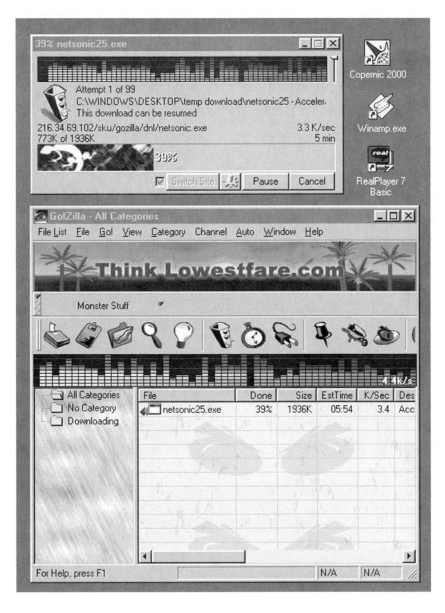

If something urgent comes up and you need to reclaim your CPU or bandwidth, you can put the download on hold by clicking the Pause button—remember, the download, if interrupted, can be resumed at any time.

A good download manager starts working for you before the download starts. Figure 9.20 shows Go!Zilla's server selection window. In this example, you want to download IrfanView (see Section 5.8.1). As you can see, it's available on a number of servers, many in Japan (notice the `jp` domain name). After you specify the file to download, Go!Zilla uses a specialized search engine to search public FTP servers and locate copies of that file on other FTP servers. After Go!Zilla locates the candidate servers, it pings each (see the Trip column) to find out how quickly each server responds. Each server is then given a rating—Excellent, Good, Average, Little Slow, Slow, Poor, No Response—based on projected download times. You can see the DNS address for each server as well as the number of intermediate hosts (hops) needed to get the download from there to here. You can try to minimize your download time by picking a site with an excellent rating and a small number of hops.

Figure 9.20:
Go!Zilla Pings Servers and Rates Their Responsiveness

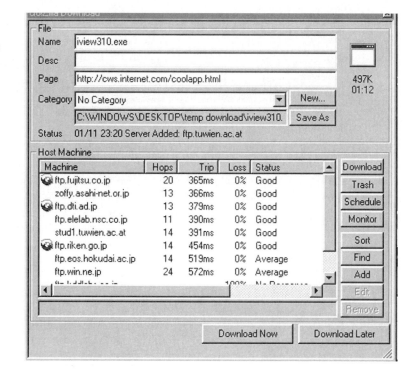

Alternatively, if none of the servers look promising, you can schedule the download for later. Go!Zilla makes it easy to schedule the download for a more convenient time (see Figure 9.21).

Because Go!Zilla usually can find the same file on multiple servers, you can start a download on one server but continue it on a different one. If you're having a lot of bad luck with the available servers, you might need to switch to other servers in order to complete the download. Go!Zilla has a minimal transfer rate setting that it uses to optimize downloads after they start. If the current transfer is not proceeding at the minimal transfer rate, Go!Zilla will automatically switch to the next best avail-

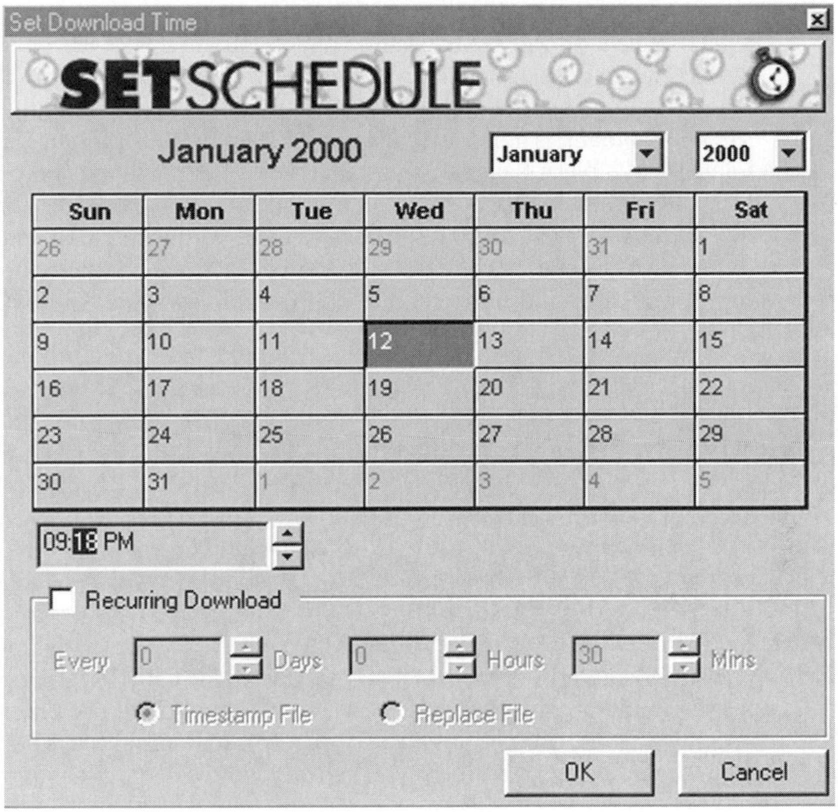

Figure 9.21:
Go!Zilla's
Download
Scheduler

able server in an effort to speed up the remaining transfer. It also tells you whether a server can resume an interrupted download. If you're downloading a very large file, you can check to see whether the server you're using can resume an interrupted download at the start of the download. If it can't, then you might want to select a different server.

Some Popular Download Managers

Here are some popular download managers that you can investigate.

Site Name	Type of Software	URL
Go!zilla Free (Windows)	Freeware	`http://www.gozilla.com/`
GetRight (Windows)	Shareware	`http://www.getright.com/`
Download Deputy (Mac)	Shareware	`http://www.ilesa.com/`

If you're interested primarily in downloading MP3 files, special search engines are available just for MP3s. MP3 search clients, such as MP3 Fiend, integrate a specialized meta search engine along with some features for managing MP3 downloads. Napster, Gnutella, and Wrapster (Macster for the Mac) use a different approach to MP3 downloads. They are really *file-trading applications* because all of the file transfers take place between Napster clients. Napster servers help client users establish file-sharing connections with other client users. However, there are no servers that archive files like an FTP server. This massive file-sharing capability has resulted in an RIAA lawsuit against Napster. However, the technology behind Napster has been duplicated and distributed as open source software, so it will be very difficult to contain.

9.6 PASSWORD MANAGERS

Some of the best Web sites are available to registered users only. These include sites that feature news from the **New York Times Online**, computer help forums for members at **ZDNet**, music downloads at **mp3.com**, and countless Web-based e-mail services. If you visit sites such as these often, you might have a problem because each requires a unique ID and a password. If you give each site an ID and password, you'll find it difficult to remember which pair goes with which site. However, if you keep things simple and use the same pair at each site, you're not practicing good online security. If your logon information is ever cracked at one site, you can be cracked at all of the other sites for which you've supplied the same ID and password.

Passwords are an important component in maintaining secure systems, and you should do everything you can to keep your passwords secure. Commercial sites that have collected your credit card account information will release that information to anyone who successfully enters your ID and password (see Figure 9.22). Similarly, sites that have collected sensitive personal information (for example, health-related sites) will release that to anyone who logs on as you. Ideally, you will use a different pair of ID and password for each site, even if you're dealing with dozens of password-protected sites and you use a *password manager* to manage them.

A **password manager** is a small program that keeps track of logon information for you. It's like an address book, except with information needed to visit protected Web sites. You might have tried to create your own form of password manager by keeping notes of your IDs and passwords in a text file. The text file solution is better than nothing if it encourages you to use unique IDs at each site. However, if that file is compromised due to a security lapse on your local host, then you're in trouble.

These complications might have discouraged you from registering at many Web sites. Avoiding these sites is a solution of sorts. However, by so doing you deprive yourself of some good online resources. A password manager is the best solution. Figure 9.23 shows a Web site entry from the freeware password manager **Password Prompter**.

Figure 9.22:
Many E-Commerce
Sites Ask Customers
to Sign In

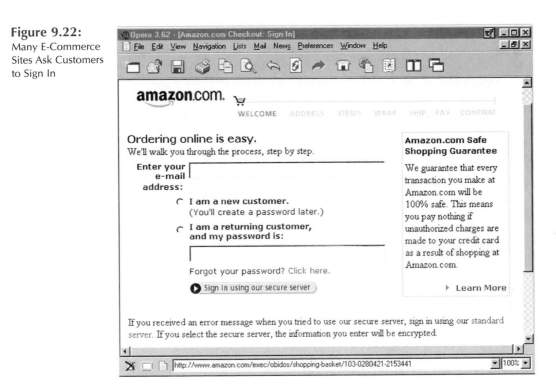

Figure 9.23:
Password Manager
Organizes and
Protects Sensitive
IDs and Passwords

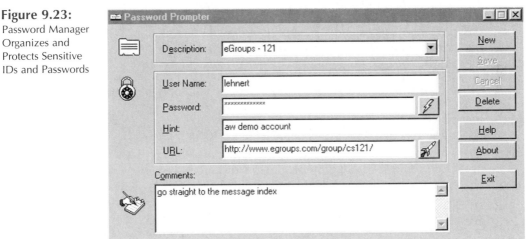

Each time that you register at a Web site, you create a new directory entry for that site. When you want to return to that site, you look up the directory entry for the site in the password manager's directory and transfer the password with a copy-and-paste command. Note that the asterisks in Figure 9.23 only mask the actual password characters in the directory display; if you copy and paste those asterisks to a text editor, the actual password will be visible. A good password manager will protect this information with encryption (see Chapter 11), as well as its own password protection on start-up, illustrated in Figure 9.24. The password that gives you access to all your other passwords is called a *master password*.

Figure 9.24:
You Still Need to
Remember One
Password

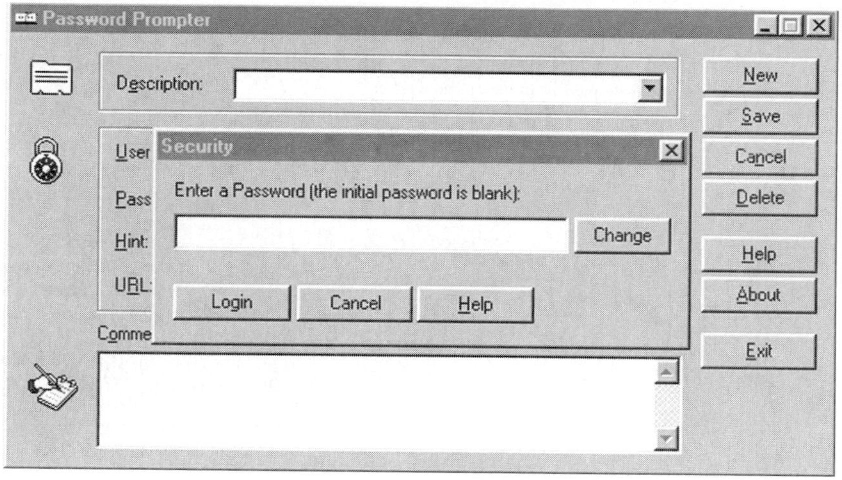

A nice feature to have in a password manager is a *random password generator*. When you register at a site for the first time, you can ask your password manager for a random password instead of making up one yourself (see Figure 9.25). Random passwords are usually more secure than human-generated passwords because they don't contain any recognizable words. Because you don't need to remember any passwords, you don't need a password that's easy to remember.

Applications such as Password Prompter are easy to find on the Web (use the search query "password manager" at a software clearinghouse) and will save you from ever having to remember passwords—just be careful not to forget the master password. However, they do need to be launched each time that you need a password and the password that you want must be manually copied from the password directory and pasted onto the Web page. If this proves to be too annoying, look for a password manager that can be integrated into your browser as a browser add-on.

Is Your Credit Card Account Number Stored on Your Computer?

If you do a lot of online shopping, you might find it convenient to have your credit card account information in a file for easy look-up. If yours is in a text file, however, you subject yourself to some risk each time that you connect to the Internet (with more risk if you have broadband connection). You can eliminate all such risk by storing sensitive information like this in a password manager. Password Prompter gives you a comment field for each entry, so you can create entries for anything that you want. Anything that you store in a password manager will be encrypted for safety against prying eyes (including your roommates, officemates, and inquisitive children). Only you will be able to retrieve it, by using your master password.

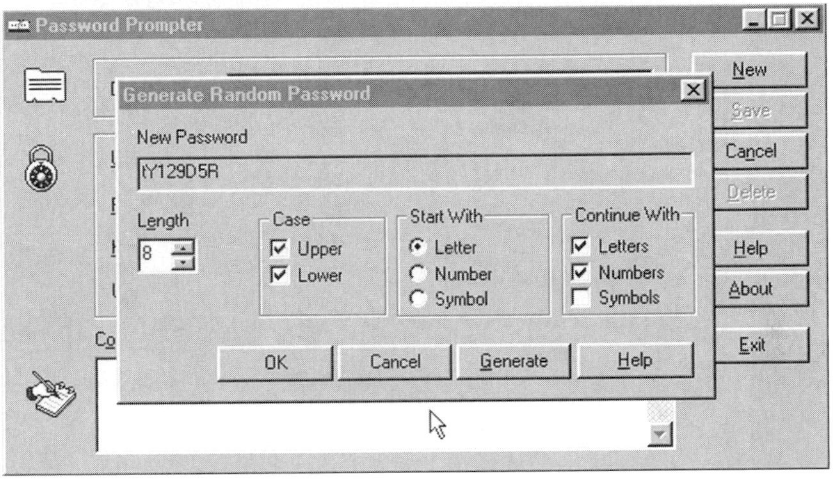

Figure 9.25:
A Random
Password Generator

Gator is an example of a Web-page form assistant that manages sensitive information for Web page forms in general. It records site IDs, passwords, and other frequently required information each time that you visit a Web page that requests them. Subsequent visits to one of those pages causes Gator to pop up and offer to complete the form for you. Instead of typing 10 to 20 characters, you click one button and you're done. You can control to which sites Gator responds (see Figure 9.26), and you can change Gator's entries for any site at any time. Gator is password–protected, and all of its data is encrypted for maximal security, like Password Prompter. To find programs such as Gator, use the search query "form fill" at a software clearinghouse.

Whatever you do, avoid using the same password in a dozen different places. With the right software in place, you can maintain separate passwords for all your Web registrations. It's always easier to prevent a security problem than it is to fix one.

9.7   DESKTOP PORTALS

A **desktop portal** (also called a **navigational toolbar**) is an application that strives to put all of your most important Internet resources a mouse click away. Many are available, and they vary quite a bit. Some strongly emphasize news updates, where-

Figure 9.26:
A Customized Site
Directory in Gator

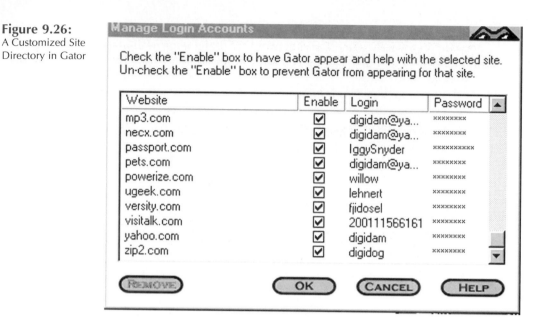

as others make searching the Web their central activity. Figure 9.27 shows EntryPoint's toolbar with a few of its features in action. All of the windows shown in the figure appear on your desktop. If you want to scan the news headlines, you go to your personalized directory and click a headline to see the full story. For the local weather, you roll your mouse over the weather button. And to hear an MP3 or a CD selection, you start EntryPoint's MP3 player to set a playlist or use the player controls.

Desktop portals offer fast access to the resources that they support. Many can be personalized like Web portals can and can be changed as needed depending on your interests. If you have a daily routine on the Web that can be handled through a desktop portal, you'll probably enjoy the convenience of finding everything that you need in a point-and-click environment.

If you spend most of your time on the Web searching for information, try **AltaVista Discovery**. This very popular application brings the AltaVista search engine to your desktop. With its toolbar, you can conduct searches as you can from the AltaVista home page, except that you have access to features that aren't available at AltaVista on the Web. For example, you can display any Web page in your browser, click an icon that depicts, say, a pair of apples, and get back a list of hits from AltaVista based on relevancy feedback (a "find documents just like this one" search). Clicking another icon gives you a list of hits that contain links to the target page. You can also generate an automatic summary of the current page (an interesting technology to see in action) and conduct a search that is limited to those Web pages that are on the same server as the target document.

Figure 9.27:
EntryPoint Desktop
Portal

You can also set up Discovery to index a local database for your own personal documents. Then you can conduct AltaVista-style searches on your own hard drive, with all of the special and advanced search features that are usually reserved for searches on the Web (see Figure 9.28). This is very useful if you're working on a large writing project that is split into multiple files.

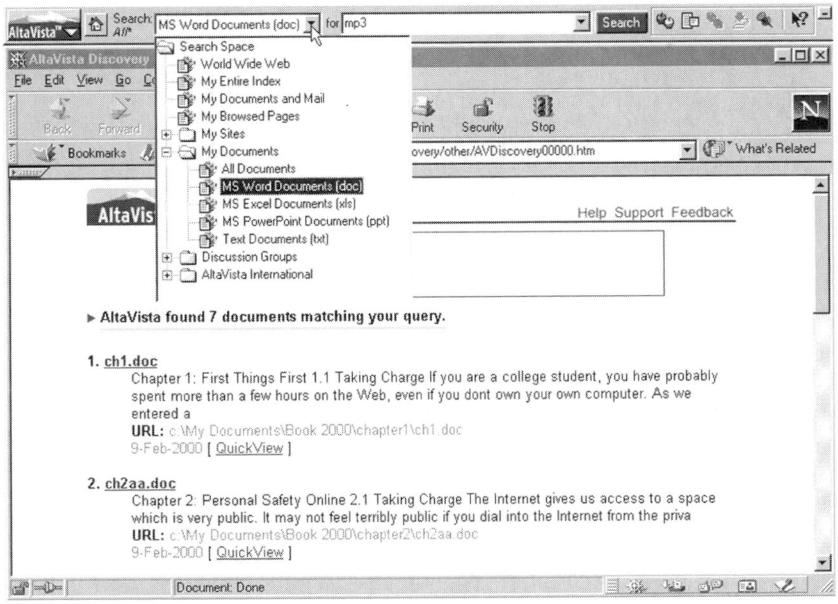

Figure 9.28:
AltaVista Discovery
Goes Beyond
AltaVista on the
Web

Another powerful desktop portal that emphasizes searching is **Naviscope**. The Naviscope viewbar acts as a portal with convenient icons for search engines, ping, traceroute, an online dictionary, thesaurus, and a bevy of animated Net monitors to keep you on top of your Internet connection. With one mouse click, you can synchronize your computer's clock with an atomic clock. By selecting Website Information at the search portal, you can look up the owner of a Web server at Internic. If you spend a lot of time on the Web and want to see what's happening behind the scenes, Naviscope is a great choice (see Figure 9.29). In fact, it has so many features, it's difficult to categorize. It's a browser add-on that does the work of at least three or four separate add-ons. It filters ads, blocks cookies (see the following Above and Beyond), accelerates pages with a configurable prefetch feature, and creates site maps that are faster to navigate than the original Web pages.

Figure 9.29:
Naviscope Is the
Swiss Army Knife of
Desktop Portals

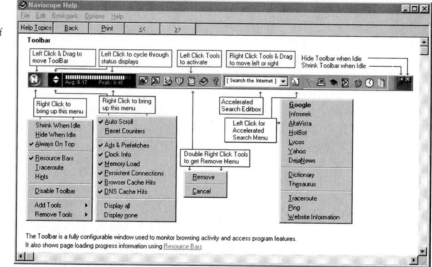

Naviscope's site map feature is a browser add-on that can significantly accelerate your Web navigation and viewing (see Figure 9.30). Using this map, you can easily traverse links within a single Web site and get a far view of all of the links available on a single page. You can create a site map for any site that you want, and you can save those maps from session to session. If you visit a site often and are familiar with its general layout, you'll find it faster to navigate Naviscope's site map rather than the actual Web pages in your browser window. Clicking links in the site map moves you around the site instantaneously because Naviscope's prefetch feature anticipates your next move and minimizes the amount of time that you spend waiting for pages to download.

The Naviscope toolbar offers access to many features; you'll probably need to consult the online documentation to make sense of it all. But it's time well spent if

Figure 9.30:
Naviscope Site Map
Feature

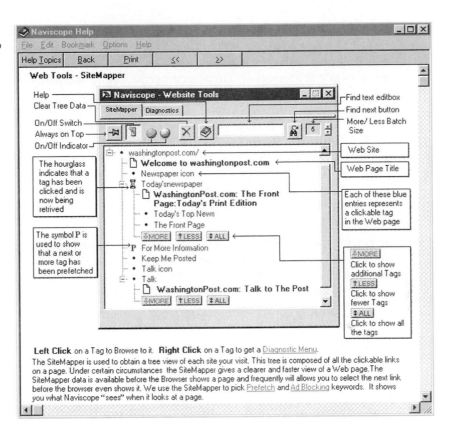

you're online a lot. This is probably not the best place to start for a newbie, but it's a great tool for those who are a bit more knowledgeable about the Net and looking for ways to streamline their time spent searching and browsing.

Desktop portals are not for everyone. However, if you find one that you like you'll probably stay with it. Some desktop portals even pay you to surf the Web in exchange for being able to display banner ads on your desktop (the going rate at AllAdvantage is $.50/hour).

9.8   ALTERNATIVE WEB BROWSERS

Many people are surprised to learn that alternative browsers are available. Chances are, you're still using the browser that came with your computer, and it never occurred to you to switch to another. If, for some reason, you did switch, it was probably because your next computer came with the *other* browser. Navigator and MSIE are the two main contenders in the world of browsers; if you're happy with one of them, great. However, if you want to check out the competition, you can have more than one browser installed on your computer—they will coexist quite nicely. Until recently, users didn't install a second browser because of the amount of memory that they consume. However, with 18GB hard drives becoming the norm, you can afford to install as many browsers as you like.

Can Competing Browsers Get Along?

If you install a second browser, the new one might at first appear to have clobbered the old one. It might take over as your default browser, and that will affect other HTML-enabled software such as e-mail clients. This doesn't mean that you can't have more than one browser on your computer. You can designate one or the other as your default browser and then can experiment with the nondefault browser as you wish.

Removing a browser from a PC, however, is not always as easy as installing a second one. For example, MSIE is more or less welded into the Windows OS and Microsoft has no desire to help anyone get rid of it. However, you can install Navigator if you already have MSIE, run them both at the same time, and even make Navigator your default browser. Windows will not self-destruct.

If you're accustomed to Navigator and want to try out MSIE, MSIE will try to make the transition as smooth as possible (see Figure 9.31).

Figure 9.31:
MSIE Welcomes Converts from Navigator

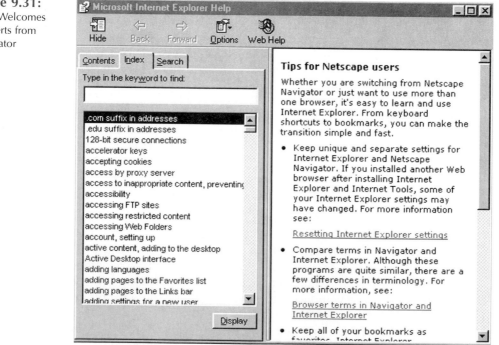

If you're moving from MSIE to Navigator, Navigator will help you reassign Navigator as your default browser any time that you launch Navigator (see Figure 9.32).

Figure 9.32:
Navigator Wants to
Be Your Default
Browser

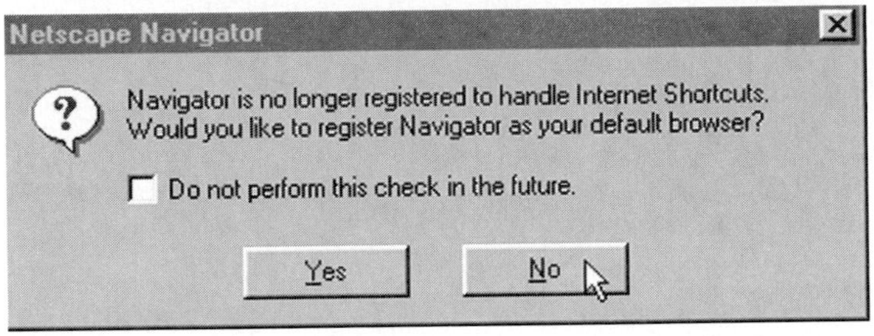

If you're seriously curious about other browsers, consider trying Opera instead of simply switching to the *other* popular browser. Opera, originating from Norway, is a true alternative to its two big American cousins. MSIE and Navigator are not really very different from each other; Opera is another story. You'll notice the difference before you even start the installation. Whereas Navigator and MSIE each consume from 15MB to 25MB on your hard drive, Opera consumes no more than 1.7MB. It is also less memory-intensive when you run it. It launches quickly and lets you open multiple windows without crashing your machine. You might also notice a speed up in the time to display Web pages. Opera is streamlined to keep everything as fast as possible. Many beginners also find Opera easier to learn and live with, particularly because it has excellent online documentation. Moreover, Opera's commands and options seem to be easier to find than those of the other two browsers. Making Opera your default browser is easy, as illustrated in Figure 9.33.

For more information about Opera and its unique features, visit **Opera's Home Page**. In general, Opera distinguishes itself by its small size, some unique features, the fact that it's highly configurable (see Figure 9.34), and a large assortment of keyboard shortcuts. If you don't have broadband and you want to speed up your browsing time, you'll be surprised how much faster a browsing session can be if you stop using your mouse and start using keyboard shortcut commands instead. You need not learn them all at once—choose one or two new ones to learn each week (the mouse is still there for you). Opera will help by showing you a Tip of the Day each time you launch it.

Opera is not free, but you can download a full-featured version of it from the Web and try it out during a free-trial period. It costs $35 but offers a 50% educational discount for students and teachers.

Figure 9.33:
Making Opera Your
Default Browser

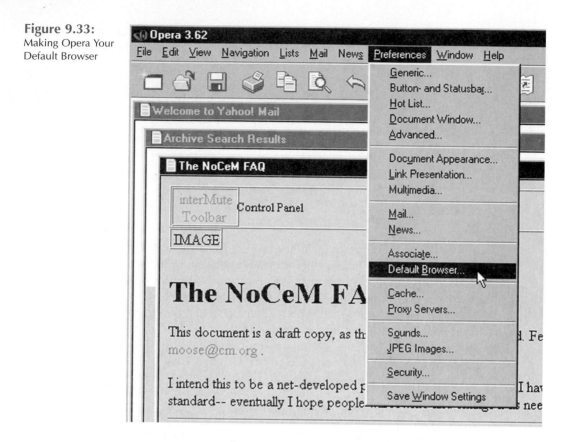

Figure 9.34:
You Decide When
Opera Should Be
Launched by
Default

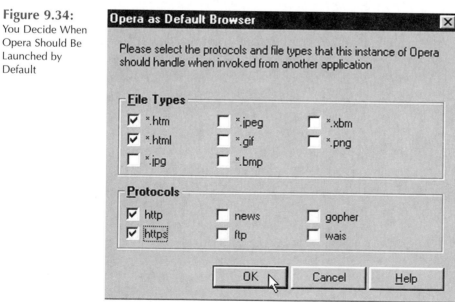

9.9 ▌ FTP CLIENT POWER FEATURES

A good FTP client is an essential tool for anyone who works with files on multiple computer accounts. This includes anyone who maintains a Web site as well as people with multiple Internet accounts. FTP servers and clients were introduced in Section 8.7. If you don't do a lot of file transfers, you might have been getting along with a comprehensive Web page construction kit (for file uploads) and a browser or a browser with a download manager (for file downloads). It's possible to get along in this world without an FTP client. As with many things on the Internet, it's a question of whether you are doing what you need to do as quickly and easily as possible. A good FTP client will have timesaving features that can't be found elsewhere. Read on to find out about these features.

- **File Type Detection and Selection**

  The business of moving a file from one Internet host to another is relatively simple. Your software needs to know if it's working with a binary file or an ASCII file—the wrong file type can scuttle a successful transfer. A good FTP client should be able to determine the file type automatically. However, it should also give you an opportunity to set the file type manually, in case the automatic method gets it wrong.

- **File Queues and Thread Counts**

  When you need to move multiple files, you need to create a *file queue*. The files will transfer faster if your FTP client can download a few at the same time, instead of working through the list one file at a time.

  You should also be able to edit the file queue. At the very least, you should be able to remove a file from the queue. Some FTP clients also make it easy to rearrange the queue elements.

  Each file transfer consumes a resource called a thread (which should not be confused with the conversational threads described in Chapter 7). You should be able to specify how many threads that you want running at once. A high-bandwidth connection can support more threads than can a slower telephone line connection.

- **Auto Resume**

  Just as a good download manager makes it possible to resume a download if the transfer is interrupted for any reason, a good FTP client will be able to resume a partial file transfer where it left off. This feature can save a lot of time if you're dealing with an unreliable Internet connection. Some FTP clients will reconnect automatically when they are disconnected from the server.

- **Desktop Integration**

  An intuitive user interface is a real plus for beginners, as well as a convenient feature for more experienced users. For example, most users appreciate drag-and-drop capabilities. If you see a file in a directory on the local host, you should be able to drag it over to a directory on the remote host for a file upload. Most FTP clients support drag-and-drop operations. When a piece of software uses the same interface capabilities as your OS, the software meshes better with your overall computing environment and seems easier to use.

- **Keep Alive**

  When you work with a remote host, you need to maintain your Internet connection to avoid frustrating delays and interruptions. If your ISP likes to disconnect you after a certain amount of time without network activity, you'll appreciate a **keep-alive option**. This option allows you to pick a time interval for periodic network activity (a single ping is all that it takes) to keep your ISP's auto-kill at bay. For example, if your ISP shuts down the connection after 10 minutes of no activity, pick a 9-minute setting and turn on the keep-alive option.

- **Customizable Toolbars**

  You've likely seen customizable toolbars on other applications. Whenever an application is too complicated to display icons for all of the commonly used commands, a customizable toolbar is a good feature to have. Different users probably will use different commands, and it's helpful to have the right toolbar for only the operations that you use. If you end up spending a lot of time with your FTP client, this might be a nonnegotiable requirement.

- **Search and Sort Options**

  Large file directories need to be navigated. No one wants to scroll through every file in a very large directory, looking for one specific file (you might someday happen upon a remote directory that contains thousands of files). This is when you need searching and sorting options to help you move to files as quickly as possible.

- **Bookmarks and Macro Recorders**

  If you maintain a Web site or work regularly with a remote directory, you might find yourself going through much the same routine each time that you do either. If some parts of the routine are really constant, you might be able to automate large segments of your routine by defining macros. Recall that a **macro** is a sequence of commands that you specify and name. It is like a small computer program that you write to take some of the drudgery out of your work routines.

  Once you've defined a macro, you can execute the entire sequence of commands contained in the macro by simply clicking the macro. If you have many routine activities, you can create a library of macros to streamline them.

  You can also save some steps in your routines by using bookmarks. A **bookmark** makes it possible to move into a specific file directory with a single mouse click instead of entering a series of directory navigation commands. Pathing a directory's tree structure is one of the more time-consuming tasks associated with FTP sessions. Something as simple as a good bookmark collection can save you a lot of time.

FTP Servers: Let the Pros Run Them

It's one thing to install an FTP *client* and quite another to install an FTP *server*. If you have a broadband connection to the Internet and you're connected around the clock, it might occur to you to set up a password-protected FTP server so that you can share files with your friends and family, such as files containing photographs. Please don't. An FTP server can constitute a major security risk if it is not set up correctly. If you want to make files available to the general public (or perhaps a restricted group of friends and relatives), try one of the family photo album services on the Web or a more general file hosting service on the Web. They are free and are a lot less work than an FTP server.

If you decide to ignore this advice and set up an FTP server anyway, make sure that you don't give anyone *write privileges* for *file uploads*. Write privileges are inherently risky, even if all of the visitors to your server are benign and clueless. It's easy to crash an FTP server by uploading more bytes than the server's hard drive can handle.

Beware of Zucchini

If you'll let anyone write to your disk, then anyone can fill your disk. This is not a hack, by any stretch of the imagination. It's more like forgetting to close your car windows during zucchini season and ending up with more squash than any mortal could ever desire.

David Fisher, Lab Manager; University of Massachusetts

Things to Remember

- It's a good idea to back up your system files before each software installation.
- Plug-ins and add-ons are often easier to set up than are helper applications.
- The maximal prefetch setting on a Web accelerator speeds up your Web sessions, but it hogs a lot of bandwidth.
- Filtering the ads from your Web pages can speed up your Web sessions.
- Banner ads can collect data from you even if you don't click them.
- All password managers should encrypt your sensitive data and restrict access via a master password.
- Some Web portals offer powerful features that you won't find anywhere else.
- Don't install an FTP server on your computer unless you're planning first to take a course on computer security.

Important Concepts

ad filter—a browser add-on that turns off some, but not all, of the graphical components in a Web page.

browser add-on—an application that works alongside and complements a Web browser.

browser helper—an application that can be launched by a Web browser.

browser plug-in—an application that expands the capabilities of a Web browser.

desktop portal—fast access to frequently visited Web servers from your desktop.

download manager—software that facilitates file downloads from Web pages and FTP servers.

password manager—software that helps you keep track of unique userids and secure passwords for multiple Web sites.

Web accelerator—software that leverages the available bandwidth so that you spend less time waiting for Web pages to download.

Where Can I Learn More

Help! Plug-Ins   `http://www1.sympatico.ca/help/Plugins/`

Web Browser Enhancements for Sound   `http://www.geocities.com/`
`~stratguitar/webtutor_music.html`

Browser Reviews   `http://netforbeginners.about.com/internet/`
`netforbeginners/msubbrowserchoose.htm`

Cookie Central   `http://cookiecentral.com/`

Junkbusters   `http://www.junkbusters.com/ht/en/links.htm`

Problems and Exercises

1. People are often warned about the dangers of drug interactions. A medication that is perfectly safe by itself can become dangerous if combined with certain other drugs or sometimes even herbal supplements. What is an analogous danger with computers? What potential dangers do computer owners have to worry about?

2. Explain the difference between a plug-in and a helper application. Which is generally easier to set up? If an application has a setting for a default browser, does that make it a browser plug-in? Explain why or why not.

3. Gator (`http://www.gator.com/`) is a popular freeware program that runs in the background and pops up whenever you download a Web page that contains a blank form. Once you've completed a form, Gator remembers that form and will fill it out for you automatically the next time you visit that same Web page. Is Gator a browser plug-in or a browser add-on? Explain your answer.

4. A friend claims to understand how Web accelerators work and says that he can achieve the same level of acceleration simply by changing the size of his browser's cache to 200MB. Explain why this can't be correct.

5. Describe two prefetch options for Web accelerators. What conditions will produce the greatest benefits when you can prefetch your Web pages?

6. Explain why there's no real harm if one person uses a Web accelerator, but a large problem could result if everyone started using them. Are some accelerator users more of a problem than others? Explain your answer.

7. What is a proxy server? Name one class of browser add-ons that requires the use of a proxy server.

8. What is an ad server? How much Internet traffic do ad servers produce?

9. Explain why ad servers are in a good position to compile extensive user profiles. How can you prevent someone from creating a detailed user profile based on your Web surfing? Is it enough to turn off the graphics in your Web browser? Explain your answer.

10. Name four things that a download manager can do that a Web browser can't.

11. How can you create password protection for sensitive credit card account information on your home computer? Name one software program that is useful for doing this.

12. Compare desktop portals with Web portals (such as Yahoo! and Excite!). Are there any advantages or disadvantages to one or the other? Explain your answer.

13. How does a download manager differ from an FTP client? Does anyone need both? Explain your answer.

14. [Hands-On] Select, download, and install a plug-in for your browser that you would like to try. Test it on a suitable page to make sure that it works. Keep a log of your activities so that you can answer the following questions.

    a. How long did it take you to decide which plug-in to try?

    b. How long did it take to download the plug-in?

    c. How long did it take to install it?

    d. Did it work right away?

Describe any difficulties that you experienced with this exercise. (You might find it useful to visit one of the sites listed previously under Where Can I Learn More?)

15. [Hands-On] Select, download, and install a download manager that you would like to try and make sure that it works properly with your browser (when you click a file to be downloaded, your browser should automatically launch the download manager). Go to Project Gutenberg (see Chapter 8), and download some files. Section 9.9 described eight features found in fully featured FTP clients. How many of these does your download manager have? List the ones that you can verify. Of the features that aren't present, how many would make sense for your download manager?

16. **[Hands-On]** Download and install both AltaVista Discovery and Alexa. (*Note*: If you're running Navigator, you should already have Alexa installed. An icon representing it should be on the Navigator toolbar.) Conduct five Web searches first using Alexa to find similar sites and then using Discovery's similar site feature. Make up your own open-ended search queries for this exercise, or use some queries from the Hands-On exercises for Chapter 6. Did one application do a better job on all five searches? Did they seem to be comparable or can you say anything about how they differ? Do you have a preference for one or the other? Explain your answers.

17. **[Hands-On]** Download Naviscope, and create a site map for a large Web site that you visit often. Then revisit the site and try to navigate it by using the Naviscope site map instead of your browser. Is the site map a good substitute for the actual Web pages? Do you think it's useful to have a site map like this? Can you think of situations in which the site map would be more desirable than the Web pages? Explain your answers.

18. **[Find It Online]** Aaron West wrote an article entitled "Will Banner Ad Blocking Software Kill Internet Marketing?" (See `http://www.w3nation.com/features/columns/aaron/adblock.htm`.) In this article, he suggests that the appeal of ad filters will eventually die out. What is the reasoning behind this claim? Defend the claim, then propose and defend a counterargument.

19. **[Find It Online]** Ad filtering can speed up your Web page downloads. Name four Web accelerators that offer an ad filtering option. (*Hint*: See `http://www.junkbusters.com/ht/en/links.html`, and do some keyword searching. The answer is in that document.)

20. **[Find It Online]** Find reviews for the Opera Web browser by visiting the site `http://netforbeginners.about.com/internet/netforbeginners/msubbrowserchoose.htm`. Compare Opera to the browser that you currently use (if you already use Opera, compare it to Navigator or MSIE). Find five things that make Opera different from those two browsers.

Power Tools for the Internet: Above and Beyond

Cookie Managers

A **cookie** is a text file or an entry in a text file that is created by your browser when you visit a Web page designed to create cookies. It can store any sort of information that is available to the Web server: your IP address, the OS that you use, the browser that you run, which (if any) search engine brought you to the site. It also includes any information that you might have made available to the server via Web forms, such as your name, address, telephone number, credit card account information, recreational activities, income, and education. Cookies are commonly used to store registration information for automatic entry to a protected site (see Figure 9.35) or credit card account information to save you from having to enter it each time that you want to place an order at an e-commerce business. For more details, see the Above and Beyond in Chapter 2.

Figure 9.35:
Check the Box, and
Get a Cookie

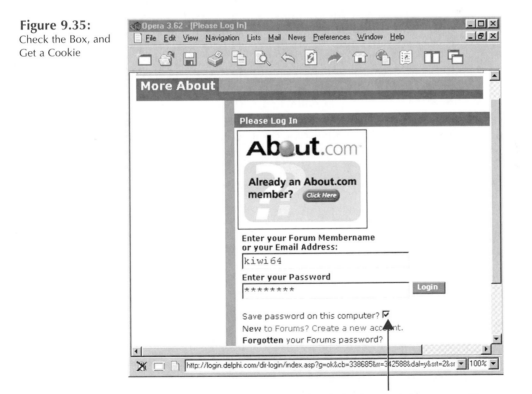

Check this box and the server will
put a cookie on your hard drive.

Cookies are safe in terms of system security. No one can get a virus from a cookie, and cookies are encrypted for security.

Cookies Can Be Useful

Cookies make the following things possible:

- Online shopping carts for e-commerce sites
- Automatic logons to restricted sites (for example, Web-based discussion groups and e-mail accounts)
- Personalized Web portals that show you only the information you care about

If you disable all cookies, you won't be able to use any of these features.

The controversy over cookies arises from concerns about user profiling, consumer consent, and privacy violations. A cookie can be read only by a server from the domain of the Web site responsible for the cookie. However, a cookie created by one Web server at yahoo.com can be read only by other servers at yahoo.com. It would be reassuring to know that personal information stays within the confines of the site that collected it and is not being sold to marketers and third-party vendors.

Privacy policies at many e-commerce sites have begun to address consumer concerns. Responsible e-commerce sites post notice-and-consent check boxes by which visitors can opt out of data resale operations (see the Above and Beyond in Chapter 2). Whereas these policies might protect data collected by in-house Web servers, most commercial data collection is done by ad servers (see Section 9.4). Few consumers understand how ad servers operate, let alone how to track them down in order to opt out of their notice-and-consent option (if the ad service even has one). Ad servers and their privacy policies still worry privacy advocates, especially since the general public is largely unaware of the fact that banner ads can collect data about you even if you never click them.

When you visit a page at yahoo.com, you might view a banner ad from a third-party ad server such as **DoubleClick**. (DoubleClick is the largest supplier of banner ads on the Web.) Banner ads from ad servers are often paired with cookies. If you accept a cookie from an ad server, that same cookie can be accessed and read by the server whenever new material (such as another banner ad) is downloaded from that ad server or any other server in the same domain (see Section 9.4). None of this is explained to the user, and few users take the time to learn about cookies and how ad servers use them.

Proponents of user profiling often argue that no identifying information is associated with the data collected by cookies. That is, the cookie ID numbers that make it possible to collect user profiles don't reveal user names, addresses, or other information. Each time a new piece of information is sent to a server under one ID, it can be added to a collection of all the information ever seen under that same ID, but that profile need not include identifying information, *if* none was ever collected. However, personal identifiers can be captured by Web forms and passed along to a third-party data broker, with or without the use of cookies. You might therefore conclude that you can protect your identity by not telling your browser your name or e-mail address and by checking the privacy policies for any site that requests identifying information. As long as you withhold information from all sites that don't promise to keep that information confidential, you should be safe, right? Unfortunately, the answer is no.

If you read your e-mail with an HTML-enhanced e-mail client, your user profiles have probably already been connected to your e-mail address. If the data brokers have your e-mail address, they probably have your name and physical address as well (have you ever filled out a form for a store that asks for your e-mail address?) Here's how it works.

It begins when you open a piece of mail from a mail spammer. If that message contains a 1-[multi]-1 pixel GIF image located on ad servers, you've just handed your e-mail address over to the ad server. Suppose that the spammer is an outfit named SPAM-O-RAMA and the company that runs the ad server is named TRACKER. Before SPAM-O-RAMA sends out one of its mailings to 30 million e-mail addresses, it sells one pixel of space in its message body to TRACKER. This means that TRACKER can insert a URL to its ad server in the e-mail message. One pixel is all of the space that TRACKER needs because TRACKER will insert an invisible GIF located on its ad server. Each time that SPAM-O-RAMA sends this e-mail message, the URL for TRACKER's GIF can be modified to include the e-mail address of the current recipient, much like URLs can be modified to include keywords from search engine queries (as described in Section 9.4). Then, when the recipient opens this message with an HTML-enabled e-mail client, the GIF file is downloaded and the recipient's e-mail address is sent back to TRACKER's ad server. When the URL request arrives at TRACKER's ad server, the server extracts the address from the URL and launches a script to collect more information from the recipient's Web browser (the recipient's HTML-enabled e-mail client is running a Web browser to read this message). The script asks the browser for any cookies from TRACKER's domain. Any that the browser finds are then sent back to TRACKER, and the cookies' ID numbers are connected to the recently obtained e-mail address. If a user profile is available for an ID number, then the e-mail address can now be added to that profile (see Figure 9.36).

A 1-pixel banner ad is sometimes called a **Web bug**. Web bugs don't threaten your system security, but they are a blatant violation of your privacy. You can foil Web bugs by doing any of the following.

1. Never read anything that looks like spam.
2. Set up ad filters for all of the biggest ad server operations.
3. Set up cookie filters for the biggest ad server operations.

4. Turn off the graphics for your browser (see Section 1.10) when you read your e-mail messages. If that 1-pixel GIF image is never downloaded from the ad server, it cannot send your e-mail address back to the server.

Figure 9.36:
Spammers Rent Out Pixels for Single-Pixel Ad Banners

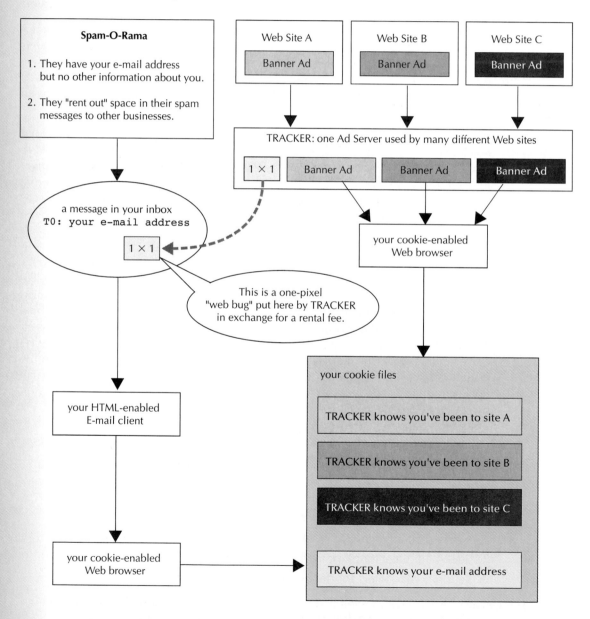

Some cookies are useful, for example if you want to do online-shopping, whereas others are nothing but a threat to your privacy. Unfortunately, Web browsers don't offer users an adequate strategy for managing cookies. If you set your browser preferences to reject all cookies, you won't be able to use shopping carts at e-commerce businesses. If you set your browser to accept all cookies, ad servers will compile a user profile on you. If you tell your browser to ask you what to do with each cookie that is offered to you by a Web server, you'll go crazy with all of the pop-up windows.

Happily, there's a solution to the problem of cookies: a cookie manager. A **cookie manager** is software that enables you to apply a default policy for cookies in general and specifying individual policies for specific Web sites. In this way, your default rejection policy will protect you from the ad servers while your favorite e-commerce sites and members-only discussion groups can be handled differently (see Figure 9.37).

Figure 9.37:
The Cookie Pal
Cookie Manager

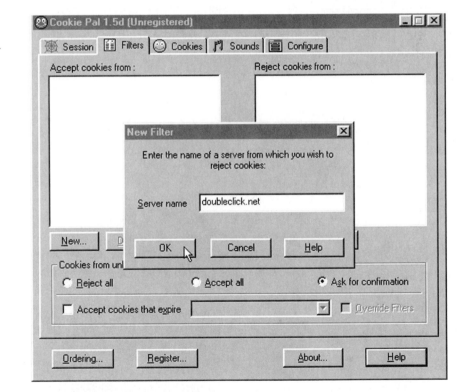

Cookie managers can also show you a world of Web activity that is normally hidden from your view. Most cookie managers will collect a log of their activities for you to review, if you're interested. Figure 9.38 shows a log generated by AdSubtract after a single browsing session. AdSubtract can filter both ads and cookies—this makes seeing the ad servers at work easy. Notice how **DoubleClick** generated a cookie for each ad, and **herring.com** generated more cookies than ads.

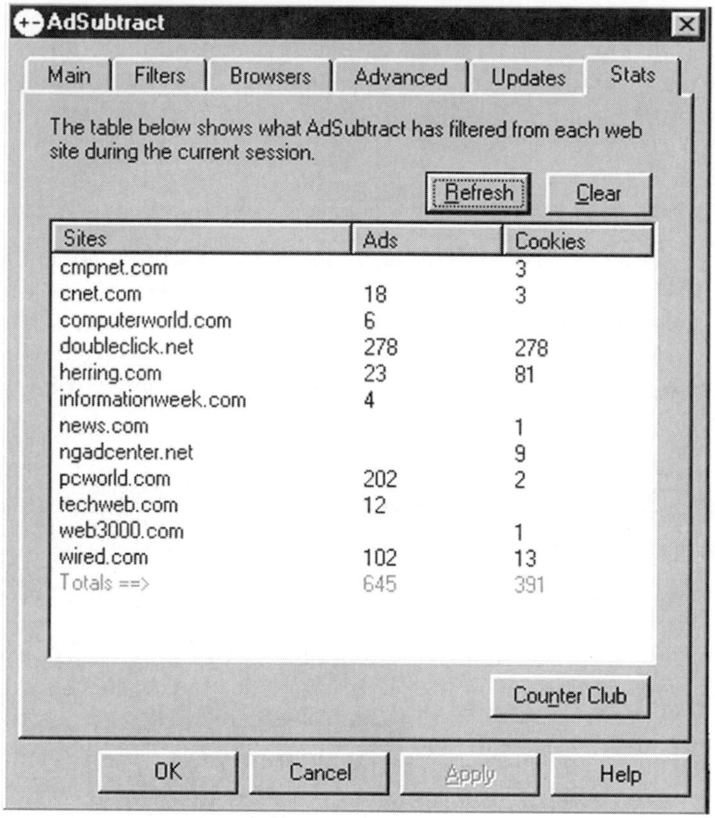

Figure 9.38:
A Look behind the
Scenes at a
Browsing Session

Many cookie managers are available on the Net. The freeware options are some-what more limited than their shareware counterparts, but all give you more control than your Web browser's preference settings. Some cookie managers can block ads as well as cookies so that you can minimize the amount of work needed to set up all of the different filters.

The best cookie managers will not ask you to set a policy for each site that you visit because doing that becomes very tedious if you visit many different Web sites. It's much easier to set up a default policy that will be applied to all sites unless you choose to create a filter for a specific site (see Figure 9.39). This minimizes the amount of work needed to create a customized plan for cookie management. Dealing with cookies might seem like an inconvenience and an annoyance, but using the right software makes the process quite painless. Don't settle for the first cookie manager that you find, as they are not all the same. Research the most pop-ular cookie managers, read their reviews, and test drive one or two before you decide. Once you get your cookies under control, they will never bother you again.

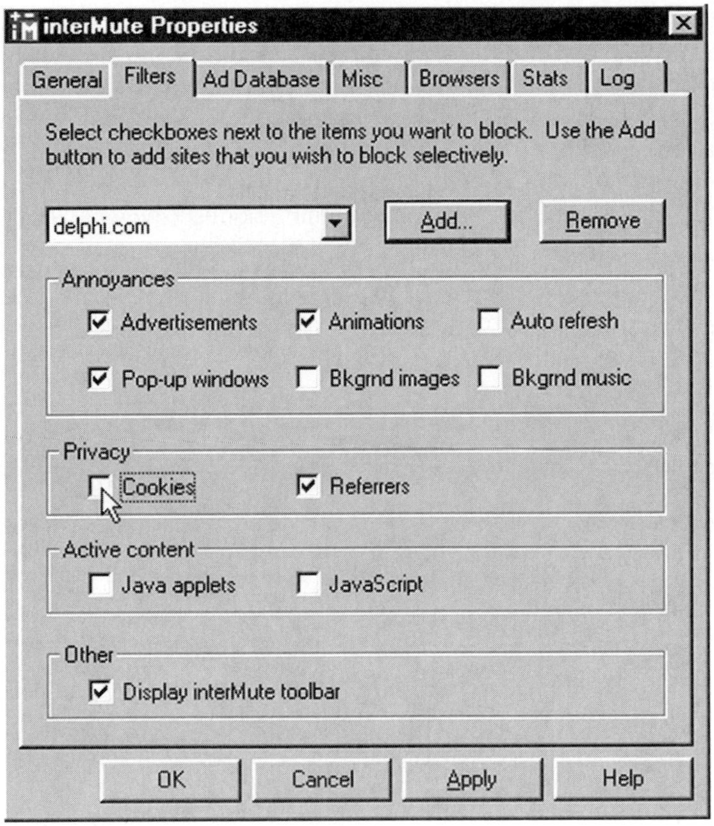

Figure 9.39:
The interMute
Cookie Manager

Some Popular Cookie Managers

Here are some of the popular cookies managers that you can explore.

Software	Type of Software	URL
CookiePal (Windows)	Shareware	http://www.kburra.com/
Cookie Crusher (Windows)	Shareware	http://www.thelimitsoft.com/
AdSubstract SE (Windows)	Freeware	http://adsubtract.com/
MagicCookie Monster (Mac)	Freeware	http://www.angelfire.com/il2/drjsoftware/

Firewalls

A **firewall** is software that monitors all attempts to move bytes over the Internet in either direction and notifies you when such movement is attempted. Firewalls previously were used only by large corporations, but no longer. Anyone with a computer connected to the Internet can set up a firewall to prevent a Trojan horse from sending sensitive files on your hard drive to a remote host (see Chapters 2 and 8) or to stop an E. T. application from "phoning home" (see Chapter 8).

Windows users can try out a freeware firewall called **ZoneAlarm**. When an outgoing transmission is attempted, the user is asked to give permission to the application in question (see Figure 9.40). When an incoming transmission is attempted, the user is alerted (see Figure 9.41).

Figure 9.40:
With ZoneAlarm, Applications Need Your Permission to Access the Net

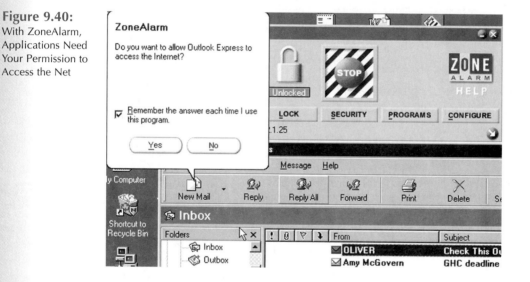

Figure 9.41:
ZoneAlarm Blocks Unauthorized Communications with Your Computer

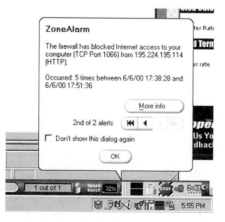

ZoneAlarm keeps track of how you answer its various alerts in order to customize a detailed security policy for your host (see Figure 9.43). You can reset these application-specific settings at any time.

Figure 9.42:
Default Preferences for Two Zones and Three Possible Security Levels

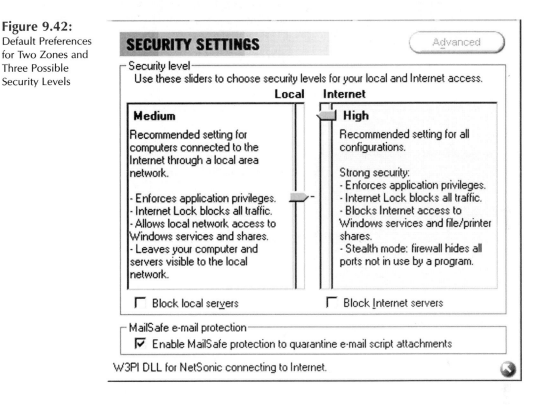

To get you started, ZoneAlarm offers some basic default policies that are easy to put into effect. You can select one of three security levels for your LAN and a different level for the Internet at large (see Figure 9.42). If you aren't sure which defaults to take, ZoneAlarm recommends a medium level of security for the LAN and a high level for the Internet. These default settings will keep you safe while ZoneAlarm collects additional preferences from your responses to ZoneAlarm alert boxes.

The program's control panel includes a dynamic display that shows all uploading and downloading activities (see Figure 9.44). In this way, you always know when data is moving in either direction into and out of your computer and the application that is responsible for the traffic.

In case of an emergency, clicking the Stop button will shut down all Internet activity as soon as possible.

Figure 9.43:
Applications Need
Permission to
Communicate with
Servers on the Net

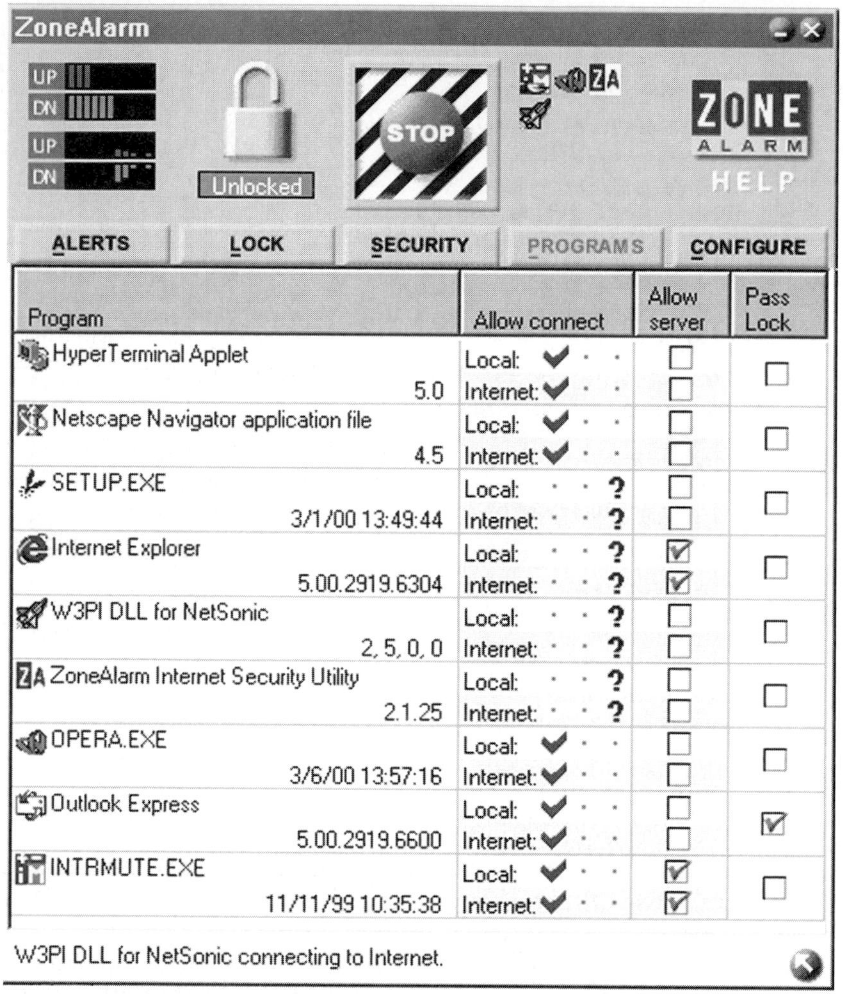

Figure 9.44:
Uploading and
Downloading
Activities are
Visible in the
ZoneAlarm Toolbar

Net Monitors

Anyone who spends a lot of time on the Internet will experience problems at times. For example, your browser might wait indefinitely for pages to download even though your modem appears to be connected. Or, your e-mail client might not be able to connect to your e-mail server even though your dial-up connection is transmitting bits. Two solutions come to mind in these situations. You can either

1. go away, do other things, and come back later to discover whether the problem has gone away by itself, or

2. call your service provider's technical support personnel to ask whether it's aware of any network problems regarding its server. If a network problem is causing your difficulties, it will eventually fix itself (with the help of one or more network administrators).

In some cases, however, the problem is at your end. For example, a local proxy server might not be communicating with your Web browser. No Web pages will download no matter how many different sites you try, and the problem won't fix itself (although restarting your computer might fix it).

If you don't like to call technical support whenever you run into a glitch of some sort, you might want to install a *network monitor* so that you can diagnose some of these problems on your own. Chapter 1 described the ping and traceroute utilities. These are two examples of network monitors and they can give you useful feedback when you're trying to pinpoint a problem. For example, if you attempt a traceroute and can't take even one hop out from your local host, then you know that the problem is on your machine. Either the modem is not transmitting, or the settings for a local proxy require attention.

For more bells and whistles, look for a graphical version of traceroute that can show you, on a world map, how your packets are moving around (this is fun, although it won't give you new information). Also try **NetMedic**, which is prepared to give you more data about your Internet activities than you really need. Although NetMedic promises to both diagnose and solve your Internet problems, there's really little that it can do that you can't do on your own. However, you might enjoy seeing all of the graphs and gauges in action—they're interesting to watch (see Figure 9.45). And if for some reason, you really need to know how many times you've logged on to the Net over the last year, how long you were connected each time, and what percentage of that time was idle, then this is the utility for you.

Telnet Clients

It's no longer possible to stick one's head through the doorway of a computer lab and surmise anything about the workloads of the machines there. A room containing 20 computers might support the activities of 400 remote users. And each of those people might be running their own Internet applications that take them to additional hosts running servers that are, in turn, capable of reaching even more

servers on demand. Users, data files, computers, and computer programs no longer need to be in close proximity to each other. One's sense of distance is quickly forgotten on the Internet. Some of this magic is accomplished with *Telnet*.

One way to share computer resources is to give programmers remote control access, or *remote logon privileges*. The idea of remote logons is as old as the original ARPANET. In 1969, an early version of Telnet was developed. A user running Telnet on one host can log on to a second host and run programs on the second host remotely. Telnet and FTP were thought to be the most important software developments of their time.

In a Telnet session, the local host acts like a computer terminal connected to another computer that happens to be very far away. A Telnet user reestablishes a continuous connection to a remote host and operates software on the remote host. Think of Telnet as a remote control device for distant computers. Many libraries first posted their online card categories on the Internet via Telnet. Interactive gaming sites such as online chess clubs also relied on Telnet connections in combination with graphical user interfaces (GUIs). People accessed these Telnet servers via guest Telnet sessions. A **guest Telnet session** is a session that is open to anyone and that allows users to perform some restricted set of operations on the remote host.

Most libraries and game sites have since moved their online resources from Telnet servers to Web servers. However, Telnet is still used extensively by computer programmers who need to run their own personal computer programs in remote locations. A programmer who connects to a remote host to run the programmer's own software is probably running a full-privilege Telnet session. A **full-privilege Telnet session** is a session that requires a userid and a password but imposes no restrictions on the user once the user is logged on.

Telnet Gateways and Web Browsers

You can initiate a Telnet session with your Web browser by clicking a link whose URL begins with the prefix `telnet://`. A hyperlink to a `telnet://` URL is called a **Telnet gateway**. When your browser sees a link to a Telnet gateway, it has found a Telnet server that is (presumably) available for guest Telnet sessions. It needs a *Telnet helper application* in order to establish a connection with the Telnet server. Your Web browser needs such an application in order to handle these URLs, so your browser must be properly configured in order to link you to a Telnet server.

Sometimes Web browsers and Telnet interfaces don't cooperate very well. If you find yourself experiencing a lot of problems with a Telnet URL, obtain the Telnet address from the HTML source file and try visiting it from inside of a Telnet client instead of a Web browser. Telnet sessions sometimes behave badly when they are nested inside of other applications.

You might still run into a Telnet gateway on the Web, but the future will see increasingly fewer. If you do need the feature, recent versions of Navigator and MSIE are configured to run a default Telnet program. Older versions of these made it easy to specify an option for a preferred Telnet client. However, current versions no longer support a Telnet helper option, although the Opera Web browser still does (see Figure 9.46). Chances are, if you need to use Telnet you'll want to run a full-privilege Telnet session, in which case you'll be launching your Telnet client as a stand-alone application.

Figure 9.46:
Setting Up a Telnet Helper Application for the Opera Web Browser

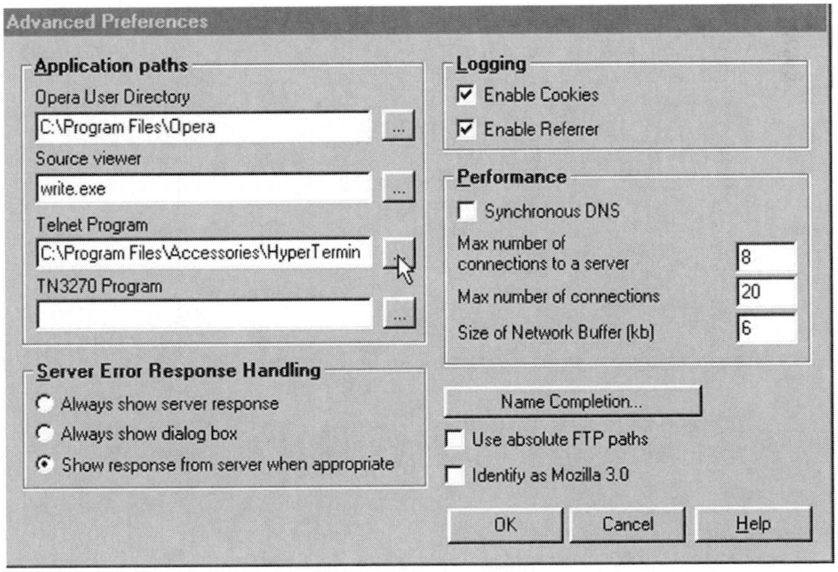

Telnet is a text-based application, so launching Telnet from a graphical Web browser won't add graphics to your Telnet sessions. You will have to deal with either a command mode interface or a menu-driven interface, depending on the site.

To initiate a full-privilege Telnet session, you need

1. a Telnet client,
2. the DNS or IP address of a remote UNIX host on which you have an account, and
3. your userid and password for the remote account.

Telnet couldn't be much simpler. You log on as if you were connecting to a local host, and then you do your work as if you were working on the local host. When you're finished, you log off and disconnect from the remote host (see Figure 9.47). Telnet negotiates multiple hardware platforms and different OSs by itself so that you don't have to. Cross-platform compatibility via Telnet is one of the technical achievements that gives the Internet an illusion of effortless connectivity.

Many people generally use Telnet because they have some space on a Web server. Many Web servers are UNIX hosts, and UNIX has a number of powerful file management, string matching, and text manipulation tools. If you know how to use these tools, you can do a lot of quick Web page edits (for example, a global replace) via

Figure 9.47:
The Circle of Telnet

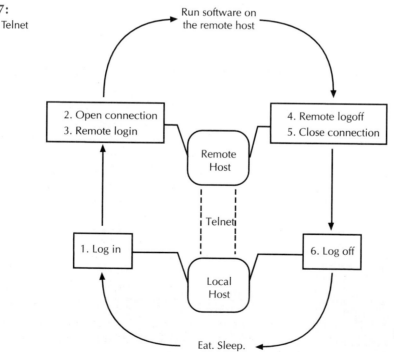

Telnet without having to download the entire site, edit it locally, and move it back up to the Web server. Then again, special Internet applications such as **CuteHTML** will also help you edit your HTML files remotely on a Web server, and with no UNIX required.

Once Is Enough

In case you have, say, six different computer accounts and it occurs to you that you can nest multiple Telnet sessions (as you hop from one host to another and then another, and so on), be warned: Nested Telnet sessions can produce strange behavior. A control character might mean one thing to one Telnet session and something else to a different Telnet session. This can create all sorts of bizarre confusion. The solution is simple: Do not nest Telnet sessions. If you need to visit many different hosts, disconnect from each one before you move to another.

Many people who work on computers at work and at home need remote access when a crucial application runs on one machine but not both. If you ever need to access your home computer from work or your work computer from home, investigate commercial software options such as **pcAnywhere** for Windows or **Timbuctu** for the Mac.

Above and Beyond: Problems and Exercises

A1. Name five kinds of information that a cookie can contain.

A2. If you allow the Web server `foo23.little.com` to place a cookie on your hard drive, will you be able to see what is stored inside of the cookie? Who will be able to retrieve the contents of that cookie?

A3. A major security problem was discovered in May 2000 that affected all users of MSIE working on the Windows platform. Because of a problem with MSIE, cookies could be returned to Web servers outside of the domains that created the cookies. You can read more about the problem at `http://www.peacefire.org/security/iecookies/`. Explain how this security hole could be exploited by someone who wanted to steal a credit card account number. If cookies are always encrypted, why should you be concerned if one falls into the wrong hands?

A4. What is a Web bug? Explain how data collection operations use Web bugs to connect e-mail addresses and otherwise anonymous user profiles. Name three things that you can do to keep your e-mail address safe from Web bugs. Are any of these options 100% effective? Are any of them something that you would be willing to do for the sake of personal privacy? Explain your answers.

A5. Which would be more useful if you wanted to protect yourself from a Trojan horse: ZoneAlarm or NetMedic? Why? Can either protect you from all possible Trojan horses? Explain your answers.

A6. Which two applications described in this section require extensive preference settings for a thoroughly customized installation? Explain how these preferences are acquired, in each case, over a period of time. Which application is relatively passive about new preference settings? Which is relatively aggressive about new preference settings? Explain your answers.

A7. How do a guest Telnet session and a full-privilege Telnet session differ?

A8. [Hands-On] You need to receive commercial e-mail messages in order to do this exercise. Monitor your incoming e-mail messages for one week, looking for Web bugs. Collect as many bugs as you can. While you're watching for bugs, pay attention to how many e-mail messages you're examining. How many messages did you examine? How many Web bugs were you able to find? Were they easy to spot? Which ad servers were the cause of your Web bugs? Can you see what information was being returned to the ad servers? Expand on your answers whenever you can add an explanation or observation.

A9. [Hands-On] Select and install a cookie manager. Live with it for a week, and then answer the following questions. How distracting is it? Do you wish anything about it is done differently? Is this an application that you would like to keep? Explain your answers.

A10. [Hands-On] Install ZoneAlarm, and live with it for a week. How distracting is ZoneAlarm? Did it detect any unexpected intruders during this time? If so, were they something you should be worried about? Explain your answers.

CHAPTER 10

E-Commerce

CHAPTER GOALS

- Understand what you can do as a consumer to protect yourself when you make purchases online.

- Find out how to ensure that sensitive data is encrypted before you send it over the Net.

- Learn how to check a digital certificate for an e-commerce business.

- Find out how to check a secure Web server to see how strong its encryption is.

- Understand what it means for commercial sites to be self-regulating.

- Learn about different kinds of online auctions.

10.1 TAKING CHARGE

When retail operations went high-tech, there was little for the consumer to do but sit back, watch the big guys duke it out. Amazon.com started in 1995, and there's been no looking back. At first, online shopping sounded like dreams come true for retailers: no rent, no sales staff, no storefront maintenance, and minimal inventory. Just set up some software and go. But then they discovered the first rule of online retail: If someone undercuts your prices, you're dead. Amazon started by offering 30% off the listed price of best-selling books. Then Barnes & Noble went online in 1997 and offered 40% off its bestsellers' list. Wal-Mart created its online output with a 45% discount off its bestsellers, and then Buy.com joined the circus with 50% discounts. The shopping bots are in the consumer's corner, and big e-commerce operations (e-stores, for short) must stay on top of the online marketing game in order to stay in business. Profit margins are low; most online operations don't turn a profit. Brick-and-mortar stores that go online often see their traditional profits eaten up by their new online storefronts.

Even so, few retailers are willing to sit on the sidelines without some sort of "Web presence." Over 100,000 e-commerce businesses were operating at the end of 1999, and online sales have soared (see Figure 10.1). If you have a computer, a credit card, and Internet access, you'll find that shopping is a whole new ball game. Even if a sale is not consummated on the Web, the Web has changed the world of sales in brick-and-mortar stores.

Figure 10.1:
The Growth of
Online Sales

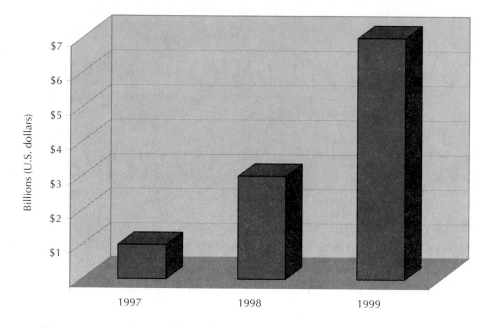

10.1.1   Buying Cars

Consider the act of buying a car. This is no longer a matter of who blinks first on the sales floor. It has been replaced by an exercise in Web research. A prepared buyer can go into a dealership today armed with crucial knowledge that used to be the dealership's secret weapon. For example, the buyer can know what the dealership paid for the car and with how much profit margin the dealership has to work. Further, it takes only a minute or so to know what the competition has to offer on the exact same model and whether it makes sense to shop a little further afield in order to get a better deal.

10.1.2   Buying Books

Suppose that you want to buy a book and you want it right now. You can visit your local bookstore and pay a little more for the privilege of taking it home today. However, what if the local retail store is out of that book? What do you do? Wait one week or more for them to place a special order for the book and call you when it arrives? Or visit Amazon.com and get the book in two days—and probably for a lower price? Knowing that you have other options, you might forgo a visit to the local store altogether and just give them a call to find out about the book in question. If the book you want is out of stock, the store not only loses a sale. It also loses the opportunity to tempt you with their aisles of specials and impulse buys. Browsing online is not the same thing as browsing in a retail bookstore. However, if the retail bookstore can't get you in the door, the everything else is moot.

10.1.3 Buying Unusual Items

Sometimes, you must cope with an unusual one-time purchase. For example, suppose that you have a teenager who wants an air hockey table for Christmas—it's one of those non-negotiable teenager fixations. You've likely never seen an air hockey table outside of a recreational center, and you've certainly never seen one in a store. You have no idea what they cost, what's wrong with the lower-priced models, or how hard it's going to be to find one in stock in a local store. You know that shipping costs will probably prohibit an online sale (air hockey tables are big and heavy). However, that shouldn't stop you from doing a little online research on the Web, where you can learn all that you need to know about the leading manufacturers, their product lines, and their relative merits. With a little surfing, you can learn that air hockey tables typically are sold by stores that sell pool tables and that it's easier to find local retail stores that sell them if you conduct a search for "pool tables" instead of "air hockey." If you're very lucky, you might even find a deal on a used air hockey table at eBay, a well-known auction site. In any case, you can research the situation in one day, possibly over your lunch hour, before you even make your first telephone call.

10.1.4 Shopping for Supplies

Then there are the routine shopping trips for items that you need regularly. Everyone purchases certain items periodically: office supplies, camera film, disposable contact lenses, pet food, vitamins (especially that hard-to-find kind for the iguana). You can probably buy most of these items locally. However, consider the advantages of using an online supplier.

1. You can comparison shop to find the best prices and discounts (be careful to take shipping costs into consideration).

2. You can use sites that let you maintain a personal account. With a personal account, you can maintain a list of the items that you need periodically so that you don't need to track them down at the site each time that you place an order.

3. After your first order, all of the information for your account will have been collected, so you can probably choose **one-click shopping**, which allows you to order items without going through a registration page and without having to re-enter credit card account information that you entered previously on the same site (thereby by-passing all possible hurdles between you and a fast impulse buy).When all goes well (no overloaded servers or Net congestion), you can place a standing order at an e-store in about two or three minutes over a slow

modem and in less than a minute over a broadband connection. You might have to wait two to seven days for the selected items to reach you, but that's not likely to be a problem with recurring purchases because most people stock up on items that need to be purchased frequently and with a little planning, you can place an order a week before you actually need your order.

Whereas e-commerce might be no piece of cake for the e-stores, it's hard to imagine a better world for consumers. Brick-and-mortar stores are still an option and will continue to be available for traditional shopping trips—the shopping mall will not disappear any time soon. However, the Web offers additional options and information to make consumers better educated, more aware of their choices, and better prepared to spend wisely. Marketing experts are studying the buying patterns of consumers online to understand what it takes for a business to succeed online. The data is relatively easy to collect, since every consumer leaves a digital trail (see Figure 10.2).

Online shopping can be wonderful. However, it has some risks. If you understand how things can go wrong, you'll find it easier to protect yourself. All consumers need to learn a few basics for safe shopping online.

Figure 10.2:
E-Commerce Data Collection Is a Business All Its Own

Nielsen//NetRatings

Top 10 Web Advertisers
Week end of July 02, 2000, U.S.

Home ▾ | GO!

BACK TO HOT OFF THE NET

Advertiser	Impression	Reach %
1. TRUSTe	492,819,854	24.51
2. AllAdvantage	220,339,137	4.19
3. Microsoft	213,392,549	34.85
4. Yahoo!	176,266,973	26.13
5. Amazon	123,778,425	31.44
6. Next Card	117,289,641	24.06
7. Casino On Net	92,563,352	11.76
8. eBay	87,667,248	14.99
9. America Online	85,884,218	24.65
10. Barnes and Noble	77,026,896	21.24

10.2 ONLINE SHOPPING RISKS AND SAFEGUARDS

This section picks up where Section 2.6 left off, delving deeper into the risks and safeguards regarding online shopping. Please take a minute to review Section 2.6 before reading this section. The technology that protects sensitive information on the Internet is discussed in Section 10.3 and Chapter 11. This section concentrates on practical advice.

Here's a list of safeguards to keep in mind.

- Shop with merchants whom you know and trust.
- Look for and read each site's delivery, return, and privacy policies.
- Never enter, and relay, sensitive information on a page that does not have both a URL that begins with `https://` and either a locked padlock or an unbroken key icon.
- Make all online purchases with a credit card and not a debit card.
- Be careful not to hit the ORDER NOW button more than once.
- Never send credit card account information via e-mail.
- Keep a record of your transactions, and save all online receipts until your shipment arrives and checks out as complete and ok.
- Use a shopping bot to comparison shop for big-ticket items.

If you follow these safeguards habitually, you'll probably never have a bad e-store encounter as far as the electronic end of things is concerned. Do take the time to read the policy statements for each e-store with which you're considering doing business. They are not all the same; after you've seen a few, you'll get a feel for what's typical. Figure 10.3 shows a policy page from **Priceless-Inkjet.com** that goes into more detail than most do. For example, this e-store says that they delete all credit card account information after it is no longer needed, since on-site security breeches are the most common cause of credit card data theft online. This is good news for consumers concerned about security and indicates that this site cares about its customers.

Unfortunately, many things can go wrong even when people do their jobs well and all of the support technology is working correctly. The e-store might ship the wrong item, and you'll have to exchange it. You might order the wrong item and want to return it. You might get what you ordered, but it might be defective or otherwise unacceptable. This is when you'll be glad that you read the return policy *before* you placed your order. As with any business, serious customer service begins when something goes wrong. So, listen to friends who've had experience with e-stores. You might want to avoid any site that has a tale of woe associated with it.

Figure 10.3:
A Reassuring
Security Policy

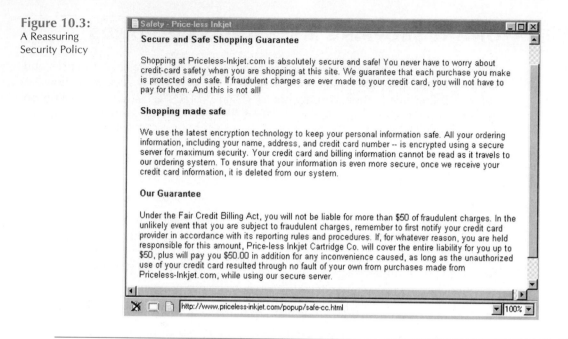

Rating the E-Stores—and Everything Else

If you're considering buying from an e-store that you don't know, first check out what other shoppers have to say about their experiences. Here are some sites that rate e-stores for you.

BizRate.com	`http://bizrate.com/`
PC Data Online	`http://www.pcdataonline.com/`
Gomez.com	`http://gomez.com/`
Media Metrix	`http://www.relevantknowledge.com/`

You can also find sites at which consumers sound off about the products that they've bought (online and off). For example, Amazon.com displays book reviews by readers, and CNet.com collects user reviews for computer software and hardware. Check out **Epinions.com** for a massive collection of consumer reviews on everything that's ever been bought or sold.

Consumer product reviews can be instructive and might alert you to potential concerns that you'll want to consider when researching your options. People love to talk about their experiences with beloved (or cursed) consumer products on the Internet—it seems that everyone wants to be a reviewer for something in their lives.

Some sites give you on-site updates regarding your order (see Figure 10.4). If an e-store ships its orders via UPS, you can track your shipment by using the **UPS Package Tracker.**

Figure 10.4:
Your Dog Food's In
the Mail

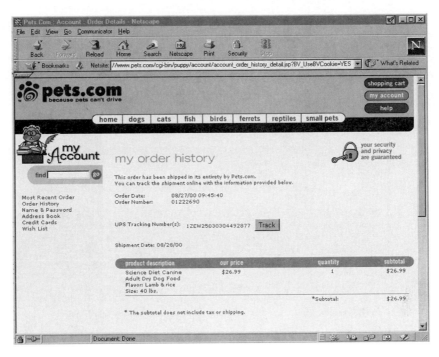

UPS's order tracking is especially nice if you must wait a week or more for something (see Figure 10.5). At the very least, your e-store should confirm your order via e-mail within 24 hours of receipt. It should also send you a note to let you know when your item has left its warehouse.

If you want to take online security one step further, you can check certain additional information about your e-store before you place an order. A Web server that is set up to protect sensitive data that is being sent over the Internet is assigned a digital certificate. A digital certificate makes it possible to send sensitive information out onto the Internet safe from prying eyes. Your browser watches for a digital certificate whenever a Web server asks for a secure connection. It needs the digital certificate in order to encrypt your personal data. Unencrypted data sent over the Internet is called **in the clear**. This is like sending a message on the back of a postcard—anyone along the way can read it. Sensitive information should always be *encrypted* before it goes out over the Net. Encrypted data is safer on the Internet than is unencrypted data. If a server has a digital certificate, then your data headed for that server can be encrypted for safe passage. If no certificate is available, then the data cannot be encrypted. Encryption on the Internet is discussed in detail in Chapter 11.

Your Web browser is prepared to accept a digital certificate that is issued by a recognized *certification authority* (CA). A **certificate authority** is an organization that

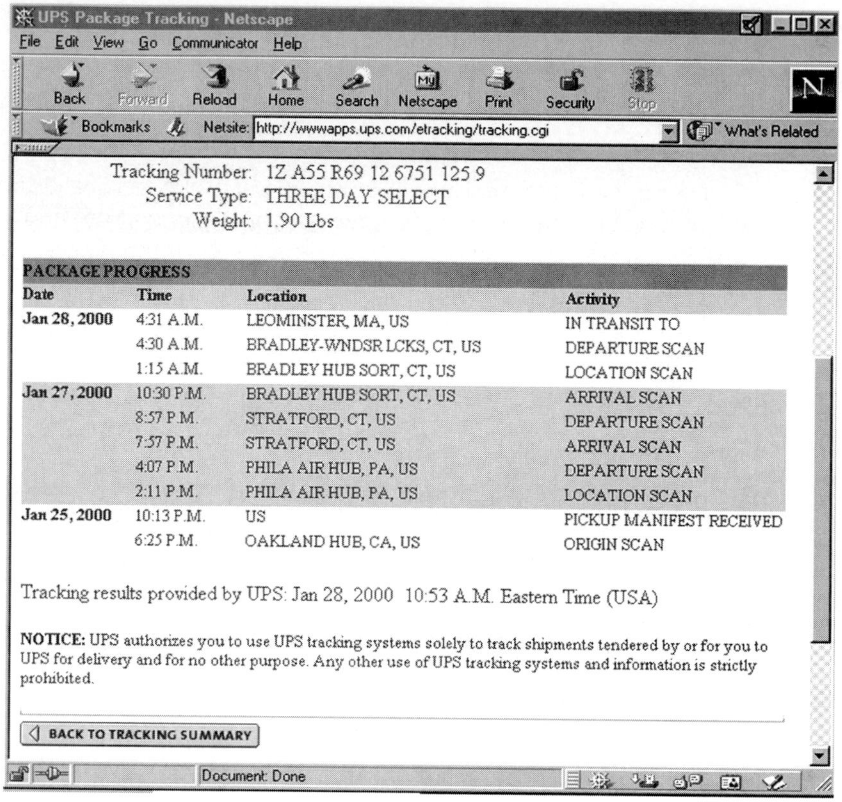

Figure 10.5:
The UPS Online
Tracking Service
Keeps You Informed
while You Wait

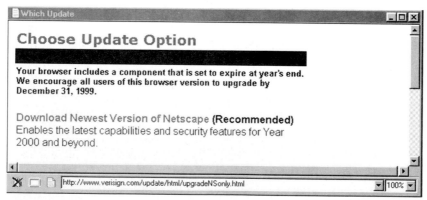

can certify the identity of a certificate holder, much as a notary public vouches for the legitimacy of a notarized signature. From time to time, your browser might need to update its database of recognized CAs. Figure 10.6 shows how Navigator users were instructed to upgrade their old browser at the end of 1999 in order to maintain maximally secure communications. The key component in this upgrade was an updated database of CA information.

Figure 10.6:
Navigator Users
Needed to Update
Their CA Databases
Before 1/1/2000

With the browser's doing certificate checking, what remains for the user to worry about? Only one thing: Users should check to ensure that they are actually interacting with the site that they think they are. The site named on the digital certificate should match the URL that the browser is reading. A certificate that does not match the site named is suspicious.

MSIE and Navigator will show you everything that you need to know to check an e-store's digital certificate. Click the *closed padlock* at the bottom of your browser window. If you're running MSIE, you'll next see a window (see Figure 10.7) that displays the following:

- The CA that issued the certificate for the site that you're viewing: Thawte Server CA
- The name of the site that owns the certificate: priceless-inkjet.com
- The time period for which the certificate is valid (from 3/17/00 to 3/31/01)

If you're considering sending your credit card account information to this e-store, ensure that the domain for the current URL matches the domain listed for the certificate's owner, priceless-inkjet.com. If they match, then everything is in order.

Figure 10.7:
A Digital Certificate
(viewed in MSIE)

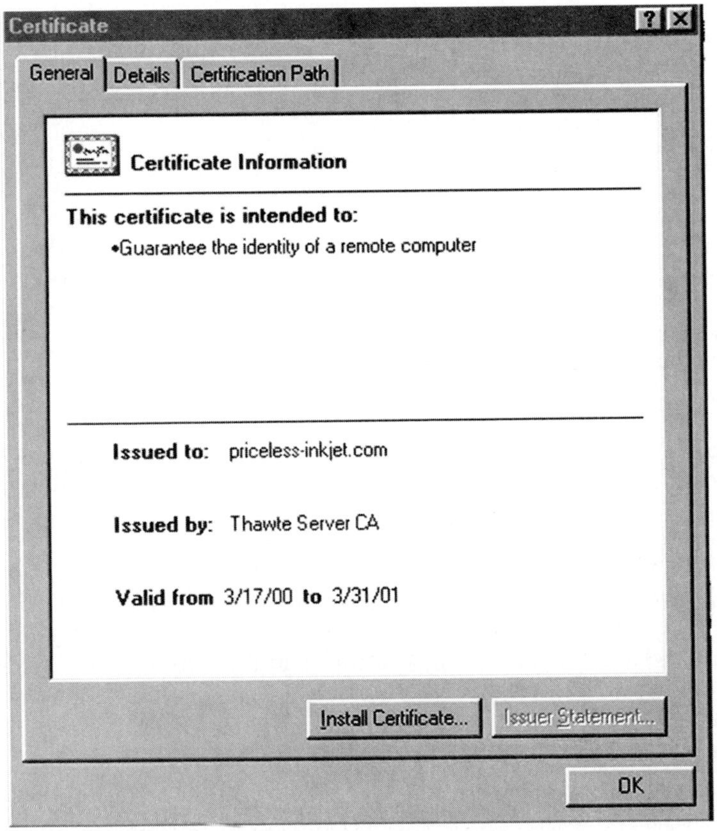

In Navigator, you click the closed padlock to reveal Navigator's security window. Click View Certificate, and a display like that in Figure 10.8 appears. Navigator's view shows more information than MSIE's (in Figure 10.7). However, the MSIE display offers additional tabs that you can click if you want more information.

Figure 10.8:
A Digital Certificate (viewed in Navigator)

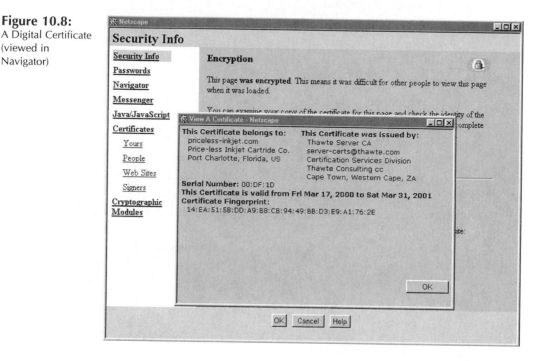

If you do a lot of online shopping, you might encounter a problem with a site's digital signature. Even if you aren't checking the certificates on your own (we'll show you how shortly), you can configure your browser to detect discrepancies and warn you about possible problems before you transmit any sensitive data (see Figure 10.9).

Click More Info to see the actual certificate being used by reno.onsale.com (see Figure 10.10). The dates are fine, and the CA looks fine. However, notice that the domain names don't match. The server was named reno.onsale.com, but the certificate it presented was issued to a host named reno.egghead.com.

In general, avoid a site that doesn't have its certificate in order. A problem with a digital certificate might be the result of an administrative error (similar in severity to someone forgetting to send off a bill payment on time), but a solid e-store operation should be attending to details like this with the utmost care. In this example, a little online research was able to shed some light on the situation. According to an Egghead press release, Egghead and OnSale merged November 3, 1999, and integrated their online sales operations. The original Egghead server was probably named reno.egghead.com (the one listed on the certificate). After the merger, the

Figure 10.9:
Navigator Is
Concerned about
This Site's Digital
Certificate

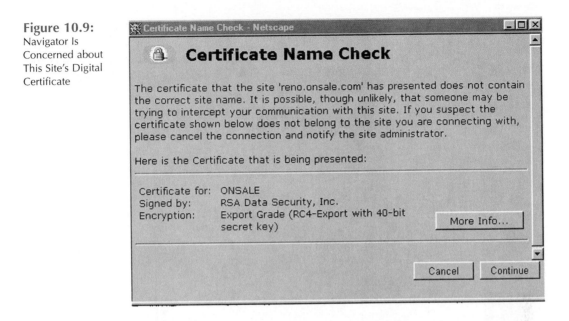

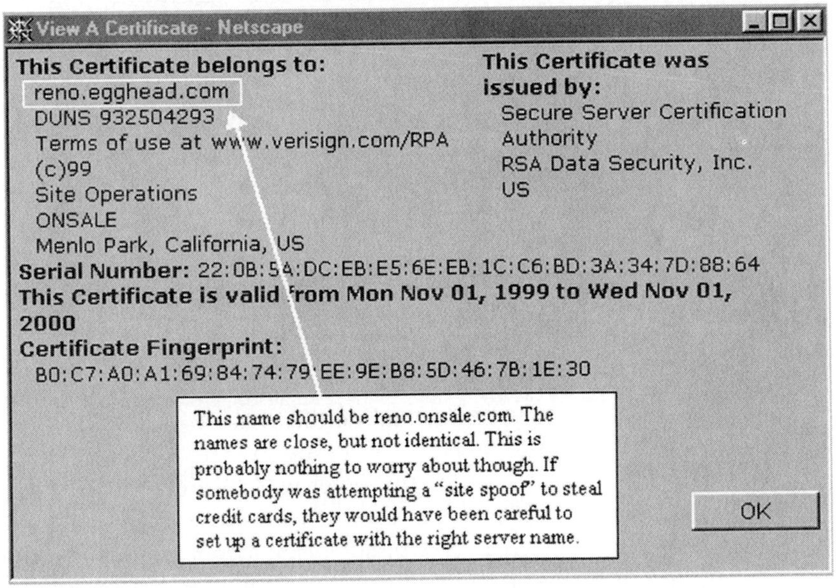

Figure 10.10:
reno.onsale.com Is
Using a Certificate
Issued to
reno.egghead.com

e-store either renamed its server or started using a new server named reno.onsale.com. Note that this certificate was created November 1, 1999, very near the time of the merger. The host name mix up probably happened when Egghead and OnSale merged their online operations and forgot to think about their changing server names when they set up this certificate.

In other cases, it may be very difficult to know what's going on with an irregular certificate. For example, Figure 10.11 shows an unusual comment about a certificate for us.buy.com. The host names check out and the dates are current, However, the comment, "This certificate has failed to verify for all of its intended purposes," is puzzling.

Figure 10.11:
MSIE Is Not Happy
with This Certificate

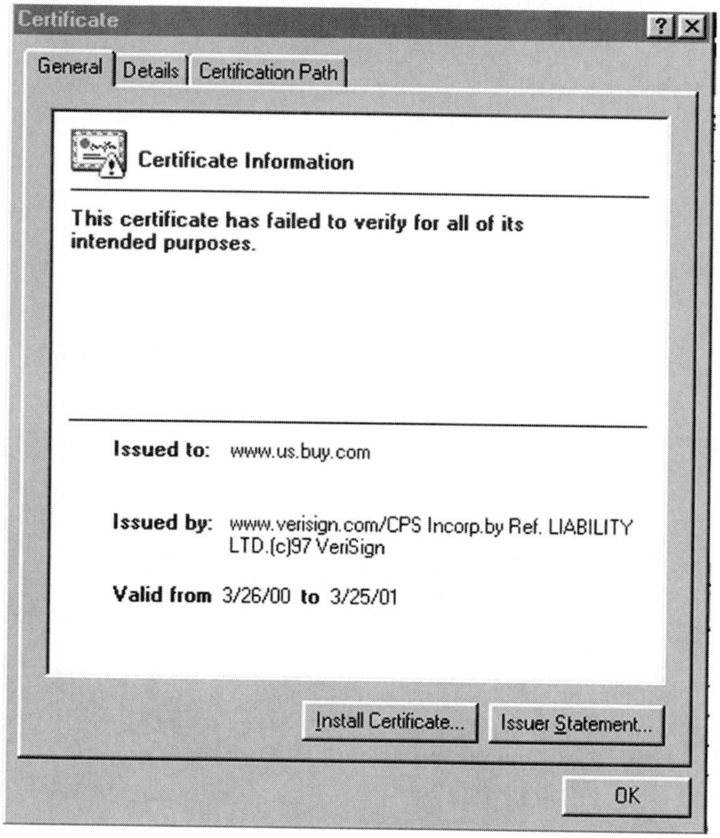

If you click the Certification Path tab, you are told, "This certificate is OK" (see Figure 10.12). So what should you do?

In a situation like this, you might want to get a second opinion. If you used Navigator to ask for security information at the same Web page at us.buy.com, you would see no warnings about the certificate. Netscape Navigator says the certificate checks out. In this case, buyers will have to decide for themselves how safe they feel about completing the sale. If you lose sleep over uncertain situations, then you should either take your business to another e-store or contact us.buy.com via telephone and ask for their certificate's fingerprint (see "Asking for Fingerprints").

Figure 10.12:
MSIE Gives Some
Mixed Signals

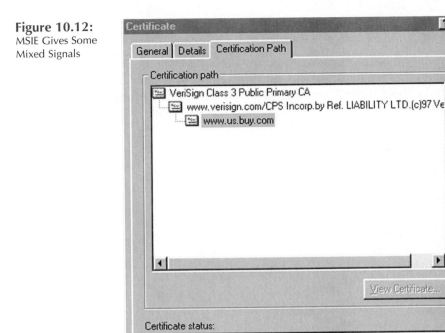

Asking for Fingerprints

If you contact technical support with a question about a digital certificate, ask them to tell you the *fingerprint* for the certificate. A **fingerprint** is a sequence of numbers and letters that uniquely identifies each digital certificate. To find the fingerprint for a digital certificate that your browser has received, examine the browser's certificate display (in MSIE, look under the Details tab). If someone at the site gives you a fingerprint that is identical to the fingerprint for the certificate that your browser is viewing, you can be assured that the certificate is legitimate.

Chapter 11 explains CAs, certificates, and fingerprints in greater detail. For now, remember the following.

- Each e-store should send a digital certificate to your browser.
- You can view these certificates with your browser.
- Before sending your credit card account number to a site, check the site's current digital certificate.

- The name of the certificate owner should match the domain name of the current URL.

Your browser will also be looking for problems with digital certificates, so a transaction that doesn't prompt a browser alert is probably safe. However, if your browser warns you about a certificate and asks you what to do, consider aborting the transaction. If you have any doubts, it may be best to be cautious.

10.3   SECURE SERVERS AND SECURE WEB PAGES

In 1995, Netscape introduced the Secure Sockets Layer (SSL) protocol for transmitting private documents securely via the Internet. SSL has been instrumental in the growth of e-commerce on the Web and is now an industry standard. The installation of SSL on an e-commerce site eliminates a number of potential security problems, as follows.

- Site spoofing

  Site spoofing is the deceptive art of setting up a counterfeit Web site that looks identical to some other legitimate Web site. Anyone with a basic knowledge of Web page design can spoof a site. Even the site's URL can be engineered to look familiar, if only at a glance. A wary user, however, might notice what appears to be (but isn't) a typographical error in the URL. If unwary consumers can be routed to the counterfeit Web site, many credit card account numbers could conceivably be collected before anyone is likely to recognize and report a problem.

- Unauthorized disclosure

  Unauthorized disclosure is the practice of sending data from a browser to a Web server in the clear (that is, unencrypted), thereby enabling hackers to intercept the transmission and obtain sensitive information.

- Unauthorized action

  Unauthorized action is an intrusion associated with unauthorized access to and modification of the pages on a Web server in subtle and destructive, or obvious and embarrassing ways.

- Data alteration

  Data alteration is the interception of data sent from a browser to a Web server in the clear and alteration of that data en route, either maliciously or accidentally.

All modern Web browsers support SSL, so users don't have to use Navigator in order to benefit from the protocol. A Web page URL that begins with the prefix `https://` (note the addition of an "s" before the colon) indicates that the Web server is prepared to offer a secure connection to your browser. Recall that if your browser is SSL-enabled, a closed padlock in the browser's window notifies you that you have a secure connection. An open padlock indicates that the connection is not secure. You might also see an alert box like that shown in Figure 10.13.

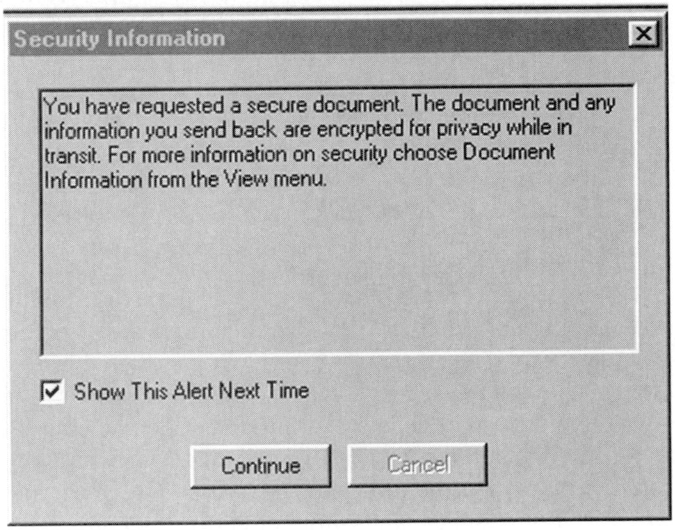

Figure 10.13:
You Might or Might Not See This Notice When You Enter a Secure Site

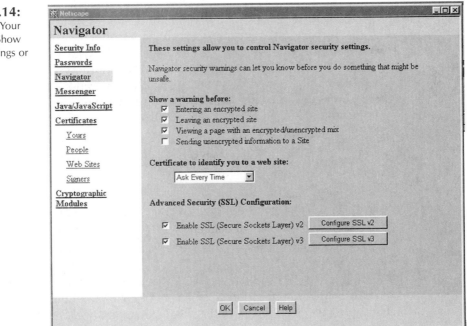

However, the alert box occurs only if your browser is configured to display one each time that you access a secure Web site (see Figure 10.14).

Figure 10.14:
Configuring Your Browser to Show Many Warnings or None

A secure SSL connection guarantees the following operations.

- Authentication

  Users can verify the actual owner of the Web site by checking the site digital certificate (as described in Section 10.3).

- Message privacy

  SSL encrypts all information moving between a Web server and a browser by using *public key encryption* and *unique session keys* (the details of how this works will be covered at length in Chapter 11).

- Message integrity

  When a message is sent, the sending computer generates a signature code based on the message content and sends that code along with the message. The receiving computer generates its own signature code for the file content just received. If the message was not altered in route, then these two signature codes will agree. If even a single character in the message was altered en route, the receiving computer will generate a different code and sound an alert—the software responsible for decrypting the message will issue a warning about the legitimacy of the document. When the two codes agree, the result is *message integrity* and both parties can be confident that they are working with unaltered messages.

The mechanisms underlying message privacy and message integrity are explained in more detail in Chapter 11. For now, you need to understand only that SSL is the right protocol for moving sensitive information via the Internet (see Figure 10.15).

The SSL protocol for secure Web-based communications can be used in combination with different *encryption algorithms*. An **algorithm** is a set of instructions spelled out in sufficient detail so that a programmer can write a working computer program based on those instructions. As you will see in Chapter 11, some encryption algorithms are harder to break than others. If you're curious about the strength of the encryption algorithms that a specific e-store uses, you can always check the digital certificate to find out how strong their encryption is. Encryption strength is measured by bit counts. More specifically, these bit counts refer to the *length* of something called a *session key* (see the Above and Beyond section in Chapter 11). Here is a guide to the relative levels of encryption strength:

- 128-bit encryption

  This is the strongest level of encryption found in commercial sites. Normally used by banks, insurance companies, and health delivery services. No one in the world can break this level of encryption. This is also called *strong encryption*.

- 64-bit encryption

  It's not the best, but it's strong enough for e-commerce. Only the U.S. National Security Agency (NSA) can break this level of encryption (the NSA doesn't disclose their code-cracking capabilities, but cryptography experts believe that the

Figure 10.15:
A Web Browser and
a Web Server
Establish a Secure
Channel via SSL

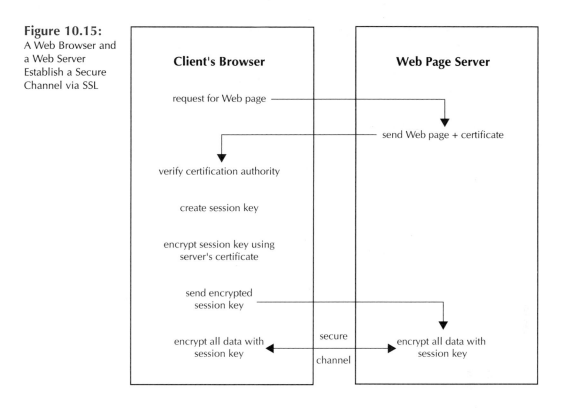

NSA must have this capability). This level was approved for general use in the United States in January 2000. If it's not the industry standard by the time that you read this, it will be soon. Meanwhile, give the browsers and servers until 2001 or so to upgrade. 64-bit encryption is also called *medium-level encryption*.

- 56-bit encryption

  Still reason to feel safe—but not for long. In a few more years, this level of encryption will be too weak to be of any use on the Internet. A hacker can crack a 56-bit key today, but only with the help of a very expensive, special-purpose code-breaking computer. During the late 90's, U.S. restrictions pertaining to the commercial use of encryption prohibited vendors from using 56-bit encryption without special permission. You might see this level of encryption at a few of the larger e-commerce sites who have not yet made the switch to 64-bit encryption. Like 65-bit encryption, 56-bit encryption is also called medium-level encryption (but leaning toward weak encryption).

- 40-bit encryption

  This is the weakest encryption level seen in commercial use. At one time, 40-bit encryption was safe and the industry standard. However, that's no longer the case. Before January 2000, most U.S. CAs were not allowed by law to distribute certificates that contained encryption stronger than 40-bits. As a result, thousands of U.S. e-commerce sites are still stuck with their old 40-bit certificates until they can upgrade their certificates. We'll be seeing increasingly less 40-bit encryption on the Web. This is also called export-level encryption or weak encryption.

Discovering How Strong the Encryption Is

To discover, using MSIE, how strongly encrypted a site is, hold your mouse over the locked padlock for a second. A pop-up window will appear, displaying the bit length, for example 40 bits or 128 bits. In Navigator, click the locked padlock to open the security page. Then click Open Page Info and look in the bottom frame for the encryption type (see Figure 10.16.)

Figure 10.16:
Viewing Encryption Details by Using Navigator

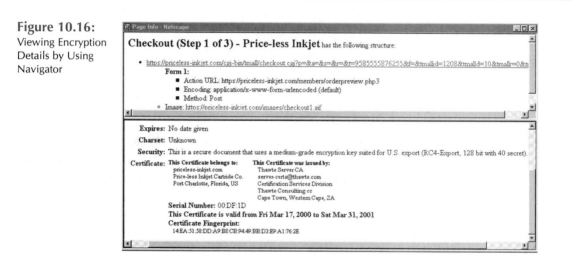

Now that you've read more than you ever wanted to know about credit card account number security on the Web, you need to gain some perspective. While it's interesting to see which sites use 40-bit encryption and which use 128-bit encryption, the essential thing is to ensure that your sensitive data is being encrypted. As long as an SSL connection is in place (check for the closed padlock and the `https://` address), even 40-bit encryption should be fine. (Someday, you might hear about a cyberthief who stole many credit cards account numbers by cracking a 40-bit encryption algorithm. After that happens, it will be time to reject any e-stores still using 40-bit encryption.)

A Little Knowledge Is a Dangerous Thing

Before you read this chapter, you might have felt safe about using your credit card on the Web, but now the idea is making you nervous. This makes sense—ignorance is bliss. However, you really needn't worry. Sending your credit card account number over an SSL connection is safer than sending it over a telephone line to a mail-order catalog, giving it to a waitress in a restaurant, or giving it to a clerk in an upscale retail store. The chances of its being stolen in those more traditional scenarios is much greater than during an SSL transfer. This is true even if an SSL transfer uses weak encryption. Some encryption is always better than no encryption.

If you want to feel nervous about something, do so about all of the *nondigital* transfers of your credit card account information. It makes no sense to worry about giving out your credit card account information over the Net if you aren't at least a little worried about doing so everywhere else.

You should verify a site's certificate before you send it sensitive data. Counterfeit Web sites (the site-spoofing scam) can purchase server certificates from reputable CAs, so the mere existence of a CA does not guarantee security. However, a site-spoofer probably won't bother to falsify the information on a site certificate, since so few people know to check them. Now, you do know to do this.

Some sites offer one-click shopping in an effort to make transactions proceed as fast as possible for you. In a one-click interaction, you have agreed to allow the site's server to store your credit card account number and expiration date, as well as billing and shipping information, in a cookie on your computer. Then, when you want to place a new order, you can log on to the site by using a userid and password; you don't have to enter any additional information. This is convenient and secure, as long as your password for the site is not compromised. If you can't remember the password, use a password manager to remember and encrypt all of your passwords for you (see Sections 2.3 and 9.6).

Be careful if you use MSIE in connection with a one-click shopping site. MSIE might offer, in a pop-up window, to remember your logon password to a particular site (see Figure 10.17). If you click the Yes button, then that password will be automatically entered for you the next time that you visit that particular site. As long as your computer is secure and no one else can ever visit that site on your computer without your knowledge, this is fine.

However, consider what could happen if your computer were stolen (a plausible scenario particularly for a laptop). Anyone using your computer could stumble on

Figure 10.17:
Be Careful How
You Answer This

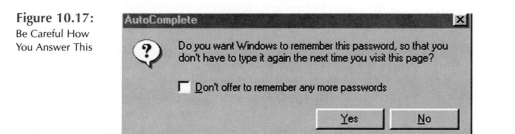

the sites for which you've set up automatic password entries and one-click shopping: with a little luck, all they have to do is visit your browser's history list. If you told your computer to remember your ISP password, a thief could be charging items to your online accounts in less than a minute. Once someone gets past the password protection for an e-store, they could change your shipping address, buy all sorts of things, and charge it all to you. How hard would it be to find those convenient one-click Web sites? Not hard at all if your system were being monitored by a *Trojan horse* (see Section 2.4) prior to the theft. Alternatively, a hacker could examine your cookies to find out which sites put them on your computer. If you use one-click shopping, you must vigilantly protect the passwords that protect your information. If you have some bad luck, those passwords could be all that stand between you and credit card fraud.

10.4 COMMERCIAL SITES AND SELF-REGULATION

The world of e-commerce is advancing at a breakneck pace. Dot-com start-ups are springing up like dandelions, and Wall Street investors are in love with them all. Although security, privacy, and taxation prompt many difficult questions, the U.S. government has been very reluctant to intervene in the evolution of e-commerce. The No-Electronic Theft Act was passed in 1997, and the Digital Millennium Copyright Act went into effect in 1998. The Children's Online Privacy Protection Act and the Electronic Signatures in Global and National Commerce Act went into effect in 2000. These are the major laws that Congress has passed to shape the behavior of U.S citizens and institutions online, although it has debated many more.

Why is the federal government so cautious about passing laws to regulate online businesses and business practice? What is the rationale for this hands-off attitude toward the Internet? The answer seems to be based on a commitment by federal legislators to the concept "less is more." Many politicians believe that U.S. citizens want less interference from big government and more freedom to let businesses regulate themselves. They think that businesses know better than anyone what the American consumer wants and the businesses will not engage in business practices that are offensive or otherwise unwanted by the general population. It is, after all, in the best interests of businesses to give consumers what they want. Government has no business regulating American businesses. But is this right? Can businesses be trusted to regulate their own behavior on behalf of consumers? Is what's best for business compatible with what's best for consumers?

The FTC (Federal Trade Commission) acknowledged in 1997 the concerns about the adequacy of self-regulation on the Internet. In that year, the FTC held a hearing to explore the problem of privacy on the Internet and to determine whether government regulation was needed. There were arguments both pro and con. At the close of the hearings, FTC Chairman Robert Pitofsky commented:

> There has been some talk, especially in the last hour or so, about whether voluntary guidelines ever work . . .. Believe it or not, there are some people who think government regulation doesn't work all that well either. And in an era in which all of government must do more with less, you cannot afford to ignore the possibility that cooperation and collaboration will lead to the appropriate result.

People who view government regulations as intrusive prefer to see industry adopt self-regulating standards. Indeed, the desire to avoid federal privacy regulation was so great that Microsoft Corp. and Netscape Communications Corp., bitter rivals in the Internet market, pledged to work together on voluntary industry standards.

Advocates for self-regulation point to some notable instances in which industry has demonstrated that it can be responsive to public opinion. For example, in 1990 Lotus Development Corp. teamed with the consumer credit bureau Equifax to produce a database, called the Marketplace, of 120 million consumer profiles consisting of names, marital status, estimated income, and purchasing habits. Lotus planned to market the data on a CD-ROM for $700. Word of this got out on the Internet, and privacy rights advocates initiated a letter-writing campaign to stop the project. In a short time, Lotus received 30,000 letters from angry Internet users who objected to the project. Sensing a public relations disaster, the company quietly dropped the project.

More recently, AOL in 1997 reversed itself regarding a plan to sell subscriber telephone numbers. AOL reserves the right to sell personal information about its subscribers to direct marketers, and it was about to add telephone numbers to their data sales. Word got out, the media voiced widespread criticism of the plan, and AOL backed down.

This shows that at least some companies are sensitive to public opinion and want to comply emerging industry standards on a voluntary basis. On the other hand, voluntary self-regulation could be easily side-stepped by smaller companies struggling to survive, larger companies that maintain a low public profile, or very large corporations that are simply not worried about public opinion. Whenever an industry relies on voluntary compliance, inevitably some of its members will violate the guidelines to gain a competitive advantage.

Privacy policies are an interesting case study of the effectiveness of self-regulation on the Internet, if only because the goals of commercial marketing departments are at odds with the privacy rights of consumers. Consider the case of DoubleClick, Inc., the largest ad server and consumer profiling operation on the Internet. In 1999, a proposed merger between DoubleClick and Abacus Direct Corp., a marketing firm that maintains databases on consumer buying habits, attracted media attention and opposition from many privacy advocacy groups, including the **Electronic Privacy Information Center**, **Junkbusters**, and **Privacy International**. At issue were the potential privacy violations that such a merger would enable, violations that would not be tolerated in many European countries in which nonconsensual data collection is illegal. DoubleClick argued that it offers consumers an opt-out option and that only ten people, out of 75 million ad viewers, choose to opt out each month. The obvious explanation for this is that perhaps only ten people in 75 million know enough about what's going on to track down the opt-out page at DoubleClick's Web site. Moreover, DoubleClick claimed that it is in compliance with the self-regulation policies promoted by the marketing industry (this presumably consists of offering notice and consent to users). The proposed merger between DoubleClick and Abacus was completed at the end of 1999 without government interference. DoubleClick is unlikely to alter its extremely successful consumer profiling operation for the sake of placating a few privacy advocates.

Personal Privacy Is Respected in Europe

Personal privacy rights are well established in Europe. Within the European Union, businesses accept the dictum that personal data released to one organization, for one purpose, should not be distributed to other organizations without the permission of the individual being described. This is a simple rule of conduct that gives Europeans much more control over their personal information than we have in the United States.

When consumer interests and business interests collide, the best weapon for the consumer is a widespread boycott. A boycott backed up by a visible public protest is one way to promote stronger self-regulation and voluntary controls. However, in the case of the Internet, many business practices are embedded in the technologies of the Web (for example, ad banners) and people can't boycott DoubleClick unless they know what cookies are and how to block them. It takes time to educate the consumer. DoubleClick retains the upper hand, thanks to a largely ignorant user population.

On the other hand, self-regulation does seem to work admirably when the best interests of business and consumers do not collide. The widespread adoption of data encryption for sensitive online communications is a good example of industry self-regulation that is in step with basic economic survival. No one had to pass a law requiring e-commerce sites to use encryption for credit card transactions, and the adoption of SSL by commercial Web sites was an obvious win for both businesses and consumers.

10.5 ONLINE AUCTIONS

Online auctions are an increasingly popular feature on the Internet. People flock to sites such as eBay to buy and sell and hunt for bargains (see Figure 10.18). Auction sites are a virtual flea market for used goods, found treasures, and the occasionally

Figure 10.18:
All Sorts of Things
Are Sold at eBay

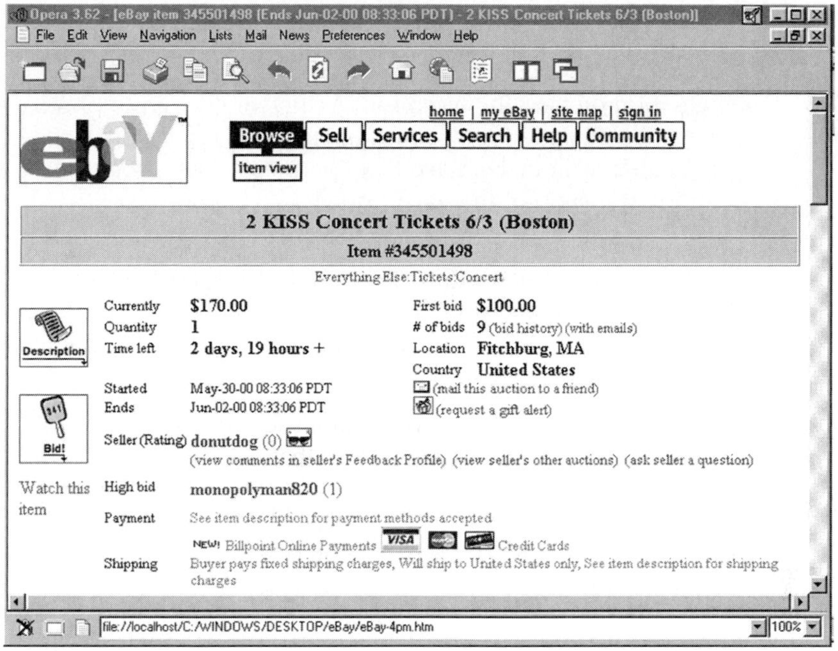

bizarre item. They also top the list of reported incidents of Internet fraud. An overwhelming 87% of all complaints reported to **Internet Fraud Watch** in 1999 were related to online auctions. If you intend to participate in an online auction, review the safety guidelines described in Section 2.9. The current section looks at online auctions from more of a business perspective.

Although there are hundreds, possibly thousands, of online auction sites at this time, **eBay** is the largest and most visible. At any given time, it lists over four million items in more than 4,000 categories. It draws eight million visitors each month and actually turns a profit (unlike so many Internet companies that depend on venture capital and air to get by). eBay seems to have struck a chord in a commercial world dominated by shopping malls, brand recognition, and ubiquitous advertising by offering its visitors a completely different shopping experience. The variety of products is there, but not the stores. Detailed information is available, but not the sales personnel. Convenience is clearly a factor, although most purchases have to be delivered, and delivery costs can add up if you do a lot of online shopping. Impulse buys are tempered by the fact that each item remains "on the block" for some fixed period, during which time other people can bid up the price over a period of days. Whatever the appeal of the online auction is, it's definitely unlike anything else in the world of commerce.

How Does eBay Work?

A seller pays $.25 to post an item. The listing is created when the seller fills out a simple form on the eBay Web site. A file that contains a photograph of the item can also be uploaded to eBay for inclusion in the listing. If the seller wishes, the listing can appear in boldface type for an extra $2 or be listed under Featured Auctions at the top of the page for $99.

Buyers find items by browsing the categories or conducting keyword searches. A fixed amount of time (usually 5 to 12 days) is set for each auction and the highest bidder at the end of that time period wins the auction. The buyer and seller mutually arrange for payment and shipping. The buyer can expect to receive the purchase in a week or two.

In general, there are three types of e-commerce:

1. Customer-to-customer (C2C) interactions
2. Business-to-customer (B2C) interactions
3. Business-to-business (B2B) interactions

eBay is primarily a C2C operation, although a few small businesses appear on eBay for B2C contacts. For a small B2C business getting off the ground or testing the waters for a new product, eBay makes product marketing and pricing experiments possible.

UBid.com is an interesting counterpoint to eBay and a good representative of a C2C online auction Web site. Unlike eBay, on which goods pass directly from sellers to buyers, UBid either purchases its goods outright or attains the rights to sell them for the manufacturer on a percentage basis. This is a much more costly model for an auction site because the site must handle all of the shipping and storage, as well as assume liability for unsatisfactory products. However, buyers can be confident that the merchandise will meet a fixed set of standards. Therefore buyers likely place more trust in a UBid auction.

Amazon.com is experimenting with online auctions. It links users to used books in its online auction site when a book search leads to an item that is available as both new or used. It also supports **LiveBid.com**, an online auction that telecasts all of its auctions live, so users can watch and hear an online auction take place in real time. Anyone who wants to participate is welcome to join in remotely from the Web and place bids online.

Online auctions will be one of the most exciting e-commerce areas to watch in coming years. Sites are likely to experiment with more-creative placements of goods and services, with possible forays into the realm of information and intellectual property deliveries. Many "get rich quick" schemes based on online auctions likely will be launched (the genre is already established), but the strongest trend appears to be away from C2C models toward B2B models. Industry analysts predicting that the B2B market, valued around $131 billion at the start of 2000, will reach between $2.7 trillion and $7.3 trillion by 2004. A number of B2C companies have already begun to retool in this direction. **Priceline.com**, **CMGI**, **Beyond.com**, and even **eBay** are all repositioning themselves to produce B2B e-commerce solutions.

Things to Remember

- Keep a record of all of your online transactions.
- Use credit cards on the Internet; never use debit cards.
- Do not send sensitive information over the Internet to a nonsecure Web page (look for `https://` and the locked padlock to confirm that a site is secure).
- Check an e-store's digital certificate before you send sensitive data to that e-store site.
- If you're unsure about a digital certificate for any reason, proceed with caution or back off completely.
- SSL is the industry standard for secure communications on the Web.
- Don't worry about what type of encryption you have. Do make sure that all of your transactions are being encrypted.
- Online auctions are the number one source of Internet-related consumer fraud complaints (by a landslide).

Important Concepts

digital certificate—a document on a Web server that can be checked to verify the identity of the server.

online auction—a popular way for individuals to buy and sell items of all kinds.

Secure Sockets Layer (SSL)—a protocol to establish secure (encrypted) communications between a Web browser and a Web server.

40-bit encryption—a weak level of encryption that was the government standard for e-commerce until January 2000.

56-bit encryption—the strongest level of commercial encryption approved by the U.S. government prior to January 2000.

64-bit encryption—a medium level of encryption approved by the U.S. government (as of January 2000) for e-commerce in the United States.

128-bit encryption—the strongest level of encryption used by commercial sites in the United States.

Where Can I Learn More?

E-commerce Times `http://www.ecommercetimes.com/`

ecommerce-guide.com `http://ecommerce.internet.com/`

Understanding Digital Certificates and SSL
  `http://www.entrust.net/products/digitalcerts/index.htm`

A Framework for Global Electronic Commerce
  `http://www.ecommerce.gov/framewrk.htm`

About > Industry > E-business `http://ebusiness.about.com/industry/ebusiness/mbody.htm`

Problems and Exercises

1. List three ways that e-stores give consumers the upper hand when a sale depends on negotiation (hint: consider the process of buying a car).

2. Why should a consumer check the digital certificate for an e-store?

3. Explain why digital certificates have fingerprints and how they are used.

4. What is site spoofing?

5. Can a site with a digital certificate be a spoofed site? Explain your answer.

6. How can you tell whether you have an SSL connection to a Web site?

7. Will your browser always show an alert box when you establish or break an SSL connection? Explain your answer.

8. How does SSL ensure that the data that you send to a Web server is not altered en route?

9. Why do some e-stores still use weak encryption?

10. What is one-click shopping? Where is personal information stored for one-click shopping?

11. Why is it a bad idea to let your computer remember all of your e-store passwords by using cookies?

12. Name four federal laws that have been passed to address Internet-specific issues. Which ones apply to e-commerce?

13. What types of companies are likely to ignore industry guidelines when an industry is self-regulating?

14. Why do privacy advocates object to the business practices of DoubleClick?

15. Why is it difficult to mount a consumer protest against DoubleClick?

16. What simple guideline for privacy rights has the European Union adopted?

17. Why isn't the practice of notice and consent an adequate policy for protecting personal privacy online?

18. How are online auction sites useful to small businesses?

19. Explain how eBay differs from UBid.

20. What is the current trend in online auction sites?

21. **[Find It Online]** Visit Nielson//NetRatings at `http://www.nielsen-netratings.com/`, and find its most recent list of the top ten advertisers on the Net. Which of those companies are also present in the top-ten list in Figure 10.2?

22. **[Find It Online]** eBay imposes some restrictions on the items that people can sell. In particular, restrictions apply to the sale of concert tickets. Describe those restrictions.

23. **[Find It Online]** eBay auctions run for a fixed period of time. When that time is up, the highest bidder wins. What is the shortest possible time period for an eBay auction? What is the longest possible time? How do proxy bids work at eBay?

24. **[Find It Online]** Some auctions at eBay are "Dutch" auctions. What is a Dutch auction? Explain how it differs from a regular auction, and describe how it works.

25. **[Find It Online]** PayPal (`http://www.paypal.com`) is a service that many eBay users rely on for electronic funds transfers (EFTs). If both the buyer and the seller have PayPal accounts, the buyer can use a credit card to send a payment to the seller's PayPal account. The seller then can confirm the receipt of the payment in minutes and immediately dispatch the purchased item. Without EFTs, the seller would have to wait for the buyer's check to arrive in the mail and then wait for the check to clear the buyer's bank, a process that can take a week or more. How much does PayPal charge users for its service? How do PayPal users convert money in their PayPal accounts into cash? How long does it take to get cash back from PayPal? How does PayPal turn a profit?

Take a Closer Look: Above and Beyond

E-Commerce, National Security, and Hackers

The Above and Beyond in Chapter 2 explored the origins and evolution of the hacker culture. In particular, you saw that although the media tends to portray all computer hackers as brilliant, alienated, and potentially dangerous, no monolithic stereotype fits all hackers. Of course, the media has a vested interest in stories that sell, so you can't be too be shocked if reporters tend to emphasize the "weird kid with frightening powers" angle. Similarly, Hollywood would have little interest in hackers if the hacker stereotype was closer to reality: a bored teenager of average intelligence dabbling in activities that are no more threatening than trespassing or shoplifting.

What Is CERT?

A tracking center for computer security problems (CERT) was set up by the Department of Defense in 1988 after Robert Morris, Jr., a graduate student in Computer Science at Cornell University, released a network worm that crippled thousands of computers connected to the Internet. The purpose of CERT is to research and compile information about the technology behind hacker attacks (see Figure 10.19).

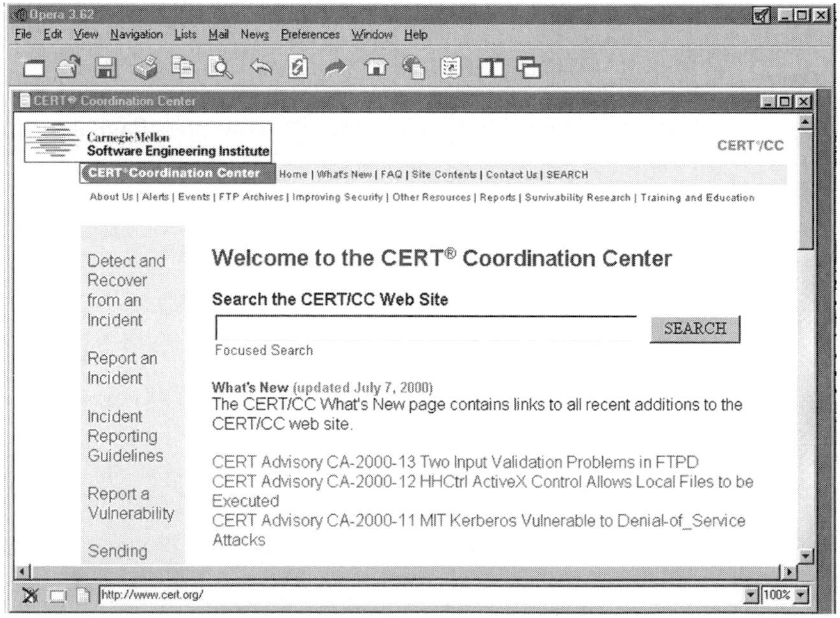

Figure 10.19: CERT Is a Timely Computer Security Clearinghouse

When the Internet was primarily a tool for programmers and researchers, hackers were accepted as an inevitable annoyance and a good reason to take system security seriously. In those days, no one equated hacker attacks with billion dollar losses. Today, when many people hear the word "hacker" they think of credit card theft and extortion. They worry about the security of their personal information on the Internet. The use of the Internet by myriad elements of our economy has elevated the hacker problem to new heights. But how real is this threat to the nascent world of e-commerce? Could hackers pull down the global economy like a house of cards? Should hackers be handled like any other criminal element, even if they are minors? Or is the whole business of computer hackers primarily media hype, with no more real impact on society than the older and more traditional methods of corporate theft?

As always, the media shapes public perceptions for events that most people don't experience first-hand. Stories in the press can be written to cause a stir, or low-level anxiety, and a single incident can galvanize public opinion. For example, one could tell people that there are 16,000 known computer viruses or explain that only 300 different computer viruses are active **in the wild** (making the rounds outside of research laboratories). Both statements are true. However, to scare readers the first is much more effective.

Regarding the subject of computer hackers and their impact on e-commerce, you can find pronouncements by many people with a professional stake in hackers and hacking. To fully understand the truth of the matter, you need to look at some hard facts, which are sometimes buried beneath the rhetoric. Consider the following quotations.

Hackers and the World Economy

The very same means that the cyber vandals used a few weeks ago [in the denial-of-service cyber attacks on several major Web sites in February 2000] could also be used on a much more massive scale at the nation-state level to generate truly damaging interruptions to the national economy and infrastructure.
—Daniel Kuehl, National Defense University of the Pentagon

If there's one lesson both the government and the private sector can learn from the world's continuing million-dollar bout with various strains of the "Love Bug" —as the "I LOVE YOU" virus is known alternatively—it is that a group of teenage students and fresh college graduates can pose a threat to a nation's economic well-being.
—Fidel R. Anonuevo, Jr., National Security Council

Are these statements of fact? Or is this simply arresting rhetoric designed to shape a political agenda? Let's check the facts. The Federal Bureau of Investigation (FBI) estimated that the denial-of-service attacks in February 2000 cost affected businesses hundreds of millions of dollars. The LoveLetter virus released in May 2000 was estimated to cost $2.6 billion worldwide. If attacks of this kind were leveled at essential businesses and communication backbones (for example, airlines and telephone companies) on a nonstop basis, the economic loss would qualify as a national emergency.

Should we expect to see more of these types of high-profile attacks? Has there been a general increase in overall hacking activities in recent years? Or is the press simply reporting more of them now because so many people depend on the Internet? **CERT** says that the number of reported attacks is increasing explosively. In 1988, they logged six attacks. In 1998, 3,743 attacks. In 1999, nearly 10,000. And during the first quarter of 2,000, there were 4,266.

NIMBY (not-in-my-backyard) Hackers

According to the FBI, only 210 Fortune 1000 companies reported attacks on their computer networks during 1999. However, an estimated 65% of all corporate cybercrime victims don't report their attacks, out of a fear of negative publicity. The FBI also estimates that 85% to 95% of all intrusions into corporate and private networks are never detected.

For a blow-by-blow account of what hackers are up to daily, drop by **InfoWar.com** and read about the latest security breaches, software alerts, and reports from the front lines. Then keep in mind that most security breeches are not reported.

Hackers who target military and government operations pose a different type of risk. Shutting down e-commerce sites can cost millions of dollars. However, hacker attacks designed to damage military security or halt infrastructure operations can cost more than money. They could cost lives.

Hackers and Military Operations

During the Gulf War, Dutch hackers stole information about U.S. troop movements from U.S. Defense Department computers and tried to sell it to the Iraqis, who thought it was a hoax and turned it down.
                    —John Christensen, CNN Interactive

We are detecting, with increasing frequency, the appearance of doctrine and dedicated offensive cyber warfare programs in other countries. We have identified several [countries], based on all-source intelligence information, that are pursuing government-sponsored offensive cyber programs.
                    —John Serabian, Central Intelligence Agency

What are the chances that a serious cyberterrorism attack will someday result in death and destruction? Once again, let's look at some facts. In 1997, the NSA hired 35 hackers and launched simulated attacks on the U.S. electronic infrastructure.

The exercise was called "Eligible Receiver," and the hired hackers managed to achieve privileged access to 36 of the Department of Defense's 40,000 networks. The simulated attack also turned off sections of the U.S. power grid, shut down parts of the 911 network in several cities, including Washington, D.C., and gained access to systems aboard a Navy cruiser at sea. Later that same year, Senator Jon Kyl (R-Arizona), chairman of the U.S. Senate Subcommittee on Technology, Terrorism and Government Information, reported that nearly two-thirds of U.S. government computers systems have security holes. These facts suggest that we're living on borrowed time.

Why are there more incidents of cybercrime, and what can we do about it? Do we need more laws? Stronger law enforcement? Are we digging our own grave by protecting hacker sites under the First Amendment? An estimated 30,000 Web sites are written for hackers by hackers, on which software tools can be found along with mini-tutorials on topics such as denial-of-service attacks and encryption cracking. These tools of destruction are distributed freely, like recipes for cheesecake, in the name of free speech and intellectual inquiry. Anyone can learn the tools of the trade.

How hard is it to be a hacker? Does it require superior intelligence? A technical background? Extensive programming expertise? Widespread agreement exists among security experts regarding these questions.

No Wonder So Many Kids Are Hackers Nowadays

A few years ago, hacking took a lot of time and study. While expert hackers still abound, the Internet has entered a new era. Using almost any search engine, average Internet users can quickly find information describing how to break into systems by simply searching for keywords like hacking, password cracking, and Internet security. Thousands of sites publish step-by-step instructions for breaking into or disrupting service to Windows NT systems, Web servers, UNIX systems, etc. The sites often include tools that automate the hacking process. In many cases, the tools have easy-to-use graphical interfaces.

—Robert A. Clyde, AXENT Technologies, Inc.

Today, it's all too easy to exploit known vulnerabilities. The Internet has placed the best cracker tools within easy reach of anyone who knows how to use the World Wide Web. The tools can be found using any common, free search engine.
  —ITATF Security Working Group, University of California at Berkeley

I think that these attacks [the denial-of-service cyberattacks on several major Web sites] have been inevitable. The Internet is totally vulnerable to this kind of thing. It was just a matter of time before the automated attacking tools became so easy and widespread that everyone started using them.

—Avi Rubin, AT&T Laboratories

This situation seems to resemble the problem of children with guns. When guns are easily available in many households, some number of children invariably pick up one. Once in a while, the outcome is tragic. Adults also pick up guns and kill people. However, in those cases, the intent is usually criminal, and the legal system holds adults accountable for their actions. As the gun analogy suggests, we must address several different problems. How should we punish a minor for an intentional act of destruction and mayhem? How should we punish an adult for committing an act of destruction if the adult did not fully comprehend or intend the consequences of that act? How can we prevent these acts of destruction from occurring in the first place? Should we hold the software (gun) manufacturers responsible for making their software (guns) too easy to use? Should we sue a software (gun) manufacturer for the monetary losses associated with its products? Should we blame our schools and places of work for not maintaining secure environments in which people are safe from cybercrimes (violence)? Should we blame parents or teachers or television for not teaching our children to stay away from hacking software (guns)? Should we blame society for producing people who see cybercrime (violence) as the solution to their problems? For both software and guns, the problems are thorny and not prone to quick fixes.

Like many analogies, the hacker/gun analogy breaks down if you examine it closely. In the case of guns, you're dealing with physical objects. Gun production can be regulated, and gun distribution can be limited. In the case of hackers, the weapons are intellectual property. Software and algorithms cannot be regulated, and their distribution cannot be controlled, at least not in a free society. In addition, we would never blame the victims of shooting incidents for not defending themselves better. But that is exactly what proponents of better system security do when corporations and institutions are hurt by hackers. They blame the victims' software for being poorly designed, and they blame the victims for not being vigilant enough about system security.

Consider the case of ProMobility Interactive, a wireless telephone merchant in Ontario, Canada. ProMobility was one of nine e-commerce sites in the United States, United Kingdom, Canada, Thailand, and Japan that were attacked by two 18-year-olds in Wales, Ireland. The sites were infiltrated, and credit card account records for more than 26,000 accounts were stolen. Credit card account data was posted on a Web site; credit card losses were estimated to exceed $3 million.

ProMobility said that hackers had infiltrated its site through a two-year-old security hole in a Microsoft e-commerce software package. Microsoft posted a patch for the problem in July 1998 on its security update site. It issued a second warning on the site in July 1999. Promobility failed to install this patch and they were attacked in February 2000.

Security through Obscurity Doesn't Work

Eric Geiler, Vice President Information Systems at ProMobility Interactive, was puzzled as to why the hackers went after Promobility. "How the hell did he even find us? We are nobody. Why did he pick us?" Sensitive data at small e-commerce sites often is at risk. Thus small e-commerce sites have become very popular targets for hackers because they are less likely to have up-to-date security software and adequate maintenance routines. "In a lot of companies, you have one system/admin guy who goes around and fixes computers, and you can't keep up to date with all of the patches," explained Geiler. (See

```
http://cnn.com/2000/TECH/computing/03/24/hackers.wales/
index.html.)
```

Many e-commerce sites don't realize how vulnerable they are—even less, how much work is required to secure an e-commerce site. Those that do might decide that it's more cost-effective to remove some of their most sensitive operations offline rather than attempt to maintain good security on their computers.

Back to the Future

Selwyn Gerber, a managing partner with the offshore banking firm PrimeGlobal USA, said his company considers the Internet so insecure that it won't use it to transmit sensitive customer data.

We're back to using faxes, and we find that much more secure. We use FedEx [Federal Express]. In fact, if there were ponies still travelling across Europe we'd probably use those, too.

Why not hold the software manufacturers responsible for software that does not better protect private data? Servers, routers, firewalls, and database programs all can be susceptible to attack. Disclaimers protect software manufacturers from legal liability. However, why can't those manufacturers produce better software and thereby close security gaps at the source? Buyers would certainly pay more for software that didn't require patches and updates in order to stay one jump ahead of hackers.

Unfortunately, software manufacturers are under at least as much pressure to produce and release products as are the e-commerce sites that rely on those products. The e-commerce sites often are racing to establish an online presence before their competition does. Along the way, they suffer from a relentless sense that everything must be done as fast as possible. In this rush to be first, concerns about security are often set aside.

E-Commerce, Security, and the Bottom Line

Often times they're going for the money-maker, that's getting the product out there, getting the site up. And security is often an afterthought.
—Elinor Abreau, *The Industry Standard*

If you have a choice of spending a million dollars on getting 250,000 new customers, or a million dollars on serving the ones you already have, better, that's a difficult value proposition.
—William P. Crowell, Chief Executive Officer, Cylink Corp.

You wouldn't build a swimming pool in the center of town and not put a fence around it, and I think that's what the software companies are doing.
—Glenn Tenney, Pilot Network Services

Easy access to hacking tools, inadequate resources on the part of e-commerce sites, pressure on software manufacturers to cut corners, and people with criminal intent as well as kids looking for thrills—all conspire to keep hacking a major problem for e-commerce. Eliminating hackers is probably impossible without a major overhauling the Internet's underlying architecture. Some Net observers accept hackers as an inevitable and compelling force in the Internet's evolution.

Hackers and the Evolutionary Process

Technology advances. In the process you get a little lax about security. Hackers come in and remind us about the problem. Companies respond appropriately and the system gets tighter. [Describing the "safety cycle" that becomes the Internet's learning curve.]
—Paul Saffo, Institute for the Future

In an arms race, there are two sides. Each side is constantly building up its forces to try to outdo the other side. We typically see this with the nuclear capabilities of various countries. On the Internet, there's a similar situation. The attackers move several steps forward by coming up with new ways of penetrating systems, and the protectors come up with new things, such as firewalls, to counter that. Unlike a typical arms race, however, the security specialists can only respond to the new attacks. There's very little you can do proactively.
—Avi Rubin, AT&T Laboratories

Meanwhile, the problems are very real, the potential for disaster is great, and the situation will probably get worse before it gets better. We can't censor software, and we can't expect security problems to go away entirely. We could, perhaps, try to dispel the notion of hacking as a "cool" activity, thereby making it no longer trendy. Hackers will always exist. However, they don't have to be viewed as folk heroes or a manifestation of alienated youth. Indeed, the personal lives and psychological profiles of criminal hackers don't deserve media attention at all.

Perhaps the most hopeful message on this subject comes from a member of the media who has investigated the hacker culture and found it remarkably lacking in dramatic figures. Charles Platt, of *Wired Magazine*, argues that the best thing that we can do is give the hackers a lot of media attention. Write exposés, conduct interviews, create weekly columns, and let television work the concept to death. Give hackers and hacking too much media, too much exposure, too much air time. The interest of the establishment is a sure-fire way to deflect young people from anything remotely countercultural. Media overexposure, he claims, conceivably could reduce the hacker of the 1990s into an adolescent icon and lunchbox theme for the 2000s. It's a proven method, he claims.

How to Destroy the Hacker Mystique

Any small group of diehard nonconformists tends to lose its power when the barriers come down. Hackerdom could turn into a harmless fad in the same way that radical hippie activism in the 1960s degenerated into a fashion statement after it received sufficient media exposure.

—Charles Platt, *Wired Magazine*

Digital Telephony and Convergence

For the cost of a $20 headset and an Internet connection with any of various telephony clients, any two people can now engage in **Internet telephony**, that is, computer-to-computer telephone calling. Also called **IP telephony** or **voice-over IP**, Internet telephony in 1998 used 310 million minutes of calling time. In 1999, the number of minutes leaped to 2.7 billion minutes.

As with e-mail, Internet telephony works only if the people whom you want to call use it, too. Early adopters had to grapple with the absence of interoperability. In the context of telephony, **Interoperability** means that people using different telephony clients will still be able to talk with each other. Without interoperability, either everyone whom you want to talk to over via telephony must use the same software (an unlikely scenario) or you must install several different clients (a cumbersome solution). For the telephony industry to achieve interoperability, it must adopt an industry standard for shared telephony protocols. It's not at that point yet, but it's making progress.

IP telephony gateways are a big success story in telephony. An **IP telephony gateway** is a device that translates voice signals into IP packets for transmission via TCP/IP. Telephony gateways also connect traditional Public Switched Telephone Network (PSTN) and TCP/IP networks, thereby allowing voice telephone calls to move seamlessly across both POTS (Plain Old Telephone Service) networks and digital networks. Telephony gateways have made computer-to-phone connections possible.

Users are attracted to Internet telephony because it offers, in essence, toll-free long distance telephone service. They pay few or no additional fees beyond the cost of

Internet access, so the savings on long distance calls can be significant. Users are also attracted to other features, including these:

- Real-time video
- Conference calls for group conversations
- File transfer capability
- Virtual whiteboard support
- Support for collaborative projects

Telephone calls on the Internet are not only cheaper than traditional telephone company services, but also more powerful—for example, instant messaging is easier to implement in a telephony environment than voice mail is in the old POTS environment. Someday, all of these capabilities will combine with wireless handheld devices that connect to the Internet. We'll end up with cellular telephones on steroids.

Digital Convergence Internet telephony is one of the hottest Internet applications under development. However, it's only one example of a large class of Internet applications involved in digital convergence. **Digital convergence** is the morphing of existing high-tech technologies into hybrid communications technologies, hybrid consumer electronics, and hybrid computers. Computers that act like telephones are an example of digital convergence at work. Another example is the television set-top box such as WebTV, which causes your television to act like a Web browser. The PDA (Personal Digital Assistant) is the result of combining the electronic address book with a Web browser. Cable companies are morphing into ISPs, and ISPs are morphing into telephone service providers. To compete successfully in the computer industry, companies must have a strong understanding of digital convergence and, if possible, a crystal ball.

Soccer and Convergence

Someone once asked Brazilian soccer player Pele (Edson Arantes do Nascimento) what made him a superior soccer player. He said, "I don't go to where the ball is. I go to where the ball will be." With that kind of eye for the future, Pele should have been a chief executive officer for a telecommunications start-up company.

The ongoing convergence of the information and communication technologies will affect individual users by blurring the lines between work and play and between play and learning. Many people have already seen how Web browsing for pleasure can quickly turn into an educational expedition. When it's so easy to dig a little deeper, curiosity can lead an inquisitive mind in many different directions, opening up new avenues of learning along the way.

Internet Appliances

If you think that the world is wired now, stick around for the next ten years. Networks are coming out of the office and into the home at the same time that microchips are showing up in every conceivable place (and a few inconceivable ones). Many consumer products will rely on smart devices that have access to a network and, in some cases, access to the Internet. We're seeing this already with PDAs, whose wireless Internet access is a sign of devices to come.

An **Internet appliance** is a device that uses the Internet for some special purpose. Two key features distinguish Internet appliances from personal computers.

1. Unlike a general-purpose personal computer, an Internet appliance has limited functionality. It can perform only one or two functions, and it cannot run general software applications.

2. Internet appliances are designed to do things that personal computers can't (or at least can't do with the same panache). Because of their limited functionality, they can be produced and marketed more cheaply than a personal computer.

Here are some examples of Internet appliances.

- **Ceiva**: An LCD picture frame that downloads and displays photographs from the Web. While your personal computer can do this, too, Ceiva looks like a traditional picture frame that you hang on a wall. $249.

- **Rocket eBook**: An electronic book (e-book) reading device that displays electronic books. It includes convenient search and bookmark features, as well as a built-in dictionary for point-and-click word look-up. The eBook can hold up to ten books at one time, as well as newspapers and magazines. $199.

- **i-opener**: A 10-inch flat-screen LCD panel with keyboard that supports a built-in Web browser and e-mail client. $99.

The world of Internet appliances is just getting started. Imagine standing in a store with a wireless device that can help you to do some quick comparison shopping before you buy. Maybe you're a sports buff and you want fast access, anyplace, anytime, to team schedules and player statistics for all of your favorite teams (but especially at the stadium while you're watching a game). Are you a hiker or a wilderness buff? Wouldn't a single device be great that contains a cellular telephone and a global positioning unit that offers detailed trail and topographical maps on demand? Internet appliances are the stuff of dreams. If you can imagine it, it probably can be built, and a visionary e-commerce company can corner the market by building the best one or maybe simply the first one.

Above and Beyond: Problems and Exercises

A1. Name three new devices (things that didn't exist five years ago) that are products of digital convergence.

A2. Define interoperability. What would e-mail be like if all of the different e-mail clients were not interoperable? Is Internet telephony interoperable? What does a communication medium need in order to be interoperable?

A3. Describe an Internet appliance that you would like to own. Explain how you would use it and why you think it would be worth having. (You can pick an Internet appliance that already exists, one that is still under development that you read or heard about, or one that you thought of on your own.)

A4. **[Find It Online]** Find a current estimate for how much hacker attacks are costing the global economy. (*Hint*: Visit `http://www.ecommercetimes.com/`, and conduct a site search.)

A5. **[Find It Online]** Software manufacturers have enjoyed strong legal protection from lawsuits associated with software failures. Are any organizations or politicians working to create a law that would force software manufacturers to assume more responsibility for product failures? Report on any effort that you can find along these lines and its current status.

A6. **[Find It Online]** The music industry is looking for new business models that involve digital technologies. Find a proposed business model that the record companies might possibly adopt. Describe it in detail, and evaluate it from the consumer's perspective.

A7. **[Find It Online]** Can companies buy insurance to cover losses in the event of a hacker attack? (*Hint*: Visit `http://www.ecommercetimes.com/`, and conduct a site search.) Explain your answer.

A8. **[Find It Online]** Cyberterrorism is a difficult threat to evaluate. Some studies argue that the United States is living on borrowed time, whereas others suggest that the news media has overemphasized the possibility of cyberterrorism. Conduct a search on the Web for papers about cyberterrorism, and decide for yourself which side is more credible. (*Hint*: Conduct your searches by using such queries as "cyberterrorism," "cyberwarfare," "Electronic Pearl Harbor," and "Electronic Waterloo.")

A9. **[Find It Online]** Net2Phone supports computer-to-telephone connections worldwide. What is its per-minute rate for calls within the United States?

A10. **[Find It Online]** Visit InfoWar.com, and click Surveys and Studies (in the navigation menu). Scan the titles of the available reports, and pick a report that interests you. Read the report, and summarize it in one paragraph.

Encryption and the Internet

CHAPTER GOALS

- Understand how private-key and public-key encryption work.
- Learn how digital signatures protect document integrity.
- Understand how key authentication is needed to protect people from counterfeit keys.
- See how the web-of-trust approach to key authentication works.
- Find out how digital certificates and certificate authorities solve the problem of key authentication.
- Understand the difference between strong and weak encryption.

11.1 TAKING CHARGE

Most of us never encounter the word *cryptography* outside of spy movies and espionage novels. **Cryptography** is the study of secret codes associated with classified information and intelligence gathering. You might know something about the important role of cryptography in World War II, but chances are you know only if you went out of your way to read a book about it. Even though everyone has probably heard of clandestine operations associated with the Central Intelligence Agency (CIA), many Americans have never heard of the National Security Agency (NSA). The NSA is responsible for developing and applying secure communication technologies in the service of national security. Cryptography used to be a science whose applications were of interest only to the military. Now, as we move into a new era of digital communication, cryptography and government interest in cryptography is touching all our lives.

Cryptography is of great interest to client/server software developers, anyone interested in digital commerce, and all Internet users who want to keep their personal communications private. In the absence of special safeguards, sensitive personal communications, legal contracts, valuable data, proprietary documents, insurance records, digital monetary transfers, medical records are all at risk on the Internet and on any digital medium. Cryptography offers us good options for protecting this information; it will become increasingly commonplace in business environments. It will eventually permeate all digital media as we come to appreciate the importance of secure communication.

When TCP/IP was adopted as the standard communication protocol for global networked communication, secure communication was not a high priority. Open software design, open resource sharing, and public information were the forces driving early network research. The Internet has succeeded as a highly accessible and expandable public network, but our priorities are slowly shifting. As the Internet becomes more commercialized, vendors need to conduct secure business transactions to allay the fears of consumers who are nervous about the risks of online shopping. We have yet to see a high-profile scandal unfold as the result of an Internet "wiretap," but it's probably just a matter of time before some technically inclined investigator figures out how to surreptitiously tap into the e-mail of some unsuspecting individual. Private investigators and lawyers are already examining back-up files as a potential source of legal evidence, but the general public is just beginning to ask about legal protections that pertain to privacy rights.

Companies must insist that sensitive information is not up for grabs just because it is stored on a computer, and citizens should feel reassured that tax returns and other private documents are not available to random individuals for recreational browsing. Online medical records must be handled with care so that employers and insurance companies can't review sensitive information without authorization. Credit records should be safe from the prying eyes of newspaper reporters and private investigators.

With so much public information going online, we've been a little slow to appreciate just how much sensitive personal information has also been going online. The technologies that promote public access were never designed to protect private data. The public has embraced the Internet without fully understanding exactly how it differs from relatively private communication channels, where safeguards for privacy are taken for granted.

The military has always understood that security is a big problem on computer networks. Sensitive military computers are carefully shielded from potentially invasive network connections. Large corporations followed suit by opting for intranet connectivity as an alternative to Internet access. An **intranet** is an internal computer network that is carefully segregated from all external computer networks such as the Internet. Internet access from an intranet is possible, but only through a secure gateway called a *firewall* (see the Above and Beyond section in Chapter 9) that is designed to keep sensitive data within organizational walls. A firewall is like a wall around a castle. As long as the wall works, everyone feels safe and sound. But a wall that is not carefully designed and maintained might be breached. So constant vigilance is needed. A castle wall without sentries is no better than a wall with a gaping hole in it.

Intranets and firewalls afford good protection and work well for large organizations. But many of our communications are not circumscribed by institutional boundaries. We also want privacy safeguards when we contact friends, acquaintances, and business contacts all over the world. Today's Internet does not have any privacy safeguards built into it. However, as time goes on we will see more and more applications incorporating privacy measures. It is not necessary to understand all of the technical foundations that enable digital privacy, but some understanding of the basic ideas will help you evaluate the available choices.

As we explain how encryption algorithms work, we will demonstrate key concepts with screen shots of encryption software in action. In particular, we will show some software traces from a command-mode version (running under UNIX) of an encryption program called **Pretty Good Privacy (PGP)**. Later on, we will see screenshots of PGP working in a point-and-click environment (under Windows). The command-mode traces actually offer a better picture of what's going on because there is a lot of explanatory text in these traces. Once you understand what the software is doing, the point-and-click environment is quicker and easier to work with. But the explanatory text in the command-mode version is very nice for beginners, which is why we've chosen to include some older PGP traces in this chapter.

11.2 PRIVATE-KEY ENCRYPTION

There was a time in the 1950s when it seemed like every kid in America wore a big purple plastic ring with white and yellow lightning bolts on it. It had a large dial on top covered in letters and symbols. Captain Midnight Decoder Rings were hot, and countless 7-year-olds deftly used these coveted artifacts to unscramble secret messages issued straight from Captain Midnight through the magic of television.

A key for a simple substitution code is just a map that tells you how to substitute one character for another. When you receive a coded message, you trade each character for a new one according to the instructions in the key. For example, suppose your coded message says this:

```
IUUJ IU JNIN66N0 KJ C2I ?95U6 JAU IK23U J6UUL
```

After applying the key in Figure 11.1 to each symbol in the encoded message, you see the unencoded message:

```
MEET ME TOMORROW AT 4PM UNDER THE MAPLE TREE.
```

The process of creating a coded message is called **encoding** (or **encrypting**). The process of unscrambling a coded message using a key is called **decoding** (or **decrypting**). To encode a message, you can use the same key that you use for

Figure 11.1:
A Substitution Code Key

A → H	F → 7	K → A	P → 5	U → E	Z → ?	5 → D	/ → W
B → C	G → 0	L → .	Q → F	V → S	1 → X	6 → R	. → Q
C → 4	H → B	M → V	R → 1	W → Z	2 → P	7 → K	! → G
D → I	I → M	N → 0	S → !	X → J	3 → L	8 → Y	? → U
E → 6	J → T	0 → 3	T → 9	Y → 2	4 → 8	9 → N	

decoding but you have to reverse the key (that is, think of all the arrows in Figure 11.1 going in the opposite direction). When the same key is used for both encoding and decoding, the code is called **private-key encryption** (also "single-key encryption" or "symmetric encryption"). See Figure 11.2.

Figure 11.2:
Private-Key (Single-Key) Encryption

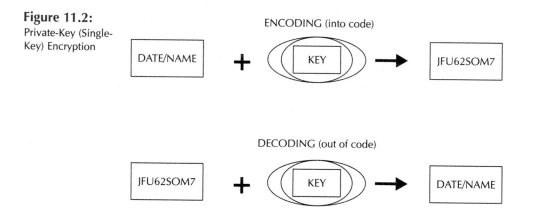

If you have the key for a code, it is easy to decode messages. If you don't have the key, you can try to break the code, but this requires some work. If you have enough encoded messages, you can study those encoded messages and try to figure out the key. You start by identifying the most frequently used characters and character sequences in the encoded messages. Then you need to know some helpful facts about the English language. For example, we know that the letter "e" is the most frequently used letter in the English alphabet. Chances are, one of the frequently used characters in the encoded messages is the encoding for "e." The most frequently used three-letter word is "the." If you see the same three-letter character sequence over and over again, it might be "the." These sorts of observations make it possible to break simple substitution codes.

An effective code is one that transmits messages to its intended recipients—and only its intended recipients. No one else should be able to decode the messages. However, one should always assume that coded messages will be intercepted by people who will try to break the code. So every effort must be made to confound the code breakers. A substitution code is one of the easiest ones to break and is never used for serious applications of cryptography. There are many other methods that are far more satisfactory, but we won't pursue them here. Interested readers will find opportunities to learn about other private-key methods in Where Can I Learn More?

A very important problem associated with private-key encryption is the problem of ensuring key security. If a code breaker can somehow steal the key for a code, the code is broken. To keep your diary safe from your snoopy big brother, you can use Captain Midnight's Decoder Ring to encode your diary entries. But then you better make sure your ring is safely hidden where big brother can't find it. The most sophisticated code in the world is of no use if the key cannot be held securely. Every precaution must be taken to keep code keys out of the wrong hands.

Private-key encryption methods are potentially risky because the same keys have to be shared by too many people. At the very least, the sender needs the key to encode messages, and the receiver needs the key to decode messages. Even when just two people share a key, you could have a problem because the key must be passed from one person to the other person. Each time a key is transferred, you take a chance that it might be intercepted. How can you make sure no one intercepts the key? Should you trust the U. S. mail? Federal Express? A telephone call? An e-mail message? A military courier? Some options are safer than others, but they all entail some risk.

If the information you want to encode is not a matter of life and death, you might decide that the risks associated with private-key encryption are acceptable (it was good enough for Captain Midnight, after all). But some applications for cryptography are very sensitive and require the best possible safeguards. To convince a few million consumers that their credit-card numbers can be safely used on the Internet, we need the best safeguards available. Indeed, concerns about the security of digital funds have been a major stumbling block in the commercialization of the Internet. No one wants to broadcast their credit-card number to the world. The solution to this dilemma is called **public-key encryption** (also known as "double-key encryption" or "asymmetric encryption").

In the next section we will explain how public-key encryption works, but we won't forsake private-key encryption altogether. Private-key encryption algorithms tend to run much faster (about 1,000 times faster) than public-key encryption algorithms. If you encrypt a lot of documents (or Web forms or e-mail), this is a significant slowdown. So while public-key encryption is superior to private-key encryption with respect to key safety, private-key encryption is superior to public-key encryption with respect to speed. When public-key encryption is used for practical applications, a little trickery makes it possible to combine private-key encryption with public-key encryption and end up with the best of both worlds. We won't digress to explain this cleverness right now, but we will cover this later in this chapter, in the Above and Beyond section, when we talk about session keys. Right now, it's more important to understand how public-key encryption works.

11.3   PUBLIC-KEY ENCRYPTION

The major weakness in private-key encryption is the problem of key security. **Public-key encryption** is an alternative to private-key encryption that addresses the problem of key security. The trick is to use two keys instead of one: One key is used for encoding and one key is used for decoding. These two keys are generated as a special key-pair that can only work together. If one key is lost, the other key is useless by itself. One of the two keys is designated as the public key. A public key can be freely distributed to anyone and everyone. The remaining key becomes the private key. A private key is held by only the owner of the key-pair. Now here's the really clever part. Although the two keys are uniquely connected to one another, having the public key doesn't make it possible to deduce the private key. Let's see how public-key encryption works by looking at an example.

How Safe Is the Private Key When Everyone Knows the Public Key?

Public-key encryption was first proposed in 1976 by Martin Hellman and Whitfield Diffie. In 1977 three computer scientists (Ronald Rivest, Adi Shamir, and Leonard Adleman) published a specific public-key encryption scheme known as the RSA Public Key Cryptosystem. At the heart of RSA is a patented method for generating secure asymmetric key-pairs. RSA key-pairs exploit the fact that while it is relatively easy to multiply two large prime numbers together, it is much harder to take that same product and find its prime factors. Although no one can prove that RSA key-pairs are unbreakable, the method has been studied extensively since 1977 and thus far, no efficient factorization algorithms have been found for very large numbers (we are talking about *very* large numbers here). RSA is one of the most widely used public-key algorithms in use today, and it is embedded inside many encryption programs used on the Internet.

If you want me to send you an encrypted message, you first need to create a pair of keys that will enable me to encode the message. You give me a copy of your public key, and you keep your private key to yourself. I can then use your public key to encode the message, and you can use your private key to decode it. This system is very secure because your private key is the only key that can decode messages encoded by your public key. Then, if you are the only person with access to your private key, you are the only person who can read messages encoded for you. It doesn't matter how many people hold the public key because it is only used for encoding messages. Figure 11.3 shows the basic idea behind public-key encryption.

For you to send me an encoded message, another pair of keys is needed. I need to create my own pair of keys, with a public key that I can distribute to anyone and a private key that only I can access. I give you a copy of my public key so that you can encode messages for me. Then when I get an encoded message from you, I use my private key to decode it. You and I can now exchanges messages back and forth, using our public keys for all the encoding and our private keys for all the decoding.

Figure 11.3:
Public-Key
(Double-Key)
Encryption

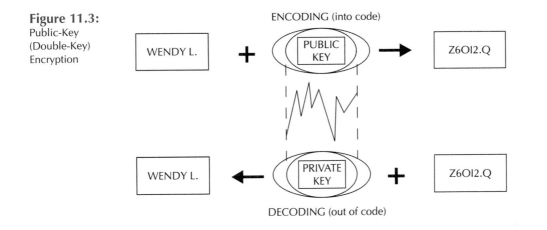

Let's consider the implications of public-key encryption a little further. If everyone on the Internet wanted to communicate with everyone else using public-key encryption, we would all need to own a personal key-pair and we would all need to access everyone else's public keys. This may not sound very practical, but all of this key management and key-related bookkeeping could be automated by communications software. For example, a central directory for public keys could be

How Hard Is It to Crack a Private Key?

A key is just a string of ones and zeros (a bit string). If someone can figure out the bit string, they've cracked the key. Assuming that no one can deduce private keys from public keys (so far so good for RSA), there is not much left to do but try a brute-force search. In a brute-force search, you simply generate and test each of the possible strings of ones and zeros until you find the right one. A shorter string is easier to crack than a longer one because there are fewer possibilities. Keys become much harder to crack as they get bigger:

10-bit keys 1,024 possibilities

20-bit keys 1,048,576 possibilities

40-bit keys 1,099,511,627,776 possibilities

56-bit keys 72,057,594,037,927,936 possibilities

In 1995 a programmer in France with access to 120 workstations cracked a 40-bit key in 8 days. (Note that today, a 600MHz Pentium III PC can crack a 40-bit key in 4 days.) In 1998, a special-purpose computer built by EFF (the Electronic Frontier Foundation) for $250,000 demonstrated that it could crack a 56-bit key in less than a week. 64-bit keys are still reasonably secure, but slipping into reach for cracking. Now it would take the EFF computer a year or two to crack a 64-bit key. By comparison, 128-bit keys are very safe. The EFF computer would need about 1,971,693,055,818,000,000,000 years to crack a 128-bit key.

created for the distribution of public keys. Once your public key goes into the directory, anyone could look it up and make a copy for their personal use. Even better, your software could go out on the net and do the directory look-ups for you automatically. If you wanted to send e-mail to someone, your mail program could look up the required key in the public-key directory. Then that key would be used to encrypt your mail message before it is sent. It could also be saved to a virtual key-ring of useful public keys for future reference, just as e-mail addresses are saved in virtual address books for future reference. The phrase **public-key infrastructure (PKI)** refers to the business of establishing and maintaining a system of public-key servers (a problem that is not unlike the challenge of maintaining domain-name servers for the entire Internet). All of the overhead associated with locating public keys and encoding outgoing e-mail must be handled by PKI software running quietly behind the scenes and requiring no extra effort on the part of the user.

At the receiving end, your mail program could be smart enough to recognize an encoded message when it sees one, in which case it would apply your private key and decode the message for you automatically. All of this would take place only when you read your e-mail, so as to maintain maximal security. Everything needed to realize this scenario exists today, including mail programs that automate message encryption and decryption. All of the technical know-how is there to secure our e-mail from prying eyes. **Privacy-enhanced e-mail (PEM)** and similar e-mail enhancements are available today and may be commonplace in a few more years (see Section 11.8.2).

11.4 DIGITAL SIGNATURES

Signatures of one kind or another are probably as old as written language. When a document is signed, we know who wrote it and who should be given credit for its contents. In the case of legal contracts, signatures are backed up by laws. Signatures are routinely written on receipts, prescriptions, grade transcripts, business correspondence, certificates of achievement, works of art, bank checks, income tax forms, loan applications, traffic tickets, photographs, notarized documents, fishing licenses, and hall passes. It's hard to get through a day without crossing paths with a signature of some kind. Sometimes a signature is forged, and when a forgery goes undetected, the outcome is rarely good.

As we move into a digital millennium we can now add a new kind of signature to the list: the **digital signature**. At first glance, it may seem that a digital signature would be especially vulnerable to forgery. If we have to use a keyboard instead of a freehand writing device, how can we possibly create distinctive signatures that offer some resistance to forgery?

In fact, digital signatures are even more distinctive than a traditional handwritten signature, but we have to use public-key encryption to make digital signatures unique and forgery-resistant. Encryption is not only important for maintaining privacy online—it is also the only way to know for sure just who is on the receiving end of your outgoing communications and who is behind each incoming communication. Safe digital signatures are crucial for e-commerce and other sensitive communications online, so digital signatures are important to everyone who intends to conduct business online.

If you understand how public-key encryption works with public and private keys, you will be able to understand how digital signatures are generated and verified. Consider the following scenario. You want to post a document on the Web, and you don't care who reads it, but you do want everyone to know that you are the original author. You don't need an encoded document—you just want to add a digital signature to a plain-text document. You can create this digital signature with the private half of a public crytography key-pair and some special software designed to generate digital signatures. When you launch the software, it asks for the file that you want signed and the private key that you are signing it with. The signature program identifies you as the source of this signature based on the fact that you are using your private key to create the signature.

Now suppose you post your document and someone else wants to make sure your signature is legitimate. To verify the signature, they will need the public key of your key-pair and some special software designed to verify digital signatures. They can retrieve your public key (perhaps from a public-key library) and use their own encryption software to see if the public key from the library and the key that signed the document are a valid key-pair. The software can tell if the keys are paired by trying to use the public key to decode the signature block generated by your private key (see Figure 11.4).

Figure 11.4:
Digital Signature
Verification

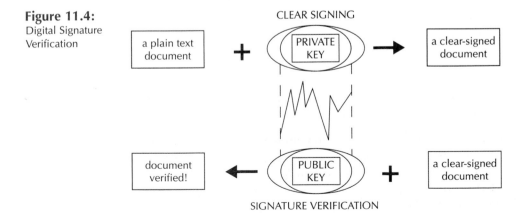

Digital signatures can be found on Web pages, in mailing list archives, and in Usenet newsgroups. People have been using an encryption program named PGP (Pretty Good Privacy) ever since it was first distributed online in 1991 (see Section 11.9.1). In Figure 11.5 we can see the encrypted PGP signature block at the bottom of a short plain-text document. A digital signature attached to a plain-text file is called a **clear signature**, and a document signed with a clear signature is called a **clear-signed document**. Digital signatures can also be added to encrypted documents, in which case the document is referred to as **encrypted and signed**.

Figure 11.5:
A Plain-Text Document Signed with PGP

```
-----BEGIN PGP SIGNED MESSAGE-----

5/12/97 voting results

Smith 27
Jones 23
Fox   16
Webb  12


-----BEGIN PGP SIGNATURE-----
Version: 2.6.2

iQBVAwUBM3en5sY2EipHoMxpAQGLXgH/ahfFSW/7uwBGHslozlDiLQWC23gNm2S7
B6kIusLnYH2v/BkIAKUu5+ULTLb3QBRMNmLC1DD3ld1FxslsYYuyHQ==
=p1dn
-----END PGP SIGNATURE-----
```

Notice how the process of generating and verifying a digital signature is similar to the process of encrypting and decrypting a file. Other people use your public key to encrypt a file for you, and then you use a private key to decrypt it. But for a digital signature, you use your private key to sign the file, and then other people can use your public key to verify the signature.

Digital signatures differ from handwritten ones in one very important way: A digital signature changes from document to document. Not only does a digital signature contain information about the person behind the signature, it also contains information about the document being signed. This makes it impossible to forge a digital signature by copying a signature from one document and inserting it into a different document. A transplanted digital signature cannot fit any document other than its original one.

Let's look more carefully at the example document in Figure 11.5. The body of the text that was present at the time of the signing is marked "BEGIN PGP SIGNED MESSAGE"; the digital signature appears at the end of the text body and is marked by the lines "BEGIN PGP SIGNATURE" and "END PGP SIGNATURE." If this clear-signed document went out via e-mail to 100 people, each of those recipients could (if they chose to) verify the authenticity of the message contents by running a PGP signature check on the document using PGP software and the author's public PGP key.

Let's see how someone on the receiving end could verify this message by checking the signature. Assume that the receiver already has a copy of the author's public PGP key. If the signed message resides in a file called comm.txt.asc, a single PGP command can check the signature and verify the message. We can see this verification process in Figure 11.6, which shows a trace of an old command-line version of PGP running on a UNIX platform.

Figure 11.6:
PGP Can Be Used to Verify Digital Signatures

```
el19:~/.pgp> pgp comm.txt.asc
No configuration file found.
Pretty Good Privacy (tm) 2.6.2 — Public-key encryption for the masses.
(c) 1990-1994 Philip Zimmermann, Phil's Pretty Good Software. 11 Oct 94
Uses the RSAREF (tm) Toolkit, which is copyright RSA Data Security, Inc.
Distributed by the Massachusetts Institute of Technology.
Export of this software may be restricted by the U.S. government.
Current time: 1997/05/12 23:32 GMT

File has signature. Public key is required to check signature. .
Good signature from user "Prof. Lehnert <lehnert@elux3.cs.umass.edu>".
Signature made 1997/05/12 23:30 GMT
```

PGP not only identifies the signature as legitimate, but also guarantees that the body of the message was not altered after the signing. Let's see what would happen if I edited comm.txt.asc and then tried to verify the altered document. I'll change the vote count for Smith from 27 to 20, changing nothing in the file but the 7 in 27. After that one minor edit, let's try to verify the document to see if everything is still ok. Figure 11.7 shows the resulting trace.

PGP warns us that the signature on this file does not match the file's contents. This tells us that the file we're looking at is not the file that the author signed. Clear signatures are a good way to make sure that information moves across the Internet untouched and unscathed. We do not need UNIX to run the PGP software. Point-

Figure 11.7:
Tampered Documents Won't Pass a Signature Verification Test

```
el19:~/.pgp> pgp comm.txt.asc
No configuration file found.
Pretty Good Privacy (tm) 2.6.2 — Public-key encryption for the masses.
(c) 1990-1994 Philip Zimmermann, Phil's Pretty Good Software. 11 Oct 94
Uses the RSAREF(tm) Toolkit, which is copyright RSA Data Security, Inc.
Distributed by the Massachusetts Institute of Technology.
Export of this software may be restricted by the U.S. government.
Current time: 1997/05/12 23:36 GMT

File has signature.  Public key is required to check signature. .
WARNING: Bad signature, doesn't match file contents!

Bad signature from user "Prof. Lehnert <lehnert@elux3.cs.umass.edu>".
Signature made 1997/05/12 23:30 GMT
```

and-click versions of PGP are also available for Windows and Macintosh computers. In these versions, the user selects "decrypt/verify" from a toolbar of PGP command options (see Figure 11.8). Then PGP asks the user which file to open (not shown), and locates the public key needed for that file (not shown). The results of the verification are recorded to a log report (see Figure 11.9). In this case, we verified a legitimate version of a file, and then we tampered with the contents of that file before attempting a second verification. The second verification fails.

Figure 11.8:
A PGP Toolbar

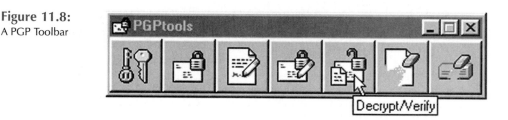

Note that a clear signature is created by one person with the expectation that anyone should be able to verify it. An encrypted document can be created by anyone with the expectation that only one person can read it. Clear-signed documents are like an inverse of encrypted documents. You use a private key to create a signature, and a public key to verify it. You use a public key to create an encrypted document, and a private key to decode it. Note that with RSA key-pairs, either key can be used to unravel an encoding created by the other key. It's just convenient to encode with one key (the public key) all the time and decode with the other (the private key)

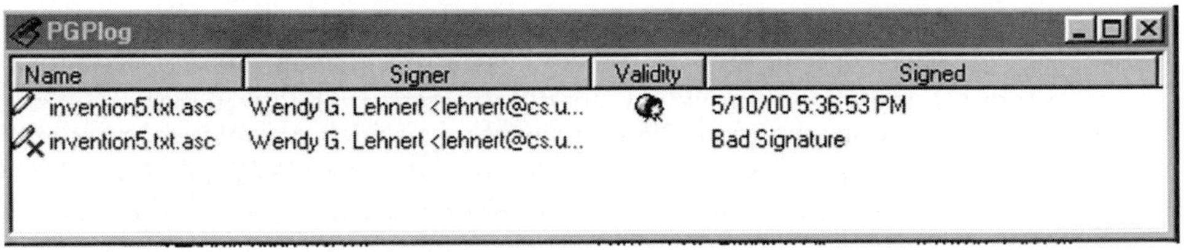

Figure 11.9:
A PGP Log File

because that makes the most sense. If the owner of the key-pair wanted to encode something with the private key, she could do that. Then anyone with the public key could decode it. But that scenario is a little silly: Why encrypt a document that could be decrypted by anyone? On the other hand, the duality of the key-pair is very handy when we want to add a digital signature to a document. Signature generation with the private key and signature verification with the public key is exactly what we want for public documents. This makes RSA an elegant solution to the dual demands of document encryption and digital signatures.

When I place a clear signature on a document, PGP asks me for a passphrase before it allows me to use my private key (see Figure 11.10). As long as I am the only person who knows my passphrase, my PGP signature is secure. No one else will be able to generate PGP signatures using my private key, even if they somehow get their hands on my private key. For maximal security, I could clear-sign a document and then encode it using my recipient's public key. Then my recipient would use her private key to decode the message and a copy of my public key to verify my signature. PGP makes it possible for my recipient to do all of this with a single command (see Figure 11.8). A communication that is both signed and encrypted using PGP is very secure.

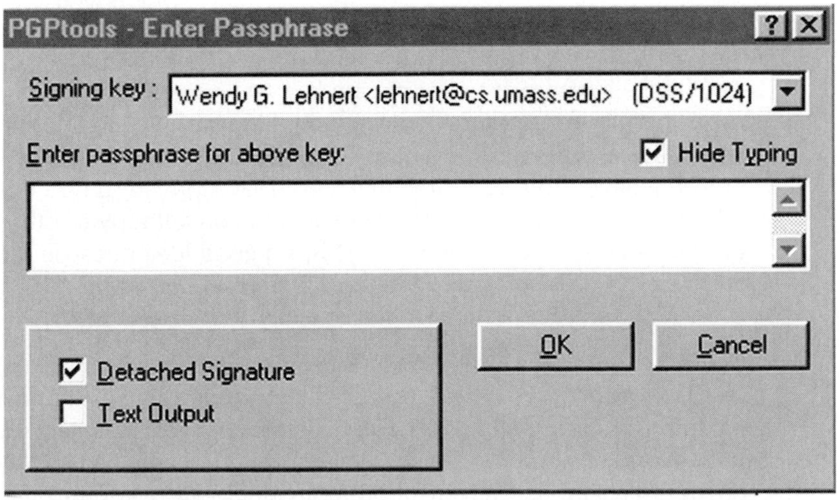

Figure 11.10:
Private Keys Are
Protected with
Passphrases

Clear signatures can't be copied and moved to different documents by someone who wants to forge a signature because each signature contains a profile of the document being signed. In this respect, digitally signed documents are even more secure than handwritten signatures, which are relatively easy to forge. In 2000, the Electronic Signatures in Global and National Commerce Act was signed into law, recognizing the crucial role of digital signatures in e-commerce, digital communications, and legal documents in a digital environment. Digital signatures may be implemented with the use of "smart cards" or other devices, but public-key encryption is always at the heart of the enterprise. Digital signatures can now be used for legal purposes, and will gradually become more commonplace as people begin to trust and accept the technology.

11.5   KEY MANAGEMENT

Public-key encryption makes it easier to keep a private key private, but safeguards must still be taken. If a private key is stored on a computer, care must be taken to protect that key if the computer's security is broken. If a private key were stolen, then encrypted documents intended for the owner of that key would be compromised, and digital signatures by the owner of that key could be forged. Although public-key encryption is generally safer than private-key encryption, the whole system still hinges on the security of the private keys.

What's to prevent someone from stealing your laptop computer and rooting around all your files in search of your private key? The simple answer is very simple: Private keys are password-protected. When you generate a key-pair for yourself, you are asked to enter a password—actually a passphrase. Then whenever you need to use your private key to decode a document or generate a digital signature, you will be asked to enter your passphrase. If you forget your passphrase, or don't know it (because the key isn't your key), you won't be able to use that private key.

Any hackers who want your private key will have to get past two hurdles: (1) they need the file that contains your private key, and (2) they need the passphrase for your private key. The problem of keeping your file secure is the same problem you face whenever you have anything sensitive or private on a computer (see Section 2.15.6). Some people store their private keys on a floppy or other removable media in case of an attack over the Net. This is a good idea because it does thwart hacker attacks, and a floppy can always be hidden in any number of unlikely places (or even stored in safe-deposit box for maximal security).

But let's assume for the moment that safeguards were not taken, and your private key has been appropriated by an unknown party. How hard is it to crack your passphrase? Once again, we can only hope that you have taken to heart the advice in Section 2.3 about password security. If you have never written your passphrase down anywhere and never told it to anyone, your passphrase will be very hard to crack. Brute-force attacks won't work on long passphrases because the number of possibilities is too large. However, someone could conceivably watch you at your computer and hope to see you type in your passphrase. This is why computers never echo back passwords when you enter them. But even if no one is standing over your shoulder to study your every keystroke, or bugging your work area with a video camera, a Trojan horse could be recording every key you type (including the ones for your passphrase) if someone were really out to get you. So good computer security is, once again, your best line of defense.

If all else fails, a wiley hacker might still hope to get your passphrase directly from your computer. After all, your passphrase must be stored on your computer so the encryption software can check your passphrase when you type it in. Of course the people who design encryption software have thought of this too. So when your encryption program stores your passphrase, the system is careful not to store your original passphrase at all. Instead, it stores a coded version of your passphrase. It uses a special type of code for this called a "hash code." A **hash code** is an encoding algorithm that converts an input string into a numerical signature for that string. (It's the same idea as a parity bit, but the possible output values are more complicated.) Then when you type in your passphrase, the same hash code is applied to what you've typed. If the resulting hash code matches the one stored in memory, your passphrase is accepted. If a hacker managed to steal the hash code for your passphrase, he would still be locked out because he won't be able to deduce the original password from the hash code for the password. Whenever passwords are stored on a computer, the actual passwords should never be stored directly: It is much safer to store only hash-codes for passwords.

In the end, the whole business relies on passphrase security, and everything that can be done to keep your passphrase secure is already being done for you by your software. All you have to do is keep your passphrase to yourself.

11.6 ▮ COUNTERFEIT KEYS

Public-key encryption has a lot going for it. We've seen how key-pairs make public-key encryption safer than private-key encryption. We've seen how digital signatures cannot be forged and signed documents are impervious to tampering as long as private keys are held securely. But there is still one soft spot in the system that needs to be addressed. What is to stop a hacker from generating a key-pair under your name and then intercepting messages intended for you using the bogus key-pair? How can we stop people from generating and using counterfeit keys?

This problem is called the *man-in-the-middle-attack* and you have to think like a criminal to grasp it. So let's pretend to be hackers for the sake of understanding the problem. Imagine for a moment that you have no scruples and you want to read John's e-mail. Intercepting John's e-mail is fairly easy for you if you know your way around computers, so while we're at it, let's pretend you also know all about packet sniffers. With a packet sniffer you could grab all of John's incoming mail before it ever gets to him. All you need is access to John's mail server or any of the hosts that feed mail to his mail server. You probably have to access one of these machines illegally, but that won't deter someone with criminal tendencies. So let's suppose you've got access to an appropriate host machine and you've got the software needed to intercept John's e-mail. If John's e-mail is not encrypted, you can read it, of course. But suppose the e-mail you want to read is encrypted with John's public key. Then you need to work a little harder.

It's probably too hard to break the code once a message has been encrypted, so you'll have to find a way to stop people from using John's public key in the first place. This might sound impossible, but this is where a devious imagination comes in handy. All you need to do is plant a counterfeit key wherever John's key has been posted for public consumption. For example, suppose John has posted his public key in a public directory. Then you have to break into that directory and replace John's public key with a counterfeit public key that is actually part of a key-pair that you own. Leaving aside the question of exactly how you might manage this, let's assume that you somehow manage to plant your counterfeit key under John's name in the key directory. Then anyone looking up John's key will have no way of knowing that a counterfeit key has been substituted for his legitimate key. Hang on to a copy of John's real public key—you'll need it later.

Now suppose someone decides to send John an encoded message. They (and/or their mail client) look up John in the key directory and unknowingly grab a copy of the counterfeit key. They use the counterfeit key to encode a message, and then they mail the message to John. You are intercepting all of John's incoming e-mail, so you get this message before it reaches John. Since you have the private key that decodes messages encoded by the counterfeit key, you can decode the message and see what it says. If that's all you care about, then you're done.

But chances are you really want to monitor a steady stream of incoming mail, and you know John is going to become suspicious if he gets no mail for one or two days. You need to make sure John thinks everything is normal. In particular, you have to ensure John gets all of his mail. You can do this. You take the decoded message that was intended for John and encode it using John's real public key (this is why you saved a copy of that key). Now all you have to do is send the newly encoded message on to John, with a forged e-mail header so that it looks like it came from the original sender. When John finally receives the message, he will decode it with his private key, and everything will appear to be as it should. John won't have a clue that his e-mail has been tampered with. Figure 11.11 illustrates how all this is done.

You can now monitor all of John's incoming e-mail and never cause any suspicion. Once the packet sniffer has been set up and the counterfeit key has been planted, everything else you need to do can be totally automated so that no significant delays slow down the delivery of John's incoming mail. John will have no way of knowing

Figure 11.11
A Counterfeit Public
Key Can
Compromise
Encrypted E-mail

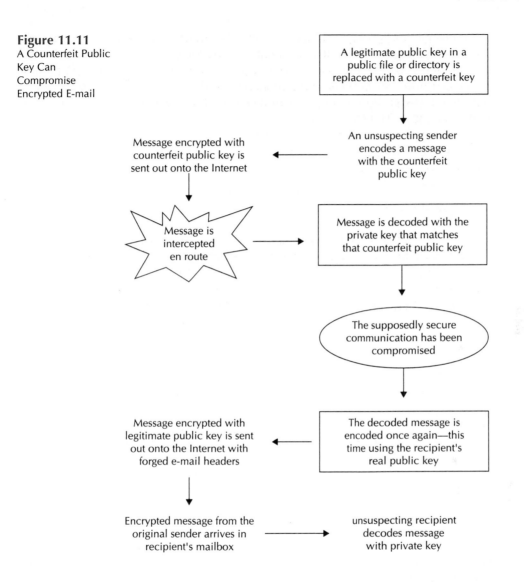

that his privacy has been violated unless he realizes that the key in the public directory has been altered. In the meantime, you are getting a copy of everything that John gets at the same time he gets it (although you could program a little delay into John's mail stream if it's important to know about something before John knows about it).

The interception of encrypted e-mail is no small undertaking. It requires technical expertise as well as a willingness to break a host of state and federal laws. So the scenario described here is highly unlikely. But it can happen. If secure communications are crucial to the operation of a business or a military operation, there can be no room for sabotage. Organizations like CERT (originally named for the Computer Emergency Response Team) that monitor computer viruses and other security threats on the Internet require reliable communication channels in order to minimize misinformation and disinformation. CERT uses PGP for secure communications and places its digital signature on all official announcements, warnings, and alerts (see Figure 11.12).

Figure 11.12:
CERT is a Target for Counterfeit Keys

```
Our PGP Key Has Changed

On October 4, 1999, the PGP key for the CERT/CC was replaced with a
new PGP key.  For information about using PGP to communicate with us,
please see our page about sending sensitive information.

WARNING! There is a forged CERT PGP key. Be sure to validate keys.
```

The solution to this problem lies in the integrity of the public keys. All public keys must be subject to careful scrutiny. You need to know who really owns all of these keys. If the actual owner of a public key cannot be determined with a high degree of reliability, that key may be a security hazard and should not be used.

The process of identifying a person as the legitimate owner of a public key is called *key authentication*. A lot of thought has gone into this process. Different levels of authentication have been identified, ranging from risky (unprotected) digital distributions to highly secure distributions made at public meetings in the presence of colleagues and associates who are willing to vouch for the identity of anyone distributing a public key. Many rituals have been proposed for secure key exchanges (see Section 11.7).

Key authentication is a special case of a more general problem related to the concept of signatures. When you pen a written signature on paper, your signature should be recognizable to at least those correspondents who know you well enough to know your signature. Your written signature is actually quite useless in the hands of someone who has never seen you sign anything in person. How could anyone know if the signature before them is really yours without having seen the genuine article? It is an imperfect system, but it does offer some degree of security, at least among friends. If more security is needed, you can sign papers in the presence of a notary public, who stamps the paper with a unique impression and signs off on the document as a trusted agent. The notary public's signed stamp tells the world that whoever signed this document at least had a copy of something that looked like a

legitimate driver's license complete with an ID photograph when they presented the document to be notarized. This is a good system, as long as no one steals the notary's stamp or tricks the notary with a false ID. Most reasonable systems can be breached if someone really wants to.

When someone accepts a public key and uses it for encoding a message, they need to understand the level of risk associated with that key. If the level of risk is too great, the key shouldn't be used. Each person should decide individually how much risk is acceptable. As we will see in the next section, steps have been taken to make that decision as easy as possible for the general public.

11.7 KEY CERTIFICATION

In the previous section we explained how counterfeit keys could be used to break a seemingly secure communication channel if people are too quick to trust the public keys available to them. A system of key authentication is needed to help people decide how much risk is associated with any given public key. Let's start by imagining the safest key authentication possible. Suppose you want to use a public key that belongs to your best friend. You friend hands you a floppy disk with a public key on it and says "Here. This is my public key." One can imagine your friend making a mistake or having his floppies switched on him by a malicious elf, but if you trust your friend at his word, this key transfer is as secure as it gets. You can take the floppy, add it to the virtual key-ring on your computer and feel confident that this is a legitimate public key. If everyone could collect all of their public keys this way, the world would be a very safe place. In fact, PGP keys used to be traded in just this way, between friends in person. If your world is relatively small and you never need to communicate with anyone outside of a close circle of friends, this is a good system.

Now let's extend this world beyond a close circle of friends to a world that includes friends of friends. Suppose you want a key for someone you don't know but who is a friend of your best friend. Suppose your best friend handed you a floppy and said, "Here. This is George's public key." Chances are you would feel pretty safe about it. You are one step away from getting the key from George directly, but your best friend is the step in the middle, and you trust your best friend to give you a legitimate public key for George. In the jargon of key authentication, we would say that George's public key was *certified* for you by your best friend. If you trust your best friend to give you a legitimate key, this certification is quite trustworthy. It may not be quite as good as getting the key from George directly, but it's still pretty good.

Key **certification** refers to a process through which someone can vouch for the legitimacy of a public key.

When a key is certified by a trusted friend, that person can add their digital signature to the public key being certified. Then if the key is sent to you over the Net, you can

verify the digital signature and feel confident that the certification is legitimate. Public keys can be certified by anyone who uses them. That way, if you receive a public key for someone you don't know, you could look at all the key certifications and see if anyone you trust has certified the key. If a trustworthy certification can be found (and verified), you can feel safe about the key. If no trusted friends have certified the key, the key is a security risk.

The model for key certification based on friends and friends of friends is called a **web of trust**. Public keys get passed along from friend to friend, accumulating certifications as they go. When you receive a key you can assess the certifications on that key and make a decision for yourself about the authenticity of the key based on whom you know and how well you trust them. The web-of-trust model works well in small worlds or highly interconnected worlds. But what if you receive a public key for someone you don't know? There are no trusted certifications on the key, and you really need to determine the authenticity of the key as quickly as possible. That's where digital fingerprints come in.

A **digital fingerprint** for a key-pair is a unique sequence of integers associated with that key-pair. Digital fingerprints are generated when a key-pair is created, based on random conditions that cannot be manipulated by the key's owner (much like a biological fingerprint). The fingerprint is built into the key and cannot be tampered with (using digital signatures). If a key owner knows the fingerprint for their key-pair, then you can check a key's authenticity by contacting the (alleged) owner and asking him or her for the key's fingerprint. Fingerprints for public keys can be confirmed with a phone call, which is a safe and convenient substitute for handing off floppy disks in person. So even if a key is not certified by anyone, you can still trust it by confirming its fingerprint. If you were to accept a key's authenticity based on its fingerprint, then you might also choose to certify it yourself in order to start a web of trust for that particular key.

PGP relies on the web of trust, key certifications, and fingerprints to help people assess the authenticity of public keys. Whenever you add a public key to your public key-ring, you need to guard against counterfeit keys. So PGP asks a lot of questions whenever you add a new key to your key-ring. Following is a trace of PGP accepting a new public key. For this example, assume that Lee Cunningham has acquired a public key for Ann Rodak and stored that key in a file named arodak.key.pgp. The key may have come from a public directory or an e-mail message sent (supposedly) by Ann herself. Here is what happens when Lee adds this new key to his key-ring:

```
el18:~> pgp -ka arodak.key.pgp
No configuration file found.
Pretty Good Privacy(tm) 2.6.2 - Public-key encryption for the masses.
(c) 1990-1994 Philip Zimmermann, Phil's Pretty Good Software. 11 Oct 94
Uses the RSAREF(tm) Toolkit, which is copyright RSA Data Security, Inc.
Distributed by the Massachusetts Institute of Technology.
Export of this software may be restricted by the U.S. government.
Current time: 1997/05/16 13:02 GMT
Looking for new keys...
pub 512/80B7AF61 1996/12/03 Ann Rodak <arodak@edlab.cs.umass.edu>
Checking signatures...
...
Keyfile contains:
1 new key(s)
One or more of the new keys are not fully certified.
Do you want to certify any of these keys yourself (y/N)? y
Key for user ID: Ann Rodak <arodak@edlab.cs.umass.edu>
512-bit key, Key ID 80B7AF61, created 1996/12/03
Key fingerprint = 38 57 B7 43 D8 46 FB 33 76 44 13 11 CE 72 FA A0
This key/userID association is not certified.
```

At this point Lee could call Ann on the phone and verify the key's fingerprint in order to make sure this is a valid key. A counterfeit key won't have the same fingerprint as Ann's real key. If Lee doesn't want to go to that much trouble, he can just accept the key and take his chances:

```
Do you want to certify this key yourself (y/N)? y
Looking for key for user 'Ann Rodak':
Key for user ID: Ann Rodak <arodak@edlab.cs.umass.edu>
512-bit key, Key ID 80B7AF61, created 1996/12/03
Key fingerprint = 38 57 B7 43 D8 46 FB 33 76 44 13 11 CE 72 FA A0
READ CAREFULLY: Based on your own direct first-hand knowledge, are
you absolutely certain that you are prepared to solemnly certify that
the above public key actually belongs to the user specified by the
above user ID (y/N)? y
```

When Lee answers yes, he is indicating his willingness to certify this key and put his own PGP signature on it. Lee's signature has now been added to this copy of Ann's key and will be there if Lee ever passes the key to someone else. Lee should think carefully before putting his signature on the key. His good reputation as a trustworthy key certifier is on the line here. If he has any doubts about the key, he should not certify it. (He can still use it if he feels confident enough about the key for his own purposes.) Whenever you are asked to certify a key, you are being asked to act like a notary public and take that responsibility very seriously. If people certify public keys too casually, the web of trust breaks apart.

In this scenario, Lee says that he is willing to certify Ann's key. That means he is going to place his digital signature on the key. He is "signing off" on the validity of the key.

```
You need a pass phrase to unlock your RSA secret key.
Key for user ID "Lee Cunningham <lcunning@elux3.cs.umass.edu>"
```

Lee's private PGP key is used to generate Lee's signature. So Lee needs to enter his password or phrase before his signature can go on the key:

```
Enter passphrase: Passphrase is good. Just a moment....
Key signature certificate added.
Make a determination in your own mind whether this key actually
belongs to the person whom you think it belongs to, based on available
evidence. If you think it does, then based on your estimate of
that person's integrity and competence in key management, answer
the following question:
Would you trust "Ann Rodak"
to act as an introducer and certify other people's public keys to you?
(1=I don't know. 2=No. 3=Usually. 4=Yes, always.) ? 1
```

Now Lee has to decide how meaningful Ann's signature is when it appears on other public keys. If Lee ever acquires another public key signed by Ann, PGP will check to see if Lee considers Ann a trustworthy key certifier and then remind him about how he answered this question when he certified her key.

All this care is taken because key integrity and the web of trust is a potential weak spot in PGP. As long as all the public keys that we use are valid, PGP keys will be impossible to crack. If a security failure ever occurs, it is likely to happen as a breach in key authentication.

When you view the contents of a key ring, you can see all of the signatures associated with each key and the level of security that applies to each signature (in the opinion of the key-ring owner):

```
el18:~> pgp -kc
No configuration file found.
Pretty Good Privacy(tm) 2.6.2 - Public-key encryption for the masses.
(c) 1990-1994 Philip Zimmermann, Phil's Pretty Good Software. 11 Oct 94
Uses the RSAREF(tm) Toolkit, which is copyright RSA Data Security, Inc.
Distributed by the Massachusetts Institute of Technology.
Export of this software may be restricted by the U.S. government.
Current time: 1997/05/16 13:05 GMT
Key ring: '/users/users3/fac/lehnert/.pgp/pubring.pgp'
Type    bits/keyID    Date         User ID
pub     512/80B7AF61  1996/12/03   Ann Rodak <arodak@edlab.cs.umass.edu>
sig! C2309975 1997/05/16 Lee Cunningham <lcunning@elux3.cs.umass.edu>
pub 768/C2309975 1997/05/16 Lee Cunningham <lcunning@elux3.cs.umass.edu>
 KeyID       Trust      Validity   User ID
 80B7AF61    unknown    complete   Ann Rodak <arodak@edlab.cs.umass.edu>
c                       ultimate   Lee Cunningham <lcunning@elux3.cs.umass.edu>
* C2309975  ultimate   complete   Lee Cunningham <lcunning@elux3.cs.umass.edu>
```

An ultimate level of trust is given to any keys signed by the owner of the key ring.

The Web of Trust Is Delicate

Never certify a PGP key unless you are absolutely confident that the key is valid. If you transfer your copy of the key with your signature validating the key, your reputation for credibility automatically goes with it. A PGP key that passes through many hands can accumulate a number of signatures with different authentication values. Each new user can examine the available signatures and decide whether the key seems to be a good risk. One trusted certification that is not based on proper precautions can sink the whole system.

The web-of-trust model is used successfully by communities of people who sign each other's keys with due care. Unfortunately, this model does not scale well when we need a web of trust for millions of Internet users who want to conduct safe e-commerce transactions with trusted keys. All you need is one counterfeit key with trusted certifications on it and the whole system falls apart. As the Internet evolved into a foundation for a global economy, a new system for key authentication was created, and the web of trust became institutionalized through the use of "trusted agents" or "certification authorities." We will explain this model in the next section.

11.8 ▌ DIGITAL CERTIFICATES

The problem of key authentication had to be solved before public-key encryption could be used for e-commerce on the Internet. Without a system for certifying valid public keys, counterfeit Web pages could masquerade as legitimate e-stores and dupe visitors into placing credit-card orders with bogus operations. It was not enough to add encryption to the Web. Digital signatures also had to be used in order to validate the identity of any operation collecting credit-card orders.

A *digital certificate* is a digital signature attached to a public key, just like the digital signatures that are attached to a public key in the web-of-trust model. The purpose of the certificate is to reassure users that the public key they are about to accept is an authentic key and not a counterfeit key. But now we will use the **certification-authority (CA)** model of key authentication, instead of the web-of-trust model. In the CA model, there are only a few trusted institutions who can generate digital certificates, and any key carrying a certificate generated by a trusted CA can be immediately trusted without question. All the user has to do is decide which CAs can be trusted.

If you have ever placed a credit-card order on the Web, your browser was probably checking server certificates for you and you never even knew it. That's because your Web browser already has a list of trusted CAs built into it, and it will accept any public key certified by a recognized CA. You can intervene in this process if you wish, but most people just want to be reassured that everything is under control. If you want to see the CAs recognized by your browser, however, you'll have to hunt around under the security settings. In Netscape Communicator, go to the Communicator menu, click on Tools, click on Security Info, then look at the pop-up window and Follow the navigation menu on the left to Certificates/Signers. You'll see a list of CAs that looks something like the one in Figure 11.13. Internet Explorer has a similar list of CAs that you can examine.

In the context of the Web, you are sending sensitive information to the Web server, so we only need to encrypt data going from your browser to the Web server. That's fine, because a secure Web page will offer your browser a public key that it can use to encrypt the data. But your browser is going to be careful about using any public

Figure 11.13:
A List of CAs
Recognized by
Netscape
Communicator

Certificate Signers' Certificates

Security Info

Passwords

Navigator

Messenger

Java/JavaScript

Certificates

  Yours

  People

  Web Sites

  Signers

Cryptographic
Modules

These certificates identify the certificate signers that you accept:

Thawte Personal Freemail CA
Thawte Personal Premium CA
Thawte Premium Server CA
Thawte Server CA
Uptime Group Plc. Class 1 CA
Uptime Group Plc. Class 2 CA
Uptime Group Plc. Class 3 CA
Uptime Group Plc. Class 4 CA
VeriSign Class 1 Primary CA
VeriSign Class 2 Primary CA
VeriSign Class 3 Primary CA
VeriSign Class 4 Primary CA
Verisign/RSA Commercial CA
Verisign/RSA Secure Server CA

Edit

Verify

Delete

OK   Cancel   Help

keys it finds on the Web. Your browser will examine the key and look for a certificate from one of its trusted CAs. Figure 11.14 shows the security information window in Netscape Communicator that will take you to a view of the public key associated with a secure Web page at amazon.com. If the amazon.com server presents a certificate from a recognized CA, then communication can commence. In Figure 11.14 we can see the public key from the amazon.com server, and we can also see that this key was certified by RSA's Secure Server CA. If we check the list of recognized CAs in Figure 11.13, we can see an entry for "VeriSign/RSA Secure Server CA." This means that the browser recognizes the CA who signed the public key, and it will therefore accept this key as an authentic public key for amazon.com. If this certificate had not been recognized or was somehow inconsistent with the server under consideration, your browser would notify you of a problem. You will probably have to do a lot of online shopping before you are likely to see any such notification. Most of the time, the certificate checks out, your browser accepts the public key, and you can send encrypted data on to the approved server with confidence. It's reassuring to know that all this work is going on inside your browser to keep your credit-card transactions secure.

Casual users will normally never need to see the CAs in Figure 11.13. But it's there in case you ever have reason to remove a trusted CA. (Make sure you have a good reason before you do this. It will limit the number of e-commerce sites you can interact with). If you add a new CA to the list, again, be careful. Make sure you know what you are doing before you decide to trust a new CA.

Figure 11.14:
Your Browser will
Show You Any
Public Key It Is
Considering

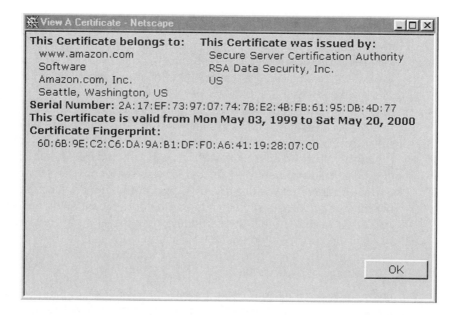

Is My Credit Card Number Safe on the Internet?

Chances are your credit card may be safer in transit than it is once it reaches its final destination. If 128-bit encryption is used to move your credit-card information across the Net and nothing goes out without a trusted CA check, that transmission is safer than any other available mode of communication. If your credit card is stolen online, it will probably be the result of a security breach on site. For example, the database that stores customer information might not have been adequately secured against security breaks and cyber theft. It is impossible to know which sites are handling their in-house security correctly and which are not. In general, a large, established operation should have the resources to maintain good computer security on site. Smaller businesses and start-ups may not have the resources to take care of computer security correctly. It is not really possible to assess all the risks associated with e-commerce transactions because you can't know what's going on inside an e-store operation. But keep one thing in mind: Traditional credit-card transactions off of the Net are far from 100% safe either. If you feel safe placing a credit-card order over the phone or if you allow store clerks to discard your credit-card carbons without tearing them up in front of you, then you have no reason to worry about credit card transactions over the Internet. There is some amount of risk in all of these scenarios, but most of us live with a reasonable level of risk as a fact of modern life.

11.9 STRONG AND WEAK ENCRYPTION

When people worry about whether they can trust encryption, they generally are concerned about how hard it is to break the code. If someone can crack the code that's being used to protect credit cards online, that's a catastrophic failure. We know that 40-bit keys can be broken, and broken by run-of-the-mill personal computers in a matter of minutes. The amount of time needed to crack a code is important. Any key that can stand up to thousands of years of computing time on the world's fastest computers is safe enough. The term **strong encryption** refers to encryption methods that are safe in this practical sense. A code that can be broken in a practical time frame is called **weak encryption**.

Anything that can be done using a large number of conventional computers over a period of weeks or months will be reproducible using special-purpose hardware within a period of minutes or hours, so the question of practical time frames should always be approached by asking what could be done with a special-purpose computer? A casual hacker with a $3,000 PC is in no position to pick off credit-card numbers encoded with 56-bit keys. But if someone starts to sell black market "black boxes" designed to crack 56-bit keys, then any transaction relying on 56-bit keys are in trouble.

Strong encryption steadily becomes weaker over time. According to Moore's law, computer processors double in speed every 18 months. Each time a processor doubles in speed, it can take on one more bit in an encryption key and break the key in the same amount of time. 56-bit encryption was cracked in 1999, so according to Moore's law, 64-bit encryption will be weak by the year 2011 and 128-bit encryption will be weak by 2107. It is, of course, impossible to predict these milestones with any real confidence. Moore's law might stop working, or a dramatic breakthrough in microchip technologies could change everything. It is simply impossible to say anything about the limitations of future computer technologies with any real certainty.

Although much is made of the line between weak and strong encryption, security breeches are rarely the fault of inadequate technologies. More often, the most exploitable link in the chain is a weak link due to human error. Someone failed to secure a database correctly, or failed to monitor ongoing network activities, or neglected to secure a backup file, or failed to do some other task. You can learn all you want about weak and strong encryption in an effort to reassure yourself about the relative merits of 64-bit or 128-bit encryption, but security will still be at the mercy of humans in the loop. If they all do their jobs correctly, the system will work. But if there is a slip-up anywhere along the line, that's when disaster can occur.

Things to Remember

- Public-key encryption is safer than private-key encryption.
- Public keys are used to encrypt and private keys are used to decrypt.
- Private keys are used to create digital signatures; public keys are used to verify digital signatures.
- 64-bit keys may not be very secure in a few years. 128-bit keys are very secure and will remain secure for quite some time.
- Strong encryption becomes weaker over time.
- Never certify a public key unless you are absolutely sure the key is authentic. The web of trust depends on cautious key certification.
- A certification authority can be trusted to authenticate public keys for e-commerce.
- Your browser does not accept any public keys for encrypted communications unless the key has been certified by a recognized certification authority.
- Digital signatures are safer than traditional signatures if a reliable model of key authentication is in place and people are careful to validate the signatures.

Important Concepts

certificate authority (CA)—a trusted agent who certifies public keys for general use (typically a corporation or a bank).

counterfeit key—a public key that does not belong to who it says it belongs to.

digital signature—an encoding of a document with a private key to preserve document integrity and document ownership.

document integrity—in the context of document transfers, this refers to the original form of the document, free from subsequent alterations during transit.

encrypted document (via private-key encryption)—an encoding of a document with a private key that can be decoded only with that same private key.

encrypted document (via public-key encryption)—an encoding of a document with a public key which can be decoded only with a private key.

key authentication—the general process of verifying the owner of a public key.

key certification—the process of placing a digital signature on a public key in order to vouch for its authenticity (a form of key authentication).

private-key encryption—an encryption strategy based on a single key.

public-key encryption—an encryption strategy based on a pair of keys.

strong encryption—encryption that cannot be cracked by brute-force means within a reasonable period of time.

weak encryption—encryption that can be cracked by brute-force means within a reasonable period of time.

web of trust—a key-authentication model based on key certification by friends and friends of friends.

Where Can I Learn More?

Public Key Encryption for Dummies

http://www.nwfusion.com/news/64452_05-17-1999.html

Basic Crytography in a Nutshell

http://www.itsc.state.md.us/info/InternetSecurity/Crypto/
    CryptoIntro.html

Hacking Lexicon

http://www.robertgraham.com/pubs/hacking-dict.html

Crypto-Gram Newsletter

http://www.counterpane.com/crypto-gram.html

The Metaphor Is the Key: Cryptography, the Clipper Chip, and the Constitution

http://www-swiss.ai.mit.edu/6095/articles/
    froomkin-metaphor/text.html

Problems and Exercises

1. Explain the difference between private-key and public-key encryption. Is one better than the other? Explain your answer.

2. What does it mean to crack a key by brute force? Explain the process and why it can take a long time.

3. If you want to send me an encrypted message, do you need your own key-pair? Do you use my public key or your own private key?

4. If you want to place a digital signature on a document meant for me, do you need your own key-pair? Do you use my public key or your own private key?

5. If you want to verify a digital signature on a document from me, do you need your own key-pair? Do you use my public key or your own private key?

6. If you want to certify my public key by adding your own digital signature to my key, do you need your own key-pair? Do you use my public key or your own private key?

7. Describe a method of key authentication that does not rely on certificate authorities.

8. Explain how hash codes are used to protect passwords and passphrases.

9. Explain how a man-in-the-middle attack works. Is it possible to set up one of these attacks without breaking the law?

10. Explain how people use digital fingerprints in connection with public keys. When are they useful?

11. 40-bit keys were first cracked in 1995. Given this fact and Moore's law, when would you have predicted 56-bit keys to be first cracked? Does your prediction appear to be on target? Can you draw any conclusions about encryption predictions from this exercise?

12. Explain how the web of trust works to solve the problem of key authentication.

13. What is a certification authority (CA)? Explain why a system of CAs is better than the web of trust for e-commerce. When is the web of trust still a useful model of key authentication?

14. If your credit card information is stolen on the Net, is it likely to be because someone broke a weak encryption code, or for some other reason? Explain your answer.

15. Suppose your browser rejects a digital certificate found on a Web server, but the same certificate is accepted on your friend's computer. Suppose you are both running the exact same browser (same version, same platform). What could explain this difference?

16. What is the difference between weak encryption and strong encryption? Why does the dividing line between them change over time? Where is the line being drawn today? (Note: You may have to research this question on the Web to see if the information given in this chapter is outdated.)

17. [**Find It Online**] Visit `http://www.netsurf.com/nsf/v01/03/nsf.01.03.html` and find out what steganography is. Is this technique better suited to military applications or e-commerce? Explain your reasoning.

18. [**Find It Online**] Companies periodically announce a "crypto challenge," complete with a prize for the winner, in order to see how long it takes the public sector to break a key of a certain length. Look to see if there is an outstanding crypto challenge going on right now. If so, describe who is sponsoring it, how long it has been running, and the length of the key to be cracked.

19. [**Find It Online**] Visit a secure Web site and examine the digital certificate for that site. If you have a Web-based e-mail account, use the server that handles your mail. If you have an e-store that you frequent, use their server. List the URL of the secure server, the owner of the server's certificate, the CA who issued the certificate, the certificate's expiration date, and its fingerprint.

20. [**Find It Online**] DES is a 56-bit private key encryption system used extensively by government and business. It was first cracked in 1997 by the DESCHALL project. Visit `http://www.interhack.net/pubs/des-key-crack/` and find out how many computers were used by DESCHALL. How long did it take them to crack the key? How many keys could be tested by a 200 MHz Pentium system in one second?

Encryption and the Internet: Above and Beyond

Pretty Good Privacy (PGP)

The most popular implementation of public key encryption is **Pretty Good Privacy (PGP)**. PGP is freeware for noncommercial use, and is significant as a "grassroots" technology. The story behind PGP is very interesting and might even make a good movie. But in this section, we will focus on the software itself. Earlier in this chapter, we saw some traces of PGP operating in a command-mode environment (on a UNIX platform). In this section we will see what PGP looks like in a point-and-click environment (Windows). PGP is also available for the Mac, where it looks very much like the Windows version. If you are not interested in installing PGP or running it on your own computer, you can skip this section.

Encrypted messages can be rendered in plain text for transport via e-mail or Usenet (see Figure 11.15). Once an encoded document has been saved to a file, PGP can apply the appropriate private key to the file in order to decode it.

Figure 11.15:
An Encoded Message Using PGP

```
-----BEGIN PGP MESSAGE-----
Version: 2.6.2

hEwD8136i4LX0zkBAf4q261Umb4Wgx8758C2r14EsQUA3fQLoc3CQEYprweaQP3N
JpguCEvhf+lVxzTok8NdiU+SENMfzOxk5U6GbeW0pgAAAN3Oa1zKWvoXIPWid6rz
+pn4KqY0Q+s4kNSDXZPWSn26Y/iG77MxIYwcxmt/uwe+FqB99avYcPN6rJkUZMvc
OjuBlVKNTTXdJQoHl49rE8Ylu9603pFslmv7QHG27i7Yew/oj9VXnwaCOsjnjwwG
BAdLLJgQ5hGMYPKDMfbcFIFP04ftGCP94UdsqiY4UNs7ImL2y5yLJ+EOIz6xxbri
We2uWNGj63Ka3BgdNnwO5bT1ZDxF0p55RaDiHGzl4BU2lhF0LJ5bumga6U23j5O
Ex+nw/+Qula6+gWblFefjA==
=6d5D
-----END OF PGP MESSAGE-----
```

Anyone can download PGP from the Web and generate a key-pair (see `http://web.mit.edu/network/pgp.html` for download links). PGP downloads come with executable installers and are very easy to install on both PCs and Macs. Once you have installed the software, you can execute a program named PGPkeys and create your own key-pair (see Figure 11.16).

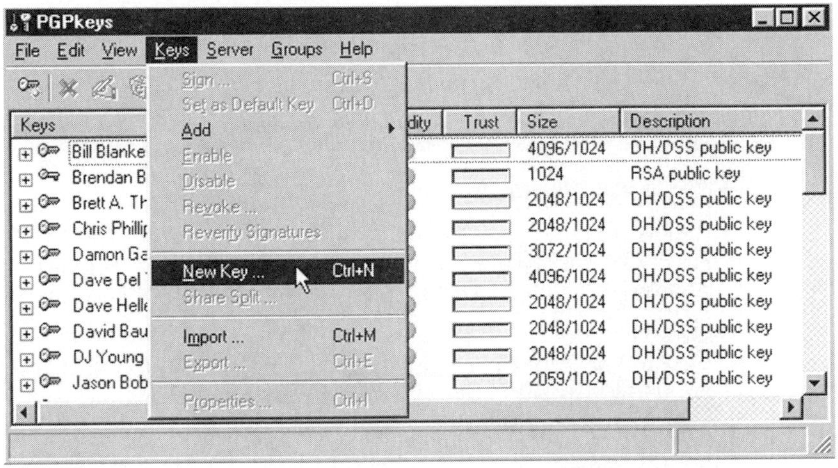

Figure 11.16:
The "New Key"
Command Adds a
New Key-Pair to
Your Virtual Key-
Ring

The key generation process requires you to answer some simple questions, such as who you are and what e-mail address you want associated with this key. Answer these questions carefully. You probably only want to generate one key-pair to keep life simple. It is best to choose an e-mail address for a POP or IMAP account rather than a Web account. If you decide to hook PGP up with your mail client (a very nice feature), the e-mail address on your key will have to match the address used by your send mail server (see Figure 11.17).

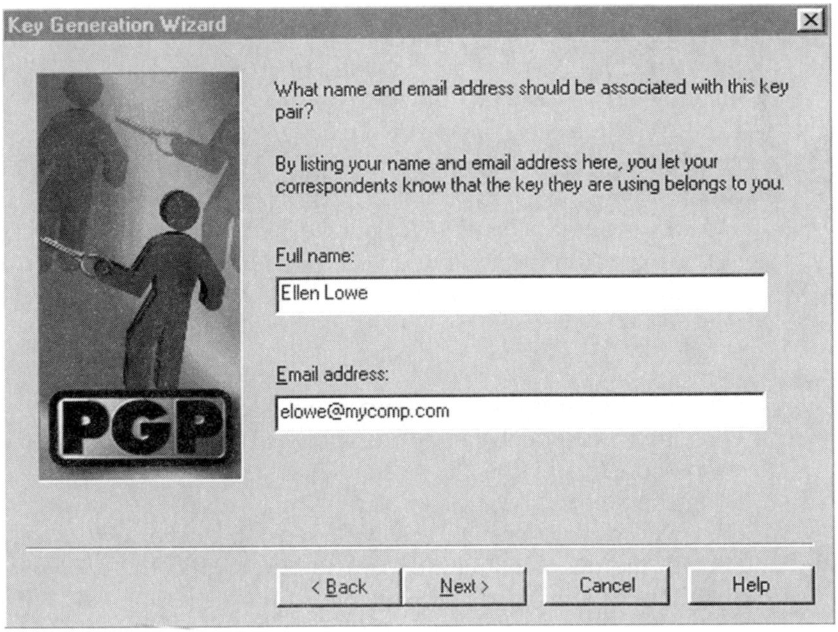

Figure 11.17:
Enter an E-mail
Address That
Friends and
Associates Will
Recognize

If you aren't sure how to answer a technical question, just take the installer's recommendation (see Figure 11.18).

PGP will give you choice of key sizes (see Figure 11.19). Note that there are actually two keys in each choice, a Diffie-Hellman key and a DSS key. (Although it's not given here in its entirety, the first choice is really called 1024 Diffie-Hellman/1024 DSS). Why are there two keys? Diffie-Hellman produces a key-pair for public-key encryption. DSS produces a second private key for a private-key encryption algorithm. When PGP encrypts a document, it speeds things up by using this second private key in conjunction with public-key encryption. The private DSS key is called a *session key*. You might have to read the next paragraph two or three times in order to understand session keys, but the idea is not too complicated—once you get it.

A **session key** is a private-key encryption key that is used in conjunction with public-key encryption for the sake of making document encoding and decoding more efficient. The session key is not a fixed key—a new one is generated for each encrypted document (hence the name). Each session key is only good for one encryption. In addition, the session key is a private key for some private-key encryption scheme (in this case, an algorithm called DSS). First we create a session key, then we use it to encrypt the document. We never use public-key encryption to encrypt the document at all. We use only public-key encryption (in this case, an algorithm called Diffie-Hellman) to encrypt the session key. When all this encoding is done, we package the two items together (the encrypted session key and the encrypted document) and send them off. When the recipient of the package wants to decode the message, PGP must use a private key to decode the session key. (Recall that the session key was encoded using public-key encryption.) Then, once the session key is decoded, PGP then uses that key and DSS to decode the original document. (Recall that the document was encrypted with the session key.)

Figure 11.19:
You Have a Choice of Security Levels

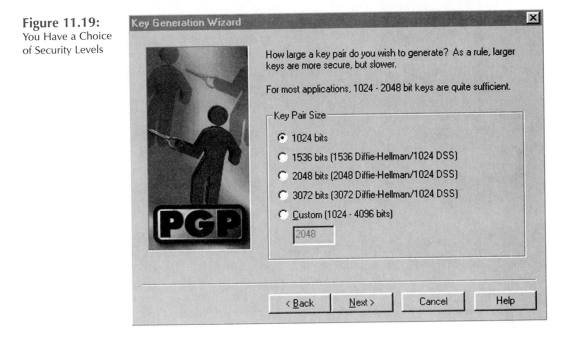

Why go through all the extra work of a session key? The session key is used for the sake of keeping things reasonably fast. Public-key encryption algorithms tend to run about 1,000 times slower than private-key encryption algorithms. So if we use public-key encryption sparingly (for just the session key), we can still ensure the safety of the message without slowing things down too much. Of course, we want to pick a session key that's large enough to be unbreakable. But that's why PGP gives us only 1,024-bit DSS keys in our list of choices (see Figure 11.19). A 1,024-bit DSS key is more than adequate. Now the only question remaining is how strong the encryption of the session key should be. It makes sense to pick a key that is at least as complex as the DSS key, but does it matter if we choose 1,024, 1,536, 2,048, 3,072 or more? The larger keys are more secure, but they will also slow you down a little each time you need to encrypt or decrypt something. So you have to decide how to balance security against time. Most users opt for a 1,024-bit Diffie-Hellman key.

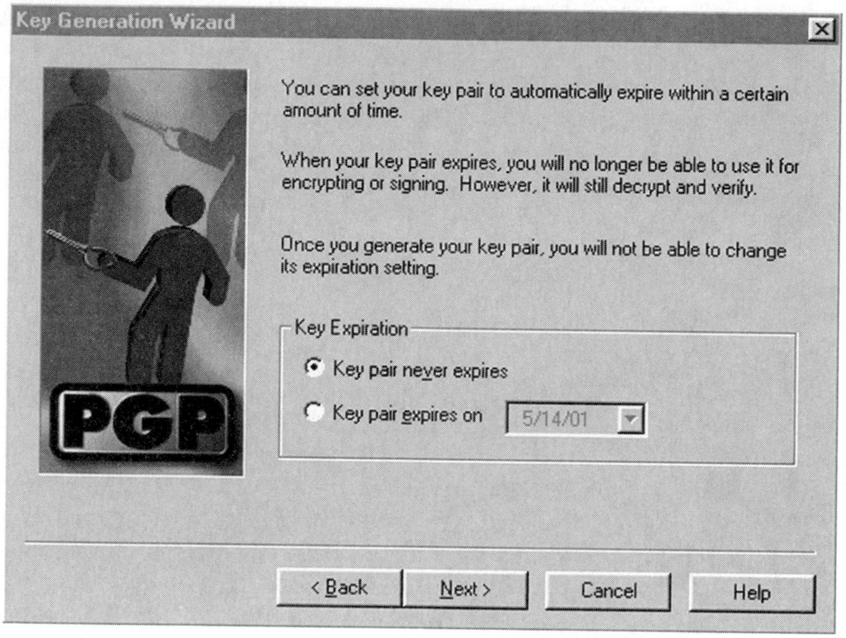

Figure 11.20:
You Can Decide if
You Want an
Expiration Date

Next, you'll be asked about an expiration date for your key (see Figure 11.20). If you examine the keys used for e-commerce, you'll see that they tend to expire after a month or a year. Expiration dates are an extra security measure. If you replace your public key once a month, you'll be protected against any special-purpose cracking computers that might be able to crack your key—for a few months of computation. If this key is not being used for financial transactions, you can skip the expiration date.

Finally, you are asked to enter a passphrase for your key-pair (see Figure 11.21). Pick one you can remember, and don't make it too short. 25 to 30 characters is a good length. Be careful to remember your passphrase after you enter it. If you forget it, it cannot be recovered, and this key-pair will have to be revoked.

You will have to wait a little while for your key-pair to be generated (see Figure 11.22). If you asked for a large key size, this step will take longer. Once your key has been generated, it is added to your virtual key-ring and you will be given an opportunity to send your key to a public-key directory (see Figure 11.23).

It is important to take good care of your key-pair. Always have a back-up copy of your key on a floppy in case something happens to the one on your hard drive. If people start sending you encrypted messages using your public key, you will want to make sure you can read them no matter what. PGP reminds you to back up your key right after you create it (see Figure 11.24).

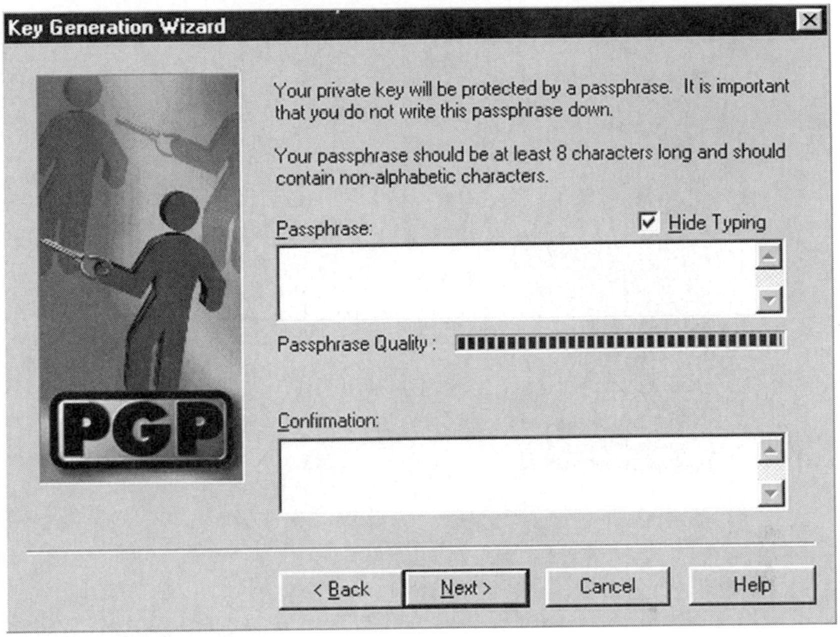

Figure 11.21:
PGP Shows You if
Your Passphrase Is
Long Enough

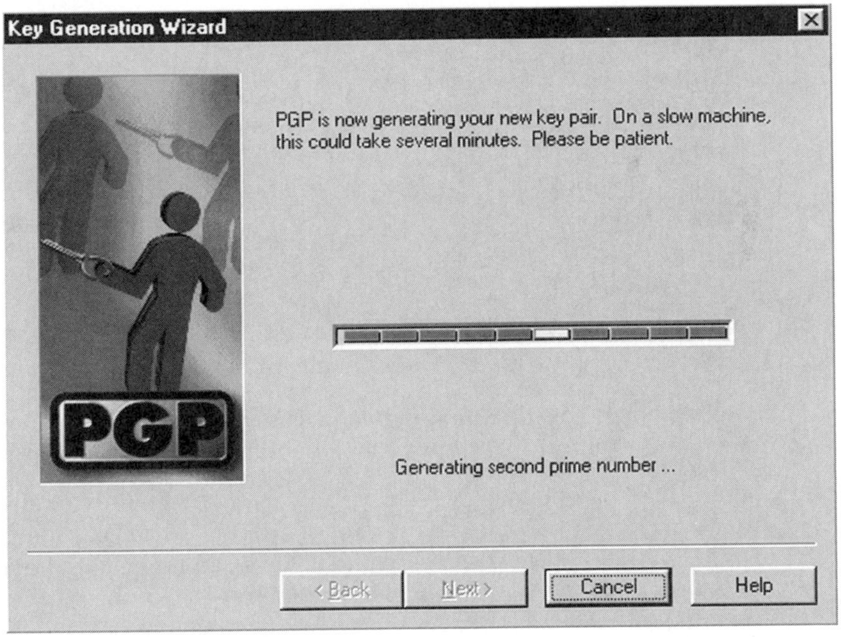

Key Generation Wizard   ✕

Your private key will be protected by a passphrase. It is important
that you do not write this passphrase down.

Your passphrase should be at least 8 characters long and should
contain non-alphabetic characters.

Passphrase: ☑ Hide Typing

Passphrase Quality : ▮▮▮▮▮▮▮▮▮▮▮▮▮▮▮▮▮▮▮▮▮▮▮

Confirmation:

< Back   Next >   Cancel   Help

Figure 11.22:
It Will Take a Little
Time to Create Your
Key-Pair

Key Generation Wizard   ✕

PGP is now generating your new key pair. On a slow machine,
this could take several minutes. Please be patient.

Generating second prime number ...

< Back   Next >   Cancel   Help

Figure 11.23:
You Don't Have to
Put Your Key in a
Public Key
Directory if You
Don't Want to

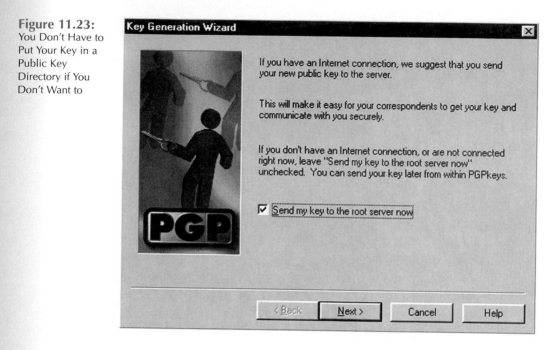

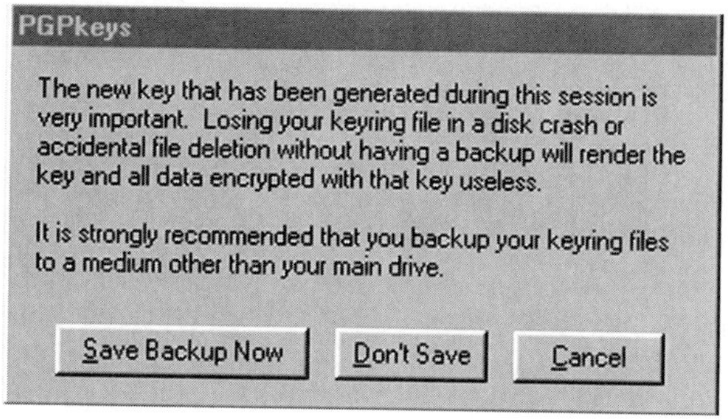

Figure 11.24:
Back Up Your New
Key-Pair

Some people advertise their public PGP key on the Web, so you may have already seen one. Figure 11.25 shows a PGP public key in plain text:

A key like the one in Figure 11.25 can be added to your virtual key-ring if you first copy and paste it to a text file on your hard drive. Then use the "import" command in PGP to add it to your key-ring. PGP keys can be acquired many different ways. Someone might hand their public key to you on a floppy. Or you might find one appended to a mail message or a Web page. If you need a public key for a particular individual, you could look for it in a public-key directory (see Figure 11.26).

Figure 11.25:
A PGP Key in Plain Text

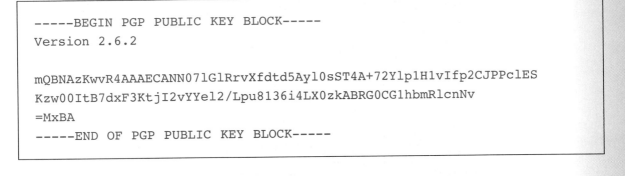

```
-----BEGIN PGP PUBLIC KEY BLOCK-----
Version 2.6.2

mQBNAzKwvR4AAAECANN07lGlRrvXfdtd5Ayl0sST4A+72Ylp1H1vIfp2CJPPclES
Kzw00ItB7dxF3KtjI2vYYel2/Lpu8136i4LX0zkABRG0CG1hbmRlcnNv
=MxBA
-----END OF PGP PUBLIC KEY BLOCK-----
```

Figure 11.26:
A Public PGP Key
Directory at pgp.net

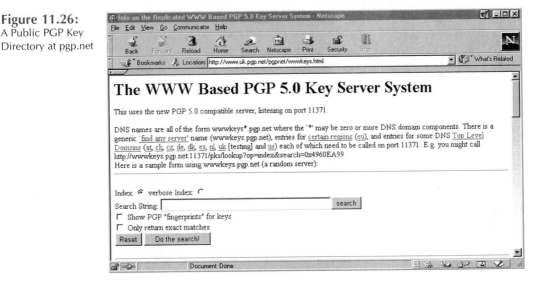

Public-key directories let you conduct keyword searches. If you know the name or e-mail address of your key owner, you can search for that person's key in the directory. Figure 11.27 shows a single hit for the keyword "aseltine" at the **www.pgp.net server.**

When we click on this key entry, we'll see a plain-text rendering of the key, just like the one shown in Figure 11.25. If we copy and paste that text to a local file, we can ask PGP to add the key to our virtual key-ring (see Figure 11.28).

PGP then reads the file, checks for legitimate key block and displays any keys that it finds before adding them to the virtual key-ring (see Figure 11.29).

Figure 11.27:
The Directory Finds
a Key for "aseltine"

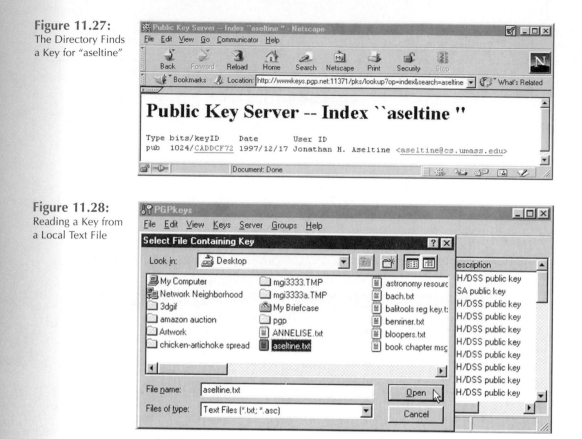

Figure 11.28:
Reading a Key from
a Local Text File

To actually add a key to our virtual key-ring, we just highlight the key or keys that we want, and click on "Import" (see Figure 11.29). Once the key has been added to the key ring we can choose to certify it (see Figure 11.32). A key from a public server could be counterfeit, so it would not be wise to certify it without first checking its fingerprint. We can view a key's fingerprint on either the key server or from inside PGP once the key is on our key-ring (see Figure 11.30).

PGP displays the key's properties including its fingerprint (see Figure 11.31).

Once we have the fingerprint for this key, we can contact the owner (a telephone call is convenient) and ask him to read off the fingerprint for his key. If the owner can produce the same fingerprint, we'll know the key is legitimate. Then we can go ahead and sign the key if we want (see Figure 11.32).

Before we can add our signature to the key, we have to enter our passphrase (signatures are generated by private keys). A secure passphrase prevents other people who may have access to this key-ring from forging our digital signature (see Figure 11.33).

Figure 11.29:
PGP Shows Any
Keys Found in the
File

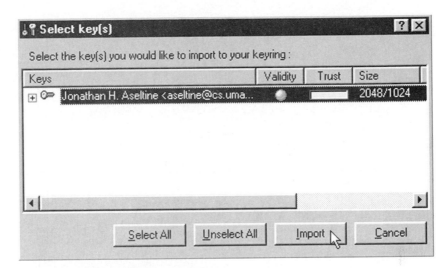

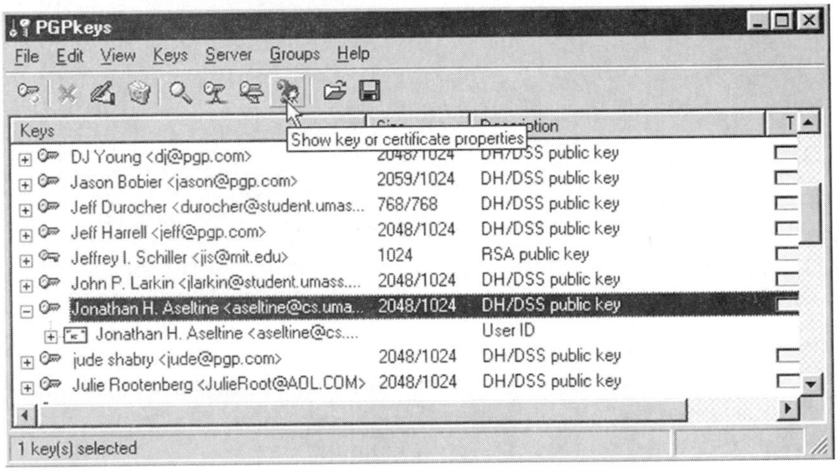

Figure 11.30:
Highlight a Key and
Ask for Its
Properties

Once we've added our signature to the key, we'll be able to see it on the key (see Figure 11.34).

We can export keys from our key-ring and pass them on to others, including any key that we've certified. When the key is exported, our signature goes with it, indicating that we can authenticate the key for anyone who trusts us to make that determination.

PGP is easy to use once you understand the basic operations of public-key encryption, key management, and key certification. PGP can also be integrated with newsreaders and mail clients to expedite the processes of encoding and decoding when encrypted documents are encountered in newsgroups or incoming e-mail. In the next section we'll look at PGP-enhanced e-mail.

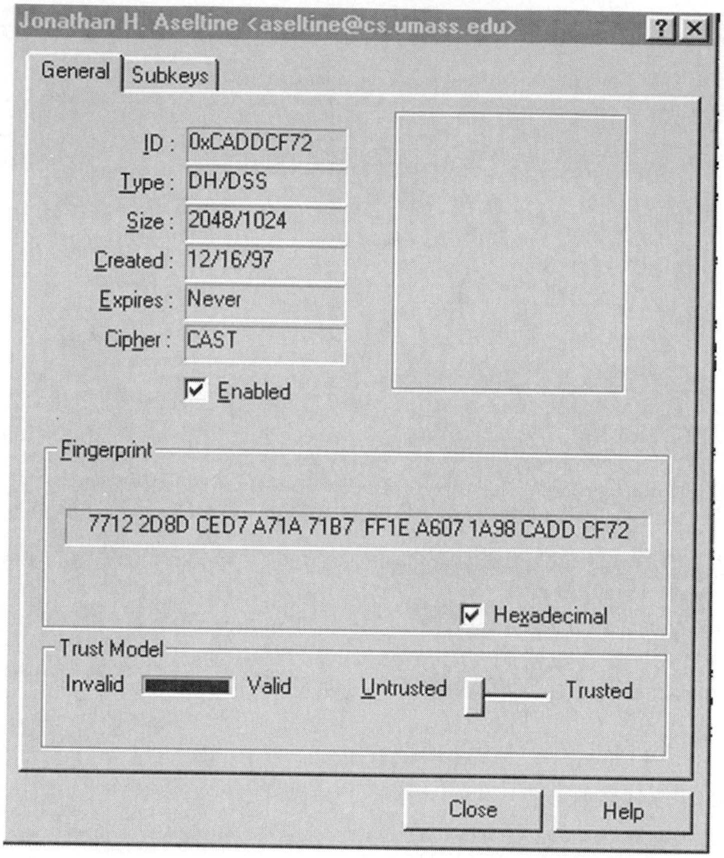

Figure 11.31:
Viewing the Key
Fingerprint

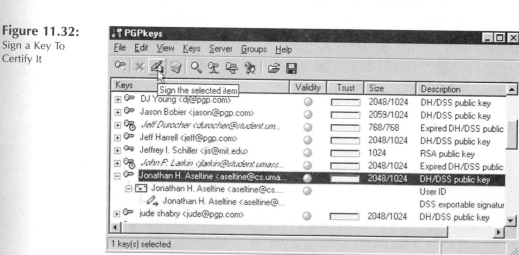

Figure 11.32:
Sign a Key To
Certify It

Figure 11.33:
A Signature
Requires a
Passphrase

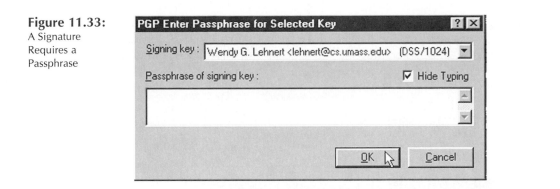

Figure 11.34:
Signatures Are
Visible on Keys

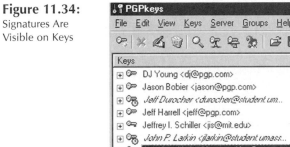

Privacy-Enhanced E-mail

One way or another, strong encryption will eventually make its way into our mail software. The technology exists, but there is no uniform standard. For example, Outlook Express supports both S/MIME (secure MIME) encryption using the CA authentication model and PGP with its web-of-trust certification model. If you use PGP, but your your friends are using S/MIME, then you've got a problem.

The popularity of PGP and its availability as a plug-in for many popular mail clients makes it an excellent candidate for users who are knowledgeable about PGP. Unfortunately, most e-mail users know nothing about PGP and will not use encrypted e-mail until it is more or less forced on them by the big-name software manufacturers (e.g., Microsoft). It is hard to be an "early-adopter" when it comes to encryption because of interoperability issues, but if you are in an environment (probably a work environment) where some encryption standard has been adopted, encrypted e-mail may be the norm, at least for e-mail within that environment.

If you install PGP, you can experience the benefits of secure e-mail communications with anyone else who has a PGP key-pair. During the PGP installation, you will be asked what optional plug-ins you wish to install (see Figure 11.35).

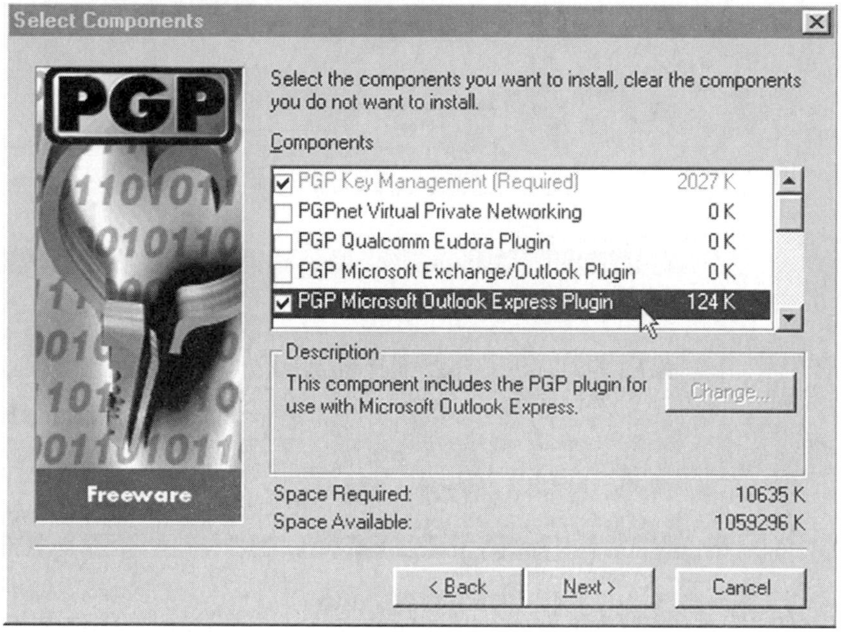

Figure 11.35:
PGP Offers a
Number of
Optional Plug-Ins
for Other Clients

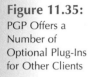

Once installed, a PGP plug-in integrates with your existing software to add encryption operations as needed. If you want to encrypt an outgoing e-mail message or add a digital signature, a single mouse click will do the job (see the upper right-hand corner in Figure 11.36). If an incoming message contains a PGP-encoded block, it will be detected and decoded automatically using available keys on your PGP key ring.

If everyone used the same encryption standard for e-mail, the only extra overhead would be for key management: where to find keys on an as-needed basis, when to accept a given key as legitimate, when to replace a key that has expired, and so forth. Much of this can be automated and hidden from view. The rest would not be very different from managing an e-mail address book. It is hard to say when encryption will become a commonplace e-mail enhancement, but the technology is available today for anyone who wants it. The rest is just a matter of commercial adaptation and public acceptance.

Fighting Spam with Encryption

In the Above and Beyond section in Chapter 7 we looked at some attempts to control spam on Usenet newsgroups. The basic idea was to identify offending articles and filter them out, but great care was needed to avoid censorship. Since the line

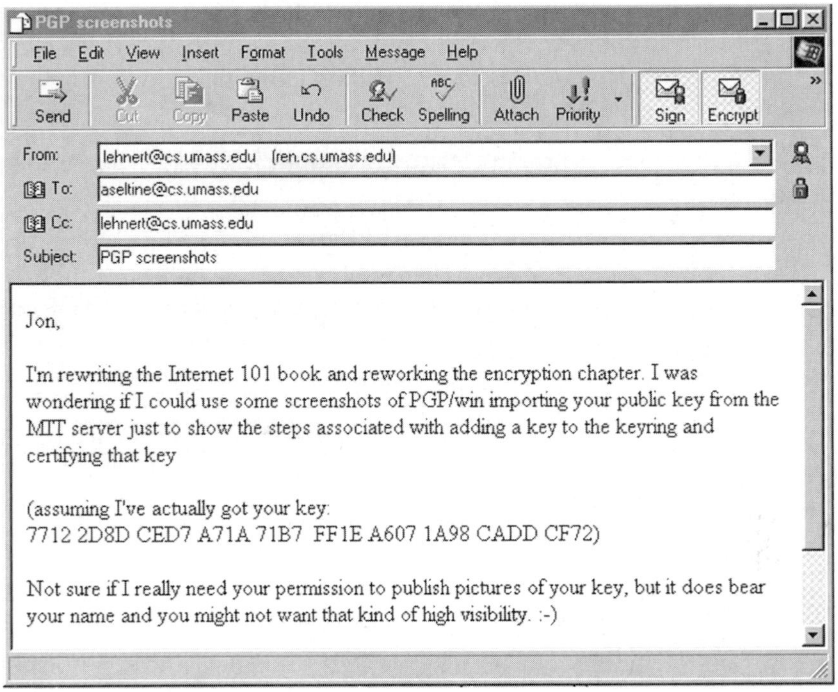

Figure 11.36:
Clicking on Icons to
Encrypt or Sign
Outgoing Mail

between legitimate filtering and unwanted censorship may be drawn differently by different people, filters on Usenet must be designed and managed with care. Although the connection between spam filters and strong encryption may not be immediately obvious, encryption has made it possible to fight spam without infringing on anyone's right to read what someone else might consider to be unwanted spam. If spam is in the eye of the beholder, then everyone must have the right to make that distinction for himself. The trick is to minimize the number of people who have to make those judgement calls, so that others can benefit from the efforts of a few. Suppose, for example, that one person could be trusted to identify spam for one segment of the Usenet community. Then it should not be necessary for everyone in that group to reproduce those judgement calls individually: It would be better to broadcast the decisions of that one trusted person, and let others accept those filtering decisions (or not). This is something like having different CAs for key authentication. But here we are talking about trusted agents for spam filtering.

Trusted agents for spam filtering are at work right now battling spam on Usenet. NoCeM (pronounced "No see 'em") is a Usenet client that can be installed by end users or applied by a Usenet administrator on a Usenet server. Here's how it works. People watch for spam on Usenet. When somebody sees spam, they can post a notice describing the offending article on a special newsgroup called news.lists.filters (see Figure 11.37). Anyone can post to news.lists.filters, but posts from unrecognized agents will be ignored. When someone launches a NoCeM-enabled news reader, it checks news.lists.filters for spam notices and kills off any targeted articles that it is authorized to kill. Authorization is needed lest censors place notices on news.lists.filters in an effort to kill random articles.

Figure 11.37:
The news.lists.filters Newsgroup

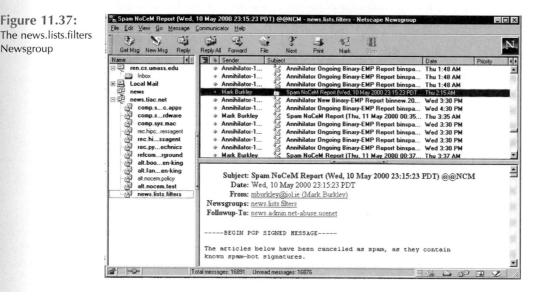

To authorize a NoCeM action, each NoCeM user creates a file of authorized signatures representing individuals whom the user trusts to issue spam notifications. Then the NoCeM software acts on only those notices posted with authorized signatures. These signatures are encoded using PGP in order to prevent forgeries. If you have located one trusted agent who monitors all of your favorite newsgroups for spam, then you simply collect that one agent's signature. Once the signature is installed, your newsreader automatically kills any articles deemed to be spam by your trusted agent. If one agent cannot cover all of your newsgroups, you can add others.

Setting up a signature file takes some extra effort on the part of the users, who must identify and collect appropriate signatures. Certainly, the agents who monitor the newsgroups expend ongoing effort to watch over the newsgroup articles and post notices to news.lists.filters (although each agent is probably using a spambot of his own design to automate the process). This may seem to be a lot of work to free Usenet users from the curse of spam. But if NoCeM were used by everyone who read Usenet, the audience for spam would be reduced to zero and there would be no incentive to post spam on Usenet anymore. Note also that NoCeM software also operates at the level of a local news server, thereby saving everyone on that server from having to manage NoCeM signatures on their own.

Encryption plays a crucial role in NoCeM. Without digital signatures, no one would be able to trust any of the posts to news.lists.filters. Counterfeit posts could be placed by censors, and legitimate articles would be effectively removed from Usenet. NoCeM is an excellent example of a technological solution to a problem that may defy legislative intervention.

Strong Encryption and the Culture of the Internet

Some software is written by professional programmers because they are paid to write it. Other software is written by students who are playing around and having fun. Programmers learn their craft by experimenting and playing with ideas that interest them; some highly innovative programs take shape when programmers are just playing around. So a lot of wonderful software is not created within corporate environments as a part of someone's job description. When software is created by programmers working on their own time and their own equipment, those individuals own the resulting creations and can sell them or give them away as they wish. If all of your software has come from your neighborhood computer store, you may wonder why programmers would ever give away their software. The answer lies in the origins of the Internet and the culture of the programming community.

In the Internet culture, software is never truly finished. Powerful software lives, evolves, and benefits from the contributions of multiple caretakers. One person codes up a nice tool and then passes it on to anyone who wants it, for free. A second person picks it up, adds some nice features to it, and then makes this newer version available to anyone who wants it. Then a third person—you get the idea. This tradition of free-style software development makes perfect sense in academic environments, where ideas are freely shared and no one is being paid to produce shrink-wrapped software.

Free-style software development is not consistent with corporate models for productivity, but it does explain why so much progress on the Internet seems to have happened by accident. Some of the best ideas on the Internet (e.g., e-mail, Usenet, and the Web) were never anticipated by anyone in a position to authorize projects and set deadlines. Some software is available simply because somebody had an idea that was good enough to catch on. This can happen only in a community that shares all of its ideas openly.

It helps to keep this cultural Zeitgeist in mind when considering Phil Zimmermann. Phil was a software specialist with an interest in cryptography and privacy. He wrote PGP and gave it to the Internet community just as thousands of programmers have written programs and handed their code off to anyone who wanted it.

Phil Zimmermann often explains PGP via an analogy involving letters and postcards. He argues that encrypted e-mail is like a letter in an envelope. A letter in an envelope is a private communication, and everyone takes that privacy for granted. An e-mail message that is not encrypted is like a message on a postcard. Anyone can read what you write on the back of a postcard, so people don't put a lot of sensitive personal information on postcards.

No one needs to defend their right to put a letter in an envelope. No one assumes that you are engaged in an illegal activity just because you choose to put a letter in an envelope. In the same way, no one should assume that you are up to something suspect if you prefer to encrypt your e-mail. You are just asking for the same level of privacy that an envelope affords you. If someone denies you that level of privacy, they are effectively saying you must put everything you write on postcards for all the world to see.

The letter/postcard analogy is provocative for anyone who thought that e-mail communications were private or secure. Phil is right about the lack of security inherent in unencrypted e-mail. If you wouldn't want to write something on a postcard, you shouldn't put it in unencrypted e-mail. But the postcard analogy is not quite accurate when you consider that the Postmaster General can open envelopes containing letters when authorized by a court order. PGP is not like a letter in an envelope because no one can inspect a PGP file unless they hold the one and only private key that can decode the file.

The encryption war is fundamentally a battle between centralized control and distributed control. As we will see in the following sections, key escrow schemes and export restrictions depend on centralized power and institutional controls. Throughout the ages, governments have feared transforming communication technologies. Literacy was restricted to the ruling classes in the Middle Ages, and the invention of the printing press represented a serious threat to that status quo. The very concept of public education is a democratizing force that enables upward mobility and lessens the advantages of social class distinctions. Special interests have always resisted certain technologies out of self interest and a legitimate desire to maintain social stability. When a technology promises profound social change, the status quo will be affected. For better or for worse, encryption threatens our status quo today, and many social forces are stumbling and colliding over the question of unregulated encryption technologies.

Strong Encryption and Law Enforcement

Suppose that strong encryption is available for general use. Anyone can generate his or her own pair of keys, post a public key in a public directory, and exchange encrypted e-mail with anyone else. The codes for these keys cannot be cracked. This means that terrorists can safely communicate with one another and say anything without fear of discovery. Criminals can plan robberies and plot murders. Right-wing militia leaders can debate the best way to stage a retaliation for the attack on the Branch Davidians in Waco, Texas. Religious extremists can talk about which abortion clinic to bomb next. A plot to assassinate the President can be fine-tuned. In short, communications that used to require face-to-face meetings in very private settings can now be conducted with blinding speed over unimaginable distances. Material that wouldn't be trusted to a phone conversation or a mail service is perfectly safe on the Internet, because powerful encryption is available to anyone who wants it.

Before the advent of computer-based communications, law-enforcement agencies had technological capabilities that enabled them to eavesdrop on certain conversations. With a court order, the police can tap a phone line or a local postmaster can open a piece of mail. The FBI has a variety of surveillance techniques used to listen in on private conversations. Although these powers can and have been abused on occasion, they also provide law enforcement personnel with legitimate weapons for combating crime and terrorism. Some people believe that the loss of these powers would be tantamount to pulling the plug on law enforcement.

Powerful encryption on the Internet pulls the law enforcement plug in a big way. As long as the codes can't be cracked, there is no way for the FBI to monitor an encrypted e-mail conversation between suspected criminals. Encrypted communications would make it much harder for the police to collect evidence in a criminal investigation. Drug dealers, organized crime, terrorist organizations, and random criminals can all use strong encryption to great advantage. So the government has a strong vested interest in cryptography. Digital communications and strong encryption open the door for problems unlike anything seen before. The distribution of PGP over the Internet has brought strong encryption into the hands of the masses, good and bad alike. People who use PGP today routinely create 1,024-bit keys, thereby ensuring a level of security like that of top-secret military communications.

What can the government hope to do about this technology? One possibility is to outlaw the use of strong encryption. Encryption software would be restricted and distributed only to authorized personnel, probably through some sort of government licensing. The good guys could have it, but the bad guys couldn't. This is the only scenario that gives law enforcement agencies a fighting chance against strong encryption.

There are problems with this, however. One is that, naturally, some people would oppose laws outlawing strong encryption based, at least in part, on the First Amendment. Another problem is the global nature of the Internet. A law that applies to U.S. citizens would not be enforceable for messages exchanged by non-U.S. citizens. We might be able to prohibit our own citizens from using strong encryption, but how can we hope to control the behavior of the rest of the world's population?

In a preemptive strike, the U.S. government has made a highly controversial attempt to limit the spread of strong encryption by making it illegal to export it outside of the United States and Canada. Encryption software has been categorized as "munitions," and hence the unregulated export of encryption programs is prohibited under the International Traffic in Arms Regulations (ITAR), a set of laws usually used against illegal arms dealers. Advocates of Internet free speech and others find fault with this restriction. Commercial software vendors claim that it ties their hands with respect to all software development involving encryption. Other countries are selling products with strong encryption (128 bits and more), but U.S. companies can sell only products that use inferior encryption (the limit at the time of this writing is 64 bits). No laws have been passed to limit the use of strong encryption within the

United States, and steps have been taken by the government to insert classified encryption software into all digital communication devices manufactured in this country.

Governmental control of digital communications could be quietly accomplished with the cooperation of major hardware manufacturers in the absence of legislation and public debate. Here's how. Public-key encryption could be hard-wired into all computer chips inserted into modems, cable boxes, and other network communication devices. Then any communications going out onto the Internet would have to pass through a government-approved encryption chip. Packets going to the net would automatically be encoded using strong encryption approved by the government, and files coming off the Internet would be automatically decoded using the same technology. Everything would be handled behind the scenes by ubiquitous encryption chips. The casual user wouldn't have to know anything about it.

Each embedded encryption chip would be programmed with its own unique key-pair. This is where the government's "back-door" comes in. To give law enforcement the power to monitor encrypted communications, the government must be able to access all of the private keys in all of the embedded encryption chips. This would be accomplished with a key escrow system. Whenever an encryption chip was manufactured, a copy of its private key would be indexed by its serial number and handed to the government for safekeeping. No one would have access to any of these private keys except by a court order (the necessary authorization for a digital wire tap). Then the serial numbers of the relevant devices would be collected and used to retrieve the necessary private keys for the proper authorities. This would effectively give law-enforcement personnel a back door into all Internet communications.

A key escrow system is the government's best bet for digital wiretapping. Unfortunately, anyone who wanted to protect themselves from all wiretaps (authorized or otherwise) could get their hands on their own encryption software and encode messages using keys that aren't held in escrow. This would sabotage the whole key escrow system. So the government's back door can work only if powerful encryption software is not available to the general public. A war on unauthorized encryption seems unlikely to stem the tide of PGP users and other software hobbyists who cannot resist the urge to tinker with their own software implementations of published encryption algorithms. And now that PGP has been given permission to be exported freely, it seems highly unlikely that U.S. citizens could ever be legally prohibited from using PGP. In spite of persistent lobbying efforts, it appears that law enforcement has lost its bid for centralized control over strong encryption.

U.S. Export Restrictions

In 1992, the U.S. government placed an export restriction on encryption software so that U.S. software vendors could not incorporate encryption keys stronger than 40 bits in their products. Strong encryption was added to the list of munitions covered by ITAR, placing it in the same category as nuclear missiles and other weapons of mass destruction.

Privacy advocates have strongly objected to any governmental restrictions on encryption on the grounds that citizens have a right to protect personal materials on personal computers and private communications on the Internet. Although the ITAR restrictions did not affect most U.S. citizens at home, it did make it illegal to take a laptop computer out of the country if it had PGP installed on it. Computer science professors could not post course notes describing strong encryption on the Internet without violating ITAR restrictions. Protesters pointed out how impossible it was to enforce the ITAR restrictions and how pointless it all was since the rest of the world already had strong encryption anyway.

If you visit the **ITAR Civil Disobedience Web site**, you will find a button you can click if you want to become an international arms dealer. When you press the button, a three-line RSA computer program will be sent to Anguilla, and you will be guilty of exporting strong encryption. Thousands of people have pushed the button and added their names to this public protest. You might still want to visit the site even if you don't want to push the button. You'll find a lot of amusing observations about the ITAR restrictions on encryption.

However persuasive many arguments against ITAR might seem, the protests that made their mark in Washington came from the business sector. U.S. software manufacturers were unable to compete in the global markets because of ITAR. U.S. companies couldn't add strong encryption to products destined overseas, while European manufacturers were free to use strong encryption technologies (many of which came from the United States) without restriction. ITAR had tied the hands of American software manufacturers, and they lobbied hard in Washington to change that. The voice of American business was loud and clear on the subject of ITAR, and Washington was under pressure to respond.

In 1996, ITAR software restrictions were relaxed under certain conditions so that selected vendors could receive permission to go up to 56 bits. (This meant that DES-based encryption could be exported.) Although a step in the right direction, this was not much help to U.S. software companies. They were still competing with European manufacturers who were free to incorporate 128-bit encryption in all of their products. Eventually, the software lobbyists began to gain ground.

In 1997, the United States Department of Commerce granted Netscape permission to export a strong (128-bit encryption) version of Netscape Navigator. At the same time, permission was also given to VeriSign Inc., a leading certification authority, to issue 128-bit certificates to banks and large-scale e-commerce operations. Ever since 1997, Netscape Navigator has been establishing 128-bit communication channels with sites bearing a Verisign certificate. Sites without the Verisign certificate were still restricted to 40-bit encryption. Internet Explorer upgraded to 128-bit encryption in 1999.

In 1999, as the Clinton administration struggled to meet international standards for privacy protection and address controversial issues in intellectual property rights, Washington observers began to sense a shift in Congress over the encryption debate. At the end of 1999, Network Associates Inc. was given permission to distribute industrial-strength PGP worldwide with 1,024-bit session keys. Shortly afterwards, U.S. software manufacturers were allowed to add 64-bit encryption into all software products without restriction. 64-bit encryption is not as good as 128-bit encryption, but the government had at least admitted that the old boundary line between weak and strong encryption has shifted since 1992, and export restrictions must move with it.

With browsers handling e-commerce transactions with strong encryption, and random individuals using strong encryption for private communications, the Internet is gradually moving in the direction of a heavily encrypted medium. It's only a matter of time before encryption becomes the norm for all private and sensitive communications over the Net.

Above and Beyond: Problems and Exercises

A1. Explain how session keys are used. Why are they needed?

A2. Explain how a key escrow system would make it possible for the government to conduct digital wiretaps on the Internet.

A3. Explain what is meant by the saying "When privacy is outlawed only outlaws will have privacy."

A4. [**Find It Online**] Read "Jackboots on the Infobahn: Clipping the Wings of Freedom" by John Perry Barlow (`http://www.eff.org/pub/Publications/John_Perry_Barlow/ HTML/infobahn_jackboots.html`) and "Resolving the Encryption Dilemma: The Case for the Clipper Chip" by Dorothy E. Denning (`http://web.mit.edu/techreview/www/articles/july95/ Denning.html`). Describe three concerns raised by Barlow and explain how Denning would respond to them. Who presents the most compelling arguments? Do you think this controversy can ever be resolved in a way that will satisfy everyone?

A5. [**Hands-On**] Install PGP on your personal computer. Visit the public PGP key server at (`http://www.keyserver.net/en/`) and download my public key (search for "Wendy G. Lehnert"). Send me an encrypted mail message. Send it to `lehnert@cs.umass.edu` with the subject header "Chapter 11— A5." Ask me a question, tell me about a great Web site, let me know what you think of this book, or just say hello. I will send you a reply. Plus, if you tell me where to find your public PGP key, I'll encrypt my reply to you.

CHAPTER 12

Making It All Work for You

CHAPTER GOALS

- Identify your goals and the role of the Internet in helping you achieve them.
- Understand how the Internet challenges us with choices—at all possible levels.
- Review some tips for telecommuters; these apply to everyone who works online at home.
- Be aware of ways the Net really does save us time.
- Develop a plan for staying on top of new Internet developments (the learning never ends).
- Find out about careers in information technology and who gets them.
- Check for signs of Internet addiction—are you in danger?
- Consider one very positive impact of the Internet on the truth and our ability to find it.

12.1 TAKING CHARGE

If you've taken the time to read this book and spent some time online putting what you've learned into action, you should have a good working knowledge of the Internet. You've seen what the Internet has to offer, and you've seen how software tools can help you take advantage of the Internet. Never stop learning about the Internet: The Internet will continue to evolve and change. As long as you are active on the Net, there will always be new resources to explore and new technologies to evaluate. The learning never stops. But now is a good time to step back, take a deep breath, and ponder an important decision.

From here on out, you need to consider your long-term goals and how the Internet fits into that picture. If you want to pursue an information technology (IT) career, then the Internet should be a central focal point in your life. You will probably be spending many, if not most, of your working hours online. If you want to pursue a career in an area *other* than IT, you should think of the Internet as a powerful tool that can help you achieve your goals, but then get out of the way while you get on with the rest of your life. It is important to be clear about this IT vs. non-IT distinction because it will help you evaluate your time online and whether you are using that time wisely.

12.2 ▌TRAPS AND PITFALLS

Most people who spend a lot of time on the Internet enjoy the Net and are convinced that they are spending their time wisely. They might feel that the Net is crucial for their work or continuing education. They might feel that the net is enriching their personal lives with superior information access, online relationships, or entertaining diversions. This is a transforming technology, and one that has the power to change each of us and our society. It might prove to have more impact on our lives than the automobile, and some observers have gone so far as to say that the Internet will rival Gutenberg's printing press in terms of its ultimate impact on the world. Can anyone expect the introduction of such a powerful technology to be completely positive and psychologically harmless?

One problem is information overload. It takes time to deal with a daily load of e-mail, favorite newsgroups, and Web-based forums. The Web also exerts its seductive pull on a remarkably wide range of people. People with intellectual interests can lose themselves in educational explorations. Music lovers can spend long stretches of time downloading new artists and discovering new worlds of music. The lure of pornography seems to cut across all socioeconomic dividing lines.

The Internet is also exerting its influence on people in terms of speed. The Internet is fast, and it seems to suck people into working fast, too. This desire for speed is not limited to daily routines of e-mail replies and one-click shopping. Our entire economy is trying to adjust to forces of globalization in rapid order. E-commerce is not just a business option, it's a business option that demands an immediate online presence and immediate market penetration. Old ways of doing and thinking often seem to have no place in this fast-paced environment. Obsolete notions of intellectual property are of little use when creative new perspectives are needed. Slow, thoughtful deliberation seems to be at odds with hypertext and short attention spans. The speed of digital communications, along with the speed of change associated with the Net, have turned the Net into a natural home for the young. Young people are generally in a hurry to move forward and pursue a dream; the Internet can only encourage these youthful inclinations.

At the same time, inordinate amounts of time can be spent socializing, mixing, and cruising the Net for one thrill or another. Adolescents love to chat online and to establish virtual relationships with people they may never meet. When online relationships are pushed as far as they can go, we encounter the strange phenomenon of cybersex. Pedophiles and psychotic personalities mix freely with the rest of the population and are often difficult to detect. Some day traders view their enterprise as a viable alternative to full-time employment, and online auctions are drawing the crowd that used to cruise local flea markets and garage sales on weekends. There is, it seems, something for everyone, and it's all out there 24 hours a day, seven days a week. People used to move to New York City to get that rush of nonstop humanity working and playing around the clock. The same sense of hustle and bustle is on the Net. The Internet won't replace the buzz of a big city, or the relaxed pleasures of a comfortable book store, but it definitely has a hum and a pull all its own. Moreover, the Internet experience is far too diverse to be bundled up into a neat little package that we can stamp "good" or "bad."

Some people can explore the net for a couple hours on weekends while maintaining the old activities and rhythms of their pre-Internet life. For others, the transition from pre-Internet to post-Internet is more pervasive. For those of us who struggle to find enough hours in the day, it is necessary to be objective and disciplined about the time we spend online. How much time spent online is justifiable in terms of greater productivity at work? How much time is enriching our lives at a personal level? How much time can be chalked up to avoidance behavior or escapism? As the novelty wears off, people will be more realistic about what to expect from the Internet.

This is not to say that the Internet does not pose unique risks. It is credited with the destruction of at least a few marriages. More than a few grade-point averages have suffered as a direct result of Internet access. The pull of the Internet is simply too strong for some people. There are those who prefer online life to real-time life, and the consequences of this preference are not clear. If someone wants to end a marriage, withdraw from society, or self-destruct, chances are he or she will succeed with or without the Internet. Anyone who is firmly plugged into the real world will probably handle the Internet as one more ball to juggle in the daily mix of work, family, and the pursuit of happiness.

Perhaps the real challenge inherent in the Internet lies in the overwhelming number of choices it offers us. Not only do we have to decide how we want to use the Net today, we also have to revisit this decision and reevaluate it on a regular basis. Suppose you have chosen to subscribe to ten different mailing lists and online newsletters. How long will it make sense to stay with these selections? Your interests will shift, your priorities will change, and your subscriptions will have to change with you. If you don't bother to change your daily routines to match your changing self, you are giving too much of your life away to stale habits and old routines that have outlived their usefulness. Eventually, you may one day realize that you feel bored and annoyed without fully knowing why.

The importance of ongoing choices applies to all aspects of our lives, both online and off. Socrates warned us a long time ago: "The unexamined life is not worth living." Perhaps the Internet is simply amplifying that sentiment and thereby forcing us all to make our choices with greater care and deliberation. There is never enough time for everything. In the end, our lives are defined by the choices we've made along the way. We are what we eat, and we are what we click. As time goes by, we are precisely what we choose to be.

12.3 ▌ TELECOMMUTING

Over 50% of all businesses in the United States offer telecommuting options for selected employees, and over 20 million American workers are now telecommuting. Telecommuting is here to stay, and there is a good chance that you'll be a telecommuter yourself someday.

Telecommuting Is Good for the Economy, the Planet, and the Workers

If 10% to 20% of traditional commuters switched to telecommuting, savings would total $23 billion annually. It would eliminate 1.8 million tons of regulated pollutants, saving 3.5 billion gallons of gas, freeing up 3.1 billion hours of personal time from reduced congestion and automobile trips, and reducing maintenance costs for existing transportation infrastructure by $500 million.

Arthur D. Little and Associates

In the 1800s, the industrial revolution took the world of work out of the private homes and into the factories. People worked on a non-negotiable schedule, traveled between work and home, and lost a lot of autonomy in exchange for weekly wages. As the industrial economy evolved, manual labor in factories gave way to white-collar workers in office buildings, but the non-negotiable schedule, the travel, and the weekly paycheck remained much the same. Plus now there were dress codes.

In the 1990s, the era of telecommuting arrived and began to reverse the effects of the industrial revolution: The non-negotiable schedule became negotiable, no commuting was needed, workers recovered more autonomy to interleave work with other personal responsibilities, and dress codes disappeared (unless you had to do a teleconference). Even the weekly paycheck fell by the wayside for those who opted to work as contractors or temps instead of permanent employees.

People on the cusp of these social shifts have had to undergo adjustments that were not always easy, even when the change in question seemed to be a change for the good. Telecommuters soon discovered that the old division between a place of work and a private residence had come with certain advantages. Most obviously, the scope of one's daily activities defined your location. Your boss didn't call you up at home to talk about work (at least not without some discomfort) and your kid didn't call you up at work to ask about a missing pair of sneakers. The division between home and work was clean and clear.

As any telecommuter will tell you, telecommuting is not as easy as it looks. It takes a lot of self-discipline, especially if you tend to stop by the fridge whenever things get a little too boring or lonely or stressful. Part of the problem is a lack of structure. You have to impose your own structure on your work day lest entire days slip out from under you in a dull gray haze. In spite of predictable difficulties, 63% of employers do not provide formal training or manuals on how to telecommute productively. The following list describes some important techniques for aspiring telecommuters:

1. You have to schedule everything. That means you have to schedule not just your work-related phone calls and meetings, and "do not disturb" times but everything you plan to do for your family as well—shopping trips, family activities, school holidays, doctor appointments, shuttle services, special events. Everything has to go on a large calendar at least a week in advance and then be posted where everyone can see it. You should even schedule regular family meetings where everyone can discuss and negotiate the schedule. This will help everyone remember that your time is valuable, or at least important enough to schedule. Schedule everything.

2. You must consistently enforce the "Do Not Disturb" policy when your calendar says you are not to be disturbed. If someone wants to interrupt you during a do-not-disturb time, it better be for a serious emergency. If you break for lunch or a stretch, set up some sort of signal to let people know that they can talk to you during these breaks. Put up a sign or a flag or something everyone can easily see so there can be no misunderstanding. If you cannot make this work, you will probably fail as a telecommuter. There is nothing more stressful than a constant stream of unnecessary interruptions, however minor.

3. Install a second phone line so you can have one line for work that is separate from your personal line. Put an answering machine on your personal line during working hours. Do not, ever, answer your personal phone during working hours. This is very important, and an important habit to establish right from the start.

4. Subscribe to a telecommuting newsletter or discussion group when you first get started so you can learn from others and handle problems as they arise. Telecommuting may look easy until you fall into some bad habits and discover how hard it is to eliminate bad habits. If you prepare for the challenge before you start, you might be able to avoid the bad habits and save yourself a lot of trouble.

12.4 TIME-SAVING SERVICES

Whenever a new technology surfaces, there is a lot of talk about how it will change our lives, our work, and sometimes our very thought processes. Everyone knows that computers are impressive for their processing speed and memory capacity. As a result, anyone who works with computers feels pressured to work with increasingly larger amounts of data but with less preparation time and less time for reflection. The time-saving potential of these high-speed technologies has somehow produced a population of workers who feel more stressed for time and less capable of staying on top of it all.

Learning curves always take time, and new users to the Internet must expect to go through a period of learning the ropes and discovering ways to leverage their time online. Although the Internet has a reputation for being addictive and time-consuming, a more disciplined use of the Internet will reveal its potential as a time-saving device. The next time someone tells you what a waste of time the Internet is, be prepared to fight back with some good arguments to counter that assertion:

- Buying a new car used to involve trips to dealerships, piles of glossy brochures that never gave you the real information you wanted, and drawn out negotiations with car salesmen. Now you can research your options online and walk into a dealership with all the information you need to get a price that you know is fair. Estimated time savings: 1–2 weeks → 1–2 days.

- E-stores in general can save you a lot of time. A trip to a store to make a purchase in person usually takes at least an hour—possibly more if you have to hunt for the item you want. Finding it online and placing an order over the Web generally takes 5–15 minutes if you are an experienced online shopper. Estimated time savings: 1–2 hours → 5–15 minutes.

- Online research can save you trips to the library and many hours in the stacks hunting down one thing or another. Again, the time savings will vary depending on your search-engine skills, but the savings are significant. Indeed, people are bothering to track down information now that they probably wouldn't have bothered with before. We can't characterize that as a time saver, but it does speak to the amount of time that library-based searches used to require. Estimated time savings: 2 hours → 1 hour.

- The Internet has also made it possible to track timely news events in any number of specialty areas that were simply not available to the general public before the Net. Once you find the right portal site, you can receive a steady diet of news that was once available only if you were willing to travel to clubs meetings and public talks. Estimated time savings: 2 hours → 15 minutes.

Mahatma Gandhi once said, "There is more to life than increasing its speed." This is undoubtedly true, and speed should not be pursued as the Holy Grail of modern life. But if an appliance or a device of any kind can save us some time, that's a valuable contribution.

12.5 ▌ STAYING ON TOP OF NEW DEVELOPMENTS

The Internet is the perfect vehicle for continuing education if ever there was one. Happily, the Internet is also the best place to track news about the Internet. So if you want to stay informed, it won't be hard. Plus, you have a choice of delivery methods: newsletters delivered to your mailbox, desktop portals with customizable news options, an assortment of news articles from online newspapers and magazines. If you are a news connoisseur, you can customize your own daily delivery of items pulled from the best Net-news sources around.

New York Times →**Technology** (**CyberTimes**)	`http://www.nytimes.com`
CNet.com → **News**	`http://home.cnet.com`
Wired News	`http://www.wired.com/`
SiliconValley.com	`http://www.sjmercury.com/svtech/`
IDG.net	`http://www.idg.net/`

If you are new to these resources, you should try them on for size and then settle on one or two that you like. They each offer a slightly different mix, but there is a lot of overlap in their coverage so you shouldn't try to read all of them. It's also not necessary to read these pages every day in order to stay on top of things. If you get too busy and are having trouble keeping up, let your news tracking slide. You can get back into it when time allows.

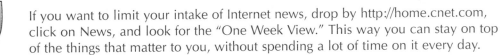

Do It Once a Week

If you want to limit your intake of Internet news, drop by http://home.cnet.com, click on News, and look for the "One Week View." This way you can stay on top of the things that matter to you, without spending a lot of time on it every day.

12.6 ▌ CAREERS IN INFORMATION TECHNOLOGY

If you know anything about IT, you've probably heard some stories about the IT job market. Companies desperate for qualified IT workers pile on the benefits on top of six-figure salaries plus stock options. Some of the standard perks include gym memberships, birthdays off, on-site dry cleaning, and leased cars. According to the Bureau of Labor Statistics, the unemployment rate of computer systems analysts weighed in around 1.3% at the start of 2000, compared to a national unemployment rate of 3.9%.

The **National Center for Education** reports one IT job candidate for every eight IT job openings. This shortage is due, in part, to the fact that the number of U.S.

college graduates in IT fields has fallen every year since 1988. Plus, the number of high-tech jobs is steadily increasing, from 4.6 million in 1996 to an estimated 6.2 million by 2006. Companies usually look for experienced computer science and engineering graduates, or technically savvy MIS graduates. Given the tight job market, companies often settle for liberal arts graduates with an interest in computer technology and a willingness to learn technical skills on the job. In a seller's market, companies can't realistically hope to land their dream candidates very often. So if you are a liberal arts major and you enjoy what you're doing, don't bother to change your major, but do take an introductory programming course from your CS department (choose an object-oriented language, if possible) and as many MIS courses as you can. If you can demonstrate a talent for technical material and show an enthusiasm for learning more, your liberal arts degree may actually be a plus to the right company.

Of course, job candidates have to be realistic too. If you are a liberal arts major who has mastered basic HTML and learned a little JavaScript, you are not going to land a $100,000 starting salary plus perks. Those jobs go to highly qualified Java and C++ programmers with Oracle or SQL experience, NT or UNIX networking skills including scripting languages like Visual Basic or perl, experience with Web site deployment (especially e-commerce applications), and solid communication skills (in English). The top salaries generally go to candidates with relevant on-the-job experience, but new MBAs from one of the **top techno-MBA programs** can expect to land a $80–$100K annual salary right out of school.

Research Current IT Trends on the Web

Go to IDG.com and enter the query "IT careers" with the "All IDG" search option. For a synopsis of current career trends, salaries, and employment prospects, consult the **Occupational Outlook Handbook** at the U.S. Department of Labor.

By the way, if you are an undergraduate contemplating a future with a .com company, you may wonder if you should even bother finishing your college degree. Internet technologies move so fast that it's hard to sit on the sidelines while others jump in. And of course, everyone knows that Bill Gates dropped out of Harvard. This question has been debated at length in various online forums with seemingly strong arguments on both sides. Colleges and universities generally acknowledge that they do not produce graduates with the exact skill sets needed by industry. It seems that a job candidate with the right skills and no college degree should be able to compete with a college graduate who is going to need extensive in-house training. But it doesn't always work that way. Companies generally expect to train new hires anyway, so they may look to the universities to develop general analytical thinking and communication skills, which is something businesses cannot do in-house. As a rule, people who finish college enjoy higher salaries, greater mobility, and more opportunities for professional advancement throughout their lifetimes.

12.6.1 Internet Addiction

Internet Addiction Disorder (IAD) is a bonafide psychiatric disorder, now recognized by the American Psychiatric Association. Psychologists are studying it just as they've studied compulsive gambling, drug addiction, and eating disorders. With the Internet available in so many college dormitories, office cubicles, and a majority of American homes, it makes sense to wonder how many people are out of control when it comes to the Internet. We all must know someone who logs on to the Internet every evening and stays online late into the night. Is 20 hours a week too much? 30 hours? 40 hours?

The experts all agree that it's not just a matter of how many hours you spend online. It's all a question of whether your time online is interfering with your ability to function and derive pleasure from other activities. It is also important to separate personal time spent online from time online in the service of work or school. If you spend 60 hours a week online because your job requires it, none of that time "counts" when it comes to assessing a possible Internet addiction. People who work the Net extensively for work or school should nevertheless try to separate time online for work and time online for recreation as cleanly as possible. If you can't separate the two (sometimes it's not so easy), it will be difficult to know if you are experiencing problems because of IAD.

Are You Addicted?

If you think you may be addicted to the Internet, visit one of these sites and take a test to assess your risk level:

The Center for On-Line Addiction	`http://netaddiction.com/`
Internet Addiction Survey	`http://www.stresscure.com/ hrn/addiction.html`

Many specialists are studying the problem and trying to help those who think they are addicted or are afraid they may be headed in that direction. Here are some questions and suggestions for those who may be struggling with this problem.

1. Look for patterns of overuse. How much time do you spend on the Internet or spend thinking about the Internet? Is this time taking you away from people and activities that you used to enjoy but no longer have time for? Have you reduced the scope of your daily activities in order to leave more time for the Internet? Have your grades suffered as a result? Is your performance at work being affected? Are your personal relationships suffering? Do family and friends complain about the amount of time you spend online? Are you unable to resist certain online acitivities such as e-mail, chat rooms, online auctions, shopping online, or interactive games? Do you ignore routine responsibilities in order to be online? Is it a big deal to be away from the Internet for a day or two?

2. Many addicts indulge in addictive behaviors because they want to escape from something else in their lives. Do you have any underlying problems that could be driving you into addictive behavior patterns? Do you think you are predisposed toward addictive behaviors? Have you battled other addictions in the past? (Most people find it easier to tackle questions like these with the help of a therapist or counselor.)

3. If you are using the Internet to escape some other problem in your life, it is crucial to confront that problem and devise a plain for handling it. The addiction itself will also need to be controlled. Cold turkey is not necessarily the best plan, but a gradually declining schedule of time online may be needed to cut back an excessive usage pattern to a more reasonable level.

As addictions go, the concept of Internet addiction is somewhat controversial. If anyone with a severe impulse-control problem qualifies as an addict, then there must be book addicts, Home Shopping Network addicts, aerobic workout addicts, crossword-puzzle addicts, and so on and so forth. Anything can be an excuse for work avoidance or psychological denial in the hands of a personality predisposed to addictive behaviors. If the Internet has attracted the attention of the psychiatric establishment, it must be because such a large percentage of the population appears to be susceptible. We will probably need a sociologist to explain why television viewing habits were never dignified with a "Television Addiction Disorder." Perhaps the potential for social disruption is minimized when an overwhelming percentage of the population succumbs to the same psychiatric disorder en masse.

12.6.2 The Truth Is Out There

It is rather premature to be putting a stamp on the Internet, proclaiming it significant because it taught us "X" or forced us to confront "Y." In another hundred years we may have the necessary perspective for that sort of thing. For now, we can only notice its effect on our own lives and speculate. A business traveler will notice how online ticket sales have made it easier to set up travel itineraries in record time. A scientist will notice how the Internet has made it easier to locate esoteric publications that were once available only in a handful of well-endowed libraries. As an educator, I have noticed how the Internet is forcing students to do something that has always been taught, but not always learned. Students growing up with the Internet are learning, out of necessity, to assess the value of everything they see.

Vinton G. Cerf, who created the TCP/IP protocol (along with Robert Kahn) wrote a short piece on the question of whether the Internet holds some intrinsic value for humankind. He suggests that the answer is yes, but only if we rise to the challenge of pursuing truth and substance over wishful thinking and expedient answers.

 Truth and the Internet

Truth is a powerful solvent. Stone walls melt before its relentless might. The Internet is one of the most powerful agents of freedom. It exposes truth to those who wish to see it. It is no wonder that some governments and organizations fear the Internet and its ability to make the truth known.

But the power of the Internet is like a two-edged sword. It can also deliver misinformation and uncorroborated opinion with equal ease. The thoughtful and the thoughtless co-exist side by side in the Internet's electronic universe. What's to be done?

There are no electronic filters that separate truth from fiction. No cognitive "V-chip" to sort the gold from the lead. We have but one tool to apply: critical thinking. This truth applies as well to all other communication media, not only the Internet. Perhaps the World Wide Web merely forces us to see this more clearly than other media. The stark juxtaposition of valuable and valueless content sets one to thinking. Here is an opportunity to educate us all. We truly must think about what we see and hear. We must evaluate and select. We must choose our guides. What better lesson than this to teach our young children to prepare them for a new century of social, economic and technological change?

Let us make a new century resolution to teach our children to think more deeply about what they see and hear. That, more than any filter, will build a foundation upon which truth can stand.

Vinton G. Cerf

Where Can I Learn More?

Catalyst (Cyberpsychology) `http://www.victoriapoint.com/catalyst.htm`

On-line Telecommuting Resources `http://smart2.svi.org/PROJECTS/TCOMMUTE/webguide/`

Time Management: A Guide for College Students `http://businessmajors.about.com/library/relatedlinks/bltimemgt.htm`

Red Rock Eater News Service `http://dlis.gseis.ucla.edu/people/pagre/rre.html`

Internet Service Providers

If you have a home computer with a modem, you can sign up with an ISP. Most ISPs offer different service packages and different types of accounts. Most people want to run a graphical Web browser such as Netscape Navigator or Internet Explorer. A SLIP or PPP account supports graphical browsers (as well as other TCP/IP applications such as FTP and Telnet). PPP can automate more of your login procedure than SLIP, but once you are connected, there is no difference between the two types of accounts. Most ISPs offer either SLIP or PPP, but not both. Some ISPs offer "shell" accounts. A shell account is a UNIX account, which is nice if you know UNIX and want to telnet into a UNIX account, but it won't be of any use for Web surfing unless you want to see what the Web looks like through the text-based browser Lynx (something the professional Web-page designers need to do).

You may also hear about POP or IMAP options, which refer to e-mail services (see Chapter 3). POP mail has been an industry standard in recent years and is the most frequently offered e-mail service. IMAP is a newer service that saves mail on the server, whereas POP users save mail on their personal PCs. IMAP is better than POP for people who need to access their mail from different locations. If you need to read mail from the office, from the house, and on the road, try to find an ISP that offers IMAP, but don't be surprised if it is more expensive than a POP option. IMAP requires more disk space and more computing power on the part of the ISP.

As for ISPs themselves, your options will vary, depending on where you live. Heavily populated areas offer more choices than rural areas, but even remote regions of the United States are sometimes covered by more than one ISP. If you can pick and choose, ask the following questions when selecting an ISP:

1. How much do they charge? (Some ISPs are more expensive than others.)
2. Is their modem pool reliable and adequate for the customer base served?
3. How good are their technical support people?
4. Will they let you try their services free for a week?
5. Do they offer any extra services?

We will discuss these questions in some detail so you can better evaluate an ISP on the basis of their answers. The first and fourth questions are the only ones that you can answer without taking a test drive. Happily most ISPs will offer a free evaluation period so you can try them out before you subscribe.

HOW MUCH DOES IT CHARGE?

If you live in an urban area, you should be able to find a service offering unlimited connect time for $20 to $30 per month. You might pay $20 per month as a baseline access charge with no connection-time charges. Or you might pay a baseline charge with additional connection-time charges for each hour after the first 40 hours. The best deals put a ceiling on those connection time charges, so you know you'll never spend more than a fixed amount each month no matter how much time you spend online. Connection-time ceilings may range from $20 to $80 per month, depending on what the market will bear. Most ISPs also charge a one-time set-up fee (usually about $20) to cover the cost of creating a new account.

What do you get for your money? Look for:

- Either a PPP or SLIP account
- An e-mail address with POP or IMAP e-mail service
- Access to 30,000 Usenet newsgroups
- 10MB storage space for a personal Web page, with
- additional Web page space for an extra charge

Keep in mind that you may also have to pay telephone charges whenever you dial into an ISP, so be sure to find a service that can be reached with a local phone call. If you select an ISP that requires a long-distance phone call, your phone bills will probably overwhelm all of your other Internet access expenses.

IS ITS MODEM POOL RELIABLE AND ADEQUATE FOR THE CUSTOMER BASE SERVED?

The answer to this question determines whether you can connect whenever you want to and then stay connected as long as you want to. Nothing is more frustrating than a busy signal from your ISP when you really need to get online. To find out how often busy signals occur, you have to try a service for a few days and see what happens each time you dial in.

A modem pool is a large bank of modems that your ISP uses to handle hundreds or thousands of incoming phone calls. Along with all the other subscribers, you rely on the modem pool for (1) an available phone line into your ISP account, and (2) a reliable connection that won't disconnect you. If a modem pool isn't large enough for the subscriber population, you may repeatedly get a busy signal when you try to connect. If the hardware in the modem pool isn't of good quality, you may also experience frequent disconnects.

Unfortunately, the adequacy of a modem pool is one of the more unstable aspects of ISP service. An ISP may be doing fine in January but grow dramatically during February—and then in March you start getting busy signals. Successful ISPs sometimes have trouble growing as fast as their customer bases. This is one reason why recommendations for ISPs must be current. *If someone gives you a recommendation for an ISP, be sure that the person is a current customer of that ISP.*

HOW GOOD IS ITS TECHNICAL SUPPORT STAFF?

Even the most self-sufficient computer user needs high-quality technical support. You may need to report a problem over which you have no control. You may hit a snag with software that isn't working. You may want to request a specific Usenet newsgroup. You shouldn't need to interact with technical support staff on a regular basis, but when you need them, it tends to be important.

Here are some indications that an ISP's technical support is up to speed:

- It has its own PC installation package for a graphical Web browser.
- It has a person who works specifically with MAC users.
- It has a 24-hour support line that's available 7 days a week, including holidays.
- It has multiple e-mail addresses for user queries (e.g., billing versus technical support).
- Its staff helps subscribers promptly with any problems during the free trial period.
- It maintains local newsgroups that subscribers can use to discuss questions and problems.

Once again, you need a trial period to assess the situation. ISPs experiencing explosive growth rates often have trouble keeping up with customer-support demand. Services that are excellent one month can be completely unsatisfactory three months later.

WILL IT LET YOU TRY ITS SERVICES FREE FOR A WEEK?

Most ISPs will give you a free account for 7 or 10 days. This is important because many questions can't be answered without first-hand experience. Your neighbors may have no problem with busy signals, but they may not be dialing in at the same times you'll want to dial in. A friend may say that the technical support is great, but your friend may have very different needs than you do. Some things you have to check out for yourself.

Any ISP should be able to help you with the necessary software installations so that you can dial up your account and establish a working connection. This is one place where you should be able to get fast and courteous help from technical support staff. If you have trouble getting connected, call for help. It's their job to get you up and running during your free trial period.

If you sign up for a free week, pick a time when you can be online as much as possible. Try to connect frequently to determine whether you get any busy signals. If you get a busy signal on the first try, can you get through on a second or third try? Install some software (e.g., a Web browser) and verify that it works smoothly. Use your newsreader to read messages on the subscribers' newsgroups to learn what people are saying about customer support. If an ISP is failing to perform, you'll see complaints from disgruntled customers. Look for problems that you can take to the technical support staff to find out how quickly, satisfactorily, and courteously they respond. Don't feel embarrassed to ask for help. They are in the business of helping people get underway with Internet access. If they make you feel like you are wasting their time, look for another ISP.

DOES IT OFFER ANY EXTRA SERVICES?

To maintain a competitive edge, some ISPs offer special services. Watch for them and weigh them in making your decision. The following are two specific options that you can ask about.

Most ISPs will offer you space for Web pages that will be accessible by anyone from anywhere. These can be personal or business pages. They may be pages of your own creation or pages that you had a professional Web-page designer create for you. If you expect to set up your own Web site, find out what your ISP can offer you. Many ISPs provide 10 MB of space for web pages as part of their standard service. Additional space should be available for an extra charge.

It is also reasonable to think about what will happen if you need to change ISPs. Chances are that you would like to have e-mail forwarded to your new address, just as the post office forwards mail for you when you change your home address. Most local ISPs will forward your e-mail for a charge, but some services don't forward any e-mail. If you expect to deal with a lot of e-mail that is important to you, ask about forwarding mail when you shop around for an ISP. This is especially important if you ever want to use an ISP for business communications.

CONCLUSION

As you can see, these questions may be difficult to answer without some experience, and even with a trial period, you may find that you haven't been able to do much more than establish a connection. If you have a number of ISPs in your area, and you're not certain that you've picked the best one, don't worry about it too much. The relative merits of the local ISPs could change six months from now anyway, making it impossible for you to be certain that your ISP is the best one available in the long run. Prices, the quality of technical support, and modem pool reliability can all change without warning. ISPs operate in the fast lane and rise or fall accordingly. If you find one whose service seems reasonable to you, be happy and turn your attention to other matters.

When to Talk to Technical Support Staff

Technical support staff are paid to help users of computing facilities work more efficiently and effectively. Increasingly, technical support staffs are also helping people who have questions about the Internet. However, one staff member may be responsible for hundreds of computer users. So it isn't realistic to expect intensive hand-holding, especially on a regular basis. It is also a mistake to assume that the only people who can help you are technical support staff.

If you're a beginner, it is relatively easy to find people who can help you because there are a lot of people who are one jump ahead of you. In fact, someone who is only a little bit more experienced may be more helpful than someone who has moved on to solve more sophisticated problems. If you ask around, you'll probably find someone who is both able and willing to help, if only because most people love it when someone asks them for advice.

The following resources are often available to college students:

- Friends and acquaintances who are experienced with computers
- Other students who use the same type of computer and software
- Any online help files or local discussion groups for beginners

When you subscribe to a commercial ISP, the rules for obtaining technical support are somewhat different. In that case, you have a right to ask for all sorts of help—whenever you need it—and, ideally, the ISP will deliver good technical support as a part of its contract service to you. Then, once you've gotten off the ground, you can peruse online bulletin boards on which fellow subscribers post questions and ask other subscribers for help with problems. Sometimes online discussions can solve your problems and sometimes they can't, but it is always worth a try, especially if you're unable to get a fast response from technical support staff.

In general, a good technical support person is a valuable resource and should be treated accordingly. If you're lucky enough to have good technical support staff available to you, remember that they're handling many problems in addition to yours. Don't take up more of their time than absolutely necessary. Many problems are easily solved, but others require extra effort and patience. Some truly nasty problems defy solution no matter how many people give it their best efforts. But most problems can be solved.

If you've decided to contact a technical support person with a question, take a few minutes to collect some relevant information before doing so. For example, suppose that you keep getting the same error message each time you try to start up a new piece of software. You can save yourself and the technical support person a lot of time if you get ready:

- Copy down what the error message said verbatim.
- Know the name of the software in question, including its version number.
- Know what operating system you're running (e.g., Win98 or MAC OS8).

It also helps if you can say whether this problem happens consistently or only some of the time. If the error appears only sporadically, try to identify any patterns that you've noticed when the error occurs:

- Does it always occur when you're trying to perform some specific operation?
- Does it happen only under certain conditions?
- Have you found a way to get around the problem, even if it's not ideal?

And whenever possible, identify anything that could have possibly contributed to the problem:

- Can you say when the problem first appeared?
- Did you upgrade any software or hardware just before the problem started?
- Did you change any settings or preferences before the problem started?
- Do you remember doing or seeing anything unusual before the problem started?

The more information you can provide, the easier it will be for the technical support person to help you solve the problem. You can't know for sure in advance whether something is relevant to your problem, but it never hurts to be forthcoming about anything that might be relevant. The better prepared you are for your conversation with the technical support person, the better the outcome is likely to be.

HTML Tags and Attributes

This appendix contains the tags and attributes described in Chapter 4. This summary is consistent with HTML 3.0 and 4.0, but it is not a comprehensive list of HTML tags and attributes. For a complete description of all HTML tags and attributes, please consult online HTML documentation or a published HTML manual.

HEAD, TITLE, AND BODY

```
<HTML>
<HEAD>     <!-- the HEAD must precede the  BODY -->
<TITLE> Web Page Title </TITLE>
           <!-- the TITLE must go inside the HEAD -->
</HEAD>
<BODY BGCOLOR=#F8F8FF
      BACKGROUND=wrinkles.gif>
           <!-- use either a background color OR a
           background pattern -->
</BODY>
</HTML>
```

HEADINGS

```
<H1 ALIGN=LEFT | RIGHT | CENTER > </H1>
                    <!-- The largest heading -->
<H2>
<H3>
<H4>
<H5>
<H6>                          <!-- the smallest heading -->
```

PRESENTATION TAGS

```
<B></B>              <!-- boldface -->
<I></I>              <!-- italics -->
<TT></TT>            <!-- teletype font -->
<U></U>              <!-- underlining -->
```

INFORMATIONAL TAGS

```
<STRONG></STRONG>    <!-- stands out -->
<EM></EM>            <!-- emphasize -->
<CODE></CODE>        <!-- monospaced font -->
<PRE></PRE>          <!--preserves all white spacing -->
<CITE></CITE>        <!-- citation -->
```

TEXT FORMATTING

```
<PRE></PRE>              <!-- reproduce all text as is -->
<BR CLEAR=LEFT | RIGHT | ALL>
                    <!-- go to next clear line -->
<P ALIGN=LEFT | RIGHT | CENTER>
                    <!-- start new paragraph -->
```

LISTS

```
<!-- an unordered (bulleted) list of three items -->
<UL>
<LI> Item X
<LI> Item Y
<LI> Item Z
</UL>


<!-- an ordered (numbered) list starting at #5 -->
<OL VALUE=5>
<LI> Item #5
<LI> Item #6
<LI> Item #7
</OL>


<!-- a list of definitions with a heading -->
<DL>
<LH> <H3> Two Important Definitions </H3> </LH>
<DT> Term X <DD> Definition of Term X
<DT> Term Y <DD> Definition of Term Y
</DL>
```

GRAPHICS

```
<IMG SRC=iggy.gif  WIDTH=30pt  HEIGHT=40pt
     ALIGN= LEFT | RIGHT | BOTTOM | TOP | MIDDLE
     ALT=[INLINE: A CARTOON IG]>
                 <!-- an inline graphic -->
                 <!-- with text alternate -->
<HR  SIZE=1,2,3,... WIDTH=25% ALIGN=LEFT | RIGHT | CENTER>
                 <!-- a horizontal rule -->
<CENTER></CENTER>
                 <!-- center justify a graphic element-->
```

HYPERTEXT LINKS

```
<A HREF=igtext.html>Basic Iguana Care for Beginners</A>
    <!-- a link to another page -->
<A HREF=http://www.repti.com/pub/info/igtext.html>
    Iguana Care </A>
    <!-- a link to another page on another Web page
    server-->
<A HREF="#food">Your Iguana Needs a Healthy Diet</A>
    <!-- a named link (to a place on the same page) -->
<A HREF="igtext.html#food">Your Iguana Needs a Healthy
    Diet</A>
    <!-- a named link (to a place on a different
    page) -->
<A NAME ="food"> Iguana Dietary Needs </A>
    <!-- an anchor for the named link #food -->
<A HREF=iggy.gif WIDTH=200pt HEIGHT=300pt >
    <IMG SRC=iggy.gif WIDTH=20pt HEIGHT=30pt> </A>
    <!-- a clickable thumbnail graphic -->
```

TABLES

```
<TABLE   BORDER=0,1,2,3,... ALIGN=LEFT | RIGHT WIDTH=
    HEIGHT= >
<CAPTION ALIGN=TOP | BOTTOM > </CAPTION> <!-- optional -->
<TR><TD WIDTH= HEIGHT= ALIGN=LEFT | RIGHT | CENTER>
</TABLE>
```

FRAMES

```
<FRAMESET ROWS="30%, 70%" COLS="50%, 50%">
    <!-- sets up a 4-frame layout split evenly down
    the middle -->
<FRAME SRC="igtext.html">
    <!-- defaults to a frame with a scroll bar -->
<FRAME SRC="igpics.html" SCROLLING="no">
</FRAMESET>
```

File Types

This appendix is a catalogue of file types commonly found in file archives on the Internet, along with the most popular file utilities needed to handle them. Most file types are platform-specific so we have grouped them under their associated operating systems. Macintosh, PC, and UNIX. This is not a comprehensive list, but it does cover the files you are most likely to encounter.

MACINTOSH FILES

File Extensions	What Is It?	Some Available Utilities
`.bin`	MacBinary is a binary format for encoding Mac files so they can be safely stored on non-Mac platforms	MacBinary II+ Stuffit Expander
`.sit`	a compressed file archive created by Stuffit Deluxe	Unstuffit Deluxe Stuffit Expander
`.hqx`	Binhex4 is an ASCII format for encoding binary files for text-based communication channels	BinHex DeHQX Stuffit Expander
`.sea`	a self-extracting archive	none needed
`.uue`	uuencoding is an ASCII format for encoding binary files for text-based communication channels	UULite UUundo
`.dd`	a file compressed with DiskDoubler	Disk Doubler Expander
`.pdf`	a Portable Document Format file	open it with Adobe Acrobat or Adobe Acrobat Reader
`.cpt`	a compressed file archive created by Compact Pro	Extractor Stuffit Expander

PC FILES

File Extensions	What Is It?	Some Available Utilities
`.zip`	a compressed file archive	PKUNZIP UNZIP WinZip WinUnZip
`.exe`	usually an executable file but can also be a self-extracting archive	none needed
`.uue`	uuencoding is an ASCII format for encoding binary files for text-based communication channels	uucode xferp wpack
`.ps`	a printable ASCII Postscript file	just send it to a Postscript printer or Postscript viewer
`.pdf`	a Portable Document Format file	open it with Adobe Acrobat or Adobe Acrobat Reader
`.wp`	a WordPerfect file	open it with a Word processor

UNIX FILES

File Extensions	What Is It?	Some Available Utilities
`.gz`	a compressed file archive created with gzip	gzip gunzp
`.Z`	a compressed file	uncompress gzip
`.tar`	a file archive (not compressed)	tar detar
`.uue`	uuencoding is an ASCII format for encoding binary files for text-based communication channels	uudecode
`.shar`	a self-extracting file archive	sh (but you must be in the UNIX Bourne shell)
`.ps`	a printable ASCII Postscript file	just send it to a Postscript printer or Postscript viewer
`.exe`	usually an executable but it can also be a self-extracting archive	none needed

`.tZ`
`.tarZ`
`.tar.Z`
	rename it as `.tar.Z` and handle it in two steps (see above)	(first uncompress it, then untar it)

`.tgz` `.tar.gz`	rename it as tar.gz and handle it in two steps (see above)	(first unzip it, then untar it)

Proxy Servers

Some browser add-ons (e.g., ad filters and cookie managers) work by creating a local proxy server. If you download software that requires a local proxy server, either the software's installer will reconfigure your browser for you, or you will be given instructions so you can reconfigure your browser manually.

The instructions given below apply to remote proxy servers. Remote proxy servers are usually available to a closed community of Internet users. For example, some ISPs offer ad filtering through a remote proxy server, so their subscribers do not have to do all their ad filtering locally. Some LANs also support a proxy server so that copies of frequently accessed Web pages can be stored locally and made available to LAN users without going out onto the Internet. In this case the proxy server speeds up at least some downloads for browser users while minimizing Internet traffic. These instructions explain how to configure your Web browser to access a remote proxy server.

To complete these steps you will need (1) the DNS address of the proxy server, and (2) a port number. You will need to get these two items from your ISP or LAN system administrator.

FOR NETSCAPE COMMUNICATOR

Load your browser and go to the Edit menu.

1. Select Preferences.
2. Hit the "+" next to Advanced.
3. Select Proxies.
4. Click on the Checkbox next to Manual proxy configuration.

5. Click on the View button.

6. Type in `<the-proxy-server-address>` next to the HTTP Proxy entry.

7. Type in `<the-4-digit-port-number>` for the Port entry.

8. Click OK twice, and you're done.

FOR INTERNET EXPLORER

For Internet Explorer:

1. Load your browser and go to the View menu.

2. Select Options.

3. Hit the "Connection" tab at the top.

4. In the Proxies area check "Access the Internet using a proxy."

5. Click on the Advanced button.

6. Type in `<the-proxy-server-address>` next to the HTTP: entry.

7. Type in `<the-4-digit-port-number>` for the Port entry.

8. Click OK twice, and you're done.

Glossary

A

absolute URL A hyperlink that uses a complete URL for its address. Absolute URLs are normally used to reference a Web page on a different Web server.

add-on An application that works alongside and complements another application (*see also* "browser add-on").

ad filter A browser add-on that turns off the graphical components of a commercial Web page that appear to be ads.

ad server A third-party server that delivers ads to commercial Web pages.

algorithm A sequence of instructions used to solve a problem.

alias An alternative name for a host machine, a server name, or an e-mail address.

all-in-one page A Web page that allows you to send search engine queries off to many different search engines, all from the same page. It is similar to, but not identical to a meta search engine.

anonymizer An Internet service that protects the identity of its subscribers while they use the Internet.

anonymous FTP A way of accessing an FTP server that does not require an account on the server. Public FTP servers allow anonymous FTP logins, but restricted (private) FTP servers require a userid and a password to login.

anonymous remailer An e-mail account designed to protect the identity of its owner.

anti-virus software A virus scanner.

applet A small Java program that is attached to a Web page.

application A computer program launched by the end-user.

ASCII characters Alphanumeric characters and other printable symbols normally found on a computer keyboard.

ASCII text file A file that contains only ASCII characters. ASCII text files can be displayed and opened by text editors (unlike binary files).

ASP (Application Service Providers) Internet services that deliver application software online from remote servers instead of local software installations.

AUP (Acceptable Use Policy) A set of rules and regulations that apply to personal computer accounts, Internet access accounts, and many other Internet-related services.

autoreply An automated e-mail reply, like the message on a telephone answering machine.

B

bandwidth A measure of digital channel capacity that describes how much data can be transferred between two locations in a fixed time interval (e.g., 28.8 kbps is 28,800 bits per second).

bandwidth bottleneck A point in the path of a data transmission where limited bandwidth slows the flow of data.

baud rate A measurement of throughput used to describe slower data transmission rates (e.g., a "1200 baud modem").

binary file A file that contains unprintable characters such as control characters. Binary files cannot be displayed or opened with text editors.

bit The smallest unit of digital data. Equivalent to an on/off switch.

bookmark file A file in which a Web browser can store favorite URL addresses. Internet Explorer calls it "Favorites" instead of bookmarks.

Boolean operators The logical operators AND, OR, and NOT. Usually supported by search engines that offer an advanced query option.

Boolean query A search engine query that uses Boolean operators.

bottom-up design A flexible strategy for Web-site design that does not require a detailed site specification at the outset (*see also* "top-down design").

broadband An Internet connection characterized by multiple channels and fast throughput.

browser add-on An application that works alongside and complements a Web browser.

browser helper application An application that can be launched by a Web browser to extend the multimedia capabilities of that browser.

browser plug-in An application that can be integrated into the operation of a Web browser in order to extend the multimedia capabilities of that browser.

browsing The process of exploring Web pages free-style as interests dictate. Browsing can be goal-oriented or purely recreational.

BubbleBoy A "proof of concept" e-mail worm that exploited the scripting capabilities of MS Outlook and Outlook Express to execute potentially malicious code.

byte A unit of computer memory that contains eight bits.

C

CA (certificate authority) A trusted third-party organization or business that issues digital certificates.

cache A block of memory that is reserved for recently accessed data or executable instructions. Information is placed in a cache in order to speed up future operations that would otherwise rely on slower forms of memory or on networked operations.

CD-ROM A read-only storage device with a 640 MB storage capacity.

CERT A government-sponsored reporting center for Internet security problems.

certificate authority (CA) *See* "CA."

clearinghouse An exhaustive collection of online resources for a specific topic.

clear signature A digital signature embedded in a clear (unencrypted) document.

clear-signed document An unencrypted document containing a digital signature.

client A software package that enables interactions with server software over the Internet. Clients typically play the role of information consumers, while servers typically operate as information providers.

compression *See* "file compression."

computer virus An executable program designed to replicate itself and spread from one computer to another. Some viruses act maliciously and damage files. Other viruses are benign and have little or no noticeable effect.

construction kit A program that helps you build Web pages or Web sites.

consumer profile Data collected by Web servers; it can include e-commerce transactions, search engine queries, and surfing activities.

cookie A small piece of text generated by a Web server, stored locally by a Web browser and made available to the originating server on demand whenever a user downloads Web pages from that Web server.

cookie manager A browser add-on that makes it easy to set cookie accept/reject policies for different Web sites.

copyright A legal claim of ownership that applies to original text, photographs, artwork, and musical works.

copyright infringement An unauthorized use of copyrighted materials that could lead to a lawsuit if the copyright holder wants to prosecute.

copyright restrictions Legal restrictions on the duplication and distribution of intellectual property.

counterfeit key A public key that does not belong to who it says it belongs to.

CPU (central processing unit) The part of a computer that can execute machine instructions in order to run a computer program.

cryptography The study of coding systems used to protect information and secure sensitive communications.

cyber-attacks Malicious attacks on host machines that are not adequately secured against intruders.

D

data rate A throughput rate.

default A value or action that is automatically invoked in the absence of more specific instructions.

default homepage A file in a user's Web server account where the server expects to find that user's homepage. Most UNIX hosts use a default homepage named index.html located in a subdirectory named public_html.

default Web page The Web page that a Web browser automatically loads when it is first launched. A user can reassign the default Web page from the Web browser's preference settings.

definition list An HTML element that formats its list elements with a place for terms and a place for term definitions.

desktop portal Software that supplies fast access to frequently visited Internet servers from your desktop.

digest A delivery option for a high-traffic mailing list.

digital certificate A document on a Web server that can be checked to verify the identity of the server.

digital convergence A computer innovation that brings two previously disparate technologies together (e.g., digital telephony brings the Internet and telephones together).

digital fingerprint A sequence of hexadecimal numbers associated with a key-pair that can be used for key authentication.

digital signature An encoding of a document with a private key to preserve document integrity and document ownership.

directory A file directory. Also, a synonym for a subject tree.

discussion group A Web-based forum where members can maintain ongoing discussions, for example, "message board."

disk cache An area of a hard drive set aside to store recently accessed data for fast access during subsequent visits.

disk memory Space available on a hard drive for long-term file storage.

DNS address A symbolic host address that can be translated by Domain Name Servers into an equivalent IP address.

document integrity In the context of document transfers, this refers to the original form of the document, free from subsequent alterations during transit.

document ranking A method of ranking documents used by search engines in an effort to show the most relevant hits first.

domain name That portion of a DNS address which specifies the site or network of the host machine. The domain name always follows the host name in a DNS address.

domain name servers Internet hosts that translate DNS addresses into IP addresses on demand.

DoS attack (denial-of-service attack) An orchestrated attack involving a massive number of simultaneous requests to a single Web server from multiple hosts—designed to overwhelm the server.

download A file is downloaded when a copy of that file is transferred from its original remote host to a local target host. A Web browser downloads Web pages from a Web server so they can be displayed by the local host running the browser (*see also* "upload").

download manager Software that facilitates file downloads from Web pages and FTP servers.

dynamic routing A strategy for finding the best pathway between two hosts given current conditions on the Net.

E

Eicar Virus Test A benign virus used to test virus scanners.

e-mail address An address of the form `<userid>@<hostname>`.

e-mail attachment A file that is sent to an e-mail address as an optional addition to a plain text message body. E-mail attachments can be either ASCII text or binary files (unlike e-mail message bodies which can only contain ASCII text).

e-mail client Software that can transfer e-mail messages between a local host and a local e-mail server, as well as display and compose messages on the local host.

e-mail distribution list A collection of e-mail addresses grouped together under a single entry in an e-mail address book.

e-mail header A set of fields that are attached to an e-mail message in order to identify the sender, recipient, time of delivery, and other useful information.

e-mail server Software that can send e-mail messages to and receive e-mail messages from other e-mail servers, as well as hold incoming messages for local e-mail clients.

e-mail virus A worm (erroneously referred to as a virus) that is spread by e-mail attachments or scripts associated with HTML-enabled e-mail.

emoticon Crude icon drawn from ASCII characters in order to communicate the emotional tone of a written message, for example, :-o (*see also* "smilee").

encrypted document A document that has been encoded using cryptology techniques such as private-key encryption or public-key encryption.

ethernet A local-area-network protocol capable of 10 Mbps throughput.

exact phrase matching A technique used by search engines to locate documents containing words in a specific sequence.

Explore.Zip An e-mail worm that tricked users into clicking an e-mail attachment by making it look like a WinZip file archive.

F

false hit A document returned by a search engine which is not what the user was looking for (*see also* "good hit").

FAQ files Compilations of frequently asked questions, originally associated with Usenet newsgroups.

file archive A single file that can be "unpacked" to create multiple files. Software files are often packed in a file archive for easy downloading.

file compression A strategy for minimizing the amount of memory needed to store the contents of a file.

file extension A suffix that follows a period in a file name. File extensions often reveal the type or format of a file.

file format A convention for encoding data in a file. File formats can often be recognized on the basis of a file's extension.

filtering A way of recognizing specific messages based on keywords in their subject headers, from fields, or message bodies.

Find command Any software application that displays text (e.g., a text editor or a Web browser) can locate a word or phrase in the current document if it supports a Find command.

fingerprint *See* "digital fingerprint."

firewall Software designed to monitor all networked communications in order to detect unauthorized host access.

flame An uninhibited display of anger or aggression online.

flame war An argument or ongoing sequence of hostile communications between two or more people in a public forum on the Internet.

frame A technique for controlling the layout of a Web page in which multiple HTML files are combined on a single Web page.

freeware Software that is publicly distributed free of charge.

frequency count The number of times a specific keyword appears in the document database of a search engine.

FTP (File Transfer Protocol) An Internet protocol that makes it possible to transfer files between two host machines.

FTP client Software designed to access FTP servers and facilitate FTP file transfers.

FTP server A server that acts as a distribution site for files, (e.g., a software archive). On many FTP servers, anyone is allowed to download files (via anonymous FTP), but only privileged users with accounts on the server are allowed to upload files.

full-privilege FTP FTP access to a host that requires a personal computer account on that host.

full-privilege telnet Telnet access to a host that requires a personal computer account on that host.

full text indexing A database indexing technique used by search engines in which all the words of a document are used to index that document.

fuzzy query An English sentence or question entered as a query for a search engine.

G

GB (gigabyte) A unit of computer memory containing 1,024 megabytes.

GIF (Graphics Interchange Format) A file format used to post drawings and artwork on the Web.

good hit A document returned by a search engine which is exactly what the user was looking for (*see also* "false hit").

gopher space A now-defunct Internet application that was very similar to the World Wide Web, and which became increasingly obsolete as the Web gained popularity.

graphical browser A Web browser that can display graphical images when they are part of a Web page.

graphical element Any picture, photograph, or background pattern on a Web page.

group reply An e-mail reply that goes out to the author of the original and everyone else who received that same message.

guest telnet session Limited telnet access to a host that is open to the general public.

H

hacker A person who searches for and exploits security holes found on Internet hosts. Also, someone who is capable of finding clever and original solutions to computer programming problems.

harassment Offensive, unwanted, and unavoidable communications or content, usually characterized by multiple or habitual incidents.

hard drive A magnetic storage device that is usually built into a computer for long-term storage.

hard-drive capacity The amount of memory on a hard drive; the size of the hard drive.

hash code An algorithm that maps text into a sequence of digits. One-way hash codes (codes that cannot be reversed) are used to store computer passwords and create digital signatures.

help desk A place where technical support personnel field questions and help users who are experiencing problems with their computers.

helper application An application that can be launched by another application (*see also* "browser helper application").

heterarchical Pertaining to a graph structure in which no nodes are more central or more important than any other nodes.

hexadecimal A notational system for the base-16 integers that uses digits 0–9 and letters A–F.

hierarchical Pertaining to a graph structure in which all nodes are organized in a tree with a common ancestor (the root node).

history list A record of Web pages recently visited in the order of their recency.

home page A Web page that acts as a "front door" or entrance to all the Web pages at that particular site.

horizontal rule An HTML element that draws a horizontal line across the page to separate blocks of text or other design elements.

host Any computer that maintains an active Internet connection.

host address An IP or DNS address used for Internet communications.

host machine *See* "host."

host name A short alphanumeric name given to a computer to differentiate it from other computers in its local area network.

HTML (HyperText Mark-up Language) A collection of formatting commands used to control the appearance of a Web page when it is viewed by a Web browser.

HTML editor A special-purpose editor designed to generate HTML files, usually through an easy-to-use graphical interface.

HTML element A segment of an HTML file that is interpreted and rendered by a Web browser in accordance with an HTML standard.

HTML source file A text file downloaded by a Web browser in order to display a Web page.

HTML tag A marker in a text file that signals the start or end of a specific HTML element. All HTML tags appear inside angle brackets. For example, `<P>` is the HTML tag that marks the start of a paragraph.

HTML tag attribute An optional directive inside an HTML tag which specifies in greater detail the proper way to render the associated HTML element. For example, `<P ALIGN=CENTER>` starts a new paragraph whose lines will all be centered on the Web page.

HTTP (HyperText Transfer Protocol) A Web-based communication protocol.

hyperlink A clickable HTML element that will direct the Web browser to display a different Web page or a different location on the current Web page.

hypertext A document that contains hyperlinks.

I

image map A way to create hyperlinks inside graphical elements.

IMAP An e-mail protocol for managing mail on a mail server.

inbox A collection of recently received e-mail messages waiting to be read.

informational element An HTML element that may be interpreted in different ways by different types of Web browsers, for example, by text-based browsers vs. graphical browsers (*see also* "physical element").

information retrieval A branch of computer science dedicated to the organization and manipulation of large text-based databases.

inline graphic A graphics file that has been inserted into an HTML file as if it were a single character in a text display.

installer A computer program that automates the installation of an application program on a computer.

instant messaging Private communication channels between people who use the same IM client software. Typically used by people who know each other and want to stay in close touch.

intelligent agent A computer program that searches the Web in order to collect and assemble information from multiple online resources.

intelligent concept extraction An information-retrieval strategy used by some search engines.

interactive mailing list A mailing list in which all subscribers can post messages to the list and interact with one another.

interlaced GIF file A GIF file that gradually "fades in" while the image is being downloaded by a Web browser.

Internet A global network of networks.

Internet abuse Antisocial behavior online that is either illegal, prohibited by AUPs, or generally frowned upon by other Internet users.

Internet Addiction Disorder A psychiatric disorder recognized by the American Psychiatric Association.

Internet appliance A special-purpose computer of limited functionality that delivers an Internet-based service.

Internet host *See* "host."

intranet A limited access TCP/IP network, usually protected by a firewall and limited to members of a corporation.

IP (Internet Protocol) A protocol for identifying Internet hosts via unique numerical addresses.

IP address A unique numerical address assigned to each Internet host. All IP addresses consist of four integers separated by periods.

IRC (Internet Relay Chat) A client/server application that supports real-time chat for multiple participants.

ISP (Internet Service Provider) A commercial business that offers Internet access to its subscribers. ISP services can be based on phone-line connections, ISDN lines, or other means of establishing a connection.

J

Java A programming language with powerful Web applications.

JavaScript A scripting language designed for the Web.

JPEG (Joint Photographic Experts Group) An image file format especially well-suited for posting photographs on the Web.

JVM (Java Virtual Machine) A platform-specific browser add-on that makes it possible for Web browsers to execute Java applets.

K

KB (kilobyte) A unit of computer memory containing 1,024 bytes. Sometimes abbreviated K.

key authentication The general process of verifying the owner of a public key.

key certification The process of placing a digital signature on a public key in order to vouch for its authenticity (a form of key authentication).

key-pair A uniquely connected public key and private key, used for public-key encryption.

key server A server that maintains a directory of public keys that can be used to verify digital signatures or generate encrypted communications.

L

label That portion of a hypertext link that is visible to the user.

libel Written statements that are damaging to the reputation of a person or a company and that could form the basis for a lawsuit.

limited edition software Commercial software distributed free of charge (or bundled with other products) in order to familiarize the customer with the product. Limited editions (also called "lite" or "special edition") usually withhold some advanced or key features that a serious user would consider vital.

link A clickable hypertext link in a hypertext document.

Linux A version of UNIX that runs on personal computers.

list command address A mailing list address reserved for subscribe and unsubscribe commands (among others). The list command address usually reaches a software program; a human might never see the messages sent to this address.

list distribution address A mailing list address reserved for messages that will be forwarded on to each list member.

listserv Software that automates mailing list management for a list owner. The term is also used to describe any host machine that is running listserv software.

local area network A network of computers that spans a limited geographical region.

LoveLetter An e-mail worm that was spread as a Visual Basic script e-mail attachment. LoveLetter deleted files from the user's hard drive.

M

macro A small program that allows users to collapse a frequently used command sequence into a single command for greater convenience and efficiency.

macro virus A virus that is triggered when a macro associated with a word-processing document or spreadsheet is executed. Many macros execute when a document is first opened, making it possible to become infected by a macro virus by simply opening a document.

mailing list A discussion forum that enables a large number of people to maintain an ongoing dialog that is visible to every list member through e-mail messages.

malicious applet A Java applet designed to crash a computer or cause other undesirable side-effects.

MB (megabyte) A unit of computer memory containing 1,024 kilobytes.

Melissa virus The first e-mail worm to propagate across the Internet by utilizing address books on host machines running Windows.

memory cache *See* "cache."

memory hog A computer program that requires a large amount of memory: either hard drive memory, RAM memory, or both.

message board *See* "Web-based message board."

message body That portion of an e-mail message in which the author enters an ASCII text message.

meta search engine A Web page that enables users to send one query out to multiple search engines for simultaneous processing.

MIME (Multipurpose Internet Mail Extensions) A standard for encoding non-ASCII files as text for reliable transport across the Internet. Almost all e-mail clients support MIME file attachments (*see also* "MIME attachment").

MIME attachment A file attached to an e-mail message. MIME attachments can be binary files, making it possible to send application files and graphics files through e-mail (*see also* "e-mail attachment").

MIPS (machine instructions per second) A measure of CPU speed.

mirror sites Alternate servers that duplicate heavily utilized public resources, as in mirrored FTP servers or key servers.

moderated mailing list A mailing list where only the list owner is allowed to post messages to the list members.

multimedia Communication based on text, graphics, audio, videos, or coordinated combinations of any such media.

multiplexing Data throughput that relies on simultaneous data transmissions over multiple channels.

N

nagware Shareware that continues to launch after the free trial-period is over, but with reminders that it's time to register.

named anchor A hypertext link that moves the user to another location on the same Web page.

Netiquette Rules of courtesy for online interactions with other people and other host machines.

Netizen An informed and responsible user of the Internet.

netspeak A telegraphic style of writing designed to minimize keystrokes through the liberal use of acronyms and emoticons.

newbie A newcomer to the Internet.

newsgroup A discussion forum available on Usenet news servers.

newsreader Client software for reading and posting to Usenet newsgroups.

news server A host machine that operates as a server for the Usenet news groups.

notice and consent A policy used by commercial vendors to protect the privacy of customer information. Consumers who do not explictly "opt out" by checking off a box on a Web page are granting the vendor the right to do whatever they want with their personal data.

O

online auction A popular way for individuals and businesses to buy and sell items of all kinds.

Open Source software Software that is freely distributed along with its source code files so that programmers are free to modify the software and distribute their modifications.

optical fiber A broadband data transport technology.

ordered list A list format supported by HTML in which each list item is numbered automatically by the Web browser.

P

packet Data formatted for TCP/IP-based transport over the Internet.

packet sharing The data transmission strategy used by the Internet.

packet sniffer Software that can be installed on a host machine in order to log the contents of all packets passing through that host en route to other destinations.

parity bit A bit reserved for a checksum test in order to verify the integrity of a byte after a data transmission.

password manager Software that helps you keep track of unique userids and secure passwords for multiple Web sites.

password security Your first and most powerful line of defense against hackers.

peak usage Maximal levels of bandwidth consumption on the Internet. Peak usage on the Internet is analogous to rush-hour traffic conditions on a highway.

PEM (Privacy-enhanced E-Mail) A mail client that encrypts and decrypts e-mail messages.

personal computer An all-purpose low-cost computer designed for a single user.

personal rich media Internet communcations that utilize multimedia (e.g., audio or video enhancements).

PGP (Pretty Good Privacy) Public-key encryption software distributed as freeware for noncommercial use.

physical element An HTML element that can be interpreted in only one way by different types of Web browsers (*see also* "informational element").

ping An Internet application that measures the time it takes to send a packet on a round-trip to a target host and back.

PKI (Public Key Infrastructure) A system of public key servers available to support encrypted communications over the Net.

plain text Readable text that is rendered without a choice of fonts, styles, or formatting options.

plug-in A software application that can be integrated into the operation of another application to extend its capabilities. (*see also* "browser plug-in").

point-and-click user interface A user interface that relies on the use of a mouse for user input.

POP (Post Office Protocol) An e-mail protocol for managing mail on a local host.

POTS (Plain Old Telephone Service) Telephone service over twisted-pair wires.

preference setting A variable setting that allows users to customize the behavior or appearance of a software application.

prefetching The downloading of Web pages before the user requests them, typically used by Web accelerators.

presentational element Another name for a physical element (*see also* "physical element").

privacy policy A statement of policy, usually associated with an e-commerce site, that explains how the site intends to use any personal data collected from visitors to the site.

private-key encryption An encryption strategy based on a single-code key.

protocol A system of communication signals that two computers can use to coordinate one-way or two-way data transmissions.

proxy server An intermediate Web server that can be used to remove ads from Web pages, or cache Web pages for a local area network.

public-key encryption An encryption strategy based on a pair of code keys.

Q

query *See* "search engine query."

R

raggy text A block of text with variable line lengths ranging from very short to very long. Raggy text is hard to read and almost always created unintentionally, usually with e-mail clients.

RAM (Random Access Memory) A fast form of computer memory reserved for data used by the CPU during a program execution.

real-time chat Public communication channels where people gather in chat rooms to exchange typed messages in real time. Often used by people who don't know each other.

relative URL A hypertext link that moves the user to a different Web page on the same Web server (and usually by the same author as well).

relevance feedback An information-retrieval technique used by some search engines.

Reload command A Web-browser command that takes the user back to the last page viewed by the browser.

rich text Text that is rendered with different fonts, styles, and formatting options.

router A server that assesses network conditions and returns an optimal pathway for packets en route to a specific destination host.

routing (e-mail) A way of directing mail to a specific folder or subdirectory for later viewing.

RTF (Rich Text Format) An ASCII-based encoding system for storing rich-text documents such as Word files.

S

S/MIME The secure MIME protocol, used to support encrypted e-mail communications.

scaling Alterations to the height and width of an image, used to enlarge or shrink the image as it is displayed on a Web page.

screen shot An image of a computer screen display or some portion of the screen display.

script A small computer program written in a scripting language.

search engine An Internet application that returns a ranked list of documents from a large database of online documents in response to a search query. Most search engines for the Web are available for free on public Web servers.

search engine query A string of text used as input to a search engine.

search query See "search engine query."

searchbot A computer program that continuously monitors multiple Web sites for information updates.

secure Web page A Web page in which it is safe to enter sensitive data like credit card numbers.

selective text indexing A database indexing technique that is used for large text databases. Selective text indexing accepts some subset of a document's text to be used as indexes for that document, while the rest of the text is ignored.

self-extracting archive A file archive that unpacks itself when you doubleclick it.

sender-only reply An e-mail reply that goes out to only the original author of an earlier e-mail message.

server A host computer which will run software on demand when it receives a request from another host computer.

session key A private key that is encoded with strong public-key encryption and sent to browsers by secure Web servers to enable encrypted SSL communications. Also used for PGP encryption.

shareware Software that can be installed and evaluated for some fixed trial period at no charge, but which requires a registration fee when the trial period ends.

shopping bot A comparison shopping service that collects pricing information for specific items at a number of e-stores on the Web.

sig file See "signature file."

signature file A small text file that can be automatically appended to the end of an e-mail message body. E-mail signatures are usually used to identify the author.

simple query A query option for a search engine that requires no special knowledge of the search engine's query features.

site maintenance The work of keeping a Web site timely and healthy.

smilee A smiling emoticon, :-) (*see also* "emoticon").

SMTP The original e-mail protocol for moving e-mail messages over the Internet.

social engineering Misrepresentations and guises used to thwart computer security by tricking people to reveal sensitive information such as passwords.

software download The process of transferring a software file or software archive from a remote host to your local host.

software installation The process of creating data files, executable files, and other support files needed to run a piece of software on a computer.

software license A legally binding contract that grants the licensee limited rights to a piece of software. Software licenses apply to freeware and shareware as well as shrink-wrapped commercial software.

software piracy The unauthorized use or distribution of software in violation of its software license.

spam Unsolicited e-mail sent out to a large number of recipients. Spam is usually commercial in nature, but it can be a plea for political action or a religious diatribe.

spambot A computer program that automates the distribution of spam via e-mail or Usenet.

special edition software An incomplete version of a commercial software package, distributed free of charge in order to attract customers who will want to upgrade and pay for the full version.

SSL (Secure Socket Layer) A protocol used to establish secure (encrypted) communications between a Web browser and a Web server.

streaming media A strategy for downloading large audio or video files so that the recipient can begin to hear or view the file while the file is still downloading.

strong encryption Encryption that cannot be cracked by brute force means within a reasonable period of time.

subject tree A hierarchical tree of topics and subjects that organizes and indexes informational Web pages.

successive query refinement A technique for working with search engines in which the user strives to formulate queries that are increasingly focused for the task at hand. Success depends on feedback from false hits along the way, and some familiarity with the features and options of the search engine.

T

table An HTML element that organizes any number of other HTML elements in rows and columns.

table column In an HTML table, data is arranged in rows and columns. Each column stretches vertically across the table (from top to bottom).

table row In an HTML table, data is arranged in rows and columns. Each row stretches horizontally across the table (from left to right).

TB (terabyte) A unit of computer memory containing 1,024 gigabytes.

TCP (Transmission Control Protocol) A strategy for breaking a digital communication into packets prior to transmission over the Internet, along with a strategy for reassembling the original transmission from multiple packets at the point of destination.

TCP/IP A combination of two protocols (TCP and IP) that mediate all communication over the Internet.

technical support A service available to computer or Internet users who need help with their software or hardware. Professional technical support is usually available through any institution or business that provides Internet access to its membership or subscribers.

telecommuting Remote work over the Internet, usually done at home.

telephony The science of translating sound into electrical signals for transmission over distance, along with a translation back into sound at the receiving end.

telnet An Internet application that allows a user to login to an account on a remote host and interact with that host as either a full-privileged user or a guest user.

telnet gateway A link on Web page to a public telnet server.

term count The number of times a specific keyword or phrase occurs in a search engine's database.

text baseline In a document display, the baseline of a text string refers to the (invisible) horizontal line on which the text characters are placed.

text file A file containing only ASCII characters (*see also* "binary file").

throughput The rate of a data transmission over a hardware device such as a telephone modem, or an I/O port.

thumbnail preview A hyperlink to a graphical image whose label is a smaller version of that same image. Thumbnail previews are used to minimize download time and give the user more control over which images are viewed. Also known as a "thumbnail sketch."

title search A search-engine query containing a term that is tagged as a keyword or phrase that should be found in the title of the document. Not all search engines support title searches.

top-down design A strategy for Web-site design that relies on a detailed site specification at the outset (*see also* "bottom-up design").

top-level domain name The final suffix in a full domain name that reveals the type of the Internet host. For example, a top-level domain name will tell you if a host machine is part of a commercial or educational site.

ToS (Terms of Service) Similar to an Acceptable Use Policy.

traceroute An Internet application that traces the path of a packet transmission between two Internet hosts.

Transmission Control Protocol See "TCP."

transparent GIF A GIF file whose background assumes the same background color or background pattern of any Web page on which it is displayed.

Trojan horse Surreptitious code, often designed to enable remote control over your computer at a later date.

U

uninstaller That part of a software application whose sole purpose is to remove the software and all of its associated files from a computer.

UNIX An operating system favored by many programmers and computer scientists.

upload A file is uploaded when a copy of that file is transferred from its original local host to a remote target host. FTP clients are typically used to upload files over the Internet, although Netscape Navigator and Internet Explorer both support file uploads (*see also* "download").

URL (Uniform Resource Locator) A unique address for Internet resources that are available through a Web browser, including files or directories on Web servers, FTP servers, telnet gateways, or news servers.

Usenet A client/server network of public message boards which predates the Web.

Usenet newsgroup A discussion forum within the Usenet hierarchy in which anyone can ask questions or post messages.

userid A unique string of characters used to identify a specific user account on a time-sharing computer or a local-area network.

uuencode An ASCII-encoding method used to move binary files across text-based communication channels (e.g., e-mail and Usenet).

V

video conferencing Multimedia communications across multiple servers. Includes real-time video and audio communications.

View history command A Web-browser command that displays hypertext links back to all the Web pages visited during the current browser session, or in some cases, Web pages from older browser sessions as well.

viewer Software used to display data files, such as image viewers or PDF viewers.

virtual community A community of people who communicate via Web-based discussion groups, mailing lists, chat rooms, or Usenet newgroups.

virus A computer program designed to install copies of itself on as many computers as possible, while delivering side-effects (often destructive) to the infected computers.

virus scanner A program that checks files to see if they have been infected with a computer virus. It is important to run a virus scanner on new software prior to installation.

W

weak encryption Encryption that can be cracked by brute-force means within a reasonable period of time.

Web accelerator Software that leverages the available bandwidth so you spend less time waiting for Web pages to download.

Web-based message board A discussion forum on the Web that normally requires you to register with the Web site if you want to post messages.

Web browser Client software used to display Web pages found on Web servers.

Web bug A 1×1 pixel image inserted into an e-mail message for data collection purposes by ad servers.

Web filter A browser add-on that removes certain types of content (e.g., ads) from Web pages before they are displayed by the browser.

web of trust A key-authentication model based on key certification by friends and friends of friends.

Web page An HTML file designed to be viewed by Web browsers. The average web page is 10 KB in size, contains 23 relative URLs, 5.6 absolute URLs, and 14.4 images.

Web-page construction kit An application designed to help beginners create simple Web pages.

Web ring A set of Web sites about a single topic that are linked together in a circle using uniform "back" and "forward" links for easy browsing.

Web server Software for posting public Web pages on the Net.

Web spider Software used by search engines to locate new Web pages for their document databases.

wide area network A network of computers that spans a large geographical region.

worm A self-replicating computer program, similar to a virus, that spreads via networked communications and commonly used software.

WWW (World Wide Web) The 17 million Web servers that make over 2 billion Web pages available to anyone with a Web browser and Internet access. 7 million new Web pages are added to the World Wide Web every day.

WYSIWIG (What-You-See-Is-What-You-Get) A feature first used by word processors and desktop publishing applications so that users could see exactly what a document would look like before it was sent to a printer. HTML editors also offer WYSIWYG page displays, although these displays may not be faithfully reproduced by different browsers.

Index

Credits

Figures 1.17, 2.3, 2.7(a), 2.7(b), 3.3, 3.9, 3.14, 4.4, 4.41, 6.9, 7.8, 8.5, 8.7, 9.4, 9.7, 9.9, 10.8, 10.9, 10.10, 10.16, 11.14, 11.37	Netscape Communicator browser window ©1999 Netscape Communications Corporation. Used with permission. Netscape Communications has not authorized, sponsored, endorsed, or approved this publication and is not responsible for its content.

Color Insert

Page I-8 (top)	Images courtesy Paul Lutus, www.arachnoid.com.
Page I-8	ImageForge is a trademark of CursorArts Company. Download the free version from http://www.cursorarts.com. CursorArts Company, P.O. Box 1370, Bend, OR 79909 USA.
Page I-9 (bottom)	Courtesy of Dr. William T. Verts
Page I-10 (bottom)	Reprinted by permission of Yuri Margolin (ufx@yahoo.com)

Chapter 1

Figure 1.4	PC Pitstop LLC. Reprinted with permission.
Figure 1.7	©2000 Matrix.Net, Inc.
Figures 1.9(a) and (b)	From www.gwbush.com. Reprinted with permission.
Figure 1.11	http://www.nua.ie.surveys/ Nua Internet Surveys, 2000. Reprinted with permission.
Figure 1.12	Copyright 2000 internet.com Corporation. All Rights Reserved. Reprinted with permission from www.thelist.com.
Figure 1.12 (bottom)	From www.isps.com.
Figure 1.13	Andover.Net, Inc. Reprinted with permission.
Figure 1.16	©1996 Peter John Harrison. Reprinted with permission.
Figure 1.17	Screen shots reprinted by permission from Microsoft Corporation.

Chapter 2

Figures 2.2 and 2.4	Courtesy of McAfee.com.
Figure 2.6	Screen shots reprinted by permission from Microsoft Corporation.
Figure 2.15	Zone Labs, Inc. Reprinted with permission.

Chapter 3

Figure 3.5	Courtesy of David Fisher.
Figures 3.6, 3.12, 3.15, 3.16, and 3.19	Reproduced with permission of Yahoo! Inc. ©2000 by Yahoo! Inc. YAHOO! and the YAHOO! logo are trademarks of Yahoo! Inc.
Figure 3.7	From Individual.com. Reprinted with permission.
Figure 3.10	From MP3.com. Reprinted with permission.
Figure 3.20	Used with permission of the Coalition Against Unsolicited Commercial Email (www.cauce.org).
Figure 3.21	Screen shots reprinted by permission from Microsoft Corporation.
Figure 3.22	Courtesy of Wayne Bishop.

Chapter 4

Figure 4.15	Reprinted with permission of Eric Mumpower, MIT
Figure 4.28	Copyright ©1994-2000 Wired Digital, Inc. All Rights Reserved.
Figure 4.28	Reprinted with permission from NewsScan Daily, www.newsscan.com.
Figure 4.32	From www.b-zone.de. Reprinted with permission.
Figure 4.41	Netscape Communicator browser window ©1999
Figure 4.43	©1998 VerySimple. Reprinted with permission.
Figures 4.46, 4.47, 4.48	Copyright 2000 NetMechanic, Inc. Used by permission.

Chapter 5

Figure 5.34	Courtesy of PY Software, Inc.
Figures 5.41, 5.42, and 5.43	Mainstream Computing, www.balitools.com. Reprinted with permission.
Figures 5.38 and 5.39	Copyright Extreme-dm.com. Reprinted with permission.
Figures 5.17, 5.18, and 5.19	From QGoo, a Java Applet developed by Steven Wittens. For more information check http://www.acho.net/qgoo/
Figures 5.20, 5.21, and 5.23	©Moondog Software. Reprinted with permission.
Figure 5.22	Screen shots reprinted by permission from Microsoft Corporation.
Figure 5.29 and 5.30	©Irfan Skiljan. Reprinted with permission.
Figure 5.27	Courtesy of Ivan Peters.
Figures 5.24, 5.25, and 5.26	From viablesoftware.com.
Figure 5.35	Imint Magic Buttons and www.imint.com are copyright of Image Intelligence Ltd., Great Britain.
Figures 5.2–5.11 and 5.32	Courtesy of Dr. William T. Verts

Chapter 6

Figure 6.1	Copyright 2000 internet.com Corporation. All Rights Reserved.
Figures 6.2–6.7	Reproduced with permission of Yahoo! Inc. ©2000 by Yahoo! Inc. YAHOO! and the YAHOO! logo are trademarks of Yahoo! Inc.
Figure 6.8	©2000, licensed to About, Inc. Used by permission of About, Inc. which can be found on the Web at www.About.com. All rights reserved.
Figure 6.9	Netscape Communicator browser window ©1999 Netscape Communications Corporation. Used with permission.
Figures 6.10 and 6.11	©1993-00 David S. Blackmar. All Rights Reserved Worldwide.
Figures 6.12 and 6.13	©The Argus Clearinghouse. Reprinted with permission.
Figure 6.14	All images from www.google.com provided courtesy of Google, Inc. All rights reserved.
Figures 6.15 and 6.16	From Ask Jeeves.
Figures 6.17, 6.18, 6.22	Courtesy of Infind.com, Inc.
Figure 6.19, 6.20 and 6.21	Copernic.com. Reprinted with permission.
Figure 6.25	©2000 by Digital Tools & Designs, Inc. Email: findspot@cmpo.com.
Figures 6.26, 6.28, 6.29, 6.30, and 6.31	From AltaVista.com. Reprinted with permission.
Figure 6.33	Reprinted with permission of IntelliSeek.
Figure 6.34	©K. Clough, Inc. Reprinted with permission.
Figure 6.36	Copyright 2000 internet.com Corporation. All Rights Reserved. Reprinted with permission from www.bots.internet.com.
Figures 6.37, 6.38, 6.39, and 6.43	Courtesy of EntryPoint Incorporated. All Rights Reserved.
Figure 6.40	From InfoPager Technologies.
Figure 6.41 and 6.42	©2000 The New York Times Company. Reprinted with permission.
Figures 6.44 and 6.45	National Research Council of Canada. Reprinted with permission.

Chapter 7

Figures 7.2–7.5, and 7.28	Reproduced with permission of Yahoo! Inc. ©2000 by Yahoo! Inc. YAHOO! and the YAHOO! logo are trademarks of Yahoo! Inc.
Figures 7.6, 7.7, and 7.19	Reproduced with permission of Yahoo! Inc. ©2000 by Yahoo! Inc. YAHOO! and the YAHOO! logo are trademarks of Yahoo! Inc.

Figures 7.20–7.24	Novell/Remarq screenshots and text Copyright © (year date) Novell, Inc. All rights reserved. Reprinted with permission.
Figure 7.25	From www.deja.com.
Figure 7.26	From Talk City, Inc.
Figure 7.27	Courtesy of Harris Interactive Inc. All Rights Reserved.
Figure 7.30	Copyright 2000, ICQ, Inc. All Rights Reserved.
Figures 7.31 and 7.32	Copyright 2000, America Online, Inc. All Rights Reserved.
Figure 7.33	Courtesy of TRUSTe.
Figure 7.34	Reproduced with permission of Yahoo! Inc. ©2000 by Yahoo! Inc. YAHOO! and the YAHOO! logo are trademarks of Yahoo! Inc.
Figure 7.35	Copyright 2000 Dialpad.com, Inc. Used by permission.

Chapter 8

Figure 8.1	Reprinted with permission of Kookaburra Software
Figure 8.2	From www.tucows.com. Reprinted with permission.
Figures 8.4, 8.6, 8.21, and 8.22	Screen shots reprinted by permission from Microsoft Corporation.
Figure 8.5	Netscape Communicator browser window ©1999 Netscape Communications Corporation. Used with permission.
Figure 8.8	Courtesy of McAfee.com.
Figures 8.9 and 8.20	Courtesy of McAfee.com.
Figures 8.10 and 8.11	Courtesy of ZipCentral.
Figure 8.12	Mainstream Computing, www.balitools.com. Reprinted with permission.
Figure 8.13, 8.14, 8.15, 8.16, and 8.17	©Go!Zilla. Reprinted with permission.
Figures 8.18, 8.19, and 8.32	Reprinted with permission of Meikel Weber (support @meikel.com)
Figure 8.23	From RealNetworks, Inc.
Figures 8.24–8.29	Reprinted with permission of Project Gutenberg.
Figures 8.30 and 8.31	Courtesy of Jan Debis.

Chapter 9

Figure 9.1 and 9.2	Reprinted with permission from Symantec Corporation.
Figures 9.6 and 9.31	Screen shots reprinted by permission from Microsoft Corporation.
Figure 9.9	Copyright © by Jakob Nielsen. All Rights Reserved.
Figure 9.10	Copernic.com. Reprinted with permission.
Figures 9.12 and 9.13	NetSonic, a division of Web3000. Reprinted with permission.

Figure 11.12	Special permission to reproduce portions of the CERT© screen shot at URL http://www.cert.org ©1999 by Carnegie Mellon University is granted by the Software Engineering Institute. CERT© and CERT Coordination Center© are registered in the U.S. Patent and Trademark Office.
Figures 11.16–11.36	Permission to reproduce screen shots from the PGP product has been provided by Network Associates, Inc. Network Associates, PGP and Pretty Good Privacy are registered trademarks of Network Associates, Inc. and/or its affiliates in the US and/or other countries.
Figure 11.37	Courtesy of Mark Burkley.